VOICE AND EQUALITY

VOICE AND EQUALITY

Civic Voluntarism in American Politics

SIDNEY VERBA

KAY LEHMAN SCHLOZMAN

HENRY E. BRADY

HARVARD UNIVERSITY PRESS

Cambridge, Massachusetts

London, England

Fourth printing, 2002

Library of Congress Cataloging-in-Publication Data

Verba, Sidney
   Voice and equality : civic voluntarism in American politics / Sidney Verba,
Kay Lehman Schlozman, Henry E. Brady.
      p.   cm.
   Includes index.
   ISBN 0-674-94292-2 (alk. paper).—ISBN 0-674-94293-0 (pbk. : alk. paper)
   1. Political participation—United States.   2. Political activists—United States.
3. Voluntarism—United States.
   I. Schlozman, Kay Lehman, 1946–   .   II. Brady, Henry E.   III. Title.
JK1764.V475   1995
323′.042′0973—dc20   95-16501

To the memory of Cesar Torres

And to Margy, Ericka, and Tina Verba,
Danny and Julie Schlozman,
Daniel and Julia Brady—
who, alas, grasp only too intuitively
the meaning of voice and equality

Acknowledgments

This book has been long in the making. We began our discussions late in the Reagan administration, gathered and analyzed the data during the Bush administration, and drafted the manuscript during the first two years of the Clinton administration. We are winding up early in 1995, a time when a Democratic President has promised to "end welfare as we know it" and to provide tax relief to the middle class, and when the newly installed Republican leadership in Congress has placed such programs as federally subsidized school lunches and assistance to homeless veterans—but not Social Security or subsidies to business—on the chopping block. Therefore, we must begin by thanking President Clinton, Speaker of the House Gingrich, and other policymakers in Washington for behaving in ways so fully consistent with the findings in these pages about what public officials hear through citizen participation and for providing such dramatic evidence that it matters who takes part.

Any project as protracted as this one incurs a lot of debts closer to home. We are grateful for all the help we have had along the way. We are particularly indebted to Norman Nie, who worked closely with us on the design and administration of this study and made invaluable contributions to it.

We have been blessed with superb research assistance. Nancy Burns and Jane Junn showed unfailing versatility, efficiency, and good humor in assisting with all aspects of the project over several years. Now that they are on their own, we can only wish for them that they should have such willing and gifted assistance. Ken Stehlik-Barry brought incomparable diligence and expertise to the preparation of the data for analysis. Demonstrating that no good deed should go unpunished, Stephen Haggerty showed the patience of Job and the craftiness of Holmes in undertaking one enormous data checking project after another. For careful and vigilant computer work, we are grateful to Tami Buhr, Anne Sartori, Natasha Unger, Bill Hoynes, Liesbeth ter Schure, Fay Booker, Chris Downing, and Martin Petrie. We would also like to thank Sharon Caldwell and Erica Grevmeyer, who helped with data cleaning; Jesse Donahue, Stephanie Easterday, and Peter Morningstar, who gathered ancillary data; and Jenny Albert, Chris Kukk, Andrea Rutherford, and Lise Van Boxel, who helped with manuscript preparation.

We are fortunate to have been able to meet occasionally with an advisory group who confront from the trenches the dilemmas that we view from academic precincts—Scott Gelzer, Mary Gonzales, David Hayes-Bautista, Joanne Howes, David Kindler, Jane Ramsey, Renae Scott, and Joan Slay. Their good works are as inspiring as their insights were acute. We are also grateful to Patricia Kates, who organized these sessions.

We would like to thank the William Benton Foundation, which sponsored a documentary about citizen participation, "The Rage for Democracy," which added a human face to the abstract themes of our study. We enjoyed working with the late Lewis Freedman and Fred Schneider of the William Benton Broadcast Project, as well as with Steve Atlas, Noel Buckner, Beth Harrington, and Rob Whittlesey, who produced and made the film. We would also like to express our appreciation to the Ford Foundation, which has made this video available for classroom use through PBS Video in Alexandria, Virginia.

Harvard University, Boston College, the Center for the Study of Politics and Society at the National Opinion Research Center, and the Survey Research Center at the University of California, Berkeley, provided institutional support of many kinds. A Boston College Faculty Fellowship provided Kay Schlozman a leave to work on the project. Over the years, Frankie Hoff, Bernardine

Pachta, Sandee MacDonald, Synita Booker, and Lyn Civitello rendered cheerful assistance in many ways.

The staff and leadership of the survey organizations that collected the data provided valuable aid. We especially want to thank Norman Bradburn, Robert Michael, and Alisu Shua-Glusberg of the National Opinion Research Center and William McCready and Ann Hildreth of the Survey Research Lab at Northern Illinois University.

Without the generous support of the Ford Foundation, Hewlett Foundation, National Science Foundation, and Spencer Foundation, this project would never have been possible. We wish especially to mention the early and enthusiastic support of the late Lawrence Cremin of the Spencer Foundation. We wish we could share with him the results of his faith in us.

Several colleagues gave our manuscript extremely careful readings. We appreciate the helpful and tough-minded advice provided by Larry Bartels, Jeffrey Berry, Derek Bok, Nancy Burns, Rodolfo de la Garza, Jane Junn, David Leege, Norman Nie, Danny Schlozman, and Merrill Shanks.

Harvard University Press moved a long and complex book through the editorial and production process with skill. We would like to thank especially Aida Donald, Mary Ellen Geer, and Elizabeth Suttell.

The authors are grateful for permission to reprint the quotation from Bertolt Brecht's *Threepenny Opera,* copyright © 1928 by Gustav Kiepenhauer Verlag, renewed 1968 by Helene Brecht-Weigel. Translation copyright for the play and texts by Brecht © 1979 by Stefan S. Brecht. Reprinted from *The Threepenny Opera* by Bertolt Brecht, published by Arcade Publishing Inc., New York, New York. This quotation is also reprinted by permission of Reed Consumer Books (Methuen, London). The authors also thank the following journals for permission to reprint published materials: *The American Political Science Review* for Sidney Verba, Kay L. Schlozman, Henry E. Brady, and Norman H. Nie, "Citizen Activity: Who Participates? What Do They Say?" in vol. 87 (1993): 303–318, and Brady, Verba, and Schlozman, "Beyond SES: A Resource Model of Political Participation," in vol. 89 (1995): 271–294; *The British Journal of Political Science* for Verba,

Schlozman, Brady, and Nie, "Race, Ethnicity, and Political Resources: Participation in the United States," in vol. 23 (1993): 453–497, and Schlozman, Verba, and Brady, "Participation's Not a Paradox: The View from American Activists," in vol 24. (1994): 1–36; and *The Journal of Politics* for Schlozman, Nancy E. Burns, and Verba, "Gender and the Pathways to Participation: The Role of Resources," in vol. 56 (1994): 963–990.

The data from the Citizen Participation Study are available on the World Wide Web on the Internet as well as from the Inter-University Consortium for Political and Social Research, University of Michigan, Ann Arbor, Michigan. The World Wide Web address is:

http://ucdata.berkeley.edu/ucdata.html

The data set and set-up instructions can be found by clicking on "Holdings" and then following the instructions.

Any academic project whose collaborators are separated by three thousand miles makes special demands. We were the beneficiaries of world-class hotel and restaurant hospitality from Cookie and Malcolm Kates, Belle Huang and Ed Blumenstock, Nancy Adler and Arnie Milstein, and Prue and Frank Beidler.

We imposed most, of course, on the folks at home. Our deepest debt is to Cynthia, Stanley, and Patricia, who gave us their support and their encouragement—and (usually) forgave us our absences.

Contents

Tables and Figures

Tables

Figures

Denn die einen sind im Dunkeln
Und die andern sind im Licht
Und man siehet die im Lichte
Die im Dunkeln sieht man nicht

Some are in darkness
And others are in light
We see those in light
Those in darkness, we do not see

> Bertolt Brecht
> *Die Dreigroschenoper*

Nemo dat quod non habet.

You cannot give what you do not have.

> Raimundus Lullus
> *Ars Generalis Ultima*

1

Introduction

Citizen participation is at the heart of democracy. Indeed, democracy is unthinkable without the ability of citizens to participate freely in the governing process. Through their activity citizens in a democracy seek to control who will hold public office and to influence what the government does. Political participation provides the mechanism by which citizens can communicate information about their interests, preferences, and needs and generate pressure to respond.

Voice and equality are central to democratic participation. In a meaningful democracy, the people's voice must be clear and loud—clear so that policymakers understand citizen concerns and loud so that they have an incentive to pay attention to what is said. Since democracy implies not only governmental responsiveness to citizen interests but also equal consideration of the interests of each citizen, democratic participation must also be equal.

No democratic nation—certainly not the United States—lives up to the ideal of participatory equality. Some citizens are active: they vote or engage in more demanding forms of participation. Others are not. In fact, a majority of Americans undertake no other political activity aside from going to the polls. In addition, those who do take part are in critical ways not representative of the citizenry as a whole. They differ in their social characteristics and in their preferences, needs, and priorities. Citizen activists tend to be drawn

1

disproportionately from more advantaged groups—to be well-educated and well-heeled and to be White and male. In consequence, the voice of the people as expressed through participation comes from a limited and unrepresentative set of citizens. The democratic ideal may be equal consideration for the needs and preferences of all, but the reality of participation is quite different.

This book is about political participation in the United States. It is about whose voice is heard. And it is about the <u>process</u> that amplifies the voice of some citizens and mutes the voice of others by differentially endowing citizens with the motivation and capacity to be active, and with access to the recruitment networks through which requests for participation are channeled. *Voice and Equality* provides a comprehensive account of the participatory process in the United States.

Understanding Participation: A Thematic Overview

In several respects, our approach to the representativeness of the participatory system is very broad. We consider numerous ways in which citizens express their voice—not only by voting but also by taking part in a range of other activities such as getting involved in campaigns, making political contributions, working informally in the community, and contacting government officials. Furthermore, our specially designed sample permits us to deal with significant activities—for example, making large campaign contributions, attending demonstrations or protests, and serving on local governing boards—in which too few citizens engage to permit analysis using ordinary sample surveys.

We also take an encompassing approach to what is being represented. The literature on participation in America has, by and large, focused on the extent to which the activists are representative of either significant demographic groups or the issue preferences of the public. We, too, consider demographic and attitudinal representation. However, we move beyond these concerns to consider other politically relevant characteristics of members of the public: their actual needs and their involvement in government programs. As we shall show, a participatory system that seems adequately representative of the public from one point of view may be quite unrepresentative from other, quite significant, perspectives. In addition, we provide unique data on the actual messages sent through the participatory process. Many studies exist of the preferences of the public—or, even, of various participant publics—as revealed in public opinion polls. We add a new component to the understanding of the voice of the people: we consider activists' participatory agendas, that is, the issue concerns they bring to their activity. Moreover, we find that different forms of activity differ in terms of the politically relevant characteristics of activists and the messages they send.

EXPLAINING CIVIC VOLUNTARISM

The model that we develop of the process by which citizens come to be active in politics is similarly comprehensive. The extent to which and the ways in which activist publics are unrepresentative of the citizenry as a whole depend upon the nature of the process of political activation. Our conception of the participatory process rests upon two main factors: the *motivation* and the *capacity* to take part in political life. A citizen must want to be active. In America, participation is voluntary activity and, thus, involves choice. However, the choice to take part in a particular way is a constrained one. Various forms of participation impose their own requirements—the time to volunteer in a campaign, the money to cover a check to a political cause, the verbal skills to compose a convincing letter. Thus, those who wish to take part also need the resources that provide the wherewithal to participate. We consider a third factor as well. Those who have both the motivation and the capacity to become active are more likely to do so if they are asked. Therefore, we consider the *networks of recruitment* through which requests for political activity are mediated.

Our analysis of the participatory process takes us deep into the basic structures of American society. We show that both the motivation and the capacity to take part in politics have their roots in the fundamental non-political institutions with which individuals are associated during the course of their lives. The foundations for future political involvements are laid early in life—in the family and in school. Later on, the institutional affiliations of adults—on the job, in non-political organizations, and in religious institutions—provide additional opportunities for the acquisition of po-litically relevant resources and the enhancement of a sense of psychological engagement with politics. Our model of the partici-patory process—which we call the Civic Voluntarism Model—considers the factors that foster political activity and demonstrates how they are stockpiled over the course of a lifetime, frequently conferring additional advantage on the initially privileged. The elaboration of this model not only establishes that such basic institutions of American society as schools, voluntary associations, and churches affect participation, but delineates how they do so.

This inquiry into the mainsprings of participation contains much that is novel. For example, we examine various civic skills—or-ganizational and communications abilities that facilitate political activity—measuring them more concretely than has ever been done before. Thus, we are able to identify the particular capacities that enhance participation and to trace their origins in early experi-ences and adult institutional affiliations.

Our investigation of civic skills leads to a deeper understanding of the role of religion in the American participatory system. It is well known that, despite the formal separation of church and state, religious institutions in America have long been involved with politics: clergy discuss political matters from the pulpit; churches provide the institutional infrastructure for political mobilization; church officials take stands on public issues. Our analysis high-lights an additional process with political consequences: even when church activists pursue endeavors with no demonstrable political content—for example, advising the church youth group or chair-ing the committee to arrange the annual rummage sale—they have opportunities to develop skills that are relevant for politics. These skill-endowing opportunities can serve a compensatory function, enhancing political resources among church activists whose edu-cational and occupational levels might otherwise predispose them to political quiescence. In this way, a distinctive feature of Ameri-can life, high rates of church attendance, has implications for citizen activity in politics.

The significance of the Civic Voluntarism Model goes beyond the introduction of factors not usually used to explain the origins of participation. In addition, we bring new understanding to rela-tionships with long pedigrees in social science analysis. An especially notable case in point is the relationship between socioeconomic status (SES)—levels of education, income, and occupation—and citizen activity, a relationship with a firm empirical footing through the decades and across polities, but with a less compelling theoretical grounding.[1] We separate SES into its constituent elements and show that its components are differentially relevant for different kinds of participation. It turns out that what matters for voting, for which educational attainment is primary,[2] cannot be generalized to all forms of activity. Not only do we demonstrate how the components of SES relate to various modes of participation, but we show why they matter. Discussions of the role of, in particular, education in producing participation tend to be accompanied by a paragraph of speculation as to the dynamics of that relationship. By dissecting the participatory process, we are able to specify in a way that has not been done before how the components of SES, especially education, interact with one another and enhance additional participatory factors such as interest in politics.

Our analysis indicates that unique configurations of participatory factors—and, therefore, unique participatory publics and sets of issue concerns—are relevant for voting, for forms of participation that require inputs of time, and for forms of participation that require inputs of money. In our analysis we pay close attention to the distinction between the latter two forms of activity—giving time and giving money. This distinction is of great significance for citizen involvement in politics. Over the past couple of decades, skyrocketing campaign costs and the use of computer-generated mailings to raise money for political causes have created an enhanced role for citizens as writers of checks. Contributors tend to

---

1. For discussion of the literature on citizen activity and extensive references, see Lester W. Milbrath and M. L. Goel, *Political Participation: How and Why Do People Get Involved in Politics?,* 2nd ed. (Chicago: Rand McNally College Pub. Co., 1977), especially chap. 4; M. Margaret Conway, *Political Participation in the United States,* 2nd ed. (Washington, D.C.: CQ Press, 1991), especially chap. 2; Stephen Earl Bennett and Linda L. M. Bennett, "Political Participation: Meaning and Measurement," pp. 160–162 in *Annual Review of Political Science,* ed. Samuel Long (Norwood, N.J.: Ablex Publishing, 1986); and Sidney Verba, Norman H. Nie, and Jae-on Kim, *Participation and Political Equality: A Seven-Nation Comparison* (Cambridge: Cambridge University Press, 1978).

2. See Raymond E. Wolfinger and Steven J. Rosenstone, *Who Votes?* (New Haven: Yale University Press, 1980), chap. 3.

differ in various ways from the public at large. Not only are they, as we might expect, more affluent, but they have distinctive motivations, needs, opinions, and priorities, with the consequence that a shifting balance among forms of participation has implications for what and from whom the government hears.

A NOTE ON DATA

This inquiry rests on a data set with special characteristics: not only is it probably the largest and most comprehensive cross-sectional data set on the nature and origins of the political activities of the American public, but it was designed to incorporate distinctive features that meet the particular requirements of studying participation and representation. To assess how well the activists represent the citizenry, a representative sample of the public is essential. However, ordinary representative samples contain very few of the most interesting activists—those who engage in relatively rare but important activities such as giving large donations, serving on local governing boards, or taking part in protests. Similarly, they provide few cases of activists drawn from politically relevant racial and ethnic minorities—African-Americans and Latinos—groups of particular interest in an investigation of participatory representation.

By using a unique two-stage sample of the American public, we achieve the twin goals of representativeness and sufficient cases of those who are truly active. The initial stage consisted of a brief telephone interview with a very large random sample of 15,000 members of the public. These screener interviews provided information about political activities as well as basic demographics and permitted us to select a sample that overrepresented activists and minorities for longer, in-person follow-up interviews. With appropriate weights the follow-up sample yields a representative sample that contains sufficient cases of those who engage in rare forms of activity, as well as African-Americans and Latinos.

Voluntary Activity and American Democracy

Let us consider the themes of the book more fully. To understand voluntarism is to understand something important about Americans—how they express their civic and humanitarian concerns and how they pursue their self-interest, for they can do both through voluntary activity. To understand voluntarism is also to understand something important about America. Voluntary activity is not only about individuals—what they do and why they do it. More than in most democracies, voluntary activity in America shapes the allocation of economic, social, and cultural benefits and contributes to the achievement of collective purposes.[3]

It is a cliché to remark upon the prevalence of voluntary activity in America. Large numbers of Americans contribute time, effort, and money to the accomplishment of public purposes in many arenas—in their neighborhoods, in campaigns, in charities and non-profit institutions, in the halls of government, in voluntary associations, and in churches, mosques, and synagogues. Some of this activity is political, some is non-political, and some is on the fuzzy border between the two.

Whether or not the American penchant for voluntary activity is, as is sometimes argued, a manifestation of a uniquely American character, there is no doubt that certain aspects of institutional arrangements in America facilitate voluntary participation—both political and non-political. First, American politics and society provide many arenas for voluntary engagement. The absence of a state church in conjunction with a churchgoing and religiously diverse population produces a circumstance with many and varied opportunities for religious involvement. Similarly, even if Americans are not, as they are sometimes touted to be, the most likely to join organizations, the number and range of voluntary associations in America are probably unsurpassed anywhere.[4] In the public realm, federalism and separation of powers imply a plurality of targets for political activity. As we shall see, citizens engage in many and varied activities aimed at different government offices. Moreover, in contrast to many democracies which narrowly circum-

---

3. On this general issue, see the essays in *Between States and Markets: The Voluntary Sector in Comparative Perspective,* ed. Robert Wuthnow (Princeton: Princeton University Press, 1991).

4. As we show in Chapter 2, low levels of union membership among American workers imply that overall levels of organizational membership in the United States may not be as high as in some Northern European countries.

scribe public expression that is potentially defamatory or compromising to national security, the First Amendment, as interpreted through the years by the courts, offers wide scope to political speech and organization. Constitutional protection has been extended by the courts to encompass acts other than speech—including monetary contributions.

Although the structures of American politics and society foster citizen activity, would-be activists have ample opportunity for participation outside the constraints of formally organized institutions. A declining party role in the nomination of candidates for office and the management of campaigns means multiple opportunities for electoral activity outside the framework of ordinary party structures—working in and contributing to campaigns.[5] In addition, much of the non-electoral activity we describe takes place outside formal organizational channels. This includes a vast number of individual contacts and communications with government officials as well as a large volume of informal, problem-solving activity among friends and neighbors in local communities. In short, as we shall document in this book, citizens who seek to become active have many ways to do so.

THE MANY FORMS OF VOLUNTARISM

Voluntary activity comes in many guises. Part of our intellectual project is to understand the many forms of voluntary activity and some of the analytical distinctions that can be made among them. One very basic distinction is that voluntary activity may be political or non-political. In this book we concentrate on the former. However, we also deal extensively with the latter both because non-political voluntarism provides a useful foil illuminating the salient characteristics of political participation and because involvement in the non-political spheres of American voluntary activity can enrich the stockpile of resources relevant to political action. In the next chapter, we discriminate more fully between the two and indicate the multiple ways in which political and non-political activity intersect. At this point it is sufficient to say

---

5. Indeed, the Supreme Court has held in *Buckley v. Valeo* (1976) that direct spending on behalf of candidates is considered an exercise of First Amendment freedoms and is, thus, exempt from the constraints of campaign finance laws.

that political participation is activity that is intended to or has the consequence of affecting, either directly or indirectly, government action.

Political voluntary activity can, in turn, take many forms. The vote has, understandably, assumed a primacy in studies of citizen participation in politics, with the result that, thanks to voting statistics and election surveys, it is the mode of participation about which we have the most information. Voting is the most common and, in a profound sense, the most basic citizen act. Although a single ballot has little impact, collectively votes provide the ultimate weapon that allows members of the public to determine who shall hold office and to hold governing officials accountable. Indeed, it is difficult to imagine a democracy in which voting would play no part. However, we consider a wide range of activities beyond the vote, activities that vary along several relevant dimensions: work in election campaigns, contributions to campaigns and other political causes, informal activity in local communities, contacts with public officials, affiliation with political organizations, attendance at demonstrations or protests, and service on local governing bodies such as school or zoning boards.

Forms of political participation also vary in the extent to which activity can be multiplied. At one extreme is the vote, the one activity for which there is mandated equality—each citizen getting one, and only one, for each election. At the opposite extreme is making campaign contributions, which is, ironically, the only other mode of participation subject to legal limitations on the volume of activity. Notwithstanding these limitations, financial giving varies more substantially in terms of quantity than any other form of participatory input: that is, the number of dollars contributed to campaigns and other political causes can vary more substantially than the number of protests attended, letters dispatched to public officials, or hours devoted to electoral campaigns. The ability to inflate the volume of political contributions is one of the principal reasons for our distinguishing modes of political involvement in which the currency is time and effort from those in which the currency is dollars.

Finally, participatory acts vary in their capacity to convey detailed messages to policymakers. Once again, the limiting case is the vote, which is capable of communicating little in the way of precise instructions. From the electoral outcome alone, the winning candidate cannot discriminate which of dozens of factors, ranging from the position taken on a particular issue to the inept campaign run by the opposition to dissatisfaction with the performance of the incumbent party, was responsible for the electoral victory. In contrast to the vote are what we call "information-rich" acts, participatory acts such as contacts with public officials that permit explicit statements of concerns or preferences.

Participation, Equality, and Representation

Democracy rests on the notion of the equal worth of each citizen. The needs and preferences of no individual should rank higher than those of any other.[6] This principle undergirds the concept of one person, one vote as well as its corollary, equality of political voice among individuals. On the presumption that those who are excluded from participation will be unable to protect their own interests and, thus, will receive less favorable treatment from the government, any system that denies equal participatory rights violates a fundamental principle of democracy.[7]

---

6. According to Robert Dahl, a crucial assumption for democracy is that "the claims of a significant number of members as to the rules, policies, etc., to be adopted by binding decisions are valid and equally valid, taken all around, and that no member's claims are, taken all around, superior or overriding in relation to this set of members" ("Procedural Democracy," in *Philosophy, Politics and Society,* 5th Series, ed. Peter Laslett and James Fishkin [New Haven: Yale University Press, 1979], p. 100). In his thorough analysis of the meaning of political equality, Charles Beitz (*Political Equality: An Essay in Democratic Theory* [Princeton: Princeton University Press, 1989], pp. 4–5) points out that this principle is asserted by most democratic theorists as "so obvious a truth as not to require systematic defense" and cites the formulation of this idea in roughly these terms in the works of such democratic theorists as Carole Pateman, Jane Mansbridge, John Rawls, and Robert Dahl. However, Beitz finds this approach overly simple and provides a deeper philosophical account and justification for political equality. For another analysis of the weaknesses in a simple assumption of intrinsic equality, see Robert A. Dahl, *Democracy and Its Critics* (New Haven: Yale University Press, 1989), pp. 86–88. Nonetheless, echoing Churchill's famous aphorism about democracy, Dahl argues (p. 86) that, although the principle has several weaknesses and can be rejected without self-contradiction, it is a sounder principle than its opposite. "[T]o reject it is to assert, in effect, that some people ought to be regarded and treated as *intrinsically* privileged . . . To justify such a claim is a formidable task that no one, to my knowledge, has accomplished."

7. It is useful to note the reciprocity between the principle of equal worth and the principle of equal rights to participate. The former justifies the latter. However, citizenship

Throughout history, most polities—including the United States—have not adhered, even in rhetoric, to principles of political equality. In most modern democracies, however, overt barriers to universal political rights have fallen. And, at least since the voting rights reforms of the 1960s, political rights have been universalized in the United States. With relatively insignificant exceptions, all adult citizens have the full complement of political rights. Equality in political rights does not, however, create substantive equality in their effective use. Individuals and groups differ significantly in terms of whether they take part at all and, if so, how much and in what ways. Since public officials are likely to be differentially responsive to citizens who exercise their voice—that is, make their wishes known by participating in politics—the fact that disparities in political involvement are so substantial and that so many citizens are not active at all potentially compromises democracy.

In addition, unequal participation has consequences for what is communicated to the government. The propensity to take part is not randomly distributed across politically relevant categories. As we shall show, disparities in political activity instead parallel the fault lines of significant political and social division in America. Thus, the voices that speak loudly articulate a different set of messages about the state of the public, its needs, and its preferences from those that would be sent by those who are inactive. Were everyone equally active, or were activists drawn at random from across the population, an unbiased set of communications would emerge. What this means is that, even in the absence of legal barriers to political rights on the basis of property, race, or sex, participatory inequalities have implications for politics.

Our concern with participatory equality in the name of equal protection of interests represents a somewhat different emphasis from that traditionally adopted in the literature on participatory

---

rights also validate the intrinsic worth of those who possess them. Denial of equal political rights to a category of citizens is an implicit assertion that they and their interests are less worthy of consideration. See Jane J. Mansbridge, "The Limits of Friendship," in *NOMOS XVI: Participation in Politics,* ed. J. Roland Pennock and John Chapman (New York: Lieber-Atherton, 1975), pp. 248–251.

democracy.[8] Participation can have many consequences: among them, promoting the development of individual capacities, building community, and legitimating the regime. Although we shall refer to these themes, they are lesser concerns. Our principal focus is on the role of participation in communicating information about citizen preferences and needs to policymakers and creating pressure on them to heed what they hear.

PARTICIPATORY ACTS AND PARTICIPATORY EQUALITY

If political equality is hard to achieve, it is almost as hard to define. Citizens have complex preferences across a myriad of issues; they hold these preferences with varying degrees of intensity; and they can express these preferences by engaging in any of a variety of participatory acts. How, then, do we recognize participatory equality?

All democracies use elections as a great simplifying mechanism for dealing with the problem of political equality. Elections constitute a scheduled opportunity to register citizen preferences. Elections provide citizens, who have many different concerns on their minds, with a limited number of choices and thereby produce a decisive outcome from a complexity of voices. In addition, because each voter casts a single ballot and because each vote has equal weight when the results are tallied, elections are an equalizing device. Indeed, political equality is often defined in terms of voting, and much of the literature equates the notion of one person, one vote with political equality.[9]

In spite of the unambiguous capacities of the electoral mechanism to guarantee some measure of equality among citizens, even elections pose dilemmas for political equality. Procedural conflicts over enfranchisement, districting, and the rules governing the elec-

---

8. See, for instance, Carole Pateman, *Participation and Democratic Theory* (Cambridge: Cambridge University Press, 1970); and Benjamin R. Barber, *Strong Democracy: Participatory Politics for a New Age* (Berkeley: University of California Press, 1984).

9. In his discussion of the criteria for political equality in electoral systems, Jonathan W. Still points out that many of the basic writings in democratic theory consider equality to be simply that each person has one vote, and the vote is equally weighted; he cites a number of authors—among them Robert Dahl and Charles E. Lindblom, Giovanni Sartori, Austin Ranney and Wilmoore Kendall, and Carole Pateman—as taking essentially this position. "Political Equality and Election Systems," *Ethics* 91 (1981): 375–394.

toral system make clear that even in the simplified world of voting, the equal power of each voter is uncertain. Furthermore, the effect of non-voting on the nature and equality of the expression of citizen preferences remains an open issue.[10]

Whatever the complexities of understanding what political equality would look like with respect to voting, however, matters become much more complicated when we move beyond voting to the multiple other forms of citizen participation. No longer is each citizen given a single, anonymous unit of input that counts equally. Instead, all the other modes of activity contain the possibility for variation in the amount of input: the campaign worker can devote many or few hours to the campaign; the protester can attend several demonstrations or a single one; the contributor can write a big check or a small one; and so on. Furthermore, the metrics differ. How do we compare the weight of participatory input measured in letters to that measured in hours or in dollars? In addition, in contrast to votes, the units of participatory input are not necessarily counted equally. A letter that is thoughtful and carefully reasoned may have a greater effect than a pre-printed postcard signed by an indifferent organization member. Moreover, unlike votes, other forms of participation are not anonymous. When public officials interpret what they hear, it matters who is speaking. For example, a phone call from the CEO of a major employer in the district may carry considerably more weight than one from an unknown constituent.

Finally, while votes, on their own, communicate little information about the concerns and priorities of the voter, many other kinds of participation arrive with specific issue concerns attached. Participants may be active on one issue or several, but certainly not the entire range of potential policy matters. And those who do express themselves on a specific issue are more likely to care deeply about it. Taken together, these factors—the variation in

---

10. On the question of whether non-voting makes a difference in interpreting the consequences of elections see, for example, Wolfinger and Rosenstone, *Who Votes?*; Stephen Earl Bennett and David Resnick, "The Implications of Non-Voting for Democracy in the United States," *American Journal of Political Science* 34 (1990): 771–802; Michael M. Gant and William S. Lyons, "Democratic Theory, Nonvoting, and Public Policy: The 1972–1988 Presidential Elections," *American Politics Quarterly* 21 (1993): 185–205.

both the volume of participation and the units in which it is measured, the fact that participatory inputs are not necessarily counted equally and are associated with the politically relevant attributes, and even the names, of activists, the multiplicity of issues that are the subject of participation, and differences in intensity of preferences among activists and between activists and non-activists—all imply that, with respect to any particular issue, it is very difficult to specify what political equality would look like. This poses the challenge for our book. We shall find a good deal of political inequality, using almost any criterion. Our goal is not to achieve some overall encompassing evaluation of the degree of inequality, but rather to show where and when it appears.

REPRESENTING WHAT?

In providing a rationale for participatory equality, we have argued that, because political participation is the mechanism by which citizens communicate concerns to public officials and attempt to control what they do, inequalities in activity are likely to be associated with inequalities in governmental responsiveness. In any real polity, it is clearly unrealistic to expect even to approximate the ideal of participatory equality. Therefore, it becomes critical to investigate whether activists are representative of inactive citizens with respect to their *politically relevant characteristics,* for, to the extent that participatory inequalities are random across citizens, they are less threatening to norms of democratic equality.

We understand politically relevant characteristics quite broadly to include any attribute of an individual that would be germane to public policy or other government action. Put another way, any characteristic of a participant is politically relevant if it would be deemed noteworthy by a public official at whom activity is targeted. Were we to list politically relevant characteristics, the list would be neither short nor fixed. As the content of political conflict is altered over time and as issues come and go, what constitutes a politically relevant characteristic changes as well. The literature on participation tends to focus on the representation of policy preferences and, sometimes, to argue that if policy preferences are represented accurately by participants, demographic differences between activists and inactives are irrelevant. We do consider the representation of policy preferences. However, when we treat these issues at length in Chapter 4, we argue that what matters is not simply what participants think but who they are; consequently, demographic distinctions are potentially important—especially when demography hews to the fault lines of political cleavage in America. Moreover, we look beyond policy preferences and demography in several ways. In comparing those who take part with those who do not, we consider their actual circumstances, their economic needs, and their receipt of various forms of government benefits. In addition, we consider their participatory agendas—the issue concerns that animate political activity and, thus, determine what the government hears.

PARTICIPATORY DISTORTION

We combine concerns with the form of participation and the politically relevant characteristics of activists in our basic measure of political *inequality: participatory distortion. Participatory distortion exists when any group of activists—such as protesters, voters, or contributors—is unrepresentative of the public with respect to some politically relevant characteristic: for example, preferences on issues, needs for government assistance, demographic attributes, or participatory priorities. As we shall see, the extent to which participant publics differ from the citizenry at large varies with the mode of activity as well as the characteristic being represented.

Explaining Participation

The meaning of participatory inequalities depends in part upon their source. In order to analyze the processes by which citizens come to be politically active—and, thus, to account for the ways in which participants represent, or fail to represent, the public at large—we develop an explanatory model of political activity that rests on three factors. In thinking about why some people are active while others are not, we find it helpful to invert the usual question and to ask instead why people do *not* take part in politics. Three answers immediately suggest themselves: because they can't; because they don't want to; or because nobody asked.

"They can't" suggests a paucity of necessary *resources*—time to take part, money to contribute to campaigns and other political causes, and skills to use time and money effectively.

"They don't want to" focuses attention on the absence of political *engagement*—little interest in politics or little concern with public issues, a belief that activity can make little or no difference, little or no knowledge about the political process, or other priorities.

"Nobody asked" implies isolation from the networks of *recruitment* through which citizens are mobilized to politics.

We give serious attention to all three factors in our analysis. We find that they are all helpful in predicting participation: both access to resources, or the capacity to take part, and political engagement, or the motivation to take part, seem necessary for activity; recruitment, or requests for activity, seems to act as a catalyst for participation among those with the wherewithal and desire to become active. In addition, we demonstrate that different configurations of participatory factors are significant for different forms of activity. Various modes of participation demand particular mixes of resources and engagement or particular kinds of resources. We also show that these participatory factors are not independent of one another. Instead, they interact in complex ways. In fact, the initial conditions that lead to the accretion of political resources—in particular, well-educated parents and a high level of educational attainment—also lead to psychological engagement with politics and to being in a position such that requests for political activity are likely.

Of the three factors, we place special emphasis on resources such as money, time, and civic skills. As we show, resources are earlier in the causal chain that leads to political activity and are less likely than either psychological engagement in politics or requests for political activity to be the result, rather than the cause, of activity. Thus, focusing on resources provides a powerful and theoretically satisfying explanation of disparities across individuals and groups in the extent to which they take part in political life. And since resources are differentially available to groups with differing needs and preferences, paying attention to resources provides an important link to our concern with political equality.

THE ROLE OF INSTITUTIONS

An important part of our intellectual project is to trace the origins of the three participatory factors in non-political experiences and commitments. As we show, the institutions with which individuals are associated as they move through life—the families into which they are born, the schools they attend, the families they form as adults, the jobs they take, and the non-political organizations and religious institutions with which they become affiliated—produce the factors that foster participation. In this way, our analysis links political life to social life.

It is well known that social institutions play a major role in stimulating citizens to take part in politics by cultivating psychological engagement in politics and by serving as the locus of recruitment to activity. Any of these settings can serve as the site for exposure to political cues—for example, an argument about politics around the dinner table, a sermon on a public issue at church, a political discussion with a fellow worker or organization member. Similarly, requests for political participation often arise in these settings from relatives or acquaintances made in school, in organizations or church, or on the job. Furthermore, institutions themselves frequently take the initiative: solicitations for political activity of a somewhat more formal nature may arise from supervisors at work, from church leaders or clergy, or from organization officers or staff. We explore these requests, considering who gets asked, who does the asking, and whether the request is met with assent. We discover that activity frequently takes place in the context of rich interpersonal networks, a finding that seems at odds with much that we know about contemporary politics. In an era in which so many political communications are delivered electronically, it nonetheless seems that personal connections among acquaintances, friends, and relatives—often mediated through mutual institutional affiliations—are still crucial for political recruitment.

Involvement in these institutions facilitates political participation not only by providing exposure to political cues and recruitment networks but in another way as well, one that has received less attention from scholars. We show how ordinary and routine activity on the job, at church, or in an organization, activity that has nothing to do with politics or public issues, can develop organizational and communications skills that are relevant for politics and thus can facilitate political activity. Organizing a series of meetings at which a new personnel policy is introduced to employees, chairing a large charity benefit, or setting up a food pantry at church are activities that are not in and of themselves political. Yet, they foster the development of skills that can be transferred to politics.

In our analysis we highlight the role of an institution that has been receiving increasing recognition from students of American politics: the church.[11] Compared with citizens in other countries, Americans are more likely to be affiliated with a religious institution, to attend services, and to take part in educational, charitable, or social activities in conjunction with their churches.[12] American churches have long been involved in politics and political movements. The role of southern Black churches on behalf of civil rights and the role of White fundamentalist Protestant churches on behalf of conservative causes are two recent cases in point. We explore this well-known aspect of political mobilization through religious institutions but add another consideration as well: the importance of churches as places where citizens can learn civic skills.

We pay special attention to the role of religious institutions in enhancing political participation for another reason. In many respects, the effects of institutions in stimulating political involvement serve to reinforce initial advantage. As we shall see, education plays an important role in this process of resource accumulation: not only is education itself a resource for politics, but those with high levels of educational attainment are likely to be slotted into the kinds of prestigious and lucrative jobs and organizational affiliations that provide further political resources. Only religious institutions provide a counterbalance to this cumulative resource process. They play an unusual role in the American participatory system by providing opportunities for the development of civic skills to those who would otherwise be resource-poor. It is com-

---

11. For a representative sampling of this growing literature, see David C. Leege and Lyman A. Kellstedt, *Rediscovering the Religious Factor in American Politics* (Armonk, N.Y.: M. E. Sharpe, 1993).

12. See the data and references in Chapters 3, 10, and 12 below, as well as Leege and Kellstedt, *Rediscovering the Religious Factor in American Politics*, chaps. 1, 2, 12, and 14.

monplace to ascribe the special character of American politics to the weakness of unions and the absence of class-based political parties that can mobilize the disadvantaged—in particular, the working class—to political activity.[13] Another way that American society is exceptional is in how often Americans go to church—with the result that the mobilizing function often performed elsewhere by unions and labor or social democratic parties is more likely to be performed by religious institutions. Because this substitutes a relatively conservative set of institutions for what are elsewhere institutions of the left, this distinctively American pattern has implications not only for who is active, but also for what the government hears.

BEYOND SES

The analysis of the origins of participatory factors and their consequences for various kinds of participation will take us well beyond the standard SES model of political activity to a richer understanding of how socioeconomic position leads to political activity. As we discuss in Chapter 9, the standard SES model is empirically powerful: study after study in the United States and elsewhere confirms that those who are advantaged in socioeconomic terms—who have higher levels of education, income, and occupation—are more likely to be politically active. However, the SES model is weaker theoretically. The Civic Voluntarism Model provides a richer theoretical interpretation of the SES model by specifying in detail how socioeconomic position is linked to political activity. Our analysis permits us to distinguish among the several components of socioeconomic status. A pioneering analysis has demonstrated that, with respect to voting, what really matters among the constituents of SES is educational attainment.[14] When we consider multiple forms of political activity, however, we discover a more complex circumstance: although education has premier position among the socioeconomic determinants of activity, the relative importance of education, income, and occupation varies across modes of participation.

---

13. See Chapter 13 for discussion and references.
14. Wolfinger and Rosenstone, *Who Votes?*, chap. 3.

The Civic Voluntarism Model also allows us to trace political activity from generation to generation. We will isolate several distinct paths from the family of origin to political activity. One effect comes through direct politicization. Early exposure to political stimuli—by virtue of having parents who are politically active in politics or who discuss politics at home—inculcates interest in politics later in life. Similarly, those whose parents were religious are more likely to attend church as adults and, thus, to acquire the civic skills associated with church activity.

The main path across the generations is socioeconomic, however. Our analysis demonstrates how parental educational level affects the respondent's educational attainment which, in turn, affects almost every other participatory factor—for example, interest in politics, family income, and the occupational and organizational commitments that provide opportunities for political recruitment and the practice of civic skills. In the process we gain greater understanding of how the components of SES relate to one another. Moreover, we see that what we just described for explanatory purposes as three distinct sets of participatory factors are, in fact, interwoven: initial advantages with respect to resources are associated with psychological engagement in politics and with placement in networks of political recruitment. In short, the Civic Voluntarism Model illumines the inner workings of the SES model: we have long known that high levels of SES produce political participation; our model provides a deeper understanding of how and why.

It should be clear by now that, in encompassing resources, engagement, and recruitment, the Civic Voluntarism Model accommodates a rich array of explanatory factors. It is not, however, exhaustive. Our analysis does not include all aspects of the political system that have been found to be significant for political participation: for example, the correspondence between public officials and constituency in terms of race or ethnicity;[15] the role

---

15. See, for example, Lawrence Bobo and Franklin D. Gilliam, Jr., "Race, Socio-Political Participation, and Black Empowerment," *American Political Science Review* 84 (1990): 377–393.

of legal institutions and requirements such as registration and voting laws;[16] and the strategic calculations of political elites.[17]

We do, however, expand our model to take into account a significant feature of American politics not captured by our analysis of the institutional basis of political activity: the intensity of response to a particular political issue. Although we cannot account for the process whereby issues that arouse strong feelings get on the political agenda, we do assess the role of issue commitments in bringing people into politics. We find that, apart from other participatory factors, strong views on the subject of abortion—the issue most likely to elicit intense opinions during the period of our research—produce higher levels of political activity.

The Rational Activist

Over the past decades social scientists have questioned whether it is rational to take part in most forms of civic activity. The problem of the rationality of participation, which has been raised in particular with reference to voting and to organizational membership, is that since the probability is extremely low that a single vote will make any difference in the outcome of an election, or that one person's efforts on behalf of a widely shared goal will contribute appreciably to securing that goal, the rational individual will not waste resources by bearing the costs of taking part but will instead take a free ride on the efforts of others. No study trying to explain voluntary civic activity can avoid confronting the question of the

---

16. Wolfinger and Rosenstone, *Who Votes?*; and G. Bingham Powell, "American Voter Turnout in Comparative Perspective," *American Political Science Review* 80 (1986): 17–43.

17. See Steven J. Rosenstone and John Mark Hansen, *Mobilization, Participation, and Democracy in America* (New York: Macmillan, 1993). Their model—which we consider complementary to the model presented here—uses longitudinal data to trace the rise and fall of participation as it relates to changing political factors, among them changing issue salience and the strategic calculations of elites. Our model probes more deeply into the circumstances that determine which citizens will be brought into politics at a particular time. The two approaches differ in no small part because of the data bases used. Rosenstone and Hansen have assembled an impressive longitudinal data base encompassing many time points but relatively few variables at any one point. We have much richer information about respondents for only a single time point.

rationality of political participation. Our concern with rationality runs throughout this book; we deal with it at some length in Chapters 7 and 9.

Our approach has several components. For one thing, we consider the rationality of participation from the perspective of the many ways in which citizens can be active. Because they have tended to focus primarily on only two forms of activity, voting and organizational membership, analyses of the rationality of participation may have given us a distorted picture. Voting is the least demanding form of political activity. In fact, the costs of voting are sufficiently low that a rational calculus of costs and benefits may not be necessary. In contrast, organizational membership exacts more in the way of resources. However, unlike many other forms of participation, organizational involvement may be especially rich in the sorts of selective benefits—that is, rewards available to activists and only to activists—that theorists of rational action assert must accompany any political participation on behalf of a widely shared objective. When we look across a variety of forms of activity we find that the logic of participation looks different from the perspective of different political acts.

Focusing on the benefit side of the calculation, we find that the problem of the rationality of participation may be exaggerated. We asked our respondents the reasons for their participation. This is not an easy question to pose, but, as we hope to demonstrate, there is much to learn from the answers. Our results will show that citizens offer many reasons for their political activity. Some invoke the kinds of narrow selective material benefits emphasized by the proponents of the narrow version of the rational actor perspective. A striking number mentioned selective social benefits—for example, enjoying the other people involved—which are compatible with this perspective but receive less attention in the literature. Many more activists, however, describe their participation as guided by a desire to influence public policy, a motive that is considered self-delusive and irrational by theorists of rational action. And many participants mention satisfying a sense of civic duty or seeking to do their share. Civic-minded motivations are technically compatible with a rational actor approach to political participation. From that perspective, all that matters is that the benefit be selective: pursuit of a lucrative city contract for the firm or a sense of satisfaction at having helped to make the community a better place to live do equally well to explain participation. However, we believe that the mix of gratifications pursued through political activity makes a difference. It matters for the political life of the community whether citizens seek self-interested material goals rather than what are, from the point of view of rational actor theory, equally self-interested civic goals.

The standard approach to the problem of rational participation is to search for benefits presumed to be sufficient to justify bearing the costs of activity. Costs figure in the discussion only as a reason for inactivity since the benefits seem insufficient to justify any costs. We turn this logic on its head. Because we find that people can identify many benefits from participation, we pay attention to the cost side of the cost-benefit calculus, considering what is required in the way of time, energy, or money for various participatory acts. By so doing, we are able to give somewhat greater empirical content to this approach and, thus, to understand the implications of the costs of activity for who is likely to be active in what ways.

The Uniqueness of the Vote

A recurrent theme in our discussion so far—and throughout the analysis that follows—is the uniqueness of the vote as a political act. Because casting a ballot is, by far, the most common act of citizenship in any democracy and because electoral returns are decisive in determining who shall govern, political scientists appropriately devote a great deal of attention to the vote.

As should be clear by now, however, it is incomplete and misleading to understand citizen participation solely through the vote. As we move through our analysis we shall see that, with respect to every single aspect of participation we scrutinize, voting is fundamentally different from other acts. Voting is, for example, distinctive in its properties as a political act. In contrast to other forms of participation which can be multiplied in volume and which are capable of communicating detailed messages about citizen concerns, the vote is the single mode of participation for which the maximum input is equalized across actors, and it is a singularly blunt instrument for the communication of information. In addition, the unambiguous decline in electoral turnout is not matched by decreases in all other forms of activity. Moreover, not only is voting the most common form of activity, but voters are, of all activist publics, the most representative of the citizenry at large. Furthermore, the origins of voting are different. Compared with those who engage in various other political acts, voters report a different mix of gratifications and a different bundle of issue concerns as being behind their activity. Finally, the configuration of participatory factors—that is, the mix of resources and motivations—required for voting is unique. To repeat, on every dimension along which we consider participatory acts, voting is *sui generis*. For this reason, it is a mistake to generalize from our extensive knowledge about voting to all forms of participation.

Participation, Political Science, and American Politics in the 1990s

There is an old dispute as to whether political science ought to be about real places and people or about abstractions and variables. Political science was once largely about the former. It was about specific countries, specific people, and specific events: a particular election in Japan and the campaign, candidates, and issues associated with it; or the emergence of a particular policy in France and the attendant processes of negotiation, contending interests, and winners and losers. This kind of analysis was located in a particular place and a particular time. Contemporary social science is less and less likely to partake of this style. Analytic categories and the search for abstract principles substitute for proper names and understanding of the uniqueness of particular events; sophisticated statistical models substitute for detailed narrative about who did what to whom.

As is probably obvious by now, this book is in the contemporary mold. We describe modes of participation rather than any particular protest or political campaign; we are concerned with resources such as money or skills, not about any particular campaign contribution or especially clever tactic that was successful in eliciting a concession from a particular official; we develop a model of the way in which people come to be politically active rather than describing any particular registration drive or citizen mobilization. Indeed, we would argue that we have provided a road map for the understanding of political participation in any democracy. Of course, one would need to tailor the content of the model to the polity to which it was being exported: the politicizing role played by American churches would be assumed by other institutions, perhaps unions and other employees' organizations, in Denmark; participation based on political cash would assume distinctive forms in Italy; and so on. Nonetheless, we aspire to analysis of general significance.

Still, the abstract style of our analysis should not obscure that it is, crucially, about the substance of American politics. Our concern with the nature, sources, and consequences of disparities in political activity across politically significant groups in America forces us to pay attention to the fundamental cleavages and issues of American politics. In delineating the extent to which participant publics are representative of American citizens we concentrate on "politically relevant characteristics," that is, attributes that are germane to politics and political contention. We focus on groups with divergent claims on the government, with different political needs and preferences, groups arranged around some of the enduring fault lines of political conflict in America. To be specific, we consider the participatory profiles and agendas of groups defined by their economic position, race and ethnicity, gender, and religion—comparing the poor and the affluent, African-Americans, Latinos, and Anglo-Whites, women and men, and those with varying religious commitments. In so doing we assess the extent to which the government hears a distorted set of messages about such basic issues as government responsibility for the poor or for minorities, as well as social issues such as abortion.

Our work touches on themes in contemporary American politics in another way as well. We conducted our study just after the close of the 1980s, a decade often characterized as dominated by self-interest and greed and by public cynicism toward the major institutions of American life, especially government.[18] Our findings are, in part, at variance with this stereotype of the era. We find a great deal of voluntary participation, both political and non-political. Moreover, it appears that the decline in voter turnout has not been matched by erosion in all other forms of political activity. Furthermore, although citizens seem to view politicians as selfish, they do not view their own political engagements from such a perspective. As we shall show, citizens sometimes see their own activity as animated by narrow, self-interested concerns. More often, however, they describe it, in ways that are convincing, as aimed at the common good. Voluntary activity in America is—more often than popular descriptions or social theory might lead us to believe—about civic matters.

Activity, Resources, and Equal Representation

As well as describing and explaining political participation, this book also provides a framework for judging the fairness of participation. One of the enduring puzzles of normative democratic theory is how we are to understand and evaluate political inactivity, especially when there are differences in participation across groups with conflicting political needs and preferences. While the consequences of disparities in participation for governmental responsiveness may have nothing to do with their origins, our evaluation of participatory inequalities may depend on the reason for inactivity—in particular, whether inactivity reflects a lack of motivation or a lack of resources.[19]

If some citizens do not participate because they freely choose not to be active—because they do not care about politics, have no taste for political life and prefer to devote their spare time to other pursuits, place the claims of religion, family, or work above poli-

---

18. See, for instance, Seymour Martin Lipset and William Schneider, *The Confidence Gap: Business, Labor and Government in the Public Mind* (Baltimore: Johns Hopkins University Press, 1987), and E. J. Dionne, Jr., *Why Americans Hate Politics* (New York: Simon and Schuster, 1991).

19. On these themes, see Ronald Rogowski, "Representation in Political Theory and in Law," *Ethics* 91 (1981): 396–398.

tics, think that it would make no difference in the outcome if they did take part, or expect that others will take up the cudgel on their behalf—then participatory inequalities do not compromise democracy.[20] The American people, however, do not subscribe to this view. It is well known that their commitment to equality in the economic domain extends only to unequivocal support for equality of opportunity and entails unequivocal rejection of equality of results. When it comes to politics, however, Americans consistently express more egalitarian views, expecting not only equal rights but equal governmental responsiveness to all citizens.[21] In short, whatever the views of the political philosophers, the American political culture bears an unmistakable egalitarian strain.

However, if differential rates of political activity reflect, not differential motivations, but differential resources, there is more reason for concern. That is, if all are free to get involved politically, but the failure of some individuals—or some kinds of individuals—to become active is the result of unequal stockpiles of the resources necessary for participation, then any resulting unevenness of governmental response is potentially unfair.[22] Our analysis

---

20. Indeed, on the basis of the lesser capacities of ordinary citizens, their lack of interest in politics, or the weakness of their commitment to the norms of democracy, some observers of democracy have argued either explicitly or implicitly that lack of participation by ordinary citizens (or disproportionate participation by elites) may have beneficial consequences for politics. For different versions of this argument, see Joseph A. Schumpeter, *Capitalism, Socialism, and Democracy* (New York and London: Harper and Brothers, 1942), especially chap. 22; Bernard R. Berelson, Paul F. Lazarsfeld, and William N. McPhee, *Voting: A Study of Opinion Formation in a Presidential Campaign* (Chicago: University of Chicago Press, 1954), chap. 14; Walter Lippmann, *Public Opinion* (New York: Free Press, 1965); Samuel Stouffer, *Communism, Conformity, and Civil Liberties* (New York: John Wiley, 1966).

21. See, for example, Jennifer L. Hochschild, *What's Fair? American Beliefs about Distributive Justice* (Cambridge, Mass.: Harvard University Press, 1981), especially chap. 6; Herbert McClosky and John Zaller, *The American Ethos: Public Attitudes Toward Capitalism and Democracy* (Cambridge, Mass.: Harvard University Press, 1984), especially chap. 3; and Sidney Verba and Gary Orren, *Equality in America: The View from the Top* (Cambridge, Mass.: Harvard University Press, 1985), chaps. 1, 8, 9. Philosophical justification for this position is given in Michael Walzer, *Spheres of Justice: A Defense of Pluralism and Equality* (New York: Basic Books, 1983).

22. Much may depend on the nature of the alternative preference. One individual decides not to attend a community meeting because he does not want to miss a favorite television program; another misses the meeting because she does not want to give up time from work which is needed to earn a living. Though each involves a tradeoff, the two situations are

shows that disparities in participation do not arise solely because some people have the inclination to be active and others do not. Instead, participatory inequalities derive not only from differences in motivations but also from differences in access to the resources of time, money, and skills that facilitate activity. In this case, inequalities in participation pose a potential challenge to democracy.

In our assessment of the relative importance of resources and motivations in inspiring political participation, we find that, of the various forms of activity, the one for which resources matter most and motivations matter least is making contributions to political campaigns and causes. What is more, of the several political resources that facilitate political activity, only one—family income—affects political donations. Variables that prove important for other kinds of activity—educational attainment, civic skills, political interest or information—are nearly irrelevant when it comes to political giving. Our data also demonstrate that money is the political resource most unevenly distributed across citizens, especially in comparison to time. Moreover, making contributions is the form of activity for which the volume of activity can vary most substantially. This configuration of circumstances suggests that, in comparison to modes of participation based on giving time, modes of participation based on giving money are especially worrisome from the perspective of political equality.

The nature of the dilemma can be highlighted by referring to the popular debate about campaign giving. In discussing the abuses of the current system of campaign finance, advocates of reform in the public, the media, and citizens' groups (though not necessarily scholars, even reform-minded ones) tend to stress three themes:

---

substantially different: the resource constraint implied in the latter is clearly more serious. See on this, Beitz, *Political Equality,* p. 109. In addition, even cases in which the lack of activity appears to reflect a lack of motivation might require closer scrutiny of the source of the lack of motivation. Citizen preference to be active in politics or to engage in some other activity is itself the result of social processes and social learning. Such a choice might be based on experience with unresponsive officials. Or it might be based on socialization experiences that systematically discourage the participation of some groups. The choice to stay out of politics may be based on experiences of having been *kept out* of effective politics or having been told that one could not or should not be active. In such a situation, the lack of motivation might be more serious.

1. Even with existing limits, the system is awash with money; that is, the process is too expensive.
2. Money buys elections; that is, the candidate who is able to raise the largest war chest will inevitably win the election.
3. Money buys public officials; that is, winners will adjust their comportment in office to conform to the wishes of the big givers who pay the bills.

The latter two of these concerns, though differing in substance, partake of the normative concern we have been discussing, the extent to which those who choose to, and are able to, make generous donations enhance their influence over political outcomes, thus compromising the norm of political equality in a democracy.

The special problems raised by money as a resource for political action become apparent if we apply the logic above to campaign work instead of to campaign giving:

1. In a system in which there are no limits on the amount of time that individuals can devote to campaigning, we are wasting too much precious leisure time on political campaigns.
2. Campaign work buys elections; that is, the candidate who can field the most, and the most active and effective, campaign volunteers will inevitably win the election.
3. Campaign work buys public officials; that is, winners will adjust their comportment in office to conform to the wishes of the volunteers who made the campaign run.

Why does the second set of concerns sound so much different—and so much less serious—than the first? Put another way, why would the American public be more comfortable with the fact that only a few people spend a lot of time as campaign volunteers, while most spend very little time or none at all, than with the fact that some give a lot of money while others give little or none? As we said before, the challenge to democratic equality is not as serious if those who are not active abstain voluntarily and choose freely to put their eggs in another basket. If, however, those who are inactive cannot take part—because they lack the means or face intimidation or other barriers, rather than because they do not want to—then participatory inequalities constitute a more serious affront to democratic norms.

Does Participation Matter?

Political scientists sometimes distinguish between political inputs, which emanate from the public, and political outputs, which are the policies produced by the government. Our book deepens and enriches what we know about inputs—elaborating their origins and content. However, detailed analysis of citizen inputs—whether votes, messages, efforts, or dollars—would hardly be worth the effort if they did not have an appreciable effect on the outputs. Perhaps governing officials do not need to consider participatory inputs because they get all the information they need from public opinion surveys, from the media, or from their own efforts to gauge public preferences. Or perhaps they act as trustees and do not deem it necessary to pay attention to what they hear.

To demonstrate that policymakers are responsive to what they hear from citizens is well beyond the scope of this volume and demands a different research strategy from what is required for investigating the nature and sources of citizen inputs. Nonetheless, a vast literature in political science—including, for example, studies of congressional representation, interest groups, and the politics of particular policies—indicates that, while policymakers are not necessarily equally sensitive to all constituents, they are sensitive to citizen inputs.[23] Moreover, commentaries by journalists and other observers of politics at all levels are predicated on the notion

---

23. Systematic studies that link input to output are both difficult and rare. Examples include Kim Quaile Hill and Jan E. Leighley, "The Policy Consequences of Class Bias in State Electorates," *American Journal of Political Science* 36 (1992): 351–363; and Walter Mebane, "Fiscal Constraints and Electoral Manipulation in American Social Welfare," *American Political Science Review* 88 (1994): 77–95. Hill and Leighley use Census data to show a relationship between the turnout rate of the poor and the spending by a state for welfare. Mebane shows that given a choice, an incumbent administration will, in times of fiscal constraint, favor tax relief coupled with a cut in benefits, a policy that falls most heavily on the poor.

that public officials, especially elected officials, monitor and care about the views and responses of citizens. For example, the success of the elderly in protecting their government benefits in an era of belt-tightening is frequently attributed to the effectiveness of the American Association of Retired Persons and to high rates of participation, especially electoral turnout, among senior citizens. Their activity is contrasted with the political quiescence of the poor, a group whose government benefits have fared less well during the same period. Another example would be the fundamental changes that have followed in the wake of the civil rights movement and the enfranchisement of African-Americans in the South.[24]

The Citizen Participation Study

Our data come from a large-scale, two-stage survey of the voluntary activity of the American public. Several unusual aspects of this study make it especially well suited for investigating the questions we have posed. First, the study focuses on voluntary activity not simply in politics but also in churches and organizations. In addition, we construed political participation quite broadly. We inquired about voting and other forms of electoral activity such as working in campaigns and making financial contributions, modes of participation that receive substantial coverage in other surveys. However, we also asked about other kinds of activity not ordinarily included in surveys: contacting public officials, attending protests, joining or otherwise supporting organizations that take stands in politics, and getting involved either formally or informally in local issues.

We also included in our survey a very rich set of questions about the extent and nature of individual involvement in non-political

---

24. James M. Button's study of six southern communities shows the multiple ways in which public services improved for Blacks as they became participants in political life. See *Blacks and Social Change: Impact of the Civil Rights Movement in Southern Communities* (Princeton: Princeton University Press, 1989), chaps. 4–5. See also William Keech, *The Impact of the Negro Voting: The Role of the Vote in the Quest for Equality* (Chicago: Rand McNally, 1968).

institutions: voluntary associations and religious institutions. These data are interesting in their own right as evidence of the voluntary activity of the American public. They also enrich our understanding of political involvement.

Beyond the kinds of activity in which citizens engage, we added other measures of participation less common in the literature. One is the measure of the volume of participation: how many times a participant engaged in an act or the amount of time or money devoted to it. This permits us to assess how much political input originates from whom.

An especially noteworthy set of measures deals with the substance of activity. Each time a respondent indicated having taken part in a particular way, we asked whether there were any issues or problems that led to the activity. Where the activity is what we call "information rich"—that is, where it has the capacity to communicate relatively explicit information about what is on activists' minds—the issues or problems discussed by activists constitute the actual content of the messages sent to public officials through participation. There are whole industries devoted to the analysis of public attitudes as revealed in opinion surveys. Similarly, a good deal of effort goes into monitoring the content of what is presented by the media. Our work is the first devoted to looking closely at the issue agendas of political activists.

The Citizen Participation Study is also unique in the nature of its sample. Since one of our overriding concerns is representation—the extent to which activists reflect accurately the politically relevant characteristics of the public as a whole—we needed a representative sample of both the public and activists and enough cases for analysis. A sample survey of ordinary size contains very few cases of individuals who engage in important but relatively infrequent political acts—who give large contributions or attend protests or serve on local community boards. This kind of sample is especially inadequate in providing sufficient cases of African-American or Latino respondents—especially African-American or Latino political activists. In light of our concern with the representation of disadvantaged groups, this defect is especially damaging.

We devised a special two-stage sample in order to generate

larger pools of citizens who engage in relatively rare activities as well as African-American and Latino respondents. The first stage consisted of a random telephone survey of 15,053 members of the American public. These short screener interviews provided a profile of political and non-political activity as well as basic demographic information. This survey produced 1,400 African-American and 894 Latino respondents as well as substantial pools of citizens who engage in rare activities. We then conducted longer, in-person interviews with 2,517 of the original 15,053 respondents, weighting the sample so as to produce a disproportionate number of both activists and members of the two minority groups. The follow-up survey yielded 295 respondents who had taken part in a protest, 420 who worked in a campaign in the 1988 election year, 273 who gave contributions of $250 or more, and 168 who had served on a local government board. It also included 478 African-Americans and 370 Latinos. With appropriate weights this sample can be treated as a representative sample of the population. The screener survey was conducted in the summer and fall of 1989; the follow-up survey in the spring and summer of 1990.

Overview of the Book

Our overall concern is with the way in which the participatory process operates to communicate information about the politically relevant attributes of the public. The book has four parts. Part I (Chapters 2–5) describes the world of participation: the ways in which citizens take part, how active they are, and the subject matter that animates their activity. In addition, we look at what participation means to the activists and explore the recruitment networks that generate political activity. Part II (Chapters 6–8) relates participation to the representation of citizen needs and preferences. It deals with the extent to which participatory input reflects accurately the politically relevant characteristics of the public. Having described how participation works to represent the public, we turn in Part III (Chapters 9–15) to the task of explaining why people participate. There we develop and test a model—the Civic Voluntarism Model—of the factors that foster participation, tracing these factors back to the basic institutions of society. In Part IV (Chapters 16 and 17) we tie the various parts of the argument together. We show how the participatory process elaborated in Part III produces the representational outcomes described in Part II. As we shall see, the process by which people are brought into the participatory system amplifies the voices of some citizens and mutes the voices of others.

I

The World of Participation

Fundamental to our analysis are the modes of participation in which citizens engage: the political acts that carry the information about the public. In Chapter 2 we survey the many varieties of voluntary activity, both political and non-political, and make some critical distinctions among them. Chapter 3 continues this enterprise, elaborating upon the many kinds of participation and providing data about the amount of voluntary activity and the issue agendas that animate it.

The following two chapters elaborate the world of participation as experienced by activists. Chapter 4 explores, from the perspective of activists themselves, their interpretations of why they participate. We demonstrate that participants get involved for a variety of reasons, that the mix of gratifications varies with the nature of the participatory act, and that civic and policy motivations figure more importantly in activists' retrospective reconstructions of the reasons for their activity than might be expected from the literature on the paradox of participation. Chapter 5 inquires into the process by which citizen activists are recruited. We examine who is asked to do what by whom and, since many requests for activity are denied, the circumstances under which solicitations are likely to be met with assent. We pay particular attention to the extent to which attempts at recruitment emanate from friends or from strangers and to the non-political institutional settings that mediate and generate requests for participation.

2

Defining Political
Participation

Political participation affords citizens in a democracy an opportunity to communicate information to government officials about their concerns and preferences and to put pressure on them to respond. Americans who wish to take part politically have an array of options: they may express their views directly by communicating with public officials or indirectly by attempting to influence electoral outcomes; they may give time and effort or contribute dollars; they may work alone or in concert with others; they may be active at the national, state, or local level. Since different forms of political activity are differentially effective in conveying information or exerting pressure, it matters how citizens take part.

In this part of the book we lay the groundwork for both an explanation of why people are active politically and an understanding of what and from whom the government hears by looking closely at the nature and scope of participation in America. In this chapter, we explicate somewhat more fully what we mean by voluntary political participation and how various kinds of activity fit into the democratic process. In the chapter that follows, we add descriptive detail about the many ways in which citizens take part. In a discussion that encompasses a wide variety of political activities, we go beyond a catalogue of the kinds of political acts to consider other important aspects of the world of participation. We take into account the *volume* of activity—not only whether or not

37

people take part in various ways, but how much they do. The analysis of volume will allow us to elaborate the extent to which various activities can apply pressure on the government. In addition, we use our unique data set to describe the *subject matter* of political activity—the issues and problems that animate the various activities in which citizens engage—and thus to shed new light on the information that citizens communicate when they participate. In this way, we provide a richer picture of the state of the voluntary participatory system in America than has heretofore been available.

Voluntary Political Participation

Although we shall have frequent occasion to consider voluntary activity in realms outside politics, our principal concern in this book is the *voluntary political participation* of the American public. Let us begin by discussing briefly what we mean by this. Our purpose in this section is both to set out some of the analytical distinctions that allow us to differentiate voluntary political participation from other forms of human endeavor and to acknowledge the fuzziness of the empirical boundaries that separate various domains of activity. No matter how sophisticated our understanding, however, what really matters are the actual measures. For example, in contrast to what we do here, other analysts have defined involvement in voluntary organizations to encompass membership in a local church or to exclude membership in a union, decisions that have implications for findings about the amount and distribution of organizational affiliation. Therefore, as we proceed, it will be important to make our measures explicit and point out the discretionary decisions about the classification of specific activities that sit on the borders of what are analytically distinguishable domains.

VOLUNTARY POLITICAL ACTIVITY

By *political* participation we refer simply to activity that has the intent or effect of influencing government action—either directly by affecting the making or implementation of public policy or indirectly by influencing the selection of people who make those policies. By *voluntary* activity we mean participation that is not obligatory—no one is forced to volunteer—and that receives no pay or only token financial compensation. Thus, a paid position on a big city school board or a Senator's re-election campaign staff does not qualify under our definition.[1]

The distinction between voluntary activity and paid work is not always clear. It is possible to serve private economic purposes through social and political activism. As we shall see, many people seek to do well while doing good. They undertake voluntary activity for which they receive no compensation—in their churches, in charities, in politics—in order to make contacts or otherwise enhance their jobs or careers. Furthermore, for many of those who participate in politics, the policy issues that animate their activity have consequences for their pocketbooks. Conversely, many people get involved in genuinely voluntary activity that is an extension of their paid employment. For example, an accountant may lend his or her professional expertise as part of unpaid service on a hospital or museum board. Those who work for non-profits or political organizations often extend their commitment with additional volunteer work on behalf of the objectives pursued through their paid employment. In all these cases, the border between voluntary participation and paid employment is blurry.

Finally, we focus on *activity:* we are concerned with doing politics, rather than with being attentive to politics. Thus, we exclude certain activities that might have been embraced by a more encompassing definition. The umbrella of our definition, therefore, does not extend to following political events in the news or watching public affairs programs on television. We have also excluded communications—political discussions among friends, letters to

---

1. Max Weber distinguished between those for whom politics is an avocation and those for whom it is a vocation. The former enter political life as occasional politicians, who "cast a ballot or consummate a similar expression of intention, such as applauding or protesting in a 'political' meeting, or delivering a 'political' speech, etc."; the latter make politics their major vocation. Max Weber, "Politics as a Vocation," in *From Max Weber: Essays in Sociology,* ed. and trans. H. H. Gerth and C. Wright Mills (New York: Oxford University Press, 1946), p. 83. We are interested in those for whom politics is an avocation. It is, of course, possible that some for whom politics is a vocation do not earn the bulk of their income that way. However, as long as it is their main occupation, they fall outside of our volunteer category. Senators Jay Rockefeller and Edward M. Kennedy are full-time professionals, not volunteers, even though their income may not depend on a government salary.

the editor, calls to talk radio shows—in which the target audience is not a public official.[2]

POLITICAL AND NON-POLITICAL ACTIVITY

Although our main concern is with political activity, our survey gathered extensive information about non-political voluntary activity. The latter is crucial to our analysis because, as we shall see later, it is central to understanding political participation. Indeed, one of the main themes of this book is the embeddedness of political activity in the non-political institutions of civil society.

The boundary between political and non-political activity is by no means clear, an aspect of political and social life in America that complicates the analysis of political and non-political participation. Voluntary activity in both the religious and secular domains outside of politics intersects with politics in many ways. First, as we shall see over and over, participation in these spheres is in many ways a politicizing experience. For one thing, undertaking activities that themselves have nothing to do with politics— for example, running the PTA fund drive or managing the church soup kitchen—can develop organizational and communications skills that are transferable to politics. In addition, these non-political institutions can act as the locus of attempts at political recruitment: church and organization members make social contacts and, thus, become part of networks through which requests for participation in politics are mediated. Moreover, those who take part in religious or organizational activity are exposed to political cues and messages—as when a minister gives a sermon on a political topic or when organization members chat informally about politics at a meeting.

Furthermore, the institutions that provide a context for non-political voluntary participation have a complex relationship to politics and public purposes. For example, churches and, especially,

---

2. We did measure these activities at the border of political activity and can investigate whether the 60 percent of respondents who indicated discussing national politics and national affairs, or the 52 percent who indicated discussing local community politics and affairs, at least once a week, the 41 percent who watch some type of public affairs program on television at least once a week, or the 4 percent who have called in to express their views on a radio talk show are especially politically active.

non-profit organizations undertake many activities—ranging from aiding the homeless to funding cancer research to supporting the symphony—that are also undertaken by governments here and abroad. Indeed, the sharing of functions among a variety of private, non-profit, and public institutions is one of the hallmarks of the peculiar American political economy.[3]

Involvement in politics extends beyond the functional overlap with public institutions, however. Many voluntary associations and even churches get involved directly in politics, and their attempts at influencing policy outcomes constitute a crucial source of input about citizen views and preferences. Support of an organization that takes stands on public issues, even passive support or support motivated by concerns other than government influence, represents a form of political activity. For many citizens it may be the main form of political participation—albeit often at second hand. The substantial variation among organizations in the extent to which they maintain an ongoing presence in politics and mix political and non-political means of furthering their members' interests presents a challenge for an inquiry like this one. Voluntary organizations range from those like a local softball league or garden club that eschew political involvement to those like the Children's Defense Fund or the Committee on the Present Danger that are deeply involved in politics. Making matters more complicated is the fact that nominal categories that are sensible to respondents frequently include organizations having very different levels of political involvement. For example, most of the organizations that would fall under the rubric of "a hobby club, sports or country club, or some other group or club for leisure time activities" do not take stands in politics; the National Rifle Association, however, is very active politically.

A final source of ambiguity in differentiating political from non-political participation is that the reported motives for activity may be at variance with the outward appearance of the act. For example, many people who engage in activity the effect of which is to influence either directly or indirectly what the government does—who campaign for candidates, donate to corporate PACs,

---

3. On this theme, see *Between States and Markets: The Voluntary Sector in Comparative Perspective*, ed. Robert Wuthnow (Princeton: Princeton University Press, 1991).

join organizations that take stands in politics, or sit on local governing boards—cite non-political reasons for their participation. Among other things, they may indicate that they enjoy the other people involved, that they want to take advantage of recreational opportunities or direct services provided by an organization, or that they want to further their careers. Conversely, as we shall see, some of those who take part in educational, charitable, or social activities associated with their churches indicate that one of the reasons for that activity is to "influence government policy."[4]

The unclear distinction between political and non-political activity is a fact of life in American politics, a fact with significant consequences for how politics operates. It is a fact that, at times, also complicates our analysis since we wish to differentiate between the domains in order to see how they relate to each other. Because it is so difficult to distinguish what is political from what is not, we shall need to proceed cautiously.

What Kind of Political Activity?

Americans who wish to take part in politics can be active in many ways. Studies of political participation traditionally have begun with—and too often ended with—the vote. Although voting is an important mode of citizen involvement in political life, it is but one of many political acts. In this study we move well beyond the vote to consider a wider range of political acts, including working in and contributing to electoral campaigns and organizations; contacting government officials; attending protests, marches, or demonstrations; working informally with others to solve some community problem; serving without pay on local elected and appointed boards; being active politically through the intermediation of voluntary associations; and contributing money to political causes in response to mail solicitations.[5]

---

4. A fuller explication of respondents' retrospective interpretations of the reasons for becoming involved in voluntary endeavors is found in Chapter 4.

5. Sidney Verba and Norman H. Nie explored some of these additional forms of activity in *Participation in America: Political Democracy and Social Equality* (New York: Harper and Row, 1972). Of the activities included in the present study, they discussed voting,

This list covers many important ways in which American citizens take part in politics.[6] Moreover, within each of these activities, the possibilities proliferate. A citizen can, for example, do campaign work in a primary or a general election; contribute to a candidate or to a PAC; contact an elected or an appointed official; or protest on a national, state, or local issue. Hence, the range of acts about which we have information is even broader than might appear at first glance.

Differences among the Political Acts

Political acts differ in a variety of ways. Rather than propose yet another typology of political acts, we shall set out three main analytical distinctions among those we study, distinctions that will recur repeatedly throughout our analysis.[7] We focus on these particular distinctions because we think that they are crucial to understanding how different acts function politically. One distinction focuses on what a particular form of participation requires of the

---

campaigning, individual contacting, and informal community activity. There is a large literature on protest activity, a category not covered in Verba and Nie. See, for instance, Samuel H. Barnes, Max Kaase, et al., *Political Action: Mass Participation in Five Western Democracies* (Beverly Hills, Calif.: Sage Publications, 1979).

6. Our list of acts is, however, not exhaustive. Among the excluded activities that would fall under our definition of voluntary political participation are attempting to persuade someone to vote a particular way and publicly supporting a candidate or a cause—for example, by wearing a button or displaying a bumper sticker. We were unable to examine another form of participation—activity on referendum issues—because opportunities for this kind of participation depend upon state laws governing ballot propositions and are, thus, distributed unevenly. In addition, James C. Scott *(Weapons of the Weak: Everyday Forms of Peasant Resistance* [New Haven: Yale University Press, 1985]) has written of the variety of ways in which the powerless can assert themselves: by malingering, sabotage, gossip, and humor.

Although we did ask about protest, we did not ask specifically about forms of protest—violent demonstrations, rioting, terrorism, illegal activities—that clearly remain outside the mainstream. Obviously, such activities would be difficult to ask about in a survey like ours. Moreover, although not totally foreign to the American context, they are sufficiently rare that it would be difficult to find sufficient cases for analysis—even if people were willing to discuss such activities in an interview.

7. Discussions of the variety of political acts can be found in Verba and Nie, *Participation in America;* Lester W. Milbrath and M. L. Goel, *Political Participation: How and Why Do People Get Involved in Politics?*, 2nd ed. (Chicago: Rand McNally College Pub. Co., 1977); Jack H. Nagel, *Participation* (Englewood Cliffs, N.J.: Prentice-Hall, 1987); and Barnes, Kaase, et al., *Political Action.*

activist in terms of the mix of resources of time, money, and skills. The other two distinctions focus on the factors affecting what a participatory act can produce in the way of response. Citizen participation influences political elites by communicating information about activists' circumstances, preferences, and needs and by generating pressure—whether the promise of support or the threat of opposition—to pay attention. The combination of what an act requires and what an act can produce is basic to how participation achieves—or fails to achieve—voice and equality in American politics. Let us consider these distinctions more closely.

TIME, MONEY, AND SKILLS: THE REQUIREMENTS FOR PARTICIPATION

The first distinction among participatory acts is what is required for activity—time, money, or skills. All forms of political activity demand an input, of either time or money. Which one is required is, as we shall see, significant in determining whose voice is heard. Indeed, the contrast between time and money, one not usually dealt with systematically in the empirical analyses of participation, is one of the most important distinctions informing our analysis. There is also variation in the extent to which participatory acts demand skills. The citizen who goes to the polls, attends a demonstration, or writes a check does not need to be especially articulate or well-organized or to be capable of exercising leadership. In contrast, activists who contact public officials, work in campaigns, serve on local boards, or work with others on community problems (or who accompany a contribution with a communication or attempt to organize a demonstration) will be more effective if they are skilled. We have no direct measure of how skillful respondents are—for example, how effectively they write or speak. We do, however, have extensive measures of prior skills: the extent to which respondents undertake in non-political contexts activities such as writing letters and organizing meetings that permit them to practice skills relevant to politics.

INFORMATION: SENDING MESSAGES

Participatory acts vary in the extent to which they convey information about the circumstances and preferences of the participant.

As is well known, the vote is a rather blunt instrument for the communication of what is on citizens' minds. In contrast, a sign carried at a protest can convey a precise message as to the substance of the issue at hand; a communication from an organization can be even more detailed about the nature of the problem and the action desired; and a direct contact from an individual to a policymaker can add further information about the circumstances of the individual. Electorally-based acts are ambiguous with respect to the information they carry. Campaign workers or contributors may accompany their support with an explicit message about their preferences, but they may also remain silent and invisible. At several points in our analysis, we distinguish information-rich activities that allow the participant to transmit detailed instructions from other activities conveying less explicit information. Although we infer the capacity of an act to carry information from its intrinsic nature, we also have data about the issue concerns, if any, that animated such participation.

Even when the act itself does not convey a precise message, there may be implicit information to policymakers in the politically relevant characteristics of those who take part. Public officials know who is paying attention to what they do. When citizens with identifiable, politically relevant attributes become visible through political activity, they transmit information even if the act itself—in particular, the vote—is not one that accommodates precise instructions.

THE VOLUME OF ACTIVITY: EXERTING PRESSURE

Political acts vary in the extent to which they generate pressure on policymakers to pay attention. The ability of participatory input to turn up the political heat depends upon many factors, including the position, security, resources, and psychological makeup of the public official at whom it is aimed. Therefore, we cannot measure it directly. However, we can—as has not been done in the past—measure a characteristic of political participation that is surely related to its capacity for clout: the volume of activity.

Political acts vary in the extent to which it is possible, or even legal, to multiply the amount of participatory input. When it comes to the volume of political input, the vote is at one extreme.

Although Americans go to the polls more frequently and cast ballots for more offices than do citizens of other democracies, in any particular election, each citizen has one and only one vote. No other political act has this characteristic. Indeed, all other kinds of participation can be described as forms of multiple voting. A citizen may contact many public officials, few, or none at all, devote many hours to working in campaigns, few, or none at all, donate many dollars to political campaigns and causes, few, or none at all, and so on through all the other activities.

Because the metrics are different—hours devoted to activity, dollars contributed, communications dispatched, protests attended—it is difficult to make comparisons across activities with respect to the extent to which it is possible to increase the amount of activity. Still, in spite of legal restrictions on the amount that an individual can contribute to a particular candidate, it is clearly possible to multiply the number of dollars donated to political campaigns and causes to an extent not feasible with other forms of activity. The ceiling imposed on contributions by campaign finance laws is higher than the natural limitation placed on the number of hours that can be devoted to electoral campaigns, writing letters to public officials, community activity, serving on a local governing board, or attending demonstrations by the fact that no one's day has more than twenty-four hours.

To a certain extent, augmenting the volume of activity produces an increase in pressure on policymakers to respond. Although the force of the collective vote outcome is definitive, a single vote has little potential leverage. A candidate for office can ignore an individual voter and suffer no consequences. The stakes are higher when it comes to the campaign volunteer who works many hours or the donor who has written a large check. Under these circumstances, the level of support may be sufficient that the individual participant gains clout.

OTHER DISTINCTIONS

There are additional bases upon which to classify political acts even though they do not form an important touchstone in our analysis. We can, for example, differentiate forms of participation that are ordinarily undertaken alone, such as contacting a public official or writing a check to a candidate or political cause, from those that are typically performed in concert with others, such as attending a demonstration or serving on a local governing board. Although this distinction is not one of our continuing concerns, it will arise when we consider the gratifications provided by various activities. In addition, we could distinguish unconventional from mainstream activities. This distinction, about which much is made in the literature, may not, however, be very significant for our concerns.[8] At the outset, we should recognize that what is considered to be unconventional activity varies substantially with time and place. Many of the citizen activities that are routine in America and other established democracies occasion prison sentences in authoritarian regimes. We do have, as we mentioned, one measure of what might be thought of as unconventional participation: attending a demonstration, march, or protest. Given the variety of groups and causes that adopt these tactics, however, we could argue that protest has, at this point, joined other forms of political participation as a relatively mainstream activity. Although only a small proportion of the American public engages in protest, our sampling technique allowed us to generate sufficient cases for analysis of those who have protested within the past two years.

Summary

In this chapter we have introduced a variety of forms of political activity in which citizens can engage and differentiated them along several critical dimensions. Table 2.1 summarizes our argument by showing for each activity its capacity for conveying detailed information, the extent to which the volume of activity can be multiplied, and the resources of time, money, and skills required for effective participation. It is possible to quibble with the judgments made. For example, it could be argued that the number of communications to public officials can vary as much as the number of hours devoted to campaigns. However, the broad outlines are consistent with the preceding argument.

---

8. See, for instance, Barnes and Kaase, *Political Action,* and Alan Marsh, *Political Action in Europe and the U.S.A.* (London: Macmillan, 1990).

Table 2.1 The Attributes of Political Activities

Activity	Capacity for Conveying Information	Variation in Volume	Requirements
Vote	Low	Low	Time
Campaign Work	Mixed	High	Time, Skills
Campaign Contribution	Mixed	Highest	Money
Contact an Official	High	Medium	Time, Skills
Protest	High	Medium	Time
Informal Community Work	High	High	Time, Skills
Member of a Local Board	High	High	Time, Skills
Affiliation with a Political Organization	Mixed	High	Time, Skills, Money
Contribution to a Political Cause	Mixed	Highest	Money

It is interesting to note the extensive variation in the patterns for particular activities. Two pairs of activities do exhibit similar configurations: the two forms of community activity, working informally with others and serving on a local governing board; and the two kinds of financial contributions, to campaigns and to political causes. Otherwise, there is tremendous diversity among modes of activity along these three dimensions. This alerts us to the fact that when we consider the wellsprings of activity, as well as the gratifications attendant to it, we must consider not only overall political participation but also particular activities with distinctive sets of participatory characteristics.

3

Political Participation:
How Much? About What?

Journalistic accounts yield contradictory stereotypes of the citizen in contemporary American politics. Are Americans still the nation of joiners observed by visitors from nations with less participatory cultures and fewer opportunities for citizen engagement? Or are they too busy getting and spending to divert themselves from individualistic pursuits in order to devote time, effort, or money to common ends? Or are they so politically disaffected that they are disinclined even to get involved? Depending upon what is being scrutinized—citizen attitudes or behavior, voting or other political activities, political participation or voluntary involvement in domains outside of politics—each of these seemingly contradictory characterizations may, in fact, be apt.

In this chapter we describe political activity in America, elaborating the various kinds of activity and considering their volume. In addition, in order to assess whether there is a lot of, or a little, political activity we will apply several comparative yardsticks: comparing activity in the United States with that in other countries, activity today with activity in the past, and activity in political life with non-political activity. Finally, we will look at the subject matter of political activity. This chapter presents a rich array of descriptive information. These data are intrinsically interesting as an elaboration of the state of participation in the United

States. The data presented are also the raw material for the analysis that follows of the participatory process in this country.

How Much Political Activity?

How many people are active in politics in any given year? Figure 3.1 presents the proportion of respondents who report having engaged in each of a variety of political acts. It shows substantial variation across acts.[1] Voting stands out clearly as the most commonly reported activity: well over half the population indicates having voted in the last presidential election.[2] More intensive involvement in the electoral process is much less frequent. Fewer than one in four respondents reported making a campaign contribution, and a much smaller share—fewer than one in ten—indicated having worked as a volunteer in an electoral campaign. Interestingly, the more frequent activities are ones outside of the sphere of electoral activity. Almost half of the respondents (48 percent) reported being affiliated with—that is, being a member of or making a contribution to—an organization that takes stands in politics. These data testify to the important role of voluntary associations as a channel for citizen activity. Other relatively common modes of participation illustrate the importance of activity outside of formally organized institutions. Thirty-four percent of the sample reported having initiated contacts with a government official. In addition, about a sixth reported having worked infor-

---

1. For the wording of political activity items, see Appendix B.1.

2. As is always the case in surveys, the reports of voting are exaggerated: only about 50 percent of the public voted in 1988. Our figures are consistent with those obtained in other public opinion surveys, including the American National Election Studies. See Warren E. Miller and Santa A. Traugott, *American National Election Studies Data Sourcebook, 1952–1986* (Cambridge, Mass.: Harvard University Press, 1989), p. 299. For a discussion of the overreporting of turnout, see Ruy A. Teixeira, *The Disappearing American Voter* (Washington, D.C.: The Brookings Institution, 1992), Appendix A.

For participatory acts other than the vote, there is no analogue to the local records that make it possible to validate reported turnout. Although we would expect there to be overreporting of other forms of activity, we have no independent measure of its dimensions. Because other forms of activity are both less frequent than voting and less firmly attached to notions of civic duty, it is possible that the problem is less severe for other activities than it is for voting. For an analysis of the issue of overreporting and its consequences for the study of participation, see Appendix D.

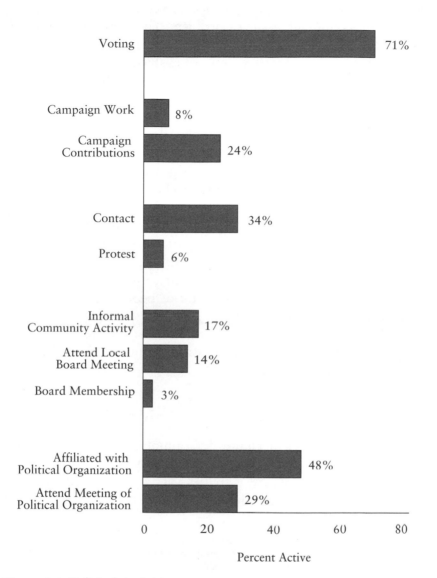

Figure 3.1 Political Activities.

Effective sample size is 2,517 weighted cases. See Appendix A for information about the sample.

mally with others in the neighborhood or community to try to deal with some community issue or problem. The importance of informal activity is highlighted by the fact that fewer respondents reported attending a meeting of an official local board in the same time period. Finally, much smaller proportions have served in a voluntary capacity on a local governmental board or council such as a school or zoning board, or attended a protest, march, or demonstration on some national or local issue.[3]

Do these figures support an image of the American public as active or passive? Whether the numbers are high or low depends, in part, on the standard of comparison chosen. Later in the chapter we present comparative data of several kinds that help in making an assessment. At first glance, however, the proportions do not appear to be high. There is no form of participation, aside from voting, in which a majority of the public engages. It is worthwhile to note, however, that, in a large country, even small proportions of the population translate into a lot of people. Consider a rare act: only 3 percent of respondents indicated serving as a volunteer on a local governing board. Yet this means that several million people, serving without compensation, assume a formal role in running their local communities.

Probing Political Activity

The bare-bones data in Figure 3.1 cannot do justice to the rich variation in the kind of activity in which citizens engage. As mentioned earlier, political activities vary in the extent to which their volume can be multiplied. Moreover, the complexity of the

---

3. In asking about political activity we were faced with a choice of a proper time frame. Consistent with the recommendations of experts in polling (for example, Seymour Sudman and Norman M. Bradburn, *Asking Questions* [San Francisco: Jossey-Bass, 1982]), we used the past twelve months as the referent. In deference to the periodicity of the electoral calendar, for electoral activities we asked about the most recent cycle beginning in January of the last presidential election year. For two of the least frequent acts—serving on a local governing board and attending a protest, march, or demonstration—we report data about the proportion having taken part in the past two years. For a further discussion of time frames, see Appendix B.1.i.

American political process proliferates the possibilities for different kinds of participation.

THE VOLUME OF ACTIVITY

We pointed out in Chapter 2 that the vote is unique in that each citizen is limited legally to a single ballot for each election. For any other mode of participation, in contrast, the activist is free to multiply the volume of participatory input: contactors can get in touch with government officials once or frequently; protesters can attend a single demonstration or many of them. The volume of activity is even more variable when it comes to giving time or money—say, to a political campaign. A contributor can give few or many hours, few or many dollars. We can elaborate the data in Figure 3.1 by probing further the volume of activity.

We begin with electoral activity, focusing on the amount of time and money given to political campaigns. Table 3.1 shows, both for the whole sample and for activists only—that is, for those who gave some time or some money—the average amounts of time and money contributed and the proportions making a substantial donation of time (five hours or more a week during the campaign) or money ($250 or more a year). This permits us to distinguish the level of commitment of the society as a whole, including those who are not involved at all, from the level of commitment of those who are at least minimally active.

Considering the public as a whole, we find that the average American gave about 36 minutes a week and about $58 to campaign activity during the 1988 campaign season. Only 4 or 5 percent of the public made what might be considered substantial contributions—more than five hours a week or more than $250. The picture changes somewhat when we consider the amount given by the activists, especially with respect to time. Although only a small share of the public works in political campaigns, those who do take part give substantial time during the campaign: half dedicate more than five hours a week to campaign activity; and not insignificant proportions give more than ten, or even twenty, hours per week during the campaign. On average, those who work in a campaign devote seven and a half hours per week to it. Among

Table 3.1 Time and Money Given to Political Campaigns

	Among All Respondents[a]	Among Active Respondents[a]
TIME		
Mean given per week	0.6 hours	7.5 hours[b]
% Giving 5+ hours per week	4%	49%[b]
MONEY		
Mean contribution per year	$58	$247[c]
% Giving $250+ per year	5%	19%[c]

a. N = 2,517 weighted cases: see Appendix A for information about the sample.
b. Among those who gave some time (N = 213 weighted cases).
c. Among those who gave some money (N = 593 weighted cases).

financial donors, the volume given is also not unsubstantial. About one in five of the donors gives over $250, and the average contribution is $247.[4]

THE NATURE OF ACTIVITY

There are several other dimensions along which forms of participation can vary. For example, citizens who take part in electoral activity can take part in primaries or in general elections or both. Discussing the campaign to which they gave the most time and effort in the 1988 electoral cycle, forty-seven percent of the campaign activists indicated that it included both a primary and general election, 30 percent a general election only, and 23 percent a primary only. As shown in Table 3.2, fully half of the campaign workers were active in a local campaign; the remainder were divided evenly between national and state campaigns.[5] Table 3.2

---

4. There is also variation in how often citizens engage in such acts as contacting and protesting. Those who get in touch with government officials tend to do so relatively often. In the initial screener survey, only 19 percent of those who indicated having gotten in touch with a public official within the past twelve months made only one contact, and 39 percent indicated having done so four or more times. In contrast, those who report protesting are likely to do so only once. Over half, 53 percent, of the protesters had done so only once, and only 16 percent had done so as many as four times—even though the period covered by our question was two years rather than just one.

5. The figures change somewhat if we consider only those respondents who hail from the fourteen states that had a gubernatorial election in the period covered. In these states

Table 3.2 Targets of Campaign Activity

	Campaign Work[a]		Campaign Contributions	
NATIONAL	22%		29%	
President		12%		14%
U.S. Senator		5		10
U.S. Representative		5		5
STATE	22		39	
Governor		6		12
State senator		4		12
State representative		10		12
Other state official		2		3
LOCAL	50		30	
County official		18		10
Mayor		11		6
City councillor		10		8
School board member		8		3
Other city official		3		3
OTHER	4		2	
WORKED FOR TICKET	2			
	100%		100%	
	(N = 212)[b]		(N = 595)[b]	

a. Respondents who were involved in more than one campaign were asked about the one to which they gave the most time and effort.

b. Weighted cases: see Appendix A for information about the sample.

also shows to whom campaign activists gave as well as for whom they worked. Local campaigns recede in relative importance when it comes to campaign finance: 30 percent of those whose largest donation was to a candidate funded a local candidate; 39 percent contributed to a candidate for state office; and 29 percent to a candidate for national office.

Aside from voting, more citizens initiate contacts with public officials than engage in any other political act. Contacts can go to elected or non-elected officials and to officials on the national,

---

11 percent of the campaigners worked for a gubernatorial candidate. Because there were contests for the Senate in thirty-four states during the period covered, there is much less change when we consider respondents from these states only: 6 percent of campaign activists in these states worked for a senatorial candidate.

Table 3.3 Contacts with Public Officials

A. Percentage reporting contacts with public officials during past 12 months:

NATIONAL	
Elected official (or staff)	13%
Non-elected	8
STATE OR LOCAL	
Elected official (or staff)	25
Non-elected	13
	(N = 2,517)[a]

B. Most Recent Contact with a Public Official (among contactors):

NATIONAL	32%	
President		2%
U.S. Senator		15
U.S. Representative		10
Other national		5
STATE	26	
Governor		3
State senator		8
State representative		11
Other state official		4
LOCAL	41	
Mayor		9
City councillor		10
School board member		5
Other city official		17
		99%
		(N = 855)[a]

a. Weighted cases: see Appendix A for information about sample.

state, or local level. Table 3.3 presents data showing where these contacts were directed. The figures in part A of the table indicate that citizens are more likely to get in touch with state and local officials than with national officials and with elected officials (or members of their staffs) than with appointed officials. Part B of Table 3.3 gives further information about these contacts (or, if there was more than one in the past year, the most recent contact). We can see the relative weight of contacts to local officials and note the unexpected greater frequency of contacts to U.S. Senators than members of the U.S. House—a finding that does not hold at the state level.[6]

It is interesting to note, further, how widespread and significant are networks of personal acquaintanceship in the process of citizen contact. A third of the contactors in our survey reported that they knew personally the public official with whom they got in touch. Again, the findings demonstrate the relative accessibility of local officials: the more local the office, the more likely it is that the contactor personally knew the target of the contact. Sixty-nine percent of those who contacted the mayor's office personally knew the person they were trying to reach, compared with 16 percent of those who contacted a U.S. Senator or Representative and 4 percent of those who contacted the White House.

Contacts also vary with respect to the scope of the concern. As part of the battery of items about any participatory act, we inquired whether there were any issues or problems that led to the activity and, if so, who was affected: only the respondent or the respondent's family, the community, or the nation.[7] Contacting was the only activity for which particularized concerns—that is, concerns that pertain only to respondents themselves or their immediate families—figure at all importantly as an animus for involvement: the subject of about one in five contacts at each level of government was a matter of particularized concern. Not surprisingly, however, within any level of government not all public officials are equally likely to be the targets of particularized contacts. The differences are especially pronounced at the national

6. In contrast to contacting, the much smaller number of citizens who reported having attended a protest, march, or demonstration within the past two years were more likely to specify a national target. Forty-two percent of the protesters indicated that the issue at stake in the protest (or most recent protest if more than one) was local in character, 50 percent that it was national, and 8 percent that it was international in scope. As we shall see later, the important role of abortion in protests has an effect on the focus of protest activity.

7. In this way, we were able to delineate more accurately the scope of concern of individuals who mentioned "Social Security" or "high property taxes"—problems that would affect many people in circumstances similar to theirs, but could be either particularistic or policy concerns. The actual question was somewhat more complex. See Appendix B.3.

level, where none of the contacts directed to the White House, in contrast to 62 percent of those directed to an official in a national board or agency, involved particularized concerns.

Finally, we can elaborate the range of kinds of voluntary local boards on which citizens sit. About one-quarter of the board members are on elected boards and the remainder are appointed. These boards cover the range of services provided within most local communities, with school boards, general local councils, and zoning boards as the most frequent types.

Affiliation with Political Organizations

A final and important form of political participation—one that once figured prominently in interpretations of American politics[8]—is involvement with the voluntary associations that represent citizen interests in politics. The range of organizations that Americans can join is vast. Indeed, the roster of known American organizations fills several fat volumes and includes organizations as well-known as the Girl Scouts and as little-noticed as the U.S. Hang Gliding Association.[9] What is more, such a listing does not begin to include the myriad locally-based organizations that escape the attention of those compiling a national register.

Organizational involvement intersects with political participa-

---

8. Following the approach originally put forth by Arthur Bentley, *The Process of Government: A Study of Social Pressures* (Bloomington, Ind.: Principia Press, 1908), analysts of American politics during the 1950s—in particular, David B. Truman, *The Governmental Process; Political Interests and Public Opinion* (New York: Alfred A. Knopf, 1951), and Earl Latham, *The Group Basis of Politics: A Study in Basing-Point Legislation* (Ithaca, N.Y.: Cornell University Press, 1952)—tended to view American politics in terms of the interactions of a plurality of contending groups and to find their influence on policymaking to be determinative. This perspective was criticized by, among others, Lester W. Milbrath, *The Washington Lobbyists* (Westport, Conn.: Greenwood Press, 1963), and Raymond A. Bauer, Ithiel de Sola Pool, and Lewis Anthony Dexter, *American Business and Public Policy: The Politics of Foreign Trade* (New York: Atherton Press, 1963). For contemporary views see, for example, Paul E. Peterson, "The Rise and Fall of Special Interest Politics," in *The Politics of Interests: Interest Groups Transformed*, ed. Mark P. Petracca (Boulder, Colo.: Westview Press, 1992), pp. 326–341, and Robert H. Salisbury, "The Paradox of Interest Groups in Washington," in *The New American Political System*, ed. Anthony King, 2nd version (Washington, D.C.: AEI Press, 1990), pp. 203–229.

9. Deborah M. Burek, ed., *The Encyclopedia of Associations*, 27th ed. (Detroit: Gale Research Co., 1992).

tion in complicated ways.[10] Most fundamentally, many voluntary associations take political stands, and their attempts at influencing policy outcomes constitute a crucial source of input about citizen views and preferences. Support of such organizations, even passive support, thus represents a form of political activity. However, as we pointed out in Chapter 2, the diverse organizations with which Americans are affiliated vary substantially in the extent to which their objectives and activities involve influencing political outcomes.

MEASURING ORGANIZATIONAL INVOLVEMENT

Measuring involvement in organizations—especially involvement in political organizations—is complicated. What appear to be relatively technical decisions have implications for both the definition of the subject and the results obtained. Several issues arise: how to define what constitutes organizational affiliation; how to determine whether an organization is political; and how best to elicit full information from a respondent—by asking about organizational membership in general or by presenting a list of organizational categories and, if the latter, which categories to include. In Appendix 3.1 to this chapter, we discuss our rationale for the way we handled these dilemmas. To summarize briefly, we consider either membership or financial contribution to be evidence of organizational involvement. We define as political any organization that, according to the respondent, takes stands on public issues either nationally or locally. And we asked about a long list, shown in Table 3.4, of twenty specific types of organizations. In addition to this organizational census, we asked a longer series of questions about the single organization to which the respondent gives the most time and money—or, if different, the organization that is most important to the respondent. We refer to this battery

---

10. For a review of relevant literature, see David Knoke, "Associations and Interest Groups," *Annual Review of Sociology,* 12 (1986): 8–9. See also Sidney Verba and Norman Nie, *Participation in America: Political Democracy and Social Equality* (New York: Harper and Row, 1972), chap. 11; Frank R. Baumgartner and Jack L. Walker, "Survey Research and Membership in Voluntary Associations," *American Journal of Political Science* 32 (1988): 908–928; and Bonnie H. Erickson and T. A. Nosanchuk, "How an Apolitical Association Politicizes," *Canadian Review of Sociology and Anthropology* 27 (1990): 206–219.

Table 3.4 Types of Organizations

A. Service clubs or fraternal organizations such as the Lions or Kiwanis or a local women's club or a fraternal organization at a school
B. Veterans' organizations such as the American Legion or the Veterans of Foreign Wars
C. Groups affiliated with [the respondent's] religion such as the Knights of Columbus or B'nai B'rith[a]
D. Organizations representing [the respondent's] *own* particular nationality or ethnic group such as the Polish-American Congress, the Mexican-American Legal Defense and Education Fund, or the National Association for the Advancement of Colored People
E. Organizations for the elderly or senior citizens
F. Organizations mainly interested in issues promoting the rights or welfare of women—an organization such as the National Organization for Women, or the Eagle Forum, or the American Association of University Women
G. Labor unions
H. Other organizations associated with [the respondent's] work such as a business or professional association, or a farm organization[b]
I. Organizations active on one particular political issue such as the environment, or abortion (on either side), or gun control (again on either side) or consumer's rights, or the rights of taxpayers, or any other issue
J. Non-partisan or civic organizations interested in the political life of the community or the nation—such as the League of Women Voters or a better government association
K. Organizations that support general liberal or conservative causes such as the Americans for Democratic Action or the Conservative Caucus
L. Organizations active in supporting candidates in elections such as a party organization
M. Youth groups such as the Girl Scouts or the 4-H
N. Literary, art, discussion, or study groups
O. Hobby clubs, sports or country clubs, or other groups or clubs for leisure time activities
P. Associations related to where [the respondent] lives—neighborhood or community associations, homeowners' or condominium associations, or block clubs

Table 3.4 (continued)

Q. Organizations that provide social services in such fields as health or service to the needy—for instance, a hospital, a cancer or heart drive, or a group like the Salvation Army that works for the poor[c]

R. Educational institutions—local schools, [the respondent's] own school or college, or organizations associated with education such as school alumni associations or school service organizations like the PTA

S. Organizations that are active in providing cultural services to the public—for example, museums, symphonies, or public radio or television

T. Other organizations[d]

---

a. Instructions to interviewers specified that this category was intended for religiously based fraternal organizations not associated with a particular congregation. It was not intended to include activity within or contributions to a congregation, which were covered in a separate section of the questionnaire. As is so often the case in the world of voluntary action, the boundary is not always clear in particular cases.

Some previous surveys of organizational membership have considered—erroneously, in our view—membership in a church or synagogue as a voluntary association membership. For a discussion of this issue and extensive bibliographical references, see David Horton Smith, "Voluntary Action and Voluntary Groups," *Annual Review of Sociology* 1 (1975): 249; and Aida K. Tomeh, "Formal Voluntary Organizations: Participation, Correlates, and Interrelationships," *Sociological Inquiry* 43 (1973): 96.

b. Respondents were instructed to include their activity in any organizations of which their employers were members. For example, a corporate manager who is an officer of a trade association would have recorded that activity in this category even though it is the firm, rather than the respondent, that is the actual member of the organization.

c. For the organizations in categories Q–S, respondents were asked about giving time as well as about membership and making donations.

d. Instructions to interviewers specified that if respondents insisted upon a particular categorization, their wishes were to be honored. To the extent that respondents sought assistance or were open to suggestion in placing organizations in categories, however, interviewers were advised to suggest that respondents put an organization in the first category on the list for which it was appropriate when, as is often the case, it straddled two categories.

of detailed follow-up questions about the respondent's most important organization at various points in the analysis.

HOW MUCH INVOLVEMENT IN POLITICAL ORGANIZATIONS?

Organizational involvement is very widespread in America. In response to the list of organizations with which they were presented, fully 79 percent of the respondents reported organizational involvement—either membership or financial contribution—and 41 percent indicated four or more affiliations.[11] And many respondents reported affiliation that is political in nature. Sixty-one percent of those indicating organizational involvement (or 48 percent of all respondents) are affiliated with an organization that takes stands in politics.

This definition, of course, requires a rather low level of commitment as evidence of organizational involvement. We have more detailed information on the degree of involvement. Of those indicating some kind of affiliation with at least one organization, 65 percent reported that they have attended a meeting within the past twelve months; 42 percent reported that they are active members, that is, that they have served on a committee, given time for special projects, or helped organize meetings; 28 percent reported that, within the past five years, they have served on the board or been an officer of an organization with which they are still involved. As a mode of activity by which individuals take part in political life, voluntary organizations are clearly a significant factor.

Table 3.5 decomposes these aggregate figures into the twenty categories of organizations and gives a good deal of basic infor-

---

11. As is so often the case in survey research, when it comes to organizational involvement, how questions are asked matters greatly for the results obtained. Our initial telephone screener included a general question about membership in organizations—"for example, unions or professional associations, fraternal groups, recreational organizations, political issue organizations, community or school groups, and so on." Respondents who indicated membership in any organizations were asked how many and whether any of them ever take any stands on any public issues—either nationally or locally. Only 49 percent of respondents indicated organizational membership in answer to the general question contained in the screener, and a mere 8 percent indicated four or more memberships. Thirty percent reported membership in an organization that takes political stands.

Table 3.5 Types of Organizations and Nature of Affiliation

| | Among All Respondents[a] | Among those Affiliated[b] | | |
| | | | | |
Organizational Type	% Affiliated[c]	% Attend Meetings	% Give Money but No Meetings	% Say Organization Takes Political Stands
Service, Fraternal	18	50	35	30
Veterans'	16	16	70	59
Religious	12	63	30	27
Nationality, Ethnic	4	45	32	61
Senior Citizens'	12	25	20	61
Women's Rights	4	33	52	79
Union	12	52	16	67
Business, Professional	23	66	13	59
Political Issue	14	20	65	93
Civic, Non-partisan	3	60	21	59
Liberal or Conservative	1	20	71	95
Candidate, Party	5	39	49	94
Youth	17	42	50	18
Literary, Art, Study	6	72	15	16
Hobby, Sports, Leisure	21	52	17	18
Neighborhood, Homeowners'	12	66	11	50
Charitable, Social Service	44	14	79	16
Educational	25	50	34	43
Cultural	13	14	71	25
Other	4	32	44	30
All Organizations	79	65	55	61

a. N = 2,517 weighted cases: see Appendix A for information about the sample.

b. To determine weighted case base for percentage attending meetings, percentage giving money but attending no meetings, or percentage indicating that organization takes stands in politics, multiply percentage affiliated (in first column) by 2,517.

c. Affiliation: member or contributor.

mation about the distribution of memberships and the nature of involvement. It shows the proportion of the sample that is affiliated with each type of organization (defined as being either a member or a contributor to an organization). It also provides information about the extent of involvement, showing the proportion of those affiliated who attend meetings as well as the proportion whose affiliation is limited to monetary contributions—that is, who give money but reported never attending a meeting. Finally, it reports the proportion of affiliates who said the organization takes political stands.

Across the categories there is, not surprisingly, a broad range in terms of the proportion of respondents who are affiliated, the nature of the affiliation, and the proportion of those affiliated who indicated that the organization takes political stands. We will highlight a few of the many details. In terms of involvement, a near majority, 44 percent, indicated affiliation with a charitable or social service organization. In general, these are minimal affiliations with organizations such as the United Way. The bulk of participation in charitable or social service organizations—nearly 80 percent—is limited to a contribution. At the other extreme, a mere 1 percent reported involvement with an ideological organization that supports general liberal or conservative causes. This is, once again, an example of what is basically checkbook membership: nearly three-quarters of the affiliates give money but never go to a meeting. Similarly, two-thirds of those involved in cultural organizations and a majority of those involved in veterans' groups and youth organizations are donors but not members. At the other extreme, at least half of those involved in fraternal, religious, non-partisan civic, literary, art, or discussion groups, hobby or sports clubs, neighborhood or homeowners' associations, business, professional, or farm groups, and unions indicated having attended a meeting in the six months preceding the interview.

The variation in the share of those affiliated who indicated that the organization takes stands on public issues seems to reflect in a reasonable way the differing purposes of the various types of organizations. Nearly all the respondents in a political issue organization, a general liberal or conservative group, or an organization that supports candidates—in contrast to fewer than one in every five in a literary, art, or discussion group, a charity or social service organization, or a hobby or sports club—reported that the organization sometimes takes stands on public issues.[12]

---

12. There is some question as to whether respondents, especially those whose commitment is limited, really know whether their organizations take stands in politics. Like

Thus, the evidence is mixed as to whether Americans are a nation of gregarious organizational activists or have retreated to the privacy and relative inactivity of checkbook participation. For many kinds of organizations, citizen involvement is limited to writing checks. Many of these are the kind of charitable cause for which making contributions is a traditional form of involvement. Nonetheless, it is interesting that other organizations also fall into this category. Still, nearly two-thirds of those affiliated with an organization devote the time and effort necessary to attend a meeting.

Patterns of Political Involvement

We were concerned to investigate, from several points of view, the way in which political participation is patterned. Is most of the political participation the work of a small group of activists, each of whom engages in several activities? Or are most activists specialists who take part in only one way? Seventeen percent of the public does nothing at all in politics, and another 18 percent does

---

hypothesis testers, they might make two kinds of mistakes: imagining organizational activity in politics where it does not exist or failing to know about it when it does. Presumably, the latter error would be more common than the former. Reading actual interviews, which contain the names of organizations mentioned by respondents, provides some evidence of their failure to recognize the political activities of organizations. From time to time an organization that has been prominent on the political scene is recorded as not taking stands in politics.

In accounting for the perception of an organization's engagement in politics, Frank Baumgartner and Jack Walker suggest that the actively involved are more likely to report that an organization takes political stands ("Survey Research and Membership in Voluntary Associations," p. 923). At first glance, our data lend substantial support to this contention: among those affiliated with at least one organization, 70 percent of those who had attended a meeting within the past six months, but only 44 percent of those who had not, reported affiliation with an organization that takes political stands. However, these data do not make any provision for ensuring that respondents—who, if affiliated at all, are likely to be affiliated with more than one organization—are finding politics in the *same* organizations whose meetings they have attended. Indeed, when the data are disaggregated and analyzed separately for each organizational affiliation, the relationship is much more modest: using the affiliation as the unit of analysis, when respondents indicated attendance at meetings, they reported political stands in 44 percent of the cases; when they indicated no attendance at meetings, they reported political stands in 39 percent of the cases.

nothing beyond voting. Thus, just over one-third of respondents do nothing in politics other than, possibly, go to the polls.[13] Another 9 percent engage in a single activity, and the remaining 57 percent undertake more than one political act, beyond voting.

We were also curious to know whether there are particular people who do a lot of one kind of activity and nothing else, or particular kinds of participation such that those who undertake them are specialists in that activity only. For example, if protesters are alienated from the political process and convinced that mainstream activity is useless in eliciting concessions from an unresponsive system, we might expect them to concentrate on protesting and eschew other forms of involvement. Similarly, some citizens might specialize in informal community activity, preferring the neighborhood as a locus of activity and avoiding partisan political campaigns.

In fact, the data lend little support to the idea of such specialization. We have already seen that only a small proportion of those who are politically active beyond voting engage in only one other political activity. Nor are there particular activities for which we find specialization. We might have expected protesters to be specialists, but the vast majority of them (93 percent) engage in some other activity beyond voting. The same is true for other kinds of activists as well.

We considered specialization from one additional, and quite different, angle. For each activity we asked whether the focus—the official to whom a contact was addressed, the issue at stake in the protest, and so on—was local, state, or national. It turns out that, while a substantial portion of those active beyond voting concentrate solely on local politics, there are very few specialists in national politics. Fully 92 percent of those who are in any way politically active beyond voting engaged in some activity with a state or local focus—for example, campaigned for a state or local candidate, contacted a state or local official, or sat on a local governing board. However, while only 8 percent of political activ-

---

13. Our definition of what constitutes a voter is not a very demanding one. Anyone who voted in the preceding presidential election or who reported having voted in all or most presidential or local elections is considered to be a voter.

ists focused their voluntary efforts in politics exclusively on the national scene, 51 percent focused solely on state and local politics. Forty-one percent combined activity at the state or local level with national-level participation. In summary, then, there is greater evidence for local specialization than for act specialization.

CHECKBOOK PARTICIPATION

It may be useful to consider one kind of activity specialization—checkbook participation—somewhat further. Throughout this inquiry we shall be concerned with the distinction between modes of activity that demand contributions of money and those that require giving time. As we shall see when we consider changes in the amount of political activity over the last two decades, one mode of participation that seems to have increased is making campaign contributions. Rapidly rising campaign costs, the enhanced role of paid professionals—rather than amateur volunteers—in managing campaigns, and the development of sophisticated telephone and mass mail techniques of raising money have conspired to augment the role of the citizen as a writer of checks.[14] As we shall see throughout this book, making contributions is, in many respects, distinctive as a mode of citizen activity. Hence, if money were to replace time as the primary medium of citizen input, the consequences for politics would be substantial.

Has America become a nation of contributors whose political activity is limited to giving money rather than time and effort? The data do show a great deal of checkbook participation. If we consider the proportions who donate time or money or both to political campaigns, we find that many more people give only money than give only time or give a combination of time and money. Of those who take some part in political campaigns, there are more than twice as many people (69 percent) who limit their involvement to check writing than there are people who give only time or who give both time and money. (Twelve percent of the campaigners give time but not money, and 19 percent give both.) It is, in fact, difficult to give time without also being expected to give

---

14. Corresponding changes are taking place in the world of non-profits and charities outside politics, as well.

money—but the opposite is not true. For many people, political activity consists of giving money and nothing else.[15]

How Much Participation?
Some Benchmarks of Comparison

Although the language used so far gives clues to whether we consider the amount of political activity we have uncovered to be a lot or a little, there is clearly no absolute answer to the question of whether Americans are active or passive. We can get some purchase on the issue, however, by considering some comparative benchmarks. One point of reference is the comparison between the United States and other democracies. Another is variation over time within the United States. A third standard by which political participation in America can be measured is one less often referred to, the level of voluntary activity in organizational and religious domains outside of politics.

In making these comparisons, it is critical to understand the extent to which the particular results, although not their broad outlines, depend upon the definitions used. It is not simply that, as always, question wording has implications for survey results. In addition, the placement of the threshold of activity—that is, how much activity is necessary before it is counted as activity—has consequences for how much activity we find. Finally, the unclear boundaries between various realms of voluntary activity complicate the matter. As we have indicated, we differentiate political, secular non-political, and religious domains of voluntary participation. These three domains interpenetrate in ways that are substantively important but that render indistinct the borders between them. Findings about the rates of activity, therefore, depend upon how this complex terrain is divided and which kinds of voluntary activity fall under which rubrics. As we proceed, we shall attempt

---

15. If we were to consider all political activities, including those where giving money is not usually an option—contacting officials, informal community activity, protesting, and the like—we would have to qualify our conclusion somewhat. If we consider all political acts beyond voting—most of which demand time but not money—we find that more than twice as many citizens give time only to politics than give money only.

to make clear the definitions that underlie our findings and the possible implications of those definitions for the results.

Participation in Cross-National Perspective

Figure 3.2 provides data for cross-national comparison, showing the proportions of citizens in the United States and four other industrialized democracies who engage in various kinds of political activity. The data confirm a point often made about citizen political activity: the United States lags far behind other democracies when it comes to voting turnout. However, this difference is not evidence of generalized American laziness, but rather reflects the peculiarities of American institutions—voter registration requirements and the weakness of American political parties as agents of mobilization.[16] When it comes to the other political activities shown in Figure 3.2—campaigning, attending political meetings, becoming active in the local community, and contacting officials—Americans are as active, or substantially more active, than citizens elsewhere. The differences in community activism and contacting are especially striking, with Americans two or more times as likely to be active.[17]

Changes over Time

Longitudinal data tell a confusing story about political participation in America. We might be led to contradictory expectations with respect to changes in political participation. On one hand, the past few decades have witnessed a remarkable increase in levels of educational attainment within the American public, which would suggest concomitant increases in political activity. On the other, it is common to observe that American citizens have abandoned politics over the past several decades. This perspective is buttressed by public opinion polls showing that Americans are alienated from

---

16. See G. Bingham Powell, Jr., "American Voting in Comparative Perspective," *American Political Science Review* 80 (1986): 23–37.

17. The proportions active in the United States differ somewhat from other data in this chapter because the data come from a different study at a different point in time.

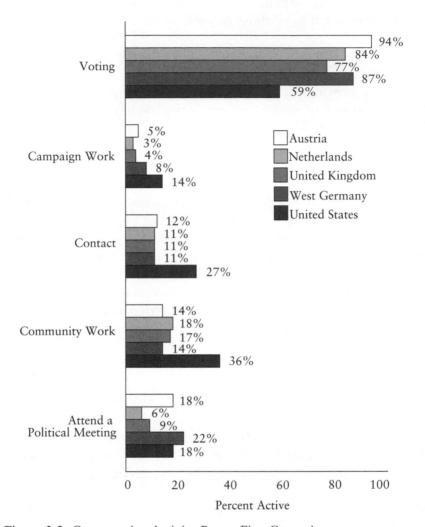

Figure 3.2 Comparative Activity Rates: Five Countries.

Sources: Average voting rates: Calculated for elections after 1945 (except for the
Netherlands where the vote is for elections after 1967 when compulsory voting was
eliminated). From Ivor Crewe, "Electoral Participation," in *Democracy at the Polls,* ed.
David Butler, Austin Ranney, and Howard Penniman (Washington, D.C.: American
Enterprise Institute, 1981), pp. 234–237.

Other activity rates: Samuel H. Barnes, Max Kaase, et al., *Political Action: Mass
Participation in Five Western Democracies* (Beverly Hills: Sage, 1979), pp. 541–542.

politics and fed up with politicians.[18] Of a piece with this interpretation of political withdrawal are the well-known data on the
decline of electoral turnout in America. From a recent high of 63
percent in the 1960 election, voting in presidential elections diminished gradually to the point where it was just over 50 percent in
1988 before rebounding somewhat in 1992.[19] As is sometimes
pointed out, many more eligible voters abstain than vote for the
winning candidate.

Data about a wider range of political acts suggest that the falloff
in voter turnout may not be part of a general erosion in political
participation. Table 3.6 presents the data from Verba and Nie's
Participation in America study in 1967 and from the National
Opinion Research Center's 1987 General Social Survey (GSS) that
replicated the 1967 questions on the proportion of the public
engaging in various political acts. The basic message is one of
continuity. The data point, once again, to the well-documented
decline in voting turnout. However, they also indicate that the
drop in turnout has not been accompanied by a general decrease
in citizen activism. In 1987, citizens were about as likely to report
involvement in electoral politics—persuading others how to vote,
working in a campaign, or attending a political meeting—as they
had been two decades before. The frequency of two activities has
changed substantially, but in opposite directions: there has been
an increase in the proportion reporting having contributed to a
political campaign and a decrease in the share mentioning mem-

---

18. Among the many examples, see Seymour Martin Lipset and William Schneider, *The
Confidence Gap: Business, Labor, and Government in the Public Mind* (New York: The
Free Press, 1983); and E. J. Dionne, Jr., *Why Americans Hate Politics* (N. Y.: Simon and
Schuster, 1991).

19. The literature on this phenomenon is voluminous. See, for instance, Richard A.
Brody, "The Puzzle of Participation," in *The New American Political System*, ed. Anthony
King; Paul R. Abramson and John H. Aldrich, "The Decline of Electoral Participation in
the United States," *American Political Science Review* 76 (1982): 502–521; Lee Sigelman,
et al., "Voting and Non-Voting: A Multi-Election Perspective," *American Journal of Politi-
cal Science* 29 (1985): 749–765; Ruy A. Teixeira, *Why Americans Don't Vote: Turnout
Decline in the United States, 1960–1984* (New York: Greenwood Press, 1987); Carol A.
Cassel and Robert C. Luskin, "Simple Explanations of Turnout Decline," *American Political Science Review* 82 (1988): 1321–1330; Warren E. Miller, "The Puzzle Transformed:
Explaining Declining Turnout," *Political Behavior* 14 (1992): 1–43; and Teixeira, *The
Disappearing American Voter.*

Table 3.6 Percentage Engaging in Fourteen Acts of Participation, 1967 and 1987

Specific Activity	1967	1987	Absolute Change	Relative Change
VOTING				
Regular voting in presidential elections	66	58	−8	−12
Always vote in local elections	47	35	−12	−26
CAMPAIGN				
Persuade others how to vote	28	32	+4	+14
Actively work for party or candidate	26	27	+1	+4
Attend political meeting or rally	19	19	0	0
Contribute money to party or candidate	13	23	+10	+77
Member of political club	8	4	−4	−50
CONTACT				
Contact local official: issue-based	14	24	+10	+71
Contact state or national official: issue-based	11	22	+11	+100
Contact local official: particularized	7	10	+3	+43
Contact state or national official: particularized	6	7	+1	+17
COMMUNITY				
Work with others on local problem	30	34	+4	+13
Active membership in community problem-solving organization	31	34	+3	+10
Form group to help solve local problem	14	17	+3	+21

Source: 1967 data, Verba and Nie, *Participation in America,* data file. 1987 data, National Opinion Research Center, General Social Survey.

bership in a political club. The former nearly doubled while the latter was cut in half.

When it comes to non-electoral political participation, the GSS data point in directions that are not inconsistent. While local community activity rose slightly, the proportion indicating having contacted local or national government officials increased much more substantially. Both proportionately and absolutely, the growth was largest for issue-based contacts—that is, contacts about matters of public policy rather than particularistic concerns. Nevertheless, the latter have risen as well, especially on the local level.

The over-time data are consistent with recent changes in the institutions that mobilize citizen activity and represent citizen interests. What we see at the level of the individual may reflect, in part, the widely discussed decline of political parties and invigoration of interest groups. However, it probably reflects as well a parallel transformation of both sets of institutions, whereby nationalization and professionalization have redefined the role of citizen activist as, increasingly, a writer of checks and letters. The rise of mass mail and electronic communications and the concomitant rise of citizen groups and political action committees dovetail with an enhanced responsiveness to constituency concerns among electorally insecure legislators to provide an institutional context for growth in the proportion of citizens who contact government officials and make campaign contributions. The obverse of these developments, the relative weakening of parties as local organizations, is reflected at the citizen level in the erosion of the numbers who are members of local party or political clubs.

The data in Table 3.6 are somewhat at variance with data presented by Steven J. Rosenstone and John Mark Hansen.[20] On the basis of an impressive data set that encompasses a much larger number of time points but a somewhat more restricted set of activities, they report a more general decline in activity. Their data are consistent with the data comparing 1967 and 1987 with respect to the increase in campaign contributions, although they note, as others do, a decline in giving in the late 1980s.[21] The sharpest difference between the data in Table 3.6 and Rosenstone and Hansen's data concerns citizen contacts with government officials. While Rosenstone and Hansen report a decline in the proportion writing to Congress, Table 3.6 indicates an increase in the proportion contacting government officials, an increase that is consistent with the available information from the recipients of such communications.[22]

---

20. *Mobilization, Participation, and Democracy in America* (New York: MacMillan, 1993), chap. 3.

21. On this point, see also Frank J. Sorauf, *Inside Campaign Finance: Myths and Realities* (New Haven: Yale University Press, 1992), chap. 1.

22. Congressional offices report a major increase in the flow of such communications. See Orval Hansen and Ellen Miller, *Congressional Operations: The Role of Mail in Decision-Making in Congress* (Washington, D.C.: Center for Responsive Politics, 1987); and

Unfortunately, accurate longitudinal data are not available for another important form of political participation, involvement in political organizations. However, observers of interest groups in Washington have documented an unambiguous increase in the number of organizations active in national politics and the birth of many new citizens' groups.[23] While the number of organizational involvements has presumably risen with the number of active organizations, it is less clear how actively engaged members are in staff-run organizations that require of members only the commitment of writing a check.

Although we are not in a position to make any kind of definitive evaluation of these discrepant data, several conclusions do seem possible. Since 1960, there has been an unambiguous decline in voter turnout. At the same time rates of other kinds of political participation have not eroded so sharply. Indeed, over the period some forms of activity—making contributions to electoral campaigns and political organizations and, probably, contacting public officials—have actually increased. As for the remaining kinds of participatory acts, the trajectory is less clear. However, what is unambiguous is that, in toto, political activity has not grown at rates that we might have expected on the basis of the substantial increase in levels of educational attainment within the public.[24]

Voluntary Activity outside of Politics

A final way to evaluate Americans' engagement in political activity is to compare it with their involvement in voluntary activities outside of the political realm. The broad terrain between the individual and family, on the one hand, and the institutions of public authority, on the other, is populated by an abundance of non-po-

---

Stephen E. Frantzich, *Write Your Congressman: Constituent Communications and Representation* (New York: Praeger, 1986).

23. See Jack L. Walker, "The Origins and Maintenance of Interest Groups in America," *American Political Science Review* 77 (1983): 390–406; and Kay Lehman Schlozman and John T. Tierney, *Organized Interests and American Democracy* (New York: Harper and Row, 1986), chap. 4.

24. See on this, Norman H. Nie, Jane Junn, and Kenneth Stehlik-Berry, *Education and Citizenship in America* (Chicago: University of Chicago Press, forthcoming).

litical institutions connected with almost every aspect of life: a multitude of voluntary associations that never get involved in politics as well as the rich array of churches and other religious institutions.

Non-political activity is widespread—indeed, more widespread than political activity—in America. The data in Figure 3.3 make this clear. Fully 68 percent of the respondents in our survey reported affiliation—either membership or contribution—with an organization that does not take stands in politics. Moreover, citizens are active in these organizations. Among those who are affiliated with non-political organizations, more than half indicated having attended a meeting in the past year; one-third reported being active members, that is, serving on a committee, giving time for special projects, or helping organize meetings; and 22 percent reported having, within the past five years, served on the board or been an officer of an organization with which they are still involved.

The analogous figures for religious involvement show an equivalent level of commitment. Fully 69 percent of our respondents either consider themselves members of a local church, synagogue, or other religious institution or attend services regularly in the same congregation. Only 13 percent of respondents never attend religious services; in contrast, 32 percent attend at least once a week, and 57 percent at least once a month. Furthermore, those who are affiliated with religious institutions tend to be active. Thirty-six percent of church members (or a quarter of all respondents) reported having given time within the past year to educational, charitable, or social activities associated with their churches—over and above attending services.[25]

Figure 3.3—which also contains data from the screener survey

---

25. As with political activity, there is some likelihood that non-political activity is exaggerated. Analyses of religious affiliation and attendance suggest systematic overreporting in these domains. See Kenneth D. Wald, Lyman A. Kellstedt, and David C. Leege, "Church Involvement in Political Behavior," in David C. Leege and Lyman A. Kellstedt, eds., *Rediscovering the Religious Factor in American Politics* (Armonk, N.Y.: M. E. Sharpe, 1993), chap. 6; and C. Kirk Hadaway, Penny L. Marler, and Mark Chaves, "What the Polls Don't Show: A Closer Look at U.S. Church Attendance", *American Sociological Review* 58 (1993): 741–752.

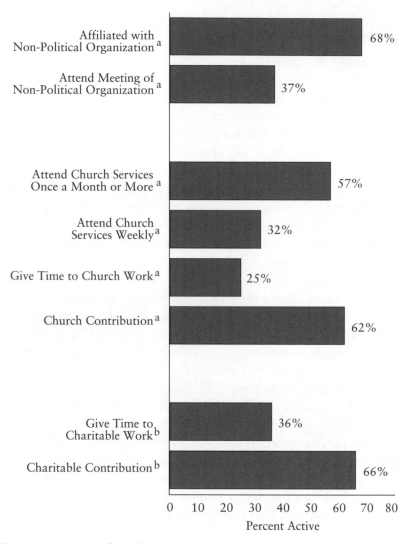

Figure 3.3 Non-Political Activities.

a. N = 2,517 weighted cases: See Appendix A for information about sample.
b. Screener sample: N = 15,055.

on contributions of time or money to charity—shows clearly that the level of participation in these forms of extra-political voluntary activity is quite high and is more or less equivalent across the domains of church, secular non-political organization, and charity.[26] In addition, beyond nominal membership, Americans are more likely to make financial contributions than to donate time. This generalization, which holds for contributions to religious institutions, secular non-political organizations, and charities, is one to which we shall return frequently. The figures about the relative importance of giving money are consonant with data that show—on the basis of a variety of indicators ranging from PTA memberships to participation in bowling leagues—a decline in non-political connectedness.[27]

A comparison of Figures 3.1 and 3.3 underlines several themes. Overall, a higher proportion of citizens take part in non-political than political activities. More citizens reported giving some time to church-related or charitable activities than indicated contacting a government official or working informally on a community problem, two of the most frequent forms of political participation beyond the vote. Comparing attendance at meetings of political and non-political organizations, we see a similar pattern. Likewise, by a substantial margin, more citizens give some money to charity, a secular non-political organization, or a religious institution than contribute to a political campaign or a political organization—and the year in question was a presidential election year.[28]

The greater commitment of citizens to non-political voluntary activities is seen most clearly if we reconsider the volume of activity—the amount of time or money given. Table 3.7 repeats data

---

26. The questions about charity asked in general about time spent or money contributed over the past twelve months to "charitable or voluntary service activities . . . in some way to help others." Because a great deal of charitable effort emanates from religious institutions, we specifically asked about donations of time or money other than those made in church. There is, therefore, a great deal of overlap between the activity referenced by these questions and that covered in the extensive section on voluntary organizations in the follow-up interview.

27. Robert C. Putnam, "Bowling Alone: America's Declining Social Capital," *Journal of Democracy* 6 (1995): 65–78.

28. Estimates by other surveys of the amount of voluntary non-political activity in the United States vary widely. See Appendix B.2.c for a discussion.

Table 3.7 Time and Money Given to Political and
          Non-Political Activity

	Campaign	Charity	Church
AMONG ALL RESPONDENTS[a]			
TIME			
Mean given per week	0.6 hours	1.7 hours	0.9 hours
% giving 5+ hours per week	4%	8%	6%
MONEY			
Mean contribution per year	$58	$191	$402
% giving $250+ per year	5%	16%	31%
AMONG ACTIVE RESPONDENTS			
TIME[b]			
Mean given per week	7.5 hours	4.5 hours	3.1 hours
% giving 5+ hours per week	49%	23%	20%
MONEY[c]			
Mean contribution per year	$247	$283	$634
% giving $250+ per year	19%	24%	49%

a. N = 2,517 weighted cases: see Appendix A for information about sample.
b. Active respondents are those who give some time. See Appendix B.1.
c. Active respondents are those who give some money. See Appendix B.1.

from Table 3.1 on the amounts given to political activity and compares them with the amounts given to charity and church. Considering the public as a whole, we find a sharp difference in the level of resources dedicated to charitable and church activities, on one hand, and political campaigns, on the other. With respect to time, the average American gave about 36 minutes per week to campaign activity during the 1988 campaign season but about 102 minutes per week to charitable activity and 54 minutes per week to church activities throughout the year. A parallel—but much sharper—distinction holds for financial contributions. In that election year, the average American gave over three times as much to charity—and seven times as much to a religious institution—as to political campaigns.

The picture changes somewhat when we consider the activists only, especially with respect to time. Although a smaller share of the public takes part in political campaigns than gives time to church or charitable work, their involvement during the campaign season appears to be more intense. Those who work in a campaign give more time during the campaign: on average, they devote seven and a half hours per week, and half dedicate more than five hours per week to campaign activity. The weekly commitment of time is smaller for those who are active in charity or church work. However, the figures for religious and charitable voluntarism are still substantial—especially since the figures for the time spent on work associated with a church or charity represent the weekly average for the entire year, while the figure for campaign activity is the average per week during the campaign only. Among financial donors, in contrast, those who make charitable or church contributions give on average more than does the average member of the much smaller group of campaign contributors—with those who contribute to church giving more than twice as much as those who contribute either to campaigns or to charity.

These data underscore a well-known fact about the public: politics is not at the heart of the day-to-day life of the American people. Beyond the domains of work and the family, which are the main concerns of most people, politics takes a secondary place to church and to other voluntary activities. Although Americans are relatively active in politics, the bulk of voluntary participation in this country takes place outside of politics.

NON-POLITICAL ACTIVITY IN CROSS-NATIONAL PERSPECTIVE
Cross-national data underscore these themes. Americans are known as joiners, and associational life in America is probably unparalleled in the number of organizations and the diversity of their concerns. We have already seen that—with the exception of voting turnout, which is lower in the United States than elsewhere—citizens of other democracies are no more active, and in some respects are less active, than Americans. As shown in Figure 3.4, this tendency holds for voluntary involvement outside of politics as well: Americans have a deserved reputation for high levels of participation in voluntary associations and, especially, religious institutions. Figure 3.4 indicates that Americans are more likely to be members of voluntary associations, in general, and religious organizations, in particular, than are citizens of other nations. What is more, not

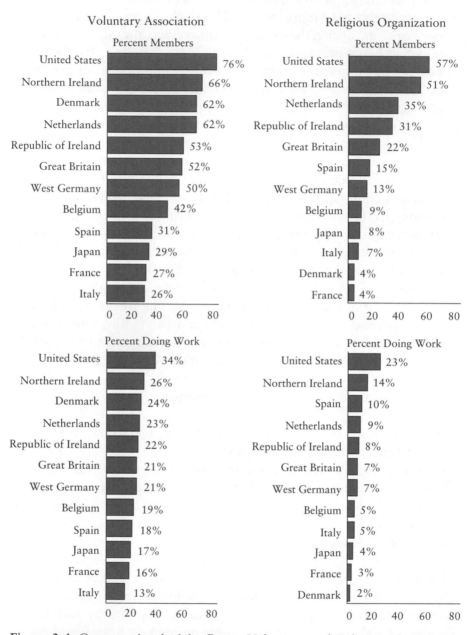

Figure 3.4 Comparative Activity Rates: Voluntary and Religious Organizations.
Source: Gallup Poll, 1981, Survey Conducted for the Leisure Development Center.

only are they more likely to be members, but they are correspondingly more likely to do work within these organizations.[29] Thus, once again, we see evidence both of the relatively high levels of participation in the United States and of the strength of the non-political voluntary sector. Because of the intrinsic significance of voluntary action outside politics, and because of the complex relationship between political activity and voluntary participation in other domains, we shall return to these themes over and over as we proceed.

The American Public: A Profile

In spite of the contemporary image of Americans as a nation of passive spectators mesmerized before their television screens, these comparative metrics suggest that there is a great deal of voluntary activity in the United States both within and, especially, outside politics. The activity may be intermittent and peripheral to Ameri-

---

29. Because of the complexity of these domains, the absolute numbers derived from surveys about voluntary participation are dependent upon the precise referent of the question. The reader may note that the data from our study contained in Figure 3.3 indicate that almost one-third of Americans reported doing some work in their churches—over and above attending services. The Gallup study reported in Figure 3.4 indicates that about one in four Americans does work for a religiously connected organization. The discrepancy reflects differences in the focus of the questions. Similar discrepancies emerge from data about participation in voluntary associations. Robert Dahl cites cross-national data showing that, because membership in such occupationally related organizations as professional associations and, especially, trade unions is very high in many northern European nations, particularly the Nordic democracies, Americans are not the most likely to be members of organizations. See Robert A. Dahl, *Dilemmas of Pluralist Democracy: Autonomy vs. Control* (New Haven: Yale University Press, 1982), pp. 67–68. See also Graham K. Wilson, *Interest Groups in the United States* (New York: Oxford University Press, 1981), pp. 132–144, and Schlozman and Tierney, *Organized Interests and American Democracy*, pp. 59–63.

There seems to be no dispute, however, about the number and variety of associations in the United States and the particular American propensity for involvement in non-economic organizations. Moreover, the 79 percent figure for organizational affiliation (both political and non-political) obtained by using our detailed list of organizations puts the United States on a par with the levels reported by Dahl for Sweden. The sensitivity of results to question wording, however, suggests that cross-national comparisons must be treated with caution. Curtis, Grabb, and Baer provide data from a number of countries that show a very high level of religious involvement in the United States. They offer, however, some qualifications to the view that Americans are at the top in terms of membership—especially active membership—in general. See James E. Curtis, Edward G. Grabb, and Douglas E. Baer, "Voluntary Association Membership in Fifteen Countries: A Comparative Analysis", *American Sociological Review* 57 (1992): 139–152.

cans' basic concerns, but it is activity nonetheless. The amount of activity, however, does not necessarily tell us how many activists there are. For many activities, especially the more difficult political acts, the percentage who have been active is quite small. Only in voting, attending church, and making cash contributions to charities and religious institutions is a majority of the public active. If activity were clearly hierarchical—that is, if all those who engaged in an activity carried out by a smaller proportion of the population could be counted on to engage in those activities carried on by a larger proportion—we might find a fairly large proportion of the population engaging in no voluntary activity, either political or non-political, and a small proportion accounting for the major share of the activity by taking part in multiple ways.

It makes sense, then, to see how members of the public sort themselves into types of activists. Figure 3.5 provides an overview of the distribution of the public across the three domains of voluntary activity: political, religious, and secular non-political. We have used the following definitions of activity in each of the domains:

Political. Engaged in at least one political act beyond voting.
Secular non-political. Member or contributor to a non-political voluntary organization or charity.
Religious. Gave time to church activities (beyond attendance at services) or gave money to church (beyond school fees).[30]

This is a quite inclusive definition. Anyone who belongs to a non-political organization or has written a check to a church or to a charitable or political cause is considered to have crossed the

---

30. Political activity includes: worked in an electoral campaign; made a campaign contribution; contacted a public official; attended a protest, march, or demonstration; served without pay on a local community governing board or attended meetings of such a board on a regular basis; worked informally with others to deal with some community issue or problem; is a member of or made a contribution beyond dues to an organization that takes stands in politics.

Secular non-political activity includes: member of or contributor beyond dues to an organization that does not take stands in politics; spent time on charitable or voluntary service activities to help others or contributed money to charitable or voluntary service activities and organizations (outside of church).

Church activity includes: spent time on educational, charitable, or social activities associated with church (aside from attending religious services); contributed to religion (aside from school tuition).

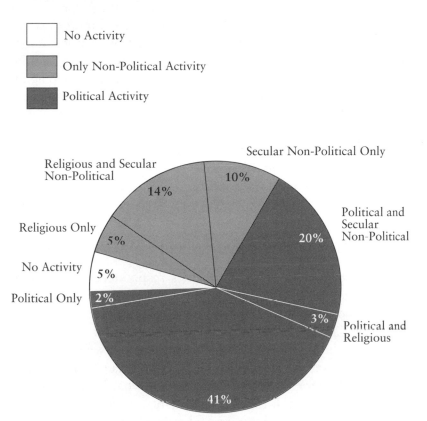

Figure 3.5 Types of Activists.
N = 2,517 weighted cases. See Appendix A for information about sample.

threshold to activity. Still, the definition is not as inclusive as it might be. Someone who just voted and did nothing else would not be counted as engaging in political activity; similarly, attending church services but doing nothing else in one's church does not make one active in church in this definition. The definition, however, seems useful in locating those who take almost no role in religious, organizational, or political life. Using this definition, we find only a very small proportion of the public, 5 percent, to be totally inactive.[31]

31. This group is genuinely inactive. Not only do they not take part in any of the activities subsumed under the umbrella of the definition, but they are much less likely than

Considering separately the three domains of voluntary activity, we find the following: 65 percent of the sample reported some kind of political activity beyond voting; 64 percent some kind of activity in a religious institution beyond attendance at religious services; and fully 85 percent some kind of secular non-political activity. What is more, most of these activists do not confine themselves to a single domain of involvement: a mere 2 percent of the sample indicated political activity only; 5 percent reported church activity only; and 10 percent secular non-political activity only. At the other end of the continuum, 41 percent of the respondents reported at least some activity in all three domains.

The Subject Matter of Political Activity

Surveys often ask about the difficulties respondents face in their personal lives, the problems they believe face the nation, or the issues they consider important in an election. However, no survey before the Citizen Participation Study has inquired about the issues that animate citizen activity. In our survey, we asked about the subject matter of political activity. These data give us a unique opportunity to enrich our understanding of what is behind voluntary participation. Each time a respondent reported having taken part in political activity, we asked whether there were "any issues or problems ranging from public policy issues to community, family, or personal concerns" that led to the activity. For the 63 percent of participants across all political activities who replied that there was such an issue, we followed up with an open-ended question about the content of those concerns and a closed-ended item about who was affected.[32] We received a range of replies, the bulk of which, 86 percent, contained recognizable public policy issues.[33] In terms of who is affected by the issue or problem, across

---

other members of the public either to vote or to attend church services regularly. Half of the inactive group as defined in the text is totally disconnected from voluntary activity in that they reported neither voting in 1988 nor going to church regularly nor any other activity. If one were looking for true isolates who take no part in political, religious, or organizational life, it would be this group, which constitutes 2.4 percent of the public.

32. See Appendix B.3. If more than one issue or problem was listed in response to the open-ended item, the closed-ended question was asked about the first one mentioned.

33. The 14 percent of responses that did not contain recognizable policy issues were distributed as follows. A small proportion—4 percent across all the political activities—

all political activities—except for contacting public officials—the overwhelming majority of participants indicated that the issue at stake affected others beyond themselves and their families. About one-fifth of those who contacted a public official indicated that the activity was aimed at an issue limited to the individual and his or her family. Otherwise, most political activity is described—in proportions that reflect quite reasonably the nature of the activity—as affecting either the entire community or the entire nation. The point is worth underlining. Political activity, in general, is not about personal problems but about public issues.

Reading the verbatim responses indicates that respondents can make these kinds of distinctions. Appendix 3.2 to this chapter contains a random sample of responses about the issues and problems behind four kinds of contacts: those to local officials defined by respondents as affecting either the whole community or themselves and their families; and those to members of Congress defined by respondents as affecting either the whole nation or themselves and their families. These are unexpurgated "word bites," transcribed as recorded by interviewers: we have not filled in the obvious blanks, spruced up the grammar, or, most important, corrected miscategorizations in respondents' self-codings. These answers give us confidence that respondents can distinguish quite well—although not perfectly—between particularistic concerns and matters of policy and between issues affecting the whole community and issues affecting the whole nation.

THE NATURE OF THE SUBSTANTIVE CONCERNS

A closer look at the range of substantive concerns yields a better understanding of the nature of these policy concerns. We coded the verbatim responses into the following categories, which reflect the dominant policy concerns of citizen activists:[34]

---

could not be coded either because the respondent was confused and inarticulate or because the interviewer was sloppy in recording and editing. Another 10 percent represented coherent and "codeable" problems or concerns that did not constitute public policy issues. Examples include the following statements describing the issues or problems behind campaign work:

To see New York have its first black mayor.
My husband was running for office. He was the best-qualified candidate.
We needed another conservative.

34. Let us clarify a few aspects of the coding. First, a single political act may have been

Basic human needs: various government benefits (welfare, AFDC, food stamps, housing subsidies, Social Security, Medicare, and Medicaid); unemployment (either as an economic issue or in terms of the respondent's own circumstances); housing or homelessness; health or health care; poverty or hunger; aid to the handicapped or handicapped rights.

Taxes: all references to taxes at any governmental level.

Economic issues: local or national economic performance; inflation; budget issues or the budget deficit; government spending; other economic issues.

Abortion: all references to abortion, whether pro-choice, pro-life, or ambiguous.

Social issues: traditional morality; pornography; family planning, teenage pregnancy, sex education, or contraception; school prayer; gay rights or homosexuality.

Education: educational issues (school reform, school voucher plans, etc.); problems or issues related to schooling of family members; guaranteed student loans.

Environment: specific environmental issues (e.g., clean air, toxic wastes) or environmental concerns in general; wildlife preservation; animal rights.

Crime or drugs: crime; gangs; safety in the streets; drugs.

International: relations with particular nations or to foreign policy in general; defense policy or defense spending; peace, arms control, or international human rights issues.

It should be noted that the categories differ with respect to whether they encompass respondents who disagree with one another. Those mentioning abortion have sharply differing opinions on the issue. In contrast, those mentioning the environment tend to agree in favoring environmental preservation. Those opposing

---

inspired by more than one issue concern. The contactor who expressed concern about "public housing, teenage pregnancy, and the child care bill" would have been coded as mentioning three separate issues. In addition, these categories are not exhaustive. Issue concerns ranging from gun control to local economic development for which we have codes have been omitted from this list because they were mentioned by so few activists.

environmental regulation would be more likely to express their concern by citing an issue like the need for economic development.

For each political act for which a codeable policy concern was expressed, Table 3.8 summarizes the subject matter. The entries in the cells represent the proportion of those activists discussing any codeable policy concern who mentioned, among other things, an issue that fell under the rubric of one of the above categories. In interpreting Table 3.8, it is critical to recall that the data reflect, in part, the era and the place in which the survey was conducted. If we had collected data two decades before, different issues—for example, the war in Vietnam or civil rights—would have figured prominently, especially in conjunction with acts such as protesting. Moreover, the data clearly represent the American political agenda. The prominence that activists give to the issue of abortion, for instance, would presumably not have appeared had the data been collected elsewhere.

The data make clear that different modes of political participation serve as the vehicle for carrying different kinds of messages to public officials in ways that might not have been fully anticipated. Because there is so much variation among participatory acts in the issue concerns they convey, we shall examine each act separately.

Electoral Activity. Reflecting the common wisdom that informs electoral politics today—that is, that matters related to economic performance are dominant—nearly half of the voters who gave a codeable policy response discussed economic issues or taxes. Interestingly, the concern about the economy and taxes that voters bring to the polls does not extend to other forms of activity. Activists are less than half as likely to report these concerns in connection with other kinds of participation, including other acts related to elections. Indeed, only 12 percent of campaign workers cited economic concerns and 7 percent mentioned taxes. Beyond these issues, voters identified a variety of others: more than a quarter cited educational issues, presumably in connection with local elections; and nearly one in six discussed abortion. With respect to working in campaigns or making campaign contributions, no one set of issues took precedence and a variety of issues were cited. The data illustrate a point we shall make many times: the danger of generalizing from voting to other participatory acts. Votes appear to turn on the economy much more than do other acts.

Table 3.8 Issues and Problems behind Political Activity (percentage mentioning particular issues)[a]

	Electoral Activity				Contacts			Protests		Community Activity	
	Vote	Campaign Work	Money to Candidate	Money to Organization	Particularized	Local	National	Local	National	Informal	Board
Human Needs	11	14	19	7	25	7	13	10	2	6	11
Taxes	32	7	6	5	13	10	2	9	0	5	1
Economy[b]	20	12	18	13	2	8	6	14	0	2	2
Abortion	17	18	13	22	0	1	17	4	45	2	0
Social Issues[c]	1	3	5	4	0	1	6	6	3	2	0
Education	28	26	19	11	9	15	7	29	1	8	29
Environment	9	6	7	22	3	5	15	10	18	8	16
Crime, Drugs	7	11	17	3	1	8	3	5	6	22	8
International	15	4	7	12	1	1	8	0	9	0	0
Weighted N:	700	97	53	138	147	272	190	39	77	351	53

a. Among those respondents who mentioned a codeable policy concern when asked about the issue or problem connected with their activity.

  b. Not including taxes.

  c. Not including abortion.

Contacting Public Officials. More than any kind of activity, contacting is distinguished by the control the participant can exercise over the timing of the activity and the content of its message. In Table 3.8 we differentiate among contacts on a particularistic issue, on a community issue, and on a national issue. In descending order of frequency, the particularistic contacts focused on three matters: basic human needs, taxes, and education. It is interesting that, in comparison to all of the more "public" modes of participation, particularized contacting is the most likely to convey concerns related to basic human needs—even though concerns about such needs can be framed as policy issues like homelessness or spending on welfare instead of particularistic concerns like the need to straighten out a Social Security payment or establish disability eligibility. Contacts on issues affecting the community focused most heavily on educational issues and taxes. Contacts on issues affecting the nation were varied in substance. The most frequent topic was abortion, followed by concerns about the environment and basic human needs.

Protesting. As with contacting, the subject matter of protests differs substantially depending on whether the issue is seen as affecting the community or the nation. With respect to issues affecting the community, education predominated followed by economic issues. Considering that protest is a political act that requires little in the way of resources and, therefore, is often characterized as the weapon of the weak, what is noteworthy is how little of the protest activity dealt with issues of basic human need: one in ten of the protesters on issues of local import and only 2 percent of the protesters on issues of national import mentioned basic human needs. Environmental concerns did figure prominently among the subjects of protests on issues affecting the nation. We were not prepared, however, for the extent to which abortion forms the subject of demonstrations about issues affecting the nation: nearly half the protesters on issues affecting the nation mentioned abortion as the subject. Of them, nearly three-quarters, 72 percent, hold pro-life views as registered on a seven-point scale measuring attitudes toward abortion.

Community Activity. Those who engaged in informal community activity mentioned a variety of issues, the most frequent of which were crime and drugs. The issues identified by members of local governing boards—educational and environmental concerns—reflect the boards on which most of them sit, school boards and zoning boards or park commissions.

THE SUBJECT MATTER OF POLITICAL ACTIVITY: A SUMMARY

Our findings about the subject matter behind political participation are a reflection, in part, of the particular time when the survey was conducted, but several general conclusions are possible about the many and varied issues to which activists referred. There is a division of labor among political acts in terms of the substantive messages they carry to policymakers. The subject matter of these messages usually appears to be linked to the appropriate act. For example, the kinds of issue concerns mentioned by particularized contactors—a personal tax problem, help for a relative—could hardly be dealt with in the context of another form of participation. In addition, there are differences in the subject matter of activity directed at local, as opposed to national, officials—differences that are clearly related to the substance of local and national politics.

Beyond that, however, the different concerns associated with different political activities are somewhat surprising. For example, there is no particular reason to have expected that crime and violence should have ranked so much higher on the agenda of informal community activists than of protesters or contactors with community-level issue concerns, or that voters should have been so much more attuned than campaign workers to economic issues and taxes. With respect to the findings about voting, it seems that voting is unique when it comes to the issue concerns behind it—just as it is unique in so many other ways.

Another striking finding is how much participation, across activities, is inspired by the issue of abortion. Those who protested on an issue affecting the nation were especially likely to have mentioned abortion, but other activists also cited abortion as an issue. In contrast, concerns about basic needs weigh heavily among the issues mentioned in conjunction with the activity that is least concerned with the making of general policies, contacting on particularistic issues. Activity aimed at influencing policy—as opposed to the handling of a particular case—is much less likely to convey a message about basic human needs. This is most notable in relation to protesting. Although it is purportedly the mode of participation available to those with few resources, it is striking that issues of basic human needs were mentioned so infrequently in connection with protests.

Conclusion

Along with the preceding one, this chapter provides a preliminary conceptual map to the terrain of voluntary political participation—activity that is undertaken without threat of coercion or promise of financial compensation and that has the intent or effect of influencing what the government does. Although this is a domain of human endeavor that can be distinguished analytically, the empirical boundaries that define it are in reality quite fuzzy: in practice, it is not always easy to differentiate what is political from what is non-political; what is done without financial reward from what is done in the expectation of future career enhancement; or what is activity from what is evidence of psychological involvement with politics.

We employed several comparative standards in order to get some purchase on the question of whether the amount of political activity in the United States is a lot or a little. Although Americans are less likely than citizens of other democracies to go to the polls, they are otherwise as active, or more active, than citizens elsewhere. However, when one uses the comparative standard of the level of participation in the secular and religious domains of voluntary activity outside politics, the level of political participation in the United States looks less impressive. Americans give more time and money to charity and to their churches than they do to politics. The data underscore the important role of non-political secular and religious institutions in the United States.

Appendix 3.1:
Measuring Organizational Involvement

As we indicated, measuring organizational involvement raises complex issues.[35] One issue is whether to ask about organizations in

---

35. For the organization questions, see Appendix B.1.g. For a fuller discussion of the issue of measuring organizational affiliation as well as for an explication of the measures

general or to present a more detailed list of types of organizations. We did the latter and asked about a long list of types of organizations, twenty categories in all. These types—for which examples were given to jog the respondent's memory—covered the full range of kinds of organizations to which individuals can belong. The categories, presented to our respondents on a card, were selected to make sense to respondents. Since these categories were designed to be readily understood by respondents, they often combine organizations with similar substantive focus, but very different organizational characteristics. Although these organizational categories are useful for illustrative purposes, we shall ordinarily find it more illuminating to consider analytical dimensions than actual organizational categories. The list as presented to our respondents is shown in Table 3.4.

Another issue in measuring organizational involvement is the definition of affiliation with an organization. Membership, in the usual sense in which one joins the Masons or the American Medical Association, is not a prerequisite for organizational involvement. Besides card-carrying membership, there are two other avenues to organizational involvement. First, citizens can support an organization simply by writing checks without ever becoming members. In an era in which organizations take advantage of computerized mass mailings and cheap long-distance rates to raise money, organizational affiliations that are confined to making financial contributions are increasingly common. Moreover, it is possible to give time in an organizational setting—by, for example, volunteering in a hospital or a school—without any kind of formal membership. Thus, in order to discern organizational affiliations that are not memberships in the ordinary sense, we inquired, for each of the twenty types of organizations, about membership and about making financial contributions as well as, where appropriate, giving time.[36]

---

used to determine both organizational involvement and whether organizational involvement entailed political activity, see Kay Lehman Schlozman, "Voluntary Associations in Politics: Who Gets Involved?" in *Representing Interests and Interest Group Representation*, ed. William Crotty, Mildred A. Schwartz, and John C. Green (Lanham, Md.: University Press of America, 1994).

36. A similar approach was employed by Frank R. Baumgartner and Jack L. Walker,

Finally, we had to deal with the fact that organizations fall along a long continuum in terms of the extent to which their goals and activities are politically relevant. Organizations that resemble one another in many respects—substantive concerns, organizational forms, the amount and kinds of support emanating from members—may differ substantially in the level of their involvement in politics. What this means is that the boundary between political and non-political organizational involvement is very indistinct, and an important form of *political* participation is difficult to distinguish from analogous voluntary activity that is not germane to politics. Especially when an organization combines political and non-political means of furthering members' goals and interests, those who are affiliated may not be motivated by political concerns or attentive to its political activities. Still, their support of the organization constitutes a significant, though perhaps latent, kind of political action. In order to establish whether an organization is politically engaged, we relied on the perceptions of our respondents. For each organization mentioned, we asked whether it sometimes takes stands on public issues—either nationally or locally. We define as political any organization that, according to the respondent, takes stands on public issues.

Appendix 3.2:
Examples of Open-Ended Responses on the Subject of Citizen Contacting

A. CONTACTS TO LOCAL OFFICIALS ON A PARTICULARIZED ISSUE

Mosquito problem in standing water on my street.
It was a personal concern. The water department had me

---

who brought many of these concerns to the construction of a battery of items about organizational involvement that was used in the 1985 pilot to the National Election Study. Although they did not inquire about donations of time without formal membership, they asked about contributions as well as membership and used a list of ten types of organizations that had been designed to provide categories for the political issue and citizen advocacy groups that have become increasingly prominent in American politics since the 1960s. Their results are reported in "Survey Research and Membership in Voluntary Associations." Unfortunately, their questions were not included in the subsequent full National Election Study.

down for $2,500 for a 4-flat building with only 5 people and I sent this problem to him . . .

My husband was in the process of getting a taxi license from the city, problems with bureaucratic process.

Permit for a family outing.

A better job. That's it.

A problem with the dock at our cottage. We needed his help to get the Dept. of Natural Resources to move quicker so we could rebuild our dock.

That I don't get my mail correctly. It has zip codes & address correct but still doesn't send my mail and I do a lot of mail contact.

Damage to our property from neighbors, lack of gutters.

Change of schools for my two boys.

Crime; yes, we have a family business and it was broken into and that's why I contacted the mayor to see what could be done to prevent it from happening.

I had a complaint. I had a complaint about another business. It was not political.

Was getting information about a rehab program. Housing rehabilitation.

Assessment. Property assessment.

Policy issue, being evicted, having the town help you make delays.

This had to do with zoning laws in the borough. Nothing else.

To fix my driveway—school bus turns around in it.

B. CONTACTS TO LOCAL OFFICIALS ON A COMMUNITY ISSUE

A plan to redevelop our area with large skyscrapers of mixed use.

Appointment of commissioner of health.

Transfer a principal of a school to another school—did not want this to happen.

It was the drug problem in this building and on the block.

Transportation issue.

Community problems; planning and gang violence.

A community project for AIDS.

About zoning problems in Glendale.

The public policy issue involving the entire community. The realignment of school district boundaries as it relates to race in Pasadena.

Community, economic development, housing, more improvements in plans for, ideas by who, that's about it.

Getting permits for buildings.

We had a lot of problems with trash in my neighborhood and I wanted some help to get it cleaned up.

Drugs, housing, poverty, more community participation, creating new programs for kids, recreation centers.

I want to improve Chinatown.

C. CONTACT TO A SENATOR OR REPRESENTATIVE ON A PARTICULARIZED ISSUE

I needed help with a refugee. I work with refugees. That's it.

Some problems with the IRS, that was enough.

Apply for temporary residence in the U.S.

Compensation for a relative; gov't agencies could help; several environmental and health issues that are coming for vote; that's it.

Passes to Government buildings.

Social Security problem for my mother.

The problem with the IRS. To do with taxes. My personal taxes. My error but I didn't know it. IRS wouldn't listen to me.

I was bidding on building a U.S. Marshall's holding facility and contacted them to get a list of the bidders.

Boundary dispute with the state. The state said part of our house was on state-owned property.

Poor mail service. That's it. It took me 5 days to get your letter mailed from Columbus, Oh. to Ft. Wayne. That's too long.

Personal problems. Just personal.

We couldn't find my Vietnamese kid's green card and he had to go to immigration.

I had to ask him to send birthday greetings to a relative who
    turned 100.
Personal concern. Concerning the taxes on cigarettes and
    beer and a new post office. That's it.
I was looking for information about a book I needed.

D. CONTACT TO A SENATOR OR REPRESENTATIVE
ON A NATIONAL ISSUE

Policy—environmental concerns.
Women's rights to choose.
Public housing, teenage pregnancy, the child care bill.
Banking, something to do with putting a cap on interest rates.
The oil industry.
This was a post-card campaign to the congressman stating I
    did not want my tax $ to go to Defense.
U.S. Senator about Pro-choice.
Abortion.
El Salvador. Our continuing high level of support for the mili-
    tary in El Salvador; a million and a half a day and my con-
    cern about that.
Art censorship.
Amendment to the constitution protecting the flag. I am
    against it, I wrote the White House.
Involved in the U.S. govt.'s refusal to participate in an interna-
    tional resolution regarding the improvement of worldwide
    air quality.
The legislation before Congress regarding Israel—Jackson
    Bannock Act, 400 million deficit.
El Salvador's persecution and ousting of Bishop Garcia.
Public policy issue, has to do with agricultural imports per
    my board position as University of Illinois trustee.
The Clean Air Act; I wanted it to pass and be strengthened;
    that's it.
The treatment of veal calves; it was about the veal calf protec-
    tion act.

4

Interpreting Political Activity:
A Report from Activists

In this chapter, we bring our analysis closer to the world of political participation as experienced by the activists. Social scientists often deal with the issue of what leads a person to engage in some activity in terms of a statistical relationship between various characteristics of the individual and the conduct in question. In Part III of this book, we adopt this strategy—using a large array of social and psychological characteristics to explain political activity within the framework of a complex causal analysis. Here we approach the problem more directly by asking respondents to tell us why they were active. How do they understand what animated their activity? What did they expect to achieve from it? This approach provides a richer understanding of the meaning of political participation to those who take part.

The common characteristic uniting the activities about which we are concerned is that they are voluntary. Nobody is forced to engage in them. While social norms may support citizen involvement in its various forms, they hardly make it obligatory in the ordinary sense of the word. Moreover, this is, by definition, activity that is not paid. Under the circumstances, it makes sense to ask why people invest their time and their money in voluntary activities. In this chapter we do just that: we not only ask *why* people participate—a question that underlies a large portion of this book—but we ask *them* to tell us. We explore voluntary activity from the perspective of the activists: their interpretations of their activity and the motivations they report. The exploration allows us to shed light on the significant question of the rationality of participation.

In our survey, we asked those who had taken part in any of the array of voluntary activities to recollect the reasons for their participation. By asking about a wide variety of possible gratifications across a number of acts, we are able to consider in a way that has not before been possible the question of why citizens participate from the perspective of the activists themselves. In so doing, we contribute to the understanding of not only the mainsprings of voluntary action but also the nature of American politics. It is tricky to ask activists to reconstruct the reasons that led to their participation. However, we shall argue that these questions can be asked and that the responses they elicit are meaningful. Across different forms of participation, the patterns of gratifications cited are so clearly related to the nature of the act and the policy goal on behalf of which it was undertaken as to suggest that respondents were not simply giving answers designed to satisfy an interviewer's queries.

These retrospective interpretations help us to understand what activists' participation means to them and, implicitly, how they understand its rationality. What we find suggests that some obvious and straightforward aspects of political activity may have been underestimated. The logic that has been imputed to activists on the basis of their revealed preferences has relatively little to do with the language they use to give retrospective interpretation to the decision to take part. In discussing their activity, voters, campaign workers, community activists, protesters, and other participants frequently recall gratifications that are self-interested in the narrow sense of the word. More often, however, their reconstructions reflect a concern for civic involvement, for the welfare of the larger community or nation, or for issues of public policy.

We do not claim that our data explain participation. Instead, they constitute a systematic account of how those who take part explain their activity, an account that gains credence by virtue of the fact that what the respondents say varies so sensibly across different modes of activity. Moreover, even if activists' reports about the reasons for their activity cannot be considered the "real" reasons, these retrospective interpretations carry additional significance. First, activists' recollections of the rewards associated with participation presumably have implications for future decisions to take part. In addition, the rhetoric of participation has consequences for the nature of politics. That civic motivations and substantive policy goals figure so importantly in activists' recollections of their reasons for their involvement and the substantive policy concerns behind it contributes to the character of political discourse and the nature of the political agenda in America.

The Puzzle of Participation

The fact of voluntary activity in collective endeavors has long been a challenge to rational actor models. According to rational actor theories of collective action, it makes little sense to take part in politics. Briefly, the logic is as follows: since governmental policies are collective goods—affecting citizens whether or not they are active in promoting or opposing them—the rational, self-interested individual has no incentive to invest scarce resources of time, money, or effort in political participation. Because the efforts of any single individual are unlikely to have a significant effect on whether the desired policy outcome is achieved, the rational individual will hitch a free ride on the activity of others and, thus, will reap the benefits of the preferred policy without expending resources on its attainment. The result of these calculations by rational, self-interested individuals is that all will refrain from joint activity on behalf of a collective goal—even one that is widely shared and intensely preferred.[1]

The puzzle of participation, thus, becomes: how are we to

---

1. The classic statements are Anthony Downs, *An Economic Theory of Democracy* (New York: Harper, 1957), chaps. 3 and 14; and Mancur Olson, Jr., *The Logic of Collective Action: Public Goods and the Theory of Groups* (Cambridge, Mass.: Harvard University Press, 1965). Downs (chap. 14) focuses on the rationality of abstention based on the very low likelihood that a voter could cast the deciding vote, while Olson (pp. 1–16) emphasizes the collective nature of the good sought. A lucid comparison of Downs and Olson is S. I. Benn, "Rationality and Political Behaviour," in *Rationality and the Social Sciences: Contributions to the Philosophy and Methodology of the Social Sciences,* ed. S. I. Benn and G. W. Mortimore (London: Routledge and Kegan Paul, 1976), pp. 246–267. For more extended discussion of the various scholarly approaches to these issues, see Kay Lehman Schlozman, Sidney Verba, and Henry Brady, "Participation's Not a Paradox: The View from American Activists," *British Journal of Political Science* 25 (1995): 1–36.

explain the fact that millions of citizens, in apparent defiance of this elegant logic, vote or take part in various kinds of voluntary activity on behalf of collective ends? Indeed, many social scientists—including some of our acquaintance who espouse the rational choice perspective—not only vote but also devote time, effort, and money to favored candidates and political causes that range from environmental preservation to U.S. policy toward human rights violations in faraway places. The puzzle of participation has been described as "the major example of the failure of rational choice theory."[2]

This logic, which has been applied most explicitly to voting and interest group activity, pertains to any voluntary, collective, goal-oriented activity—recycling cans, contributing to the church's famine-relief fund, helping to stage a costume ball to raise money for cancer research—regardless of whether it is political. Of the activities on which we focus, only particularized contacting—in which the subject of the contact is germane only to respondents themselves or their immediate families—is exempt from the dictates of the logic of collective action. The respondent who seeks to clear up a tax problem or to get a pothole fixed does not have the option of free riding. Moreover, the collective goal need not be a public good like clean air or national security that, if achieved, is available to all in a society. On the contrary, the joint goal can be of the sort that is ordinarily termed "self-interested."[3] Thus, the puzzle of collective action pertains to collective efforts by ranchers seeking grazing rights, veterans requesting increased benefits, or parents in a school district holding a bake sale to buy new playground equipment. In each case, the goal sought would be of particular benefit to some smaller group in the community or nation. Still, if rational and self-interested, the potential beneficiaries will not lend their support to the collective effort but will instead leave it to other ranchers, other veterans, or other parents.

The puzzle has spawned a voluminous scholarly literature. Vari-

---

2. John H. Aldrich, "Rational Choice and Turnout," *American Journal of Political Science*, 37 (1993): 247.

3. On the nature of the interests pursued through collective action in organizations, see Kay Lehman Schlozman and John T. Tierney, *Organized Interests and American Democracy* (New York: Harper and Row, 1986), pp. 23–37, 123–132.

ous explanations have been proposed to account for the vast amount of seemingly irrational collective action.[4] However, the dominant approach to solving the puzzle—and the one most relevant for our concerns here—focuses on the selective benefits, benefits available only to those who take part, that accompany collective action. Consistent with a perspective that equates rationality with self-interest narrowly construed,[5] the initial search for the selective benefits that would render joint activity rational focused on material benefits such as low-cost insurance policies, travel opportunities, business contacts, or patronage jobs. Often, however, material selective benefits could not be found to account for support of a collective endeavor.[6]

The failure to find material rewards has led to a recognition of the variety of additional, often intangible, rewards associated with voting,[7] organizational support,[8] and other kinds of political ac-

---

4. These explanations focus upon, among other things, the size of the group involved, individuals' estimates of the impact of their own participation, and, with respect to voting, the closeness of the election. See, for example, Olson, *Logic of Collective Action;* Russell Hardin, *Collective Action* (Baltimore: Johns Hopkins University Press, 1982), esp. chaps. 2–3; Morris Fiorina and John A. Ferejohn, "The Paradox of Not Voting: A Decision Theoretic Analysis," *American Political Science Review* 68 (1974): 525–535; and John A. Ferejohn and Morris Fiorina, "Closeness Counts in Horseshoes and Dancing," *American Political Science Review* 69 (1975): 920–925.

5. See the discussion in Jane J. Mansbridge, "The Rise and Fall of Self-Interest in Explanation of Political Life," in *Beyond Self-Interest,* ed. Jane J. Mansbridge (Chicago: University of Chicago Press, 1990), pp. 11–13.

6. Moreover, even when they are present, material benefits are more effective for inducing rational individuals to join a collective effort than to work on its behalf once they are members. In addition, tangible benefits are more useful for explaining the persistence of an ongoing organization than for explaining its inception. On this point, see, for example, James Q. Wilson, *Political Organizations* (New York: Basic Books, 1973), chap. 3.

7. William H. Riker and Peter C. Ordeshook emphasize the satisfaction of performing a citizen duty in their classic attempt to solve the paradox of voting, "A Theory of the Calculus of Voting," *American Political Science Review* 62 (1968): 25–42. Subsequent analyses have added a variety of other psychic gratifications—for example, the desire to support a particular candidate or party, group identification and loyalties, social benefits, and the desire to avoid the social costs of not voting. See, for example, Morris Fiorina, "The Voting Decision: Instrumental and Expressive Aspects," *Journal of Politics* 38 (1976): 390–415; Carole J. Uhlaner, "Rational Turnout: The Neglected Role of Groups," *American Journal of Political Science* 33 (1989): 390–422; Stephen Knack, "Civic Norms, Social Sanctions, and Voter Turnout," *Rationality and Society* 4 (1992): 133–156; and Aldrich, "Rational Choice and Turnout."

8. There has been extensive empirical work on the benefits provided to members of political organizations. Jack L. Walker reviews the relevant literature and presents data in *Mobilizing Interest Groups in America: Patrons, Professions and Social Movements* (Ann

tivity.[9] These intangible benefits are of several types. Joint activity can bring social rewards—the chance to interact with other people or to gain respect from others involved—or can be fun or exciting. Moreover, performing the act may be intrinsically gratifying: participants may derive a sense of satisfaction from promoting a cause in which they believe, doing their share, or fulfilling a civic duty. These benefits are sometimes termed "expressive" rather than "instrumental"—the benefit deriving from the performance of the act, not from the consequences of the act.[10] In these cases, costs and benefits are hard to disentangle, for paying the cost becomes itself a benefit. Finally, the desire to affect policy seems to motivate activity.

When the benefit derived from political activity includes—and we show that it does—the satisfaction of performing a civic duty or doing one's share to make the community, nation, or world a better place, the greatest reward is not necessarily achieved by the

Arbor: University of Michigan Press, 1991), chaps. 3 and 5. See also Wilson, *Political Organizations;* John Mark Hansen, "The Political Economy of Group Membership," *American Political Science Review* 79 (1985): 79–96; and David Knoke, *Organizing for Collective Action: The Political Economies of Associations* (Hawthorne, N.Y.: Aldine deGruyter, 1990).

9. The historical emphasis upon the selective material benefits offered by the patronage-oriented urban party machine has yielded to an understanding of party activism rooted in a more diverse set of rewards. See, for example, James Q. Wilson, *The Amateur Democrat: Club Politics in Three Cities* (Chicago: University of Chicago Press, 1962); M. Margaret Conway and Frank B. Feigert, "Motivation, Incentive Systems and the Political Party Organization," *American Political Science Review* 62 (1968): 1159–1173; and Samuel J. Eldersveld, *Political Parties in American Society* (New York: Basic Books, 1982), chap. 9.

Survey data also demonstrate the importance of intangible rewards in motivating collective action. See Karl-Dieter Opp, "Soft Incentives and Collective Action," *British Journal of Political Science* 16 (1986): 87–112; and Edward N. Muller and Karl-Dieter Opp, "Rational Choice and Rebellious Collective Action," *American Political Science Review* 80 (1986): 471–487.

Carole Jean Uhlaner develops a formal model to explain political participation in general in "Political Participation, Rational Actors, and Rationality: A New Approach," *Political Psychology* 7 (1986): 551–573; and "'Relational Goods' and Participation: Incorporating Sociability into a Theory of Rational Action," *Public Choice* 62 (1989): 253–285.

10. In "A Theory of the Calculus of Voting," Riker and Ordeshook argue that fulfilling a sense of civic duty provides such a direct benefit. This position is elaborated in Geoffrey Brennan and James Buchanan, "Voter Choice: Evaluating Political Alternatives," *The American Behavioral Scientist* 28 (1984): 185–201. For a recent elaboration that explains much of voting behavior in terms of the direct consummatory benefits of political action, see Geoffrey Brennan and Loren Lomasky, *Democracy and Decision: The Pure Theory of Electoral Preference* (Cambridge: Cambridge University Press, 1993).

least cost. Instead, a goal that has been realized as the result of struggle against hardship gains meaning while a cheap victory sometimes seems trivial or, at least, unearned. Under such circumstances, the more time, money, or effort given, the higher is the level of gratification.[11] In short, bearing the cost becomes part of the benefit.[12]

Finally, despite the argument that a single individual cannot have any significant impact on a collective outcome, the desire to influence policy may motivate political activity. This may rest on activists' overestimation of their potential impact. When it comes to voting, where the probability at stake is the small chance that the individual will cast the tie-breaking vote, the belief that one's vote counts is surely such an overestimation. But for some acts where the input is large (a large campaign contribution) and the scope of the desired outcome not too large (a local election, a specific policy affecting the actor), the belief that an individual can make a difference may be less unrealistic.

Clearly, narrow versions of rational choice do not suffice to explain citizen participation. That these theories are not, as some claim, universally applicable does not negate their validity, however. In fact, they have been shown to be relevant to broad realms

---

11. Roger Finke and Rodney Stark's analysis of an analogous domain of activity, religious involvement, illustrates this point well. They ask why the more demanding, fundamentalist and evangelical denominations have been growing in membership while mainline denominations have been declining. They find the answer in the very demands that the former put on their members. "[R]eligious organizations are stronger to the degree that they impose significant costs . . . on their members. . . . People tend to value religion on the basis of how costly it is to belong—the more one must sacrifice in order to be in good standing, the more valuable is the religion." Roger Finke and Rodney Stark, *The Churching of America, 1776–1990: Winners and Losers in Our Religious Economy* (New Brunswick, N.J.: Rutgers University Press, 1992), p. 238.

12. Albert O. Hirschman makes this point with a distinction between "striving and attaining." He notes that "the neat distinction between costs and benefits of action in the public interest vanishes, since striving, which should be entered on the cost side, turns out to be part of the benefit." Albert O. Hirschman, *Shifting Involvements: Private Interests and Public Action* (Princeton, N.J.: Princeton University Press, 1982), pp. 85–86. Edward N. Muller and Karl-Dieter Opp ("Rational Choice and Rebellious Collective Action," p. 485) find that those who "believe that rebellious behavior is likely to be costly show a somewhat greater tendency to participate than those who believe that it is unlikely to be costly." Brennan and Lomasky (*Democracy and Decision,* p. 97) point out that the call to sacrifice is common in politics, the reward of political action deriving, at least in part, from having borne heavy burdens.

of human activity—for example, market behavior in economics and the strategic calculations of legislators in politics. The issue is to specify the domains in which they apply.[13] In light of their failure to predict the substantial amount of voluntary political participation that does take place, narrow versions of rational choice can be salvaged by enlarging the theory to specify a much wider range of benefits that can enter the utility calculus of the potential activist.[14] From the perspective of rational choice theory, any of the selective rewards—whether material, social, or civic—can function to provide benefits sufficient to justify the costs of activity for a rational actor.

From our perspective, however, the gratifications of participation are not interchangeable. It matters fundamentally what kind of rewards citizens associate with their activity. There is a significant difference between citizens whose activity is motivated by a desire to further their careers or to have fun by mingling with the mighty and those whose gratification emanates from the feeling of having helped others or having made the community a better place to live. In terms of the explanation of individual behavior, such civic gratifications can be fit into an approach predicated on the calculation of costs and benefits: the participant balances the benefit of feeling good about helping the community against the costs of taking part.[15] In terms of the quality of civic life in the

---

13. Brennan and Lomasky (*Democracy and Decision*, p. 2) make a similar point. They take a "two-hats" position, that "actors have two personae: one for markets and a different one for the ballot box (and analogous collective activities)."

14. This approach is taken by Riker and Ordeshook in "Theory of the Calculus of Voting"; they add the gratification of fulfilling a civic duty to the cost-benefit analysis of voting. This preserves the theory but makes it so encompassing that it borders on tautology. However, as Brian Barry (*Sociologists, Economists, and Democracy*, p. 33) who first commented on the dilemma, points out, the theory is "still a quite potent tautology." For discussion of the problems with this expansion, see also S. I. Benn, "Rationality and Political Behaviour," pp. 256–260.

In *Political Participation* (Canberra: Australian National University, 1978), p. 77, Benn presents a justification for political action that draws on a "notion of non-instrumental rationality" which includes consideration of a broad range of principles.

15. Amartya Sen suggests that it is more appropriate to consider this to be behavior based on normative commitments. See his classic statement in "Rational Fools," reprinted in *Beyond Self-Interest*, ed. Jane J. Mansbridge. For arguments from many disciplinary perspectives about the significance of altruism and cooperation in human behavior and extensive bibliographical references, see the essays in that volume.

community or nation, however, surely the mix of motivations that citizen participants bring to politics makes a difference.

Our survey data give empirical content to a wider range of gratifications. Whenever a respondent indicated having been active in a particular way, we administered a battery of items designed to measure the relative importance of a range of possible rewards in animating the activity. Thus, we can consider—across a broad range of voluntary activism—what activists say about the reasons that led to their activity. These data permit us to investigate in a way that has never before been possible how political acts differ in terms of the gratifications they provide.

Analysis of the rewards that accompany political activity has generally focused upon voting, a form of participation of sufficiently low cost that the threshold for the logic of collective action is not reached,[16] and support of political organizations, a form of participation for which it is somewhat easier to provide social and material selective benefits. Other modes of collective action have received less attention. We are able to juxtapose all these forms of participation, probing the rewards of modes of activity that have received less attention and making systematic comparisons among all of them. As we shall show, different acts provide different gratifications. The data illuminate not only the content of the benefits that flow from collective action and the meaning of participation to activists but also the nature of the different political activities in which citizens engage. The varied content of the selective gratifications associated with different political activities tells us something important both about the nature of political activity and the nature of politics in the United States.

Can We Ask about Reasons?

Although it seems relatively straightforward to ask why a voluntary action was undertaken, some psychologists warn that we must treat retrospective reconstructions of reasons or motivations with caution. They argue that people may not be able to identify

---

16. This point is made by, among others, Aldrich, "Rational Choice and Turnout," p. 261.

the factors that influenced them. In the absence of explicit memories of thought processes, respondents will generate plausible responses of what they must have thought at the time, responses that may or may not represent accurately what determined their original action.[17] Yet other students of mental processes take a less negative view toward verbal reports of the influences on an individual's actions, arguing that they can provide insight, and even explanations, of the actions people take.[18] And philosophers such as Donald Davidson and Jon Elster have argued that having reasons is the essence of rationality.[19] We cannot resolve this debate, but we can specify its relevance for our enterprise, asking about reasons within the context of political participation. We shall argue that, when handled with care, questions about reasons can yield useful information.

Our subject matter, voluntary activity, does give us cause for caution in interpreting respondents' reports about their motivations. First, the dictates of social desirability give respondents an incentive to emphasize civic-minded motives at the expense of selfish ones when being interviewed. Hence, we would expect a certain inflation in the proportion of respondents reporting that they were active in order to do their share or make the community

17. The strongest statement of this point of view is Richard E. Nisbett and Timothy DeCamp Wilson, "Telling More Than We Can Know: Verbal Reports on Mental Processes," *Psychological Review* 84 (1977): 231–259.

18. Nisbett and Wilson's original claim has been modified somewhat in the substantial literature inspired by their influential article. See, for example, Eliot R. Smith and Frederick D. Miller, "Limits on Perception of Cognitive Processes: A Reply to Nisbett and Wilson," *Psychological Review* 85 (1978): 355–362; Peter White, "Limitations on Verbal Reports of Internal Events: A Refutation of Nisbett and Wilson and of Bem," *Psychological Review* 87 (1980): 105–112; K. Anders Ericsson and Herbert A. Simon, "Verbal Reports as Data," *Psychological Review* 87 (1980): 215–251; John Sabini and Maury Silver, "Introspection and Causal Accounts," *Journal of Personality and Social Psychology* 40 (1981): 171–179; Peter Wright and Peter D. Rip, "Retrospective Reports on the Causes of Decisions," *Journal of Personality and Social Psychology* 40 (1981): 601–614; Robert E. Kraut and Steven H. Lewis, "Person Perception and Self-Awareness: Knowledge of Influences on One's Own Judgments," *Journal of Personality and Social Psychology* 42 (1982): 448–460; and Igor Gavanski and Curt Hoffman, "Awareness of Influences on One's Own Judgments: The Roles of Covariation Detection and Attention to the Judgment Process," *Journal of Personality and Social Psychology* 52 (1987): 453–463.

19. See Davidson, *Essays on Actions and Events* (New York: Oxford University Press, 1980), especially "Actions, Reasons, and Causes," and Jon Elster, *Sour Grapes* (Cambridge and New York: Cambridge University Press, 1983).

a better place to live and a diminution in the proportion indicating a desire to get help with personal or family problems or to advance in their careers. Moreover, those who become active as volunteers may discover unanticipated gratifications in the process. For example, those who volunteer in a campaign in the hopes of getting patronage jobs or who help to organize a protest out of concern with a particular issue may find along the way that they enjoy the other people involved. After-the-fact reconstructions of reasons for participation might easily include reference to these unexpected benefits of activity.

In other respects, however, we have reason for confidence that our respondents' reports of their motivations constitute useful information. In most cases, we were able to ask about specific acts of participation within the recent past. Moreover, there is general agreement that answers about reasons gain significance to the extent that the matters at stake are important ones. In contrast to voting, a relatively low-cost activity scheduled by the government rather than by the activist, most of the activities about which we inquired demand individual initiative in deciding whether, when, and how to get involved and entail investment of more substantial resources.[20] Under the circumstances, we would expect those who take part to be more self-conscious about their intentions.

In short, while we cannot be certain that activists' responses to the battery of items about possible reasons for participation constitute an accurate depiction of the mental state that preceded a decision to undertake voluntary action, the pattern of responses across activities is so compelling that we are sure that respondents did not simply fabricate answers randomly in order to please an expectant interviewer. Since the reasons cited by activists vary systematically across different kinds of activity in ways that are

---

20. In addition, in order to avoid giving respondents the occasion to invent reasons for relatively inconsequential activity—very small political donations or nominal church memberships or organizational affiliations—we imposed a minimum level of commitment below which we did not ask about the reasons for participation. Those whose campaign contributions did not total more than $50, whose church activity did not include being a board member or an officer, serving on committees or helping with special projects, or giving at least two hours each week, or whose activity in their most important organization entailed giving neither time nor money were not asked about their reasons for getting involved.

sensibly connected to the nature of that activity, we construe these reports as being, at a minimum, meaningful contemporary interpretations of past activity, respondents' current understanding of the gratifications attendant to participation. As such, these interpretations have intrinsic significance. As we have mentioned, they surely have implications for activists' decisions to get involved again in the future. Furthermore, this "rhetoric" of participation tells us more generally about the culture of citizen activity in America—the shared associations surrounding modes of voluntary activity.

Interpreting Political Activity

To capture the broad range of possible gratifications that can flow from voluntary activity, respondents who participated in a particular way were presented with a long list of possible motivations for that activity and asked whether each reason was very, somewhat, or not too important in the decision to become active—or, in the case of ongoing participation such as organizational affiliation or membership on a local governing board, in keeping them active.[21] The theoretical underpinnings of the lists derive from James Q. Wilson's typology of the incentives provided by political organizations,[22] modified to reflect what we learned during our extensive pre-tests about the language and categories that citizen activists actually use in explaining and interpreting their activity.[23]

---

21. It has been suggested to us that the way to ask about gratifications is to use open-ended rather than closed-ended questions. We did not do so for several reasons. Pre-testing indicated that respondents tend to mouth clichés when an open-ended question about rewards of participation is posed. In addition, they are more likely to acknowledge the importance of selfish motives when self-interestedness is legitimated in closed-ended items. Moreover, we followed up the battery of closed-ended items about the relative importance of various gratifications with an open-ended, "Anything else?" Most of the replies to this question simply restated something already covered in the closed-ended questions.

22. *Political Organizations,* esp. chaps. 2–3. Other typologies of the gratifications attendant to organizational support have many elements in common with Wilson's. See, for example, Robert Salisbury, "An Exchange Theory of Interest Groups," *Midwest Journal of Political Science* 13 (1969): 1–32; or Knoke, *Organizing for Collective Action.*

23. In constructing items about the reasons for activity, we were not always able to frame them in such a way that they would hew to the lines of Wilson's analytic categories.

We consider four kinds of motivations. Three of these are selective benefits—selective material benefits, as well as two less tangible selective benefits: social gratifications and civic gratifications. In addition, we consider the desire to influence collective policy.

Selective gratifications are available only to those who take part and, thus, bypass the free-rider problem. *Selective material benefits,* such as jobs, career advancement, or help with a personal or family problem, were the lubricant of the classic urban machine. They continue to figure importantly in contemporary discussions of congressional constituency service and incentives for joining organizations. The selective nature of these material benefits implies that only those who participate receive them; they are rewards in what is a market-like transaction. They are, however, not organically related to the activity itself. The situation differs for the two kinds of intangible selective benefits. *Selective social gratifications,* such as the enjoyment of working with others or the excitement of politics, cannot be enjoyed apart from the activity itself. Without taking part, there is no way to partake of the fun, gain the recognition, or enjoy other social benefits. Similarly, *selective civic gratifications,* such as satisfying a sense of duty or a desire to contribute to the welfare of the community, also derive from the act itself.[24] In this case, however, we are concerned that social norms give respondents an incentive to emphasize the desire for these psychological rewards in order to please the interviewer.

Some of the formulations that recurred as respondents talked about their activity in pre-tests were not readily identifiable in terms of Wilson's typology. For example, across almost all the acts relatively high proportions of activists—ranging from 40 percent in the case of contributing or contacting to 70 percent in the case of protesting—reported that "the chance to work with (contribute along with, add my vote with, etc.) people who share my ideals" was very important. In Wilson's terms, it is not clear whether this should be considered a "solidary" gratification deriving from the association with like-minded people or a "purposive" one dependent upon the ideals to which the activist is committed.

Because the way in which activists actually talk about politics does not always correspond to Wilson's conceptually distinct categories, we posit our categories, not as a theoretical breakthrough, but rather as a version of Wilson's categories altered for utility in a survey. Because our survey items could not always preserve Wilson's analytic distinctions, we do not use his labels—even though we derive our understanding from his categories.

24. These are what Wilson calls "purposive" gratifications, "intangible rewards that derive from the sense of satisfaction of having contributed to the attainment of a worthwhile cause" (*Political Organizations,* p. 34).

While there is no reason to expect respondents to exaggerate the social gratifications of voluntary activity, they might overstate the extent to which they were motivated by civic concerns.

Finally, we consider collective outcomes, the gratifications that come from the enactment or implementation of desired public policies or the election of a favored candidate. Unlike the previous motivations, these are subject to free-rider problems. This is the case even when the goals are "self-interested"—in the sense that they would advantage some smaller group of which the participant is a member—so long as the benefits, once available, are available to all members of that group regardless of whether they worked to achieve them.

According to the rational choice approach, activists who consider that they got involved in order to promote a collective policy goal are deluding themselves in imagining that their contributions would enhance appreciably the probability of achieving the joint end. At best, activists motivated by a desire to realize some policy objective can only hope for the kind of civic reward that derives from doing one's share and expressing oneself along with others who are like-minded. Because respondents cited this category so frequently in recalling the reasons they got involved, however, we consider the "irrational" desire to affect policy separately from the intangible rewards that we group under the rubric of civic gratifications.[25]

As mentioned, for each voluntary activity, activists were asked about the relative importance of a series of possible motivations in their decision to become or, in the case of ongoing activity, to stay active. In constructing the lists for various kinds of activity, we attempted, insofar as possible, to make a complete matrix— that is, to ask each item about reasons for each voluntary act—but we were not always able to do so.[26] In assigning items to categories

---

25. David Knoke follows a similar approach when he specifies a separate dimension for "lobbying incentives" in "Organizational Incentives," as does Hansen, who discusses "political collective benefits" in "The Political Economy of Group Membership."

26. The difficulty in using a common set of reasons for all participatory acts grows out of the profound differences among the modes of activity. When pre-tests elicited reactions indicating that respondents considered an item simply too far-fetched ("I went to the protest for the chance to meet important and influential people? Give me a break!"), we omitted it from the list. In so doing, we avoided alienating respondents but risked missing a possible

of analysis, we attempted to use items germane to many kinds of participation and to include only items that were unambiguous as indicators of the theoretical dimension in question.[27] In addition, we used factor analysis to confirm our approach. The results were generally consistent with our categorizations.[28] The items that fall under the four rubrics are as follows:

Selective material benefits:
   The chance to further my job or career.
   I might want to get help from an official (from the organization, etc.) on a personal or family problem.
   I might want to run for office someday.
   I might want to get a job with the government someday.
   The direct services provided to (church or organization) members.
   The recreational activities offered by the organization.
Selective social gratifications:
   I find it exciting.[29]
   The chance to be with people I enjoy.
   The chance to meet important and influential people.

---

motive for activity. In addition, certain items are significant for a single context—but relevant only there. For example, a higher proportion, 76 percent, of the church activists cited the desire to affirm their religious faith as very important than any other item on the list for religious activity. Not to have included this item—one that is, obviously, germane only to one kind of activity—would have been to overlook one of the fundamental wellsprings of religious activity. For a complete listing of the items used for each of the acts, see Appendix B.4.

27. It is certainly possible to question the judgments made in assigning items to categories. Although we settled on a strategy of including under a particular rubric only items that unambiguously belong there, we experimented with more expansive definitions of several of the categories. The effect of defining the categories more broadly by including items germane to relatively few acts or ambiguously related to a particular theoretical dimension was only to raise the proportion who cited at least one of the components as very important but not to change in any way the pattern of responses reported below.

28. We factor analyzed the gratifications from each political act separately. We consistently found three dimensions: civic gratifications, collective policy outcomes, and a dimension that combined selective material and social gratifications. In the absence of clear guidance from the factor analysis, we separated the latter dimension into two—material and social—based on our reading of what the questions were about. For a description of the analysis and its results, contact the authors.

29. Because activities undertaken alone can be exciting, this is not technically a "social" gratification. However, this is a gratification cited relatively frequently across acts, and it seems to fit in with the other reasons we call "social," all of which involve gratifications derived from an association with others.

The chance for recognition from people I respect.

I did not want to say no to someone who asked.

Selective civic gratifications:

My duty as a citizen.

I am the kind of person who does my share.

The chance to make the community or nation a better place
    to live.

Collective outcomes:

The chance to influence government policy.

The Gratifications of Voluntary Activity

Voluntary activities vary substantially in the number and kinds of
gratifications they provide. Of all the modes of citizen involvement, church activity seems to be the most rewarding. Considering
simply the number of gratifications, church activists cited an average of 7.5 of the reasons on the list as being "very important"
in explaining why they stay active. At the other end of the scale,
those who contacted a government official about an issue of concern only to themselves or their families reported an average of
2.4 reasons as being "very important." Given the attention paid
in the literature to the selective benefits provided by organizations,
it is not surprising that those affiliated with organizations reported
a relatively high level of reward—an average of 5.3 for those
whose most important organization takes stands in politics and
4.9 for those whose most important organization does not take
political stands.[30] However, the rewards of organizational involvement depend upon what is invested: those who gave money but
no time to their most important organization reported an average
of 3.7 reasons as very important if the organization takes stands
in politics and an average of 3.5 if it does not; in contrast, those
who devoted some time to their most important organization
reported averages of 5.9 reasons for organizations that take po-

---

30. The questions about gratifications from organizational activity are about the single
organization to which the respondent gives the most time and money or, if different, the
one he or she considers most important.

litical stands and 5.5 for organizations that do not take stands. The data for other political activities teach the same lesson. It is clear that modes of participation requiring an input of time furnish greater rewards than those in which the investment is money.[31]

WHICH GRATIFICATIONS?

Our main goal is to compare gratifications across political activities. We report, therefore, on a range of political activities and, for contrast, also provide data on non-political activity in churches and non-political organizations. The political activities include voting, campaign work, campaign contributions, community board membership, informal activity in the community, protests, contacts to officials, and involvements in political organizations. For a few activities we have made even finer distinctions. Among contributors to electoral organizations, we differentiate among those whose largest donation was to a party organization, a political action committee (PAC) concerned about a particular political issue, and a work-related PAC, such as a PAC associated with a union, company, or professional association.[32] Although each of these

---

31. It might be argued that, since the lists of possible reasons varied in length across the acts, the average number of items deemed "very important" is not the appropriate measure. After all, the respondent was given more possible reasons to consider important for church activity than for voting. This line of reasoning suggests that a more appropriate measure would be the average proportion considering each reason important for the various acts. By this measure, church activity still stands out as the most rewarding. Among political acts, protest scores high with respect to the proportion of activists rating each of the possible reasons as very important. Before accepting this alternate measure, however, we should note that, as mentioned earlier, the lists varied in length because certain gratifications are simply not plausible for certain acts. Thus, in each case the length of the list says something about the approximate number of potential benefits.

32. Of those whose electoral contributions were directed to an organization rather than a particular candidate, 39 percent donated to a party organization, 52 percent to a PAC, and the remainder to some other kind of organization. The PAC donations were directed as follows:

Work-related	38%
Political issue	40
General liberal or conservative	12
PAC associated with a politician	7
Other	4
	101%

activities is similar in being a campaign contribution, the differences among the organizations and the relation of the individual to them should have an effect on the gratifications associated with them. Among contactors, we distinguish those who contacted on an issue of personal or family concern from those who contacted on an issue of community or national concern.

With respect to citizen involvement in politics through organizational affiliation: organizations that get involved politically vary substantially in the extent to which they concentrate exclusively on political means of promoting their members' interests or use non-political means as well. Therefore, we report data on organizations that take stands on political issues (although they may do other things as well) and a narrower category of explicitly political organizations. This category is an amalgam of four kinds of organizations: organizations active on one particular issue; multi-issue organizations that support general liberal or conservative causes; organizations, such as party organizations, that are active in supporting candidates in elections; and women's rights organizations.

Table 4.1 reports on the specific reasons given for these various activities. It shows the proportion of activists who cited at least one of the reasons in each category as "very important." Clearly, respondents report a variety of motivations associated with their activity, and acts differ in the mix of gratifications they provide.

Selective Material Benefits. Selective material benefits—the kind traditionally associated with machine-style politics—are given precedence in the literature on political organizations as the means for circumventing the free-rider problem. Although we asked about a variety of such benefits, the logic of collective action leads us to consider all of them together since only a single selective benefit

---

The distribution among types of work-related electoral organizations is as follows:

Union	32%
Company or firm	27
Trade association	4
Professional association	29
Other	8
	100%

Table 4.1 Gratifications Reported for Various Activities: Percentage Mentioning a Gratification (among activists)[a]

	Material Benefits	Social Gratifications	Civic Gratifications	Policy Gratifications
VOTE	7%	20%	93%	61%
WORK IN A CAMPAIGN	25	48	85	48
CONTRIBUTE				
Candidate	18	22	80	46
Party Organization	8	5	86	37
Work-Related PAC	46	14	63	64
Issue Organization	1	6	88	84
CONTACT				
Particularized	75	24	40	19
Community Issue	31	20	87	57
National Issue	24	12	87	79
PROTEST	b	44%	89	80
COMMUNITY ACTIVITY				
Informal	17	35	85	39
Board Member	14	49	87	42
ORGANIZATION				
Takes Political Stands	53	45	69	33
"Political" Organization[c]	25	29	85	62
Takes no Political Stands	58	54	59	6
CHURCH	40	68	83	6

a. See Appendix B.1.i for information about sample number for activists.

b. Material benefits item not asked of protesters.

c. "Political" organization: organizations active on a single issue; general liberal or conservative; organizations active in supporting candidates; women's rights organizations.

(of sufficient size) is needed to obviate the free-rider problem. Hence, it is appropriate to ask whether the respondent mentioned *any* selective material benefit as being very important in explaining activity. As Table 4.1 shows, three-quarters of those who contacted on a matter germane to themselves or their families considered at least one of the material benefits to be very important. Reflecting the potential career benefits accruing to contributors to work-related PACs, 46 percent of them mentioned at least one material benefit. Regardless of whether the most important organization is one that takes stands in politics, over half of those affiliated with an organization mentioned at least one material benefit as being very important.[33] Otherwise, the proportions who reported a selective material benefit as being very important are relatively low, below one-third across all the other political acts.[34]

It is interesting to note that, even though activists were given plenty of opportunity to do so, a surprisingly small proportion of them mentioned the most traditional of material benefits—job and career advancement—as animating their activity. For only one kind of participation, making contributions to a work-related PAC, did an appreciable share of activists, 44 percent, mention the chance to further their job or career as very important in the decision to become active. Otherwise, the proportions mentioning career benefits were much lower, ranging downward from the 14 percent for the campaign workers. Similarly, only 7 percent of the campaign workers indicated that they might want to get a job with the government someday, the highest for any political activity. And 8 percent of the members of local governing boards reported that they might want to run for office someday, again the highest for any mode of political participation. In short, the data show that selective material benefits are quite infrequent and seem inadequate to explain the volume of political activity. We must look

33. With respect to the kinds of selective material benefits in which organizations are said to specialize, 15 percent of those whose most important organization takes stands in politics and 29 percent whose most important organization does not take political stands mentioned the recreational opportunities provided by the organization as very important in keeping them active. The analogous figures for the proportions mentioning the direct services provided to members are 36 percent and 33 percent.

Considering the narrower group of organizations that are more exclusively political, we see that the proportion mentioning any selective material benefit as a reason for involvement is much lower, only 25 percent. Similarly, among those whose most important organization fell into the narrower category of explicitly political organizations, only 4 percent cited recreational opportunities and 15 percent cited direct services as very important in keeping them involved.

34. The proportion of church activists reporting at least one material benefit as very important is relatively high, 40 percent. Church activists rarely cited career-oriented motivations, however. Rather, they were much more likely to report that the recreational opportunities, the possibility of getting help on a personal or family problem and, especially, the services—for example, child care or marriage counseling—provided by the church were very important in keeping them active in their churches. If we were to include the desire for a religious education for their children as a selective material benefit, then the proportion of church activists mentioning at least one such benefit would soar to 73 percent.

elsewhere. The obvious place is the other selective, but less tangible, benefits of a social and civic nature.

Social Gratifications. Overall, the proportion of activists who reported that at least one of the social gratifications was very important in explaining their activity is fairly high, higher than might be expected on the basis of the emphasis on material benefits that emerges from some of the literature on the problem of collective action. Given the differences among voluntary activities in the opportunities they provide for social interaction, however, it is not surprising that the share of activists rating social gratifications as very important varies substantially across acts. For political activities ordinarily undertaken solo—voting, making campaign contributions to candidates or organizations, and contacting—fewer than one-quarter of the activists mentioned any social gratification as being very important. In contrast, those who engaged in political activities usually performed in a social context—campaigning, protesting, getting involved in an informal community effort, or serving on a local governing board—were much more likely to mention some kind of social gratification as very important, more likely indeed than to mention a material benefit. The distinction between campaign workers and campaign contributors is particularly striking: those who gave time to a campaign were more likely than those who gave money to mention both material benefits and social gratifications; however, the discrepancy between the two forms of electoral activity is much wider for social, rather than material, benefits. Not unexpectedly, church and organization activists are especially likely to have indicated social rewards.

Civic Gratifications. The proportion of activists who mentioned some civic purpose—the desire to do their duty as a member of the community, to make the community or nation a better place to live, or to do their share—is remarkably high. Indeed, for all forms of voluntary participation except particularized contacting, a larger share of activists reported at least one civic gratification as being very important than mentioned a material benefit or social gratification. In fact, the tendency for activists to cite some civic gratification extends even to activity outside politics in non-political organizations and churches. Since efforts to "make the community or nation a better place to live" can be undertaken by religious, non-profit, and charitable institutions as well as by governments, this is not unreasonable.

How should we interpret these civic replies? Since civic motivations are socially appropriate, we may be receiving answers that respondents think they ought to give. Data in Figure 4.1 on the frequency with which respondents mentioned civic reasons for the various acts shed some light on this issue. The bars show the proportion of activists who make some mention of civic gratifications as well as those who mention *only* civic gratifications—that is, who reported neither material nor social benefits as very important in explaining their activity even though they were given a number of opportunities to do so. If respondents were merely paying lip service to civic-minded platitudes, then we would expect no differentiation in the interpretations placed on various kinds of voluntary participation by activists. In fact, this is not the case. Even though mention of civic gratifications was virtually universal across all political activities except for particularized contacting, the proportion of activists who cited civic gratifications but not material or social ones differs substantially across participatory acts in a pattern that reflects the nature of the acts themselves. At one extreme, 71 percent of the voters mentioned civic gratifications but neither material nor social benefits; at the other, only 9 percent of particularized contactors did so.

In short, respondents surely find it socially appropriate to cite civic gratifications in interpreting their voluntary activity. That norms of civic responsibility and voluntary service are embedded in American political culture, in itself, says something about the peculiar nature of American individualism. Moreover, selective benefits of a material or social nature go only so far in activists' retrospective understandings of their participation. Some activities—in particular, voting and making campaign contributions to candidates, parties, or issue PACs—offer few such benefits. Those who engage in such activities, as well as substantial proportions of those who engage in activities offering more in the way of selective benefits, interpret their activity in terms of the psychological rewards of doing their share.

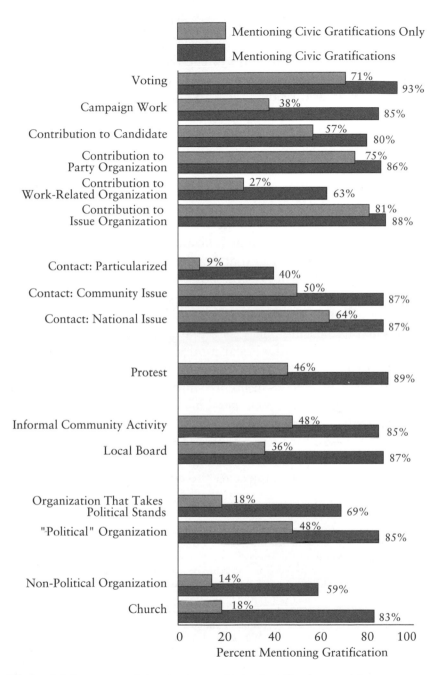

Figure 4.1 Percentage Mentioning a Civic Gratification and Percentage Mentioning Civic Gratifications Only.

The mix of selective benefits is significant. From the perspective of theories of rational choice, *any* selective benefit—material, social, or civic—will do to confirm the theory that individuals will not be active for collective purposes. But, as we said earlier, it makes a great deal of difference to the nature and substance of politics whether activists pursue narrow material benefits, seek the social rewards of political engagement, or are motivated by a sense of civic responsibility.[35]

Collective Policy Outcomes. For a supposedly irrational motivation, a quite high proportion of activists interpreted their activity as inspired, at least in part, by a desire to influence government policy. Of course, the acts range widely in terms of the extent to which respondents see them as relevant for government policy. At one extreme are three acts that are very high in their capacity to carry policy-oriented messages. For these three acts—protesting, making a donation to a political issue PAC, and contacting on a problem affecting the nation—roughly four out of five activists mentioned influencing policy as a reason for taking part.[36] At the other extreme are non-political modes of voluntary activity such as activity in a non-political organization or church, for which only 6 percent cited a desire to influence policy. In addition, contactors concerned about personal or family matters are, not unexpectedly, unlikely to have mentioned public policy as a very important reason for their activity. The other political acts are in the middle range. Interestingly, although voting as a form of participation is especially subject to the collective action problem, a

---

35. In a study of conceptions of citizenship, Pamela Conover, Ivor Crewe, and Donald Searing find less emphasis on participation as a citizen duty than we do. Part of this may be due to a different format of study—focus groups rather than interviews. But some is probably due to the fact that we are studying people who have been active and asking about that activity. Their analysis of citizen duty focuses on citizens in general, active and inactive. See "The Nature of Citizenship in the United States and Great Britain: Empirical Comments on Theoretical Themes," *Journal of Politics* 53 (1991): 800–832.

36. Our data on the high proportion of contacts that refer to policy issues are consistent with data based on analyses of the mail to Congress. Frantzich reports that the largest share of that mail—about 50 percent—contains opinions on issues of the day. Stephen E. Frantzich, *Write Your Congressman: Constituent Communications and Representation* (New York: Praeger, 1986), p. 13.

relatively high proportion of voters, 61 percent, cited a desire to influence government policy as very important in their decision to go to the polls.

Not only do activists indicate that their activity was motivated by a desire to influence policy but—free-rider problem to the contrary—they believe that their activity did make at least some difference.[37] Among the respondents who reported contacting a government official, four out of five said they received an answer, and about two-thirds of the group that received an answer were satisfied with it. Among those who took part in a protest, two-thirds thought the protest made a difference and 15 percent thought it made a great deal of difference. Among campaign workers, three-quarters thought their activity affected at least some votes, and 16 percent thought they influenced a large number of votes. In sum, citizens are active in relation to policy issues reasonably associated with their mode of activity, and they often believe—perhaps, not unreasonably—that their activity can make a difference.

The "Gratification Space"

Table 4.1 focused our attention on the varying gratifications associated with activity. By combining the dimensions treated separately in Table 4.1, we can get a better sense of the bundle of gratifications associated with particular participatory acts. Figure 4.2 locates the various kinds of voluntary activity in a single "gratification space." Since we wish to consider simultaneously four different kinds of gratification, the figure is "four-dimensional." Each act is located on a plane in which the north-south axis is the proportion of activists who cited influencing government policy as a very important reason for the activity; the east-west axis is the proportion who mentioned at least one of the items about civic gratifications as very important; the height of the bar located on that plane indicates the proportion who cited at least one material

---

37. On the issue of perceived effect, see Terry M. Moe, *The Organization of Interests: Incentives and the Internal Dynamics of Political Interest Groups* (Chicago: University of Chicago Press, 1980).

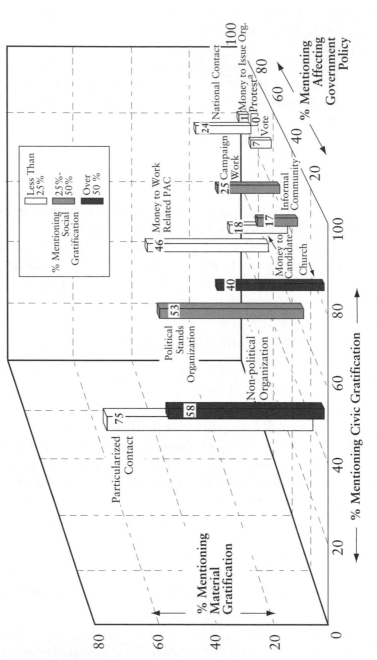

Figure 4.2 Gratification Space for Political and Non-Political Acts.

a. Protesters not asked about material benefits. 44% mention social gratifications.

selective benefit as very important; and, finally, the shading of the bar reflects the proportion who mentioned a social gratification as very important.

Figure 4.2 makes visually clear that voluntary activities differ substantially in the mix of rewards they provide. Most *political* acts are clustered in the right-hand section of the plane, with overwhelming majorities citing civic gratifications. Among these "civic" acts, the proportion reporting a desire to influence policy varies substantially. The three acts in the upper-right corner— where citizens cite civic gratifications *and* a desire to influence policy—are quite varied. One involves writing checks (to an issue organization) and one involves direct contact with an official (on a national issue). Both of these are generally undertaken alone. Also in this space is protest, an activity done in concert with others. In short, not only can citizens select from many forms of political activity, but they have many choices that allow them both to satisfy a sense of civic obligation and to attempt to influence public policy.

The acts that provide civic gratifications (in the right-hand section) are diverse with respect to the frequency with which activists mention social gratifications: very few of those who made a donation (to a campaign or issue organization) or who contacted an official (about a national issue) mentioned any social benefits; a substantial proportion of the campaign workers, members of a political organization, and protesters did. On average, these acts elicited fewer mentions of material benefits. Again, however, there is a range, with none of the protesters and very few of the voters mentioning material gratifications, in contrast to somewhat higher proportions of the campaign workers, members of political organizations, and contactors on community and national issues.

A few kinds of political activity stand outside the upper-right-hand section of the gratification space. Contacting on an issue of particularized concern is the most distinctive. Among all acts, it is by far the least likely to be described in terms of civic gratifications and the most likely to be described in terms of material benefits. Furthermore, particularized contactors were very unlikely to have referred to the chance to influence policy as very important. The contrast on these dimensions between contacting on an issue of particularized concern and contacting on an issue of national import is especially striking. Yet these are the *same act* in the service of *different substantive concerns,* and those who engage in any kind of contacting are unlikely to have mentioned social rewards.

Another political activity that stands apart is making contributions to work-related PACs. Among political participants, contributors to work-related PACs are relatively unlikely to have mentioned civic gratifications—and relatively likely to have mentioned material benefits, usually benefits associated with job and career. In this case, the contrast with making contributions to issue PACs is especially noteworthy. Those who made contributions to issue PACs were more likely to have reported a desire to influence policy and to have mentioned civic gratifications and much less likely to have cited economic benefits than were contributors to work-related PACs.[38] As with the various kinds of contacts, we are dealing with the same act, writing a check, a form of participation very rarely described as yielding social rewards. Still, the mix of other expected benefits differs substantially depending upon what kind of electoral organization opens the envelope. When individuals make a campaign donation to a PAC at work, they have something quite different in mind than when they make a donation to a candidate, a party organization, or an issue PAC.

According to our respondents' reports, established institutions like organizations and churches seem to provide a richer array of gratifications to activists, both because they are in a position to offer members the kinds of services and recreational opportunities that are referred to so often in the literature on collective action and because they bring people together on a continuing basis and, thus, create the possibility for social engagement. Interestingly, the pattern of gratifications from organizational involvement does not seem to depend upon whether the organization takes political stands. Compared with those who engaged in other types of vol-

---

38. The item asking the kind of electoral organization to which the contribution was made was separated from the battery of items about the reasons for the contribution. Hence, we believe that the difference in the patterns of reported gratifications is not simply a function of question ordering.

untary activity, those affiliated with organizations are especially likely to mention economic benefits and social rewards, regardless of whether the organization gets involved in politics.[39] What does distinguish those whose most important organization takes stands in politics from those whose most important organization does not is only the greater extent to which the former cite a desire to affect policy as a source of their ongoing organizational activity.

The rewards of organizational affiliation are, however, differentiated by whether individuals invest money or time in their organizations. Compared to those who give money only, those who give some time to an organization—whether political or non-political—are more likely to cite each kind of benefit as being very important. Considering those whose most important organization takes stands in politics, the pattern is especially clear for social benefits: 52 percent of those who gave time, as opposed to 27 percent of those who gave only money, mentioned a social benefit as being very important. However, it is quite striking for civic benefits (80 percent and 65 percent respectively), for material benefits (56 percent and 35 percent) and for policy benefits (36 percent and 26 percent) depending upon whether the respondent gives time or only money.

Like activists in non-political organizations, church activists are quite unlikely to have reported a desire to influence government policy. In contrast to those affiliated with either kind of organization, however, church activists were somewhat more likely to have mentioned civic and social gratifications and somewhat less likely to have mentioned material benefits.

SUMMARY
Those who engage in different kinds of voluntary activity interpret the potential rewards of that activity in different ways. Contrary to expectations, selective material benefits play a relatively small role in the reasons given for political activity. Although they are mentioned frequently in conjunction with particularized contacting and, somewhat less often, support for work-related PACs, they

---

39. The profile for the narrow category of explicitly political organizations is, of course, quite different and more similar to that for most political activities.

are mentioned relatively rarely in conjunction with other kinds of activity. In contrast, selective social gratifications and, especially, civic gratifications are invoked frequently. Finally, attempts to influence policy are discussed much more frequently than one would expect on the basis of the logic of collective action.

Interestingly, it is not simply the nature of the act—whether it is undertaken alone or with others, whether it involves time or money, whether it is ongoing or temporally defined, whether it takes place in the context of an established institution like a church or organization, and so on—that is related to the mix of reported gratifications. In addition, the subject matter has implications for the way that activity is interpreted. Thus, those who contacted on matters of concern only to themselves or their families described their activity very differently from those who contacted on matters of community or national concern. Similarly, those who contributed to work-related PACs reported very different potential rewards than did those who contributed to party organizations or issue PACs.

In each case, the profile is related so reasonably to the activity at stake that we are convinced that the responses indicate something real about the way activists understand the gratifications attendant to various forms of activity and that these understandings have potential consequences for decisions to get involved as volunteers in the future. Although we cannot be certain that the retrospective reconstructions of what animated voluntary participation constitute accurate accounts of the activists' thought processes at the time they decided to get involved, we are sure that the pattern of responses we have delineated demonstrates that their interpretations are related in sensible ways to their activity. The mix of material, social, and civic selective gratifications that citizens attribute to various acts fits neatly with the varying nature of the acts.

Policy gratifications are, perhaps, the most problematic. That citizens say they were active in order to influence public policy runs counter to much contemporary theorizing. However, the credibility of these reports of the gratifications associated with various activities is further strengthened by the data reported in Chapter 3 concerning the subject matter associated with various activities. As we noted, the nature of the act seems quite consistent with the issue or problem that respondents reported to have animated the act. Whether or not it is rational to cite a desire to influence policy in connection with political participation, consideration of the open-ended replies discussing the policy concerns behind activity suggests that these are real responses about genuine policy concerns. The actual language used by respondents to describe what their activity was all about buttresses our conclusion that we are examining a real and significant aspect of citizen activity.[40]

The Other Side of the Coin: Interpreting Inactivity

Just as important as understanding how those who get involved politically interpret their activity is understanding how those who do not take part interpret their political inactivity. However, if it is tricky to ask people why they did what they did, it is far trickier indeed to inquire of them why they did not do what they did not do. Since those who do not take part can hardly be expected to know and report on what they have been missing, it is hard to ask questions of the inactives that parallel the items posed to participants. Such questions would not only be difficult to write but might, in fact, jeopardize the rapport between interviewer and respondent.

Although our ability to elicit respondents' understandings of why they stay out of politics is constrained, it is critical to try. About half of our respondents reported that they took no part in political campaigns (gave neither time nor money) and that they had neither contacted, nor protested, nor had they done anything in the community. The reasons for their inactivity matter fundamentally for our interpretation of American democracy. They may withdraw out of fear of reprisals or other damaging consequences,

---

40. Data on citizen motivations from a different perspective are consistent with our analysis. In a study of the incentives for organizational participation, David Knoke found that those members who were attracted to an organization for normative or social inducements were more likely to be active participants in the organization, while those who were attracted to more selective benefits were less likely to be active in the organization. See David Knoke, "Organizational Incentives," *American Sociological Review* 53 (1988): 311–329.

or out of a sense that they lack the wherewithal to take part. Or they may be inhibited by a feeling that they would accomplish little. Or perhaps they consider politics irrelevant to their lives, or are simply not interested in politics, or do not enjoy taking part.

Although the explanation of political activity—and, therefore, of political inactivity—requires multivariate analysis and occupies a major portion of this volume, we did seek to give those who do not take part politically an opportunity to discuss directly the reasons for their inactivity. Those who had undertaken no political activity beyond voting within the past twelve months had relatively short interviews because they were not asked the follow-up questions posed to participants about the specifics of activity. Near the end of the interview—after rapport had been established and most of the questions had been asked—we asked inactive respondents to consider a long "list of reasons people give us for not being active politically" and to indicate which apply to them.[41] The list covered a wide range of reasons for not taking part. Many items, though not all, were the obverse of those presented to activists. (For example, we asked participants if they found political activity to be "exciting" and inactives if they found it "boring.") Once again, we understand the replies not necessarily as explanations for inactivity, but as reflections of the way in which those who do not take part interpret their inactivity to themselves.

Table 4.2 presents the proportion of non-participants who said

---

41. We actually had two different lists of potential reasons for activity, one for inactive respondents and the other for currently inactive respondents who told us that there had been a time in the past when they had been more active in politics than they are now. The items on the two lists were actually identical. Only the preface differed. Interestingly, the responses of the two groups—the always inactive and the currently inactive—are remarkably similar. The only differences are that the currently inactive were less likely to say that they had never thought about being involved and more likely to say they felt burned out. Given the similarity, we have combined the responses of the two groups in reporting data below.

After they had dealt with the items on the list, respondents were asked an open-ended question about any other reason not already mentioned. Although various other reasons—for example, having been ill or having been active in college—were discussed, the open-ended responses do not suggest that we omitted from the list any factor pertaining to more than a few respondents. In fact, most of the "other" reasons mentioned were simply repetitions of or elaborations on items included on the closed-ended list. For the full list of questions, see Appendix B.5.

Table 4.2 Reasons for Political Inactivity: Percentage of Inactives
Saying a Reason Was Very Important for Their Inactivity[a]

Reason	Percent
I don't have enough time.	39
I should take care of myself and my family before I worry about the community or nation.	34
The important things of my life have nothing to do with politics.	20
I never thought of being involved.	19
Politics is uninteresting and boring.	17
Politics can't help with my personal or family problems.	17
Politics is too complicated.	15
As one individual I don't feel I can have an impact.	15
For what I would get out if it, politics is not worth what I would have to put into it.	14
Politics is a dirty business.	13
I feel burned out.	9
It is not my place.	9
I don't like the people.	7
It is not my responsibility.	6
There are no good causes any more.	6
I might get into trouble.	3

a. N = 1,285 weighted cases: see Appendix A for information about the sample.

that a particular item was "very important" in explaining why they are not very active politically. Clearly, no single interpretation dominates all others. The most frequent response, cited as very important by 39 percent of the inactives, is that they do not have enough time.[42] Beyond that, the statements eliciting most frequent agreement are those that refer to the irrelevance of government to

42. Those who cited insufficient time as an explanation for political inactivity appear to have somewhat less time to spare than do other respondents. Our survey included a series of time budget questions about the number of hours devoted on a typical day to such obligatory activities as paid employment, necessary household work, and the like. (These measures are discussed more fully in Chapter 10.) Inactives who indicated that they do not have time for political involvement do, in fact, have less time left over after accounting for these necessary activities. They average 5.6 hours each day of spare time not committed to necessary activities. In contrast, political activists average 6.4 hours, and inactives who did not cite time constraints as an explanation average 7.3 hours of free time each day. Nevertheless, the time-pressured inactives watch a bit more television (an average of 2.7 hours per day) than do political participants (who average 2.5 hours each day). Inactives who did not mention time constraints watch an average of 3.2 hours of television daily.

the respondent's life or to a general lack of interest. Thirty-four percent of the inactives indicated they ought to take care of themselves and their families before getting involved in politics, and 20 percent stated that the important things in their lives have nothing to do with politics.

Each of the items that probed for a lack of efficacy also received some mention: that politics is too complicated to understand (15 percent); that one individual cannot have an impact (15 percent); or that it is not their place to be involved in politics (9 percent). Interestingly, fear of reprisals does not loom large in the interpretations of lack of political participation. We had expected that a sizeable proportion of inactive citizens would eschew politics out of fear of the consequences. As we have seen, many of those who do not take part politically are economically marginal or depend upon government programs. For them, the perceived dangers of political action might be substantial. In fact, however, only about 3 percent mentioned concern about getting into trouble as very important—the lowest frequency for any of the statements on the list. This finding is confirmed by answers to questions elsewhere on the questionnaire. We asked respondents how worried they would be that they would get into trouble with the authorities—"maybe the police, school authorities, or an office that deals with public housing"—if they were to take a public stand on a controversial issue. Twenty-four percent of the inactive citizens indicated that they would be somewhat or very worried. This figure, which is slightly higher than the 18 percent of activists who expressed such concerns, is lower than we had expected—although sufficiently high as to be worthy of note.[43]

---

43. Quite small percentages—6 percent for the inactives and 2 percent of the actives—indicated that they would be very worried. Where the two groups differ appears to be on the positive side—that is, in terms of enjoying political involvement rather than fearing political engagement. Activists (40 percent) were nearly twice as likely as inactives (22 percent) to have reported that they enjoy political discussions.

During the design phase of our research, we were told by community organizers who work with disadvantaged groups that disadvantaged citizens would fear retaliation from school or housing officials if they were too outspoken. We were, in fact, surprised that we found so little mention of this reason. It is perhaps the case that this is a question that those who are truly fearful might avoid. If we look at the small group of Latino non-citizens—a group whose members might be expected to be fearful—we find that 9 percent said that

In short, no single explanation predominates among the factors cited by those who do not take part. Some indicated that they do not have time for political involvement. Others reported that politics is just not relevant to their lives, that politics does not interest them, or that they can use their time better in other ways. Feelings of political inefficacy and fears of damaging consequences figure rather less importantly among the potential explanations.

Citizens and the Meaning of Political Activity

Our journey through the data on citizens' interpretations of their political activity brings us to conclusions at variance with some of the major current theories of citizen activity. A great deal of citizen political participation is interpreted by activists as having been motivated by civic concerns or a desire to influence government policy. If we add to this a finding reported in Chapter 3—that the bulk of citizen activity is about issues affecting the community and the nation, rather than affecting only themselves—we wind up with a portrait of a citizenry involved in politics in order to influence public policy. A high proportion of political participation is animated by concern about community and national issues. It is not simply about the pursuit of narrow self-interest by political means.

Our results speak not only to social science issues associated with the interpretation of political participation but also to the

---

fear was a reason for staying out of politics and 34 percent said they avoided political discussions so as to stay out of trouble. These figures are higher than for the public in general. We do not have information as to the legal immigration status of the non-citizens.

Fear, of course, is contingent on the circumstances of the individual and the social context. There can be little doubt that fear was a major factor in suppressing the participation of African-Americans in the pre–civil rights legislation era. For an analysis of data arguing that fear continued to suppress voting among Mississippi blacks, see Lester M. Salamon and Stephen Van Evera, "Fear, Apathy, and Discrimination: A Test of Three Explanations of Political Participation," *American Political Science Review* 67 (1973): 1288–1306. They use indirect measures of fear based on occupational insecurity. For a critique of this approach, see Sam Kernell, "Comment: A Reevaluation of Black Voting in Mississippi," *American Political Science Review* 67 (1973): 1307–1318.

Fear that is perhaps too subtle to pick up in our surveys may inhibit those who do not want conflict with friends and neighbors from becoming active on controversial local matters. For several case studies that illustrate the personal attacks that can leave a residue of fear among citizens pursuing causes they believe just, see Laura R. Woliver, *From Outrage to Action: The Politics of Grassroots Dissent* (Urbana: University of Illinois Press, 1993).

nature of contemporary civic involvement. The images associated with American politics are many and disparate, some of them loftier than others. One is the Constitutional Convention of 1787, in which the exercise of republican virtue yielded the framework for a new civic order. Another is the congressional roll call vote, in which the laws that will govern the nation are enacted. Another is the urban political machine, a form of governance in which the making of policy was secondary to the dispensing of patronage and in which the pursuit of self-interest, narrowly defined, took precedence. Still another is the nineteenth-century torchlight parade—politics as spectacle and noisy entertainment, exciting for its own sake.

In an era when surveys show Americans to be disillusioned about politics, distrustful of politicians, and impatient with the level of political debate, we might have expected that activists would either characterize their own political involvement in cynically self-interested terms or see themselves as spectators at an exciting, if sometimes foolish or dirty, sport. To the contrary, their retrospective interpretations of their activity are replete with mentions of civic motivations and a desire to influence policy. Of course, many participants also report selective material or social gratifications. Still, it is striking to note both the extent to which references to doing one's share and making the community or nation a better place to live run as a thread through activists' reports of the concerns that animated their involvement, and the number of participants who discuss nothing but civic motivations for their activity.

5

Recruiting Political
Activists

Often political activity arises more or less spontaneously from individuals when they become excited about issues, connect politics to their basic interests, or get involved out of a sense of civic duty. Frequently, however, they become active because someone asked. In this chapter, we explore the networks through which individuals are recruited to participation.[1] We cannot understand the process of political activation without considering the role played by requests for participation.

Linking appeals for participation to participation is, however, not a straightforward task. Just as requests might beget activity, so, too, activity might beget requests. That is, citizens might become engaged in some public activity as the result of having been asked to do so; however, the opposite process can take place as well when those seeking to recruit activists search for likely prospects among those known to have taken part in the past.[2] At this

---

1. In political science we usually use the term "recruitment" to signify the process by which citizens are selected for inclusion among political elites. We use it, in much the same sense, in relation to citizen activity. Other terms, in particular "mobilization," have multiple meanings and, therefore, might lead to misunderstanding concerning the process we are discussing.

2. In an analysis of the sources of political information, Huckfeldt and Sprague argue that the "direction of influence obviously runs both ways." Individuals construct political networks that are compatible with their political preferences, but there are also autonomous social forces that affect the networks people are in. Robert Huckfeldt and John Sprague,

point we shall not attempt to unravel the complex causal nexus between being asked to participate and being politically active—reserving that task for Chapter 13 where we treat the subject in the context of the Civic Voluntarism Model.

Instead, in this chapter, we concentrate on mapping the largely uncharted terrain of requests for political participation—considering the frequency of solicitations, their source, and the likelihood that they will be met with assent.[3] Our description of networks of recruitment will demonstrate that, contrary to what seems like a blitz of entreaties for political involvement ranging from the mass-market phone appeals for political donations to requests from neighbors for help in dealing with some community issue, many people never receive requests to get involved. Moreover, inclusion in a recruitment network is not a random process but is highly structured by several characteristics that are also related to activity. Furthermore, to seek is not necessarily to find. A substantial share of requests are denied, especially if they come from strangers. We shall also see that patterns of recruitment vary according to what is being asked. Hence, as we have found so often, it is critical to distinguish among different forms of political participation.

Requests for Participation: How Many? What For?

Our survey contained four batteries of questions designed to probe experiences with requests for activity. We asked respondents whether,

---

"Networks in Context: The Social Flow of Political Information," *American Political Science Review* 81 (1987): 1198.

3. The domain has been largely neglected. Although there is ample research on contextual effects in politics, none of it focuses on the specificities of the networks through which individuals are mobilized. For a review of contextual studies, see Robert Huckfeldt and John Sprague, "Citizens, Contexts, and Politics," in *Political Science: The State of the Discipline,* ed. Ada W. Finifter (Washington, D.C.: The American Political Science Association, 1993), pp. 291–304. Steven J. Rosenstone and John Mark Hansen stress the important role of mobilization in explaining activity. Their focus, however, is on the role of strategic elites in mobilizing citizens, not on the more proximate interpersonal networks within which citizens live. See *Mobilization, Participation, and Democracy in America* (New York: MacMillan, 1993). For a work that does deal with the effects of close interpersonal networks on participation, see David Knoke, "Networks of Political Action: Toward Theory Construction," *Social Forces* 68 (1990): 1041–1063.

Table 5.1 Recruitment to Politics: Percentage Asked to Be Active and Percentage of Those Asked Who Say Yes

	Percentage Asked[a]	Percentage of Those Asked Who Say Yes[b]
Campaign Work[c]	12	48
Campaign Contribution	22	27
Contact	29	57
Protest	11	28
Community Activity	19	50

a. N = 2,517 weighted cases.
b. N = 2,517 multiplied by percentage who were asked.
c. Or work in a campaign and contribute to it.

over the past twelve months, they had received any requests to take part in a campaign (either to work in the campaign, to contribute money, or both); to contact a government official; to take part in a protest, march, or demonstration; or to take some active role in a local, public or political issue. If so, we followed up by inquiring whether they had received more than one such request and whether they said yes to the request.[4] In addition, we probed the characteristics of people making requests and the nature of their connections to respondents.

Requests for political activity are quite common but far from universal. Just over half of our respondents (52 percent) reported having been asked to be politically active in some way over the past year. About half of those who were asked to do something were asked in relation to only one of the activities about which we have recruitment information. A mere 1 percent received requests to do all of them.[5] Not surprisingly, as we look across kinds of political involvement, the higher the proportion who actually do a particular activity, the higher the proportion who are asked to do so. As shown in Table 5.1, 12 percent of our respondents were asked at least once to work in a campaign; 22 percent to contribute; 29 percent to contact a government official; 11 percent

---

4. If there had been more than one request for a particular kind of activity, we asked about the most recent one. See Appendix B.8.a.
5. For a description of how we arrived at these figures, see Appendix B.8.a.

to take part in a protest; and 19 percent to become active on a local issue in the community.[6]

Interestingly, more often than not these appeals for political involvement do not bear fruit. Taking all requests together, only 44 percent of those asked said yes.[7] Considering the activities separately, in no case do respondents grant as many as 60 percent of the requests for participation. However, as the data in Table 5.1 make clear, these activities vary considerably in the degree to which a solicitation will be met with assent. Among those asked to work in a campaign, or to contact, or to get involved in community affairs, roughly half say yes. Among those asked to make a campaign contribution or to go to a protest, about a quarter say yes. Thus, the proportion of the sample successfully recruited—a function of the likelihood of being asked and saying yes, if asked—varies across political acts and ranges from a high of 17 percent for contacting to a low of 3 percent for protesting, an activity for which the relatively small number of requests are relatively unlikely to generate accord.

SPONTANEITY OR MOBILIZATION?

Contemporary political observers often emphasize the way in which political organizations generate political activity among the rank and file. Although there are many case studies of the unambiguously successful use of the techniques of grassroots mobilization by interest groups, there has been less in the way of systematic

---

6. In presenting the data for campaign work and contributions, we have combined requests for both work and contributions with requests simply to work in campaigns into a single category. The proportion listed as being asked to contribute are those who were asked to give money but were not asked to work. When we considered these categories separately, we found that, when compared to requests for campaign work, requests for contributions tend not only to be much more frequent but also to show distinctive patterns. Requests for both work and contributions, however, seem to resemble requests for work. It is interesting to note how rare are requests for campaign work only. About two-thirds of the requests for campaign work were linked to a financial solicitation. Only 28 percent of the appeals for contributions were connected to requests for campaign work.

7. Indeed, it is striking that 66 percent of those who received any requests for activity denied at least one of them. In a small proportion (2 percent) of the responses, the respondent indicated spontaneously that he or she acceded in part to the request. In presenting the data we have not considered these qualified answers to be "yes" responses. We did, however, analyze the data both ways with no appreciable effect on the results.

Table 5.2 Spontaneous and Mobilized Activity

Type of Activist	Spontaneous[a]	Mobilized[b]
Campaign Workers	52	41[d]
Campaign Contributors	38	33
Contactors	51	38
Protesters	49	43
Community Activists[c]	60	30

a. Respondent either received no request or received one request and denied it. See footnote 9 for discussion.

b. Respondent received at least one request to which he or she said yes. See footnote 9 for discussion.

c. Informal activists, board members, and regular attenders of meetings of local boards.

d. Rows do not add to 100% because of ambiguous cases not included.

study. We can use our data to estimate roughly how much political activity occurs as the result of a positive response to a direct request. The left-hand column of Table 5.2 presents for several forms of activity the proportion of participants who acted spontaneously—that is, who either received no requests to become active in that particular way or who were asked once but did not say yes when asked.[8] The right-hand column shows the proportions of those engaging in the various activities who assented to the most recent solicitation.[9] The data indicate that, across all activi-

8. Thus, in this context we are considering political activity triggered by media reports, though not by a specific request, to be spontaneous.

9. These data have been analyzed conservatively with the effect that we have surely underestimated the proportions of activists who received no requests to which they said yes. We asked all respondents, whether or not they had been active in a particular way, if they had received any requests for that activity. As indicated, if there had been more than one request, we asked about the details of the most recent one only. From these data we cannot, therefore, discern whether a respondent who had had more than one request might have acceded to a previous request even though he or she said no to the most recent one. We have omitted these respondents (who received more than one request and responded to the most recent one negatively) from the table. This means that the proportion of respondents for whom we have no evidence of successful mobilization is even higher than is represented in Table 5.2. Because the unit of analysis in this case is the activist rather than the request, we consider contributors who received a request both to work in a campaign and to give to it as having received a request for a contribution. Eliminating requests for both work and money for contributors has the effect of boosting the proportion of campaign givers who acted spontaneously.

ties, appeals for activity figure importantly. Thus, any attempt to understand the roots of participation must take into account the impact of requests from others.

Nevertheless, the real message of Table 5.2 may be how much spontaneous activity there is. Only for contributors—only 31 percent of whom received no requests for cash and 29 percent of whom received more than one solicitation, the most recent of which they rejected—is the proportion who acted spontaneously well under half. Perhaps most interesting are the data on contacts. Recent observers of American politics have argued that new technologies permitting interest groups to contact their supporters and the supporters, in turn, to contact public officials are responsible for a flood of communications—mail, telephone calls, faxes, e-mail messages—to the government. Estimates run well over 100 million items a year. On specific issues, millions of messages can appear within days.[10] It is generally assumed that a very high proportion of these communications are not spontaneous.[11]

The data in Table 5.2 give clues as to the extent to which the torrent of mail and other contacts to the government is spontaneous or arises in response to requests. Thirty-eight percent of all contactors had acceded to at least one request, and 51 percent acted spontaneously. However, if we consider just those whose most recent contact was directed to an official on the national level, the situation is somewhat different.[12] Forty-four percent of those who contacted an official on the national level indicated

---

10. See Orval Hansen, *Congressional Operations: The Role of Mail in Decision Making in Congress* (Washington, D.C.: Center for Responsive Politics, 1987), and Stephen Frantzich, *Write Your Congressman: Constituent Communications and Representation* (New York: Praeger, 1986). For specific examples, see Sidney Verba, "The Voice of the People," *PS: Political Science and Politics* 26 (1993): 677–686.

11. On the basis of analyses of specific campaigns, Rosenstone and Hansen (*Mobilization, Participation, and Democracy in America,* p. 107) argue that "In most cases . . . the issue mail Congress receives is 'inspired'—mobilized by political interest groups"—an impression they report as shared by many of the recipients in Washington.

12. Note that, because our questions about requests for activity were posed to all respondents and, therefore, not tied to the performance of particular acts, we cannot be sure that the most recent participatory act (say, a contact with a government official on the national level) was undertaken as the positive response to the most recent request.

that, in the past year, they had been asked to make a contact and had agreed to do so while slightly more—48 percent—contacted a national official spontaneously.[13] In contrast, of those whose most recent contact was with a local official, only 26 percent had received at least one request to which they said yes, and 60 percent had either never been asked (58 percent) or had been asked only once and had denied the request (2 percent).

These data indicate that the massive volume of requests for political action plays a significant role in inspiring communications to public officials. Consistent with reports of an inundation of mobilized communication on policy issues, this phenomenon is particularly prominent on the national level. Nevertheless, the data also make clear that a remarkably high proportion of the contacts to the government are the more or less spontaneous acts of individual citizens.

The Social Nexus of Requests

Requests for political activity are not random. Those who ask others directly to get involved in politics are apt to target likely prospects before making appeals. On a more impersonal level, organizations that solicit through mass telephoning or mass mailings invest large resources in developing lists of probable donors. We consider three dimensions along which these networks of recruitment might be structured. The first is the degree of personal connection between the askers and the asked: Do solicitations come from people who are known personally or from strangers dialing from a computer-generated list? The second aspect of recruitment networks is their location in the life space of the individual: Do requests for involvement come from neighbors, co-workers, or fellow organization members? A final concern is the demography of recruitment networks: Do the people who make appeals share the race or ethnicity or the sex of those they ask? In each case we will consider both the likelihood of being solicited and the likelihood of saying yes, once asked. This material

---

13. This 48 percent is apportioned as follows: 45 percent had never been asked and 3 percent received a single request which they denied.

provides a rich description of the social networks within which political activity is embedded.

FRIENDS AND STRANGERS

An unambiguous trend in the politics of the second half of the twentieth century has been the impact of electronic technologies and the consequent impersonalization of certain modes of citizen involvement. We were curious to know whether—just as the torch-light parade has given way to the sound bite and the photo op—the process by which potential activists are recruited to political activity has been transformed by the electronic revolution. That is, are the networks of recruitment that bring people into politics rooted primarily in personal ties to friends and neighbors or in the impersonal world of computer-generated mailings and mass-market telephone solicitations?

Each time a respondent indicated having received a request for involvement, we asked a series of questions designed to learn whether networks of personal acquaintanceship underlie these efforts to generate political activity. We asked first whether the respondent knew the person making the request and, if so, whether he or she was a close friend or relative. If the respondent was not acquainted with the person making the request, we asked whether that person was someone who knew someone the respondent knew, someone whose name the respondent recognized, or a complete stranger. Overall, personal connections form the underpinnings for a large share of these requests: nearly half arise from someone the respondent knows personally—either a close friend or relative (24 percent) or a more distant acquaintance (23 percent); just under a third emanate from a circle of secondary ties—friends of friends (11 percent) or others whose names are recognized (20 percent). Just under a quarter (23 percent) come from strangers.

Figure 5.1 indicates the variation among political acts in terms of the sources of recruitment. For most acts, appeals from people who are known personally are significant. About two-thirds of the requests for community involvement or attendance at a protest involved someone known personally by the respondent. This is true as well for over half of the requests to give time to a campaign

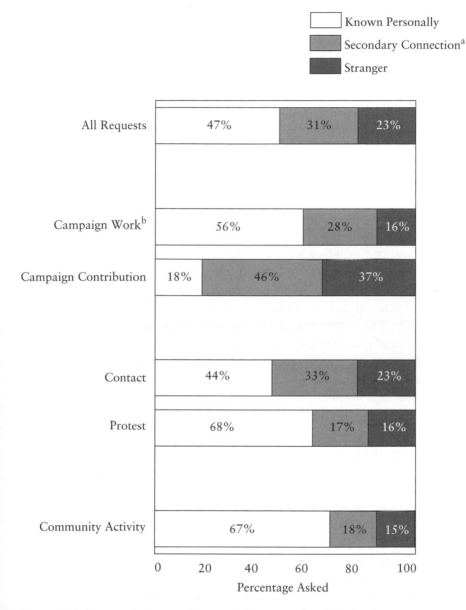

Figure 5.1 Personal Connections and Requests for Activity (percentage of requests emanating from people known personally, secondary connections, and strangers).

a. Secondary connection: someone who knows someone the respondent knows or someone whose name the respondent recognized.

b. Or work in a campaign and contribute to it.

and just under half of the requests to contact an official. Requests for monetary contributions to a campaign present a much less personal picture than do other activities: only 17 percent of the requests for money originated from friends or acquaintances, and fully 37 percent derived from total strangers. The difference from the parallel proportions for solicitations for campaign *work*—59 percent arising from friends or acquaintances and only 17 percent from complete strangers—highlights the fact that requests for time and requests for money move through different channels, with the latter being much less personal.

Not surprisingly, across all acts, those who know the people who attempt to recruit them are much more likely to give a positive answer than those solicited by strangers. When the personal connection was present, respondents acceded to requests for involvement 58 percent of the time—regardless of whether the appeal came from a close friend or relative or from an acquaintance. Those in the secondary network fared less well, with 35 percent of their attempts at recruitment successful. Strangers, 26 percent of whose requests elicited a positive response, had a somewhat less enviable track record still. This is particularly relevant in relation to solicitations for monetary contributions, since most come through impersonal sources. The proportion saying yes to requests for money from strangers is quite low—8 percent.[14]

REQUESTS THROUGH THE MAIL
Given what appears to be a growing role of money as the medium of political participation, it is useful to pursue its special characteristics a bit further. As we have seen, requests for campaign donations are distinctive in their frequency, in the likelihood of coming from strangers, and in the likelihood of being turned down. These special characteristics of requests for monetary contributions are underscored in relation to another, very common mode of request for political involvement: mail solicitations for donations to political campaigns or causes.[15] We did not ask whether

---

14. Requests for money from those known personally do better, but not especially well: fewer than half (46 percent) receive assent.
15. The questions about mail solicitation were not followed up with a full battery about

the respondent was personally acquainted with the source of the request—on the presumption that these requests are usually impersonal, the result of a name having been included on a promising mailing list. These appeals are frequent though not ubiquitous: a full 68 percent of the sample reported receiving at least one such request in the past year. However, those whose mailboxes groan under the weight of computer-generated mail may be surprised to learn that they come as often as once a week to only 7 percent of respondents.

There is considerable overlap between these networks. Those who are asked directly are more than twice as likely to receive impersonal mailed requests as those who receive no personal solicitations. As is well known in the direct-mail industry, these requests produce a low yield: only 10 percent of those asked reported responding with a contribution, a figure lower than any we have viewed so far.[16]

FRIENDS, STRANGERS, AND REQUESTS FOR POLITICAL ACTIVITY: A SUMMARY

Attempts at political recruitment are widespread and important as a means of eliciting political activity but less common than they are sometimes assumed to be. Requests are differentially likely to meet with assent depending upon whether the requests come from those personally connected (close friends or relatives as well as more distant acquaintances), from a secondary network, from strangers, or through the mail. Differences among various participatory acts in terms of the success rate of appeals are related, at least in part, to disparities in the proportion of such requests deriving from personal connections. However, there are clear differences among types of political involvement with respect to our respondents' willingness to agree to requests for participation, even when those entreaties come from relatives or close friends.

---

the sources of these requests. Hence, we cannot engage in the full analysis we do for other sorts of requests for political activity.

16. This figure is, appropriately, higher than the single-digit figures usually quoted for the expected yield from a political mailing. Those who reported making a contribution in response to direct-mail solicitations need not have sent money *each* time they received a request.

Whether those doing the asking are personal friends, friends of friends, or mere strangers, they are more likely to be successful in their efforts at recruiting others to take part in politics if they ask someone to contact a government official or take part in a community activity rather than to give a campaign contribution or attend a demonstration or protest. One of the clearest patterns is the comparative impersonality of the network for soliciting funds. Campaign solicitations arise infrequently from friends or acquaintances—coming more often from strangers or through the mail. These impersonal requests rarely generate positive responses, but the volume is sufficient that the payoff is presumed to justify the effort.

THE LOCUS OF RECRUITMENT

Another feature of the networks of political solicitation is their location: are Americans recruited to political life in their neighborhoods, at work, or through organizational connections? One of the reasons sometimes given for the weakness of class politics in America is that politics tends to be organized by residence rather than work.[17] We were thus curious about the location of political solicitations, and asked those respondents who had been recruited whether the person making the appeal was a neighbor, someone who works where the respondent works—and, if so, someone in a supervisory capacity—and/or someone who belongs to an organization to which the respondent belongs.[18] Consistent with the notion that citizen involvement in American politics is more likely to be based in the home and neighborhood than in the workplace, more requests come from neighbors than from fellow workers. Of all the requests for political involvement, 18 percent were made by neighbors compared with 13 percent by fellow workers. Interestingly, nearly a third (30 percent) of workplace-based requests came from supervisors. The organizational nexus is, however, by far the most important: fellow organization members are responsible for fully 48 percent of the requests. Not surprisingly, the

---

17. See Ira Katznelson, *City Trenches: Urban Politics and the Patterning of Class in the United States* (New York: Pantheon Books, 1981).

18. Unfortunately, we did not also inquire whether the person making the request was a member of the respondent's church congregation.

requests arriving through all of these channels rarely came from total strangers: 81 percent of those asked by neighbors, 86 percent of those asked by fellow workers, and 63 percent of those asked by fellow organization members indicated having some connection to the individual who made the request.

Reflecting these personal links, requests through neighborhood, workplace, and organizational networks have a relatively high probability of success. Supervisors at work have the highest success rate: fully 70 percent of those asked by a supervisor acceded. However, this figure is not substantially higher than the 60 percent who said yes to neighbors, the 61 percent who said yes to workmates, and the 57 percent who said yes to fellow organization members.[19] These data underscore once again the personal basis of recruitment to political participation. Despite the supposed impersonality of a political world dominated by television and computer-generated solicitations, a remarkably high proportion of the political recruitment—and an even higher proportion of the successful recruitment—comes from people who are known personally.

INVITATIONS TO POLITICS IN INSTITUTIONS

We have some additional data that allow us to refine our understanding of the institutional context in which recruitment takes

---

19. We can also look at the proportion assenting to a request from someone known personally in each of the domains. Sixty-two percent of those asked by a fellow organization member whom they knew personally acceded to the request—a figure almost identical to the 60 percent who said yes to neighbors whom they knew personally and 63 percent who said yes to a workmate whom they knew personally. These proportions are analogous to the overall figure of 57 percent of respondents who assented when asked by someone they knew personally to take part. Supervisors at work, not surprisingly, get somewhat better results. Seventy-five percent of those asked by a boss whom they knew personally agreed to the request.

When these figures are disaggregated, we find few distinctive patterns for requests for particular kinds of activity. As we might expect, appeals for participation on community issues are more common in the neighborhood than are requests for any other form of activity. Even with respect to requests for participation on community issues, however, the organizational nexus takes precedence—as it clearly does for other forms of activity. Requests for community involvement are slightly more frequent from fellow organization members than from neighbors. Also, the probability of getting assent is related less to whether the source of appeal is a neighbor, a workmate, or a fellow organization member than to what is being asked: appeals for campaign contributions and, to a somewhat lesser extent, for attendance at a protest are especially likely to be denied.

place. As part of the battery of items about experiences in the workplace, church, or organizations, we asked about efforts by these institutions to stimulate political activity. These questions differ from those just discussed in that the thrust was not simply to assess whether those who ask others to take part are connected by common institutional affiliation to the targets of their requests, but rather to discover whether these institutions themselves attempt to recruit citizens to activity. Thus, we inquired of those in the paid work force whether, within the past five years, the organization they work for or one of their superiors had ever asked them to vote for or against a candidate in an election for public office or to take some other action on a political issue—sign a petition, write a letter, or get in touch with a public official. Analogous questions were directed to regular church attenders and those affiliated with a local church congregation with respect to requests from a member of the clergy or someone in an official position in the church and to those involved in an organization with respect to requests from the organization they designated as their most important or from one of its officers or staff.[20]

Table 5.3, which summarizes the responses to these items, shows several patterns: that requests for political activity are neither the norm nor exceptional in work, church, or organizational settings; that requests to vote for a particular candidate are less common than requests for other kinds of activity; and that requests are more frequent in churches and organizations than at work. Overall, in the past five years 20 percent of all respondents have been asked to vote for or against a candidate in an election and 38 percent have been asked to take some other political action in one or more of these settings. Considering not the total sample, but only those affiliated with these institutions, we find relatively few requests to vote for a candidate for office in any of the three settings. Requests to take some other political action are more

---

20. With respect to requests in the workplace, we also asked about requests for contributions both to election campaigns or political action committees and to charitable campaigns such as the Community Chest. We did not, however, ask these questions with respect to requests in church or organizations. The questions about requests for political activity in organizations were asked only about the respondent's most important organization. For the questions, see Appendix B.8.b.

Table 5.3 Percentage Reporting Being Asked to Be Active in Institutional Settings[a]

	All Respondents	Institutionally Affiliated[b]
ON THE JOB		
Asked to Vote	5	9
Other Acts	11	18
Either Vote or Act	13	22
IN AN ORGANIZATION		
Asked to Vote	11	14
Other Acts	20	26
Either Vote or Act	22	28
IN CHURCH		
Asked to Vote	8	12
Other Acts	21	30
Either Vote or Act	23	34

a. N = 2,517 weighted cases for all respondents: see Appendix A for information about sample. For weighted numbers of cases for workers, see Appendix B.11.a, for members of non-political organizations, see Appendix B.2.c, and for church members, see Appendix B2.b.

b. On the job: working full or part time; with a job but not at work due to vacation, illness, etc. In an organization: member of or contributor to an organization. In church: member of or regular attender of services at a local church.

frequent. For both kinds of requests, we find fewer in the workplace than in churches or organizations.[21]

The extent to which these institutions incubate requests for political activity is related to the extent to which they otherwise get involved with politics or provide political cues. When the organization is one that takes stands on public issues, these requests are very frequent: 32 percent of the affiliates reported electoral recruitment and 52 percent indicated recruitment for some other kind of political activity. In contrast, when the organization is one that does not take stands, appeals for political participation are actually less common than in church: 4 percent

---

21. In addition, of those in the paid work force 8 percent indicated having been asked for a campaign contribution and 40 percent having been asked for a charitable contribution at work.

reported having been asked to vote for a candidate and 11 percent indicated having been asked to take other political action.

Not surprisingly, the likelihood of recruitment is increased when institutional affiliation is coupled with some kind of political exposure within the institution. Of the church affiliates who reported that the clergy in their churches never discuss local or national political issues from the pulpit, only 4 percent indicated that they had been asked to vote in their churches and 11 percent that they had been asked to take other political action. In contrast, of those reporting that clergy sometimes or frequently discuss political issues, 23 percent indicated that they had been asked to vote and 50 percent that they had been asked to take other political action. As would be expected, the figures are even higher for those who had, within the past five years, attended a meeting about some local or national political issue at their church: 30 percent indicated having been asked to vote and 66 percent to take some other political action by their churches.

Similarly, those who reported that there is informal chat about politics or government at meetings of their most important organization were more likely to have been asked by those organizations to vote for a particular candidate or take other political action. Once again, however, the more fundamental distinction is whether or not the organization takes stands on public issues. Recruitment is much less likely in organizations that do not take stands on public issues, even when members reported informal chat at meetings, than in organizations that do take stands. When these characteristics are combined, however, recruitment is quite likely: of those reporting informal political chat in an organization that takes political stands, 36 percent reported having been asked to vote and 61 percent to take some other political action by the organization or one of its officers or staff.

These data indicate some of the consequences for political participation of experiences at work, in church, and in organizations. Those who are involved in each of these contexts are exposed to political cues and become the targets of efforts to recruit them to political activity—both because they meet people and, thus, broaden the networks through which requests for involvement are filtered and because these institutions (and the people who run and staff them) themselves seek to generate political activity. We shall revisit these data in Chapter 13 when we consider the causal process by which citizens become active.

The Demography of Political Recruitment

Given the importance of class, race, and gender to American politics, we were curious to investigate the demographic roots of political recruitment—in terms of both who is asked and who does the asking. We begin with economic circumstances and proceed to examine race or ethnicity and gender. What we find is that the process by which people become the targets of requests for activity is socially structured, and that much of what we find when we consider who solicits whom to take part will hold when we look directly at the demography of participation.

FAMILY INCOME

We begin our investigation of the kinds of people who are likely to be the targets of solicitations for political participation by considering family income. Figure 5.2 shows the relationship between family income and the likelihood of being asked to take part in politics. It reports data about requests for activity of any sort—as well as requests for campaign contributions or attendance at protests. Figure 5.2 indicates clearly that the well-heeled are much more likely than the poor to report ever having been asked to take part.[22] Requests for attendance at protests, marches, or demonstrations are less structured by income than are requests to give money—although, even for protest, those in the lower three income categories are less likely to be asked than are those in the upper three categories.[23] More substantial disparities in the frequency of requests emerge when it comes to contributions. Compared to the poor, the affluent are more than four times as likely to be asked for contributions but only one and a half times as likely to be asked to protest.

---

22. The pattern is even more pronounced for education: those with limited education are much less likely to be recruited to activity.

23. Other activities tend to resemble contributions more than they resemble protests.

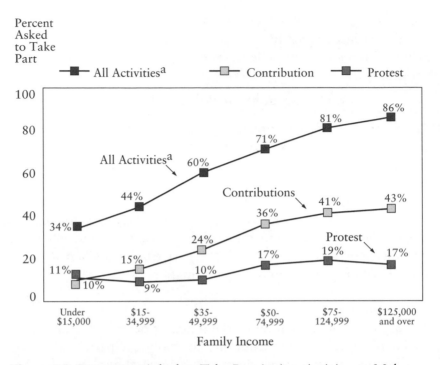

Figure 5.2 Percentage Asked to Take Part in Any Activity, to Make a Contribution, or to Take Part in a Protest: by Income.

a. Asked to work or contribute to a campaign, contact, protest, or to take part in community activity.

Although the relationship between income and being asked to be active is strong, it is interesting to note that—except at the bottom and the very top—there is no consistent relationship between income and the probability that an attempt at recruitment will be successful.[24] In the broad middle range that accounts for more than three-quarters of all respondents, family income has no

---

24. This generalization holds for education as well. Considering all requests for activity across categories of family income, the proportion that are met with assent is as follows:

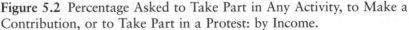

	Family Income:						
Low	1	2	3	4	5	6	High
	34%	44%	46%	43%	44%	54%	

bearing upon whether a request for activity will bear fruit. Thus, the social structuring of requests to take part in politics occurs in the sorting out of who gets asked rather than in who says yes. The critical threshold is the request.

RACE, ETHNICITY, AND GENDER

We have analogous data on who is asked to be active with respect to race or ethnicity[25] and gender. Anglo-Whites are considerably more likely than Blacks or, especially, Latinos to be asked to get involved in politics. Fifty-six percent of the Anglo-Whites, as opposed to 40 percent of the African-Americans and 25 percent of the Latinos, reported receiving at least one request for political participation.[26] In fact, when it comes to being asked to take part in politics, the gap between Anglo-Whites and African-Americans is wider than we shall find when we look at actual political activity. The gender differences are less pronounced: men are slightly more likely than women to be asked to get involved politically—55 percent of the men, as opposed to 50 percent of the women, reported being asked.

Information about the characteristics of the person making the request, derived from the battery of questions administered each time a respondent reported having been asked to participate in a particular way, permits us to inquire whether requests for political activity originate from within racial, ethnic, or gender groups or cross a divide. We can also probe whether those who are solicited to take part in politics are more likely to agree to the request when it comes from someone with whom they have race, ethnicity, or gender in common. In terms of who asks, we find a repetition of the results about who is asked—although, in the case of gender, with greater bias. Overall, Anglo-Whites (who represent 82 percent of respondents) are the source of 91 percent of the requests for activity; Blacks (9 percent of the respondents) are responsible

---

25. See Chapter 8 for discussion of the measures used to categorize the racial or ethnic groups—Anglo-Whites, African-Americans, and Latinos.

26. Although Latinos who are not citizens are even less likely to be recruited to political activity than are Latino citizens, when we consider Latino citizens, a large gap remains. Only 28 percent of Latino citizens received any requests for participation.

for 7 percent of the requests; and Latinos (6 percent of the respondents) make 2 percent of the appeals for political activity. Differences between men and women—rather minimal with respect to being asked to take part—are more pronounced when it comes to making requests. Sixty-six percent of all requests emanate from men (who constitute 47 percent of the sample); reciprocally, women (who constitute 53 percent of the sample) are responsible for only 34 percent of the requests for political participation.

WHO ASKS WHOM?

Although attempts at recruitment to participation do cross lines of race or ethnicity and gender, they are much more likely to cluster within groups—especially within groups defined on the basis of race or ethnicity—than would be expected on the basis of chance. Taking into consideration the relative size of the groups as well as the differences among racial or ethnic and gender groups in rates of asking and being asked, and making the assumption that anyone who asks someone else does so randomly with respect to race or ethnicity or to gender, we can estimate that roughly three-quarters of all attempts to get someone else to become active would be expected to involve persons of the same race or ethnicity, and about half would involve persons of the same sex. In fact, with respect both to race and to gender, the extent to which requests for activity bring together people with shared characteristics is higher than would be expected on the basis of chance.[27] The disproportion is greater in relation to race or ethnicity: instead of the expected figure of about 75 percent, we find that 91 percent of the requests are within the race and ethnic borders. For gender, we find 62 percent of requests—rather than the expected 50 percent—to be within gender boundaries.

---

27. This discussion uses the proportion of each group within the sample as the basis for the probabilities that attempts at recruitment will involve people of the same or different ethnicity. The implicit postulate, however, ignores a fundamental aspect of life in America: the fact that the neighborhoods, churches, and organizations from which requests for political involvement originate are segregated by race and—less so—by ethnicity, thus diminishing the opportunities for recruitment across group lines. This, of course, suggests an explanation of the high level of within-group recruitment that goes beyond individuals' preferences for dealing with their own kind, but it does not help us to understand why Anglo-Whites are more likely to ask Blacks or Latinos than vice versa.

Table 5.4 Who Asks Whom to Get Involved?
Race or Ethnicity and Gender

	Race or Ethnicity of Survey Respondent		
	Anglo-White	African-American	Latino
RACE OR ETHNICITY OF PERSON MAKING REQUEST			
Anglo-White	96%	38%	72%
African-American	3	61	4
Latino	1	1	24
	100%	100%	100%

	Gender of Survey Respondent	
	Men	Women
GENDER OF PERSON MAKING REQUEST		
Male	77%	54%
Female	23	46
	100%	100%

We pursue this theme further in Table 5.4, which presents these data separately for Anglo-Whites, African-Americans, and Latinos and for men and women. The columns show for Anglo-White, African-American, or Latino respondents and for male or female respondents the racial or ethnic or gender characteristics of the people who solicited their political activity. Anglo-Whites tend to be targeted by other Anglo-Whites—at a level even higher than their share of the public. Put another way, it is very rare for an Anglo-White to be asked to get involved politically by a Black or a Latino. The pattern is quite different, and more complicated, for African-Americans and Latinos. Anglo-Whites are more numerous, and African-Americans are asked by them to get involved. Thus, a substantial proportion of requests to African-Americans come from Anglo-Whites. Still, African-Americans are disproportionately likely to receive requests for political participation from other African-Americans.

Like Blacks, Latinos are asked by Anglo-Whites to take part in political activities; still, they are disproportionately likely to be asked to become active by other Latinos. This pattern, however, is much less pronounced than it is for African-Americans—even taking into account that Latinos constitute an even smaller share of the public than African-Americans. Indeed, across all political activities, Latinos are more likely to receive requests from Anglo-Whites than from other Latinos. In contrast to the situation for African-Americans, it is clear that the difference between the relatively large number of Anglo-Whites who ask Latinos to get involved and the infinitesimal number of Latinos who make reciprocal requests of Anglo-Whites represents more than simply the fact that Latinos are a small minority. Clearly Latinos feel inhibited from asking Anglo-Whites to get involved politically.

Because men and women constitute roughly equal shares of the public and residential patterns are not segregated by gender, analogous data about gender are more easily interpreted. As we saw before, men are, in general, more likely to make requests for political activity than are women. In addition, as shown in Table 5.4, when women do make attempts to recruit others to participate, they are disproportionately likely to focus their efforts on other women. These data, therefore, show considerable evidence of social structuring in recruitment attempts. Requests for political involvement are overwhelmingly segregated by race or ethnicity. Requests that cross these lines are much more likely to involve Anglo-Whites asking Blacks or, especially, Latinos rather than vice versa. Recruitment across gender lines is more common but is similarly non-reciprocal, with men much more likely to ask women than women to ask men.

WHO SAYS YES TO WHOM?
When we consider the success of efforts to recruit within and across racial and gender groups, the results are perhaps unexpected. Despite the structuring of requests, respondents, once asked, are not systematically more likely to accede to requests from those who share their race or ethnicity or their gender than to requests from outsiders. The data in Table 5.5 indicate that Anglo-Whites are no more likely to respond positively to Anglo-Whites than to African-Americans and that African-Americans are only slightly

Table 5.5 Who Says Yes to Whom? Race or Ethnicity and Gender
(percentage who said yes to request)

	Race or Ethnicity of Respondent		
	Anglo-White	African-American	Latino
RACE OR ETHNICITY OF PERSON MAKING REQUEST			
Anglo-White	48	46	44
African-American	53	57	a
Latino	a	a	43

	Gender of Survey Respondent	
	Men	Women
GENDER OF PERSON MAKING REQUEST		
Male	47	44
Female	50	53

a. Insufficient cases.

more likely to say yes to African-Americans than to Anglo-Whites.[28] Latinos are equally likely to grant requests from Anglo-Whites and from other Latinos.

With respect to gender, solicitations from women—relatively few though they are in number—meet with slightly greater success than requests from men regardless of whether the target of the request is male or female. In particular, women are somewhat more responsive to appeals from other women. However, what is especially striking about the data in Table 5.5 is the absence of differentiation in terms of the probability that a request will elicit assent.

---

28. It is worth noting, however, that when we consider requests for particular kinds of involvement, the pattern for Blacks becomes more complex. African-Americans are considerably more likely to grant requests from other African-Americans when it comes to campaign assistance, contacts with government officials, or involvement on community issues. However, with respect to requests for attendance at demonstrations or protests, African-Americans are—for reasons we do not understand—actually more likely to say yes to Anglo-Whites than to Blacks.

Conclusion

Our consideration of the processes by which invitations to become
involved in politics are extended has suggested several themes
germane to the understanding of political participation. First, requests for political activity are frequent, but not universal. Nearly
half our respondents could not recall having been asked by someone else to take part within the preceding twelve months. Moreover, although over two-thirds reported receiving at least one
mailed request for a political contribution in the past year, only
28 percent indicated receiving such requests as often as once a
month.

What is more, not all these appeals meet with success. In fact,
in a majority of cases the answer is negative. This suggests that to
elaborate our understanding of the processes of political recruitment we need to probe not only who gets asked by whom but also
who says yes to whom. That so many requests are turned down
also suggests that we cannot make a simple assumption that the
solicitation is the parent to the act. Instead, alternative processes
are possible: requests for political participation can stimulate activity; reciprocally, political activism invites further requests for involvement by demonstrating that the participant is a likely prospect.

Throughout this analysis, both the pattern of requests and the
likelihood of assent are affected by what is being asked. As is often
the case, attendance at protests or demonstrations—the political
act that is both least frequent and least mainstream—is distinctive.
Furthermore, echoing a theme that will surface regularly in our
analysis, political participation through financial contribution differs in many ways from other forms of activity.

We have also seen that, in spite of the profound influence
electronic technologies exert on our politics, personal connections,
embedded in the main institutions of life, play a significant role in
the civic life of citizens. Although direct-mail solicitation has become widespread as a tool for raising money for political campaigns and causes, nearly half the requests for political activity
discussed by our respondents emanated from those they know
personally—either family and close friends or more distant ac-

quaintances—and only a small proportion came from complete strangers. Furthermore, when appeals arrive through these personal channels, they are more likely to elicit a positive response.

Underlying this discussion has been another theme that will recur throughout this inquiry: the multiple ways in which the non-political institutions of adult life—the workplace, voluntary association, and church—serve to enhance political participation. In this context we saw that these institutions are frequently the locus of attempts to stimulate political involvement both because those affiliated with these institutions develop the personal networks from which requests for activity often spring and because these institutions, or those who run them, frequently make explicit attempts to recruit political participation. Moreover, involvement at work, in organizations, or in church brings exposure—both formal and informal—to political conversations and messages. This exposure is, presumably, a politicizing factor on its own. Beyond this, however, is a synergy such that an institution that provides political cues to those affiliated with it provides a nurturant context in which attempts to recruit political activity also proliferate.

The data in this chapter also suggest several important themes about the social structure of recruitment. There is a bias in terms of who asks whom to get involved in politics. In terms of being recruited, the poor and those with little formal education, as well as African-Americans and Latinos, are less likely to be asked to get involved. When it comes to asking others to become active, women and Blacks—who, as we shall see, have overall rates of participation not much lower than those of men and Anglo-Whites—are less likely to make overtures to others or to cross the boundaries of gender or race when they do. Latinos are especially unlikely to make requests for political activity—particularly requests directed at non-Latinos. However, when requests are made, social structuring plays a relatively minor role in determining whether they are successful.

This echoes a theme in the literature about organized interests in the political process. According to one interpretation, one factor that matters significantly for political outcomes is not a systematic bias among policymakers in favor of a particular set of interests—for example, a privileged position for business—so much as who is in the game. Hence a critical step is gaining an established role as a legitimate player. Those interests that are poorly endowed with traditional political resources are not doomed forever to lose—if they manage to get over the threshold and become accepted as contenders. The interests that come up short in the end are those that are so deprived of resources that they never even establish a foothold in the process.[29] So it is with efforts to get others involved in politics. The winnowing process occurs with respect to who asks whom and not with respect to who says yes to whom.

We conclude by repeating a caution with which we began. Implicit in our discussion is the notion that requests to take part lead to political activity. Yet we must recall that the causality probably does not run in a single direction. While appeals for activity do presumably beget activity, political activists are obvious targets for recruitment attempts. After all, who has not gotten involved in some form of voluntary activity—often one that, while not uncongenial, might not otherwise have been undertaken—because somebody asked? A strong relationship between political participation and political recruitment might result from the fact that many people get involved because someone asked; however, it might also result from a reciprocal process by which people are asked to take part because they are already active. Those who are politically active develop networks of acquaintanceship that lead to additional requests. Just as the surest way to get more catalogues through the mail is to buy something from a catalogue, previous activists become more likely as prospects. As most of us

---

29. This view is advanced in Kay Lehman Schlozman and John T. Tierney, *Organized Interests and American Democracy* (New York: Harper and Row, 1986), chaps. 4, 14, and 15. See also John P. Heinz, Edward O. Laumann, Robert L. Nelson, and Robert H. Salisbury, *The Hollow Core: Private Interests in National Policy Making* (Cambridge, Mass.: Harvard University Press, 1993), chap. 11. They analyze major policy controversies in four policy domains and find that multivariate analysis predicts remarkably little about success in achieving policy goals. In short, once at the table, the variables that might be expected to make a difference seem not to matter. What does matter is getting to the table.

know, the only certain "reward" for a contribution of time or money to a political cause is a request for another contribution. Moreover, not all of those who are asked to take part say yes. Presumably, other factors structure the process by which some people accept invitations to take part politically—and others send their regrets. We return to these themes in Chapter 13, where we attempt to sort out the relationship between recruitment and participation.

II

Participation and Representation

Part II focuses on representation: the extent to which participatory input reflects accurately the politically relevant characteristics of the public. Chapter 6 provides a theoretical introduction to the subject. We discuss the peculiar ways in which dilemmas about representation present themselves with respect to citizen participation and the nature of the politically relevant characteristics that are communicated through the participatory process. In addition, we develop some indices of participatory distortion—ways of measuring the extent to which the politically relevant attributes of activists match those of the public. The two chapters that follow apply the concepts introduced in Chapter 6 to the many modes of participation. In Chapter 7 we consider the extent to which participant publics are representative in terms of their economic circumstances and needs—for example, family income, receipt of government benefits, and attitudes on economic issues. In Chapter 8, we raise these issues of representation with respect to groups defined by their race or ethnicity (African-Americans, Latinos, and Anglo-Whites) and their gender.

6

Thinking about Participatory
Representation

Questions of representation, long central to democratic theory, present themselves in several contexts in empirical studies of American politics. They constitute one of the fundamental theoretical anchors in studies of legislatures and other deliberative bodies. They arise in considerations of what kinds of organizations—and what kinds of interests—are active in pressure politics. And they inevitably surface when we ask how well or badly political participation connects the mass public to organized interests, legislatures, and other political institutions. Through political activity citizens have an opportunity to communicate their concerns and wishes to political leaders and to influence public outcomes. Those in public life are more likely to be aware of, and to pay attention to, the needs and preferences of those who are active.[1] Thus, it

---

1. In this chapter, we consider the representativeness of the participatory input from the perspective of a concern with its impact on the communication of citizens' needs and preferences to political elites and thus a concern with equal protection of interests. Participation may also perform other functions—for example, legitimating a regime, increasing popular commitment to democratic values, developing the capacities of those who take part and enhancing their self-esteem. On these themes, see Carole Pateman, *Participation and Democratic Theory* (Cambridge: Cambridge University Press, 1970); Geraint Parry, "The Idea of Political Participation," in *Participation in Politics,* ed. Geraint Parry (Manchester: Manchester University Press, 1972); Peter Bachrach, *The Theory of Democratic Elitism: A Critique* (Boston: Little, Brown, 1967); Jane J. Mansbridge, *Beyond Adversary Democracy* (New York: Basic Books, 1980), chap. 17; and Benjamin Barber, *Strong De-*

must matter for the democratic principle of equality that studies of citizen participation in America find political activists to be unrepresentative of the public at large.

In this chapter we develop a framework for thinking about participation and representation. In the succeeding two chapters, we use this framework to understand from whom—and about what—the government hears. The focus is on the representation of some of the basic demographic groups in America: in Chapter 7, groups defined by their economic circumstances, and in Chapter 8, by their race or ethnicity and gender.[2]

Our purpose in this part of the book is not to *explain* who is active and who is not. That concern forms the core of Part III of this volume, in which we develop and test a model of the factors that lead to political activity. Instead, our task is to *describe* the differences among groups in the amount and kinds of participation in which they engage. These variations have political implications—regardless of whether the source of the group's particular participatory profile derives from group membership per se or from some characteristic, for example, distinctive levels of education, associated with group membership. It matters for politics whether public officials hear disproportionately from the rich or the poor, from African-Americans, Latinos, or Anglo-Whites, and from men or women, no matter what the explanation for the disparity.

Dilemmas of Representation

Because the consequences for democracy of disparities in participation rest so heavily upon how well and in what ways political activists are representative of the citizenry, let us begin by review-

---

mocracy: Participatory Politics for a New Age (Berkeley and Los Angeles: University of California Press, 1984). With respect to voting in particular, see Stephen Earl Bennett and David Resnick, "The Implications of Nonvoting for Democracy in the United States," *American Journal of Political Science* 34 (1990): 771–803.

2. Our demographic answer to the question, "Who is represented through citizen participation?" is necessarily incomplete. We have been forced to be selective from among the many demographic characteristics of an individual. With greater space we might have considered other cleavages as well—for example, religion; region; urban, suburban, or rural residence; or, most important, age. We have chosen to focus on economic circumstances, race or ethnicity, and gender because these categories are so politically salient.

ing briefly the findings of the rich literature on representation in legislatures and other deliberative bodies.[3] Empirical studies of representation in many contexts show again and again that, in demographic terms, elected representatives are not descriptively representative of the populations from which they are drawn. Instead they are more likely to be male, affluent, educated, and of the dominant racial and ethnic groups.[4]

These studies also demonstrate the difficulty of achieving descriptive representation among political elites. Since all societies are divided in complex ways along multiple axes of cleavage, descriptive representation on all relevant demographic dimensions probably cannot be realized within the confines of a legislature of manageable size. The efforts by the Democratic Party to make its nominating convention more descriptively representative of Democratic voters illustrate this dilemma. Although greater numbers of Black, female, and young delegates rendered the 1972 Democratic convention more representative than its predecessor in terms of race, gender, and age, the delegates were not at all representative of the rank and file in terms of education, income, religion, or policy preferences.[5]

This example illustrates not only the difficulty of achieving descriptive demographic representation but also a final point made

3. The literature on representation is voluminous. The classic theoretical statement is Hanna Pitkin, *The Concept of Representation* (Berkeley and Los Angeles: University of California Press, 1967). There are several noteworthy studies of delegates to presidential nominating conventions: Jeane J. Kirkpatrick, *The New Presidential Elite: Men and Women in National Politics* (New York: Russell Sage Foundation, 1976), esp. chap. 10; John S. Jackson, III, J. C. Brown, and Barbara Leavitt Brown, "Recruitment, Representation, and Political Values: The 1976 Democratic National Convention Delegates," *American Politics Quarterly* 6 (1978): 187–212; John S. Jackson, III, J. C. Brown, and David Bositis, "Herbert McClosky and Friends Revisited: 1980 Democratic and Republican Elites Compared to the Mass Public," *American Politics Quarterly* 10 (1982): 158–180; Warren E. Miller and M. Kent Jennings, *Parties in Transition: A Longitudinal Study of Party Elites and Party Supporters* (New York: Russell Sage Foundation, 1986). A general account of the role of leadership and representation is Robert D. Putnam, *Comparative Study of Political Elites* (Englewood Cliffs, N.J.: Prentice-Hall, 1976). See also Carol M. Swain, *Black Faces, Black Interests: The Representation of African-Americans in Congress* (Cambridge, Mass.: Harvard University Press, 1993) which deals with these issues in relation to the representation of Black interests.

4. On this issue in general, see Putnam, *Comparative Study of Political Elites,* and Kenneth Prewitt and Alan Stone, *The Ruling Elites: Elite Theory, Power, and American Democracy* (New York: Harper and Row, 1973), chap. 6.

5. See Kirkpatrick, *The New Presidential Elite,* chap. 10.

by the literature on legislative representation: there is no necessary correspondence between the demographic characteristics and the behavior of an elected representative. For one thing, social characteristics are an imperfect predictor of policy positions, especially among elected representatives. Furthermore, even if elected representatives do not share the characteristics of their constituents, they may still act "in the interest of the represented, in a manner responsive to them"—to use Pitkin's definition of political representation.[6] In other words, a failure of descriptive representation in relation to elected officials—the fact that they do not match their constituents in important demographic characteristics—does not necessarily imply a failure of substantive representation of the needs and interests of their constituents.

THE SPECIAL CASE OF PARTICIPATORY REPRESENTATION

Many of the findings with respect to representation in legislatures and other deliberative bodies are germane to the understanding of citizen participation. It is well known that citizen activists, like elected representatives, are not descriptively representative of the population as a whole, but are instead more likely to be well-educated and well-heeled, of the dominant racial or ethnic extraction, and male.[7] Moreover, just as the demographic characteristics of elected delegates are very imperfect predictors of either their policy views or their conduct in office, a gap in policy preferences between active and inactive citizens does not follow inevitably from

---

6. Pitkin, *The Concept of Representation*, p. 209. On the relationship between the social characteristics of political elites and their views, see Putnam, *Comparative Study of Political Elites*. We should not overstate the case, however. The literature makes clear that, while there is no *necessary* connection either between a representative's social characteristics and policy views or between personal policy views and the policies pursued while in office, personal characteristics, ideology, and comportment in office are, in fact, not independent of one another.

7. There is an extensive literature on the demographic characteristics of those who are active in politics. For extensive references, see Lester W. Milbrath and M. L. Goel, *Political Participation: How and Why Do People Get Involved in Politics?*, 2nd ed. (Chicago: Rand McNally College Pub. Co., 1977); Stephen Earl Bennett and Linda L. M. Bennett, "Political Participation," in *Annual Review of Political Science*, ed. Samuel Long (Norwood, N.J.: Ablex, 1986), and M. Margaret Conway, *Political Participation in the United States*, 2nd ed. (Washington, D.C.: CQ Press, 1991).

the fact that political activists are not descriptively representative of the public at large.

In their study of voting, Raymond E. Wolfinger and Steven J. Rosenstone confirm the demographic differences between voters and non-voters, but they also demonstrate that these demographic differences do not necessarily imply parallel differences in their policy positions. With the exception of party identification, where there is a genuine, although not terribly large, Republican electoral advantage among voters in comparison with the public as a whole, differences between the public and the voters on such issues as government welfare policy, health care, and abortion are negligible.[8] Furthermore, any small differences between voters and non-voters in attitudes on these policy issues are not systematically skewed in a liberal or conservative direction. On issues of domestic economic policy, other researchers find some tilt in a liberal direction among non-voters but agree that the differences are not very great.[9] All in all, this research confirms that, as with representative bodies, a gap in policy preferences between activists and non-par-

---

8. Raymond E. Wolfinger and Steven J. Rosenstone, *Who Votes* (New Haven: Yale University Press, 1980), pp. 105–114.

9. With respect to presidential elections, data and conclusions similar to Wolfinger and Rosenstone's are contained in Stephen Schaffer, "Policy Differences Between Voters and Non-Voters in American Elections," *Western Political Quarterly* 35 (1982): 496–510. Using data from several elections (1984, 1986, and 1988), Bennett and Resnick, "Implications of Nonvoting," p. 799, modify the Wolfinger and Rosenstone conclusion somewhat. They find that, although non-voting "does not skew most foreign policies" and "non-voters are not more egalitarian than voters, or more hostile to business, or more in favor of extensive government ownership and control of key industries," non-voting "does have an impact on some domestic policies, especially spending on welfare state programs." Michael M. Gant and William Lyons ("Democratic Theory, Nonvoting, and Public Policy," *American Politics Quarterly* 21 [1993]: 185–204) and Jerry Calvert and Jack Gilchrist ("The Social and Issue Dimensions of Voting and Nonvoting in the United States" [paper presented at the annual meeting of the American Political Science Association, September 1991, Washington, D.C.]) draw similar conclusions. All authors agree that the impact of nonvoting per se does not skew the policy debate very much.

According to Austin Ranney, primary elections do not adhere to this pattern. His data indicate that voters in primaries tend to have more extreme preferences than the public at large. See *Curing the Mischiefs of Faction: Party Reform in America* (Berkeley: University of California Press, 1975), p. 129. More recent data, however, indicate that primary voters are more representative than earlier writers had suggested. See Barbara Norrander, "Ideological Representativeness of Presidential Primary Voters," *American Journal of Political Science* 33 (1989): 570–587.

ticipants is not always the consequence of differences in descriptive demographic characteristics.

In certain other respects, however, issues of representation present themselves in special ways when it comes to citizen activity. We have indicated that descriptive representation along multiple dimensions is an unattainable goal in the context of elected deliberative bodies: elected assemblies—even big, unwieldy ones—are finite in size and unchanging in composition for a fixed term, so that they are inevitably limited in how closely the members can resemble the public—if that were deemed desirable. In contrast, there is no limit to the number of citizens who can become politically active. The active public can change from issue to issue. Therefore, over time, as different publics are mobilized to take part on different issues, or even on a single issue if enough people get involved, representation on a variety of dimensions—impossible in a legislative setting—becomes feasible for the population of political activists.

In another respect, representation is distinctive when it comes to citizen participation. Elected representatives have an incentive to represent more than their own narrow, selfish interests—at least if they wish to be retained in office. When it comes to citizen activity, however, there are no such incentives. Citizen activists face no costs for behaving in a narrowly self-interested fashion; indeed, they are expected to represent their own interests. Even when their activity is a response to an institutionally based request, under ordinary circumstances citizen participants are free to speak for themselves and are presumed to do so.

Beyond Voting, Beyond Attitudes

In our exploration of participatory representation, we begin with the important insights derived from Wolfinger and Rosenstone's study of voting, but we extend them in several ways. First, we consider a variety of political acts in addition to voting, acts that have the capacity to convey more precise messages and to generate more pressure to respond than does a single vote. In addition, we encompass a broader array of characteristics, including not only attitudes but also other characteristics—even demographic characteristics—that are relevant to politics. Moreover, we go beyond activists' opinions about issues presented to them by survey researchers to probe the policy concerns behind their participation; that is, we consider not just what participants think but what they say when they take part.

AN ARRAY OF POLITICAL ACTIVITIES

One of the themes of this book is that the vote is *unique* among political acts. Generalizations that hold for voters and non-voters may not obtain for those who engage, or fail to engage, in other forms of participation. For one thing, the vote is the one participatory act for which there is mandated equality: each citizen gets one and only one. Other forms of activity, as we have seen, necessitate no such equality of inputs. Individuals may make as many phone calls to public officials, spend as many hours campaigning for as many candidates, and attend as many demonstrations as their time and inclination permit. Within certain limits, they can even write as many checks as their bank balances allow. Moreover, for some forms of participation, when the volume of activity is multiplied, the possibility that it will be accompanied by pressure to respond is enhanced. A candidate can ignore with impunity a single voter or a single letter-writer, even one letter-writer who writes a lot of letters. The campaign volunteer who works many hours, or the donor who makes a large contribution, has potentially greater leverage. Finally, the vote also differs from many kinds of activity in being a rather blunt instrument for the communication of information about the needs and preferences of citizens. In contrast to the vote, many acts are what we have labeled "information-rich": a letter to a Senator, a sign carried at a protest, a conversation between members of a neighborhood group and a city councillor all permit the transmission of much more precise messages about citizen concerns. Thus, our consideration of participatory representation will be based on the full array of political activities described earlier and will entail examination of the amount of political activity—not just how many people are active but how much they do when they get involved.

POLITICALLY RELEVANT CHARACTERISTICS

Our investigation of the representativeness of participatory input involves consideration of characteristics other than positions taken on standardized survey questions. In the chapters that follow, we base our understanding of participatory representation on a wide range of *politically relevant characteristics.* These are characteristics whose visibility to a public official might make a difference in their responses to citizen participation. They can be anything about an activist that might have an effect on government action. Politically relevant characteristics naturally include policy preferences. However, they also encompass a broad range of social and economic characteristics that make government policies relevant to an individual—among them certain demographic characteristics as well as needs for government assistance as revealed by actual economic circumstances and receipt of various kinds of means-tested and non-means-tested government benefits.

The range of politically relevant characteristics is quite broad and the content ever-changing. It is well known that the political agenda varies over time. Temperance, child labor, and the gold standard are issues that once engaged passionate debate but now, having been replaced by other concerns, do not figure in our political discourse. Analogously, what constitutes a politically relevant characteristic changes with new times and new circumstances. Indeed, new groups with shared politically relevant characteristics are being created all the time. A natural disaster like a hurricane, a new government program supporting medical research for a particular disease, an emerging social movement, and decisions by foreign governments are but a few examples of the kinds of developments that leave in their wake groups of individuals who have common interests in or preferences for government policies.[10]

---

10. The literature on political agenda setting provides important insights into the multiple sources, and ever-changing nature, of politically relevant characteristics. See, for example, Peter Bachrach and Morton S. Baratz, *Power and Poverty: Theory and Practice* (New York: Oxford University Press, 1970); John W. Kingdon, *Agendas, Alternatives, and Public Policies* (Boston: Little, Brown, 1984); Nelson W. Polsby, *Political Innovation in America: The Politics of Policy Innovation* (New Haven: Yale University Press, 1984); and Roger W. Cobb and Charles D. Elder, *Participation in American Politics: The Dynamics of Agenda-Building* (Baltimore: Johns Hopkins University Press, 1983).

We cannot dismiss demographic characteristics from the list of characteristics that are potentially politically relevant. When demographic distinctions are pertinent to political conflict—and they often are—disparities in participation of demographic groups may be significant. Apart from the explicit demands made by activist publics, there is implicit information in their social characteristics. When a group is active—especially one with identifiable, politically relevant characteristics—it becomes visible to an elected representative and is incorporated into his or her salient constituency. Politicians attend to their constituencies and know who is watching what they do. (As a former representative is said to have remarked about the town in which two of us live, "One-tenth the votes. Half the mail.") Even in the absence of explicit directives—and constituents often do not send detailed messages—elected officials anticipate the needs and make inferences about the preferences of potentially active constituents.[11] Thus, it matters not only how participants differ from the non-participants in their opinions—whether they want lower taxes, greater restrictions on

---

11. There are many linkage studies that combine data about constituents and representatives. On the disputes in the measurement of linkage see, for example, Christopher Achen, "Measuring Representation: The Perils of the Correlation Coefficient," *American Journal of Political Science* 21 (1977): 805–815; and Heinz Eulau and Paul D. Karps, "The Puzzle of Representation: Specifying the Components of Responsiveness," *Legislative Studies Quarterly* 2 (1977): 233–254. Robert S. Erikson and Gerald C. Wright, "Voters, Candidates and Issues in Congressional Elections," in *Congress Reconsidered*, 4th ed., ed. Lawrence C. Dodd and Bruce I. Oppenheimer (Washington, D.C.: CQ Press, 1989), provide citations to the many studies that find a positive relationship between constituent characteristics and preferences and the roll-call behavior of legislators. Other studies, using a variety of approaches, demonstrate the responsiveness of elected officials to the views of active constituents, especially activists who have supported them. See, for example, Sidney Verba and Norman H. Nie, *Participation in America* (New York: Harper and Row, 1972); Gregory B. Markus, "Electoral Coalitions and Senate Roll Call Behavior," *American Journal of Political Science* 18 (1974): 595–607; David R. Mayhew, *Congress: The Electoral Connection* (New Haven: Yale University Press, 1974); Richard F. Fenno, Jr., *Home Style: House Members and Their Districts* (Boston: Little, Brown, 1978); Charles S. Bullock and David W. Brady, "Party, Constituency, and Roll-Call Voting in the Senate," *Legislative Studies Quarterly* 8 (1983): 29–43; and Louise Huddleston, "The Influence of Constituency Opinions on Representatives: A Study of the 1980 Congress" (paper presented at the annual meeting of the Midwest Political Science Association, Chicago, April 1984). Although these studies are suggestive for the issues raised here, they do not provide a definitive characterization of the characteristics—attitudes, economic circumstances, demographic characteristics—that an official is likely to note in observing the constituency and trying to infer its needs and preferences.

handguns, or protection from foreign trade competition—but who they are.

BUNDLES OF POLITICALLY RELEVANT CHARACTERISTICS

Politically relevant characteristics rarely travel on their own. Instead, they ordinarily come bundled together. Often, to know that a set of people with a particular attribute is active is to know something about the other characteristics that are being well represented through participation. For example, being elderly carries with it, on average, a number of other characteristics. Therefore, if the elderly in a community take part, it also means that there is activity coming from people who benefit from Social Security or Medicare and who support these programs politically.

That politically relevant characteristics are often packaged together complicates the problem of participatory representation. Accurate representation of a group sharing one politically relevant characteristic does not guarantee accurate representation with respect to other group attributes because it also matters *which* group members are active. Senior citizens, those over sixty-five, might be proportionally represented among activists. However, if elderly activists are drawn disproportionately from those who are between sixty-five and seventy-five, then participatory input from the aged would underrepresent the preferences and needs of what are sometimes called the "old-old," a group that is less healthy and less well-off financially than those whose Medicare cards are more recently acquired. This brings us to our next consideration in relation to participatory representation.

REPRESENTING POLITICALLY RELEVANT GROUPS

Once the understanding of participatory representation is opened up to include groups like the elderly that have several characteristics in common, questions parallel to those we have been discussing arise about whether and in what ways group activists represent fellow group members who do not take part. The implicit model is that it matters not only whether activists resemble the population at large in terms of a particular attribute that defines a group—say, a demographic characteristic—but also whether activists drawn from a politically relevant group resemble more quiescent group members on other politically relevant dimensions.

This is a familiar question raised with respect to organizational democracy in political interest groups. Students of organized interests have proposed conflicting answers to this question of group representation. Earlier in this century, Roberto Michels proposed an "Iron Law of Oligarchy" to demonstrate that leaders of social democratic parties would inevitably moderate their positions, thus selling out, and failing to represent accurately, a more radical rank and file.[12] More recently, analysts have drawn the opposite conclusion, arguing that group leaders, animated by their ideological concerns and rewarded by the purposive benefits that accrue to those who fight for causes in which they believe, are likely to be less mainstream than the membership and to be forced to moderate their views only in order to satisfy a rank and file whose support is needed to keep the organization in business.[13] However, when it comes to citizen activity, these constraints, which place limits on the extent to which organization leaders can simply act on their own political views, do not operate. As we mentioned earlier, even if their activity has been stimulated by a request from an institution with which they are affiliated, ordinary citizens who participate in politics are expected to speak their own minds and not to represent a constituency.

The most common form in which this issue of participatory representation presents itself is with respect to whether activists who share some politically relevant demographic characteristic are representative of inactive group members in terms of their opinions on policy. This question can also arise, however, in terms of whether activists drawn from a group defined demographically are representative with respect to their economic or social needs. Thus, even if minority group members are accurately represented from a demographic point of view, we would need to inquire

---

12. Roberto Michels, *Political Parties: A Sociological Study of the Oligarchical Tendencies of Modern Democracy* (1913) (Glencoe, Ill.: Free Press, 1958).

13. See, for example, James Q. Wilson, *Political Organizations* (New York: Basic Books, 1973), chap. 3.

whether African-American or Latino activists are representative either in their opinions on issues having to do with poverty or programs to aid minorities or in their actual circumstances—for example, their homelessness or reliance on government benefits. Similarly, in their views on issues of gay civil rights are gay activists representative of those who share their sexual orientation but do not take part in politics? The dilemma can present itself with respect to any two politically relevant characteristics. Survey data reveal that members of the public who express pro-life sentiments about abortion are a gender-balanced group. If protesters at pro-life demonstrations are disproportionately male—or disproportionately female—then similar questions about participatory representativeness are raised.

THE VISIBILITY OF POLITICALLY RELEVANT CHARACTERISTICS

We have often made the point that political acts vary in their capacity to convey information. Votes tell little about the preferences of voters, but a sign carried at a demonstration or a telephone conversation with a public official can communicate more. Analogously, some characteristics are more immediately apparent to those at whom activity is targeted. A group of handicapped citizens who arrive at city hall in wheelchairs with concerns about regulations for access to buildings have a more visible set of characteristics and needs than a group of dyslexic citizens with concerns about special school programs. Thus, in evaluating the messages that activity sends to policymakers, we need to consider both the nature of the politically relevant characteristic and the nature of the participatory act.

The question of the visibility of politically relevant attributes is particularly important for characteristics that are bundled. The problem is how much can be inferred about less visible characteristics such as policy preferences or issue priorities by observing visible characteristics such as race or gender. Public officials constantly make such inferences, sometimes inaccurately, about activist publics—often using polling results as an aid. In our study, we have information about activists, not about the targets of their activity. Therefore, we cannot probe the conclusions public officials draw about less obvious attributes from the apparent characteristics of activists. Nonetheless, an ongoing concern will be to understand how politically relevant characteristics are connected to one another and, therefore, how the over- or underrepresentation of a particular characteristic, especially a visible one, affects the representation of the characteristics with which it is associated.

WHAT DO THEY SAY? THE PARTICIPATORY AGENDA
We can extend the understanding of participatory representation in another way as well. When it comes to the representativeness of participatory input, what matters is not simply what activists think about various political issues but what issues they make the subject of their activity. We can use our data about the issues and problems associated with activity to investigate what participants actually say when they take part. As important as it is that the set of citizen activists reflects accurately the opinions of those who do not take part, it is critical to recall that the attitudes expressed by activists in surveys are not necessarily equivalent to the set of messages communicated through their participation. A full assessment of the representativeness of citizen activity requires consideration of its actual issue content. In the context of a survey, Whites may register their concern about civil rights, or affluent liberals their concern about homelessness, but are these the issues about which they protest or write letters? Or is their political involvement animated by concern about the environment, foreign affairs, or a narrow issue connected with work? Hence, we shall be concerned to delineate the actual issues behind activity and to raise questions about the extent to which politically relevant groups have distinctive participatory agendas.

The Possibility of Proxy Representation

By now it is clear that many politically relevant groups are underrepresented among participant populations. Somewhat surprisingly, however, even when group members themselves are not active, if the group's issue positions and participatory priorities are represented by others not in the group, there can be a fairly accurate representation of the group's position. This would be the case when there is proxy or surrogate representation. Activists from the rest of the population—with policy views and a participatory agenda similar to that of the inactive group members—counterbalance the inactivity of the group or the internal distortion caused when the group activists are not representative of the group.

Proxy representation is sometimes the only representation available. Where individuals cannot speak for themselves, secondary advocates constitute the only option: adults lobby on behalf of children; civil libertarians on behalf of prisoners. And even where the affected group enjoys citizenship rights but is relatively inactive, surrogates might be effective advocates: for example, middle-class liberals might lobby for the homeless, employed labor leaders for the unemployed, or university administrators for recipients of federal student loans. Sometimes, the advocacy is altruistic—such as efforts on behalf of the developmentally disabled by those who are not themselves disabled or are not related to persons who share the disability; sometimes it is self-interested—such as support by builders for public housing projects or by teachers for federal aid to schools. Whatever the motivation, it can be argued that proxy representation can often be a useful way for some groups to achieve representation.[14]

Such second-hand representation is sometimes necessary, but it may be less effective than direct participation.[15] For one thing,

---

14. In addition, organized groups lobbying for some broader public can deploy resources such as access and expertise much more effectively than a more dispersed and unorganized grassroots movement. For this reason, public interest groups usually spend more time and effort lobbying and litigating than mobilizing local constituents. See Jeffrey M. Berry, Kent E. Portney, and Ken Thompson, *The Rebirth of Urban Democracy* (Washington, D.C.: Brookings Institution, 1993), pp. 42–43.

15. Studies of interest groups in American politics have dealt inconclusively with the question of the consequences for the representation of the interests of the inactive when other organizations are active on their behalf. For contrasting emphases, see Kay Lehman Schlozman and John T. Tierney, *Organized Interests and American Democracy* (New York: Harper and Row, 1986), pp. 401–405, and Jack L. Walker, Jr., *Mobilizing Interest Groups in America: Patrons, Professions and Social Movements* (Ann Arbor: University of Michigan Press, 1991), pp. 13–16. Kay Lehman Schlozman and Sidney Verba discuss the role of activist liberals on behalf of the unemployed who were themselves relatively inactive in *Injury to Insult: Unemployment, Class, and Political Response* (Cambridge, Mass.: Harvard University Press, 1979), pp. 338–344. They argue that surrogates—union leaders, heads of liberal organizations—play a significant role in unemployment policy, but they have a large agenda of concerns and, therefore, often abandon the unemployment issue for other priorities.

surrogates who purport to communicate the needs and interests of some group may not tell quite the same story that group members would tell. Needs and preferences are complex. Especially when the surrogates are self-interested, but even when they are not, communication by a proxy is likely not to be identical to what would have been communicated by the relevant subjects themselves.[16] In addition, surrogates may prove to be fair-weather friends as they abandon those for whom they serve as secondary advocates in pursuit of other policy concerns having a higher priority. Furthermore, advocacy by others often lacks the dramatic impact carried by direct testimony from those most affected. For example, when the case for handicapped rights is made by those who are themselves handicapped, the message has an urgency that cannot be captured by social service personnel acting on behalf of the handicapped.

The fact that participation makes citizens visible even in the absence of articulate expression of their preferences is germane to another point made by studies of representation. Those who have searched for the link between citizens and their representatives have to contend with the fact that citizens rarely if ever make clear, detailed policy demands. Their preferences are ill-formed or nonexistent, and their information about policy issues and the options faced by public officials is very limited.[17] This characterization—clearly accurate, although sometimes overstated—underscores the point being made here: by making their representatives aware of their life circumstances, activity—even by citizens who lack information about policy alternatives and do not articulate clear policy

16. For examples of this tension between lobbying organizations and disadvantaged population groups in the area of toxic waste regulation, see Carmen Sirianni, "Civic Discovery and Discursive Democracy: Social Movements, Civil Associations, and Social Learning in Citizen Participation Programs" (paper presented at the Annual Meeting of the American Political Science Association, Washington, D.C., August 1993).

17. The classic statement of the public's lack of knowledge of its congressional representatives is Donald E. Stokes and Warren E. Miller, "Party Government and the Salience of Congress," *Public Opinion Quarterly* 26 (1962): 531–546. This has led scholars to call for an approach to representation that does not depend upon government response to citizen demands. See John C. Wahlke, "Policy Demands and System Support: The Role of the Represented," *British Journal of Political Science* 1 (1971): 271–290; and Eulau and Karps, "The Puzzle of Representation," pp. 233–254.

preferences—can communicate important information about their needs and interests.

Conceptualizing Participatory Distortion

We have discussed several sources of potential distortion in the representation of politically relevant characteristics through participatory input: activists with particular characteristics may on average differ from members of the public in terms of the amount of their activity; the issues on behalf of which activists take part may depart from the participatory priorities of those who are less active; participants may differ in significant ways—including having different policy preferences—from more quiescent members of the group from which they are drawn.

With this discussion as background, we can now treat more rigorously the concept of participatory distortion—the circumstance in which political activists do not reflect accurately the larger population from which they come with respect to some politically relevant characteristic. This circumstance results when some politically relevant sub-group within the population—environmentalists, recipients of veterans' benefits, farmers, trial lawyers, poor people, or proponents of school prayer—is more or less active on average than members of the public at large, with the result that public officials hear disproportionately from people with particular sets of attitudes, needs for government assistance, demographic characteristics, or participatory priorities.

We can note certain circumstances under which participatory distortion is likely to be enhanced or muted. For any group, the degree of participatory distortion depends on how far it is from the mean of the population on whatever shared politically relevant characteristic defines it. When it is far from the mean, then participatory distortion is likely to be exacerbated. For example, consider an issue like abortion where public opinion is relatively polarized. If one of the extreme groups, either pro-choice or pro-life, does not get involved in abortion politics, the opinions on abortion expressed by participants will be substantially skewed from the average for the population by the underrepresentation of one of the two polar groups. If, in contrast, those with moderate views on abortion are quiescent but those at each extreme are very active, the average position of the public will be accurately represented. However, the message will be distorted by its shrillness, as only those at the ends of the issue continuum express their opinions.

The *size* of the under- or overrepresented group will also have implications for overall participatory distortion. For a group that constitutes only a very small fraction of the population, especially high, or low, levels of activity in comparison with the population as a whole can have only minor consequences for the extent to which activists deviate from the average for the population as a whole. In contrast, smaller deviations from proportionality can have much more substantial effects on overall distortion if the group is a large one.[18] In short, one consequence of focusing on overall distortion for the population as a whole is to deemphasize the situation of a small minority. It is interesting to note, by the way, that these two circumstances do not ordinarily reinforce each other. Overall participatory distortion is amplified by the over- or underrepresentation of groups that are far from the population mean on some politically relevant characteristic or that are large. However, a really large group cannot deviate substantially from the average for the population; the larger a majority group as a proportion of the population, the less distinctive it can be relative to the population of which it is a part.

SIZE, INTENSITY, AND EQUAL REPRESENTATION

Questions of participatory distortion and group size raise for citizen activity a thorny issue in democratic theory: how to steer between the twin dangers of majority tyranny and minorities' rule. In order to consider this dilemma, we must raise explicitly a consideration that has been implicit in our discussion of equality

---

18. This analysis helps us understand the asymmetrical position of majorities and minorities. Huckfeldt and Sprague, in an analysis of the sources of political information, comment on the fact that minorities are fully aware of the position of the majority but majorities often ignore the position of the minority. Robert Huckfeldt and John Sprague, "Networks in Context: The Social Flow of Political Information," *American Political Science Review* 81 (1987): 1197–1216.

of participatory representation: the problem of intensity.[19] Across the myriad issues that occupy a position on the political agenda, there are inevitably some about which particular individuals, or groups, care especially deeply and others about which they are relatively indifferent. Auto workers, concerned about the potential migration of their jobs abroad, are likely to feel much more strongly about trade policy than are surgeons. Surgeons, in turn, are more likely than auto workers to have deeply held preferences when it comes to federal health care policy.

We have defined equal representation as a circumstance such that the activist portion of the population matches the whole population in those characteristics that are politically relevant. However, if this condition is imposed on an issue-by-issue basis, then participatory equality might produce a situation in which a small group can never prevail no matter how passionate it might be about the outcome on a particular issue and no matter how lukewarm the majority. In short, achieving participatory equality for each successive political controversy would seem to risk tyranny of the majority—a circumstance that has caused concern to observers of American politics at least since Madison.

We must recognize, however, that tyranny of the majority is not the only concern. Students of interest groups sometimes argue that American politics is uniquely hospitable to rule by groups representing narrow publics—so long as those small groups are well organized and well endowed with political resources.[20] According to this interpretation, the extent to which power is dispersed by federalism and the separation of powers, reinforced by the weakness of various governing institutions and the political parties, produces a circumstance in which minorities' rule is much more likely than majority tyranny. An analogous circumstance can arise

---

19. For a discussion of this issue, see Robert A. Dahl, *A Preface to Democratic Theory* (Chicago: University of Chicago Press, 1956). The issue is discussed more recently in Lani Guinier, *The Tyranny of the Majority: Fundamental Fairness in Representative Democracy* (New York: Free Press, 1994).

20. Analyses in this tradition include Grant McConnell, *Private Power and American Democracy* (New York: Alfred A. Knopf, 1966), and Theodore J. Lowi, *The End of Liberalism: Ideology, Policy and the Crisis of Public Authority* (New York: W. W. Norton, 1969).

with respect to citizen participation. A small part of the public can, in fact, dominate the participatory communications in relation to a particular issue if one, or both, of two things happen: the rest of the public is quiescent or the small group amplifies its voice by multiplying the volume of its activity. Indeed, in such a circumstance, the average position of the public at large can be very different from the average position as conveyed by the activists, even though the latter are a quite small proportion of the public.

Can our construction of equal representation be reconciled with some deference to intensity of preferences? One way to resolve this dilemma is to allow individual activists to apportion their participatory eggs as they will—selecting the issue baskets about which they feel most strongly—and to require only that, *across all issues,* the activist portion must reflect accurately the politically relevant characteristics of the entire population. This solution preserves the norm of equality in that, in the aggregate, activists are representative on all politically relevant dimensions; however, it makes no stipulations as to how activists divide their participation across many or few issues depending upon how much they care about each one. Yet it is important to recognize that, on any single issue, the activist public may be completely unrepresentative of the public at large. Handgun control provides a well-known example. For decades, public opinion polls have shown the American public to favor stricter firearms laws. Because the minority who oppose increased gun control not only are politically active but place special emphasis upon this issue in their participation, citizen input on this issue is skewed. If gun control opponents concentrate their participatory firepower on a single issue while supporters of gun control—even if equally active overall—take on many issues, there may be no violation of participatory equality in the aggregate. On the specific issue, however, the position of the public at large will not be accurately represented.

It is possible to construe the amount of activity individuals dedicate to a particular issue as an index of how much they care about it—the political equivalent of the economists' useful concept of revealed preferences. This cannot be done in relation to the vote. As we have made clear, the vote is unique among political acts in that its volume is fixed, with each individual limited to a single vote per election. However, no such requirement for equality of input exists for other forms of activity; hence, in order to demonstrate the depth of their commitment, those who are most intensely concerned about an issue are free to multiply both the number of participatory acts and the amount of time, energy, or money devoted to activity.[21] The volume of activity is, thus, a measure of intensity of commitment—but only an imperfect one. How much someone cares about an issue is only one factor—although an important one—in determining how active he or she will become in relation to it. We cannot ignore the extent to which the *capacity* to be politically active is unevenly distributed across individuals and groups. As we shall see when we explore this issue at length in Part III, those who are not active are not necessarily unconcerned or apathetic. Instead, they may be handicapped by a deficit of the resources that facilitate political participation. If resources were distributed equally, then we could interpret the level of activity as a barometer of the intensity of preferences. However, as is well known, political resources are not apportioned equally, a fact that poses one of the greatest challenges to fairness in a democracy and one of the knottiest riddles for democratic theory.

Measuring Participatory Distortion

With these considerations in mind, let us consider some of the many ways in which participatory distortion might be measured. We need to make more precise the notion that activists might not resemble a random sample of the public or that activists drawn from a particular demographic group may not represent the relevant features of that group. One measure used in the literature is the average for some characteristic for the activists in some population minus the average for that characteristic in the population as a whole.[22] To take a simple example, and a simple statistical

---

21. In Chapter 14, we investigate the role played by deep issue commitments in generating participation.

22. See, for example, Wolfinger and Rosenstone, *Who Votes?*, pp. 104–107, esp. table 6.1, column (3). See also tables 6.2 and 6.3.

measure: suppose 40 percent of the adults in a town favor a bond issue to build a new school, but among the activists working to pass or defeat the referendum, 50 percent are in support; then the participatory distortion is 10 percent ($50 - 40 = 10$). On the politically relevant characteristic of support for the bond issue, the activists are 10 percentage points higher in their support than is the public. If, in contrast, 40 percent of both adults and activists wish to see the measure pass, then participatory distortion is zero, and referendum activists accurately represent the population's attitudes.

This "difference" measure of participatory distortion has the virtues of being simple, applicable to a variety of politically relevant characteristics, and useful (as described in Appendix C.1) for highlighting some interesting relationships among various measures of participatory distortion. However, it has the defect of having upper and lower bounds that depend on the characteristics of the population no matter what the characteristics of activists. In the example of the bond referendum above, with 40 percent of the population favoring the referendum, the maximum positive distortion is 60 percentage points (if 100 percent of the activists supported the bond issue) and the maximum negative distortion is -40 percentage points (if no activists supported the bond issue). If, however, 90 percent of the public supported the issue, the maximum positive distortion would be 10 percent and the maximum negative distortion would be 90 percent. This property limits the utility of this measure in comparing across different situations.

Given these problems with the difference measure, we created a summary index of representation, the Logged Representation Scale (LRS),[23] which is based on the *ratio* of the percentage of the activists with a characteristic to the percentage with the characteristic in the population as a whole. In the referendum example, this ratio is 50 percent over 40 percent, or 1.25. The LRS is the logarithm of this ratio, or .097. This gives us a measure of the

---

23. This measure is based on a generalization of the index developed by Wolfinger and Rosenstone, *Who Votes?*, chap. 6. A more complete explanation of the derivation of and rationale for this measure is contained in Appendix C.

extent to which a particular characteristic is over- or underrepresented within a given activist population. By taking the logarithm of the ratio, we create a measure with some useful properties. Because the LRS is a dimensionless number like a correlation coefficient or beta weight, one value can be compared with another. Furthermore, it is a symmetrical index: it ranges from plus infinity to minus infinity. An index of zero indicates that activists have exactly the same likelihood of having a characteristic as members of the population as a whole. Negative numbers mean that the characteristic is underrepresented among activists and positive numbers that it is overrepresented. An LRS score of +.30 indicates that activists are twice as likely to have a characteristic as members of the population as a whole; an index of −.30 indicates that the activists are half as likely to have the characteristic as members of the population as a whole. An LRS score of +1 indicates overrepresentation by a factor of ten; −1 indicates underrepresentation by the same amount.

We use the Logged Representation Scale in the next chapter to indicate the extent of under- or overrepresentation of various groups within different activist populations. In using the LRS, we can vary both the *characteristics* of activists and the *political activities* through which they are represented. We consider groups defined by such politically relevant characteristics as attitudes on economic issues, economic circumstances, and participation in various benefits programs; and we consider such activist publics as voters, campaign workers, campaign contributors, contactors, protesters, informal community activists, and members of local community governing boards.

Conclusion

This discussion makes clear that the understanding of participatory representation requires the simultaneous consideration of several different dimensions. In our data analysis, we shall be concerned about an array of political acts, not just voting but various forms of participation that are capable of carrying much more precise sets of instructions to policymakers and that can be multiplied in volume beyond the enforced equality implicit in one

person, one vote. Moreover, in considering over- and underrepresentation within various participant publics, we shall consider
groups defined by a variety of politically relevant characteristics,
not just attitudes as measured by surveys, but needs for government policy and, even, demographic characteristics. In addition,
recognizing that the opinions expressed in surveys are not necessarily the same as participatory priorities, we must examine the
actual issues that animate activity—in short, what participation is
about. Finally, because groups sharing a single politically relevant
characteristic—say, their age or race—are often distinctive in other
ways as well—for example, in their economic circumstances, dependence upon government benefits, or opinions on issues—we
need to examine whether the activists drawn from the group
accurately represent its more quiescent members.

7

Who Participates?
Economic Circumstances
and Needs

Although class conflict has traditionally been relatively muted in America, one leitmotif of American politics—as of the politics of all industrial democracies—has been contention over economic issues. In consequence, economic circumstances and needs, as well as preferences with respect to economic issues, are among the most fundamental of an individual's politically relevant characteristics. In this chapter, we consider the way in which such characteristics are represented through political activity and focus on the extent to which the participatory process distorts them, amplifying the voices of the advantaged and muting the voices of the less advantaged. We consider a wide range of characteristics relevant to economic stratification: basic demographic attributes—not only income but also education and occupation; more direct measures of circumstances as well as benefiting from government programs related to economic need; and opinions on these matters, in particular attitudes on how much the government ought to be doing to aid the disadvantaged. As we shall see, the degree of participatory distortion depends on what it is that is being represented— who people are, what they need, or what they think the government ought to do.

Income and Activity

Myriad government policies—ranging from taxes to welfare to labor relations to the minimum wage—affect income groups differently. It makes sense, therefore, to begin our analysis of representation with one of the most basic measures of economic circumstance, family income. In so doing, we are not making any assumptions as to whether income is the principal causal variable for activity. We leave that issue for Part III of this book, where we undertake a causal analysis and show, as others have done before, that education takes precedence over income as a predictive factor for many, though not all, kinds of participation. Instead, at this point, we are concerned with describing who is active in order to explicate the way in which politically relevant characteristics are represented throughout the participatory process.[1]

In the previous chapter we discussed that the representation of a group depends on both its rate of activity compared with the public as a whole and the extent to which activists drawn from the group are representative with respect to its other politically relevant attributes. Let us begin with the first source of potential

---

1. For our current project of describing differences in who takes part, income differences in participation would appear to matter more than differences among educational groups, because income differences are more closely linked to differences in citizens' needs for government policy. Education is, of course, an area for massive governmental activity, and educational policies often engender acrimonious debate. However, in spite of differences in political preferences between the educated and less well-educated, educational controversies do not usually pit against one another groups defined by their level of education. Instead, those at odds are more likely to be differentiated on the basis of income in a controversy over taxes; by race in a controversy over school integration or curriculum content; by language in a controversy over bilingual education; or by ideology and religious commitment in a controversy over school prayer or the teaching of creationism. In short, conflicts over educational policy are likely to be structured less by educational attainment than by other social attributes. On the relationship between social characteristics and voting in school referenda, see Frederick M. Wirt and Michael W. Kirst, *The Political Web of American Schools* (Boston: Little, Brown, 1972), pp. 102–104.

There are systematic differences in opinion between the educated and the less well educated. However, the most substantial gap in attitudes between groups defined by their educational level appears, not with respect to substantive policy issues, but with respect to procedural matters like tolerance and free speech. See also Michael Y. Nunnery and Ralph B. Kimbrough, *Politics, Power, Polls, and School Elections* (Berkeley: McCutchan, 1971), pp. 49–50. This is a theme to which we return in Chapter 16.

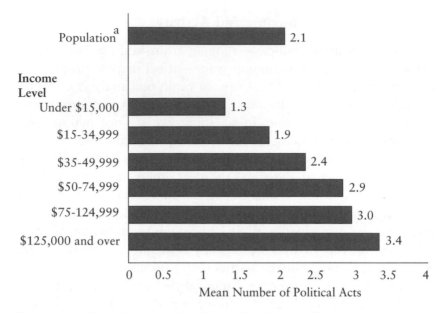

Figure 7.1 Mean Number of Political Acts by Family Income.
a. N = 2,517 weighted cases. See Appendix A for information about sample.

representational distortion, group rates of activity, by considering differences in activity rates among income groups. We consider first differences on an overall additive scale of political activity. The scale is a summary measure of the number of political activities in which the individual has engaged. It is an additive scale with each of the following counted as one act: voting in the 1988 election, working in a campaign, contributing money to a campaign, contacting an official, taking part in a protest, working informally with others in the community on a community issue, membership on a local governing board or regular attendance at the meetings of such a board, and membership in an organization that takes political stands.[2] As we have pointed out, there are numerous and significant differences across political acts. The overall participation scale masks many of these differences. It is, nevertheless, a

2. For a description of the scale including the time frame used for the various activities and a discussion of the relationship among the items, see Appendix B.1.i.

useful summary measure which we shall use often. We shall, however, supplement the summary scale with a consideration of various political activities. Figure 7.1 shows the average number of political acts performed by citizens at six levels of family income.[3] The increase in political activity with income is clear. Those in the lowest level of income average one act (usually voting); those at the top of the income scale average more than three acts.[4]

INCOME AND INDIVIDUAL POLITICAL ACTS

Because the summary measure obscures differences among acts, we can decompose it into its components. Figure 7.2 compares two income groups at the extremes—those with family incomes below $15,000 per year, that is, below or very close to the poverty line, and those with family incomes of $75,000 and above—with respect to the proportion who take part in various political activities.[5] For each kind of participation, affluence and activity go together. Of the various acts, voting is perhaps the most egalitarian. Turnout is much higher among the wealthy than the poor, but voting is the only act for which the affluent are not at least twice as likely to be active. Those with the lowest family incomes are less well represented among those who take a more active role in political campaigns. The poor are one-quarter as likely as the affluent to do campaign work and about one-tenth as likely to give a campaign contribution.

There is also a participation gap among income groups with respect to contacting, a mode of activity that might be of special relevance to the disadvantaged who depend upon government programs; with respect to informal community activity; and, es-

---

3. For the measurement of income and the income categories used, see Appendix B.13.

4. The data are, as we might expect, parallel to the data reported in Chapter 5 that showed that those with higher income are more likely to be asked to be active. Are those who are asked likely to give or those who give likely to be asked? The answer is probably both. We shall return to this set of issues in Chapter 13.

5. Focusing on the extreme groups makes the relationships especially clear. For each activity, the proportion of activists in the intermediate groups lines up in a fairly regular way between the two extremes. Definitions of the political activities are found in Appendix B.1.

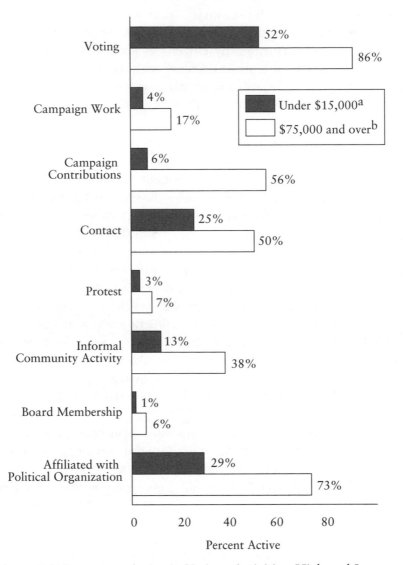

Figure 7.2 Percentage Active in Various Activities: High and Low Income Groups.

a. N = 483 weighted cases.
b. N = 224 weighted cases.

pecially, serving on a local governing board. Moreover, although the disparity is somewhat smaller than for other modes of activity, the poor are less likely to attend protests, a form of activity that is often described as the "weapon of the weak" because it is available to those with few economic resources. In short, the affluent are overrepresented among activists to an extent that varies from act to act: this overrepresentation is least pronounced when it comes to voting and, not unexpectedly, most pronounced when it comes to making campaign contributions.

The Volume of Activity

We have pointed out that, as the only act for which there is mandated equality in each citizen's input, the vote is unique among political acts. For other acts, participants can do more or less: they can give varying amounts of time or money, or engage in an activity once or many times. Thus, those who take part in any activity beyond voting make essentially two decisions: whether to become active at all and, if so, how active to be. We have just shown the inequality across income groups in the proportion who choose to act. We now consider the second of these decisions by looking across income groups at the extent of inequality in the volume of activity generated by those who decide to participate.

We begin with contributions of time and money to campaigns. Although the affluent are more likely to be active as both campaign workers and campaign donors, the pattern becomes more complicated once we move beyond the threshold of making a contribution. Figure 7.3 presents the average number of hours given by campaign workers and the average number of dollars donated by contributors to a campaign or an electoral organization. Among those who did campaign work, the amount of time given is relatively uniform across the income groups, with the only deviation being the higher number of hours given by the lowest income group of campaign workers. The data for dollar contributions could hardly provide a sharper contrast. For campaign contributions, the amount given increases with family income. The increase in the amount donated is relatively gradual through the

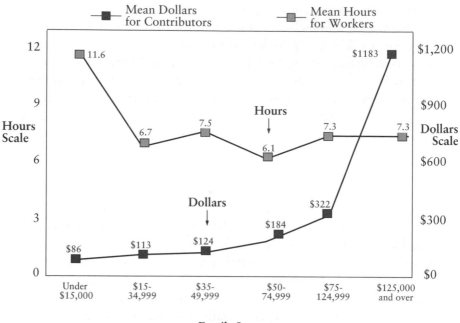

Figure 7.3 Mean Hours and Dollars Given to Political Campaigns by Family Income (among campaign workers and campaign contributors).

middle incomes and quite steep in the higher-income categories, with the result that, among contributors, the average donation from an affluent respondent is nearly fourteen times the average contribution from a poor one.

The data suggest that time and money function differently as inputs for political activity. As we have seen, for all forms of activity, the affluent are more likely than the poor to become active. Once active, however, the poor are as generous with their time as those who are better off financially. Their lack of financial resources does not appear to act as an impediment to the investment of "sweat equity." Since nobody's day contains more than twenty-four hours, the well-heeled can give only so much time— apparently not more, on average, than the poor. No such leveling occurs when it comes to money. Not only are those with higher family incomes more likely to make donations, but they give more when they do.

We can learn more about the representation of income groups through various forms of political activity by considering the volume of activity they produce. Figure 7.4 gives us a politician's-eye view of what the citizenry would look like if each income group's visibility depended on the amount of its political activity. The upper-left section of the figure presents as a baseline the distribution of various family income groupings within the population. The other graphs show the proportion of the population that falls in various income categories weighted by the amount of activity produced by that income group: by the votes cast; the number of hours worked in campaigns; the number of dollars contributed to candidates, parties, and campaign organizations; the number of contacts produced; and the number of protests attended.

The upper-right graph shows the proportion of votes coming from the various income groups in the 1988 presidential election. A citizen who voted is weighted as one; a non-voter is weighted as zero and does not appear on the figure. The other parts of Figure 7.4 show the proportion of campaign hours or campaign dollars coming from each income category as well as the proportion of contacts or protests.

Consider first the electoral arena. Those at the top of the income hierarchy produce more than their proportionate share of votes, campaign hours, and campaign dollars. However, the distortion is much less pronounced for votes than for campaign time and, in turn, much less for campaign time than for campaign money. The 3 percent of the sample with family incomes over $125,000 are responsible for 4 percent of the votes, 8 percent of the hours devoted to campaigning, and fully 35 percent of the money contributed. Indeed, when it comes to campaign dollars, the top two income groups, which together account for less than 10 percent of the population, donate more than half of the money. At the other end of the family income scale are those with family incomes under $15,000, who form 19 percent of the sample. They are somewhat underrepresented among voters and more distinctly

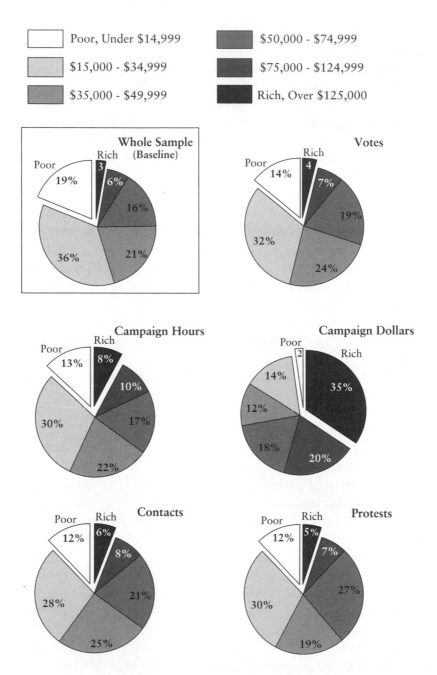

Figure 7.4 Volume of Political Activity: Percentage from Various Family Income Groups.

underrepresented among campaigners. When it comes to making electoral contributions, however, they are barely visible—donating only 2 percent of total campaign dollars.[6]

Contacting and protesting are of particular concern both because they are modes of activity that permit the transmission of relatively specific messages and because they are especially important for the less well off—contacting because contacts permit the addressing of specific individual problems and protesting because protests require little in the way of resources. Reflecting patterns we saw earlier in Figure 7.2, the bottom section of Figure 7.4 shows that the affluent produce more than their proportionate share, and the poor less than their share, of contacts and protests. In terms of the volume of activity, the poor are not as underrepresented as they are with respect to campaign contributions, but their share of the contacts and protests is lower than their proportion in the population and similar to their share of campaign work.

We have focused on a comparison of the affluent and the poor. It is important to note, however, that the difference among the modes of activity affects the representation of the middle class as well. Consider those in the $35,000–50,000 income bracket. They are somewhat overrepresented in terms of votes, campaign hours,

---

6. It might be argued that the comparison between hours and dollars donated to campaigns is unrealistic and that time given to campaigning by the more affluent has greater value than time contributed by the less well-off. Certainly the opportunity cost in forgone earnings is likely to be higher for the well-off. However, the forgone earnings of the poor, though smaller in amount, are not necessarily less important to them. Calculating the dollar value of the hours given to political campaigning (by imputing to the hours spent campaigning the earnings one would expect them to represent given the respondent's individual income), the resulting distribution resembles the distribution of campaign money more closely than it resembles the distribution of campaign hours.

Proportion of Hours of Campaigning (weighted by imputed earnings per hour)

Proportion from bottom 19% earners	2%
Proportion from bottom 55% earners	20%
Proportion from top 9% earners	37%
Proportion from top 3% earners	18%

However, this calculation rests on an assumption that is probably faulty. It is not obvious either that the campaign hours represent forgone income of equal magnitude or that the value to the campaign of work arising from different income groups is proportional to the difference in the family incomes of these groups.

and contacts, but substantially underrepresented in terms of campaign dollars. The pattern of underrepresentation when it comes to giving money is even stronger for the group that is one step further down on the economic ladder (those with family incomes between $15,000 and $35,000), who might be thought of as at the border of the poor and the middle class. The special inequality associated with monetary contributions affects the poor most strongly, but it also means that most of the middle class is underrepresented as well.

In one sense, these data merely underline the obvious: that the rich have more money. Nonetheless, the distinction among acts matters for politics. As political campaigns, and other aspects of political life, have become increasingly professionalized and dependent upon financial contributions from citizens, the stratification of political life has, presumably, become more severe. As we showed earlier, checkbook participation has grown more quickly than other forms of activity over the past two decades. As it has done so, the stratification of American politics has probably been exacerbated as well.[7]

The Volume of Non-Political Activity

The distinctiveness of political activity, particularly political contributions, becomes evident when we compare the hours and dollars devoted to voluntary political activity with the hours and dollars devoted to charities or religious institutions. To begin with, the affluent are more likely to take part in non-political activity just as they are more likely to be politically active. The differences among income groups are, however, much less pronounced when it comes to non-political secular activity and, especially, to religious activity. As we saw in Figure 7.2, compared to those in the

---

7. The difference between voting and giving money is highlighted by a consideration of a circumstance where giving money is constricted to a very limited and uniform amount. This occurs in contributions to the general fund to finance elections to which taxpayers may contribute by checking the appropriate box on their income tax forms. The amount is uniform and is low: one dollar. Above a fairly low threshold (incomes under $5,000 per year) the propensity to give is fairly inelastic across the range of incomes. See W. Mark Crain, "An Empirical Estimate of the Income Elasticity of Political Participation," *Kyklos* 30 (1977): 122–125.

lowest level of family income, those in the highest income category are about four times as likely to give time, and almost ten times as likely to give money, to campaigns. In contrast, the affluent are roughly twice as likely as the poor to give time to charitable causes or to donate money to charity. When it comes to religious activity, those with the highest family incomes are, once again, more likely to contribute money to a church, but the difference between the income groups is even less substantial. The gap in activity between income groups is reduced to the point of insignificance with respect to giving time to religious activity. In comparison to the poor, the affluent are no more likely to be frequent church attenders and only slightly more likely to give time to church activity beyond attending services. When it comes to the *amount* of time and money given by those who have crossed the threshold to give something, there is a close parallel in the non-political sphere to what we have found in politics: among the givers, poor and rich give about the same amount of time; among the givers, the rich give much more money than the poor.[8]

Since the volume of activity coming from a group depends on the proportion who become active and the average amount they contribute when active, this suggests that contributions of both time and money to politics will be more unequal than contributions in the non-political domains. Further, we would expect the contributions of money to be more unequal in all three domains than the contributions of time. Figure 7.5, which shows the proportion of campaign, charitable, and church time and money arising from different family income groups, supports these expectations. When it comes to the volume of voluntary activity, the poor are underrepresented and the affluent are overrepresented. However, the distortion is generally greater in the domain of politics than in other arenas and much more pronounced for money than for time. With respect to hours, the poor are under-

---

8. Among those who contribute, those with family incomes under $15,000 give on average $113 per year to charity, while those with incomes over $125,000 give on average $963. The figures for church giving are $331 and $1,481 respectively. For giving time, the poor actually give somewhat more hours per week to charitable and church work than the rich.

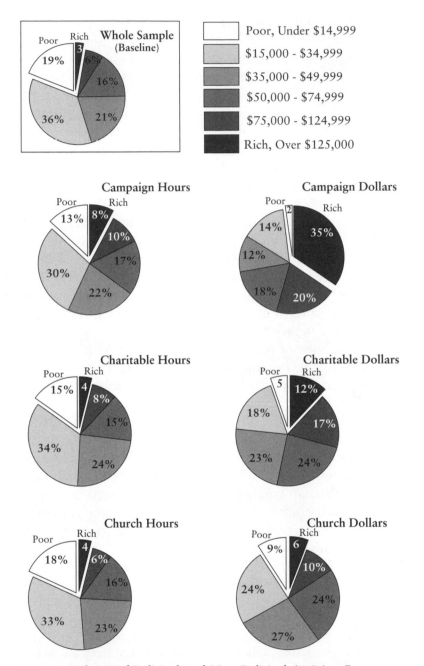

Figure 7.5 Volume of Political and Non-Political Activity: Percentage from Various Family Income Groups.

represented in all three domains, but by the largest amount when it comes to campaign activity. The affluent are overrepresented by a substantial amount in campaigning, by a smaller amount when it comes to charitable hours, and they are proportionately represented when it comes to hours devoted to church work. Note, in fact, that both the highest and lowest income groups contribute a proportional share of the church hours, reinforcing the characterization of the religious domain as the one of greatest equality. In terms of dollars, the affluent are overrepresented and the poor underrepresented in the money contributed in all three domains. However, the bias is much less pronounced for donations to religious institutions than for donations to charities. And the bias is greatest for campaign contributions.

It is hardly surprising that those who have higher family incomes are more generous in their financial contributions, but not necessarily in the amount of time they give. Not only do they have more money to spend but, in comparison to the poor, they are relatively better off with respect to money than with respect to time. It is less obvious why they should be relatively more generous than those who are less well-off in their contributions to politics than in their contributions to charity or, particularly, church—especially since democratic politics is the arena of voluntary activity with the strongest underlying egalitarian commitment. In an age when candidates rely ever more heavily on campaign contributions, the extent to which campaign dollars arise from the wealthy has implications for equality in a democracy.

THE PROPORTION OF INCOME CONTRIBUTED
We can get an additional perspective on the fact that the well-heeled contribute more than do the poor in all three domains by considering the *proportion* of family income contributed. Data comparing the proportion of income given to political campaigns, to charity, and to church are shown in Figure 7.6. Citizens give a higher proportion of their family incomes to churches than to charities and, especially, to political campaigns. What matters here, however, is the nature of the relationship between income level and the average proportion of family income contributed. There are three strikingly different patterns. When it comes to campaign

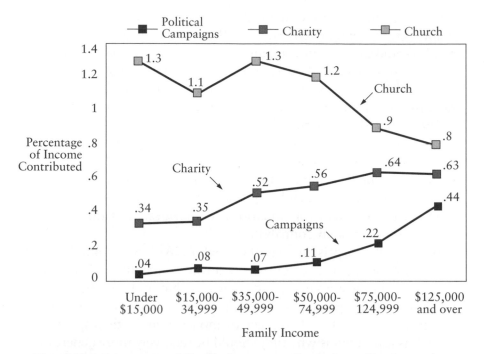

Figure 7.6 Percentage of Family Income to Campaigns, Charity, and Church by Family Income.

contributions, the average percentage of family income devoted to contributions is fairly stable across the lower three income levels, after which it rises sharply. Comparing the groups near the bottom of the income distribution with the top group, we find that those in the highest family income group contribute to political campaigns a proportion of family income about ten times higher on average than that of the least well off. Again, the biggest differences are found in the top income brackets—families with middle incomes being closer to the poorer families than to the wealthier.

Charitable contributions also show a higher proportion of income given by the affluent, but the disparities across income groups are much smaller. The proportion given rises slowly and fairly steadily with income; those in the lowest income group contribute a proportion of family income that is, on average, a bit more than half the proportion contributed by those in the most affluent group.[9] When it comes to church contributions, the pattern we observed for campaign and, more weakly, for charitable contributions is reversed: those in the lower family income category donate, on average, a higher proportion of family income.[10]

POLITICS BY MAIL AND RELIGION BY TELEVISION

Other data in our study confirm the striking distinction between political and religious contributions in terms of the amount of money contributed by more and less affluent citizens. A major trend relevant to volunteer activity in America is the explosion in solicitations that use electronic media or computerized mailings. The world of political, charitable, and religious giving has been revolutionized by the ability to communicate with vast, but targeted, audiences through television appeals, sometimes using special audience cable channels or computer-generated mass mailings. Although they are very expensive, these technologies permit the raising of substantial sums without mobilizing armies of solicitors.

In our questionnaire we asked about exposure to two forms of electronic solicitations, one religious and one political. We asked if our respondents ever watched religious programs on television and if they ever received computer-generated mail solicitations for political causes or organizations; if so, whether they ever sent in contributions in response to the television or mail solicitation; and, if they had sent money, how much. Seventeen percent of our respondents reported watching religious programs on television at least once a week, and 7 percent reported receiving a mail solicitation for a political contribution at least once a week.

---

9. The data on charity, showing that the more affluent give somewhat more of their income, appear somewhat at variance with data from the Independent Sector showing that the lowest income groups are proportionately the biggest donors. They do find an increase in giving in the top bracket, but the proportion is still smaller than that in the lower brackets. (See Virginia Hodgkinson et al., *Non-Profit Almanac, 1992–1993: Dimensions of the Independent Sector* [San Francisco: Jossey-Bass, 1992], table 2.13, p. 72). However, the Independent Sector's charitable contributions are a combined measure that includes both secular and religious giving. If we combine our measures of church and charity, a similar pattern appears.

10. The figures for regular church attenders indicate that this pattern is not the result of more regular church attendance among the poor. Among regular church attenders, the poor (with incomes under $15,000) give on average 2.5 percent of their income to a church, while the affluent (with incomes over $125,000) give on average 1.3 percent.

Table 7.1, which reports the data across income levels, shows a pattern quite similar to what we have already seen for political and religious contributions. The affluent are more involved with politics, the poor with religion: affluent respondents were more likely to indicate that they had received political requests through the mail, those with lower family incomes were more likely to report watching religious programs on television. Among those who received political solicitations through the mail, the well-heeled are somewhat more likely to make a donation in response. In contrast, among those who watched religious programs on television, there is no relationship between family income and the likelihood of sending in a contribution. When it comes to the amount contributed, however, the wealthy send more in response to both political and religious solicitation.[11]

TIME AND MONEY: SUMMING UP

We have found distinctive patterns for voluntary donations of time and money and distinctive patterns for voluntary activity in the domains of politics, secular charities, and religion. The rich are more likely than the poor to give time to charitable and, especially, political activity—although not to church activity. Among those who give time in any of these arenas of voluntarism, the most affluent give, in general, less time than do those with the lowest family incomes. As for financial contributions, wealthy respondents are substantially more likely than poor ones to make politi-

---

11. A final comparison provides additional confirmation of the patterns we have already observed. With respect to donations in response to mass-mail political requests, the affluent give, on average, a higher proportion of their family incomes than do the poor. When it comes to contributions generated by televised religious programs, the pattern is, once again, reversed: it is the poor who donate the larger proportion of their incomes. In the table below, percent of income given is calculated for all members of the income group; those who did not give are counted as giving zero.

	Income Levels					
	Under $15K	$15K– $35K	$35K– $50K	$50K– $75K	$75K– $125K	Over $125K
Percent of Income Given						
Political Mail	.01%	.01%	.01%	.02%	.04%	.05%
TV Religion	.02%	.01%	.01%	←	.01%	→

Table 7.1 Requests for Political Contributions through the Mail and Religious Contributions on Television by Family Income[a]

	Family Income				
	Under $14,999	$15,000–34,999	$35,000–49,999	$50,000–74,999	$75,000–124,999	$125,000 and over
REQUESTS						
Receive Political Mail	51%	63%	74%	84%	88%	88%
Watch Religious Programs on TV	55%	41%	36%	←	31%[b]	→
PERCENT CONTRIBUTING (AMONG THOSE ASKED)						
Political Mail	8%	8%	7%	12%	20%	26%
TV Religious Programs	7%	8%	12%	←	9%[b]	→
AMOUNT GIVEN (AMONG GIVERS)						
Political Mail	$32	$88	$83	$102	$183	$344
TV Religious Programs	$55	$94	$72	←	$263[b]	→

a. N = 2,517 weighted cases: see Appendix A for information about sample.
b. Because of the small number of upper-income respondents who watch religious programs on television, the top three income categories are combined.

cal and charitable contributions and a bit more likely to make religious donations. On average, the absolute size of their contributions in each domain is much larger. However, when we consider the proportion of family income contributed, the impression of greater generosity by the rich becomes less clear. The least affluent actually give a higher proportion of their much smaller family incomes in donations to church. They give a somewhat smaller proportion of their incomes to charity. However, only in politics do the poor devote a much smaller share of family income to contributions.

This finding is somewhat ironic: politics is the arena for which the norms of equality and the legal requirements for equality are strongest—enshrined in the principle of one person, one vote and reflected as well in campaign finance legislation. Yet it is in politics that stratification by income is most pronounced. In comparison with the religious and secular non-political spheres of voluntary activity, the political domain is characterized by the most substantial stratification by income.

Beyond Income Categories: Economic Attitudes and Circumstances

When we discussed the relevance of the literature on legislative representation to the question of the representativeness of input through citizen activity in Chapter 6, we pointed to the importance of moving beyond demographic categories and referred to Wolfinger and Rosenstone's crucial finding that, although voters and non-voters differ in their demographic characteristics, there is no corresponding difference in their attitudes as measured in surveys.[12] Our findings about voting and policy preferences are consistent with Wolfinger and Rosenstone's. Using responses to standard seven-point scale survey questions, we replicated their analysis of the representativeness of the attitudes of voters with respect to such issues as whether the government should provide all citizens with an adequate job and standard of living or let each individual

---

12. Raymond E. Wolfinger and Steven J. Rosenstone, *Who Votes?* (New Haven: Yale University Press, 1980), pp. 108–114.

Table 7.2 Attitudes of Voters and the Whole Population

	(1) Percent of Sample	(2) Percent of Voters	Difference[a] (2)−(1)	Ratio[a] (2)/(1)
GOVERNMENT PROVISION OF JOBS				
Liberal	27.7	23.6	−4.1	.85
Moderate	25.7	25.9	.2	1.01
Conservative	46.6	50.6	4.0	1.09
GOVERNMENT SPENDING FOR SERVICES				
Liberal	38.6	36.1	−2.5	.94
Moderate	29.7	29.3	−.4	.99
Conservative	31.7	34.6	2.9	1.09

a. See Appendix C for a discussion of this and related measures and approaches to tests of statistical significance.

get ahead on his or her own and whether the government should reduce social spending or maintain government services. Using Wolfinger and Rosenstone's measures of representativeness, we present the data in Table 7.2. On both measures, voters are more conservative than the public as a whole, but the differences are quite slight. In short, our data support the conclusion that voters and non-voters do not seem to differ substantially in their attitudes on public policy issues.

As we indicated in the last chapter, however, in order to understand the representativeness of citizen input, we must expand this analysis in several fundamental ways. First, we must take a broader view of activity, moving beyond electoral turnout to include various kinds of political activity that can convey more precise messages to policymakers and can be multiplied beyond the enforced equality of ballots. In addition, we must take a broader view of politically relevant attributes, encompassing not only demographics and policy positions as expressed in response to survey questions but also policy-relevant circumstances and the actual content of participatory input. And finally, we must look within groups to see how their activists represent them.

We begin by comparing groups defined in terms of their socioeconomic characteristics and their policy preferences—the same pair of attributes we just considered in relation to voting—with respect to their overall level of political activity as measured by the additive scale of political acts that we used earlier in the chapter. Figure 7.7, which considers several demographic measures and several measures of political preferences as measured by standard survey questions, shows the overall activity rates of demographic and attitudinal groups.[13] Even when we enlarge our understanding of political activity, the distinction that Wolfinger and Rosenstone make between demography and attitudes holds up. Disparities in activity across socioeconomic groups—whether defined by income, education, or occupation—are much more substantial than across attitudinal groups. Those with high family incomes score much higher in overall participation than those with incomes at the poverty line, and professional and managerial workers score higher than unskilled and service workers. The gap in overall participation between college graduates and those who never finished high school is also wide. In contrast, attitudinal differences on public issues or differences in partisan attachments are associated with less variation in political activity. There is, however, a small but consistent tendency for those who are more conservative in attitude or Republican in party identification to be more active. Although the differences are not great, they are more substantial than those associated with the vote.

ECONOMIC CIRCUMSTANCES AND NEEDS

The contrast between the similarity in the amount of activity across groups defined in terms of attitudes and ideological positions and the difference in activity among groups defined in demographic terms might suggest that participatory distortion in descriptive demographic terms is not matched by distortion in substantive representation. However, as we argued in the previous chapter, policy preferences are not the only politically relevant characteristics. Figure 7.8 presents data on the activity of respon-

---

13. We define liberals and conservatives by responses to two seven-point survey items listed in Appendix B.6: the question about government provision of a job and a good standard of living and the question about whether the government should provide fewer services in order to reduce spending. Liberals are those who were on the liberal side of the scale on both items or on the liberal side on one and in the middle on the other. Conservatives are those who were on the conservative side of the scale on both items or on the conservative side on one and in the middle on the other.

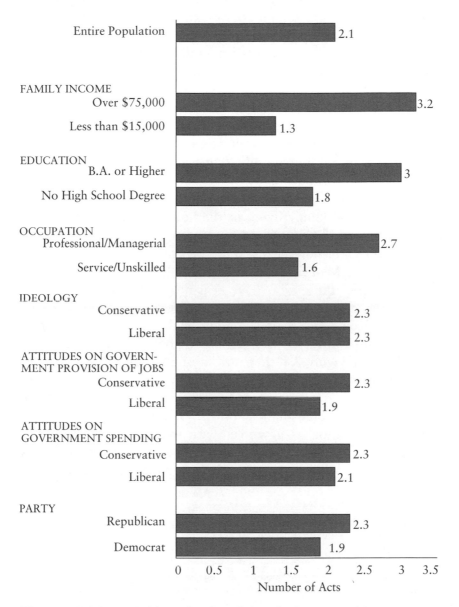

Entire Population — 2.1

FAMILY INCOME
Over $75,000 — 3.2
Less than $15,000 — 1.3

EDUCATION
B.A. or Higher — 3
No High School Degree — 1.8

OCCUPATION
Professional/Managerial — 2.7
Service/Unskilled — 1.6

IDEOLOGY
Conservative — 2.3
Liberal — 2.3

ATTITUDES ON GOVERN-MENT PROVISION OF JOBS
Conservative — 2.3
Liberal — 1.9

ATTITUDES ON GOVERNMENT SPENDING
Conservative — 2.3
Liberal — 2.1

PARTY
Republican — 2.3
Democrat — 1.9

0   0.5   1   1.5   2   2.5   3   3.5
Number of Acts

Figure 7.7 Mean Number of Political Acts by Demographic Characteristics and Attitudes.

dents who have varying economic needs and life circumstances. We concentrate on two dimensions—efforts to get by financially and receipt of various government benefits by respondents or immediate members of their families living with them. In our survey we asked whether, in order to make ends meet, the respondent or any immediate family member living in the household had to "put off medical or dental treatment," "cut back on the amount or quality of food," or "delay paying the rent or making house payments." We inquired as well about two other strategies for making ends meet: did anybody "cut back on spending on entertainment or recreation" or "work extra hours or take an extra job?"[14] In addition, we asked whether the respondent or a member of the immediate family living in the household received means-tested government benefits (food stamps, subsidized housing, Medicaid, or AFDC) or non-means-tested benefits (Social Security, veterans' benefits, Medicare, or educational loans).[15] We were thus able to identify those who have real financial needs or depend upon government programs. These measures are, of course, closely related to income, but they give additional indications of respondents' potential interests with respect to government support.

As shown in Figure 7.8, there are substantial differences in rates of political activity across groups distinguished by financial need or by the receipt of government benefits. Consider the activity of those who report some financial pinch. They are slightly less active than the population as a whole, with the divergence from the average for all citizens increasing with the severity of the financial squeeze. Those who report the relatively mild—and quite wide-

---

14. Exact wording of these questions is given in Appendix B.16.a. The question on entertainment is not used in our measure of need.

15. Note that the referent in the questions about government benefits was the respondent or any immediate family member living in the household. In the text we shall, in the name of parsimony, refer frequently to "food stamp recipients" or "those who receive veterans' benefits" when, in fact, it may be another family member in the household who receives the benefits.

We should also note that, although there is a means test for student loans, we are categorizing them with non-means-tested benefits. The level of permissible income for student loans is much higher than for other means-tested benefits such as food stamps or AFDC, and the beneficiaries are not located primarily among the poor. For the full text of these questions, see Appendix B.16.b.

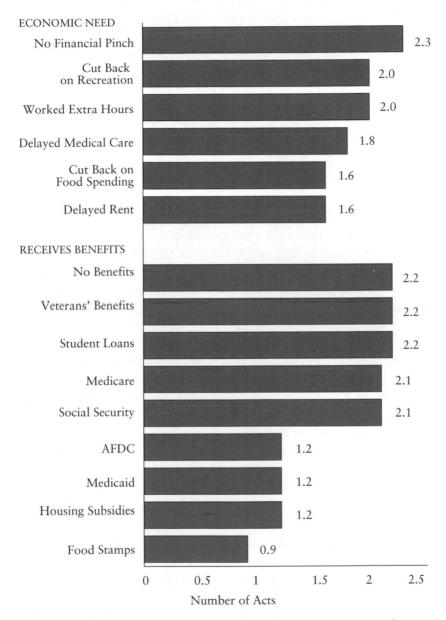

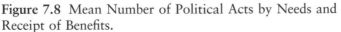

Figure 7.8 Mean Number of Political Acts by Needs and Receipt of Benefits.

spread—need to cut back on recreation do not differ from the population as a whole very much. Those who had to cut back on spending for food or who delayed paying the rent, however, are substantially less active. Clearly, those with real needs are less visible in the participatory system.

This pattern is even more pronounced if we consider those who reported that they or a member of the immediate family receive one of a number of government benefits. The receipt of benefits per se does not imply a low level of activity. Those who receive non-means-tested benefits such as student loans or veterans' benefits, Medicare, or Social Security are at least as active as the public as a whole. In contrast, those who receive means-tested benefits such as AFDC, Medicaid, food stamps, or subsidized housing are substantially less active than the public as a whole. The differences imply that those who would be most in need of government response—because they are dependent on government programs—are the least likely to make themselves visible to the government through their activity.

It is useful to decompose the data in Figures 7.7 and 7.8, in which activity is measured by a summary of several participatory acts, in order to consider the kinds of participation separately. As we have seen, voters do not differ much from non-voters when it comes to policy preferences. But what about in terms of their actual needs or their actual dependence on government programs? And do those who do more than just vote—those who engage in participatory acts that may involve a greater volume of activity or convey more information—differ from the population as a whole?

Figure 7.9 reports for various kinds of activity the Logged Representation Scale (defined in Chapter 6) for groups of individuals defined by their political attitudes on economic issues, as well as by their objective economic circumstances: by the need to cut back on necessities, by whether they receive welfare, and by whether they are poor. The degree of over- or underrepresentation is measured for several different activist groups: voters, campaign workers, campaign contributors, contactors, community activists, members of local boards, and protesters. By varying both the *characteristics* of activists and the *activities* through which they can be over- or underrepresented, Figure 7.9 thus tells us something about both

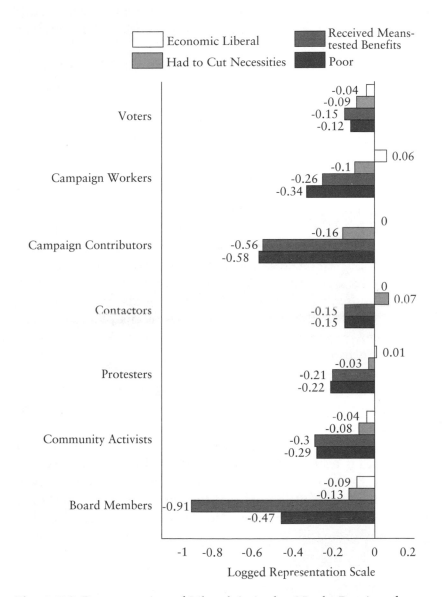

Figure 7.9 Representation of Liberal Attitudes, Needs, Receipt of Means-Tested Benefits, and the Poor: Logged Representation Scores.

parts of our puzzle: what characteristics of citizens are better represented through activity and what activities better represent citizen characteristics.[16] It also tells us something about the extent of under- and overrepresentation. For instance, the top section of the figure tells us that, among voters, liberals are very slightly underrepresented compared to their proportion in the population as a whole; those who said they had to cut necessities are a little more underrepresented; and those who receive means-tested benefits are the most underrepresented.

Across all types of activities, those who take part represent more accurately the attitudes of individuals as measured by the standard survey questions on economic policy than they represent individuals' actual needs, as measured by the need to cut necessities, by income, or by receipt of means-tested benefits.[17] Economic liberals are, in general, represented roughly proportionately among activists across the various activities. When we consider the representation index for differences based on the actual needs of citizens and, even more so, for differences based on their receipt of means-tested benefits, however, we find that the disparities are much greater.

There are also significant variations in terms of types of activity. If we look at activities associated with elections, the voting population and the population of campaign workers are, as mentioned, fairly representative of the population at large with respect to attitudes, and only somewhat unrepresentative of those who have had to cut back on necessities. However, the poor and those who receive means-tested benefits are substantially underrepresented among voters and, especially, campaign workers. It is, however, among campaign contributors that the underrepresentation of the poor and needy is most pronounced. This is hardly surprising. We would not ordinarily expect those who have severe economic

---

16. In order to move through a large amount of data, we present in Figure 7.9 the representation index for those who take a liberal position on policy and those who manifest some economic need or receive some welfare benefit from the government. The argument would not be any different if we had looked at the other side of the divide—those with conservative views and those who do not receive such benefits.

17. For a fuller discussion of the relationship between protesting and liberal attitudes, see Chapter 16.

problems to be campaign contributors. But that does not change the substantive implication of that fact for the messages that are received through participatory channels—in this case, one of the most effective and salient channels. Compared with campaign contributors, the underrepresentation of those who have had to cut back and the poor in other activist populations is more moderate. The differences, though, are still substantial compared with the representation of policy attitudes.

For three modes of activity that might be particularly relevant for needy citizens—getting in touch with public officials, attending protests and demonstrations, and being active in the community—those who felt financially strapped are fairly accurately represented in the activist population. However, for those who received means-tested benefits and for those in poverty, there is fairly severe underrepresentation. Contacting is, presumably, especially important for citizens who receive government benefits, since ensuring the flow of benefits may entail the need to deal with officials. Recipients of means-tested benefits, however, are substantially underrepresented among the contactors. Although protest should be particularly important for disadvantaged groups that lack financial resources or connections, those receiving a means-tested benefit are underrepresented in that participant population as well. And the recipients of means-tested benefits are about half as likely to be community activists as their proportion in the population would warrant.[18]

Activists among the Poor

The data we have presented make clear that activists do not match the public as a whole. The extent of participatory distortion depends upon both the nature of the politically relevant character-

---

18. We have seen that political acts vary with respect to the number of people who perform them. We might have expected that the smaller the number of people who engage in a particular form of participation, the less representative would be the activist group. Although voters are both the most numerous and the most representative of the activist groups, the pattern does not hold overall. Much larger proportions of the population reported making campaign contributions than attending protests, but the contributors deviate from the population as a whole much more than do the protesters.

istic—citizens' attitudes or their actual economic circumstances—and the mode of activity through which citizens communicate to the government. Still, the underlying theme is the distinct tilt of participatory input away from the disadvantaged.

As we have noted, however, there is another dimension to the underrepresentation of the voice of the disadvantaged. The extent to which any group is heard depends not only on the level of activity of its members but also on which of its members take part. Just as the activist portion of the public as a whole may not be representative of the public at large, so may the activists from a particular group be unrepresentative of that group. Hence, we must inquire whether the participants from among the disadvantaged reflect accurately the group from which they come.

We consider this issue for the poor in Figure 7.10. As we would expect, those with family incomes of $15,000 or less (close to or below the poverty line) and the activists among them are more likely than members of the public as a whole to favor government programs that aid the poor. Taking those citizens who are consistently and relatively strongly liberal or conservative on the issue of government aid to the disadvantaged, we find 16 percent of the public—as opposed to 28 percent of the poor—to be liberal on such issues.[19] However, there is also a difference between the poor and the activists among the poor. Only 21 percent of the activist poor take the liberal position. Moreover, the activist poor are as likely as the public at large to be at the conservative end of the spectrum on these issues.

An analogous difference between the activist poor and all the poor emerges with respect to receipt of means-tested government benefits. Nine percent of the public reports receiving means-tested benefits. Not surprisingly, a greater share of the poor—32 percent—receive such benefits. The activist poor, 24 percent of whom receive such benefits, are in between. Citizens dependent on government benefits would, presumably, need to be active. However, we find that, among the poor, recipients of benefits are, in fact, less participant. Thus, the activists among the poor do not fully

---

19. For the definition of liberals and conservatives, see Appendix B.6.b.

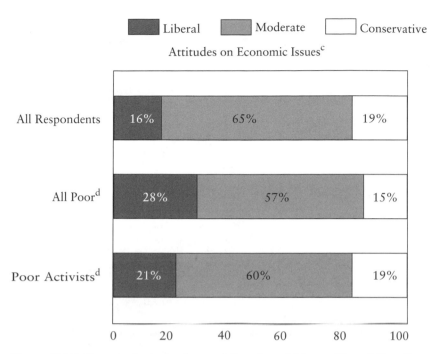

Figure 7.10 Economic Attitudes and Receipt of Means-Tested Benefits among All Respondents, the Poor,[a] and Poor Activists.[b]

a. Poor = family income under $15,000.
b. Activists = three or more political acts (including voting).
c. For definition of liberals and conservatives, see Appendix B.6.
d. N's: Poor = 446, Poor Activists = 73 weighted cases.

represent other politically relevant circumstances of the poor—their preference for and dependence on government programs. This circumstance compounds the disadvantage of the poor in terms of participatory representation: they are less likely to be active, and the activists drawn from among them do not accurately represent their level of need or their preferences for governmental help.

Sending a Message

We have noted that participatory acts differ not only in the extent to which their volume can be multiplied but also in the extent to which they can convey to policymakers detailed information about citizens' concerns. Our data allow us to investigate in several ways

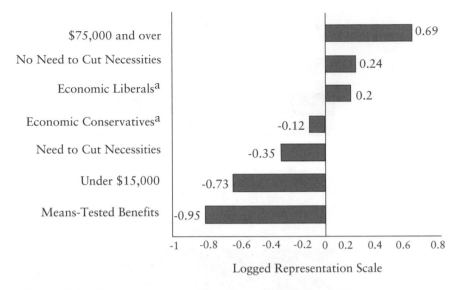

Logged Representation Scale

Figure 7.11 Representation of Big Campaign Givers Who Communicate an Explicit Message.
a. For definition, see Appendix B.6.

this largely uncharted, but crucial, aspect of citizen activity. For one thing, we can consider the characteristics of those activists who combine a substantial participatory investment with a specific message: that is, who combine a significant amount of activity with information about what they want in response. In addition, we can look at those who are active in relation to particular government benefit programs. And, finally, we can consider the actual messages sent by activists who engage in modes of participation that permit the communication of information. These data greatly enrich our understanding of what is represented through participation.

Let us begin by considering one group of activists who join an activity of substantial dimensions with an explicit message: those who contributed $250 or more to a political campaign and who reported that they "communicated to the candidate or to someone involved in running the campaign [their] views on an issue of public policy—for example, about what [they] wanted the candidate to do when in office." Figure 7.11 indicates how well various sub-groups defined by their attitudes and economic circumstances are represented within this group of participants whose activity is high in its potential both for generating pressure and for conveying information to candidates. As expected, those who make major campaign donations are more representative in terms of their attitudes on economic issues than in terms of their actual economic needs. The affluent are nearly five times as likely—and those who have had to cut back on necessities are roughly half as likely—to appear in this politically potent group as is their proportion of the population. The most marked underrepresentation is found among the poor and those in households where a family member receives a means-tested benefit. These data echo the results reported earlier concerning who is and who is not represented, but the relationships are even stronger. When it comes to an act that communicates a good deal of information and has potential clout, the less well-off are especially underrepresented.

POLITICAL ACTIVITY AND PROGRAM PARTICIPATION

We have shown that those receiving such means-tested benefits as AFDC, Medicaid, food stamps, or subsidized housing are much less active than those receiving such non-means-tested benefits as Social Security, veterans' benefits, or Medicare. We can take the analysis one step further, however, by examining whether their activity is in any way directly connected to these benefit programs and whether, therefore, the government receives more messages about benefits programs from recipients of non-means-tested benefits than from recipients of means-tested benefits. In our survey we inquired whether recipients of various government benefits had been active *in relation to* that benefit. For each government program for which the respondent (or a family member living in the household) was a recipient, we asked about the following activities: Had they taken that program into account in deciding how to vote? Had they given a campaign contribution based, at least in part, on concern about it? Had they contacted an official to complain about the program? Did they belong to an organization concerned about that program? The data in Figure 7.12 on the proportion of the recipients of each benefit who reported an activity related to the benefit program are consistent with what we know about the overall activity levels of the recipients of govern-

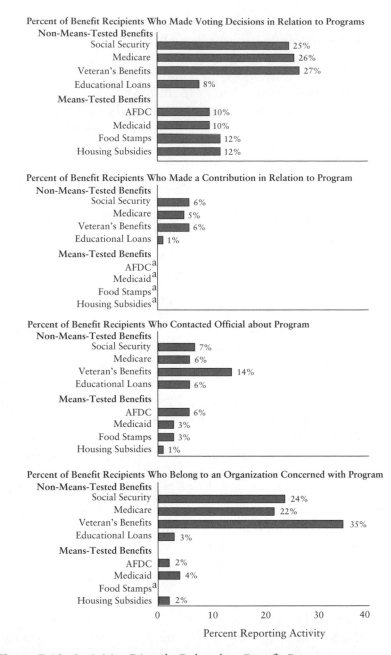

Figure 7.12 Activities Directly Related to Benefit Programs.
a. Under 1%.

ment benefits. For each kind of activity—voting, contributing, contacting, and membership in an organization—recipients of non-means-tested benefits are more likely to have been active than recipients of means-tested benefits.

The difference is especially striking with respect to membership in an organization associated with the benefit—with the AARP and veterans' organizations presumably playing a major role—and campaign donations. However, it applies as well to the considerations that enter into voting decisions.[20] The data on contacting are interesting. We might expect that inclusion in the non-means-tested programs would be more or less automatic and, thus, would require fewer contacts. Nevertheless, Medicare recipients are more likely than Medicaid recipients to contact about their medical benefits; Social Security recipients are more likely than AFDC recipients to contact about their benefits.[21] Clearly, the government hears more from those on some programs than on others, and the ones it hears from are the more advantaged citizens.[22]

---

20. It has been suggested to us that the seeming salience of entitlement programs for voting decisions is only a reflection of the fact that political leaders have drawn attention to these programs in campaigning and, thus, this tells us more about political leaders than about citizens. That candidates make promises about protecting Social Security or veterans' benefits, but not about means-tested benefits, however, tells us something about their strategic calculations and about what they are hearing from citizens and the organizations to which they belong.

21. Student loans are an exception. There is relatively little activity in relation to student loans. However, there is generally more activity in relation to student loans than there is in relation to means-tested programs.

22. One alternative explanation might be that the recipients of such non-means-tested benefits as Medicare and Social Security are elderly. For the elderly, certain private strategies for dealing with economic difficulties—for example, seeking additional employment—are less feasible, which puts a premium on political activity as a means of coping with problems. However, if we control for age and compare the level of activity between the recipients of the two kinds of benefits, a disparity remains.

Mean Activity Rate Among Benefit Recipients		
Non-Means-Tested		Means-Tested
Age		
40 and under	1.8	1.0
41–65	2.3	1.5
66 and over	2.1	1.3

The difference between the activity rates of the two types of benefit recipients is a function, in part, of education. Those receiving means-tested benefits are, on average, less

What Do They Say?

We can extend our analysis one step further by examining directly
the issue basis of citizen activity. We have probed who is active in
what ways, but we have not investigated the substantive content
of that activity. Let us now consider what activists actually say.
We have mentioned many times that political activities differ in
their capacity to convey explicit messages to policymakers. In
contrast to, for example, contacts or protests, votes are limited in
their ability to transmit precise information about citizens' priorities and preferences. As we pointed out in Chapter 3, the issues
that individuals report to have animated their activity vary across
political acts. They also vary with the economic circumstances of
the activists. Table 7.3 summarizes the subject matter behind the
political activity in which a codeable issue concern was expressed
and compares advantaged and disadvantaged respondents with
respect to the issue concerns that animate their participation.[23] In
order to ensure that what is on people's minds is actually communicated to public officials, we focus solely on those information-
rich activities in which an explicit message can be sent: contacting,
protesting, campaign work or contributions accompanied by a
communication, informal community activity, or voluntary service

---

well educated than those receiving non-means-tested benefits. Controlling for education,
we find that among those with no college education, the recipients of means-tested benefits
are less active than the recipients of the non-means-tested benefits across all four activities
measured in Figure 7.12. However, among those with at least some college, the two types
of benefit recipients are similar in their likelihood of contacting or in the likelihood that
they will take into account the position of a candidate on the benefit program when deciding
how to vote. The means-tested recipients in this educational group are, however, still
substantially less likely to make a campaign contribution or to belong to an organization
related to the program. Our point is not, however, to argue that receipt of means-tested
benefits causes low levels of activity, but rather to demonstrate that a group that is
dependent upon the government is, by virtue of its lack of education or any other factors,
less active in expressing its concerns and, therefore, less visible to public officials.

23. Both to generate additional cases for analysis and to purge the lowest income
category of a few aberrant cases of very well-educated, low-income respondents, we are
shifting our focus from the extremes in terms of family income to a more general definition
of socioeconomic advantage and disadvantage. We define the advantaged as those with at
least some college education and a family income over $50,000, and the disadvantaged as
those with no education beyond high school and family incomes below $20,000. These are
groups of roughly equal size each representing about one-sixth of the sample.

Table 7.3 What Respondents Say: Issue-Based Political Activity (information-rich activities only)[a]

	All	Advantaged[b]	Disadvantaged[c]	Receives Means-Tested Benefits
Proportion of Issue-Based Activity Animated by Concern about:				
Basic Human Needs	10%	8%	21%	32%
Taxes	6	6	4	8
Economic Issues (except taxes)	5	7	1	1
Abortion	8	11	0	4
Social Issues (except abortion)	2	1	5	6
Education	12	15	10	18
Environment	9	8	2	2
Crime or drugs	9	6	10	8
Foreign Policy	3	3	0	0
Number of respondents[d]	2,517	425	480	228
Number of issue-based acts[d]	1,556	432	123	73

a. Information-rich acts are those in which an explicit message can be sent to policymakers: contacting, protesting, campaign work or contributions accompanied by a communication, informal community activity, or voluntary service on a local board. The numbers in the cells represent the proportion of such acts having identifiable issue content for which there was a reference to the particular issue.

b. Advantaged: At least some college and family income $50,000 or more.

c. Disadvantaged: No education beyond high school and family income below $15,000.

d. Numbers shown are the weighted numbers of cases and issue-based acts. See Appendix A for information about sample.

on a local board.[24] The issue-based political act is the unit of analysis, and the figures represent the proportion of all issue-based activities for which the respondent mentioned, among other things, a particular set of policy concerns.[25]

Although the advantaged and disadvantaged are similar in having wide-ranging policy concerns, they differ in the distribution of their concerns. Compared with the issue-based activity of the

---

24. Thus, we omit voting, attending meetings of a local board on a regular basis, and campaigning for, or contributing to, a candidate when the activity is not accompanied by an explicit message.

25. A fuller description of the derivation of these categories and a discussion of these open-ended responses is found in Chapter 3.

advantaged, the activity of the disadvantaged is more than twice as likely, and the activity of respondents in families receiving means-tested benefits four times as likely, to have been animated by concerns about basic human needs—poverty, jobs, housing, health, and the like. Moreover, the activity of the disadvantaged is more likely to have been motivated by concern about drugs or crime. The activity of the advantaged, in contrast, is more likely to have been inspired by abortion, the environment, or economic issues such as taxes, government spending, or the budget.

When we consider the actual number of communications, however, a very different story emerges. Because the disadvantaged are so much less active than the advantaged, public officials actually hear less about issues of basic human needs from the disadvantaged than from the slightly smaller group of advantaged respondents—even though references to basic human needs occupy relatively greater space in the bundle of communications emanating from the disadvantaged.

These findings might suggest that, although the disadvantaged are underrepresented with respect to participatory input, their concerns and needs are, nonetheless, being expressed by others. When the disadvantaged speak for themselves on issues of basic human needs, however, their communications differ in two fundamental ways from those sent by others. First, when the disadvantaged communicate with public officials about basic human needs, they are much more likely than the advantaged to be concerned about problems that affect them personally. Even affluent citizens may have need for government assistance with respect to basic human needs: they may have health problems or a handicapped child in school; if elderly, they receive Medicare and Social Security. Still, a much larger proportion of the messages about basic human needs from the disadvantaged involve particularized communications about problems specific to themselves or their families—a question about eligibility for Social Security, a complaint about the conditions in a housing project, or a request by a disabled respondent for special transportation, to cite some actual examples from our data.

Such particularized concerns were behind 56 percent of the issue-based activity in which human-needs issues were mentioned by the disadvantaged, but only 8 percent of that in which human-needs issues were mentioned by the advantaged. Even when the human-needs issue was framed as a policy issue rather than a particularized concern, the disadvantaged were much more likely to report that the problem is one that affects themselves or their families as well as others in the community. All in all, of those who communicated to public officials about issues of basic human needs, 71 percent of the disadvantaged, but only 29 percent of the advantaged, were discussing something with an immediate impact upon themselves or their families. It is axiomatic in the literature on lobbying that public officials listen more carefully to those who are directly affected by the policies they advocate and who speak on their own behalf. Presumably, the analogous principle applies to communications from individuals: stories about basic human needs sound different to policymakers when told by those who are in need.

The responses of the advantaged and the disadvantaged differ even more fundamentally when it comes to their actual content. So far, we have concentrated solely on the subjects people talk about without considering what they actually say. The appropriate governmental role in addressing problems of basic human needs is an issue about which liberals and conservatives disagree deeply. In Table 7.4 we differentiate advantaged and disadvantaged respondents in terms of their liberalism or conservatism on economic issues. Overall, the activity of disadvantaged liberals is the most likely to be animated by concerns about issues of basic human needs. Among the advantaged, there is almost no difference between the ideological groups in terms of the proportion of their activity that is inspired by human-needs concerns. However, the activity of advantaged conservatives is more likely to spring from concerns about economic issues. Given that there are more than twice as many conservatives as liberals among the advantaged, a majority of the activity from the advantaged on issues of basic human needs comes from conservatives. And, given that the advantaged are so much more active than the disadvantaged, activity inspired by concerns about basic human needs on the part of advantaged conservatives far outweighs such activity on the part of disadvantaged liberals.

Table 7.4 What Liberals and Conservatives Say: Issue-Based Political Activity (information-rich activities only)[a]

	Disadvantaged[b]		Advantaged[b]	
	Liberals[c]	Conservatives[c]	Liberals[c]	Conservatives[c]
Proportion of Issue-Based Activity Animated by Concern about:				
Basic Human Needs	21%	17%	10%	9%
Economic Issues (including taxes)	7	7	7	17
Number of respondents[d]	168	125	98	219
Number of issue-based acts[d]	45	37	126	199

a. Information-rich acts are those in which an explicit message can be sent to policymakers: contacting, protesting, campaign work or contributions accompanied by a communication, informal community activity, or voluntary service on a local board. The numbers in the cells represent the proportion of such acts having identifiable issue content in which there was a reference to the particular issue.

b. For definitions, see Table 7.3.

c. Liberals and conservatives are defined on the basis of two questions about economic policy. See Appendix B.6 for details.

d. Numbers shown are the weighted numbers of cases and issue-based acts. See Appendix A for information about sample.

Since the largest share of activity animated by concerns about basic human needs emanates from advantaged conservatives, we should examine just what is said by the activists. Some of the policy statements about human needs clearly take a liberal point of view. Various respondents discussed the issue basis for their activity in terms of, for example, concern about "homeless plight," "Commission for visually handicapped Blind Association. To increase their benefits." Other statements were as identifiably conservative. For example, one respondent asserted that "welfare should be done away with." Another got involved in a campaign out of a "dislike of big government, welfare state, and big brothers." Not all the policy statements about issues of basic human needs could be so readily categorized, however. Unadorned references to "Social Security," "housing," or "health issues" do not reveal the direction of respondents' preferences.

Close reading of the verbatim responses shows marked differences between what liberals and conservatives say when they discuss policy about basic human needs.[26] Consistent with figures given earlier, among disadvantaged liberals a substantial share—and, among disadvantaged conservatives, nearly all—of the mentions of basic human needs involve particularized communications. The remaining statements by disadvantaged liberals are divided evenly between those that are not identifiably liberal or conservative and those that are clearly liberal; the few remaining statements by disadvantaged conservatives are ambiguous. Thus, to the extent that disadvantaged respondents—whether liberal or conservative—make policy statements about basic human needs in association with political activity, they never suggest reducing public attention to issues of basic human needs.

Among the advantaged, verbatim responses about these issues are both more numerous and more likely to focus on policy issues rather than particularized concerns. Among the liberals, brief recitations of issues without obviously liberal or conservative content account for one-third of the statements. The remaining two-thirds are unambiguously liberal. For advantaged conservatives, the pattern is very different. More than half of their issue statements have no identifiable ideological direction; the others are divided evenly between clearly liberal and clearly conservative content.

In short, with respect to concerns about basic human needs, information-rich forms of participation carry different kinds of messages from different groups. The issue-based activity of the disadvantaged and recipients of means-tested government benefits is more likely to be inspired by such concerns. However, because these groups are less active, they actually send fewer messages about basic human needs than do more advantaged respondents. The communications from the advantaged differ in two fundamental ways from those sent by the disadvantaged. First, the advantaged are much less likely to be discussing problems that they experience in their own lives. In addition, policy statements from the advantaged are not uniformly supportive of greater efforts to meet problems of basic human needs.

---

26. This paragraph, which is based on a close reading of actual verbatim responses, focuses upon policy-based activity and omits particularized activity. We do not give precise figures because we read each response as a unit without applying sample weights. Because the data are unweighted, the actual number of verbatims is higher than the numbers given in Table 7.4.

Conclusion

In this chapter we began the construction of a richly detailed portrait of from whom—and what—the government hears through the medium of citizen participation. In considering the issue of who participates, our particular perspective has been on economic characteristics, circumstances, needs, and attitudes. Consistent with our concern about matters of representation, we focused first on groups defined by their family income, not because income is the variable with the strongest causal relationship to participation but because economic conflicts have been of such fundamental importance in modern democracies.

As is well known, the affluent are more involved in voluntary activity than are those of lesser means. Nevertheless, underneath this overall regularity—the propensity of the well-heeled to take part—are variations that provide important insights into both the participatory process and the nature of politics in American democracy. One important distinction is between inputs of time and money. The participation gap among income groups is especially wide when it comes to making financial contributions. What is more, among contributors, the wealthy, not unexpectedly, write larger checks than do those of more modest means. To the extent that citizen-based political money figures significantly in campaigns and political controversies, our findings have implications for the equal protection of citizens' interests. While the tendency for those who are better endowed financially to give more money might seem obvious, it is in striking contrast to the pattern that holds for giving time. Among those who give time, those with high family incomes are no more generous with their "sweat equity" than are those lower down on the income scale.

We also observed important differences among the three domains of voluntary activity—political, charitable, and religious—in terms of the extent to which participation is stratified by income. Although the principle of equality of citizen inputs implicit in one person, one vote is fundamental to American democracy, politics is the sphere of activity in which the overrepresentation of the wealthy is most pronounced. In contrast, the religious domain appears to be the most egalitarian. The implication of this special character of religion for political life is profound.

Our analysis moved beyond demography to consider as well politically relevant attitudes, needs, and circumstances. We have shown that a relationship that holds for voting—that the electorate is unrepresentative demographically, but more representative when it comes to attitudes as measured by survey items—obtains for other forms of political activity. However, political participants differ from inactives not only in their demographic attributes but also in their economic needs and in the government benefits they receive. These disparities are exacerbated when we move from the most common political act, voting, to acts that are more difficult, convey more information, and can be multiplied in their volume. With respect to the amount of activity, the disparity is especially great for electoral contributions: the advantaged account for the overwhelming share of the dollars donated to campaigns.

When we examined the issues that animate political participation, we found that, although all groups bring diverse concerns to their activity, the particular mixture differs substantially among groups. In terms of a set of issues of particular salience to those who are economically disadvantaged—concerns about basic human needs—the disadvantaged speak with a distinctive voice. Not only do such issues weigh more heavily in their lists of concerns, but when they communicate about these matters to public officials, they are more likely to be discussing issues that touch their own lives and more likely to be prescribing greater public attention to these needs.

If those who take part and those who do not were similar on all politically relevant dimensions, then substantial inequalities in participation would pose no threat to the democratic principle of equal protection of interests. As our analysis has demonstrated, this is hardly the case. Those whose preferences and needs become visible to policymakers through their activity are unrepresentative of those who are more quiescent in ways that are of great political significance: although similar in their attitudes, they differ in their personal circumstances and dependence upon government benefits, in their priorities for government action, and in what they say when they get involved. In terms of whose concerns are expressed, it matters who participates.

8

Who Participates?
Race, Ethnicity,
and Gender

Throughout American history, conflicts over, especially, race or ethnicity but also gender have surfaced regularly in various guises. Abolition, nativism, and women's suffrage are but a few examples from the past, and the contemporary political agenda is replete with issues—ranging from affirmative action to domestic violence to bilingual education—having implications for the status and well-being of groups defined by their race or ethnicity and their gender. We turn now to a concern with these two major fault lines of political cleavage in America and ask questions, analogous to those just posed about groups defined by their economic position, about who is represented through participatory input. In this chapter, we compare African-Americans, Latinos, and Anglo-Whites[1]

---

1. There is no generally accepted nomenclature for the groups to which we refer, and what are the appropriate designations is often a politically volatile question. We use the terms "African-Americans" or "Blacks" for one of the minority groups and "Latinos" or "Hispanics" for the other. We use the term "Anglo-Whites" to denote those who described themselves as White, but not as Latino or Hispanic. The locution is admittedly awkward. Since "White" is often juxtaposed to "Black" or "African-American" and "Anglo" to "Latino" or "Hispanic," however, the conglomerate term for the majority group seems appropriate.

We differentiate racial or ethnic groups on the basis of self-identifications. (See Appendix B.12 for the questions asked.) When referring to a survey question about a particular group, we attempt, insofar as possible, to use in our prose the locution contained in the question. In addition, when quoting or paraphrasing verbatim responses, we try to use the term used

and men and women in terms of their political activity to see how differences in participation affect the expression of the distinctive opinions, interests, and needs of these groups.

We begin by focusing on the political participation of two racial or ethnic minorities in the United States, African-Americans and Latinos—the former a disadvantaged internal group that has faced centuries of political, social, and economic discrimination, the latter a newer immigrant group facing similar disadvantage.[2] Historically, these groups—especially African-Americans, but Latinos as well—have encountered many legal and institutional barriers to full participation as citizens. However, the issue today is not one of the exclusion of these groups from the rights to participate that citizens enjoy: full citizenship rights have been available to African-Americans since the passage of important civil rights measures—in particular, the Voting Rights Act of 1965—during the 1960s, and similar rights accrue to Latinos once they become citizens, a difficult but not insuperable hurdle. Instead, the issue is the use of political rights once achieved—that is, the extent to which these groups take full advantage of the opportunity to participate in political life.[3]

---

by the respondent. By the way, respondents tended to refer to "Blacks" rather than to "African-Americans," and to "Hispanics" (or "Mexicans," "Cubans," or "Puerto Ricans") rather than to "Latinos." We use the term "race or ethnicity" because African-Americans are usually referred to as a racial group and Latinos as an ethnic group. This gives "ethnicity" a restricted meaning, since we do not undertake an analysis of participatory differences among nationality sub-groups such as Irish-Americans, Italian-Americans, or Polish-Americans.

2. Although most Latinos are relatively recent arrivals to the United States, it is important to recognize that many Latinos—particularly Mexican-Americans—have been in the United States for many generations.

3. There is a large literature on the political activity of African-Americans and Latinos. For works on African-American participation that attempt to describe and explain differential activity rates see, among others, Marvin Olsen, "Social and Political Participation of Blacks," *American Sociological Review* 35 (1970): 682–697; Sidney Verba and Norman Nie, *Participation in America: Political Democracy and Social Equality* (New York: Harper and Row, 1972), chap. 10; Nicholas L. Danigelis, "Black Political Participation in the United States: Some Recent Evidence," *American Sociological Review* 43 (1978): 756–771; Susan Welch, John Comer, and Michael Steinman, "Ethnic Differences in Political and Social Participation: A Comparison of Some Anglo and Mexican-Americans," *Pacific Sociological Review* 18 (1975): 361–382; Richard D. Shingles, "Black Consciousness and Political Participation: The Missing Link," *American Political Science Review* 75 (1981): 76–91; Thomas M. Guterbock and Bruce London, "Race, Political Orientation, and Participation:

The contrast between African-Americans and Latinos is an intriguing one from the point of view of participation. Among the most significant transformations of American politics in recent decades has been the mobilization of African-Americans. During the 1950s, rates of activity for African-Americans were substantially lower than for whites. Several factors—the lowering of *de jure* and *de facto* barriers to activity, mobilization by the civil rights movement, and the dramatic increase in the proportion of African-Americans with higher levels of education and higher-status occupations—operated together to narrow the gap during the 1960s and early 1970s. Indeed, studies showed that, controlling for socioeconomic status, Blacks participated as much as and perhaps more than Anglo-Whites.[4] In addition, this period witnessed a substantial increase in the number of African-Americans in political office and an enhanced role for African-Americans in other political decision-making arenas.

Americans of Hispanic or Latino origin are among the fastest-growing segments of the American population. In some areas of the country, they constitute a major group within the citizenry. There have been significant attempts to mobilize Latinos to political activity, particularly voter turnout drives in the Southwest and California. However, we would expect Latinos to be somewhat behind African-Americans in terms of political mobilization. Like other immigrant groups, Latinos face special obstacles of language and legal status, and political movements among Latinos are of more recent vintage than the civil rights movement.

An Empirical Test of Four Competing Theories," *American Sociological Review* 48 (1983): 439–453; Carole J. Uhlaner, Bruce E. Cain, and D. Roderick Kiewiet, "Political Participation of Ethnic Minorities in the 1980s," California Institute of Technology, Social Science Working Paper 647, June 1987; Lawrence Bobo and Franklin D. Gilliam, Jr., "Race, Socio-Political Participation, and Black Empowerment," *American Political Science Review* 84 (1990): 377–393.

On Latino participation see Rodolfo O. de la Garza et al., *Latino Voices: Mexican, Puerto Rican and Cuban Perspectives on American Politics* (Boulder, Colo.: Westview Press, 1992).

4. See Olsen, "Social and Political Participation," and Verba and Nie, *Participation in America*. Bobo and Gilliam ("Race, Socio-Political Participation, and Black Empowerment") and Christopher G. Ellison and David A. Gay ("Black Political Participation Revisited: A Test of Compensatory, Ethnic Community, and Public Arena Models," *Social Science Quarterly* 70 [1989]: 101–119) argue that, while African-Americans participated at even higher rates than would have been predicted on the basis of their socioeconomic characteristics during the late 1960s, there has been convergence since then.

Political Participation of Anglo-Whites, African-Americans, and Latinos

We begin with the differences in participation among African-Americans, Latinos, and Anglo-Whites. Figure 8.1, which shows the average number of political acts for the three racial or ethnic groups, indicates that African-Americans and Anglo-Whites are fairly similar in participation. Latinos, in contrast, evince lower levels of overall activity. The difference is fairly large.[5] However, since we are considering all Latino respondents in the sample, the data may overstate the Latino participatory deficit. In our study, we interviewed respondents regardless of their citizenship status. Twenty-one percent of the Latino respondents in the sample are not citizens. Since they are barred from voting—an activity that is included in the scale—it seems reasonable to look at the activity of Latino citizens separately.[6] Considering citizens only, the mean score for Latinos rises from 1.2 to 1.4, narrowing the gap with the other groups but leaving, nevertheless, a substantial difference.[7]

Latinos are, of course, a diverse group. We can use our data

---

5. Again, the data for activity parallel the data on who is asked to take part in Chapter 5. We assume that the causality goes in both directions.

6. There are a number of philosophical questions as to whether non-citizens are appropriately part of the universe for a participation study. Although it could be argued that, from the perspective of democratic theory, this should be a study of citizens only, we did make a deliberate choice to interview non-citizens. Non-citizens are affected by American laws, and many are permanent residents (legally or illegally). They may—and do—participate in many ways even though they cannot vote. Putting voting aside, we find that 66 percent of the citizens in our sample of citizens report engaging in one political act beyond the vote. This percentage is about half as large among non-citizens (36 percent) but is far from zero. Thus, we decided to include non-citizens since they can always be separated in analysis. Garcia and Arce note that "ineligibility from voting does not totally remove the Mexican-born from the electoral process." John A. Garcia and Carlos Arce, "Political Orientations and Behaviors of Chicanos: Trying to Make Sense Out of Attitudes and Participation," in *Latinos and the Political System*, ed. F. Chris Garcia (Notre Dame, Ind.: University of Notre Dame Press, 1988), p. 147.

7. We might have expected an even larger difference between Latino citizens and non-citizens. It is likely that our sample is biased when it comes to Latino non-citizens, underrepresenting migrant workers and undocumented residents. Hence, those in our sample may well be relatively advantaged in comparison to non-citizen Latinos as a whole. Our findings about Latino citizens and non-citizens are consistent with those from the National Latino Immigrant Survey as reported by the National Association of Latino Elected and Appointed Officials in "Political Participation among Latino Immigrants," *NLIS Research Notes* 1 (October 1992).

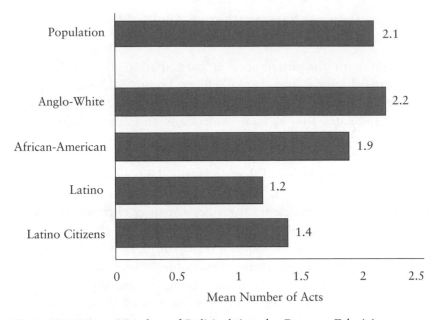

Figure 8.1 Mean Number of Political Acts by Race or Ethnicity.
See Appendix B.12 for effective sample sizes for racial and ethnic groups. For a
discussion of the sample, see Appendix A.

from the screener survey to compare average overall participation
scores for the main Latino sub-groups—the majority who are of
Mexican origin—as well as those whose roots are in Puerto Rico,
Cuba, or other parts of Latin America (usually Central America).
Americans of Cuban origin, on average, engage in about as many
political acts as the national average—indeed, somewhat more.
Those from Mexico, Puerto Rico, or other parts of Latin America
are well below the national average; they average about half the
number of political acts of Anglo-Whites.[8]

With some interesting variations, the pattern in Figure 8.1 is
replicated when we consider the various kinds of participation
separately. Table 8.1 compares the three racial or ethnic groups (plus

---

8. The differences among the Latino groups in terms of political activity are consistent
with their socioeconomic profiles, with Cuban-Americans more likely to have higher levels
of education and higher-status occupations. For an overview of social and political data
among Latino groups, see de la Garza et al., *Latino Voices*.

Table 8.1 Political Activities by Race (percent active)

Activity	Anglo-Whites	African-Americans	Latinos	Latino Citizens
Vote	73	65	41	52
Campaign Work	8	12	7	8
Campaign Contributions	25	22	11	12
Contact	37	24	14	17
Protest	5	9	4	4
Informal Community Activity	17	19	12	14
Board Membership	4	2	4	5
Affiliated with a Political Organization	52	38	24	27

Latino citizens) in terms of their involvement in various political activities. Consider first the three electoral activities: voting, campaign work, and campaign contributions. The differences between African-Americans and Anglo-Whites are small in magnitude and inconsistent in direction. African-Americans are somewhat less likely than Anglo-Whites to report voting.[9] When it comes to activity within a campaign, African-Americans are more likely to say that they have worked in a campaign but less likely to say that they have given money.[10] In each case, however, Latinos—even Latino citizens—are less active.

---

9. We have mentioned that our survey, like all surveys, overestimates voter turnout. Paul R. Abramson and William Claggett indicate that the gap between self-reported and validated turnout is especially wide for Blacks. ("Race-Related Differences in Self-Reported and Validated Turnout," *Journal of Politics* 46 [1984]: 719–738.) We are uncertain about the applicability of their findings to self-reports of other kinds of political activity.

10. The fact that African-Americans are more active in campaigning than Anglo-Whites but less likely to vote may be a function of the particular circumstances of the 1988 presidential election. We suspect that many of the Black campaigners were supporting Jesse Jackson in his primary bid for the Democratic presidential nomination. This is consistent with our data which show that African-Americans were somewhat more likely than other respondents to indicate having been involved in a primary rather than a general election. Katherine Tate shows that Blacks who favored Jackson in the 1988 primaries were less likely to vote in the presidential election. See "Black Political Participation in the 1984 and 1988 Presidential Elections," *American Political Science Review* 85 (1991): 1159–1176.

It is interesting to note how many of the African-American electoral activists were supporting Black candidates. We asked those who had either worked in a campaign or made a contribution about the race of the candidate they supported. Seventy-four percent of the 100 African-American campaign activists reported supporting a Black candidate. In

Table 8.1 also shows the proportion of these three groups engaging in the various forms of non-electoral participation. African-Americans and Anglo-Whites are approximately equally active in informal community activity, with Latinos lagging somewhat. Latinos, however, are slightly more likely to report membership on a local board. The differences among the three groups with respect to a relatively common form of political participation, affiliation with an organization that takes stands in politics, are much larger: Anglo-Whites are considerably more likely than African-Americans and, especially, Latinos, regardless of citizenship, to be involved in a political organization.

The figures for contacting and protesting bear closer scrutiny. As we have mentioned, these are both forms of political involvement that permit the communication of clear messages to policymakers; however, they differ in significant ways. While a larger proportion of the public engages in contacting than in protesting, contacting requires a higher level of communications skills than does attending a demonstration, a form of activity that was important to the American civil rights movement. Compared to protests, contacts with government officials permit the transmission of much more precise messages—including concerns about how policies affect an individual. In addition, while protests may be used as a device to promote minority group solidarity, getting in touch with a public official may require a minority group member to cross a racial or ethnic barrier: only 49 percent of the African-American contactors (N = 134) reported that the official they contacted was also African-American, and only 23 percent of the Latino contactors (N = 64) reported that the official they contacted was also of Latino origin; in contrast, 94 percent of the

---

contrast, only 31 percent of the 24 Latino activists reported supporting a Latino candidate. More than 90 percent of the Anglo-Whites reported supporting a White candidate. Because Anglo-Whites are the overwhelming majority of the population, if citizens supported candidates on a random basis we would expect a majority of Anglo-Whites, African-Americans, and Latinos to support Anglo-White candidates. Clearly, the process is not random, however: patterns of residential segregation affect the distribution of candidates, and citizens are differentially attracted to candidates who share their race or ethnicity. The bottom line is that all three groups, but especially African-Americans, supported candidates from their own group more often than we would expect on the basis of sheer probability.

Anglo-Whites (N = 691) indicated that the official they contacted was an Anglo-White.[11]

The sharp contrast in the patterns for contacting and protesting is consistent with these considerations, especially in relation to the comparison between African-Americans and Anglo-Whites. The former are less likely to contact an official and more likely to protest than are the latter. Since the two groups are quite similar in their overall levels of activity, the quite substantial difference in these two activities probably reflects the fact that African-Americans are as politically mobilized and involved as the Anglo-White portion of the population but have not received—or do not perceive themselves to have received—full acceptance. As usual, Latinos are the least active group. They are only slightly less likely than members of the Anglo-White majority to report having protested, but substantially less likely to report having gotten in touch with a government official.[12]

The Volume of Activity

As we have indicated, what the government hears depends not only on who is active but also on how much they do. Table 8.2 shows, for those who are active, the amount of time or money the three groups devote to their activity as well as the average number of contacts or protests for those who engage in these activities. As we found with economic representation, the inputs of time and money are quite different. When it comes to giving time, minority activists are not less active than their Anglo-White counterparts. Indeed, African-Americans and Latinos who get involved in electoral campaigns give more hours per week than do the Anglo-White activists. The situation is entirely different with respect to money. Among contributors, Anglo-Whites—who are, as we saw, slightly more likely than African-Americans and considerably more

---

11. Number of cases for Latinos and African-Americans is unweighted, number for Anglo-Whites is weighted. See Appendix A for a discussion.

12. Among Latinos, citizens are more likely than non-citizens to contact public officials. Consistent with the notion that protest is an outsider activity, however, Latino non-citizens are as likely as Latino citizens to protest.

Table 8.2 Voluntary Contributions of Time and Money
by Race or Ethnicity

	Anglo-Whites	African-Americans	Latinos	Latino Citizens
Mean Hours Contributed to Political Campaigns (among those who give some time)	6.8	11.4	8.9	9.2
Mean Dollars Contributed to Political Campaigns (among those who give some money)	$257	$165	$177	$194
Mean Number of Contacts (among contactors)	1.7	1.7	1.7	1.8
Mean Number of Protests (among protesters)	2.0	2.3	2.0	1.8

likely than Latinos to make campaign donations—give substantially more than African-Americans or Latinos do when they contribute.

When it comes to contacts and protests, Latinos, African-Americans, and Anglo-Whites differ relatively little in the amount of their participation, once they have crossed the threshold to some activity. This is especially clear in relation to contacting. Anglo-Whites are the most likely to have reported getting in touch with a government official. Among contactors, however, there is almost no difference in how frequently they do so. The data for protesting present a similar pattern. In this case, African-Americans are more likely than members of the other two groups to have reported attendance at a protest, march, or demonstration. Among protesters, they are also the most likely to protest frequently. However, the group differences in the amount of protest activity among protesters are not nearly as pronounced as the group differences in the likelihood of engaging in any protest.

In a pattern that is similar to the one we saw when we considered income groups, we see once again the important difference between acts that require inputs of time and those that require money. When it comes to political activity that demands time, members of disadvantaged groups (whether poor or racial or ethnic minorities) are less likely than members of advantaged groups to cross the threshold to activity. However, once over the barrier, they are as active as their more advantaged counterparts. In contrast, when it comes to giving money, there is both a threshold effect (with the disadvantaged less likely to give anything at all) and a difference among donors in how much they give.

What, then, does the American public look like in racial and ethnic terms if viewed through the lens of participation? In Figure 8.2 we use the same kind of graphs contained in the previous chapter to show the racial and ethnic composition of the citizenry if each group's visibility depended on its amount of political activity. The upper-left section of Figure 8.2 presents, as a baseline, the distribution of the three racial or ethnic groups within the Citizen Participation Study.[13] The other circle graphs in this figure show what the population would look like if the size of each group were proportional to the amount of activity emanating from its members: the number of votes cast; hours worked in campaigns; dollars contributed to candidates, parties and campaign organizations; contacts with public officials; and protests attended.

Once again, the pattern is similar to what we observed for income groups. The voting population is the closest match in racial and ethnic terms to the population as a whole. African-Americans are somewhat less well represented and Latinos substantially less well represented among voters, but the distortion is less than for other activities. In contrast, contacts and, as usual, campaign dollars come unevenly from the three groups.

Across all the acts, Latinos are the least visible in the activist populations. The disparities are particularly pronounced when it comes to contacts and, especially, campaign dollars. The patterns for African-Americans show considerable variation. With respect to two forms of participatory input—the number of hours devoted to campaigns and the number of protests attended—they are over-

---

13. We present a "population" made up of the three groups we have been considering and omit other ethnic groups such as Asian-Americans. Note that, in spite of special efforts to reach African-Americans and Latinos, the sample is not a perfect reflection of the racial and ethnic composition of the population.

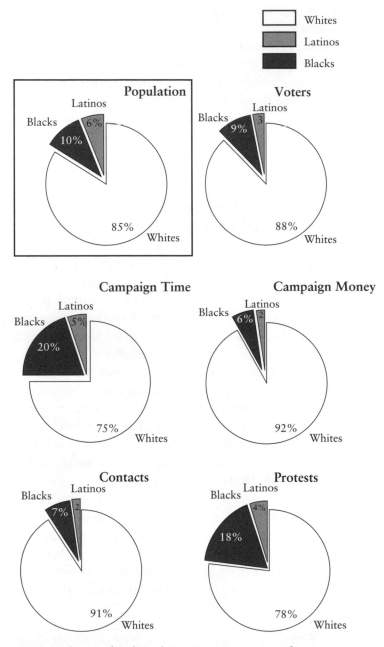

Figure 8.2 Volume of Political Activity: Percentage from Anglo-Whites, African-Americans, and Latinos.

represented. As we suggested earlier, the former may reflect the candidacy of Jesse Jackson and, thus, may be idiosyncratic to the 1988 election. The greater frequency of protest activity may reflect a tradition dating back to the civil rights era. The contrast between the political activity of African-Americans and that of Latinos is particularly striking with respect to protests. It is an activity available to those with few resources. However, African-Americans use this weapon much more frequently than do Latinos.

Black Activists, Latino Activists

When we considered the participation of the poor in Chapter 7, we noted that group activists may not represent accurately the characteristics of less active group members, for example, their attitudes or their actual social circumstances. We can raise this issue for African-American and Latino activists. Figure 8.3 presents data on the attitudes toward government efforts to assist Blacks and Hispanics[14] and receipt of means-tested benefits. Data are shown for several categories: all respondents, African-Americans, and Latinos and the activists—that is, those who engage in three or more participatory acts—drawn from each of these groups. Using as the indicator of support for government assistance to Blacks or Hispanics the proportion who take the most favorable position on the seven-point scale measuring these attitudes, we find little difference between the opinions of all respondents and all activists. (When it comes to receipt of means-tested benefits, there is—as we reported in Chapter 7—a sharper difference between activists and the population as a whole.)

African-Americans and Latinos differ from the public at large in ways that are not unexpected: they are more likely to support government programs to help their own group, and more likely to receive means-tested benefits. The proportion of African-Americans and Latinos taking the strongest position in favor of govern-

---

14. Our survey included seven-point attitude items, asking whether, on one hand, the government should make efforts to improve the social and economic position of Blacks (or Hispanics or women) or whether, on the other, the government should not make any special effort to help Blacks (or Hispanics or women) because they should help themselves.

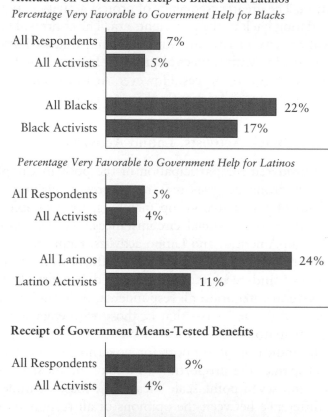

Attitudes on Government Help to Blacks and Latinos

Percentage Very Favorable to Government Help for Blacks

All Respondents — 7%
All Activists — 5%

All Blacks — 22%
Black Activists — 17%

Percentage Very Favorable to Government Help for Latinos

All Respondents — 5%
All Activists — 4%

All Latinos — 24%
Latino Activists — 11%

Receipt of Government Means-Tested Benefits

All Respondents — 9%
All Activists — 4%

All Blacks — 26%
Black Activists — 16%

All Latinos — 25%
Latino Activists — 13%

0   5   10   15   20   25   30

Percentage Favorable

Figure 8.3 Percentage Favoring Help to Minority Groups and Receipt of Means-Tested Benefits by Minority Group Membership and Activity.

Activists: Engage in three or more activities (including voting).

ment assistance to their own group is three to five times the proportion in the population as a whole. Similarly, compared to all respondents, African-Americans and Latinos are roughly three times as likely to receive means-tested benefits. When it comes to the activists from these two minority groups, are they more or less committed to government help for their group? Do they represent the better off or the more disadvantaged portion of their group? The data in Figure 8.3 show that the minority activists fall between the population in general and the members of their own group on each measure. The activists are less likely to favor government programs to help their group than are the members of the group as a whole, a difference that is especially pronounced among Latinos.[15] They are also less likely to receive means-tested benefits. Black and Latino activists are more likely to receive means-tested benefits than are members of the population in general; still, compared to all Blacks or all Latinos, they are only half as likely to do so.[16] Thus, the participatory representation of African-Americans and Latinos is diminished in two ways: they are less likely to be active, and group activists are less likely to represent the distinctive policy positions and needs of the group. Each of these patterns is especially apparent among Latinos.

Voluntary Activity outside Politics

As before, figures about voluntary activity outside of politics provide a revealing counterpoint to data about political participation. We have already mentioned the multiple ways in which involvement outside politics can have implications for political activity. For members of groups that have faced constricted opportunities

---

15. We had thought this might be due to a preponderance of Latinos of Cuban origin, who are more active and more conservative among the Latino activists. However, the pattern remains the same if one considers the data omitting those of Cuban origin.

16. A quite similar pattern is found if we consider being poor as the measure of need. About one-fifth of the sample has a family income below $15,000. While African-Americans and Latinos are about twice as likely to be in that category, the income profile for activist minority group members differs relatively little from that of the population as a whole.

Table 8.3 Secular, Non-Political Activities by Race or Ethnicity
(percent active)

	Anglo-Whites	African-Americans	Latinos	Latino Citizens
Non-Political Organizational Affiliation	71	58	40	42
Active in a Non-Political Organization	39	34	19	20
Time to Charitable Work	38	34	27	29
Charitable Contribution	71	56	47	52

for advancement in the workplace, non-political voluntary activity might assume particular significance.

We begin by considering Table 8.3, which presents data about the involvement of Latinos, African-Americans, and Anglo-Whites in non-political organizations and charities.[17] With respect to affiliation with non-political organizations we find a familiar pattern: a substantially lower level of activity for Latinos than for African-Americans or, especially, Anglo-Whites. Latinos are less likely to be involved with such organizations and even less likely to be active in or officers of non-political organizations. In contrast, the differences between Anglo-Whites and African-Americans are much smaller. A similar, although less pronounced, pattern obtains for

17. There are many studies of minority, especially African-American, affiliation with voluntary associations and a long-standing debate within sociology as to whether high levels of African-American organizational activity represent "overcompensation." See, for example, Nicholas Babchuk and Ralph V. Thompson, "The Voluntary Associations of Negroes," *American Sociological Review* 27 (1962): 647–655; Anthony M. Orum, "A Reappraisal of the Social and Political Participation of Negroes," *American Journal of Sociology* 72 (1966): 32–46; J. Allen Williams, Jr., Nicholas Babchuk, and David R. Johnson, "Voluntary Associations and Minority Status: A Comparative Analysis of Anglo, Black, and Mexican Americans," *American Sociological Review* 38 (1973): 637–646; and J. Miller McPherson, "Correlates of Social Participation: A Comparison of the Ethnic Community and Compensatory Theories," *The Sociological Quarterly* 18 (1977): 197–208. On organizational involvement among Mexican-Americans, see Garcia and Arce, "Political Orientations and Behaviors of Chicanos."

charitable involvement—both working for a charity and contributing to one.

Because they can work within a particular community, group-based organizations can play a significant role for minorities—especially where there are barriers to full and open interaction between the dominant ethnic group and minority groups. Thus, African-American or Latino organizations may be particularly significant for the provision of both services and opportunities to develop political skills and consciousness. In this connection, it is important to note that African-Americans are more likely to take part in such organizations than are Latinos. One in seven of the African-American respondents indicated affiliation with an organization specifically identified with their race or with civil rights. In contrast, only one in twenty of the Latinos indicated affiliation with a Latino-identified organization.[18]

In short, while Anglo-Whites and African-Americans are fairly similar in their secular, non-political participation, Latinos are considerably less active. In comparison to Latinos, African-Americans are not only more likely to be involved with non-political organizations, but they are more likely to be involved with organizations identified with their own race. As we shall see, this involvement in non-political organizations has implications for rates of political activity.

RELIGIOUS ACTIVITY

We have seen that, of the various kinds of voluntary activity, church involvement is the least stratified with respect to the representation of income groups. Affluent and poor are equally in-

---

18. Looking only at those with a non-political organizational affiliation, we find that 19 percent of the African-Americans with such an affiliation reported involvement in at least one that has a racial connection. The parallel figure for Latinos is 9 percent.

Among the more detailed questions we asked was an item about the racial or ethnic composition of the membership of the single organization with which respondents are most involved. A similar pattern emerges in relation to this question: 39 percent of the African-Americans reported that the membership of their most important organization is mostly or all Black; only 18 percent of the Latinos said that their organization is mostly or all Latino in membership.

Table 8.4 Religious Activity by Race or Ethnicity (percent active)

	Anglo-Whites	African-Americans	Latinos	Latino Citizens
Attend Church Services 2–3 Times a Month or More	48%	60%	53%	51%
Time to Church Activity	27	35	23	24
Church Contribution	63	72	59	58

volved. Similarly, it is not stratified by race or ethnicity. From the earliest days, the church was the only secondary institution available to African-Americans.[19] Since churches can play a significant role not only as spiritual and social institutions but also in generating political involvement, their role for African-Americans and Latinos in the United States, therefore, bears examination.

The data on religious involvement are quite different from those on participation in more secular activities. Table 8.4 presents data on attendance at church services; time spent on social, educational, or charitable activities within a church; and contributions of funds to a church.[20] In contrast to most of the other comparisons we have made, Anglo-Whites are not the most active group. By all three measures of religious involvement, African-Americans are the most active. The pattern for Latinos is especially interesting. Although they attend church less frequently than do African-Americans, their church attendance exceeds that of Anglo-Whites.

19. There is extensive literature on the history of the Black churches. For a discussion and bibliographical references, see David W. Wills, "Beyond Commonality and Plurality: Persistent Racial Polarity in American Religion and Politics," in *Religion and American Politics: From the Colonial Period to the 1980s,* ed. Mark A. Noll (New York: Oxford University Press, 1990), chap. 9. Although some dispute the role of the Black churches, arguing that their otherworldliness reduces political engagement, most agree that they are a powerful political force among blacks. See Hart M. Nelsen and Anne Kusener Nelsen, *Black Church in the Sixties* (Lexington, Ky.: University of Kentucky Press, 1975), p. 1. For the role of the Black church under slavery, see John Hope Franklin, *From Slavery to Freedom: A History of Negro Americans,* 3rd ed. (New York: Knopf, 1969), pp. 199, 310, 404–405.

20. Our measure of being a regular church attender is attending two to three times a month or more. Alternative definitions produce different numbers of church attenders but do not affect the general differences found among the groups.

However, Latinos are the least likely to take part when it comes to church activities beyond attendance at services. The pattern for Latinos is, thus, a puzzling one: a high level of church attendance coupled with a lower level of involvement in auxiliary church activities.

Part of the explanation for this pattern seems to lie in the fact that Latinos are much more likely than African-Americans or Anglo-Whites to be Catholic rather than Protestant.[21] Protestant and Catholic churches differ—and Protestant denominations differ among themselves—along several dimensions that would seem to be relevant for the extent of lay participation in church matters: Protestant congregations tend, on average, to be smaller; most Protestant denominations allow for greater lay participation in the liturgy; and most Protestant denominations are organized on a congregational rather than a hierarchical basis. Table 8.5 shows that the average Protestant is a bit less likely than the average Catholic to attend church regularly but is much more likely to engage in church-based activities.[22] The pattern holds, in general,

---

21. In our sample, 25 percent of the Latino respondents are Protestant and 66 percent are Catholic; 85 percent of the African-Americans are Protestant and 7 percent are Catholic; 62 percent of the Anglo-White respondents are Protestant and 26 percent are Catholic.

Interestingly, while Latinos are more likely than Anglo-Whites to attend church services frequently, they are slightly less likely than Anglo-Whites to be a member of a local church (or to attend services regularly in the same congregation or parish). However, this is true for Latino Catholics only. Among Latinos, 74 percent of the Protestants, as opposed to 67 percent of the Catholics, belong to a local church. For Anglo-Whites, this slight relationship is reversed: 73 percent of the Protestants and 77 percent of the Catholics are members of a local church. Church membership for the small number of African-American Catholics is analogous to that for Anglo-White Catholics. African-American Protestants, 82 percent of whom belong to a local church, have the highest levels of church membership. These data suggest that there may be some substance to the stereotype that the Catholic Church in America relates less well to the most recent Catholic immigrants than it does to more established Catholic groups. We were concerned that this might be more a function of the different meaning of "membership" among Catholics and Protestants, with Protestants being more likely to join a particular congregation, while Catholic affiliation with a particular congregation is defined by the parish in which they live. For this reason, our definition of "membership" includes individuals who, even if not claiming to be members, regularly worship in the same church.

22. This relationship holds for all Protestants and Catholics regardless of their church membership or attendance as well as for members and regular church attenders. The differences between Protestant and Catholic congregations were probably even more pronounced a generation ago. Although Catholic parishes remain, on average, substantially larger than Protestant congregations, among the important consequences of Vatican II has

Table 8.5 Religious Attendance and Activity in Church by Denomination and Race or Ethnicity

	Percent Regular Attenders[a,b] (All)	Percent Active[c]		Mean Hours of Church Activity[a]	
		All	Members[d]	All	Attenders[b]
Protestants	56	35	63	1.6	2.8
Catholics	59	20	32	.8	1.3
Anglo-Whites					
Protestants	53	35	50	1.6	2.8
Catholics	59	21	35	.8	1.2
African-Americans					
Protestants	69	39	59	2.1	2.8
Catholics	53	13	23	.8	1.6
Latinos					
Protestants	68	34	65	2.1	3.1
Catholics	63	19	32	1.0	1.5

a. Screener data.
b. Regular church attendance: 2–3 times a month or more.
c. Church activity: 2 hours a month or more.
d. Member of local congregation or regular attender in the same congregation.

for the separate race and ethnic groups. Since there are relatively few black Catholics in the follow-up sample (unweighted N = 33), where possible, we report data from the screener, which had a much larger data base of African-American Catholics (N = 87).[23] The data, shown in the two right-hand columns, indicate the number of hours spent each week on educational, social, or charitable activities in the church—beyond attendance at religious services.[24] In all three groups, Protestants are much more active in their

been increased lay participation both in the liturgy and in parish governance through parish councils. The effects of Vatican II have, presumably, been reinforced by enhanced educational levels among Catholic parishioners and the decrease in priestly vocations. See Joseph Gremillion and David C. Leege, "Post-Vatican II Parish Life in the United States: Review and Preview," *Notre Dame Study of Catholic Parish Life,* Report No. 15, 1989. Whether the unambiguous distinction between churchgoing Protestants and Catholics with respect to the number of hours they spend on other activities associated with their churches will disappear in the future we cannot speculate.

23. The data from the screener are used only when we look at religion and at race or ethnicity at the same time. Thus, the data in Table 8.4 are from the follow-up study. For this reason, there may be some apparent discrepancy between the data in Tables 8.4 and 8.5.

24. We did not ask about membership in a local church on the short screener. Hence,

churches than are Catholics. On average, the Protestant church-goer devotes more than twice as many hours each week to non-religious activities in church than does the average Catholic.[25] The lower level of Latinos' involvement in church-based educational, charitable, or social activities—despite their high rates of church attendance—appears, thus, to derive from the fact that they are disproportionately Catholic. Controlling for religious preference, Latinos are no less active than the other two groups. As we shall see in subsequent chapters, this distinction has important political implications.

What Do They Say?

The difference in participation rates among Anglo-Whites, African-Americans, and Latinos gains added significance if we look at the messages that accompany their activity. As before, we report data on the subject matter associated with "information-rich" activities—that is, those activities in which an explicit message can be sent: contacting, protesting, campaign work or contributions accompanied by a communication, informal community activity, and voluntary service on a local board.

Table 8.6, which shows the proportion of all issue-based activity for which the respondent mentioned, among other things, a particular set of policy concerns, compares the issue concerns of the three groups.[26] The data make clear both that the political activity of each group is animated by a range of issues and that there is considerable overlap in the issue concerns of Latinos, African-

---

we report the data for regular church attenders (those who attend two to three times a month or more).

25. Gremillion and Leege ("Post-Vatican Parish Life") report somewhat higher levels of participation in church activities among Catholics. Among regular church attenders, we find that 32 percent of Catholics report giving one hour or more a week to church activities (compared with 63 percent among Protestants), while Gremillion and Leege find that 45 percent of their sample of Catholics report giving this much (more than 5 hours per month in their categorization). The difference may be due to different samples and definitions of church affiliation. Their sample consists of non-Latinos, and they use a sample of names of registered parishioners. Much also depends on question wording. The absolute level is less important than the clear differences we find between Catholics and Protestants using the same questions and the same definition of affiliation.

26. Thus, the act rather than the respondent is the unit of analysis. See Chapter 3 for a discussion of this measure and the components of each of the policy categories.

Table 8.6 What Latinos, African-Americans, and Anglo-Whites Say: Issue-Based Political Activity (information-rich activities only)[a]

	Anglo-Whites	African-Americans	Latinos
Proportion of Issue-Based Activity Animated by Concern about:			
Basic Human Needs	9%	13%	13%
Taxes	7	3	3
Economic Issues (except taxes)	6	2	1
Abortion	9	3	3
Social Issues (except abortion)	2	2	2
Education	11	17	19
Children or youth (except education)	5	12	10
Environment	10	1	9
Crime or drugs	7	25	16
International	3	1	4
Civil rights or minorities	1	6	6
Number of respondents[b]	2,074	233	141
Number of issue-based acts[b]	1,341	129	50

a. Information-rich acts are those in which an explicit message can be sent to policymakers: contacting, protesting, campaign work or contributions accompanied by a communication, informal community activity, or voluntary service on a local board. The numbers in the cells represent the proportion of such acts having identifiable issue content for which there was a reference to the particular issue.

b. Numbers shown are the weighted numbers of cases and issue-based acts. See Appendix A for information about sample.

Americans, and Anglo-Whites. There are, however, some quite important differences. Anglo-White respondents are more likely to have focused on taxes and other economic issues. They are also more likely to mention abortion. In contrast to Anglo-Whites, the two minority groups are more concerned with issues of basic human needs, education and youth, and, especially, crime and drugs. Clearly, the distribution of issue concerns of activist African-Americans and Latinos reflects the real circumstances of their lives.

The particular emphasis upon issues of crime, violence, and drugs by African-Americans and Latinos deserves mention. Among candidates and public officials, these issues have been the traditional bailiwick of Anglo-White conservatives. In contrast, the minority and Anglo-White liberal politicians who represent African-American and Latino constituencies have often kept issues like drug use and crime at arm's length. It is noteworthy how importantly these issues figure on the agenda of concerns brought to politics by the citizen activists whose communities are most affected by them. Reading the actual comments of those concerned about crime, public safety, and drugs, it is impossible to distinguish the race or ethnicity of the respondent. Within each group a range of themes was mentioned. However, more systematic content analysis reveals that Blacks and Latinos were somewhat more likely than Anglo-Whites to mention drugs and to refer to their own neighborhoods or communities in discussing these issues. Anglo-Whites were somewhat more likely to discuss a neighborhood effort to set up a crime watch.

We were also interested in the extent to which the concerns associated with political activity involved civil rights issues. We include under this rubric both general references to "civil rights," "racial issues," or "discrimination" and specific concerns—for example, getting translators for Spanish-speaking prison inmates, hiring more minority teachers in the school system, establishing Martin Luther King's birthday as a state holiday, or opening up the all-Anglo cheerleading squad to Hispanics in a majority-Mexican-American high school. Table 8.6 indicates that 6 percent of the information-rich, issue-based activity of both African-Americans and Latinos involved reference to such issues. These issues figure in a very small portion, less than 1 percent, of the participation of Whites. Because African-Americans and Latinos constitute only a fraction of the population, and because African-Americans are somewhat, and Latinos are substantially, less likely to participate than are Anglo-Whites, only an extremely small proportion of the messages communicated through the medium of information-rich participation concerns policy matters germane to civil rights or racial or ethnic minorities. Moreover, public officials hear as much about these matters from Anglo-Whites as from African-Americans and Latinos combined. In terms of content, since some of the references to civil rights issues by Anglo-Whites consisted of negative views of affirmative action, what public officials hear from Anglo-Whites is more mixed than what they hear from either of the other groups.

In addition, for each codeable verbatim we noted whether there was a reference to African-Americans or Latinos—apart from mention of civil rights or a minority-related *policy* issue. For example, several respondents—not all of them African-American—discussed wanting "to elect New York's first Black mayor" in connection with campaign work; a Latino respondent mentioned "Hispanic dropouts" in the context of informal community activity on school issues. When these references are included in the tally, the proportion of codeable, information-rich activity that involves reference to minorities or to a particular group is raised to 9 percent for African-Americans and 10 percent for Latinos. (For Anglo-Whites, the results are unchanged.)

Although concerns about civil rights issues are behind only a tiny fraction of the issue-based activity of Anglo-Whites, they weigh relatively heavily in whatever policymakers hear on the subject. Thus, we should probe further. When we considered the messages sent to public officials about issues of basic human needs in Chapter 7, we scrutinized what was said by advantaged respondents—for whom concerns about issues like health, poverty, and housing are much less likely to arise from their own personal circumstances—and differentiated liberals and conservatives on economic issues. In this case, we can distinguish Anglo-Whites in terms of their responses to the two seven-point attitude items to which we referred earlier, asking whether the government should make efforts to assist Blacks (or Hispanics) or whether the government should give no special help to Blacks (or Hispanics) because they should help themselves.[27] To the extent that concerns

---

27. We should note that opinion on these questions was not completely unanimous among African-Americans and Latinos and that it could easily be argued that those who urged members of minority groups to help themselves are no less committed to their well-being. The distribution of opinion on the seven-point scales is as follows:

		Anglo-Whites	African-Americans	Latinos
Government help Blacks	1–3	18%	40%	35%
	4	31	28	30
Blacks help themselves	5–7	51	32	35
		100%	100%	100%

about civil rights or minority group issues figure at all in the participation of Anglo-Whites, they figure more importantly in the activity of those who expressed support for greater government efforts on behalf of Blacks or Hispanics than in the activity of those who suggested that they should help themselves. However, since many more Anglo-Whites urge self-reliance for minorities than support enhanced government assistance for Blacks or Hispanics, public officials receive a roughly equal number of messages on these subjects from Anglo-Whites who support and from Anglo-Whites who oppose government help for minorities.

What is the actual content of these messages? Considering the direction of issue concerns, the comments of advocates of greater government efforts to aid minorities were in every case consistent with the opinion expressed on the attitude scale.[28] The comments of those who do not support special efforts for minorities were divided: some—such as the Anglo-White who reported attending a counter-demonstration against the Ku Klux Klan—took positions on behalf of African-Americans or Latinos; others opposed affirmative action to assist minorities—either on the basis of personal experience or as an ideological issue.

Gender and Participation

We conclude our descriptive account of what, and from whom, the government hears by considering the last in a triad of politically relevant demographic characteristics, gender. Like African-Americans, women were long deprived of the basic rights and privileges of citizenship. In addition, historical and contemporary movements on behalf of women have flourished at the same time as, and learned important lessons from, movements on behalf of

		Anglo-Whites	African-Americans	Latinos
Government help Hispanics	1–3	15%	36%	42%
	4	31	32	30
Hispanics help themselves	5–7	54	32	28
		100%	100%	100%

28. Anglo-Whites often phrased their comments in general terms, discussing "civil rights," "race relations," or "minorities." To the extent that they mentioned specific groups, they referred to Blacks, but said almost nothing about Latinos.

African-Americans. However, women have never been as politically distinctive or as politically cohesive as Blacks. There is no unanimity of opinion among women on policy issues—even those issues such as abortion or the Equal Rights Amendment that affect them differentially. Instead, women's attitudes are divided along more or less the same lines as men's. Indeed, to the extent that there are opinion differences between the sexes, they tend to be more pronounced on issues like war and the use of violence than on what are often referred to as "women's issues."[29]

Early studies of the behavior of citizens in American politics discovered a gender gap in citizen participation, with men more, and women less, likely to take part in political life.[30] These findings soon came in for criticism on several grounds, among them that the disparity between men and women in political activity was overstated, exaggerating the importance of small—and, sometimes, not statistically significant—differences.[31]

29. For examples of the extensive literature on the differences between women and men in attitudes and vote choices, see, for example, Sandra Baxter and Marjorie Lansing, *Women and Politics: The Visible Majority,* rev. ed. (Ann Arbor: University of Michigan Press, 1983), chaps. 3–4; Keith T. Poole and L. Harmon Zeigler, *Women, Public Opinion and Politics: The Changing Political Attitudes of American Women* (New York: Longman, 1985), chaps. 2–3; Ethel Klein, "The Gender Gap: Different Issues, Different Answers," *Brookings Review* 3 (1985): 33–37; Robert Y. Shapiro and Harprett Mahajan, "Gender Differences in Political Preferences: A Summary of Trends from the 1960s to the 1980s," *Public Opinion Quarterly* 50 (1986): 42–61; and the essays in *The Politics of the Gender Gap: The Social Construction of Political Influence,* ed. Carol M. Mueller (Newbury Park, Calif.: Sage Publications, 1988).

30. See, for example, Angus Campbell, Philip E. Converse, Warren E. Miller, and Donald E. Stokes, *The American Voter* (New York: John Wiley and Sons, 1960), pp. 483–493; Maurice Duverger, *The Political Role of Women* (New York: UNESCO, 1955); Robert Edwards Lane, *Political Life: Why People Get Involved in Politics* (Glencoe, Ill.: The Free Press, 1959), pp. 208, 213, 354–355. In addition to the investigations of adult political behavior were socialization studies that considered gender differences in children's political orientations. See, for example, Fred I. Greenstein, *Children and Politics* (New Haven: Yale University Press, 1965), chap. 6; Robert D. Hess and Judith V. Torney, *The Development of Political Attitudes in Children* (Chicago: Aldine, 1967), chap. 8; and Dean Jaros, *Socialization to Politics* (New York: Praeger, 1973), pp. 44–45, 81–82.

31. There are numerous assessments of this literature. See, for example, Susan Bourque and Jean Grossholtz, "Politics as an Unnatural Practice: Political Science Looks at Female Participation," *Politics and Society* 4 (1974): 255–266; Murray Goot and Elizabeth Reid, *Women and Voting Studies: Mindless Matrons or Sexist Scientism?* (Beverly Hills: Sage Publications, 1975); Susan Welch, "Women as Political Animals? A Test of Some Explanations for Male-Female Political Participation Differences," *American Journal of Political*

A second line of criticism took issue with the very definition of what constitutes political activity, holding that the conceptualization of political activity was too narrow to encompass the kinds of activity in which many women specialized. Drawing on a rich body of historical literature demonstrating women's long-neglected contributions to organizational and charitable activity, critics argued that overemphasis upon voting and other electoral activities leads to the disregard of alternative modes of participation—for example, organizational, protest, and grassroots community activity—in which women have always taken part.[32] The necessary corrective is an understanding of political participation that would encompass modes of involvement less formal, less conventional, and less nationally centered than those documented in many surveys.[33] Unfortunately, systematic data have not been available to

---

Science 21 (1977): 712–714; and Vicky Randall, *Women and Politics: An International Perspective*, 2nd ed. (Chicago: University of Chicago Press, 1987), chap. 2. For a more complete discussion of the criticisms of the early studies of gender differences in citizen participation and additional bibliographical references, see Kay Lehman Schlozman, Nancy Burns, and Sidney Verba, "Gender and the Pathways to Participation: The Role of Resources," *Journal of Politics* 56 (1994): 963–990.

32. See, for example, Gerda Lerner, *The Majority Finds Its Past: Placing Women in History* (New York: Oxford University Press, 1979); Anne Firor Scott, *Making the Invisible Woman Visible* (Urbana: University of Illinois Press, 1984); Anne Firor Scott, "Most Invisible of All: Black Women's Voluntary Associations," *The Journal of Southern History* 56 (1990): 3–22; Anne Firor Scott, *Natural Allies: Women's Associations in American History* (Urbana: University of Illinois Press, 1991); Paula Baker, "The Domestication of Politics: Women and American Political Society, 1780–1920," *American Historical Review* 89 (1984): 620–647; Paula Giddings, *When and Where I Enter: The Impact of Black Women on Race and Sex in America* (New York: W. Morrow, 1984); Nancy F. Cott, "Across the Great Divide: Women in Politics before and after 1920," in *Women, Politics and Change*, ed. Patricia Gurin and Louise A. Tilly (New York: Russell Sage Foundation, 1990), pp. 153–176.

33. This general point is made by many authors. For an especially articulate and concrete exposition of this perspective, see Randall, *Women and Politics*, pp. 50ff. Some critics take the point further, arguing that our conception of politics should be broadened in either of two ways: to include all collective involvements that influence the life of the community, even those charitable and organizational activities that do not touch upon what is traditionally called the "public sector"; or to include all private relationships—for example, bosses and employees—in which power is exercised. Although historians are more likely than political scientists to call for a radical expansion of the term "political" to arenas of human action and relationship that have ordinarily not entailed government influence or involvement, scholars from both disciplines have made this argument. Among the many examples, see Kay Boals, "The Politics of Male-Female Relations: Political Science Looks at Female Participation," *Signs* 1 (1975): 171–175; and Baker, "The Domestication of

probe the extent of the gender gap for a wide range of activities. In this section we use our data to fill this gap and examine gender differences in who is active in what ways.

THE GENDER GAP IN POLITICAL ACTIVITY

We begin by using the overall scale of political participation to assess the breadth of the gender gap in political activity. This summary measure confirms the general impression that men are more active than women. However, the difference is quite small: men average 2.3 acts and women 2.0. This gap is roughly similar in magnitude to the difference in activity between Anglo-Whites and African-Americans and considerably narrower than that separating Latinos from Anglo-Whites or the affluent from the poor. To put it in perspective, the male-female difference of 0.3 political acts is about one-seventh the size of the participatory difference between a high school and a college graduate.

Figure 8.4 disaggregates these data for specific political acts. For each kind of activity except attending protests, there is a consistent gender difference with women less active than men. The differences for voting, working in a campaign, serving on a local board, or attending a protest are statistically insignificant.[34] Statistically significant gender differences are found in relation to making a campaign contribution, working informally in the community, contacting an official, and affiliation with a political organization—

Politics," pp. 646–647. It may be that the reason mainstream political science has developed a reputation for slighting non-electoral forms of citizen participation is that the single best source of ongoing data is the biennial National Election Study, which—because it is anchored in national elections—naturally emphasizes voting and other forms of electoral participation.

34. As in all surveys, the figures for voter turnout are exaggerated. Data from polls taken just after the election, for example, show the opposite result with respect to gender: for example, the 1990 *Statistical Abstract* gives figures from a large government-sponsored survey that 56.4 percent of men and 58.3 percent of women reported going to the polls in 1988. With respect to level of turnout, these figures are still inflated, but are closer to the actual turnout than the figures from our survey. With respect to gender difference, there is evidence from vote validation studies (Michael Traugott and John P. Katosh, "Response Validity in Surveys of Voting Behavior," *Public Opinion Quarterly* 43 [1979]: 359–377) that men are slightly more likely to misrepresent having gone to the polls than women are. Unfortunately, we have no analogous method of ascertaining the extent of, or gender bias in, overreporting for other activities.

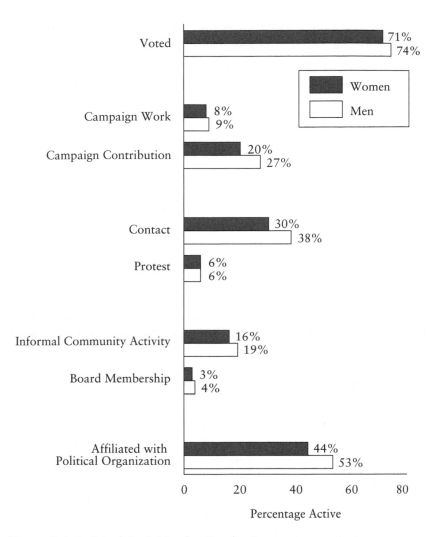

Figure 8.4 Political Activities by Gender (percentage active).

that is, membership in or contributions to organizations that take stands in politics. The differences are not very large in any case, but some of them may be of substantive significance.

Several findings emerge from Figure 8.4. If the percentage of citizens who engage in a particular political activity is a measure of how hard or easy it is, the size of the gender gap is not related to the difficulty of the act. Furthermore, gender differences do not disappear when we expand the scope of participation beyond electoral participation. The exception to the gender gap in participation is protesting; women are as likely to attend a protest as men. The data suggest that women participate a bit less than men in community activity. Contrary to what might be expected, there is less gender difference in the formal political activity of serving on a local government board than there is in more informal, ad hoc activities such as working with others in the community or getting involved in a political organization. The latter is an activity for which the not insubstantial male advantage is surprising, given some of the expectations in the literature. In short, then, the small to moderate differences between women and men persist—and, indeed, in some instances increase—even after we expand the scope of political participation.[35]

The data on organizations are particularly interesting. With respect to involvement in political organizations, the disparity between women and men is somewhat wider. Contrary to stereotype, women are slightly less likely than men to be affiliated with any organization, political or non-political: 82 percent of male and 77 percent of female respondents indicated involvement in an organization. We were curious about which of two processes is responsible for the wider gap for involvement in political organizations: do women and men join different kinds of organizations? or are men more likely than women to perceive as political more or less the same kinds of organizations? Data about affiliations with different kinds of organizations suggest that the former operates more strongly than the latter—that is, that men and women are involved in different kinds of organizations, rather than that women are insensitive to political cues—but they do not provide a definitive solution to this puzzle. With the exception of women's rights organizations (with which 6 percent of the women and 2 percent of the men reported affiliation), the categories for which

---

35. Interestingly, data not included in Figure 8.4 also call into question the notion that women are local specialists. Women are only slightly more likely than men to confine their political activity to sub-national politics: 53 percent of the women, as opposed to 49 percent of the men, who participated in any way beyond voting had no activity at the national level.

women were more likely than men to report affiliation were those in which a relatively small proportion of those affiliated (regardless of gender) reported that the organization takes stands in politics—for example, youth groups, religiously affiliated organizations, and literary, discussion, or study groups. Within any particular organizational category, there seems to be some tendency for men to be more likely to view their organizations as being political, but the gender differences are inconsistent both in magnitude and in direction.

One further way to examine this puzzle is to consider the members of the single organization in which sufficient respondents reported membership to justify further analysis, the American Association of Retired Persons (AARP). Reflecting the disproportionate number of women among the elderly, women were more likely than men to report affiliation with a senior citizens' organization, but, among those involved in a senior citizens' group, men were more likely than women to name the AARP, an organization that admits members as young as age 50. Among AARP members, there was virtually no gender difference in terms of the proportion who recognize that the AARP takes stands: 80 percent of male, and 78 percent of female, AARP members indicated that the organization takes political stands. Among those affiliated with senior citizens' groups other than the AARP, 40 percent of the men and 27 percent of the women indicated that the organization takes stands in politics, which suggests that it is differences in organizational choices rather than ability to perceive politics that is the source of the fact that men in senior citizens' groups are more likely to report that their organizations take stands on public issues.

VOLUNTARY ACTIVITY OUTSIDE POLITICS
When we consider voluntary activity in realms in which women have sometimes been thought to predominate—the non-political organizations, charities, and religious institutions outside politics as conventionally defined—the data show a different pattern. Figure 8.5 shows virtually no difference between women and men when it comes to voluntary participation in the secular domain outside politics in non-political organizations and charities. What is striking, however, is that the arena in which women are clearly

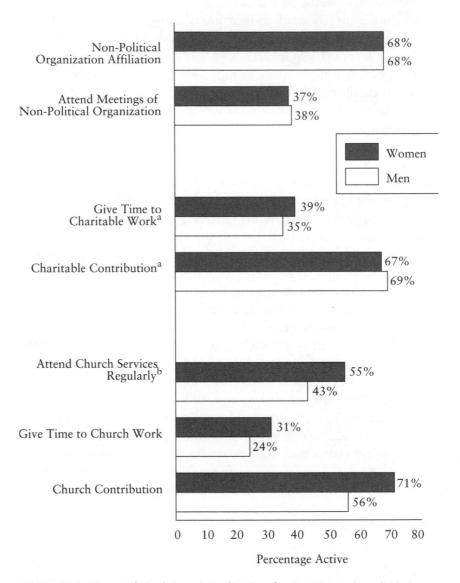

Figure 8.5 Non-Political Activities by Gender (percentage active).
a. Screener data.
b. Two or three times a month or more.

Table 8.7 Voluntary Contributions of Time and Money by Gender

	Women	Men
MEAN HOURS PER WEEK (among those who give some time)		
Political Campaigns	7.9	7.2
Charity	4.5	4.6
Church	3.1	3.0
MEAN DOLLARS PER YEAR (among those who give some money)		
Political Campaigns	$201	$285
Charity	$248	$321
Church	$588	$697

more active than men is one that is rarely mentioned in discussions of gender differences in participation: religious institutions. Not only are women more likely than men to go to services regularly, they are more likely to give time to educational, charitable, or social activities associated with their church or synagogue and to contribute money to their religion.

THE VOLUME OF ACTIVITY

What we have seen so far is a pattern of small differences, consistent in direction although not in size, with men more active than women with respect to political participation, rough gender equality when it comes to voluntary activity in the secular domain outside politics, and a feminine advantage in terms of activity in religious institutions. The data in Table 8.7, however, put a somewhat different gloss on these matters. This table shows the volume of activity—the average number of hours or dollars contributed in the political, charitable, and religious domains of voluntary participation—by women and men who are active in each realm. The striking contrast in these data is not among the three realms of voluntary activity, but between time and money as voluntary inputs. With respect to time, there is no consistent gender difference in the average number of hours dedicated to voluntary action among those who are active. Surprisingly, once active, men give on average as many hours to church activities as do women—even though women are more likely to be active in their churches. What is equally surprising is that women, once active, give more hours to politics than do men. With respect to money, however, the pattern is quite uniform. Among donors, men make larger contributions in each of the three domains—even though only in politics are they more likely than women to be donors. The patterns of difference here have less to do with whether an activity falls into the realm of conventional, formalized electoral participation and more to do with whether what is being given is money or time.[36]

WHAT DO THEY SAY?

As usual, we can investigate whether there are group differences in the nature of the concerns that animate political activity. We begin by considering the scope of the issues behind political activity, distinguishing among issues that affect the entire nation, those that affect the community, and those for which the impact is limited to the individual or the immediate family. As we have discussed, contacts to government officials may be limited to narrow personal concerns—in contrast to most participatory acts, for which the referent is usually broader. Given women's traditional role within the family as well as the particularistic orientation to politics that has been ascribed to them since the Greeks, women might be expected to bring to politics narrower, more personal or family concerns. In fact, however, this is not the case. Men and women who get in touch with public officials do not differ in their expression of personal or public concerns. Discussing their most recent contact, 22 percent of the men and 21 percent of the women indicated that the subject was a matter of particularized concern. Thirty-five percent of the female contactors indicated that the issue

---

36. Because men have, on average, higher family incomes than women do, the pattern is different when we consider the proportion of family income given to politics, charity, and church in the following table, which shows contributions as a percentage of family income:

	All Respondents		Contributors	
	Women	Men	Women	Men
Campaigns	.07%	.12%	.35%	.44%
Charity	.47%	.46%	.72%	.68%
Church	1.47%	1.00%	2.13%	1.83%

Table 8.8 What Men and Women Say: Issue-Based Political Activity (information-rich activities only)[a]

	Men	Women
Proportion of Issue-Based Activity Animated by Concern about:		
Basic Human Needs	9%	10%
Taxes	7	5
Economic Issues (except taxes)	6	4
Abortion	5	12
Social Issues (except abortion)	2	2
Education	9	15
Children or youth (except education)	5	6
Environment	9	9
Crime or drugs	8	9
International	4	2
Women	b	1
Number of respondents[c]	1,191	1,327
Number of issue-based acts	821	736

a. Information-rich acts are those in which an explicit message can be sent to policymakers: contacting, protesting, campaign work or contributions accompanied by a communication, informal community activity, or voluntary service on a local board. The numbers in the cells represent the proportion of such acts having identifiable issue content in which there was a reference to the particular issue.

b. Less than 1 percent.

c. Numbers shown are the weighted numbers of cases and issue-based acts. See Appendix A for information about sample.

affects the whole community and 25 percent that it affects the entire nation (or the whole world); the analogous figures for male contactors are 38 percent and 22 percent respectively.[37]

When it comes to the actual issues that animate activity, there is also more similarity than difference between women and men. Table 8.8 shows the proportion of information-rich, issue-based activity that arises from concern about various subjects. For both men and women, participation is about many things. The distribution is similar, though not identical, for the two groups. One

37. Interestingly, the men (36 percent) were slightly more likely than the women (31 percent) to indicate that they knew the government official with whom they got in touch before they made the contact.

gender difference is that concerns about education figure more importantly in the activity of women.

The second gender difference of note is that women are much more likely than men to refer to abortion. Abortion figures twice as importantly in the issue-based activity of women than of men, with the result that two-thirds of what public officials hear on the subject comes from women. Using a seven-point attitude scale to differentiate activists who are pro-life from those who are pro-choice, we find that the public as a whole leans in a pro-choice direction and that men are slightly more pro-choice than women.[38] Abortion figures more importantly in the activity of those who are pro-life than of those who are pro-choice: abortion was mentioned in connection with 19 percent of the information-rich, issue-based activity of pro-life women and 10 percent of the activity of pro-life men; in contrast, abortion was mentioned in 9 percent of the activity of pro-choice women and 4 percent of the activity of pro-choice men. Given the extent to which those who are pro-life concentrate a significant share of their participatory input on the issue of abortion, the net effect is that a majority of what public officials hear on the subject of abortion carries a pro-life message—even though all respondents, and political participants in particular, were more likely to express pro-choice sentiments in response to the attitude question.

Apart from the issue of abortion, women's issues—for example, sexual harassment or discrimination against women—are mentioned extremely rarely as the subject matter of activity. Women discussed these issues in connection with just under 1 percent of their information-rich, issue-based activity, and men did so even less frequently. All the messages on the subject came from respon-

---

38. The data are as follows:

A woman should always be able to obtain an abortion as a matter of choice.				By law abortion should never be permitted.		
	1	2	3	4	5	6	7
Men	40%	11	9	13	6	10	10
Women	36%	9	8	12	7	9	19

dents who indicated, in response to an attitude question, that the government should be making greater efforts to help women. Still, what is most apparent is not that the government hears more from women than from men about women's issues or that the content of the messages is uniformly in support of equality between the sexes, but rather that public officials hear so little on the subject. Clearly, these results would have been different had the data been collected fifteen years earlier when there was widespread public contention over the ERA. Still, it is noteworthy how little space on the public's agenda these issues occupy.

Conclusion

This chapter has continued the intellectual project of the preceding one—to map the demography of from whom, and what, the government hears by focusing on two sets of characteristics of obvious political relevance: race or ethnicity and gender. Much of what we have found follows the lines established when we considered economic inequality. Among activist publics, representativeness in terms of opinions as expressed in response to survey questions is not matched by descriptive demographic representation. When it comes to politically relevant groups defined by their race or ethnicity and their gender, African-Americans are slightly less active, and Latinos are considerably less active, than Anglo-Whites; women are slightly less active than men, with the overall gap of similar dimensions to that between Blacks and Whites. With respect to particular acts, the magnitude of the disparities in participation between men and women is sometimes surprising and contrary to what might have been expected.

We also compared the activists in these groups with the group as a whole to see how well the former represent the views and the needs of the latter. Both African-American and Latino activists differ from the group as a whole. They tend to be less supportive of government help for their group and tend to be less in need of such help. In this way, they present a picture that obscures the distinctive policy positions and needs of their group. This fact is especially significant for Latinos: the activists among them are decidedly less supportive of government programs to help Latinos and less in need of such programs. When this distortion of the actual position of Latinos by their activists is added to the distortion that arises from the low level of Latino activity, Latinos turn out to be rather badly represented through the participatory system.

One regularity that has emerged over and over is that, because the size of financial contributions can vary so dramatically and because the wherewithal to make donations is so unevenly distributed, the bias in participatory input is particularly pronounced with respect to money-based activity. The proportion of contacts, protests, hours devoted to campaign work, or, especially, votes coming from different income groups, from African-Americans, Latinos, or Anglo-Whites, or from men or women reflects the demographic composition of the population less inaccurately than does the proportion of dollars coming from each of these groups.

Another consistent finding is that of the arenas of voluntary activity, politics—the supposedly level playing field on which citizens compete as equals—is the one for which participatory input is most skewed in demographic terms. Activity in the secular and religious domains outside politics is much less biased in the direction of Anglo-Whites and men. In fact, African-Americans are more likely than Anglo-Whites, and women are more likely than men, to attend religious services and to be involved in educational, social, or charitable activities associated with their churches. Latinos do attend church but are less active than African-Americans or Anglo-Whites with respect to ancillary activities associated with their churches, a function of the fact that they are overwhelmingly Catholic and Catholics, regardless of race or ethnicity, are less likely to spend time on church-based activity. Even the skewing in financial contributions is less pronounced for charities and churches than it is for politics.

When we analyzed the issue bundles behind political activity, what emerged most notably was the diversity of the issues that animate participation. Every group we considered has an agenda of diverse concerns. In addition, although there were important differences among groups in terms of the priority given to particular issues, there was a remarkable amount of overlap across groups in the issues mentioned in connection with information-rich activity.

What the government hears on any particular subject is a function of the relative size of the politically relevant groups; the division of opinion within them; their differing levels of activity; and the relative weight carried by the issue in their bundles of issue concerns. As shown in this chapter and the preceding one, these variables interact in complex ways to influence the amount and the mix of communications on any topic. For example, with respect to issues concerning basic human needs, the disadvantaged are hardly a small group, and what they say on the subject is, although often grounded in their own particular circumstances, uniformly supportive of greater government efforts in meeting human service needs. However, for reasons that will be explored in subsequent chapters, the disadvantaged are not active in politics. In contrast, advantaged citizens participate at higher levels. Although they do not place especially high priority on issues of basic human needs, through their participation they actually send more messages on the subject than do the disadvantaged—messages that include many opposing government aid to the needy.

The pattern for issues having to do with civil rights and the status of minorities has somewhat similar contours. Concerns about these matters figure much more importantly in the activity of Latinos and African-Americans than in the activity of Anglo-Whites. However, in comparison to the Anglo-White majority, these are small groups and Latinos, in particular, are not especially active. The net effect is that messages about civil rights and race are as likely to come from Anglo-Whites as from African-Americans or Latinos. In terms of content, what public officials hear from Anglo-Whites is more mixed than what they hear from either of the other groups. This is a good example of an issue discussed in Chapter 6, the potentially contrary effects of the size of a group and the intensity of its concern with an issue.

Communications about analogous issues concerning women conform to a different pattern. In contrast to the racial or ethnic groups we examined, women and men are groups of nearly equal size and the gap in their overall rates of political participation is not especially large. With respect to content, the messages about women are not mixed. However, because women's issues carry so little weight on the agenda of either men or women, public officials hear very little on the subject from either men or women.

What is transmitted to government officials about abortion is characterized by still another pattern. Here the relevant groups are not simply men and women but also the opposing attitude groups. In comparison with men, women—whether pro-life or pro-choice—tend to place higher priority on abortion in the bundle of issue concerns that animate participation. Although those who express pro-choice opinions in response to an attitude question are relatively participant, the abortion issue figures much more importantly in the activity of those who are pro-life. The upshot is that, even though the population leans in a distinctly pro-choice direction in its attitudes and even though those expressing pro-choice opinions are not inactive, the government hears more about abortion from the minority that is pro-life.

In short, then, in thinking about participant publics, it is critical to inquire not only about who takes part in what ways and what their views are, but also to consider how much they do and what they actually say when they take part.

III

The Civic Voluntarism Model

Having described how participation works to represent the public, we turn to explaining why the process works as it does. Our purpose is to show how a series of participatory factors lead to political activity.

Chapter 9 provides a theoretical introduction, presenting an explanatory model of political activity—the Civic Voluntarism Model—that rests on three factors: resources, psychological engagement with politics, and access to networks through which individuals can be recruited to political life. In Chapters 10 and 11 we look closely at the main resources for political action, considering what they are, where they come from, and who has them. Chapter 10 treats money and time. Chapter 11 deals with civic skills, paying particular attention to the organizational and communications skills developed in the non-political institutional domains of adult life.

In Chapter 12 we begin the discussion of the Civic Voluntarism Model using the first two participatory factors, resources and psychological engagement with politics. We test models predicting overall activity in politics as well as particular kinds of activity. We demonstrate the importance of resources and political engagement, and show that various modes of political participation have distinctive configurations of participatory factors. Chapter 13 adds the third factor—recruitment to politics in institutions—to the explanation based on resources and engagement.

Chapter 14 adds a final piece to the model, showing how issue engagements—commitments that grow out of having a stake in some policy outcome or intense views on some issue—can raise levels of activity beyond what would have been expected on the basis of the participatory factors already considered. We use as examples the participation generated by having a stake in what the government does by virtue of having children in school or receiving means-tested government benefits, as well as the participation generated by having strong opinions on the subject of abortion.

In Chapter 15 we put together the multiple pieces of the puzzle of the participatory process. We trace the process back a generation, demonstrating how parental educational level and parental involvement in politics influence the various factors that predispose an individual to take part in politics. In addition, we consider how educational attainment ramifies through the process, affecting almost every factor—for example, income, political interest, and the exercise of adult civic skills—that explains participation.

9

Explaining Participation: Introductory Considerations

We now embark on one of the central components of our intellectual project—to understand what explains participation. We investigate why some people take part in politics and others do not and probe how activists choose particular modes of participation as the vehicles for their involvement.

Why People Participate: An Overview of Participatory Factors

We focus on three factors to account for political activity. We suggested earlier that one helpful way to understand the three factors is to invert the usual question and ask instead why people do *not* become political activists. Three answers come to mind: because they can't; because they don't want to; or because nobody asked. In other words, people may be inactive because they lack *resources,* because they lack psychological *engagement* with politics, or because they are outside of the *recruitment* networks that bring people into politics. Our analysis of the sources of political participation will focus on all three factors—resources, engagement, and recruitment—which we combine into what we label the Civic Voluntarism Model.[1]

---

1. In contrast to labels such as the "SES model" or the "rational choice model," the

All three components of the model are important. However, we place greater emphasis on the resources that facilitate participation and on the variety of psychological predispositions toward politics that we label "political engagement" than on political recruitment. Recruitment to political activity—being asked to take part—plays an important role, but participation can, and does, take place in the absence of specific requests for activity. In contrast, it is hard to imagine activity without at least a modicum of resources and some political engagement. With respect to resources and engagement, for several reasons we place greater stress on the former. First, we can measure resources with greater reliability and validity than we can measure the other factors. Second, the causal priority of resources is easier to establish. Third, a theoretical model based on resources is more interpretable. And, last, a resource-based model has significant substantive relevance for American politics. We shall explicate these reasons further as we develop our model.

In our analysis, we consider not only overall participation but particular political acts as well. As will become clear, forms of political participation vary in terms of the explanatory factors that matter most. In particular, the requirements for activities that demand inputs of money are quite different from the requirements for those that demand inputs of time.

RESOURCES

The literature on participation refers to a heterogeneous set of factors—ranging from such aspects of social position as a high level of education or income to such psychological predispositions as a sense of political efficacy or group solidarity—as resources for political activity. In the Civic Voluntarism Model, we define resources more concretely and treat their relationship to participation more comprehensively, probing their origins and investigating how they operate to facilitate participation.[2] Our approach distin-

---

Civic Voluntarism Model is not very descriptive. However, we deliberately chose an appellation that is non-restrictive in order to accommodate the range of factors that we bring to bear on the explanation of participation.

2. Our approach has strong affinities with resource mobilization theory in sociology. However, while we concentrate upon the resources available to individuals, the focus in sociological resource mobilization theory is upon social movement organizations. Still, in

guishes between the social positions from which resources derive—for instance, the respondent's family background or occupation—and the resources themselves. This allows a focus on the processes by which resources are acquired in the context of social positions.

We emphasize three kinds of resources: time, money, and civic skills. Many forms of political activity—campaign work, informal efforts to solve community problems, even voting—require time. Contributions to candidates or political causes, a mode of activism that has grown in relative importance in recent decades, obviously demand money. Finally, the citizen who possesses the requisite organizational and communications capacities—what we call civic skills—will find it less daunting to take part. Indeed, when inputs of time and money are coupled to civic skills, citizens become not only more likely to participate but also more likely to be effective when they do.

We trace the origin of these resources back to the fundamental involvements of individuals in major social institutions. Experiences in the family, at school, and in the workplace and citizens' voluntary affiliations with non-political associations and religious institutions—a function of their socially structured circumstances and the constrained choices they make about their lives—affect the stockpile of time, money, and civic skills available for politics. Depending on the nature of the institutions and the nature and extent of a citizen's involvement with them, families, schools, jobs, voluntary associations, and churches provide differential amounts of each of the three resources. Since the resources of time, money,

---

its discussion of the nature of the relevant resources and its emphasis upon the role of resources in movement success, resource mobilization theory is very relevant to our concerns. Charles Tilly suggests that land, labor, capital, and technical expertise are fundamental resources to movements in *From Mobilization to Revolution* (Reading, Mass.: Addison-Wesley, 1978), p. 69. John D. McCarthy and Mayer N. Zald refer to time and money and to "skills in lobbying, accounting, and fund raising" in "Resource Mobilization and Social Movements: A Partial Theory," *American Sociological Review* 82 (1977): 1224 and 1234.

In the literature on political participation, resources are implicit in the "socioeconomic" model of Sidney Verba and Norman H. Nie in *Participation in America: Political Democracy and Social Equality* (New York: Harper and Row, 1972). However, Verba and Nie neither explain what resources are involved and how they work to enhance participation nor delineate clearly between resources and other factors—for example, political efficacy or interest—that intervene between socioeconomic position and political activity.

and skills are differentially useful for various forms of activity, an explanation of political activity that is based on resources enables us to link basic life circumstances and choices to patterns of political activity.

ENGAGEMENT

The variety of psychological predispositions that we group under the rubric of engagement is the second component of the Civic Voluntarism Model. Measures of psychological engagement with politics have played a central role in theories of political participation. Scholars have emphasized such characteristics as the interest in politics that makes individuals want to take part; the sense of political efficacy that provides the subjective feeling that they can make a difference when they do; the civic values that imply that participation will be accompanied by the psychic gratification of having fulfilled a duty; the group consciousness that endows individuals with a sense that their fate is linked to that of others; identification with a political party; and commitment to specific policies that individuals would like to see implemented.[3]

As with resources, we shall show the way in which these various indicators of engagement relate to the non-political involvements of individuals—beginning with early experiences at home and at school and continuing into adult life. And, as with resources, we shall investigate how various measures of engagement are differentially relevant depending upon the particular mode of political activity.

RECRUITMENT

As shown in Chapter 5, requests for participation that come to individuals at work, in church, or in organizations—especially those that come from friends, relatives, or acquaintances—often

---

3. For descriptions of these various measures and how they are used in the literature, see, among others, Paul R. Abramson, *Political Attitudes in America: Formation and Change* (San Francisco: W. H. Freeman, 1983), p. 135; Steven Earl Bennett, *Apathy in America, 1960–1984: Causes and Consequences of Citizen Political Indifference* (Dobbs Ferry, N.Y.: Transnational Publishers, 1986); and Lester W. Milbrath and M. L. Goel, *Political Participation: How and Why Do People Get Involved in Politics?*, 2nd ed. (Chicago: Rand McNally, 1977).

lead to participation. Those who are asked in this way might have intended to act anyway, but the request was the triggering factor. Scholars have demonstrated the role of various institutions in mobilizing citizens to political action. In particular, they have remarked upon party efforts to get out the vote.[4] However, they have also paid attention to the role of religious institutions in mobilizing activity: both the Black churches and, more recently, White conservative Protestant churches.[5] Our data are unusual in that, as we have already seen in Chapter 5, we investigate the phenomenon across a variety of activities in several institutional settings and relate the characteristics of the respondent to the characteristics of the person making the request. We incorporate the attempts to recruit activists into our model of participation.

Resources, Engagement, and Recruitment as Explanations

No explanation of political activity will ever be complete. As with any attempt to explain human behavior, there are too many individual social and psychological characteristics, too many stimuli external to the individual, too many experiences, too many accidental events to permit us ever to explain fully the ways citizens take part in politics. Hence, we must satisfice, seeking an expla-

---

4. See, among others, Robert Huckfeldt and John Sprague, "Political Parties and Electoral Mobilization: Political Structure, Social Structure, and the Party Canvass," *American Political Science Review* 86 (1992): 70–86; and Steven J. Rosenstone and John Mark Hansen, *Mobilization, Participation, and Democracy in America* (New York: Macmillan, 1993), chap. 6. Cross-national studies are especially helpful in demonstrating the role of parties. See, for example, Sidney Verba, Norman H. Nie, and Jae-On Kim, *Participation and Political Equality: A Seven-Nation Comparison* (Cambridge: Cambridge University Press, 1978); and G. Bingham Powell, "American Voter Turnout in Comparative Perspective," *American Political Science Review* 80 (1986): 17–43.

5. Analyses that demonstrate the mobilizing role of churches include C. Eric Lincoln and Lawrence H. Mamiya, *The Black Church in the African-American Experience* (Durham, N.C.: Duke University Press, 1990); Kenneth D. Wald, *Religion and Politics in the United States*, 2nd ed. (Washington, D.C.: CQ Press, 1992); Clyde Wilcox, *God's Warriors: The Christian Right in Twentieth Century America* (Baltimore: Johns Hopkins University Press, 1992); Kenneth D. Wald, Lyman A. Kellstedt, and David C. Leege, "Church Involvement in Political Behavior," in David C. Leege and Lyman A. Kellstedt, eds., *Rediscovering the Religious Factor in American Politics* (Armonk, N.Y.: M. E. Sharpe, 1993), chap. 6; and Allan D. Hertzke, *Echoes of Discontent: Jesse Jackson, Pat Robertson, and the Resurgence of Populism* (Washington, D.C.: CQ Press, 1993).

nation that uses a limited a set of variables to account for as much as possible—in short, an explanation that is simultaneously powerful and parsimonious. However, we seek more than explanatory power. The social sciences are replete with models that are statistically powerful, but methodologically unsound or substantively trivial. Thus, we are concerned that any model we propose should be based on explanatory factors that are measurable, causally ordered, theoretically interpretable and interesting, and relevant to politics. Let us introduce each of these criteria.

Obviously, no empirical study, ours included, is sound if it is not based on *measurable factors*. We shall show that the explanatory factors included in our model of political activity are reliable (that is, they can be measured with a good deal of confidence) as well as valid (that is, they measure what we think they measure).

The factors we use to explain political activity should be *causally prior* to that activity. Causal direction is usually difficult to identify in the social sciences. Since our analysis is based on cross-sectional data, this is a particular problem for us. Although we shall make causal inferences, we shall attempt to be as clear as possible about the basis for any inference and the uncertainty surrounding it.

We also seek explanatory factors that are *theoretically interpretable and substantively interesting*. That a variable generates robust coefficients in predictive equations is insufficient. We seek factors for which the impact on participation is understandable within the framework of some more general model or theory of what leads to participation. We want, in other words, to know why a particular factor operates as it does. Furthermore, we prefer explanatory factors that tell us something interesting about participation. Interesting factors tend to be ones that are less proximate to that which is to be explained: it is, for instance, more interesting to explain an individual's vote on the basis of economic circumstances or family background than on the basis of candidate preference just before entering the voting booth. As we shall see, not all powerful predictors of participation are terribly interesting.

Finally, we seek an explanation that is *relevant to real issues of American politics*. As we have argued, political participation matters because it constitutes the voice of the people: it provides citizens with a means of communicating information about their preferences to those who govern and generating pressure to comply. The nature of that voice depends on the representativeness of the activists—whether and in what ways they differ from the population at large. To the extent that those differences hew to the fault lines of political cleavage, our explanation gains political resonance. If the factors that have an impact on the propensity of individuals to take part in politics are also related to the fundamental divisions that underlie American politics, not only do we improve our ability to predict activity but we enrich our understanding of the way in which participation shapes public outcomes in America. Thus, we will discuss both the factors that predispose citizens to be active and the way in which the distribution of these factors affects the ability of politically relevant groups defined by, for example, their race or income to add their voices to the American political debate.

We can evaluate the triad of explanatory factors on the basis of these criteria—measurement, direction of causality, theoretical interpretability and interest, and political relevance. The criteria all lead us in the direction of making resources the centerpiece of our explanatory model.

MEASUREMENT

Political motivations, such as interest in politics or a sense of efficacy or group consciousness, are more difficult than either resources or recruitment to measure in a reliable and valid manner. We depend—as survey researchers must—on the answers we receive to questions. Reports of motivations are difficult to compare reliably across individuals. The measurement of such resources as money, time, and skills rests on relatively concrete, objective questions. With respect to money, we asked about both total family income from all sources and the respondent's own earnings. In terms of time, we asked about the number of hours devoted to such activities as paid work, necessary tasks at home, and sleep. Although we know that there is error in these measures, the metrics used, dollars and hours, are unlikely to vary in meaning from respondent to respondent. Questions about skills are factual as well. We asked about actual experiences of exercising specific skills—for example, making a public presentation or organizing a meeting—rather than about subjective assessments of respondents' capacities.

Similarly, the measures of recruitment are fairly clear and concrete. As discussed in Chapter 5, we asked at separate points in the interview about mobilization attempts in three institutional settings—on the job, in church, in organizations. These measures are relatively unambiguous in meaning, and respondents had little difficulty in answering these questions or in describing the social characteristics of those making requests.

When it comes to the various indicators of political engagement, it is less clear just what is being measured. We know, more or less, what it means when a respondent has a salary of a particular size, has given a speech or presentation at work thus exercising a civic skill, or has been asked by a friend to go to a protest. We are less clear what it means when a respondent indicates being "interested in politics and public affairs" or agrees that "people like me have no say over what the government does."[6] Survey researchers that we are, we use measures of engagement such as political interest and efficacy, but we try to rest our argument on measures that have clearer face meaning and greater measurement solidity.

DIRECTION OF CAUSALITY

Direction of causality, always a problem in the social sciences, is particularly troublesome when it comes to both political engagement and recruitment. Political interest and a sense of political efficacy probably lead to political activity but, presumably, participating in politics also enhances political interest and cultivates feelings of political efficacy. Similarly, the direction of causality is problematic with respect to requests for political activity. This is particularly obvious in the case of mail and phone solicitations for

---

6. A particularly vexing problem is whether efficacy is a property of the respondent or of the system: that is, do responses to efficacy questions tell us something about the way a particular individual is constituted psychologically or something about the probability that the political system will be responsive? The distinction between internal and external efficacy helps to short-circuit this dilemma but does not eliminate all of the ambiguities of meaning. For a discussion of the literature on internal and external efficacy, see Abramson, *Political Attitudes in America*, chap. 8.

political contributions. The existence of an industry dedicated to this kind of fund raising attests to the fact that these impersonal appeals for financial support are sufficiently likely to bear fruit to justify the enterprise. However, it is well known that the quickest way to generate a mailbox full of additional solicitations is to respond favorably to the first one. Since fund raising is expensive, professionals in the field are careful to target likely prospects. Who is more likely to say yes to an appeal for money than a past donor? The same principle obtains for appeals made through personal, rather than electronic, networks. Surely activity results from requests for activity: when asked, especially when asked by a friend, people engage in political acts that they might not otherwise have undertaken. However, those who ask others to take part in politics have no incentive to waste their efforts on unlikely prospects. Once again, who is more likely to assent than a former participant?

In contrast, we are more comfortable inferring causal priority when it comes to a resource-centered explanation, for the institutional involvements out of which citizens acquire resources are, we believe, antecedent to political activity. In the absence of actual life histories collected over respondents' lifetimes, we cannot be absolutely certain that individuals make decisions about family, work, organizational involvements, or affiliations with religious institutions apart from and in advance of choices to take part politically. However, these seem to be plausible assumptions. Obviously, family background and early experiences in school, critical in their implications both for the development of resources for politics and for the future institutional commitments that permit the further enhancement of political resources, precede adult political activity. Even decisions about adult institutional involvements—the nature, direction, and extent of commitment to the workplace, religious institutions, or non-political organizations— would seem to be largely independent of political inclinations. They do not derive from voluntary political activity or, even, from anticipation of voluntary political activity.[7]

---

7. Huckfeldt and Sprague take a similar position in their careful review of the literature on contextual effects in politics. They express skepticism about "simple versions of the self-selection argument. To what extent do people choose their location in the social

It might be objected that, contrary to this line of reasoning, there are well-known—albeit infrequent—examples in which someone chose a line of work, married into a politically prominent family, or even worshipped in a particular church as the result of political ambitions. In these cases the purported causal direction is reversed, with politics dictating adult non-political affiliations. However, in all the cases of which we know, the political motivation is to run for office or to have a career in public life rather than to enhance opportunities as a *volunteer* political activist. Although it is surely possible for an aspiring political participant to make life choices on the basis of a desire for expanded volunteer opportunities, we believe that it would be a rare occurrence.

Affiliations with voluntary associations present a special challenge to this perspective. Involvements in organizations—which are much more likely than, say, church affiliations to be fluid—are often inspired by political concerns. For this reason, when discussing the development of resources for politics in non-political contexts, we confine our purview to involvements in organizations that do not take stands on public issues.[8] This permits us to make the assumption of causal priority even for voluntary organizations.

There is a final aspect to the problem of causal inference that we should consider: the possibility that there is some omitted variable that explains the relationship between experiences in non-political settings and political activity. One possible omitted variable might be a "taste" for social activities that affects all the measures we have, both the independent measures of involvement in non-political institutions and the dependent variable of political activity. However, as we shall see, it is not simply being affiliated—having a job, joining an organization, or attending religious serv-

---

structure? How many of us really choose our workplace colleagues, our coreligionists, our neighbors? To the extent that we are able to exercise control over our surroundings, do we use political criteria in exercising such choice? Or do we choose a job because it pays well? A church because our parents raised us in it? And then we take the politics that accompanies the choice." Robert Huckfeldt and John Sprague, "Citizens, Contexts, and Politics," in *Political Science: The State of the Discipline,* ed. Ada W. Finifter (Washington, D.C.: The American Political Science Association, 1993), p. 294.

8. See Chapter 3 for a discussion of our definitions of political and non-political organizations.

ices—that matters for political participation but how actively engaged the individual is in each setting. Furthermore, apart from the activity of the individual, institutions differ in their capacity to incubate the skills that facilitate political participation. For example, we shall demonstrate that it matters for political participation what *kind* of church one attends—a choice that is relatively unlikely to reflect a generalized taste for involvement.

THEORETICAL INTERPRETABILITY AND INTEREST

Most measures of political engagement are not very distant from political participation. Asking whether someone feels able to participate in politics or is interested in politics is sufficiently proximate to that which is to be explained, activity, that any relationship becomes less interesting theoretically. In contrast, the resources of time, money, and skills on which we focus—and the non-political domains in which they are nurtured—are conceptually quite different from political activity. This linking across domains—from the non-political realms of everyday life to the political—is one of the hallmarks of our approach. Since the institutions on which we concentrate are the most fundamental ones to which individuals become connected as they move through the ordinary stages of life, we believe we have an explanatory model of wide generality that is deeply grounded in the substance of people's lives. In addition, as we shall see shortly when we connect our analysis of resources to two of the principal models of political activity, rational actor theory and the socioeconomic model, resources provide a theoretically interpretable relationship between the explanatory and dependent variables.

POLITICAL RELEVANCE

A resource-centered explanation also tells us a good deal about the nature of contemporary American politics. A central concern in the study of participation is the extent to which disparities in participation are consonant with group differences in political preferences or needs. We have already seen that many groups that matter for politics in America—groups based on, for example, class, race, ethnicity, or receipt of means-tested government benefits—differ substantially in their rates of activity. They also vary in their access to the resources that facilitate political activity. The most obvious example of a resource that is at the same time the basis for differential political preferences and needs is money. Those with high incomes command an important participatory resource; they also want and need different things from the government. The complex role of money—as a factor facilitating political activity and as a politically relevant resource—serves as a leitmotif of this analysis.

EVALUATING AMERICAN DEMOCRACY

Finally, resources matter from a normative perspective. A major issue in normative democratic theory is the interpretation of political inactivity, especially when there are differences in participation across groups with conflicting political needs and preferences. How we evaluate political inactivity may depend upon its source: if individuals are not involved in politics because they do not care or because they prefer to devote themselves to private rather than public pursuits, then we are apt to be less concerned about disparities in participation than if their lack of involvement derives from resource constraints that make it difficult or impossible to take part in political life even if they are motivated to do so.

Resources, Rational Choice, and the Socioeconomic Model

We can elaborate upon the theoretical significance of the resource component of the Civic Voluntarism Model by placing it in the context of two important approaches to political activity, the socioeconomic, or SES, model and the rational actor approach. The strengths of the SES model are in its empirical power to predict activity and in the political relevance of the groups upon which the analysis is based. However, it is theoretically deficient in failing to specify the mechanism that links socioeconomic status to political participation. In contrast, the rational actor approach is theoretically rich but weak in its predictive power and relevance for politics. Our model seeks to draw on the merits of each while compensating for its shortcomings.

RESOURCES AND THE SES MODEL

The central tenet of the SES model is that people of higher socio-economic status—those with higher education, higher income, and higher-status jobs—are more active in politics. As mentioned, the sources of its strength are two-fold: it is *empirically powerful,* and it is *politically relevant.* SES has been found in many contexts to be a powerful predictor of political activity. As Milbrath and Goel put it, "No matter how class is measured, studies consistently show that *higher class persons are more likely to participate in politics than lower class persons* . . . This proposition has been confirmed in numerous countries."[9] Moreover, the analysis of political activity implicit in the SES model is rich with political implications. Since the predictor variables in the SES model are significant components of the stratification system in any society, the SES model is also a model of political inequality predicting participatory disparities across politically relevant groups—that is, groups that have differing preferences and needs for governmental action and, therefore, that are in political conflict with one another.

However, the SES model is weak in its theoretical underpinnings. It fails to provide a coherent rationale for the connection between the explanatory socioeconomic variables and participation. Numerous intervening factors are invoked—resources, norms, stake in the outcome, psychological involvement in politics, greater opportunities, favorable legal status, and so forth. But there is no clearly specified mechanism linking social statuses to activity.[10] By

---

9. Milbrath and Goel, *Political Participation,* p. 92 (emphasis in original). They cite many studies in which this result is replicated.

10. See Milbrath and Goel, *Political Participation,* chap. 4; and M. Margaret Conway, *Political Participation in the United States,* 2nd ed. (Washington, D.C.: CQ Press, 1991), pp. 21–27. In *Participation in America* (p. 133), Verba and Nie indicate a variety of factors that link socioeconomic status with activity, resources such as time, money, skills, and knowledge—the resources on which we focus—as well as subjective characteristics like efficacy: "What is it that links higher socioeconomic status with political participation? As indicated, many connective links have been suggested. Some depend on the social environment of upper-status citizens: They are more likely to be members of organizations, and they are likely to be surrounded by others who are participating. Some connecting links depend on the availability of resources and skills: Upper-status citizens have the time, the money, and the knowledge to be effective in politics. Other connecting links depend on the psychological characteristics of upper-status citizens: They are more likely to be concerned

moving from socioeconomic status to resources—which are at a higher level of abstraction and generality—we are able to define more fully the nature of the connection between SES and activity. As we shall see, resources link backward to SES and forward to political activity. The three resources of money, time, and civic skills vary in their association with SES. Money and some kinds of civic skills are closely related to SES; they are more available to those in higher socioeconomic positions. Time and other civic skills are less stratified by socioeconomic status. The three resources also vary in their forward link to participation: each is more useful for some kinds of activities than for others. By showing how resources that are differentially available on the basis of socioeconomic status affect various modes of political activity, we explain not only why some individuals are more active and others less, but also why certain kinds of people are more likely to engage in particular participatory acts. The result is a fuller and more complex picture of the sources of political activity.

A resource-centered explanation of political activity, then, enhances the SES model by providing an interpretation of the way that model works. Resources explain why people of higher education or income or occupation are, in general, more active. A resource-centered explanation, however, does more than improve upon the SES explanation of political activity. It *goes beyond* the SES model to encompass other factors not linked to SES. The new model provides an explanation of many of the *deviations* from the predictions of the SES model by isolating other social characteristics, not part of the bundle of characteristics associated with SES, that generate participatory resources.

Our prime example involves the role of religion. Religious institutions are the source of significant civic skills which, in turn, foster political activity. The acquisition of such civic skills is not a function of SES but depends on frequency of church attendance

---

with general political problems, and they are more likely to feel efficacious."

In *Who Votes?* (New Haven: Yale University Press, 1980), Raymond E. Wolfinger and Steven J. Rosenstone unpack SES into its constituent parts and demonstrate that it is education, rather than income or occupation, that has consequences for voting. However, they do not explain why education has an impact on turnout.

and the denomination of the church one attends. As we shall see, individuals with low SES may acquire civic skills if they attend church—and if the church is the right denomination. Conversely, individuals who are otherwise well endowed with resources because of their high socioeconomic status will be lower in civic skills if they do not attend church regularly—or if the church they attend is the wrong denomination. Frequency of church attendance and the kind of church one attends are, in turn, closely connected to race and ethnicity. This allows us to provide an explanation of differences in political activity across race and ethnic lines. In this manner, a resource-centered model provides a more solid theoretical foundation for the robust predictions and politically relevant findings of the SES model. And it accounts as well for some of the deviations from what the SES model would predict.

RESOURCES AND RATIONAL CHOICE

A model of political activity based on resources does just the opposite for rational actor theory: It provides greater empirical grounding and political relevance to a model of political activity that is more satisfying for its theoretical elegance than for its predictive power or its relevance to politics. Although rational actor theories have clearly specified how and why individuals might decide to participate in politics in order to pursue their self-interest, these theories have done a very poor job of predicting political participation. Rational actor theory falls short in predicting *how much* political activity there will be, and it falls short in predicting *who* will take part.

The failure to predict the volume of activity constitutes the basic paradox of participation. According to the theory, few should participate given the costs and the benefits, but many do. In Chapter 4, we considered this paradox by examining the benefits that people mention in discussing their participation. We concluded that activists can and do cite a multitude of benefits—most of which go substantially beyond self-interest narrowly defined. Far from being unable to deliver benefits commensurate with its costs, political participation seems able to provide substantial and significant benefits. Once the range of selective benefits is, as it must be, enlarged to encompass such psychic benefits as the satisfaction attendant to doing one's civic duty, political participation delivers more than enough benefits to satisfy any rational actor. The theory, however, becomes almost unfalsifiable once we enlarge the set of benefits and, thus, loses its analytical bite.

Furthermore, even if the expansion of the meaning of benefits to embrace such a wide range is acceptable as a means of making the theory predictive, rational choice approaches fail to predict *who* will participate. The theory is, for instance, ambiguous about how SES is related to participation. According to one version of the theory, people of high SES should be less active because they have the education and intellectual sophistication to comprehend the free-rider problem and because their high salaries raise the opportunity cost of participation.[11] However plausible this approach, the strongest empirical regularity for participation is that those with high levels of SES, who are not otherwise known for particular irrationality in the conduct of their lives, are the most likely to be active. Another version of the rational actor approach, dating back at least to Anthony Downs,[12] holds that lower information and transaction costs for the well educated imply that it will be easier for them to take part in politics. This approach has the virtue of fitting the facts but seems somewhat *post hoc*. Little has been done to verify whether the mechanism specified operates in the posited manner.

By moving beyond an exclusive focus on benefits and paying serious attention to the costs in the participation calculus, a resource explanation of participation makes rational actor theory more predictive of the amount and source of participation. There are real costs to participation. Money given to a candidate is not available for other purposes; time devoted to an informal community effort is time away from work, family, recreation, or sleep.[13]

---

11. See W. Mark Crain and Thomas H. Deaton, "A Note on Political Participation as Consumption Behavior," *Public Choice* 32 (Winter 1977): 131–135.

12. Anthony Downs, *An Economic Theory of Democracy* (New York: Harper, 1957), chap. 14.

13. When expended, money and time represent real costs since they are diminished when used. Civic skills are more ambiguous. The stock of skills may actually increase through their use. They are related to costs in that they reduce the effort needed for political activity.

The Civic Voluntarism Model highlights the resources necessary to bear the costs of various kinds of activity and the way in which a given configuration of resources enhances, or places constraints on, the ability to participate in politics.[14]

In focusing on resources, the Civic Voluntarism Model applies to politics an important variant of rational choice theory that is less commonly applied to economics and rarely applied to politics. The standard model of economic behavior assumes stable preferences, maximizing behavior, and budget constraints—that is, limited resources such as time, money, and skills—with the emphasis on the preferences. As we have noted, students of political participation have also emphasized the preference aspect of the model—that is, the benefits accruing from the activity—with less than satisfying results. By focusing on resources, we follow an alternative approach. The Chicago School of Economics has shown how a powerful theory of choice can be built, not upon restrictions on the motives for choice, but on the budget constraints on resources that limit choice.[15] In this approach, regardless of preferences—even random and idiosyncratic preferences—differential resource

---

For a discussion of costs as an explanation for activity, see Angus Deaton and John Muellbauer, *Economics and Consumer Behavior* (Cambridge: Cambridge University Press, 1980), chap. 1.

14. Our characterization of rational actor theory does not encompass an important strand: the role of strategic elites in mobilizing citizens to political action, an important component of models of social movements. See, for example, Dennis Chong, *Collective Action and the Civil Rights Movement* (Chicago: University of Chicago Press, 1991); and Doug McAdam, *Political Process and the Development of Black Insurgency: 1930–1970* (Chicago: University of Chicago Press, 1982). See also the model of the ebb and flow of citizen involvement in relation to particular issues or in the context of electoral contests in Rosenstone and Hansen, *Mobilization, Participation, and Democracy.*

15. The "new consumer theory" takes into account constraints on time as well as money, the production of commodities by the household, and investment in human capital. In this theory, individual behaviors are constrained by income, time, and household production capabilities. Household production functions vary from person to person depending upon accumulated skills, but production capabilities can be improved through the investment of time and goods in human capital. See Gary S. Becker, *Human Capital: A Theoretical and Empirical Analysis, with Special Reference to Education,* 2nd ed. (New York: National Bureau of Economic Research, 1975); Becker, "A Theory of the Allocation of Time," *Economic Journal* 75 (1965): 493–517; Robert T. Michael, "Education in Nonmarket Production," *Journal of Political Economy* 81 (1973): 306–327; and Michael and Becker, "On the New Theory of Consumer Behavior," *Swedish Journal of Economics* 75 (1973): 378–396.

constraints will result in predictable differences in behavior.[16] In their work on consumer theory, Angus Deaton and John Muellbauer state this position clearly:

> Consumer behavior is frequently presented in terms of preferences, on the one hand, and possibilities on the other. The emphasis in the discussion is commonly placed on *preferences,* on the axioms of choice, on utility functions and their properties. The specification of which choices are actually available is given a secondary place, and, frequently, only very simple possibilities are considered. . . . We begin, however, with the *limits to choice* rather than the choices themselves. Unlike preferences, the opportunities for choice are often directly observable so that, to the extent that variation in behavior can be traced to variations in opportunities, we have a straightforward and objective explanation of observed phenomena. It is our view that much can be so explained and that the part played by preferences in determining behavior tends to be overestimated.[17]

Substituting "political behavior" for "consumer behavior" neatly summarizes our position. That Deaton and Muellbauer focus on "the limits to choice" which are "often directly observable" rather than on preferences is the economic parallel to our emphasis on resources rather than on benefits. Because preferences are, by their very nature, subjective and, therefore, difficult to measure, it is much easier, and more productive, to base an explanation of political participation on differences in resources.

Not only does the consumer theory associated with the Chicago School demonstrate the importance of resource constraints, but it shows how different resource constraints operate in different circumstances.[18] Similarly, by analyzing the way in which multiple resources are distributed across the population, we are able to

---

16. This is the conclusion in Gary Becker's "Irrational Behavior and Economic Theory," *Journal of Political Economy* 70 (1970): 1–13. He shows that the main implication of the traditional theory, "that market demand curves are negatively inclined—can also be derived from a wide variety of irrational behavior." In his discussion of revealed preferences, Paul Samuelson has stressed that the real power of the approach comes from the budget constraint. See his *Foundations of Economic Analysis* (Cambridge, Mass.: Harvard University Press, 1947).

17. Deaton and Muellbauer, *Economics and Consumer Behavior,* p. 1 (emphasis in original).

18. Michael and Becker, "On the New Theory of Consumer Behavior."

probe the implications of resource constraints for the ability to bear the costs of different kinds of participation. By considering civic skills, we are able to understand why transaction and information costs might be lower for those of higher socioeconomic status. Incorporating income and free time as well helps to explain why participants might choose modes of activity that require inputs of time as opposed to inputs of money. Thus, by focusing on costs as well as benefits, a resource approach retains the assumption of rational choice but provides a more complete explanation of political activity. In this way, we do not contradict the calculus of rational choice; instead we build upon its basic logic to gain additional empirical insights.

In sum, the resource component of the Civic Voluntarism Model links both rational choice theory and the socioeconomic approach to political activity. Stratification theories suggest that the distribution of class and status are fundamental features of any society and often determine its politics. A resource-centered explanation of political participation shows how class and status stratification shape individual resources to constrain individual choices about political participation.

The task of the next few chapters is to develop and test the Civic Voluntarism Model of political participation. We consider each of the components—resources, engagement, and recruitment—and demonstrate how they are related both to overall political participation and to particular modes of activity. We also trace their origins back to involvements with the major non-political institutions of American society: the family, school, workplace, church, and non-political organizations. Taken together, the various factors in the Civic Voluntarism Model offer a powerful and new explanation of political participation.

10

Resources for Politics:
Time and Money

Resources are the most critical component of the Civic Voluntarism Model. In this chapter and the next, we define what we mean by resources and describe how we measure them. In addition, we put empirical flesh on our understanding by pursuing several themes. We show how the resources on which we focus—money, time, and civic skills—vary in their availability to politically relevant groups defined by their income, education, occupation, race or ethnicity, gender, and religion. This is an important enterprise because, in the chapters that follow, the stratification of resources along lines of socioeconomic and other demographic cleavages will become a principal explanation for the inequalities in participation we have described in earlier chapters. Moreover, we shall investigate the roots of money, time, and civic skills in the nonpolitical institutions with which individuals are involved throughout their lives. These institutions include the families into which they are born as well as the families they create as adults, the workplace, voluntary associations, and religious institutions. Furthermore, since various resources are differentially useful for various kinds of political participation, understanding the origins and distribution of resources will help explain not only why some people are active but why they are active in particular ways. In this chapter we consider money and time; in the next we turn to civic skills.

288

Money and Time

Money and time are the resources expended most directly in political activity. It is impossible to contribute to a campaign or other political cause without some discretionary income. Similarly, it is impossible to write a letter to a public official, attend community meetings, or work in a campaign without the free time to do so. We are able to measure both of these directly. We measure money in terms of family income.[1] We measure free time in terms of the residual time available to an individual after accounting for the hours spent doing necessary household tasks of all sorts including child care, working for pay including commuting and work taken home (for those in the work force), studying or going to school (for those taking courses toward a degree), and sleeping.[2] These resources differ in their distribution in the population and in their usefulness for political activity.[3]

Time is both more constrained and more evenly distributed than is money. Time is constrained by the fact that, unlike money, it cannot be banked for later use if not expended today. Furthermore, in contrast to money, there is a fixed upper bound on time: the best-endowed of us has only twenty-four hours in a day.[4] Because time is inherently limited, disposable time is more evenly distributed across individuals than is disposable income. Even allowing for the difference in the metrics, the gap in dollars between the richest and poorest is far wider than the gap in hours

---

1. For a fuller explication of the measure of family income, see Appendix B.13.

2. For the time use questions and a discussion, see Appendix B.15.

3. On the similarities and differences between time and money as resources, see Jacob Mincer, "Labor Force Participation of Married Women: A Study of Labor Market Supply," in *Aspects of Labor Economics,* ed. National Bureau Committee for Economic Research (Princeton: Princeton University Press, 1962); and Clifford Henry Sharp, *The Economics of Time* (Oxford: Martin Robinson, 1981).

4. There is evidence that Americans are working more and have less free time for leisure or volunteer activities. See Juliet B. Schor, *The Overworked American: The Unexpected Decline of Leisure* (New York: Basic Books, 1991). Her estimate (chap. 2) that the average American is working one extra month per year indicates how severe is the cutback in the time available for volunteer activity. See also Benjamin Kline Hunnicutt, *Work without End: Abandoning Shorter Hours for the Right to Work* (Philadelphia: Temple University Press, 1988), who argues (pp. 1–4) that the long-term trend toward a shorter work week ended around the close of the Great Depression or the beginning of World War II.

between the busiest and most leisured. Indeed, of all the resources that facilitate political involvement, money is the most stratified. Income and wealth are especially highly stratified in the United States. In comparison with other developed democracies, income and wealth are distributed relatively unequally in the United States.[5] Moreover, there is strong evidence that, after a long period of stability beginning after World War II, income inequality has grown in the last decade and a half.[6]

Money plays a dual role in our analysis of political participation: it is at the same time an important source of political conflict—one of the characteristics that defines citizens' needs and interests—and an important resource for political action. In earlier chapters we have shown how political contributions vary substantially by income group and how income is related to substantial differences in needs, circumstances, and interests. In this important respect, money functions quite differently from time. Although citizens differ in their access to free time, American politics has not involved conflicts between the harried and the leisured in the way that it has sometimes involved conflicts between the affluent and the less well-heeled. Not only are income groups themselves politically relevant, but income inequalities, not unexpectedly, hew to other fault lines of political division. As we shall see, those who are advantaged in other ways also report more income. This is another way in which money is distinguished from time as a political resource.

Whereas those with income and wealth self-evidently have more money to spare for politics, it is less obvious whether they also

---

5. For recent data that place the United States in the set of countries with the lowest income equality, see Michael O'Higgins, Gunther Schmaus, and Geoffrey Stephenson, "Income Distribution and Redistribution: A Microdata Analysis for Seven Countries," in *Poverty, Inequality, and Income Distribution in Comparative Perspective: The Luxembourg Income Study (LIS),* ed. Timothy M. Smeeding, Michael O'Higgins, and Lee Rainwater (Washington, D.C.: The Urban Institute Press, 1990), pp. 20–56.

6. On this issue see, for example, the papers and bibliographical citations in *Uneven Tides: Rising Inequality in America,* ed. Sheldon Danziger and Peter Gottschalk (New York: Russell Sage Foundation, 1993). Kevin P. Phillips makes a similar argument in *The Politics of Rich and Poor: Wealth and the American Electorate in the Reagan Aftermath* (New York: Random House, 1990).

have more free time to spare for politics. On one hand, we might guess that the rich would be better off when it comes to time because they can hire others—gardeners, accountants, and the like—to do what most people have to do for themselves. On the other, we might expect that the rich would have less free time because they manage to accumulate wealth by dint of the long hours they log at work.[7] Indeed, the ambiguity is expressed in the cliché that "If you want something done, ask a busy person." Again, the contrast between time and money is apparent. Imagine an old saw asserting, "If you want a large contribution, ask a poor person."

WHO HAS MONEY? WHO HAS TIME?

We can learn more about the distinction between money and time as political resources by considering their availability to politically relevant groups. Figure 10.1 shows the average family income and average free time for respondents differentiated by their educational attainment and, if working, their job level (that is, the education and on-the-job training required). The data in the top portion of the figure show, not unexpectedly, that average family income rises steeply with the respondent's educational level. In contrast, there is no analogous pattern of stratification when it comes to free time. Those who never finished high school (a disproportionate share, 51 percent, of whom are retired, keeping house, or permanently disabled) have more spare time; beyond this, however, educational level is not associated with differences in free time. The data in the bottom portion of Figure 10.1 repeat this pattern for position in the job hierarchy.[8] Once again, the data

---

7. In fact these conjectures reflect the contradictory predictions of economic theory which holds both that an income effect would produce more leisure for the wealthy because they are able to purchase it and that a substitution effect would produce less because their higher wages raise the opportunity cost of free time. See Mincer, "Labor Force Participation," p. 63.

8. The job level variable captures respondents' assessments of the education and/or training on the job required to handle a job like theirs. The categories range from jobs requiring no more than a high school diploma and less than one month of on-the-job training to jobs requiring either a graduate degree or a college degree and at least two years

A. Family Income and Free Time by Education

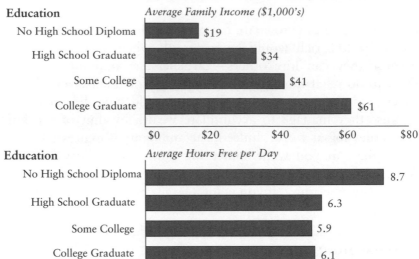

Education — *Average Family Income ($1,000's)*

- No High School Diploma: $19
- High School Graduate: $34
- Some College: $41
- College Graduate: $61

Education — *Average Hours Free per Day*

- No High School Diploma: 8.7
- High School Graduate: 6.3
- Some College: 5.9
- College Graduate: 6.1

B. Family Income and Free Time by Job Level

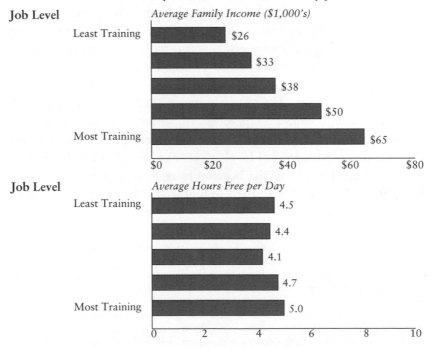

Job Level — *Average Family Income ($1,000's)*

- Least Training: $26
- $33
- $38
- $50
- Most Training: $65

Job Level — *Average Hours Free per Day*

- Least Training: 4.5
- 4.4
- 4.1
- 4.7
- Most Training: 5.0

Figure 10.1 Family Income and Free Time by Education and Job Level.

bear out our expectations with respect to income: those whose jobs require high levels of education or long periods of on-the-job training have much higher family incomes. When it comes to free time, however, we had contradictory expectations. On one hand, we hear a great deal about the long hours worked by those in high-level jobs—for example, corporate lawyers in large firms. On the other, those at the opposite end of the job spectrum often have to moonlight simply to make ends meet. In fact, free time does not vary systematically with occupation level. Those at the top may feel harried—or they may complain especially loudly—but they are not disadvantaged when it comes to time.

Similar patterns emerge when we consider the availability of money and time to Latinos, African-Americans, and Anglo-Whites and to men and women in Figure 10.2. As we would expect, Anglo-Whites and men are distinctly advantaged when it comes to family income. Once again, however, they enjoy no analogous advantage with respect to free time. Men and women are equally busy. Anglo-Whites have slightly more time than African-Americans, and Latinos report somewhat less time than the other two groups. But the differences are minimal compared with the gaps in income.

If various measures of socioeconomic advantage, race and ethnicity, and gender are not related to the availability of free time, what does influence the amount of leisure an individual enjoys? The answer is strikingly simple and, in retrospect, obvious. The data are shown in Figure 10.3. The factors that affect free time are "life circumstances." Having a job reduces free time. So does having

---

of on-the-job training. The scale has five categories. Although the job level classifications are based on what respondents told us rather than on objective assessments, examination of actual cases suggests that respondents make judgments fairly accurately. Examples of occupations at each level include:

1. Dishwasher	Janitor	Cashier
2. Bank teller	Mail carrier	Machine operator
3. Electrician	Machinist	Construction inspector
4. Insurance agent	Engineer	Elementary teacher
5. Physician	Architect	Attorney

For the questions, see Appendix B.11.b.

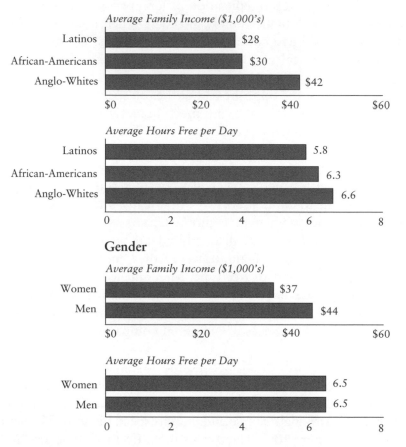

Figure 10.2 Family Income and Free Time by Race or Ethnicity and Gender.

young children at home—especially pre-schoolers—although having grown children seems to have no effect. Having a spouse with a job also diminishes free time. In addition, data not shown in Figure 10.3 indicate that among those not in the work force, the retired have the most time not committed to other activities.

PREDICTING INCOME AND FREE TIME

We can deepen our understanding of the differences between money and time by undertaking analyses that predict each of them on the

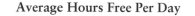

Average Hours Free Per Day

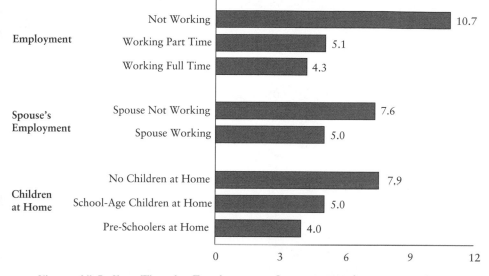

Figure 10.3 Free Time by Employment, Spouse's Employment, and Children at Home.

basis of variables measuring socioeconomic status and other life circumstances. For this purpose, we turn to multiple regression analysis. The results of a multiple regression analysis predicting income and free time are given in Table 10.1. Since this is a mode of analysis we use often in this book, we digress briefly to discuss why we use regression techniques and how to interpret the results. We hope this discussion will help readers unfamiliar with this technique to understand the data. More technically sophisticated readers may wish to skip this explication—although they may be interested in our explanation of why we use ordinary least squares multiple regression, a technique we supplement at various points with other techniques.

A Note on Multiple Regression

Multiple regression is a commonly used statistical technique that indicates which putative causes (or independent variables) are associated with a dependent variable. It was developed to deal

Table 10.1 Predicting Family Income and Free Time: OLS Regression Results

Variable	Family Income			Free Time		
	B	SE B	Beta	B	SE B	Beta
EDUCATION AND JOB						
Education	.57**	.05	.29	−.07	.05	−.02
Working	.08	.08	.02	−2.71**	.09	.54
Job level	.16*	.05	.08	.06	.06	.02
FAMILY CHARACTERISTICS						
Spouse working	.52**	.06	.16	−.48**	.08	−.10
Pre-school children	−.01	.17	.00	−1.92**	.20	−.16
School-age children	.20	.16	.03	−.97**	.19	−.09
DEMOGRAPHIC CHARACTERISTICS						
Black	−.15	.19	−.01	.10	.23	.01
Latino	−.46	.24	−.05	−.37	.28	−.02
Gender	−.33**	.12	−.05	−1.12**	.14	−.12
(Constant)	2.60**	.41		13.24**	48	
R^2		.19			.53	
Sample Size		2,445			2,463	
		weighted cases			weighted cases	

* Significant at .05 level.
** Significant at .01 level.
Note: Age is also included in the equation but not reported in the table.

with multiple overlapping causes and to distinguish those causes that are systematic across people and situations from those that are idiosyncratic to particular people and situations. Regression analysis considers a set of possible systematic determinants of the dependent variable and assigns each potential determinant a regression coefficient.

The unstandardized regression coefficient (B) in the first column of Table 10.1 measures the effect on the dependent variable of a change in the independent variable. A one-unit change in the independent variable produces a change in the dependent variable equal to the regression coefficient multiplied by the units in which the dependent variable is measured. The size of that impact is a measure of the substantive significance of the independent vari-

able. The interpretation of a regression coefficient can be illustrated by the .57 coefficient for education as a predictor of income
on Table 10.1. Because the equation contains multiple independent variables, the coefficient for the impact of education on income measures that effect while taking account of—controlling
for—the other factors included in the analysis, for instance, the
kind of job. Education is measured as eight steps that go from
grammar school education to Ph.D. or professional degree. Thus,
everything else remaining the same, a respondent whose education
increases one level obtains a .57 increase in family income. Since
income is measured in tens of thousands of dollars, this is a $5,700
increase for each of the eight steps up the educational ladder! A
respondent who moves two levels obtains $11,400 more income
$(2 \times .57 \times \$10,000 = \$11,400)$. Changes of this magnitude are
certainly substantively significant.

The change in the dependent variable, however, might be the
result of errors in our estimation of this equation which come from
having only a sample to represent the entire population of the
United States and from other uncertainties in our understanding
of the determinants of family income. The second column of Table
10.1 contains a measure called the standard error of B which tells
us how precise our estimate is. The usual convention is to use the
standard error to construct a confidence interval of possible values
for the regression coefficient. This is constructed by taking the
regression coefficient in the first column of Table 10.1 and adding
and subtracting approximately two standard errors. If that interval does not include zero, we can have some confidence that the
regression coefficient is not zero—that it has, in statistical terms,
a statistically significant impact, in contrast to the substantively
significant impact. The asterisks in Table 10.1 indicate that a
coefficient is statistically significant. Both substantive significance
and statistical significance are important—the former measuring
the amount of effect an independent variable has, the latter the
likelihood that the effect was not produced by chance. The two
forms of significance are related, but not identical. In discussing
multiple regressions, we shall refer to both meanings.

Let us illustrate by continuing with the example of the coefficient for education as a predictor of income in Table 10.1. Using

the standard errors, we can calculate the confidence interval around the regression coefficient of .57. Since two standard errors equal .10, the interval runs from .47 to .67. Since this interval does not include zero, we can be confident that the effect of education is statistically significant as well. The double asterisk indicates it is significant at the .01 level. This means that if the true value of the coefficient were zero, there would be only one chance in one hundred of finding a coefficient as large as was found. Thus, we are pretty confident in assuming that the true coefficient is not zero.

Table 10.1 also contains a third measure, the beta weight. The beta weight is a standardized measure of the effect of the independent variable on the dependent variable. It adds a piece of information that can be very useful in making comparisons across variables. One of the defects of a regression coefficient is that the coefficient for any particular independent variable depends upon the scale of that variable. In this respect, regression coefficients are somewhat arbitrary. If we were to change the number of categories into which education is divided, we would change the regression coefficient. Since the nature of the categories is not comparable across independent variables measured in different metrics, we cannot easily compare the effects of two independent variables. The beta weight provides us with a common scale so that we can compare the effects of two variables. Every variable has a standard deviation that indicates how much it varies in the population being studied. The beta weight indicates how much of a standard deviation change in the dependent variable will result from a one standard deviation change in the independent variable.[9]

To take an example from Table 10.1: the regression coefficients would seem to indicate that education (+.57) and being Latino (−.46) have effects on income of a similar size, although in the opposite direction. However, education is measured in eight categories while the variable measuring ethnicity is a dichotomy—a respondent either is or is not Latino. Thus, there are seven steps

---

9. The virtues of beta weights are also their defects. The standard deviation of a variable depends upon the population being studied, so that education, for example, would seem to matter more, everything else being equal, in a population in which there is large variance in education rather than a small amount of variance.

on the educational ladder, each of which adds to income; there is only one for the "Latino" variable. The beta—which is roughly six times as large for education as for being Latino—is a better comparison across those two independent variables. In later analyses, we will use beta weights when we wish to compare across independent variables measured in different units.

Perhaps the most fundamental issue in undertaking regression analysis is choosing which variables to include in the predictive equation and which to leave out. Systematic factors must be included; unsystematic or idiosyncratic factors can be omitted from the predictive equations. In the example in Table 10.1, education is a systematic cause: the higher the level of educational attainment, the higher the family income. An idiosyncratic characteristic might be something like winning the lottery. This kind of factor is not unimportant; rather it is unique to particular individuals. These factors are consigned to the "residual" (sometimes misleadingly called the "error term") in analysis.

Multiple regression can lead to quite misleading results if the unidentified omitted factors in the residual term are correlated with factors included in the multiple regression equation. If the omitted factors are correlated with variables in the equation, then the variables in the equation will carry the effect of—or proxy—these other causes as well as the causes they were meant to represent. This leads to misleading inferences; just how misleading depends in part on the real causal connections among the included and excluded variables. In Table 10.1, for instance, we include both a measure of the respondent's race and education to explain income. The race variable (being African-American) has relatively little effect. What seems to matter is education level. Had we left education out of the analysis in Table 10.1, the coefficient for the race variable would have been substantially larger ($-.26$ rather than $-.15$ as in Table 10.1) since race would carry the effect of education on income. This would be the result of omitting a factor correlated with the factors in the equation. It would produce a somewhat misleading result. It would be only *somewhat* misleading because whether or not one is an African-American does have a real effect on income, an effect, however, that runs in part through education. In the absence of a measure of education in the analysis, the finding as to the size of the effect of race would not be a false finding. Rather, it would be an incomplete finding.

A more serious error would emerge if the omitted variable that was correlated with the included factors truly explained income. Let us suppose for the moment that the underlying real cause of income level were a psychological predisposition to try hard—an ambition factor—that also affected education level. The results would misleadingly suggest that income was caused by educational attainment, when both income and education were the result of this psychological predisposition. As we try to explain political activity, we must pay attention to the possible existence of such predispositions.

These examples illustrate the care that must be taken in making decisions about what to exclude or include in regression equations. Ideally, we must be sure that we have included all of the most important variables so that the error term is uncorrelated with the included independent variables. In the end, theory, common sense, and some empirical testing are the only way to be certain. In presenting results, one strategy is to include all the variables considered relevant at once. We adopt this approach for income and free time in Table 10.1. On other occasions—for example, when we try to explain participation in Chapter 11—we take a more step-by-step approach in order to avoid a false sense of finality and certainty. In so doing we hope to provide the reader with a sense of how the model we develop came to have the shape it does and why we have substantial faith in it.

There is still another major problem we have to face in interpreting our regression analyses. What appears to be our independent variable may not be the cause but the effect of our dependent variable. Or, to make things worse, the causal arrow might run both ways, creating a problem of simultaneous causation. This danger will vary with the substance of the variables under consideration. The variables in Table 10.1, which seeks to explain income and free time, do not appear to pose a real problem: it seems highly unlikely that having a high family income causes a respondent to be male or to have a working spouse. In general, if we are not in doubt as to the correct causal order, we can use "ordinary least squares" (OLS) regression analysis to estimate the relationship between independent and dependent variables. At various stages of our analysis of participation, however, the danger of simultaneous causation will assume greater proportions. In these cases, we shall try to solve the simultaneity problem by using a technique called "two-stage least-squares" (2SLS). To be conservative, we often display the results from both OLS and 2SLS analyses.

We now return to the analysis of Table 10.1. Table 10.1 reports two regression equations, one for family income and another for free time. For each equation, nine regression coefficients are listed for nine different independent variables including three measures of socioeconomic status, three measures of family structure, and measures of race, ethnicity, and gender.[10] The comparison between the variables that best predict family income and free time is quite striking.

Family income is closely related to the socioeconomic stratification variables that distinguish in various ways the advantaged from the disadvantaged, in particular to education and the level of the job. Having a working spouse also increases income. In addition, even with these factors taken into account, Blacks, Latinos, and women have somewhat lower family incomes. The predictors of free time are different. Free time is a function of such life circumstances as having a job, a working spouse, or small children at home.[11] Education, so powerful a predictor of income, has no effect on free time.[12] Note that the level of the job—the education and on-the-job training needed for the job—is signifi-

---

10. The definitions of the variables for Table 10.1 are given in Appendix B. We also included dummy variables for various age categories in the equation to take into account the confounding effects of age on income and free time. In order not to overburden Table 10.1 with additional figures, we did not include the age data there.

11. If we add family income to the regression for free time, we find that it also has no impact. It is interesting to note that, as one would expect, having a working spouse increases income but diminishes free time.

12. In contrast with income, which increases by $5,700 with each step up the educational ladder, the coefficient for free time is −.07; that is, each step up in education is associated with a decline of .07 of an hour of free time (about 5 minutes). In fact, the standard error is almost as large as the coefficient, indicating that the coefficient is statistically insignificant.

cant as a predictor of family income, but whether one is working or not does not predict family income.[13] For free time the situation is reversed; what counts is having a job, while the level of the job does not seem to have an effect. What this means is that time, in sharp contrast to money, is a resource relatively equally available to the rich and the poor, to Blacks and Whites, and to the educated and the less well educated. In this busy world, the proper locution might be that it is equally *unavailable* to all sorts of people—but the equality in its availability is what counts.[14]

GENDER AND FREE TIME: A NOTE

Careful readers may have noticed a potential inconsistency in the data we have presented. Figure 10.2 shows no gender difference in terms of the average number of hours left over after accounting for life's necessary activities: paid work, household chores and child care, school, and sleep. Yet the seeming gender similarity in Figure 10.2 obscures a finding that emerged from the equation reported in Table 10.1: with other factors controlled, men have significantly more free time available than women do.

The solution to the puzzle lies in the way in which women's and men's lives have traditionally been patterned by different commitments to home and the workplace. The data on time constraints make clear that life circumstances have a different impact on free time for women than for men. Not surprisingly, those who work full time, a group that is disproportionately male, have less free time than those who work part time or are not in the work force, a group that is disproportionately female. However, the reduction

---

13. This is not to say that whether or not one works has no impact on income. Rather it says that when one takes into account the level of the job—in relation to which those who are not working are categorized in the lowest category—the fact of working per se has no impact. This is an example where the omission of a correlated variable would change the coefficient of an included variable. If we had left job level out of the equation, the coefficient for working would more than double and be statistically significant.

14. Just as the distribution of free time is not connected to class or gender, so the shrinking of free time is an "across-the-board" phenomenon. "[T]he rise of work is not confined to a few selective groups, but has affected the great majority of working Americans. Hours have risen for men as well as women, for those in the working class as well as professionals. They have grown for all marital statuses and income groups." Schor, *Overworked American*, p. 5.

in leisure deriving from full-time employment is greater for women than for men. This is not the result of greater time spent on the job, but of the fact that women who work full time continue to assume disproportionate responsibility for caring for home and children.[15] Among those who work full time, women reported working somewhat shorter hours, 9.5 hours per day, than men, who average 10.1 hours. However, the additional time spent by women on chores at home more than compensates for men's greater time on the job. Among full-time workers, men reported devoting 2.6 hours a day and women 3.7 hours a day to home and child care.[16] In short, what may once have been an advantage for women in terms of the resource of time has disappeared with women's increasing work force participation. However, we must remember that in comparison with money, for which there is an unambiguous masculine advantage, time seems in the aggregate to be relatively equally distributed with respect to gender.

To summarize, we have seen that time is more equally distributed than is money. Moreover, in sharp contrast to money, spare time is not differentially available to those who are in other ways privileged by virtue of their education, occupation, race, or ethnicity. The implications for political activity are profound. If the necessary resource for participation is money, politics will be more stratified than if the necessary resource is time. The data suggest, and we shall demonstrate, that a participatory system based on money will be more unequal than one based on time. We shall return to this theme when we look at the impact of resources on various participatory acts.

---

15. See, for example, Arlie Hochschild, *The Second Shift: Working Parents and the Revolution at Home* (New York: Viking, 1989).

16. A regression analysis of how the free time available to women and men relates to family and work circumstances shows that the same life circumstances affect the free time available to women and to men: working (especially full time), having a working spouse, and having children at home. With one exception, there are no gender differences in the coefficients. The exception is that, while having pre-schoolers at home leads to a statistically significant drop in free time for both men and women, women lose twice as much free time from pre-schoolers as men do. Looked at another way, if we consider those with full-time jobs and pre-schoolers at home, women report that, in comparison to men, they give, on average, 1.3 hours less to paid work and 1.9 hours more to housework.

11

Resources for Politics:
Civic Skills

Civic skills, the communications and organizational abilities that allow citizens to use time and money effectively in political life, constitute a third resource for politics. Citizens who can speak or write well or who are comfortable organizing and taking part in meetings are likely to be more effective when they get involved in politics. Those who possess civic skills should find political activity less daunting and costly and, therefore, should be more likely to take part. Furthermore, these capacities allow participants to use inputs of time and money more effectively, making them more productive when they are active.

In our conception, civic skills are not subjective competencies.[1] Our measures are relatively objective: they include, for example, communications skills such as possessing a good vocabulary or ability to communicate in English and experiences in exercising

---

1. There is precedent for considering the role of civic skills in facilitating participation. John M. Strate, Charles J. Parrish, Charles D. Elder, and Coit Ford III ("Life Span Civic Development and Voting Participation," *American Political Science Review* 83 [1989]: 443–467) demonstrate the importance of "civic competence" for voting turnout. However, the variables included in their measure of civic competence (for example, attentiveness to politics and level of political information) are explicitly political. Because we cannot be sure that they are not also a result as well as a source of activity, we consider them to be measures of engagement rather than skills in our model.

communications and organizational skills on the job, in voluntary organizations, and churches. Thus, we are not referring to subjective feelings of efficacy—although those who exercise these skills are likely also to feel more efficacious. Presumably, someone who routinely writes letters, gives speeches, or organizes meetings will be more likely to feel confident about undertaking these activities in politics. The individual who, for example, commands verbal skills—a wide vocabulary, an ability to formulate and articulate an argument—will be more effective and persuasive when he or she decides to speak up. Moreover, we would expect someone who has these skills—perhaps as the result of opportunities to make speeches in other contexts—to be more likely to feel capable of making a statement at a community or political meeting and, thus, to do so. In our understanding, then, those who possess civic skills, the set of specific competencies germane to citizen political activity, are more likely to feel confident about exercising those skills in politics and to be effective—or, to use the economist's term, productive—when they do.

Education and Language

Civic skills are acquired throughout the life cycle beginning at home and, especially, in school. Investigations of citizen political participation in democracies around the world inevitably find a relationship between education and activity. Various reasons are adduced for this close relationship. Education enhances participation more or less directly by developing skills that are relevant to politics—the ability to speak and write, the knowledge of how to cope in an organizational setting. Education also affects participation by imparting information about government and politics, and by encouraging attitudes such as a sense of civic responsibility or political efficacy that predispose an individual to political involvement. In addition, education affects activity indirectly: those who have high levels of education are much more likely to command jobs that are lucrative and, as we shall see later in the chapter, to have opportunities to exercise leadership and to develop politically relevant skills at work, in church, and in voluntary associations.

We return to the multiple consequences of education for participation throughout this book. At this point, however, we focus on
the skill-creating aspect of education.

The ability to communicate effectively is, obviously, critical for
most forms of political action. Hence, we were concerned with
both respondents' linguistic facility and their proficiency in English. After all, despite the existence of foreign-language media,
English speakers have ready access to many more sources of political information than do those with limited capabilities in English. There are some political activities—attending a protest, for
example—that may not depend upon knowledge of English. However, most forms of involvement—in particular, contacting a public
official or serving on a local governing board—are likely to require
mastery of English. To measure their familiarity with the English
language, we asked respondents what language they ordinarily
speak at home: English, another language, or a combination of
English and another language.[2]

In addition, to assess developed verbal ability, we administered
a 10-item vocabulary test that has been used regularly on the
National Opinion Research Center's General Social Survey (GSS).[3]
The vocabulary score is, as we might expect, strongly related to
schooling. Those who never finished grammar school defined an
average of 3.8 of the 10 words on the test correctly; at the other
end of the scale, those with graduate degrees did more than twice
as well—defining an average of 8.0 words correctly. A recent study
confirms this relationship, but shows that such scores also "corre-
late highly with tests of general intelligence—usually .8 or higher—
and are good indicators of scores on the verbal component of
standard tests of general intelligence."[4] These facts suggest that the
vocabulary score measures something more than just schooling,
but for our purposes the exact relationship between vocabulary

---

2. English was scored as 3, English plus another language as 2, and another language
as 1.

3. For the 1 percent of our sample interviewed in Spanish, this test was administered
using Spanish words. For a discussion of this measure, see Appendix B.9.b.

4. See Duane F. Alwin, "Family of Origin and Cohort Differences in Verbal Ability,"
American Sociological Review 56 (1991): 625–638, 627. The correlation with schooling is
.54 in the Alwin study and .51 in our sample.

score and education is not important: that is, it does not really matter in our analysis whether schooling develops vocabulary, people with good vocabularies stay in school longer, or both. What is important is that the vocabulary score allows us to control for verbal ability wherever or however it has been obtained. Years of education and vocabulary score are included in our model to show that both schooling and general intelligence matter for political participation and to provide additional support for our contention that civic skills matter when other factors are controlled. We do not try to answer the difficult question of whether basic ability or schooling matters more.

The Distribution of Education and Language Skills

Although minorities, especially Blacks, have made strides in education since the 1960s, we might expect that Anglo-Whites, African-Americans, and Latinos would differ in their educational level. Table 11.1 presents information about educational attainment and vocabulary skill for Latinos, African-Americans, and Anglo-Whites and for men and women. Anglo-Whites are much less likely than African-Americans and, especially, Latinos to have dropped out of school before finishing high school and more likely to have graduated from college.[5] In contrast, the gender differences in education appear to be quite small, although men are considerably more likely than women to have graduate degrees.[6]

Data about vocabulary skill within racial or ethnic and gender groups, presented on the bottom line of Table 11.1, reflect the differences in education shown in the top portion of the table.

---

5. In this context, it is interesting to note the differences among the three groups across the generations. Considering only those respondents who could report on the educational attainment of both their parents, 20 percent of the Anglo-White respondents, as opposed to 28 percent of the African-Americans and 40 percent of the Latinos, indicated that neither of their parents had gone beyond eighth grade. In contrast, 24 percent of the Anglo-Whites, 16 percent of the African-Americans, and 13 percent of the Latinos indicated that at least one of their parents had graduated from college.

6. Since women tend to be overrepresented among the elderly who have, on average, less education, it is important to consider age effects. Within each of a set of age cohorts—except for the very youngest and the oldest—male respondents report more education.

Table 11.1 Educational Attainment and Vocabulary Skill by Gender and Race or Ethnicity

	Men	Women	Anglo-Whites	African-Americans	Latinos
EDUCATIONAL ATTAINMENT					
Grammar School or Less	5%	5%	4%	9%	15%
Some High School	8	11	9	13	14
High School Graduate	34	38	36	37	39
Some College	24	24	24	26	24
College Graduate	14	12	14	8	4
Some Graduate Work	4	4	4	2	1
Master's Degree	7	5	6	4	2
Ph.D./M.D./D.D.S./J.D.	4	1	3	1	1
	100%	100%	100%	100%	100%
VOCABULARY SKILL					
Average Number of Words Correct	6.2	6.2	6.5	5.0	5.0

Anglo-Whites scored an average of 6.5—and African-Americans and Latinos 5.0—on the vocabulary test. Men and women scored identically at 6.2.

When it comes to proficiency in English, the major distinction is between groups defined by their race or ethnicity. In comparison with African-Americans and Anglo-Whites, Latinos are at an aggregate disadvantage when it comes to English. While the overwhelming majority of African-Americans and Anglo-Whites—96 percent of the former and 97 percent of the latter—speak *exclusively* English at home, only 42 percent of Latinos do so. For the remaining 58 percent of the Latinos, just over half speak Spanish and English at home, and just under half speak Spanish all the time at home.[7] Not surprisingly, the majority of those who speak Spanish all the time at home were interviewed in Spanish.

---

7. Nevertheless, a majority of Latinos can operate in a bilingual environment. Thirty-four percent of the Latinos currently speak some English as well as some Spanish at home. An additional 16 percent were raised in households in which they spoke Spanish but they now speak exclusively English at home. Another 12 percent were raised in households where only Spanish was spoken and now only speak Spanish at home, but were, nevertheless, interviewed in English. Finally, 2 percent spoke English as youngsters but now speak

Unions?

Adult Civic Skills

The non-political institutions of adult life—the workplace, voluntary associations, and churches—function in several ways to enhance citizen activity in politics.[8] First, these non-political settings provide exposure to political stimuli. People engage in informal political discussions in these settings. In addition, the agenda at a meeting of even a non-political organization may include consideration of political issues. The weekly sermon at church may cover   *have* a political topic. Not only do these settings provide exposure to political messages, but—as we have seen—they are frequently the locus of political recruitment of citizen activists. On the job, in church, or in organizations, individuals develop networks of friends and acquaintances from which requests for political involvement emerge. Moreover, leaders and staff in these settings often make deliberate attempts to mobilize the ranks to political action.

---

exclusively Spanish at home. This suggests that almost two-thirds of the Latinos can operate in a bilingual environment. About 15 percent appear to be only able to operate in Spanish, and about 20 percent only in English.

There are interesting differences with respect to language among the Latino nationality   *Wonder how their civic skills were? (cubans)* groups. The Mexican-Americans were considerably more likely to have been born in the United States than members of the other Latino groups and are somewhat more proficient in English. It is, in fact, the Cuban-Americans—who are, in terms of their level of income and education, the most advantaged Latino group—who are most likely to have been born abroad and least likely to be comfortable in English. Although they are more likely to be U.S. citizens than are the Mexican-Americans or the Latinos who come from other parts of the hemisphere, the Cuban-Americans are least likely to speak only English at home and least likely to have been interviewed in English. Indeed, 59 percent of the Cuban-Americans speak only Spanish at home, in comparison with no more than a quarter of the other Latino groups.

8. For a review of relevant literature on voluntary associations, see David Knoke, "Associations and Interest Groups," *Annual Review of Sociology* 12 (1986): 8–9. See also Sidney Verba and Norman H. Nie, *Participation in America: Political Democracy and Social Equality* (New York: Harper and Row, 1972), chap. 11; Frank R. Baumgartner and Jack L. Walker, "Survey Research and Membership in Voluntary Associations," *American Journal of Political Science* 32 (1988): 908–928; and Bonnie H. Erickson and T. A. Nosanchuk, "How an Apolitical Association Politicizes," *The Canadian Review of Sociology and Anthropology* 27 (1990): 206–219.

On the historic role of American churches as a locus of political mobilization, see, for example, Joseph R. Gusfield, *Symbolic Crusade: Status Politics and the American Temperance Movement* (Urbana: University of Illinois Press, 1963) and Aldon D. Morris, *The Origins of the Civil Rights Movement: Black Communities Organizing for Change* (New York: The Free Press, 1984).

But don't most people in these orgs already have these skills?

We consider all these effects of institutions in Chapter 13. In this chapter, we concentrate on an aspect of non-political institutional affiliation that has received less attention from scholars: the way in which these non-political settings serve to incubate civic skills. The development of civic skills does not cease with the end of schooling but can continue throughout adulthood. These non-political institutions offer many opportunities to acquire, or improve, organizational or communications skills in the context of activities that have nothing to do with politics. Managing the firm's move to new quarters, coordinating the volunteers for the Heart Fund drive, or arranging the details for a tour by the church children's choir—all these undertakings represent opportunities in non-political settings to learn, maintain, or refine civic skills. In short, those who develop skills in an environment removed from politics are likely to become politically competent.[9] Indeed, those who enter the higher levels of politics—who, for example, run for office—have almost always developed civic skills at work, in non-political organizations, or in church, regardless of their previous political experience.[10]

The chance to gain resources in a non-political context depends

---

9. Although we pay much greater attention to the importance of skills developed in adult, non-political environments than is traditional in analyses of political participation, there is precedent for this emphasis. Discussing "Religion as a Political Resource," Kenneth D. Wald mentions the extent to which "congregational organizations may serve as leadership training institutes for people who lack other means of exposure to organizational skills," in *Religion and Politics in the United States*, 2nd ed. (Washington, D.C.: Congressional Quarterly, 1992), p. 35. The studies he cites find (as we do) a strong relationship between attendance at church services and electoral turnout, but not between religious attendance and other forms of political activity. In his study of parish-connected, non-Latino Catholics, David C. Leege finds a relationship between parish activity and political activity and discusses the potential of parish activity for developing the kinds of skills we measure here ("Catholics and the Civic Order: Parish Participation, Politics, and Civic Participation," *The Review of Politics* 50 [1988]: 704–737).

In their study of voting turnout, "Life Span Civic Development and Voting Participation," John M. Strate et al. demonstrate the importance of "civic competence." As we mentioned, the components of their measure of civic competence (for example, attentiveness to politics and level of political information) are more directly connected to political activity than the skills we discuss here.

10. In our emphasis upon the cultivation of skills in non-political settings, we do not mean to imply that these skills are not also developed in the course of political activity. Those who take part in politics usually receive on-the-job training for future participation. We emphasize the skills acquired outside politics because of our concern with the consequences of inequalities of extra-political resources for equality of political participation.

upon several factors. First, an individual must be connected to the institution—must have a job or be affiliated with a secular voluntary association or a church. In addition, it depends upon the particular kind of institution: a job in a public relations firm rather than a hairdressing salon or membership in a fraternal association rather than a softball league is more likely to yield opportunities to acquire resources relevant to political participation.

There is, moreover, variation among individuals. Some people are more inclined than others to assume responsibility voluntarily and more capable than others of undertaking acts that demand—and, thus, hone—skills. To the extent that the initiative in apportioning tasks rests with leaders and staff rather than with the individual, we would expect them to be more likely to recruit workers or members with existing skills or previous experience and with demonstrated willingness to undertake activities that involve practicing civic skills. Among workers or members with similar credentials and experience, however, leaders and staff might also be more likely to call upon those with particular characteristics—say, gender or race—to take on these responsibilities. Therefore, as we consider the complex processes by which opportunities to develop resources in non-political institutions are apportioned, we shall seek to find at what point the selection occurs—in differences in institutional affiliations, in the kinds of institutions with which individuals are involved, or in the way in which opportunities to practice skills are meted out within institutions.

In order to learn about the development of these skills we asked those respondents who are employed, who give time or money to a non-political organization, or who give time to educational, charitable, or social activities in their churches beyond simple attendance at services whether, in the relevant context, they had within the past six months:

Written a letter
Gone to a meeting where they took part in making decisions
Planned or chaired a meeting
Given a presentation or speech

Table 11.2 presents data on the proportions who have engaged in each of these skill-building activities on the job, in non-political voluntary associations, and in church, for those respondents who

Table 11.2 Exercising Skills in Non-Political Settings

	On the Job (% of working)	In Non-Political Organizations (% involved)	In Church or Synagogue (% members)
Attend a meeting where decisions are made	69%	39%	32%
Plan such a meeting	35	19	17
Write a letter	58	20	12
Make a speech or presentation	40	19	18

are institutionally attached—that is, who are working, who are affiliated with a non-political association, or who are members of a church.[11] Nearly identical proportions of respondents are connected to each domain: 66 percent have jobs; 68 percent are involved in a non-political organization; and 67 percent are church members. Therefore, differences in the aggregate proportions who have exercised particular civic skills over the preceding six months represent differences among the domains rather than differences in the proportion of respondents who are institutionally affiliated.

The data make clear that these non-political settings provide many opportunities to practice skills relevant to politics. In terms of specific acts, across institutions respondents are more likely to attend meetings where they take part in making decisions than to exercise civic skills in other ways. In terms of particular domains, the workplace is especially rich in opportunities for the exercise of skills: for instance, over two-thirds report attending a meeting where decisions are made and over one-third planned such a meet-

---

11. We consider as working those who were working full or part time for pay or who were with a job but temporarily not working because of illness, vacation, or temporary layoff. We define anyone who is a member of, or a contributor to, an organization that does not take stands on public issues to be affiliated with a non-political organization. (For an extended discussion of the complexities in defining institutional involvement, see Chapter 3 and Appendix B.1.g and B.2.c.) We include among church members either those who said that they belong to a church, synagogue, or other religious institution in their community or one nearby or those who said that they attend services regularly (at least two or three times a month) in the same congregation or parish.

The questions about skills practiced in an organization were asked about the respondent's main organization—the one to which the most time or money was given or, if different, the one the respondent considered most important.

ing. Organizations and churches also provide the chance to practice civic skills: about a third attended a meeting where decisions are made and close to a fifth planned such a meeting.[12] Thus the data indicate that the job, voluntary organizations, and churches are places where citizens can learn how to be active citizens.[13]

Who Gets Adult Civic Skills?

Throughout this chapter and the preceding one we have been concerned with the way in which resources accumulate—leading to stratification in who has the wherewithal to be active, and effective, in politics. Hence we are led to inquire who gets and takes advantage of opportunities to practice adult civic skills. Opportunities to exercise skills are not distributed evenly along lines of class, race, or gender. Instead, different institutions provide opportunities for different sets of people. In some cases, the allocation of opportunities to exercise civic skills reinforces other processes that create advantage; in others, it counterbalances these processes.

We mentioned that the extent to which an individual gets the opportunity to practice a civic skill on the job, in an organization, or at church depends first upon being institutionally connected—having a job, or being affiliated with a voluntary association, or belonging to a religious institution. It also depends upon the kind of job, organization, or church, and upon the way in which the institution allocates opportunities to choose—or to be chosen—to exercise civic skills. In order to understand how the processes by which civic skills are acquired in adulthood articulate with other processes by which political resources are stockpiled, we must begin by considering who is in an institutional position to obtain

---

12. We may underestimate somewhat the exercise of civic skills by church members because of the way the questions were asked. The number of church skills may, in fact, be closer to the number of non-political organizational skills than is seen in the reported data. We do not believe it affects the overall findings that the workplace is especially rich in opportunities for the practice of civic skills and that organizations provide somewhat more opportunities than religious institutions. For a discussion of the measurement of church and other skills, see Appendix B.9.

13. For further discussion of these civic skills, their measurement, and the basis for our considering them to be a common set of skills, see Appendix B.9.a.

these skills. Table 11.3 contains data on the stratification by income, race/ethnicity, and gender of affiliation with institutions—having a job, being in a voluntary association, and belonging to a church. Some of these data were reported in Chapters 7 and 8; since they are relevant to the issue of skill acquisition with which we are dealing, we repeat them here.

THE WORKPLACE

The chance to acquire civic skills in the workplace obviously depends, first of all, on having a job. Most people must get a job to earn money, so it is no surprise to find, in Table 11.3, that the vast majority of people do work (either part-time or full-time) and that it is those with lower incomes who are less likely to work.[14] Moreover, the percentage working is not very different across Latinos, African-Americans, and Anglo-Whites. Sixty-seven percent of Anglo-Whites and 65 percent of African-Americans report working either part-time or full-time. Latinos, 60 percent of whom have full-time or part-time jobs, are slightly less likely to be in the work force. When it comes to gender, however, there is a clear distinction. Men are more likely than women to be in the work force: 76 percent of the male respondents, compared with 58 percent of the female respondents, have full-time or part-time jobs.[15]

Having a job is, of course, a necessary first step toward acquiring civic skills in the workplace, but the nature of the occupation is also important. Teachers or lawyers are more likely to have

---

14. The dropoff in the proportion working at the highest income level appears to be due to the low level of employment among married women in the highest income group. While 70 percent of the married women with family incomes between $75,000 and $125,000 are employed (N = 48), only 32 percent (N = 20) of married women in the top category are.

15. The percentages of those working full-time or part-time or out of the work force are as follows:

	Full-Time	Part-Time	Not Working
Anglo-Whites	57	10	33
Blacks	57	8	35
Latinos	50	10	40
Women	43	15	43
Men	71	5	24

Table 11.3 Institutional Involvement by Income, Race or Ethnicity, and Gender

[handwritten: why so low?]

[handwritten right margin: Better chere would be attendance p church function]

	Percent Working	Percent Involved with a Non-Political Organization	Percent Belong to a Church
FAMILY INCOME			
Under $15,000	42%	52%	63%
$15,000-34,999	67	66	64
$35,000-49,999	78	79	69
$50,000-74,999	79	80	71
$75,000-124,999	78	76	69
$125,000 and over	62	89	66
RACE OR ETHNICITY			
Latinos	60%	40%	62%
African-Americans	65	58	74
Anglo-Whites	67	71	66
GENDER			
Women	58%	68%	74%
Men	76	68	58

opportunities to enhance civic skills—to organize meetings, make presentations, and the like—than are fast-food workers or meat cutters. Occupational stratification is one of the components of socioeconomic status, and it is closely linked to educational attainment and, as we have seen, to income. In this way, resources for participation accumulate: schooling itself produces civic skills; in addition, with increasing educational attainment come opportunities for jobs that not only are more financially rewarding but also provide more chances to practice civic skills.

Access to high-level jobs—that is, jobs requiring high levels of education or on-the-job training—is highly structured by other social characteristics. It is hardly surprising that high levels of educational attainment or family income tend to go hand-in-hand with high-level occupations.[16] Among the employed, 2 percent of those who never finished high school—compared with 91 percent

---

16. In this paragraph we are defining a high-level job as one that, in the respondent's estimate, requires at least a college degree. This corresponds to the two highest levels on the five-point scale.

of those with graduate degrees—work in high-level jobs. Similarly, 9 percent of those whose family incomes are below $20,000—in contrast to 80 percent of those whose family incomes are above $75,000—are employed in high-level jobs. It is also worth noting that, in spite of remarkable changes in job opportunities for minorities and women over the past several decades, disparities remain in the kinds of jobs held by members of various groups.[17] Among those with jobs, 13 percent of Latinos, 20 percent of African-Americans, and 34 percent of Anglo-Whites hold high-level jobs. Because women are less likely to be in the work force, it is not surprising that women are, in the aggregate, less likely to be in high-level occupations. Even among the employed, however, 28 percent of the women and 34 percent of the men work in high-level jobs.

In summary, except for the lower work force participation of women and the fact that the poor are less likely to work, the imperative of having to work affects all groups. What structures the chances to engage in adult civic skills in the workplace is not work force participation, but the kinds of jobs people have. And these are highly stratified by race, ethnicity, income, education, and gender.

NON-POLITICAL VOLUNTARY ORGANIZATIONS

To gain skills in a non-political organization requires, first of all, organizational affiliation. As shown in Table 11.3, which repeats data from Chapters 7 and 8, affiliation with non-political organizations is significantly structured by income and race or ethnicity, but not gender. Unlike work, which is a necessity for most people, belonging to organizations is a luxury good and increases with income. As for ethnicity, Anglo-Whites are somewhat more likely than African-Americans, and much more likely than Latinos, to

---

17. For instance, in a study of the attitudes of important elite groups, Verba and Orren sampled leaders from various domains of life including top business leaders—CEOs or other very high officials of Fortune 500 companies. These business leaders were 99 percent White and 98 percent male. Similarly, there were few females or minorities in parallel samples of leaders in other areas of the economy. Top leaders of farm organizations were 98 percent White and 94 percent male; labor leaders 96 percent White and 95 percent male. See Sidney Verba and Gary R. Orren, *Equality in America: The View From the Top* (Cambridge, Mass.: Harvard University Press, 1985).

be affiliated with a non-political organization. In terms of activity we showed in Chapter 8 that Anglo-Whites and African-Americans are equally likely, and considerably more likely than Latinos, to be active in a non-political organization. There is no difference between men and women with respect to activity in non-political organizations, except that among those who give money, men give larger amounts.

RELIGIOUS INSTITUTIONS

Earlier we noted the irony that, although the democratic polity is the domain of human endeavor founded upon the equality of all citizens, the religious domain is in fact a more democratic arena of activity. We have also discussed the significance of the Black churches in nurturing leadership, developing skills, and providing an organizational infrastructure for political action. As shown in Table 11.3, participation in religious institutions is much less structured by income, race, or ethnicity than is political activity. Belonging to a church is even less stratified by income than is having a job.

Moreover, in the religious domain women participate more than men and African-Americans more than Anglo-Whites. Women are more likely than men both to go to services and to give time to charitable, educational, or social activities connected with a church. The only area in which men predominate is in giving money. Among those who make religious contributions, men give larger amounts to their churches. African-Americans are the most active in their churches by all measures. Latinos and Anglo-Whites are equally likely to attend religious services, but Latinos are much less likely than Anglo-Whites to be involved in educational, charitable, or social activities associated with their churches. In Chapter 8 we surmised that the disparity in church-related activity might be related to the fact that Latinos are disproportionately likely to be Catholic rather than Protestant. Later in this chapter, we explore further the implications of this distinction.

Exercising Skills

We have seen that there is variation across institutions in the extent to which institutional attachment is socially structured—with church membership distributed more evenly across groups defined by income, race or ethnicity, or gender than is organizational affiliation or, especially, access to high-level occupations. The next step is to inquire how opportunities to practice skills are apportioned. Figure 11.1 shows for groups defined by their income, race or ethnicity, and gender the mean number of civic skills practiced by those who are attached to each institutional domain—that is, those who are working, affiliated with a non-political organization, or members of a local church. Several findings emerge from this figure. First, the workplace provides, by far, the most opportunities for the exercise of civic skills but does so in the most stratified manner. The chance to practice skills on the job rises steeply with family income, much more steeply than it does in organizations. In contrast, there is no systematic relationship between family income and the exercise of civic skills in church.[18]

These patterns obtain—although they are less pronounced—when it comes to gender and race or ethnicity. The workplace is the most stratified of the three domains: among workers, women exercise, on average, somewhat fewer skills than men; Latinos exercise fewer skills on the job than do African-Americans and, especially, Anglo-Whites. Organizations replicate these patterns, although less strongly. These patterns are partially reversed, however, for the exercise of civic skills in conjunction with church activity. Among church members, there is only a minimal gender gap in the exercise of civic skills, with the advantage in a masculine direction;[19] African-Americans practice, on average, somewhat more skills in church than Anglo-Whites. Latinos, however, have the fewest opportunities across all three domains.

We can now summarize our findings with respect to the acqui-

---

18. Since the "mean number of civic skills" is not an immediately intuitive metric, it might be useful to give a concrete example of the magnitude of the differences reflected in Figure 11.1. Among those in the lowest income category who are working, 17 percent get a chance to make a speech or presentation on the job and 13 percent get a chance to plan a meeting. The parallel figures for those in the top income category are 74 percent and 82 percent.

19. Data not included in Figure 11.1 show that among all respondents, men exercise, on average, fewer civic skills in church than women do. The discrepancy results from the fact that women are more likely than men to be church members. However, as shown in Figure 11.1, among members, women exercise, on average, very slightly fewer skills than men.

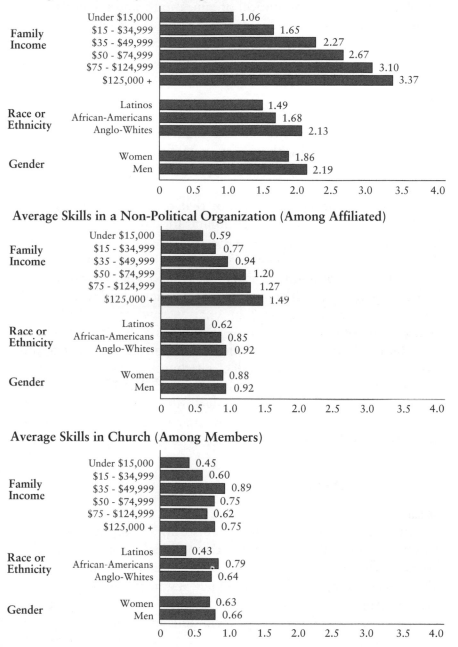

Figure 11.1 Skills Practiced on the Job, in a Non-Political Organization, and in Church, by Income, Race or Ethnicity, and Gender.

sition of civic skills in the three domains of adult non-political involvement: jobs, non-political organizations, and religious institutions. Acquisition of skills depends upon the level of skill opportunity provided by the domain; the extent to which involvement in the domain is socially structured; and the extent to which opportunities for skill development are socially structured among those affiliated.

Workplaces provide the most opportunities for the practice of civic skills, churches the fewest. In addition, access to the workplace is not associated with income or with race or ethnicity. However, opportunities to acquire civic skills are highly stratified on the job, largely because those who are otherwise disadvantaged are likely to be in the kinds of jobs that provide few chances for skill development. In contrast, organizational affiliation is stratified by income and race or ethnicity—though not by gender. Furthermore, as in the workplace, among those affiliated with non-political associations, the well-heeled and Anglo-Whites enjoy greater opportunities for the exercise of civic skills. However, the relationships are less strong than what we saw for the workplace. The domain of equal access to opportunities to learn civic skills is the church. Not only is religious affiliation not stratified by income, race or ethnicity, or gender, but churches apportion opportunities for skill development relatively equally among members. Among church members, the less well off are at less of a disadvantage, and African-Americans are at an actual advantage, when it comes to opportunities to practice civic skills in church.

Catholics, Protestants, and Civic Skills

Because they distribute opportunities for the exercise of civic skills relatively democratically, religious institutions appear to have a powerful potential for enhancing the political resources available to citizens who would, otherwise, be resource-poor. However, our data suggest that this process, which augments the resources of African-Americans, does not have the same compensatory impact for Latinos, who practice fewer civic skills in all three domains of adult activity, including church. Since, as we saw in Chapter 8, Latinos are somewhat more likely than Anglo-Whites to attend services regularly, the Latino disadvantage in the religious domain is puzzling. Why, then, do Latinos not have more chances to develop skills in church?

We begin our investigation of the roots of church-related civic skills by recalling a point we raised in Chapter 8: Latinos are much more likely than African-Americans to be Catholic rather than Protestant. In our sample, 85 percent of the African-American respondents are Protestant, while 25 percent of the Latinos are Protestant and 66 percent are Catholic. As we mentioned earlier, Protestant and Catholic churches differ along several dimensions that would seem to be relevant for the extent of lay participation in church matters: Protestant congregations tend, on average, to be smaller than Catholic parishes; compared to the Catholic Church, most Protestant denominations allow for greater lay participation in the liturgy; and most Protestant denominations are organized on a congregational basis with authority vested in the congregation itself rather than in a church hierarchy.[20] It is important to recognize that we are not asserting that Catholic churches are apolitical. On the contrary, as we shall see in Chapter 13, Catholics are no less likely than Protestants to be exposed to political messages in church. The opportunities for skill development to which we refer arise in the course of church-based activity that has no demonstrable political content—for example, serving on a committee to hire a new minister or oversee the church budget.

These differences are reflected in Table 11.4, which presents data about the average skills exercised by Protestants and Catholics and repeats data from Chapter 8 about the amount of time they give to church-related activities—over and above attendance at services.[21] Table 11.4 shows a dramatic difference between Catholic and Protestant respondents in terms of both opportuni-

---

20. We pointed out in Chapter 8 that the differences between Protestant and Catholic congregations were probably even more pronounced a generation ago. There seems to have been some convergence since Vatican II. See Chapter 8 for discussion and references.

21. Since there are relatively few Black Catholics in our follow-up sample (an unweighted N of 33), the data for church activity are derived from our much larger screener survey which has a larger data base of African-American Catholics (87). Because the screener did not include information about membership in a local church, we report these data for regular church attenders rather than for church members.

Table 11.4 Skills Exercised and Activity in Church by Denomination and Race or Ethnicity

	Average Skills Exercised in Church		Average Hours Church Activity[a]	
	All	Members[b]	All	Attenders[c]
All				
Protestants	.60	.81	1.7	3.2
Catholics	.19	.25	.8	1.3
Latinos				
Protestants	.42	.55	2.2	3.2
Catholics	.24	.35	1.0	1.4
African-Americans				
Protestants	.68	.83	2.1	3.5
Catholics	.21[d]	.29	.8	2.4
Anglo-Whites				
Protestants	.60	.82	1.6	3.2
Catholics	.18	.23	.8	1.3

a. Screener data.
b. Member of local congregation or regular attender in the same congregation.
c. Regular church attendance: at least 2–3 times a month.
d. 33 unweighted (17 weighted) cases.

ties to exercise politically relevant skills in church and time devoted to church-related educational, social, or charitable activity. Protestants are three times more likely than Catholics to report a skill opportunity; since Protestants and Catholics have roughly equivalent rates of attendance at services, this finding holds both for all members of the denomination and for the substantial proportions of each group who report membership in a local congregation or parish.

Considering Anglo-Whites, African-Americans, and Latinos separately, we see that the Protestant-Catholic distinction holds up in terms of both the amount of time devoted to church activity and opportunities to exercise civic skills in church.[22] In all three groups, Protestants are much more active, and more likely to practice civic skills, in their churches than are Catholics. Latino Protestants

---

22. We did not ask about opportunities to exercise skills on our short screener.

Table 11.5 Skills Practiced in Church by Religion and Educational Level (church members[a] only)

	Protestants	Catholics
No High School Diploma	.30	.16
High School Graduate	.75	.15
Some College	1.07	.23
College Graduate	.85	.35
Graduate Work	1.28	.55

a. Member is defined as member of local congregation or regular attender in the same congregation.

report exercising on average fewer civic skills than do African-American and Anglo-White Protestants. However, they report an average number of skills well above the average among Latino Catholics. In short, the Latino disadvantage with respect to opportunities to learn politically salient skills in church seems to derive from the fact that they are disproportionately Catholic.[23] Since many Latinos have left the Catholic Church for various Protestant sects in recent years, it will be interesting to see if they have enhanced opportunities to develop civic skills in the future.

It is important to stress that the difference between Protestants and Catholics appears to be related to the characteristics of the two religions and the way their congregations are governed rather than to characteristics of the congregants. In all three domains—jobs, organizations, and churches—those with high levels of education are more likely to exercise skills relevant to politics. However, Table 11.5 makes clear that the difference between Catholics and Protestants in the exercise of civic skills is not a function of

---

23. Readers who consider Latino Catholic churches in America to be important centers of political activity have been skeptical about our findings concerning the absence of church-based skill opportunities for Latino Catholics. They have suggested that the explanation for the apparent contradiction lies in the fact that many Latinos report themselves as Catholics, but are only nominally Catholic and rarely attend church. However, the data we presented in Chapter 8 (which were from our screener survey and thus contain large numbers of cases) suggest that Latino Catholics are certainly no less likely to attend church than are Anglo-White Catholics. It is also relevant to recall our earlier point that we are not arguing that Catholic churches are apolitical as institutions, but rather that they are less rich in the *non-political* activities that afford opportunities to develop skills.

a difference in overall educational level. The difference in skill opportunities shows up quite strongly at all educational levels.

There could, however, be a number of other reasons, unrelated to religious preference, why African-Americans and Latinos report different levels of opportunity to practice civic skills in church. Latinos might attend church less frequently; or the more restricted role of women in the Catholic church might diminish skill acquisition among Latina women; or the fact that Latinos are more likely to be newcomers to a community and to their congregations might reduce their role in church.[24] To eliminate these alternative explanations, we considered the impact of religious preferences on civic skill acquisition in church, controlling for a number of other characteristics: race and ethnicity, gender, roots in the community (measured by years in the community, home ownership, and having school-aged children), frequency of church attendance, as well as education and age.

Table 11.6 reports a multiple regression analysis predicting the number of church skills acquired for the 86 percent of the sample with a Catholic or Protestant religious preference. Several of the explanatory variables—especially the frequency of church attendance—have an impact on the likelihood of acquiring civic skills in church. However, we are especially concerned about the impact of being Protestant rather than Catholic. What is striking about the results in Table 11.6 is that the effect of religious preference is strong and statistically significant even when these other factors have been taken into account. Indeed, controlling for these other variables does not diminish at all the relationship between church preference and civic skills.[25] In short, the exercise of civic skills is related not only to individual characteristics but also to the characteristics of Protestant and Catholic churches.

---

24. These are, in fact, the conjectures of skeptical readers of our manuscript.

25. The coefficient for religious preference is a bit stronger once these other factors have been controlled than it is without taking such factors as education and frequency of church attendance into account. Taking none of these factors into account, Protestants practice .40 more skills (on a scale that ranges from zero to four) than Catholics do. Controlling for attendance at religious services, education, and other factors, the difference between the two groups (as measured by the regression coefficient) rises slightly to .43. If anything, individual characteristics such as frequency of church attendance and education mask somewhat the effect of church structure.

Table 11.6 Predicting Skills Practiced in Churches: OLS Regression
(Protestants and Catholics only)

Variable	B	SE B	Beta
DEMOGRAPHIC CHARACTERISTICS			
Gender	−0.03	0.04	−0.02
Black	.04	.07	.01
Latino	.01	.09	.01
Education	.07	.01	.10**
ROOTS IN THE COMMUNITY			
Years in community	−.00	.00	−.02
Home ownership	.13	.04	.06**
School-age children	.07	.05	.03
RELIGION			
Church attendance	.18	.01	.45**
Protestant (rather than Catholic)	.43	.04	.19**
(Constant)	−1.14	.11	
R^2		.26	
Sample size		2,204	

* Significant 0.5 level.
** Significant 0.1 level.
Note: Age is also included in the equation but is not reported in the table.

Practicing Skills at Work and in Church: A Final Look

We have argued that the kind of institution with which an individual is affiliated affects the acquisition of civic skills. However, observed differences in civic skills across different types of institutions might result from differences in the people who choose to join them rather than from differences in the institutions themselves. This is why we took pains to demonstrate that, even after controlling for individual characteristics, especially education, a large gap remains between Protestants and Catholics in the civic skills they exercise at their churches. Still, we might wonder whether we have failed to control for some crucial individual difference.

We can sort out the impact of the *kinds of institutions* to which individuals belong from the impact of the *kinds of individuals* who join such institutions by considering skill acquisition in jobs and churches together. If the two—the exercise of skills on the job and in church—work in tandem for all individuals, then we have reason to conclude that it is the characteristics of individuals rather than the characteristics of institutions that are responsible for opportunities for skill acquisition. If, in contrast, some individuals do particularly well in skill acquisition in one setting but not in another, we have reason to suspect that the institutions are having an independent impact. What matters is that the *same people* fare so differently in different settings.

The nearly 40 percent of the sample who work either full or part time and who are church members provide us with a large group within which to test this line of reasoning. The extent to which these individuals exercise skills in either or both settings will depend upon their own personal characteristics and, if institutions matter, upon the kind of church they attend and the kind of job they have. Table 11.7 contains data on the socioeconomic status—as measured by educational attainment and average family income—and the number of civic skills exercised on the job and in church for working church members who are in various occupations and several religious denominations. With respect to religion, we present data, as usual, about Catholics and Protestants. In addition, we include information about three Protestant denominations, Baptists, Methodists, and Episcopalians. We also present data on five occupational groups.

The data in Table 11.7 indicate that job and church do not work in tandem. Comparing across job levels, we see that professionals exercise nearly three times more civic skills on the job than do laborers or service workers. However, as shown in the right-hand column of Table 11.7, high occupational status confers much less advantage in church. That the increase in church skills does not track the increase in job skills as we move up the occupational hierarchy suggests that we are observing a true institutional effect. We can make a similar comparison on the basis of religious affiliation. Protestants and Catholics differ enormously in the average number of church skills practiced; however, there is no parallel difference in average job skills. The same people, once again, develop quite different levels of civic skills depending upon whether they are at work or in church.

Table 11.7 Family Income, Educational Attainment, and Skills Exercised on the Job and in Church (among working respondents who are church members)

	Average Family Income	Percentage College Graduates	Average Job Skills	Average Church Skills	Weighted N
Occupation					
Laborer/Service	$33,600	4%	.97	.60	(144)
Skilled/Operative	$36,800	4%	1.27	.62	(150)
Clerical/Sales	$42,300	13%	1.82	.70	(208)
Managerial	$48,900	28%	2.80	.70	(182)
Professional	$53,600	68%	2.89	.93	(272)
Denomination					
Catholic	$49,000	31%	2.11	.27	(309)
Protestant	$41,600	26%	2.05	.96	(657)
Baptist	$40,700	14%	1.72	.92	(201)
Methodist	$44,500	35%	2.53	.95	(112)
Episcopalian	$61,900	51%	2.84	1.29	(19)

Table 11.7 also includes information about three Protestant denominations, Baptists, Methodists, and Episcopalians. Clearly, Baptists and Episcopalians differ sharply in social status—with Methodists sandwiched between them. The gap in income and, to a lesser extent, in education is comparable to the gap between those at the top and bottom of the occupational hierarchy. Reflecting their comparatively high educational attainment and higher-status jobs, Episcopalians practice more civic skills on the job than Baptists do. In church, however, the two groups are much less distinct in the skills they practice.[26] It is also instructive to compare Catholics and Methodists. While their educational and income profiles are quite similar, Methodists exercise more than three times the number of civic skills in church. Since we are talking about the

---

26. This pattern is even more pronounced if we consider the other conservative Protestants—who belong to a variety of fundamentalist, Pentecostal, and evangelical churches. Consistent with their relatively low level of educational attainment (only 15 percent college graduates) and family incomes that average $37,000, the other conservative Protestants exercise relatively few skills on the job, an average of 1.71. However, in church they are not so disadvantaged, exercising, on average, 1.02 civic skills.

same individuals, it is thus clear that it is the institution that is the driving force.

We can underscore the point by considering two groups of church members with full-time jobs: Catholics with professional or managerial occupations and Baptists with clerical or blue-collar occupations. The two groups differ, quite obviously, in education and family income. Fifty-three percent of the Catholic professionals and managers, as opposed to 3 percent of the Baptist clerical and blue-collar workers, graduated from college. Their family incomes average $55,500 and $36,100 respectively. Consistent with everything we have seen, they have very different profiles when it comes to the exercise of civic skills at work or in church. The Catholic professionals and managers practice an average of 2.9 skills on the job and an average of .2 skills in church. For the Baptist clerical and blue-collar workers, the figures are 1.1 for work-based skills and .8 for church-based skills. In other words, high-status, high-income, and highly educated Catholics exercise more than ten times as many skills in their jobs as in church, while low-status, low-income, and relatively uneducated Baptists exercise almost the same number of skills in each place. Similarly, Catholics with high-status jobs exercise about two and a half times as many skills on the job as do Baptists with low-status jobs, but the high-status Catholics exercise only about one-quarter the number of skills in church as do the latter. Since we are looking at what happens to the *same people in two different places,* the data suggest, once again, that these are institutional effects.

Figure 11.2 gives dramatic confirmation of the special role of religious institutions in providing opportunities for the development of civic skills to those, especially African-Americans, who otherwise would not be in a position to acquire them. Once again we consider data for those who could exercise civic skills both in church and on the job: working church members. Figure 11.2 compares African-Americans and Anglo-Whites at the lowest job level with those in the top two job levels in terms of the exercise of two particular skills—making a presentation or speech and organizing a meeting—at work and in church. The data, especially those for African-Americans, are quite striking. African-Americans in low-status jobs differ markedly from their counterparts in high-

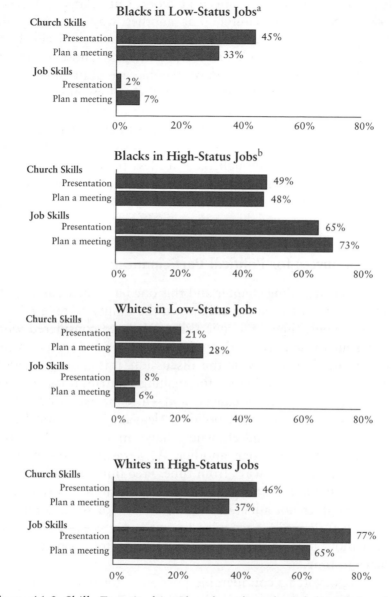

Figure 11.2 Skills Exercised in Church and on the Job by Job Level and Race (among working respondents who are church members).

a. Low-status job: lowest of 5 categories on Job Level variable. See Appendix B.11.b for definition.

b. High-status job: highest 2 of 5 categories on Job Level variable. See Appendix B.11.b for definition.

status jobs in the skills practiced at work, but relatively little in the skills exercised in church. Put another way, those in jobs requiring virtually no education or training are very unlikely to give a presentation or to plan a meeting at work. Those in jobs requiring high levels of education or training are quite likely to do so. For them, the opportunities for skill development in church supplement the greater opportunities in the workplace. For those with low-status jobs, the skill opportunities in church are the only opportunities they have—and they are not inconsequential. These relationships obtain, although they are less pronounced, for Anglo-Whites as well. In short, church activity can compensate in part for the nearly complete absence of opportunities for job-related civic training available to those in low-level jobs.

Resources for Political Participation: Summary

Together the preceding chapter and this one have focused on three resources with potential for enhancing the ability to take part in politics—money, time, and civic skills. We have considered what these resources are, where they come from, and who has them. Money figures in two ways in this discussion. It is at once a critical resource for politics, essential for making contributions to campaigns and other political causes, and—in contrast to both time and civic skills—a source of political cleavage, for political controversies in America and elsewhere have often pitted the better and worse off against one another. As a resource for politics, money differs in many ways from time. Free time is divided much less unequally than is money. Furthermore, advantage with respect to free time does not adhere to the fault lines of social stratification. Instead, those in particular life circumstances—specifically, those without jobs or children—tend to be better endowed when it comes to time.

We have devoted a considerable portion of the discussion to the organizational and communications skills that facilitate participation in politics. The acquisition of these skills begins early in life in the family and in school and continues throughout adulthood in non-political domains—at work, in organizations, and in church. These civic skills are, thus, developed in the course of activities that have nothing to do with politics: making a presentation to a client, organizing a celebrity auction for a charity, or editing the church's monthly newsletter. Once honed, however, they are part of the arsenal of resources that can be devoted, if the individual wishes, to politics.

A NOTE ON SELF-SELECTION

In seeking to understand the role of the non-political institutions with which individuals affiliate in the development of civic skills, we must constantly be wary of the possibility that the causal arrow points in the other direction. Rather than these institutions fostering political capacity, it might be that those who are politically active and competent might seek out institutions where they have the opportunity to use their political skills. Or individuals with civic skills might transform the internal structures of their institutions to make them more participatory. In other words, rather than jobs, organizations, and churches being the source of civic skills, politically skilled and involved individuals might seek jobs or organizations or churches in which they can use skills already developed.

The data presented about the variations among institutions cast doubt on a self-selection explanation of the acquisition of civic skills.[27] As we have shown, apart from the characteristics of the individuals affiliated with them, various kinds of institutions operate differently to encourage the exercise of civic skills; and the same individuals exercise different levels of civic skills on the job and in church, depending on where they work and where they worship. We saw, for example, that Baptists—who are, on average, not especially well educated or well heeled and who, consequently, exercise relatively few skills at work—are considerably more likely than Catholics to exercise civic skills in connection with their church activity. Presumably, this reflects institutional characteristics of the two denominations—for example, the fact

---

27. See on this, Henry E. Brady, Sidney Verba, and Kay L. Schlozman, "Beyond SES: A Resource Model of Political Participation," *American Political Science Review* 89 (June 1995). This article develops a different approach to the issue through a simultaneous equation learning model for civic skills but comes to the same conclusion.

that Baptist churches are smaller than Catholic ones and are organized on a congregational basis.

Even more telling are the data on race or ethnicity and religious affiliation. As we have seen, African-Americans obtain more civic skills in church than do Latinos, a difference that seems to derive from the difference in the churches they attend—Protestant versus Catholic. People choose what church to attend for many complex reasons, beginning with family background. However, we assume that very few people select a church on the basis of its potential for helping to improve their capacities as volunteer political activists. The reason African-Americans generally attend Protestant churches that are rich in opportunities for developing politically useful civic skills while Latinos attend Catholic churches offering fewer such opportunities has nothing to do with the group differences in aspirations to political participation. Rather the origins of the denominational affiliation of the two groups lie in the history of religious development in the antebellum South and in the history of the Spanish conquest of Latin America—both, surely, centuries earlier in the causal chain.

It is hardly more plausible to seek the origins of the less hierarchical internal structures of Protestant churches in variations in the participatory propensities of Protestant congregants. The roots of differences in church structures do not lie in different political agendas of the congregants—or even of church officials—but in the history of the respective churches dating back to the Reformation. The fact that Latinos practice fewer civic skills than African-Americans is a function of their religion, not their politics. In Chapter 13, we shall see analogous institutional effects that seem unlikely to come from self-selection.

SOCIAL STRATIFICATION AND POLITICAL STRATIFICATION

The institutional origins of skills have implications for American democracy because important institutional characteristics—and significant political conflicts—are linked to income, race, and ethnicity. The workplace and the church are both stratified, but they are stratified in quite different ways. A workplace with many employees usually mixes together people who vary in their education, income, and race or ethnicity. However, a diverse work force usually breeds internal stratification and the consequent apportioning of greater skill opportunities to those at the top: at a large manufacturing corporation, managers organize meetings and give speeches; assembly line workers and file clerks do not. In contrast, religious congregations tend to be relatively socially homogeneous. Those who worship together are likely to share not only their faith but also their race or ethnicity and social class. Thus, skill opportunities are more equally allocated across educational, income, or racial or ethnic groups because, within the congregation, there is a more limited range of people who can be chosen—or who can select themselves—to be active.

The relative equality with which opportunities for skill development are distributed in churches is a finding of potential significance for the understanding of American politics.[28] Among the several ways in which American politics is exceptional among the world's democracies is the attenuation of the organizations that bring disadvantaged groups to full participation in political life elsewhere. The labor unions and political parties are weak, and there are no working-class or peasant parties.[29] Less frequently remarked is the strength of religious institutions—which contrasts with the weakness of parties and unions and the frequency with which Americans attend religious services. By providing opportunities for the practice of politically relevant skills, the American churches—especially the Protestant churches—may partially compensate for the weakness of institutions that ordinarily function to mobilize the disadvantaged.

---

28. The lack of stratification in the role the churches play in relation to political participation is paralleled by the ability of church organizations as interest groups to represent all social levels. On this, see Allen D. Hertzke, *Representing God in Washington: The Role of Religious Lobbies in the American Polity* (Knoxville: University of Tennessee Press, 1988).

29. For a comparative analysis showing the consequences for political activity, see Sidney Verba, Norman H. Nie, and Jae-On Kim, *Participation and Political Equality: A Seven-Nation Comparison* (Cambridge: Cambridge University Press, 1978), chaps. 6–8.

12

Resources, Engagement, and Political Activity

In this chapter we reach the heart of our enterprise, to explain political participation as the result of politically relevant resources and psychological engagement in politics. This brings together two essential strands of our inquiry. The resources of time, money, and civic skills make it easier for the individual who is predisposed to take part to do so. The various indicators of political engagement—for example, political interest and efficacy—measure that predisposition. Taken together, these factors provide the framework for a potent explanation of political activity—an explanation we have labeled the Civic Voluntarism Model.

We have already seen how the resources of money, time, and civic skills derive from involvements in family, job, organizations, and religious institutions. The next step is to demonstrate that these resources are the basis for political activity. If we can link political activity back to resources, and resources, in turn, back to their institutional origins, we shall thus be able to establish the roots of citizen activity in the basic institutions of civil society. Furthermore, since resources are unevenly distributed along lines congruent with politically relevant divisions in society, making the connection between resources and activity permits us to explain inequalities in political participation with reference to social inequalities. In addition, we shall show that political engagement adds to an explanation of political activity based on resources without replacing resources as a significant factor in determining who is and who is not active.

Modeling the Sources of Political Activity

Demonstrating that resources and political engagement do, in fact, explain participation involves several issues. We must find some way to disentangle the many factors that might explain different levels of political activity. These include resources, measures of political engagement, and other possible explanatory variables. We turn to the method of multiple regression, which we introduced in Chapter 10, to show how these factors explain political participation. As we have noted, we must take care in designing our analysis. All multivariate techniques, including multiple regression, can be quite misleading unless the unidentified factors that are not included in the analysis—factors in the residual term—are not correlated with the factors that we include in the multiple regression equation. If these omitted factors are correlated, then the variables we include in our equation will carry the effect of these other causes as well as the causes they were meant to represent. This leads to misleading inferences.

We can illustrate how the problem of omitted variables might enter our analysis of the origins of political participation with reference to the relationship between organizational affiliation and political participation. It is well known that citizens who are involved in voluntary associations are also more politically active, but the reasons for that relationship remain obscure.[1] Possibly there are variables that intervene between organizational involvement and participation that are the more direct and proximate causes of participation. In the previous chapter, we showed that civic skills are exercised in the course of activity in non-political organizations. If the Civic Voluntarism Model is correct, it is these civic skills (among a variety of other factors), not the organiza-

---

1. See Sidney Verba and Norman H. Nie, *Participation in America: Political Democracy and Social Equality* (New York: Harper and Row, 1972), chap. 11; and Lester W. Milbrath and M. L. Goel, *Political Participation: How and Why Do People Get Involved in Politics?*, 2nd ed. (Chicago: Rand McNally College Pub. Co., 1977), pp. 110–113.

tional affiliations per se, that explain participation. Organizational involvements matter, but they matter as a step in the process that produces skills, which are then the more direct cause of participation. The same logic obtains for involvements at work and in religious institutions.

The problem of omitted variables becomes more severe when the relationship between the variables included in the analysis is spurious. Consider again the example in the previous paragraph. What if there are no links, direct or indirect, between organizational affiliation and participation, but instead both are the result of some omitted factor—say, psychological engagement with politics and social life or a "taste" for voluntary involvement? If so, the taste for involvement would be the real cause of both organizational affiliation and political participation; yet, unless we included measures of taste or engagement, we would come to the spurious conclusion that organizational affiliation mattered for participation. In the analysis that follows we build our model step by step, adding measures of resources and psychological engagement as we go along, in order to make clear the nature of the relationships we find.

We mentioned another problem in our discussion of multiple regression in Chapter 10: the possibility that the causal arrow runs in the opposite direction, from participation itself to the factors that we assume cause participation. Rather than civic skills and psychological engagement in politics fostering political activity, political activity may lead to the acquisition of skills and engagement. Or the causal arrow might run both ways, creating a problem of simultaneous causation. We have already argued that this danger is probably relatively small for civic skills and the other resources. Ordinarily, people join religious institutions, become involved with non-political organizations, or take jobs for reasons that have little to do with politics. Then they learn skills as a by-product of these institutional affiliations. Ordinary least squares (OLS) regression analysis would be adequate if we were certain of the causal direction of resources and participation. We believe the argument for the causal ordering of civic skills and activity is compelling; nevertheless, we want to be as careful as possible. We also believe that political engagement matters for political participation. The danger of simultaneous causation looms larger for political engagements because, unlike the measures of civic skills, measures of engagement have an explicitly political component. It would seem likely that measures of political engagement such as political interest or efficacy are, at least in part, the result of involvements in politics. This suggests that we should try to solve the simultaneity problem for political engagements. We do this by using a technique called "two-stage least squares" (2SLS). Because both methods, OLS and 2SLS, have defects, we display the results from each.[2] To be conservative, we use 2SLS for political engagements *and* for resources.

From Resources to Political Activity: Estimating the Model

Our main task in this section is to develop and test several explanatory models of political activity. The first step is to test the argument that affiliation in institutions leads to political activity through the development of civic resources. We begin with the link between involvement with institutions and political activity. The dependent variable is the overall scale of political activity, presented in Chapter 7.[3] The explanatory variables are measures of involvement in the major non-political institutions of adult life: attachment to the work force, measured by whether the individual is retired or is employed and, if employed, at what kind of job; involvement in non-political organizations; and attendance at church or synagogue. Two additional measures are amount of education and citizenship.[4] Table 12.1, which presents the results of a linear OLS analysis, reports regression coefficients, standard errors, and beta weights for the impact of these variables on participation.[5] Since

---

2. The strengths and weaknesses of each method are discussed in more detail in Appendix D.

3. See Appendix B.1 for a discussion of this scale and its components.

4. Most studies of participation sample only citizens. We expanded our sample to non-citizens as well, in part because of our interest in Latinos. Thus, we use citizenship as a control in our analysis. For definitions of the variables used in this regression and the others in this chapter, see Appendix B.

5. We use a linear equation because of its simplicity. The results are robust across many other functional forms including the logarithm of participation, logarithms of some of the

Table 12.1 Predicting Overall Participation by Institutional Affiliation and Education: OLS Regression

Variable	B	SE B	Beta
Education	.37	0.02	0.35**
Citizenship	1.10	.17	.11**
Working	.02	.04	.01
Retired	.29	.13	.06*
Job Level	.07	.02	.06**
Organizational Affiliation	.30	.04	.15**
Religious Attendance	.05	.01	.08**
(Constant)	−1.14	.21	
R^2		.29	
Sample Size	2,489		

* Significant at .05 level.
** Significant at .01 level.
Note: Controls for age and Catholic religious preference in the equation.

we wish to compare across independent variables we shall, for reasons outlined in Chapter 10, focus on the beta weights.

The data in Table 12.1 are consistent with the arguments we have been making. Not unexpectedly, education is an important predictor of activity. In this chapter and Chapter 15, we elaborate upon several reasons for the association between education and political participation including the fact that education produces skills. Citizenship is also related to activity.[6] Beyond this, however, institutional involvements also increase political activity. Affiliation with non-political voluntary associations and church atten-

---

independent variables such as family income, and dummy variable versions of scales for occupation, education, work status, and many other variables. See Appendix D for more discussion of these issues.

Beta weights are not a perfect way to measure the importance of a variable, but they are convenient for making comparisons across variables. (See Christopher H. Achen, *Interpreting and Using Regression* [Beverly Hills, Calif.: Sage Publications, 1982].) Although they should actually be attached to the unstandardized coefficients, we place indications of the statistical significance next to the beta weights in Table 12.1 and subsequent tables in order to make the tables easier to read.

6. Virtually all of this relationship is due to the voting component of the activity scale. Although voting is but one act on the scale, it is the one in which, by far, the most respondents engage.

dance are positively related to political activity. So is active involvement in the work force. Although working per se is not significantly related to participation,[7] the other two work-related variables—retirement and job level—are significant predictors. In general, then, institutional factors have a substantial impact on activity.

Why are institutional involvements related to political activity, even when education is controlled? Our argument is that they have their effect through the development of resources. Therefore, we add to the analysis the measures of resources discussed in Chapters 10 and 11: language skills as measured by vocabulary knowledge and use of English at home; family income; free time; and civic skills acquired on the job, in organizations, and in religious institutions. Table 12.2 presents the results of an OLS regression with these resource variables added as explanatory variables.[8] These results are quite consistent with our argument. As a measure of language skills, vocabulary matters.[9] When vocabulary is included, the impact of education is reduced substantially. In addition, family income is also a significant factor in political activity.

Each of the three measures of civic skills developed in institutions is also a strong predictor of political activity. Interestingly, when civic skills are entered into the analysis, the key measures of institutional affiliation—the level of the job, organizational affili-

---

7. This last result is somewhat surprising, but it follows from the two opposite ways in which working affects the resources available for political participation. Working increases civic skills (indeed, one can only acquire job skills if one is working), but it also reduces the availability of free time. The net result is that working appears to have no impact, even though it has substantial effects through civic skills and free time.

8. Age is also in the equation. The variables for "working," "retired," and "Catholic" are also carried in this equation and in subsequent OLS equations as controls. "Working" and "Catholic" have no direct effect on activity in this analysis and in the rest of the analyses in this chapter. "Retired" has a moderate positive effect on activity, but its inclusion does not affect the other explanatory variables in whose impact we are interested.

9. Once we control for citizenship (with which it is correlated at .48), the measure for speaking English at home has only a small impact. This continues to be true as we elaborate our model in the rest of the chapter. We shall carry "English at home" along as a control in our multiple regressions, but we do not report its impact in subsequent tables. There is a complex interrelationship among various measures associated with ethnicity, citizenship, and language which we do not explore here. More research on the interaction among ethnic features and political resources would be useful.

Table 12.2 Predicting Overall Participation by Institutional Affiliation and Resources: OLS Regression

Variable	B	SE B	Beta
EDUCATION AND LANGUAGE			
Education	.24	0.03	0.23**
Vocabulary	.09	.02	.12**
English at Home	.10	.09	.02
INCOME AND TIME			
Family Income	.07	.01	.12**
Free Time	−.01	.01	.04
INSTITUTIONAL AFFILIATION			
Citizenship	.90	.19	.09**
Job Level	.00	.02	.00
Organizational Affiliation	.08	.04	.04
Religious Attendance	.02	.01	.03
CIVIC SKILLS			
Job Skills	.12	.03	.11**
Organization Skills	.16	.03	.10**
Church Skills	.19	.03	.11**
(Constant)	−.93	.24	
R^2		.33	
Sample Size	2,415		

* Significant at .05 level.
** Significant at .01 level.
Note: Age, working, retired, and Catholic religious preference in the equation but not reported.

ation, and church attendance—become insignificant as predictors of activity.[10] Simply being involved with an institution, therefore, does not foster participation. What matters for participation is what happens in the institution—the acquisition of civic skills.[11]

One resource variable, free time, appears to have no significant impact on political activity. In part, this may be the result of the

10. Although working, on its own, has a somewhat negative effect on activity, being retired has the opposite consequence. As we shall see, these effects reflect the impact of these variables on the availability of free time.

11. Other things that happen in institutions—such as exposure to recruitment to politics—also matter. We turn to these in the next chapter. For supporting evidence on the effect of church activism on political activism, see Steven A. Peterson, "Church Participation and Political Participation: The Spillover Effect," *American Politics Quarterly* 20 (1992): 123–139.

fact that two other variables that measure amount of time available to an individual—being an active worker or being retired—are in the equation, the former having a negative impact on activity, the latter having a positive impact. In addition, free time is a measure with, we believe, a good deal of measurement error in it, which makes it hard for the multiple regression to determine its true impact. We shall return to this issue later.

The results reported in Table 12.2 are consistent with our argument about the causal effect of resources on political activity. However, as we have mentioned, OLS is an inadequate technique if causal direction is uncertain. Hence, we estimated a two-stage least squares model of political activity in which the various resources are the explanatory variables. This allows us to deal with the potential ambiguity of causal direction. In addition, 2SLS can help reduce the problems created by measurement error in the OLS equations. When a variable is measured with error, OLS typically produces regression coefficients that are closer to zero than they should be. In effect, the error makes the independent variable appear less powerful than it is. A 2SLS procedure can help to produce better estimates that correct for this error.[12] Appendix D contains the full explication of the model, including justification for the instrumental variables used.

Table 12.3, which presents the results of this analysis, indicates that all the *remaining* resource variables have a strong and significant effect on participation.[13] In particular, note the strength and the similarity of each of the three civic skill variables. This

---

12. Two-stage least squares is, however, not a panacea. If the wrong instruments are chosen or the wrong specification is proposed, then misleading inferences are possible. See, for example, Larry M. Bartels, "Instrumental and 'Quasi-Instrumental' Variables," *American Journal of Political Science* 35 (1991): 777–800. As indicated in the footnotes, we have tried many alternative specifications and obtained the same results. For still other specifications see Henry E. Brady, Sidney Verba, and Kay L. Schlozman, "Beyond SES: A Resource Model of Political Participation," *American Political Science Review* 89 (1995).

13. The specification reported uses the variables given in Table 12.3 as instruments. See Appendix B for the definition of the variables and the questions asked. An argument could be made that the variables for age should not only be used as instruments but also included in the equation because our theory does not fully account for all the possible impacts of age. The issue is whether or not civic skills and the other resources can be thought to mediate the impacts of age. If age is included in the 2SLS regression, the impact of variables measuring civic skills and free time is reduced somewhat. However, the basic pattern reported in Table 12.3 remains.

Table 12.3 Predicting Overall Participation by Resources: Two-Stage
Least Squares Regression

Variable	B	SE B	Beta
EDUCATION AND LANGUAGE			
Education	.20	.03	.18**
Vocabulary	.09	.02	.12**
FREE TIME AND INCOME			
Family Income	.06	.01	.11**
Free Time	.08	.01	.24**
CIVIC SKILLS			
Job Skills	.26	.05	.25**
Organizational Skills	.25	.06	.16**
Church Skills	.37	.06	.23**
(Constant)	−1.67	.22	
R^2		.28	
Sample Size	2,412		

* Significant at .05 level.
** Significant at .01 level.
Notes: Citizenship and English spoken at home are not reported.
Instruments for the 2SLS are: citizenship, education, vocabulary, English at home, family income, working, retired, job level, organizational affiliation, religious attendance, Catholic, number of children under eighteen at home, preschool children at home, sex, spouse working full- or part-time, Black, Latino, education of parents, and dummy variables for age groups.

suggests both that civic skills are an important factor in political activity and that opportunities to develop organizational and communications skills, no matter where they may occur, function similarly vis-à-vis political activity.[14] Furthermore, in the 2SLS

---

14. Moreover, the strength and the similarity of the coefficients for the three measures of civic skills show that skills exercised at work, in non-political organizations, and in church are all transferable to politics at about the same rate. A test for equality of the coefficients strongly supports the conclusion that the three coefficients can be treated as equal to one another. For the OLS version in Table 12.2 the appropriate test is an F-test (with two degrees of freedom in the numerator and 2394 in the denominator) which yields a value of 1.45 which is not significant even at the .25 level. For the 2SLS specification in Table 12.3, the appropriate chi-square test is described in George G. Judge et al., *The Theory and Practice of Econometrics,* 2nd ed. (New York: Wiley, 1985), p. 614, and the value of 2.45 with two degrees of freedom (highly insignificant with a probability value of about .25) strongly supports the null hypothesis that the coefficients are equal to one another.

framework, free time becomes a quite significant factor in predicting participation.[15]

Political Engagement and Activity

Resources appear to matter for political participation. Resources are, however, only one of the components of our Civic Voluntarism Model. The model pairs resources with political engagement. Both resources and political engagement would seem to be required for most forms of political participation. Hence, we must draw both under the umbrella of our analysis.[16] We are concerned about these psychological predispositions for their substantive interest: incorporating them into our analysis should provide a more nuanced understanding of political activity. As the omitted variables that are possible causes of both resource acquisition and political activity, these variables are also germane to our continuing concern with making causal connections. By adding them to the resource analysis, we subject the Civic Voluntarism Model to a more severe test. In so doing, we will also pay attention to an aspect of the problem we have bypassed thus far—the differential impact of resources on different political acts.

We have argued that the availability of resources would explain why someone might or might not be *able* to participate in politics. Political activity is, however, *voluntary* activity. Subjective factors explain why individuals might or might not *want* to participate. The resources of time, money, and skills that facilitate political activity can be put to many uses. Presumably, those who commit these resources to political purposes—rather than to going to the opera, putting in extra hours at the office, or coaching the Little League team—are likely to be engaged in politics: to be aware of, know something about, and care about politics and public issues; and to believe that they can, in fact, have a voice. These internal stimuli to political activity have figured importantly in studies of political participation under such rubrics as political interest, aware-

---

15. The story for free time is a complicated one. See Appendix D for a discussion.

16. This discussion suggests using an interactive or multiplicative specification between political engagements and resources. We have not done so for several reasons. See Appendix D for discussion.

ness, consciousness, and efficacy. For convenience, we call the bundle of these psychological orientations to politics "political engagement."

In Chapter 9 we presented several reasons for treading cautiously when considering political engagement as a cause of participation. First, issues of the ambiguity of causal direction present themselves especially starkly when it comes to measures of engagement. Presumably, being politically interested, knowledgeable, or efficacious enhances the likelihood that an individual will be active; reciprocally, being active may increase engagement as participants become more interested, informed, and efficacious.[17] Second, the fact that political engagement is so close to that which is being explained, political participation, makes an explanation based on political engagement less interesting. That people who are politically interested are politically active seems to tell us less than an explanation based on resources, which have their origins in commitments and involvements further removed from politics. Third, we have more confidence in our ability to measure resources, which are concrete and based on units having standard metrics, than in our ability to measure political engagement. With the possible exception of political information, the various aspects of political engagement are more ambiguous in meaning. Finally, resource-based explanations of participation are relevant for real issues of American politics: conflicts between the rich and the poor, or between those with rewarding, skill-producing work and those with lesser employment or no work at all, have recurred in American politics; competition between the interested and the uninterested or the efficacious and the inefficacious has not been a theme in American political life.

---

17. This, of course, is one of the basic assumptions in the participatory democracy literature: that participation leads to political involvement and interest. Classic statements are in Rousseau and John Stuart Mill. See also Carole Pateman, *Participation and Democratic Theory* (Cambridge: Cambridge University Press, 1970); and Benjamin R. Barber, *Strong Democracy: Participatory Politics for a New Age* (Berkeley and Los Angeles: University of California Press, 1984). There are few empirical studies of this relationship, but see Steven E. Finkel, "Reciprocal Effects of Participation and Political Efficacy," *American Journal of Political Science* 29 (1985): 891–913, who reports that participation enhances efficacy—at least "external" efficacy.

Even so, for several reasons, we believe that attention must be paid to these subjective factors. First, it is hard to imagine that at least some psychological engagement with politics is not required for almost all forms of political participation. Although ambiguous and hard to measure precisely, political engagement is a meaningful and important notion. Some people are involved in politics and others are not, and there is good reason to believe that differences in subjective political engagement affect political activity. Those who choose to devote scarce resources to political activity rather than to other pursuits would, presumably, differ in their orientations to politics.

As we have stressed, there is a final reason for considering the role of these orientations in relation to political activity: to rule out the possibility that we have omitted some variable that explains both resources and political activity. Various components of political engagement are good candidates for such a role. Those who care about politics (perhaps reflecting a more general involvement in the social world) or who feel that they can influence political outcomes (perhaps reflecting a more generally self-confident personality) might be more likely not only to be active in politics but also to engage in skill-creating activities in non-political settings, to earn more, or even to manage their time more effectively. By including measures of political engagement in our analysis, we can test whether they are responsible for the relationship of resources to political activity.

The literature on participation contains numerous measures of political engagement, many of them overlapping in meaning. We concentrate on four that, while all dimensions of political engagement, seem conceptually distinct: political interest, political efficacy, political information, and partisanship.

Political Interest. Citizens who are interested in politics—who follow politics, who care about what happens, who are concerned with who wins and loses—are more politically active.[18] Political interest has been measured in various ways and used as a predic-

---

18. Milbrath and Goel (*Political Participation*, p. 46) report on many studies that find this relationship. It is so taken for granted, they say, that "many authors do not bother to report it."

tor of political activity in many studies.[19] Our measure is simple and straightforward: it is an additive score of the amount of expressed interest—ranging from "not at all interested" to "very interested"—in national and local politics and affairs.[20]

Political Efficacy. According to one student of political attitudes, "Next to party identification, no political attitude has been studied more extensively than feelings of political efficacy."[21] The concept lies at the heart of many explanations of citizen activity and involvement and has been measured in many different ways.[22] In its various forms, it has been shown to vary in significant ways across social groups and to be a strong predictor of political involvement. Socialization explanations of political involvement also emphasize political efficacy.[23] Our measure, which derives from

---

19. The early Michigan election studies combined interest in the election campaign and concern with the outcome along with intensity of partisan preference, sense of citizen duty, and sense of citizen duty into a measure of political involvement. See Angus Campbell, Philip E. Converse, Warren E. Miller, and Donald E. Stokes, *The American Voter* (New York: Wiley, 1960), chap. 5. Gabriel A. Almond and Sidney Verba use measures of following politics and paying attention to political campaigns in *The Civic Culture: Political Attitudes and Democracy in Five Nations* (Princeton: Princeton University Press, 1963), pp. 88–89. Sidney Verba and Norman H. Nie combine interest in politics with political discussion and media attention in *Participation in America*, pp. 367–369. Other scholars have used various combinations of similar measures. For a thorough discussion see Steven Earl Bennett, *Apathy in America, 1960–1984: Causes and Consequences of Citizen Political Indifference* (Dobbs Ferry, N.Y.: Transnational Publishers, 1986), chap. 3. By combining interest in campaigns and a more general measure of interest, Bennett (p. 41) bases his analysis of political apathy—the other side of the political interest coin—on the Almond and Verba approach. W. Russell Neumann uses political interest as one of the components of his measure of political sophistication in his analysis of mass politics. See *The Paradox of Mass Politics: Knowledge and Opinion in the American Electorate* (Cambridge, Mass.: Harvard University Press, 1986).

20. See Appendix B.7.a.

21. Paul R. Abramson, *Political Attitudes in America: Formation and Change* (San Francisco: W. H. Freeman, 1983), p. 135.

22. The classic measure is the four-item efficacy scale used in the Michigan election studies. See Angus Campbell, Gerald Gurin, and Warren E. Miller, *The Voter Decides* (Evanston, Ill.: Row, Peterson, 1954), pp. 181–194. In *The Civic Culture*, chap. 7, Almond and Verba use a five-item "subjective competence" scale based on the respondent's self-assessment of ability to influence politics. Others have used many variations including a distinction between internal and external efficacy—the former measuring whether the individual believes he or she is efficacious, the latter measuring whether the respondent believes the political system is responsive. Abramson, *Political Attitudes in America*, chap. 8, summarizes the vast literature.

23. See David Easton and Jack Dennis, *Children in the Political System: Origins of*

Almond and Verba's approach, is an additive scale of four items about how much attention a local or national government official would pay if the respondent had a complaint and how much influence the respondent has over local or national government decisions.[24]

Political Information. Citizens vary substantially in their political information or knowledge. This information can be of many sorts—about the issues of the day, the individuals active in politics and government, the constitutional principles underlying government, the actual workings of the political system. Political information differs from the other components of political engagement in being objective rather than subjective. Indeed, since an information scale measures cognitive knowledge, rather than affective engagement, we were, at first, uncertain as to whether to include measures of information within the framework of motivations. However, we are convinced by John Zaller's argument that political knowledge—which he calls "cognitive engagement"—is a powerful predictor of political attitude formation and of the connectedness of an individual to the political process.[25] Although we label this measure "political information" rather than "cognitive awareness," we think it useful to include it in the analysis as one of the measures of political engagement. Our political information scale consists of eight items—three of which were names of public officials and five of which tested knowledge of government and politics.[26]

Strength of Party Identification. Party identification holds a special place in the study of the political behavior of the American

---

Political Legitimacy (New York: McGraw-Hill, 1969) and Robert D. Hess and Judith V. Torney, *The Development of Political Attitudes in Children* (Chicago: Aldine, 1967).

24. See Almond and Verba, *The Civic Culture*, chap. 7. For our questions, see Appendix B.7.f.

25. John R. Zaller, *The Nature and Origins of Mass Opinion* (Cambridge: Cambridge University Press, 1992), pp. 42–43. Zaller considers political information to be a measure of affective engagement with politics. Information also figures centrally in Russell Neumann's measure of political sophistication in *The Paradox of Mass Politics*. For a thoughtful analysis of the role of information in participation, see Jane Junn, "Learning about Politics: Sources of Political Knowledge in America," unpublished Ph.D. dissertation, University of Chicago, 1994.

26. See Appendix B.7.c.

public. Although it is usually used to predict the direction of the vote, as one of the fundamental political orientations, it may also play a role in engaging citizens in politics.[27] We measure it by a simple four-point scale constructed from the answers to the standard battery of party identification items. We categorize them in terms of the strength, not the direction, of their partisan leanings as strong partisans, weak partisans, partisan leaners, or non-partisans.[28]

As we might expect, political interest, efficacy, and information are all positively related to each other. Partisanship is somewhat separate, significantly related to political interest but not to efficacy or information.[29]

Who Is Politically Engaged?

Like resources, political engagements are not independent of other social cleavages. In Chapter 15 we will consider some of the roots of psychological involvement in politics. Here we ask quite simply:

---

27. Political science literature has often stressed the importance of party identification in relation to electoral turnout and activity. See, among others, Campbell et al., *The American Voter*, chap. 5; and Verba and Nie, *Participation in America*, chaps. 5, 12. One of the main explanations for the decline in turnout in America is the decline in party attachment. See, for example, Steven J. Rosenstone and John Mark Hansen, *Mobilization, Participation, and Democracy in America* (New York: Macmillan, 1993), chap. 5; and Paul R. Abramson and John H. Aldrich, "The Decline of Electoral Participation in America," *American Political Science Review* 76 (1982): 502–521. Cross-national studies also show that partisanship is a prime factor in political activity. See, for example, Sidney Verba, Norman H. Nie, and Jae-On Kim, *Participation and Political Equality: A Seven National Comparison* (Cambridge: Cambridge University Press, 1978), chap. 6; G. Bingham Powell, "American Voter Turnout in Comparative Perspective," *American Political Science Review* 80 (1986): 17–43; and Steven E. Finkel and Karl-Dieter Opp, "Party Identification and Participation in Collective Political Action," *Journal of Politics* 53 (1991): 339–371.

28. See Appendix B.7.e.

29. The following is the partial correlation matrix among the four measures. We have controlled for political activity to eliminate the relationship among these four measures that derives from the fact that they are all related to activity.

	Efficacy	Information	Partisanship
Interest	.21[***]	.22[***]	.12[***]
Efficacy		.21[***]	.01
Information			.03

Table 12.4 Political Engagement[a] by Education, Family Income, Race or Ethnicity, and Gender

	Average Scores			
	Political Interest (SD = 1.6)	Political Efficacy (SD = 2.4)	Political Information (SD = 1.9)	Strength of Party ID (SD = .9)
All	5.8	9.2	4.1	2.0
Education				
Grammar School or Less	4.5	7.5	2.2	2.0
Some High School	4.9	8.1	3.0	1.9
High School Graduate	5.6	8.9	3.7	1.9
Some College	6.0	9.7	4.4	2.0
College Graduate	6.3	10.2	5.1	2.0
Some Graduate Work	6.3	10.2	5.2	2.2
Master's Degree	6.4	10.0	5.4	2.0
Ph.D./M.D./D.D.S./J.D.	6.8	10.4	6.1	1.9
Family Income				
Under $15,000	5.2	8.4	3.3	2.0
$15,000-34,999	5.6	9.1	3.9	1.8
$35,000-49,999	6.0	9.7	4.6	1.9
$50,000-74,999	6.2	9.8	4.9	2.0
$75,000-124,999	6.3	10.0	5.0	2.2
$125,000 and over	6.6	10.5	5.4	2.2
Race or Ethnicity				
African-American	5.7	8.8	3.1	2.3
Latino	4.9	8.4	2.7	1.8
Anglo-White	5.8	9.4	4.4	1.9
Gender				
Women	5.6	9.1	3.7	2.0
Men	5.9	9.5	4.6	1.9

a. For definitions of political engagement variables, see Appendix B.7.

what kind of person is politically engaged? As we argued with respect to political resources, the potential political significance of these stimuli will vary with the extent to which politically relevant groups differ in their political interest, efficacy, or information or in their strength of party ties. Table 12.4 reports the mean scores for these variables for groups defined by their education, income, race or ethnicity, or sex. Table 12.4 shows the following:

Education: Education is related to three of these variables. Those at the highest levels of education are more than one standard deviation above those in the lowest group with respect to interest, efficacy, and information. In contrast, highly educated respondents are no more strongly identified with a political party than those lower on the education scale.

Income: The pattern for income tracks closely that for education.

Race or ethnicity: The differences among Latinos, African-Americans, and Anglo-Whites parallel those found earlier with respect to political participation. In general, Anglo-Whites score the highest, African-Americans next, and Latinos lowest across the various measures. The one variation is that African-Americans are somewhat stronger in partisanship.

Gender: The differences between women and men are rather smaller and range from almost imperceptible in the case of partisanship to considerably larger when it comes to information, with men better informed than women.

Overall, then, groups that show high levels of participation also evidence high levels of political engagement. This finding suggests that we need to take seriously the possibility that it is engagement, not resources, that explains activity. The engagement measures may be omitted variables that cause both resources and participation. Or, according to our theory, they may be variables that supplement resources in causing participation. Let us try to sort this out.

Resources, Engagement, and Activity: An Expanded Model

The next step is to add the four measures of political engagement to the original model, which included institutional affiliations and political resources as explanatory factors. This submits the resource model to an even more stringent test and should yield a richer understanding of political activity in general, as well as particular political acts. We continue to use OLS for these analyses. However, since we have reason to suspect ambiguity in causal direction—that is, that the political engagement is likely to be caused by activity as well as to cause it—we replicate the analysis using two-stage least squares regression.

Table 12.5 presents the results of a regression analysis in which the dependent variable is the overall scale of political activity and the explanatory variables are the components of the resource model plus the four measures of political engagement.[30] The results of the OLS analysis are quite strong and straightforward. Not unexpectedly, each measure of political engagement is a significant predictor of political activity. Of the four, political interest appears to have the largest effect, but the coefficients for information and efficacy are substantial as well. Strength of partisanship is also significant.

The results of this analysis provide strong support for our contention that resources and political engagement jointly matter for political participation. The coefficients for the various resources— education and vocabulary, family income, and the measures of three civic skills—remain significant after the inclusion in the model of four quite potent attitudinal predictors of political activity. What is more, including measures of political engagement does not diminish the power of the model but instead adds to it. The fact that resources, especially civic skills, continue to play a role in fostering activity even after we incorporate measures of political engagement into the model is particularly important. The data

---

30. In order to simplify the data presentation, we have not been displaying the results for every variable. In Table 12.5 we do not report the result for using English at home, a variable that has no effect on activity when the other variables are in the equation. In addition, we omit the measure of citizenship. Although Table 12.2 showed citizenship to be significant as a predictor of overall political activity, in fact, its significance derives solely from its impact on voting, an activity limited to citizens. With the other variables in the equation, citizenship affects no other mode of activity. In addition, to eliminate the possible confounding effects of age, we continue to include five dummy variables for age categories. The age coefficients are not reported in the table but are in the equation. We also do not report the coefficients for working, being retired, or being a Catholic.

We are unable to include in the analysis the measures, discussed in Chapter 4, of the perceived rewards of political participation. We measured political interest, efficacy, information, and strength of partisanship for all respondents—whether or not politically active. Because the measures of the gratifications of activity were tied to the performance of particular acts, they are not available for the inactive. Hence, they cannot be used to explain whether or not an individual takes part.

Table 12.5 Predicting Overall Political Participation by Resources, Institutional Affiliation, and Political Engagement Measures: OLS Regression

Variable	B	SE B	Beta
EDUCATION AND LANGUAGE			
Education	.17	.02	.16**
Vocabulary	.03	.01	.03
INCOME AND TIME			
Family Income	.05	.01	.10**
Free Time	−.01	.01	−.03
INSTITUTIONAL AFFILIATION			
Job Level	−.02	.02	−.02
Organizational Affiliation	.00	.04	.00
Religious Attendance	.00	.01	.00
CIVIC SKILLS			
Job Skill	.07	.02	.07**
Organizational Skill	.15	.03	.10**
Church Skill	.13	.03	.08**
POLITICAL ENGAGEMENT			
Political Interest	.25	.02	.24**
Political Information	.10	.02	.12**
Political Efficacy	.08	.01	.12**
Partisan Strength	.10	.03	.06**
(Constant)	−2.55	.24	
R^2		.44	
Sample size		2,386 weighted cases	

* Significant at .05 level.
** Significant at .01 level.
    Note: Citizenship, English spoken at home, working, retired, Catholic religious preference, and age dummies are also included in the equation but not reported in the table.

make clear that these resources are independent factors, not proxies for some other psychological engagement. Using the coefficients from Table 12.5 (or Table 12.6, which will be discussed shortly), we calculate that the exercise of a single civic skill in each of the three non-political domains leads to an increase in political activity of roughly a third of a political act (in a population which engages in an average of 2.1 political acts with a standard deviation of 1.6).

Table 12.6 Predicting Overall Participation by Resources and
Political Engagement: Two-Stage Least Squares Regression

Variable	B	SE B	Beta
EDUCATION AND LANGUAGE			
Education	.13	.03	.12**
Vocabulary	.01	.02	.02
INCOME AND FREE TIME			
Family Income	.05	.01	.09**
Free Time	.03	.01	.09*
CIVIC SKILLS			
Job, Organization, and			
Church (total)	.11	.03	.17**
POLITICAL ENGAGEMENT			
Political Interest	.48	.06	.46**
Political Information	.12	.06	.13*
Political Efficacy	.02	.09	.03
Partisan Strength	.08	.05	.04
(Constant)	−3.56	.52	
R^2		.37	
Sample size		2,380	

* Significant at .05 level.
** Significant at .01 level.

Notes: Citizenship and English spoken at home are also included in the equation but not reported.

Instruments for the 2SLS are: citizenship, education, vocabulary, English spoken at home, family income, working, retired, job level, organizational affiliation, religious attendance, Catholic, number of children under 18, preschool children at home, sex, spouse working full or part-time, Black, Latino, education of parents, age dummies, and three variables from the screener survey—political interest, information, and partisan strength.

In short, by introducing civic skills into our analysis, we have enlarged the arsenal of explanatory factors for participation.

The fact that the importance of resources holds up so well once the engagement measures are included suggests that none of the aspects of engagement is an omitted variable that explains both resources and political activity.[31] The data in Table 12.5 buttress

---

31. The Civic Voluntarism Model holds up well under other challenges as well. In our screener data we asked people how many hours they gave to charity. This might be thought of as a measure of "taste" for voluntarism. The inclusion of this variable in the model does

our view that the Civic Voluntarism Model is a powerful one for understanding political activity. However, the addition of the engagement variables raises another issue. As we have argued, political interest and the other engagement measures may be the result rather than the cause of political activity. This suggests, once again, using two-stage least squares. Using two-stage least squares also permits us to correct for measurement error in the free time variable. Table 12.6 presents an analysis using 2SLS. To simplify the presentation, we add the three skills together and report the impact of the sum of skills in Table 12.6 along with the other basic variables.[32] These results strongly support the conclusions from the OLS analysis. The resource variables and two of the engagement variables are all significant and potent predictors of political activity. As before, once we move to a 2SLS specification, free time becomes significant as well.

SUMMARY: RESOURCES AND ENGAGEMENT

Political participation, then, is the result of political engagement *and* resources. We have systematically eliminated as many alternative explanations as possible with the data and techniques at hand. Our results are robust across many different specifications and statistical estimation methods.[33] To summarize, interest, information, efficacy, and partisan intensity provide the desire, knowledge, and self-assurance that impel people to be engaged by politics. But time, money, and skills provide the wherewithal without which engagement is meaningless. It is not sufficient to know and

---

not change the results. In Chapter 15 we add another measure of engagement to the resource model—political involvement during the high school years, which may be thought of as a measure of the long-term propensity to be an activist. As we shall see, the resource variables retain their power even when subjected to that additional challenge.

32. We can sum these skills because it makes theoretical sense and because statistical tests for the data in Tables 12.2 and 12.3 (reported in footnote 14) showed that we could not reject the assumption that the coefficients for the three skills were equal. Equivalent tests for Tables 12.5 and 12.6 yield an insignificant F-test of 2.07 for the OLS specification in Table 12.5 and an insignificant result for Table 12.6.

33. In the language of econometrics, we have investigated the "fragility" of our results regarding civic skills and income and found that alternative specifications lead to the same result. Our results for free time are more fragile, but we certainly have enough evidence to suggest that free time is probably important.

care about politics. If wishes were resources, then beggars would participate. Political engagement, however, does not produce resources, and the resource-poor are less politically active than those who are better endowed with resources.[34]

A NOTE ON GROUP CONSCIOUSNESS

Since group consciousness has played such an important role in the understanding of the political participation of women and African-Americans, we had assumed that measures of consciousness would figure significantly in the bundle of political predispositions we have gathered under the rubric of political engagement.[35] So committed were we to giving group consciousness a prominent place in our analysis that we included several measures on the screener questionnaire that was administered to all 15,000 original respondents. These items asked women, African-Americans, and Latinos whether they felt close to others who share their sex, race, or ethnicity; whether they thought that group members had problems in common; and, if so, whether they thought that the government ought to help in solving joint problems. In addition, all respondents were asked three seven-point scale questions in the follow-up survey—one each on whether the government ought to help Blacks, Hispanics, or women or whether members of these groups should help themselves—as well as whether they had ever experienced discrimination on the basis of either their sex or their racial or ethnic background.

Our efforts did not produce results. Although we tried several versions of scales built from these measures, none had an effect on political activity once measures of resources and other aspects of political engagement were included in the equation. We analyzed the data for each of the groups separately as well as jointly

---

34. Some political activity, such as voting, however, is less dependent on resources. See below.

35. See, for example, Verba and Nie, *Participation in America*, chap. 10; Marvin E. Olsen, "Black Consciousness and Political Participation: The Missing Link," *American Sociological Review* 35 (1970): 682–697; Arthur H. Miller, Patricia Gurin, Gerald Gurin, and Oksana Malanchuk, "Group Consciousness and Political Participation," *American Journal of Political Science* 25 (1981): 494–511; and Sue Tolleson Rinehart, *Gender Consciousness and Politics* (New York: Routledge, 1992), especially chaps. 3, 5.

using a combined measure of consciousness. The most extensive measure, encompassing five items, produces a coefficient that approaches significance for women. For Blacks and Latinos, the coefficients are not significant for any of the variations we tried.[36] We have, therefore, omitted group consciousness from the analysis in this chapter.

Although these findings are puzzling, they are consistent with recent scholarship on the political behavior of African-Americans.[37] What is not clear is whether the absence of relationship between race consciousness and political participation that we—and other contemporary analysts—find for Blacks reflects changes in the nature of group politics in America or changes in the way consciousness is measured. One interpretation is that the findings for the 1960s reflect the unique politics of the civil rights era. In brief, times have changed. The alternative interpretation is that it is the measures that have changed. Verba and Nie based their analysis on spontaneous references to race in open-ended questions. These may be a better measure of group consciousness than the closed-ended items used in recent work, including our own.[38]

Explaining Particular Political Acts

We have focused thus far on overall political activity without considering that the path to participation may involve a different mix of motivations and resources for particular acts that are components of the overall scale. In this section, we focus on different political acts to ascertain whether they have distinctive configurations of participatory factors: acts that involve giving

36. These results cannot be explained by the large number of other variables in the equation. The zero-order relationships between political participation and measures of consciousness are not significant for Latinos or for Blacks. They are, however, significant for women.

37. See, for example, Lawrence Bobo and Franklin D. Gilliam, Jr., "Race, Sociopolitical Participation, and Black Empowerment," *American Political Science Review* 84 (1990): 377–393; and Katherine Tate, "Black Political Participation in the 1984 and 1988 Presidential Elections," *American Political Science Review* 85 (1991): 1159–1176.

38. See Jeremy Zilber, "Group Consciousness and Black Political Participation Revisited" (paper presented at the Annual Meeting of the Midwest Political Science Association, Chicago, April 1994). Using the open-ended National Election Studies "like-dislike" questions, he finds a significant relationship with political activity.

time, making political contributions, and voting. For contrast, we also consider engaging in political discussion. Because talking about politics does not, under ordinary circumstances, have a direct effect upon what the government does, it falls outside the umbrella of what we define as political participation. Therefore, we have not so far paid attention to engaging in political discussion as an activity. Since the variables that predict taking part in political discussions provide an illuminating counterpoint to the patterns for other modes of activity, however, we introduce it here. Table 12.7 reports the results of an OLS analysis in which measures of political resources and engagement are used to predict four separate forms of activity: time-based acts, voting, making political contributions, and engaging in political discussions.[39]

TIME-BASED ACTS

The rubric "time-based acts" encompasses all the forms of political participation included in the overall activity scale—with the exception of voting and giving money. Since time-based activities figure so importantly in the overall scale of participation, it is not surprising that the results for time-based acts in Table 12.7 are similar to the results for the overall scale of activity in Table 12.5. However, the data provide a good baseline for comparison with the other activities.[40]

---

39. In order to facilitate comparison across the variables having different metrics, we report only the standardized regression coefficients in Table 12.7. The full data on which Table 12.7 is based—including the unstandardized coefficients and standard errors—are contained in Appendix F. As in Table 12.6, we have combined all the three civic skill variables into a single measure for simplification.

40. Free time—in the equation but not reported on the table—has no significant effect. It is, however, worth more consideration. For each of three of the time-based acts—working in a campaign, getting involved informally on a community issue or problem, and serving on a local community board or attending its meetings—we asked activists the number of hours they give to the activity each week. When we limit the analysis to the 16 percent of our respondents who devote an hour or more per week to one of these activities (N = 393), we find a very strong relationship between the total number of hours given and the amount of free time available. Roughly speaking, each additional hour of free time per day leads to about one-third more hour of political activity per week. Thus, the amount of free time available seems especially important for the *amount of time* people give to activities. What we observe, then, is a two-stage process of political activation. Political interest and resources like adult civic skills have a major impact on the *decision* to participate (free time has a minor impact as well), but constraints on free time control the *amount* of the time-based political activity once this decision is made.

Table 12.7 Predicting Particular Political Activities by Resources, Institutional Affiliations, and Political Engagement: OLS Regressions (standardized regression coefficient)

	Time-Based Acts	Voting	Political Contributions	Political Discussion
EDUCATION AND LANGUAGE				
Education	.10**	.05	.05	−.01
Vocabulary	−.03	.05*	−.03	−.02
INCOME				
Family Income	.05*	.04*	.30**	.04*
INSTITUTIONAL AFFILIATION				
Job Level	−.05*	.00	.00	.01
Non-Political Organization	.04	.03	−.02	.03
Religious Attendance	−.02	.11**	−.03	−.06**
CIVIC SKILLS				
Civic Skills (Sum)	.20**	.01	.05	.02
POLITICAL ENGAGEMENT				
Political Interest	.21**	.25**	.06**	.54**
Political Information	.05**	.12**	.03	.13**
Political Efficacy	.13**	.06**	.01	.03
Partisan Strength	.01	.16**	.04*	.03*
CITIZENSHIP				
Eligible to Vote	.00	.13**	.01	.02
R^2	.23	.38	.13	.42
Sample size	2,386	2,384	2,286	2,386

* Significant at .05 level.
** Significant at .01 level.

Note: Free time, English spoken at home, working, retired, Catholic religious preference, and age dummies are also included in the equation but not reported.

VOTING

Voting is both the most common and the most commonly analyzed political act.[41] In light of its centrality to the study of political behavior, it is striking how much the pattern of participatory factors for voting differs from that for other political activities. A prerequisite for voting, citizenship, of course, plays a significant

---

41. The voting scale, which has values from 0 to 9, was constructed from two items, one each about voting in local and national elections.

role for voting but, strikingly, for no other activity. That citizenship matters uniquely for voting is only one way in which voting is distinctive. What is even more important, with the exception of vocabulary skill and family income, which have weak effects, resources play virtually no role for voting. When the measures of political engagement are included in the model, education is, surprisingly, not significantly related to voting. Moreover, in contrast to the configuration for overall activity (shown in Table 12.5) or time-based acts (shown in Table 12.7), civic skills are unimportant. Voting also differs from other political acts in that one of the measures of institutional affiliation, attendance at church, is a significant positive force.[42] Each of the engagement variables is a powerful predictor, with political interest being especially strong. Not unexpectedly, partisanship is also quite important, substantially more so for voting than for any other activity. The other two measures of political engagement—in particular, political information—are significant as well. In short, the path to voting is quite different from the path to other political acts.

It is interesting to contrast the relative importance of civic skills and political information with respect to time-based acts and to voting. For time-based acts, civic skills are much more important than information. For voting, information has an impact, but civic skills do not. These findings are, in fact, consistent with the nature of the two kinds of activity. Civic skills are required—or, at least, quite helpful—for several of the time-based activities, for example, working in an electoral campaign, contacting a public official, or getting involved in an informal effort to solve a local problem. In contrast, a citizen does not need to know how to speak in public or how to organize a meeting in order to cast a ballot. However, the informed citizen will find it easier to vote, as well as to be active in other ways.

Several aspects of these findings bear emphasis. Most important, these data confirm that voting is different and cannot be considered a surrogate for all forms of political activity. They also vali-

---

42. Other studies also find a strong relationship between attendance at church services and electoral turnout, but not between religious attendance and other forms of political activity. For citations, see Kenneth D. Wald, *Religion and Politics in the United States,* 2nd ed. (Washington, D.C.: CQ Press, 1992), p. 35.

date that our measures of civic skills are indeed different from traditional measures of civic competence that rely on information as their principal component. Unlike political information, civic skills are useful for time-based acts, but not for voting.

Most striking, perhaps, is the fact that education is not a significant predictor of voting once the engagement variables are taken into account. A consistent and generally accepted finding in the literature on voting is the impact of education.[43] Our data do not, in fact, contradict this finding. First, vocabulary skill—a variable closely related to education that is not ordinarily included in analysis of the determinants of turnout—is significant. Furthermore, when the measures of political engagement are omitted from the equation, education is a strong predictor of voting. In short, the inclusion of the intervening role of political engagement specifies more clearly the way in which education affects voting. The effect is not direct, but occurs through engagement.[44]

What we have seen about the determinants of the vote suggests once again that voting is *unique* among political acts. Our discussion in Chapter 4 indicated that voting provides little in the way of either social or, especially, material benefits. Instead, the gratifications are overwhelmingly civic—the desire to do one's duty as a citizen or, perhaps irrationally, to influence government policy. The analysis in this chapter indicates that not only are the rewards

---

43. See Raymond E. Wolfinger and Steven J. Rosenstone, *Who Votes?* (New Haven: Yale University Press, 1980), chap. 2. Wolfinger and Rosenstone decompose socioeconomic status into its constituent parts and demonstrate the primacy of educational attainment as a determinant of voting.

44. Most of the literature uses only a single measure of political engagement. By using several engagement measures, we encompass more of the ways in which engagements mediate between education and voting, thus helping to solve the serious problem of unreliability. When only one measure of political engagement is used, education picks up some of the impact of the omitted variables: leaving all political engagements except political interest out of our equation for voting almost doubles the apparent impact of education. Part of the reason why interest seems so anemic in this situation is that most authors do not correct for its unreliability. Once corrections are made, interest alone can turn out to be much more important than education. This issue is explored in more detail in Brady, Verba, and Schlozman, "Beyond SES." There we use 1990–1993 panel data from the National Election Studies, which has a validated vote measure and repeated measures of interest, to show that, once statistical corrections are made for the unreliability of interest, it crowds out the impact of education.

of voting different, but the requirements are as well. What matters most for going to the polls is not the resources at voters' disposal but, rather, their civic orientations, especially their interest in politics. In short, voting is the civic activity *par excellence*—civic in its demands and civic in its rewards.

MAKING POLITICAL CONTRIBUTIONS

The data in Table 12.7 on making political contributions provide a strong contrast to the findings for voting. In this case we measure activity in terms not simply of whether or how many times the respondent was active but of how much was done.[45] In accounting for the volume of contributions to politics, family income is, overwhelmingly, the dominant factor. To give money one needs money and, apparently, little else. Education, vocabulary, and civic skills play no role. Strikingly, the impact of the political engagement variables is also relatively weak. Political interest and partisanship—but not political efficacy or information—are statistically significant; however, with other factors considered, political interest has much less influence on contributions than on the other kinds of acts. Writing checks for political causes demands little political interest and political information and even less sense of efficacy.[46] In comparison to other activists, contributors are—all else being equal—affluent but not especially engaged. This has important implications for political stratification and for politics: the great bulk of the public that is not affluent—a group that has distinctive politically relevant needs—is greatly disadvantaged when it comes to a mode of activity that has increased substantially in importance in recent decades.

Maybe needs another factor to learn why people donete to Campaing

---

45. The dependent variable is the sum of the amount contributed to candidates or groups and the amount contributed to political organizations, causes, and candidates in response to direct mail requests. See Appendix B.1.k for a description of the contributions variable.

46. Parallel analyses for campaign work and protesting are generally consistent with the findings for overall activity. Political interest is a significant predictor of both kinds of activity. Not unexpectedly, partisanship is significant for campaign work but not for protesting. Interestingly, efficacy is also significant for campaign work but not protesting. It is not clear why, but it may be that those who register as politically efficacious in response to our items feel that they can be heard through traditional channels while protesters are disproportionately likely to consider the system unresponsive.

A GLANCE AT POLITICAL DISCUSSION

That there are differences among the political acts in terms of the relative importance of resources and political engagement validates the approach we take. We can highlight the fact that political acts vary in sensible ways with respect to the factors that explain them if we pause briefly to consider a mode of involvement that we have neglected so far, engaging in political discussion. Because political discussion is not an activity aimed—directly or indirectly—at influencing the government, it does not fit under our definition of political participation and we have, therefore, left it out of our analysis. However, it provides an interesting test of our model of the factors that lead to activity. To take part in discussions about politics would seem to require few resources beyond, perhaps, a good vocabulary: it demands neither money nor organizational skill nor even the capacity to make a public presentation. What would seem essential is engagement with politics—at a minimum, to be politically interested, perhaps to be informed as well, although not necessarily to be politically efficacious.

Table 12.7 also contains the results of an OLS analysis in which the dependent variable is a scale measuring how frequently the respondent takes part in discussions of local and national political affairs.[47] Our expectations are borne out: resources do not figure importantly in participation in political discussions. Even vocabulary skill does not have an impact on the propensity to chat about politics. In contrast, political engagement—especially, political interest but also political information—is critical.[48] Once again, the pattern is so sensible as to reinforce our conviction that we have captured real effects.

Our discussion makes clear that there are different paths to different political activities. The varying patterns are summarized in Table 12.8, which draws on Table 12.7 as well as on results of earlier analyses. As we have seen, voting, time-based acts, mone-

---

47. The measure is a sum of discussions of national and local politics. See Appendix B.7.b.

48. The predictors of engaging in political discussion and going to the polls are similar in the absence of significant effects of civic skills. The two are by no means identical, however. Not surprisingly, partisanship is related more closely to voting than to engaging in political discussion. It is also interesting that religious attendance is related to increased voting but decreased political discussion.

Table 12.8 The Factors That Foster Political Participation

	Substantial Effect	Some Effect	Small Effect	No Effect
TIME-BASED ACTS	Civic skills, Interest	Education, Free time, Information, Efficacy	Income	Vocabulary, Partisanship, Citizenship, Job level, Organizational affiliation, Religious attendance
VOTING	Interest, Information, Partisan strength, Citizenship	Religious attendance	Vocabulary, Income, Efficacy	Education, Civic skills, Free time, Job level, Organizational affiliation
POLITICAL CONTRIBUTIONS	Income	Interest	Partisan strength, Information	Education, Civic skills, Vocabulary, Free time, Efficacy, Citizenship, Job level, Organizational affiliation, Religious attendance
POLITICAL DISCUSSION	Interest	Information	Income, Partisan strength	Education, Vocabulary, Civic skills, Free time, Efficacy, Citizenship, Job level, Organizational affiliation

tary contributions, and—for contrast—political discussions have individual configurations of participatory factors. Table 12.8 also underlines two themes of this discussion: that it is erroneous to generalize from what is known about voting to other forms of activity; and that it is critical to disaggregate overall measures of participation into their constituent parts and consider certain participatory acts separately.

Time, Money, and the Threshold of Participation

Throughout this inquiry we have been concerned with the distinction between time and money as forms of political input. In Chapter 7 we noted an interesting contrast between time and money with respect to the threshold of activity. The affluent are much more likely both to give time and to give money to politics. However, once an individual has crossed the threshold and has given *something*, the relationship between affluence and the amount given differs: among those who give time, there is no relationship between income and the amount of time given; among contributors, the affluent give, on average, much more than those whose incomes are more limited.

In this chapter we have added a consideration of political engagement to our analysis of the role of resources. We have found that the two work in tandem, each contributing to the likelihood that an individual will participate in politics. And each adds to the political advantage of the economically advantaged. The difference between time and money provides an important elaboration of the process involved. Activity involving time is enhanced by political engagement. Political contributions, in contrast, appear to depend on available income and on little else. Political engagement is relatively unimportant for giving money. This suggests that when it comes to giving money to politics, the less well off can never compete with the affluent—no matter how deeply engaged they are in politics. With respect to giving time, however, if they are politically engaged—if they care and feel that they can make a difference—they can be as politically active as their counterparts higher on the income ladder, once they decide to take part.

The data in Figure 12.1—which echo findings from Chapter

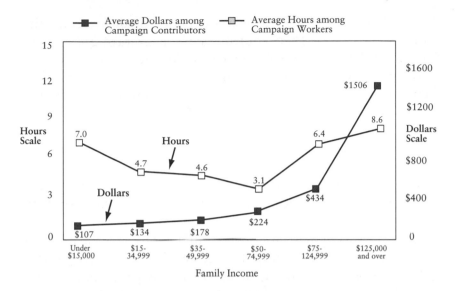

Figure 12.1 Time and Money Contributed to Politics by Highly Engaged[a] Respondents.

a. Highly engaged respondents are those in the top third of a scale based on the degree of political efficacy and political interest expressed. See Appendix B.7.

7—support this supposition. It reports data for those citizens who are in the upper third of a scale created by combining the scales measuring political interest and efficacy. The figure shows, for this group of engaged citizens, the amount of money and the amount of time given to politics by those who cross the threshold—that is, who contribute at least some time or some money to politics.[49] When it comes to giving time, there is no clear-cut relationship between family income and the number of hours devoted to politics: among the politically engaged, those at the bottom of the income hierarchy give nearly as much time on average as those at the top.[50] The contrast with money could not be more striking.

49. For money, the threshold is giving at least $25 to either a political campaign or in response to a mailed request to support a political cause. The amount given is the sum of the amounts given to campaigns or mailed requests. For time, the threshold is giving at least one hour to either a political campaign or a community activity. The amount of time is the sum of these.

50. We were puzzled as to why those in the $50–75,000 income category are so low in

Duh!

Even if deeply politically engaged, the poor cannot overcome the resource constraint. Their contributions on average are a small fraction of those of the highly engaged affluent.

The participatory system in America is sometimes described in contradictory terms, characterized as both stratified and permeable. These data illustrate both aspects. Those who are less well off are less likely to enter the participatory system by becoming active in any way. If they can muster psychological engagement to enter the system, however, they can generate a volume of participatory input not dissimilar to that contributed by those who are better endowed in socioeconomic terms—at least with respect to those activities that demand inputs of time. When it comes to time, the participatory system, although stratified, provides the possibility of equality of opportunity. This description, however, is singularly inappropriate for forms of activity that depend upon money. When it comes to making financial donations, a mode of participation that has taken on increased significance in recent decades, the resource constraints of income are determinative even among those who are active and engaged in politics.

Conclusion

This chapter has tested the Civic Voluntarism Model. In demonstrating that the resources of time, money, and skills are powerful predictors of activity, this analysis adds a good deal to our understanding of political participation in America. Our analysis has shown resources to be causally prior to political activity—deriving from the major institutions with which individuals are involved. Of particular note is the way in which the civic skills that facilitate participation are cultivated in the major secondary institutions of adult life, including churches, non-political organizations, and the workplace. In this way, the institutions of civil society operate, as Tocqueville noted, as the school of democracy.

The Civic Voluntarism Model permits us to go beyond the "standard SES model." The strength of the SES model has always been empirical: socioeconomic attributes such as educational at-

---

the time they give. Respondents in this income category are the most likely to have a working spouse, pre-school children at home, and, consequently, the least free time.

tainment and occupation are strong predictors of political activity. The Civic Voluntarism Model—especially through its resource component—provides the explanatory links that tell us why. By moving to a more general level and specifying more abstractly the resources derived from socioeconomic position that can be applied to politics, the model delineates the mechanisms that connect SES to participation. Finally, the analysis of the role of resources illumines American politics. We have seen that different resources are differentially available to various politically relevant groups and differentially critical for various kinds of activity. This permits us to understand the potential consequences for political outcomes of changing issues and changing modes of participation.

Our analysis has moved beyond resources to encompass political engagement as well. Perhaps the main finding is simply that causal analysis based on resources survives the challenge of the rival hypothesis that an omitted variable—such as a subjective predisposition to become politically engaged—might explain both resources and participation. We incorporated measures of several predispositions to political activity along with the resource variables in our equations. All the aspects of political engagement, especially interest in politics, turn out to be potent predictors of political activity. Instead of substituting for the resource variables, however, they appear to supplement them. Furthermore, there is reason to believe that participation and engagement are mutually reinforcing: taking part in politics probably enhances political interest, efficacy, and information; reciprocally, these political orientations surely have an impact on participation. In short, working together, resources and political engagement provide a powerful explanation of political activity.

We are led to have even greater confidence in our approach by the fact that the configurations of participatory factors vary across acts. The resource model, supplemented by engagement variables, is a powerful predictor of political activity in general. The patterns differ for voting and for making contributions. Voting depends on psychological engagement—especially political interest, but also partisanship—rather than resources such as money or skills. Making political donations depends on having money, and not on motivations or on other resources such as skills. Even if motivated, the poor cannot overcome the resource constraint to become contributors. As we saw in a previous section of this book, various modes of activity differentially advantage particular groups and particular interests. They are not interchangeable in their consequences. As we now see, they are not interchangeable in their origins either. The two are, of course, connected. We shall return to this theme in the last section of this book.

13

Institutions and
Recruitment

The non-political, secondary institutions of adult life—the work-place, voluntary association, or church—are windows on a wider world of civic life. In our discussion of these domains, we have already indicated that, while undertaking activities having no demonstrable political content, people develop organizational and communications skills that can be transferred to politics. Not only are these institutions the training ground for civic skills, but they also function as a site for political recruitment and nurture political engagement. Since they are the backbone of civil society—lying between the personal world of the family and the public world of politics—their role in stimulating political activity merits further investigation. This chapter expands our view of the role of these institutions and then folds what we have learned into the Civic Voluntarism Model.

We broaden our understanding to encompass two additional ways in which these institutions operate to enhance political participation. First, they serve as the locus for requests for involvement. In Chapter 5, our discussion of the processes by which activists are recruited by others noted how frequently requests for participation arise on the job, in church, and in organizations. As we mentioned, these settings incubate the social networks through which solicitations for activity are mediated. In addition, the institutions themselves generate requests for participation. On behalf of the institution itself, officers and staff sometimes ask the institutional rank and file to vote for a particular candidate or to take other political action.

These institutions bring citizens into politics in another way as well—by exposing them to political cues, even in the context of endeavors having no connection to politics. Wherever people are brought together—in the office lunchroom, at a meeting of the union local, at a church picnic—they may chat about politics.[1] Once again, the informal process has an institutional counterpart: clergy often discuss political issues from the pulpit; organizations, even those that do not take political stands, may communicate political messages. For example, without taking an official position on the issue, the local PTA might include an informational update about an upcoming school bond referendum in its bulletin or on the agenda of a monthly meeting.

The Institutional Nexus:
Direction of Causality

Our goal in considering the role of institutions in stimulating political activity is to add another set of factors to the explanatory

---

1. The literature on contextual effects on political attitudes is based on the assumption that an individual's attitudes are affected by the attitudinal composition of the surrounding environment. For evidence supporting this effect see Robert Huckfeldt, Eric Plutzer, and John Sprague, "Alternative Contexts of Political Behavior: Churches, Neighborhoods, and Individuals," *Journal of Politics* 55 (1993): 365–381; Huckfeldt and Sprague, "Discussant Effects on Vote Choice: Intimacy, Structure, and Interdependence," *Journal of Politics* 53 (1991): 122–159; and Huckfeldt and Sprague, "Networks in Context: The Social Flow of Political Information," *American Political Science Review* 81 (1987): 1197–1216. One problem of this research is that it is difficult to separate out the effects of the attitudes of those with whom the respondent associates on the respondent's own attitudes from the effects of the respondent's attitudes on the choice of network associates. That is, our friends may influence our attitudes, but we may also choose our friends on the basis of attitudinal compatibility. (Huckfeldt and Sprague, "Networks in Context," p. 1197.) We ameliorate this problem by focusing on the impact of the more or less official requests made by the institutions with which individuals are affiliated rather than the impact of more informal affiliations such as friendship networks. These commitments tend to be, in the long run, not easily changed for reasons associated with the political messages received. As Huckfeldt, Pulzer, and Sprague put it ("Discussant Effects," p. 367), "the decision to take a job or join a church is not retaken everyday."

For a work that deals with the impact of networks on participation and that shows the effect of organizational affiliation, see David Knoke, "Networks of Political Action: Toward Theory Construction," *Social Forces* 68 (1990): 1041–1063.

model. However, we face a problem analogous to that which we posed in Chapter 12 when we discussed the relationship of various measures of psychological engagement to political participation: the causal priority is uncertain. With respect to requests for activity, people do undertake political actions because they are asked. Yet, as we discussed in Chapter 5, the reciprocal is probably true as well. When volunteers are recruited for some joint political enterprise—for example, workers or donors to support a campaign, protesters to take part in a demonstration—the most likely prospects are those who have been active in the past. Hence, just as solicitations generate activity, past activity attracts subsequent requests. Similarly, when it comes to exposure to political cues, direction of causality may be ambiguous. Those who are exposed to political chat while sitting on the bench at the softball league or waiting for church choir practice to begin are likely to become more interested, and active, in politics. However, those who are interested and active in politics are also more likely to converse about political matters in these circumstances.

Given the nature of our data, there is no complete solution to this problem. Therefore, as we did in considering measures of political engagement, we shall proceed cautiously in imputing causality. However, issues of causal direction seem particularly intractable when it comes to *informal* institutional processes: requests for involvement that come through the informal social networks that develop on the job, in an organization, or at church, or political cues that arise in the course of the informal social interactions that take place in these institutions. The processes of self-selection that make it so difficult to sort chickens from eggs when it comes to the effects of institutional participation would, presumably, operate especially strongly in these informal situations. However, when it is the institution that takes the initiative—that is, when the company suggests that it might be wise to write to one's Senator about a pending piece of legislation or when the minister comments on some political issue in the course of the Sunday sermon—there is more reason to assume that institutional action is generating political participation than vice versa. Therefore, in probing the multiple ways in which institutions foster activity, we shall, whenever possible, use items that measure circumstances in which the impetus came from the institution itself.[2]

The Institutional Nexus:
Introductory Data

As part of the battery of items about experiences in the workplace, church, or organizations, we asked about efforts to stimulate political activity within these institutions. Let us begin by reviewing some data originally presented in Chapter 5 about institutional requests for activity. We inquired of those employed full- or part-time, those involved with a non-political organization, and those affiliated with a church by virtue of being members of or regular attenders of services in a local congregation whether, within the past five years, the institution or someone in an official position within it had asked them to vote for or against a candidate in an election for public office or to take some other action on a political issue—sign a petition, write a letter, or get in touch with a public official. The top portion of Table 13.1, which repeats data presented in Chapter 5, summarizes the responses to these items. The data indicate that requests for political participation—sometimes to vote for a particular candidate, more often to engage in other forms of activity—do emerge at work, in non-political organizations, and in religious institutions.

We also asked various questions about exposure to political messages in these non-political settings. Unfortunately, we did not include any measures about the workplace, and the measures for non-political organizations and churches are not completely analogous. For each category of organization for which the respondent had attended a meeting within the past six months, we asked whether there are sometimes political discussions on the agenda and whether people sometimes chat informally about politics at

---

2. We do have measures of the more informal kinds of recruitment described in Chapter 5. If we were to use these in our explanatory model of political participation, they would be very powerful as explanatory factors. By using the measures of more formal institutional recruitment, we are providing a harder test of the impact of institutions.

Table 13.1 Political Mobilization in Institutions

	All Respondents	Institutionally Affiliated[a]
A. Percentage Asked to Be Active		
ON THE JOB		
Asked to Vote	5	8
Take Other Action	11	16
Either Vote or Act	13	19
IN A NON-POLITICAL ORGANIZATION		
Asked to Vote	2	3
Take Other Action	5	8
Either Vote or Act	6	9
IN CHURCH		
Asked to Vote	8	13
Take Other Action	21	31
Either Vote or Act	23	34
B. Percentage Exposed to Political Messages		
IN A NON-POLITICAL ORGANIZATION		
Political matters on agenda	8	12
Informal political discussion at meetings	20	30
IN CHURCH		
Attended a meeting about a political issue	8	12
Clergy frequently or sometimes discuss political issues from the pulpit	16	25

a. The definitions of institutional affiliation are as follows: On the job: Working full or part time. In a non-political organization: Member of or contributor to an organization that does not take stands on public issues. In church: Member of or regular attender of services at a local church.

meetings. For churches, we inquired whether, over the past five years, the respondent had attended a meeting in the church about some national or local political issue and how often the clergy discuss political matters from the pulpit. The responses to these items, shown in the bottom portion of Table 13.1, echo what we saw for institutional solicitations of political activity: exposure to political communications in non-political organizations or in church is not frequent, but neither is it rare.

POLITICAL CUES IN ORGANIZATIONS:
A NOTE AND A REMINDER

The data in Table 13.1, especially the top portion, are subject to misinterpretation. The links between organizational involvement and political action are well known. Yet the data in Table 13.1 seem to suggest that organizations are no more politicizing than the other institutions of adult life. Indeed, when it comes to solicitations for political activity, requests are most frequent at church and least common in organizations. In considering these data, however, it is essential to recall that we have included only organizations that *do not take stands* in politics.

As we have indicated over and over, organizations in America can be arrayed along a continuum in terms of the extent to which they use political or non-political means of serving members' needs.[3] In order to make sense of this complexity, we have consistently distinguished organizational affiliations on the basis of whether respondents indicate that the organizations take stands in politics. As we have done elsewhere in reporting data on experiences in non-political institutions, in Table 13.1 we present information about organizations that do not take political stands.

Comparing the data about non-political organizations in Table 13.1 with analogous figures for organizations that do take stands in politics shows striking differences. By all measures of exposure to political stimuli in organizations, those that take stands provide more political cues than those that do not. This is especially the case in relation to direct requests for political activity. While only 9 percent of those whose most important organization does not take stands in politics indicated having been asked to get involved politically, fully two-thirds of those whose most important organization does take stands in politics did so. In addition, of those affiliated with non-political organizations, 30 percent reported that people at meetings sometimes chat about politics and 12 percent stated that there are sometimes political discussions on the agenda of these meetings. For those affiliated with political organizations, the figures are 53 percent and 46 percent respectively. The

---

3. For more extended discussion, see Chapter 3.

acquisition of civic skills, in contrast, is less affected by whether or not the organization is political. Non-political organizations do almost as well in inculcating such skills as do political organizations. Forty-four percent of those whose most important organization is non-political and 54 percent of those whose most important organization is political reported an opportunity to practice civic skills.

We should underline several conclusions that emerge from this discussion. First, the data in Table 13.1 should not be interpreted as showing that organizations are less important than jobs or churches in giving political cues. Rather, organizations that do not take stands in politics, although they might provide rich opportunities for the development of skills, are a more limited source of overtly political stimuli: requests for political participation and exposure to political discussion or informal political chat. In addition, the figures cited in this discussion make clear that differentiating organizations on the basis of whether they take stands in politics captures a real distinction. As we mentioned in Chapter 3, respondents surely make mistakes in categorizing organizations in terms of whether they take stands on political issues—with a bias in the direction of failing to see politics where it exists. Nonetheless, whatever the error, the organizations classified by respondents as taking political stands are, in the aggregate, distinctive in the cues they give. Finally, the data in Table 13.1 do point to the importance of religious institutions as a source of explicitly political stimuli. Church members may attend meetings on political topics and may hear discussions of political issues from the pulpit. In Chapter 11, we noted that the workplace is especially rich in opportunities for the acquisition of political skills. However, institutionally-based requests for political activity are somewhat more likely to arise in church than in the other non-political institutions of adult life.

WHO IS ASKED?

Within institutions, there are, as we would expect, variations based on education, income, gender, and race or ethnicity in terms of who is asked to become politically active. The patterns, shown in Table 13.2, reflect what we already saw in Chapter 5 with

Table 13.2 Recruitment to Politics in Institutions by Education, Family Income, Race or Ethnicity, and Gender (percentage asked to be active among institutionally affiliated[a])

	On the Job	In a Non-Political Organization	In Church
EDUCATION			
No High School Diploma	3	6	16
High School Graduate	13	9	29
Some College	19	8	39
College Graduate	25	10	42
Graduate Work	34	12	53
FAMILY INCOME			
Under $15,000	11	10	22
$15-34,999	16	8	34
$35-49,999	20	9	44
$50-74,999	25	10	41
$75-124,999	26	8	37
$125,000 and over	22	12	42
GENDER			
Women	20	9	32
Men	18	10	37
RACE or ETHNICITY			
Latino	12	4	16
African-American	15	9	38
Anglo-White	19	10	35

a. The definitions of institutional affiliation are as follows: On the job: Working full or part time. In a non-political organization: Member of or contributor to an organization that does not take stands on public issues. In church: Member of or regular attender of services at a local church.

respect to the more general measure of political recruitment and in Chapter 11 with respect to opportunities to develop civic skills. Those who are advantaged in terms of income and, especially, education are more likely to be asked by institutions to take part in politics.[4] The steep gradient for education and income is hardly

4. The data on who is exposed to political stimuli—informal discussion of politics and politics as agenda items in organizations as well as political meetings in church and exposure to political messages from the pulpit—are, in overall pattern, similar to those for being asked to be politically active when it comes to education, income, and gender.

There are some interesting differences on the basis of race or ethnicity. In organizations,

a surprise. However, in this case the workplace is not as distinctive as what we observed for the exercise of skills. When it comes to education, the differences are less pronounced in organizations than on the job or in church. In terms of income, the pattern is less clear both on the job and in church than it is for education. With respect to race or ethnicity, in all three settings Latinos are least likely to have received an institutionally-based request for participation. In an echo of a pattern we have seen before, Anglo-Whites are more likely than African-Americans to have been asked in the workplace. However, the patterns are not consistent for non-political organizations and church. The gender differences are fairly minimal.

The Institutional Nexus: Recruitment and Civic Training

When we considered the acquisition of civic skills, we noted that what matters is not only the characteristics of the individual but also the nature of the institution. Particular jobs, organizations, and churches vary in the extent to which they provide opportunities to practice skills. They also differ in the likelihood that an individual will be exposed to an explicit request for political activity or to other political stimuli. However, as shown in Table 13.3, the institutions that provide opportunities to develop civic skills are not necessarily the same ones that are most likely to be the locus of direct political requests or other political stimuli. In this table we list various types of occupations, non-political organizations, and churches in decreasing order of the frequency with which those affiliated reported a chance to practice a civic skill. The right-hand column shows the proportion of those affiliated

---

Anglo-Whites are similar to African-Americans in their frequency of exposure to political messages. Latinos lag behind both groups. Since Latinos are less likely to be involved in organizations, the pattern would be even more pronounced if we were to consider all respondents. In churches, however, it is African-Americans who are more likely (indeed, twice as likely) to be exposed to discussion of political matters, with very little difference between Latinos and Anglo-Whites. Interestingly, this is the single dimension for which we have not seen a Latino disadvantage, at least compared with Anglo-Whites.

The absence of a Latino disadvantage when it comes to exposure to political stimuli in church is consistent with the impression that the Catholic churches attended by Latinos are highly politicized.

Table 13.3 Skills Practiced and Requests for Activity in Institutions (among institutionally affiliated[a])

	Percentage practicing a civic skill	Percentage asked to take political action
ON THE JOB		
Professional	95	28
Managerial	92	14
Sales	79	21
Clerical	77	19
Skilled/craft	60	20
Service	59	17
Machine operative	58	10
Laborer	53	7
IN A NON-POLITICAL ORGANIZATION[b]		
Fraternal/service club	71	16
Youth	66	6
Literary, art, study	66	21
Religious	66	19
Neighborhood, homeowner	60	27
Hobby, sports, leisure	52	11
Business professional	52	11
Educational	45	17
Veterans'	40	26
Union	39	39
Cultural	24	14
Senior citizens'	21	13
Charitable, social service	17	4
IN CHURCH		
Protestant	37	35
Catholic	13	33

a. The definitions of institutional affiliation are as follows: On the job: Working full or part time. In a non-political organization: Member of or contributor to an organization that does not take stands on public issues. In church: Member of or regular attender of services at a local church.

b. Includes categories selected by at least 20 respondents (unweighted) as "most important."

who indicated an institutionally-based request for political participation.

Clearly, the rankings are not identical. Overall, the occupational rankings are similar: the more likely a job is to provide the opportunity to exercise civic skills, the greater the likelihood of being asked to be active. The discrepancy is among managers who rank higher in skill opportunities than they do in terms of likelihood of being asked. When it comes to organizations, the differences are more pronounced. Some organizations provide many skill opportunities but are relatively unlikely to be the setting for political requests: youth groups, literary and arts groups, service and fraternal organizations, and religious groups are examples. In contrast, unions and veterans' groups rank relatively low in skill opportunities but higher in the likelihood of political requests, with the disjunction particularly severe in relation to unions.[5] Finally, the data show a clear distinction between skill opportunities and political requests when it comes to religion. Protestants are no more likely than Catholics to be asked to take political action, but much more likely than Catholics to have an opportunity to develop civic skills in the course of church activity having nothing to do with politics.[6]

---

5. It is important to recall that the data in Table 13.3 are for respondents who indicated that their most important organization does not take stands in politics. Many of the categories—for example, business and professional groups—contain organizations that differ with respect to political involvement. In the case of unions, however, we surmise that some of the reports that the union does not take stands in politics represent erroneous perceptions on the part of those who are less involved and active. Union members who reported that the union does take political stands exercise more civic skills in the context of their union activity.

6. We also looked at the ranking of organizations and at church differences in terms of exposure to political stimuli—informal political chat and political issues on the agenda at meetings of non-political organizations as well as political meetings in church and exposure to political messages from the pulpit. The ranking of organizational types in terms of the frequency of reports of such stimuli is similar to that in Table 13.3 for being asked to take political action.

As for religious denomination, 13 percent of Protestants and 9 percent of Catholics report a political meeting in church; 26 percent of Protestants and 20 percent of Catholics report political messages from the pulpit. For an analysis of the variety of ways in which churches function to communicate political views and to stimulate political involvement, see Michael R. Welch, David C. Leege, Kenneth D. Wald, and Lyman A. Kellstedt, "Are the Sheep Hearing the Shepherds? Cue Perceptions, Congregational Responses, and Political Com-

In short, the distinction between these two kinds of institutional effects illustrates the variety of ways in which non-political institutions—jobs, organizations, and churches—can have an effect on the civic involvement of citizens. It is highly significant for understanding citizen participation both that there is such variation among jobs, organizations, and churches in terms of the opportunities for the development of civic skills and exposure to political stimuli, and that skill opportunities and political stimulation in non-political institutions do not necessarily travel together. With respect to opportunities to learn skills, we have hypothesized that what counts is the internal structure of the institution. Presumably, the less hierarchical and the more participatory the organization or the church, the more are affiliates able to learn skills. However, there is no necessary connection between such internal organizational characteristics and the likelihood that an organization will be a site for exposure to political stimuli. In this case, what may matter more is the substantive content of the concerns and interests of the institution and those who run it.

We can examine the multiple processes by which non-political institutions facilitate political involvement in two ways. First, we consider the two different roles of the church in bringing individuals into politics—through civic training and through political stimulation. As we shall see, the processes are not the same, but they jointly affect who is brought into political life through church affiliation. We then turn to a comparison of two institutions, labor unions and churches, that are of special relevance to working-class citizens, who may be disadvantaged with respect to such traditional political resources as income or education and whose jobs are relatively unlikely to provide opportunities for the development of civic skills. Again we shall see how such non-political institutions shape political participation in the United States.

---

munication Processes," in David C. Leege and Lyman A. Kellstedt, *Rediscovering the Religious Factor in American Politics* (Armonk, N.Y.: M. E. Sharpe, 1993), chap. 12. They show the range and variety of political cues that come through church involvement. They also show that the "otherworldliness" of the evangelical clergy does not impede their expression of politically relevant messages, especially on moral and sexual issues.

THE SKILL-PRODUCING CHURCH VERSUS
THE POLITICIZING CHURCH

We have argued that involvement in a religious institution might augment the individual's potential for political activity in two ways: by providing opportunities to practice civic skills and by providing exposure to political stimuli, either explicit political messages or requests to become politically active. However, the aspects of a religious institution that might incubate skill development are not necessarily those that would foster exposure to political stimuli. We have no reason to expect that political recruitment or political messages are more common in congregationally-organized churches than in hierarchical churches, in small rather than large congregations, or in denominations in which lay members take a larger part in religious rites.

These expectations are borne out by Figure 13.1, which contains data reported earlier on the likelihood of acquiring skills in Catholic and Protestant churches as well as figures on the likelihood of being exposed to political stimuli in these churches. There is a striking contrast between the data on practicing skills, on the one hand, and the data on being asked to be active or being exposed to political cues, on the other. As we have seen, the chance to practice civic skills is related to being Protestant or Catholic—a pattern that obtains for the population as a whole as well as for the three groups defined by their race or ethnicity.

In contrast, with respect to requests for political activity or exposure to political messages (attendance at a political meeting in church or discussions of political issues from the pulpit), what is striking is how little systematic difference there is between Catholics and Protestants. In terms of being asked to be active in politics, the small group of African-American Catholics were somewhat more likely to report such requests than were African-American Protestants. For Latinos, this weak relationship is reversed. In relation to exposure to political messages, Protestants, in general, report somewhat more exposure—with the exception of African-Americans. What emerges most clearly from Figure 13.1, however, is how small the differences are between Catholics and Protestants in terms of political recruitment and exposure to political messages

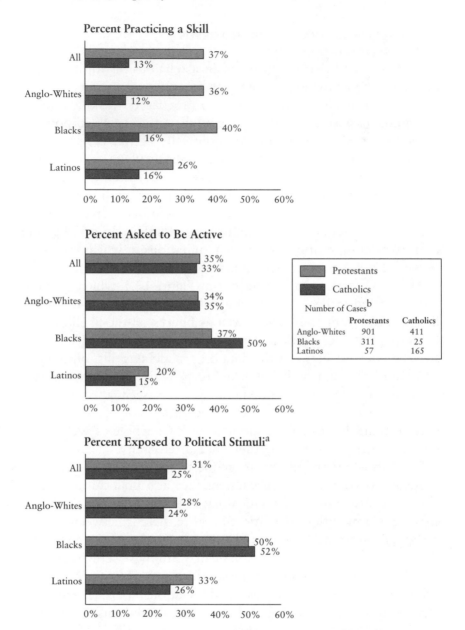

Figure 13.1 Political Impact of Church by Denomination and Race or Ethnicity (church members only).

a. Either clergy discuss political issues from the pulpit or respondent attended a political meeting at church.

b. Anglo-Whites, weighted; Blacks and Latinos, unweighted.

in church compared to those for the practice of skills. When it comes to recruitment and exposure, the biggest distinction is between African-Americans and the other two groups—Latinos and Anglo-Whites. Regardless of religious preference, African-Americans are substantially more likely to report exposure to such political stimuli.[7]

In short, for two quite different reasons, the churches that African-Americans attend have special potential for stimulating political participation. First, they belong to churches whose internal structure nurtures opportunities to exercise politically relevant skills. This process need not derive from activities that are intrinsically political. Running a rummage sale to benefit the church day care center or editing a church newsletter provides opportunities for the development of skills relevant to politics even though the enterprise in question is expressly non-political. In addition, Afri-

---

7. As we mentioned in Chapter 8, the role of the Black church has been mixed in relation to political recruitment. Some churches have stressed otherworldly orientations that would seem incompatible with a politically mobilizing church, while other churches have combined both a political and a spiritual orientation. And many have had a decidedly political and worldly involvement. On this, see Aldon Morris, *The Origins of the Civil Rights Movement: Black Communities Organizing for Change* (New York: Free Press, 1984). Since such variation probably exists among White churches as well, the issue is not whether all Black churches are political but whether on average they are more so than White churches. Our data suggest that they are. See on this, John B. Childs, *The Political Black Minister: A Study of Afro-American Politics and Religion* (Boston: G. K. Hall, 1980); Stephen D. Johnson, "The Role of the Black Church in Black Civil Rights Movements," in Stephen D. Johnson and Joseph B. Tamney, eds., *The Political Role of Religion in the United States* (Boulder, Colo.: Westview Press, 1986), pp. 13–38; Robert J. Taylor, Michael C. Thornton, and Linda B. Chatters, "Black Americans' Perceptions of the Socio-historical Role of the Church," *Journal of Black Studies* 18 (1988): 123–138; and Clyde Wilcox, "Religion, Group Identification, and Politics among American Blacks," *Sociological Analysis* 57 (1990): 271–285.

For interesting data on the political role of the Black church, see Fredrick C. Harris, "Something Within: Religion as a Mobilizer of African-American Activism," *Journal of Politics* 56 (1994): 42–68, and Harris, "Religious Institutions and African-American Political Mobilization," in *Classifying by Race,* ed. Paul E. Peterson (Princeton: Princeton University Press, 1995). In their typology of American denominations, Wade Clark Roof and William McKinney, in *American Mainline Religion: Its Changing Shape and Future* (New Brunswick, N.J.: Rutgers University Press, 1987), place Black Protestant churches in a separate category from other Protestant churches on the basis of, at least in part, the enhanced and special political role of Black churches. For evidence on the positive relationship between religiosity and participation among African-Americans, see Clyde Wilcox and Leopoldo Gomez, "Religion, Group Identification, and Politics among American Blacks," *Sociological Analysis* 51 (1990): 271–285.

can-Americans also seem to belong to more *politicized* churches where they are exposed to political stimuli, requests for political participation, and messages from the pulpit about political matters. Certainly this is consistent with the important role churches have played in issues of civil rights.[8]

Churches, Unions, and Political Stimuli

The relative equality with which opportunities for skill development and politically relevant stimuli are distributed in churches is a finding of potential significance for the understanding of American politics. Among the ways in which American politics is alleged to be exceptional among the world's democracies is the weakness of the institutions that, in other nations, bring disadvantaged groups to full participation in political life. Elsewhere, social democratic or labor parties and politically engaged trade unions play a significant role in the political mobilization of those who, on the basis of their income and education, might otherwise not take part politically. Such working-class institutions can act as agents of politicization through the processes we have been discussing. They are venues within which individuals can learn civic skills. Because these class-based institutions are deeply involved in politics, they are, therefore, likely to be the source of explicit political cues and messages. In contrast, American labor unions are relatively weak

---

8. We had considered the possibility that the extent of exposure to political stimuli in church would be related to the racial composition of the congregation. In fact, the relationship between the racial segregation of the congregation and the likelihood of being exposed to political stimuli is not monotonic. As shown in the data below, which are for African-American church members only, the mostly Black congregations are the most politicizing.

	Composition of Congregation		
	Mixed	Mostly Black	All Black
Exercise a skill	38%	38%	40%
Asked to take political action	33%	57%	30%
Exposed to a political message	41%	54%	39%

That the all-Black churches are somewhat less politicized was surprising to us. The explanation, however, may lie in the fact that the more racially segregated the congregation, the lower is the average level of the education of African-American members.

✗ Surprising since mainstream denominations are ↓. (must be compared to Europe) no data on "bible" churches.

Institutions and Recruitment   385

and enroll a relatively small proportion of the work force. In addition, American political parties are structurally fragmented, and there are no working-class or peasant parties.[9]

An aspect of American exceptionalism that receives less atten- ✗ tion in discussions of politics is the depth of religious commitment of American citizens and the relative frequency of their religious attendance. The data we have reviewed so far would indicate that, in many ways, American churches function in a manner similar to voluntary associations in nurturing politically relevant skills and exposing members to various sorts of political stimuli. Thus, it is possible that religious institutions in America partially compensate for the weakness of unions and the absence of a party of the left and play a role in bringing into politics those who might not otherwise be involved. In this section we compare the role of unions and churches in terms of their potential for political mobilization.

The extent to which churches or unions might enhance political activity is, presumably, a function of the politically relevant experiences of church and union members within these institutions— whether they develop civic skills, are recruited to politics, and are exposed to political stimuli. Table 13.4 compares—first, for all church members and all union members and, then, for blue-collar church members and blue-collar union members—religious institutions and unions in terms of the opportunities they provide for the development of civic skills (the proportion reporting the chance to practice a skill), recruitment to politics (requests for activity), and exposure to political messages (discussion of political issues from the pulpit or on the agenda at union meetings).[10] The data indicate

---

9. For an empirical analysis of the ways in which class-based institutions mobilize individuals to politics, see Sidney Verba, Norman H. Nie, and Jae-On Kim, *Participation and Political Equality: A Seven-National Comparison* (Cambridge: Cambridge University Press, 1978).

10. For both the measures of requests for political activity and the measures of civic skills, the data for churches and unions are not completely comparable. All active church members were asked these questions. However, because we could not ask a detailed battery of items about every one of twenty categories of organizations, we asked these items for a single organization only. Therefore, only union activists who are members of a single organization or (if involved in more than one organization) who designated the union as their most important organization were asked the request and skill questions about their union activity.

Table 13.4 Political Mobilization in Churches and Unions (among members)

	Church Members	Union Members
Opportunity to develop civic skills	30%	56%[a]
Request for political activity	34%	66%[a]
Exposure to political discussion	24%[b]	39%[c]

	Blue-Collar[d] Church Members	Blue-Collar[d] Union Members
Opportunity to develop civic skills	28%	50%[a]
Request for political activity	24%	68%[a]
Exposure to political discussion	21%[b]	31%[c]

a. Includes only those union members who designated it as their most important organization. See footnote 10.

b. Clergy frequently or sometimes discuss political issues from the pulpit.

c. Political issues on agenda at union meetings.

d. Employed as skilled or crafts worker, machine operative, or laborer.

that unions are potentially more politicizing than churches as institutions: whether we consider all respondents or just blue-collar respondents, union members are more likely than church members to have reported opportunities to practice skills, requests for political activity, or discussions of political issues.

However, as we have often indicated, if an institution is to have

---

Fortunately, for the skills questions, we have good reason to surmise that the number of skills reported by such members is not different from the number that would have been reported by those union members who are involved in other organizations besides the union and did not choose the union as their most important organization. We compared the two groups of union members—those for whom we have skill measures and those for whom we do not—in terms of three measures of organizational activity (whether they attended union meetings, were active in the union, or had held an official union position) that together are good predictors of the exercise of skills. We found no difference in the union activity of the two groups.

That those who say a union is their most important organization are not more active in their unions than those for whom some other organization is more important would seem to be an anomaly. However, it is important to recognize that many of the union members for whom we have union skill measures because their union is their most important organization are members of no other organizations, while union members for whom we do not have union skill measures are members of at least one other organization (that is, the one they named as most important to them instead of naming their union). Hence, the union members for whom the union is not the most important organization are somewhat more active in general—that is, they are multiple organization members—than are those union members citing their union as most important. Unfortunately, we have no way of making analogous inferences for requests for political activity in unions.

Table 13.5 Membership in Churches or Labor Unions

	Member of Church	Member of a Union
All Respondents	69%	12%
Employed	67%	14%
Blue-Collar Workers[a]	67%	26%

a. Employed as skilled or crafts worker, machine operative, or laborer.

an effect on an individual, the individual has to be affiliated. And it is in terms of affiliation that churches greatly overshadow unions in their impact. Table 13.5 presents data for the population as a whole, for those with jobs, and for blue-collar workers in order to compare the proportions of Americans involved with unions and with churches.[11] Overall, a respondent is much more likely to be affiliated with a church than with a union. This holds for the working class as well: 67 percent of the blue-collar workers in the sample reported church membership compared with 26 percent who indicated membership in a union.[12] If they were merely nominal, these memberships would mean little in terms of exposure to institutional political stimuli. However, in this respect as well, churches appear to have the advantage. Church members are more likely to attend services than are union members to attend union meetings. Of union members, 52 percent indicated having gone to at least one union meeting within the past year; 94 percent of church members—and an identical proportion of blue-collar church members—reported having attended services within the past year.

If we put together these two effects—affiliation with church or

---

11. The category of blue-collar workers includes skilled workers, machine operatives, and laborers. Not all union members fall into these categories: teachers, nurses, and government clerical workers are examples of white-collar workers who may be union members. As usual, we include among church members those who say that they belong to a local congregation or that they attend services more than once a month in the same congregation.

12. The reader should note that the data in Tables 13.4 and 13.5 are for all union members, not just the minority who reported that their union does not take stands in politics. Elsewhere in this volume, including Table 13.3 of this chapter, our concern with the politicizing effects of institutions outside politics has led us to focus on organizations that do not take political stands. Because we are interested in comparing the aggregate effects of churches and unions, we thought it appropriate in this section not to distinguish union members in terms of their perception that the union takes political stands.

union and political mobilization in these two institutions—we find
that the sheer volume of church affiliation overwhelms the fact
that there is somewhat more mobilization in unions. If we look at
the American public as a whole, we find that the average citizen
is three to four times as likely to be politically mobilized in a
church than in a union. Even if we consider blue-collar workers
only, we find them about one and a half times more likely to
develop a civic skill or to be exposed to political discussion in
church than in a union setting. Only in relation to direct requests
to take some political action are unions and churches about as
likely to have an impact on blue-collar workers—but even in
relation to direct requests for activity, churches have a slight edge.
In short, because Americans, even blue-collar Americans, are so
likely to be religiously affiliated and active, American churches
have the potential to compensate partially for the weakness of
institutions that elsewhere function to mobilize the disadvantaged.

The Institutional Impact on Activity

We can carry this story to its conclusion by examining the way in
which institutional effects combine with other factors in the Civic
Voluntarism Model to influence political activity. As presented in
Chapter 12, the basic model accounts for significant institutional
effects with the measures of civic skills acquired in non-political
institutions. As we have seen, they are powerful predictors of
political activity. We then added the measures of political engagement—political interest, information, and efficacy, identification
with a political party—and found that, while these variables, especially political interest, are strongly related to political activity,
the independent effect of the resource component of the Civic
Voluntarism Model holds up. Now we round out the explanation
by adding a measure of the exposure of the individual to direct
requests for political activity in all three institutions.[13] Table 13.6,

---

13. The measure is the sum of the number of times an individual was asked either to vote
or to take some other political action on the job, in church, or in a non-political organization.
It runs from 0 to 6. See Appendix B.8.b. We use the measure of direct requests for activity
rather than the more problematic measures of exposure to political stimuli such as conversations about politics. The former is more likely to be an independent causal effect of the
institution, whereas the latter is more likely to reflect preexisting involvement in politics.

Table 13.6 Predicting Overall Political Participation by Resources, Institutional Affiliations, Political Engagement, and Institutional Recruitment: OLS Regression

Variable	B	SE B	Beta
EDUCATION AND LANGUAGE			
Education	.15	.02	.14**
Vocabulary	.03	.01	.04*
INCOME AND TIME			
Family Income	.05	.01	.10**
Free Time	−.01	.01	−.03
INSTITUTIONAL AFFILIATION			
Job Level	−.02	.02	−.02
Organizational Affiliation	.02	.04	.01
Religious Attendance	−.01	.01	−.02
CIVIC SKILLS			
Civic Skills (sum)	.10	.02	.14**
POLITICAL ENGAGEMENT			
Political Interest	.24	.02	.23**
Political Information	.09	.02	.11**
Political Efficacy	.08	.01	.12**
Partisan Strength	.09	.03	.05**
INSTITUTIONAL RECRUITMENT	.25	.03	.14**
R^2		.45	
Sample Size		2,386	

* Significant at .05 level.
** Significant at .01 level.
Note: Age dummies, retirement, working, English spoken at home, citizenship, and Catholic religious preference are also included in the equation, but are not reported.

which presents the result of an OLS analysis of the predictors of political activity, adds to the variables discussed in Chapter 12 the measure of recruitment to politics. As such, it encompasses two different ways in which non-political institutions might enhance political participation: by fostering the development of civic skills and by acting as a source of requests for political activity.

The additional variable of institutionally based political recruitment is a significant predictor of political activity. Indeed, it is one of the strongest predictors—roughly as potent as education and civic skills. Table 13.6, however, also shows clearly that resources and political engagements are significant predictors of political activity even with this additional variable included. This is a striking finding in that the indicator of political recruitment in non-political institutions represents a potentially powerful variable that might have explained away the relationship between resources and activity. Furthermore, even with the additional variable included, the various measures of engagement—in particular, political interest—continue to have a strong positive association with political participation. In short, this model provides a quite potent explanation of the many factors that enhance political participation.

The results highlight the multiple effects of non-political institutions on political activity. These institutions of civil society provide civic training as well as direct requests for activity.[14] The non-political institutions of civil society have long been at the heart of theories of democracy. These data give an empirical grounding of unprecedented strength to their effects on democratic citizenship.[15] Thus, the analysis in this chapter lends support to our original formulation, presented in the Introduction. Why, we asked, do those who are inactive not take part in politics? We proposed three possible reasons: they can't, they don't want to, or nobody asked. What we have shown is that citizens who have *resources* can be active; those who are *engaged* want to be active; and those who are *recruited* often say yes when asked.

---

14. They also produce politically relevant cues. We have not put them in the equation for Table 13.6 because of concerns about the direction of causality. Including a measure of institutional effects that encompassed the stimulation measures discussed in this chapter would have added further explanatory power. It is interesting to note, however, that resources and engagement retain their predictive capacity—providing an even more stringent test of our model.

15. We also tested this model for several separate types of political acts: "time-based" acts, making political contributions, and voting. The recruitment measure has no effect on giving money, a moderate effect on voting, and a stronger effect on acts involving time. This is of little substantive significance since our question did not ask about monetary contributions. Furthermore, as we discussed in Chapter 5, requests for contributions are frequent—and frequently denied.

14

Participation and the Politics of Issue Engagement

According to the Civic Voluntarism Model, those who have the wherewithal to participate by virtue of the resources at their command and the desire to do so by dint of their engagement with politics are likely to become active in politics—especially in the catalytic presence of requests for participation. We can, however, add a final ingredient to the model. One of the critical components of citizen participation is concern about policy matters. Contrary to what we might expect on the basis of collective action theory, activists told us over and over that their participation was founded, at least in part, on a desire to influence what the government does.

The various factors described so far that foster participation are themselves devoid of substantive issue content. Although resources are not randomly distributed within the public, those who are well endowed with resources can put them in the service of many different political purposes. Similarly, efforts to recruit political participation may take place in the name of many different causes. Even the various forms of political engagement—political efficacy, political information, and especially, political interest—are general orientations, not concerns about particular issues. In this chapter, we move beyond these general political orientations to investigate the independent role in motivating activity played by the policy concerns that arise from citizens' differing needs and preferences—what we shall call "issue engagements."

The Sources of Issue Engagement

Issue engagements—policy commitments that might serve on their own to stimulate participation—can have diverse origins. In this chapter, we consider the implications for activity of issue engagements that come from two sources: first, having a personal stake in government policy; and second, caring deeply about a particular political issue. With respect to the former, the myriad government policies that affect citizens in different ways create potential constituencies of activists. All of us—ranging from farmers to veterans to the wheelchair-bound to auto executives—have interests in what the government does. Many of the identifiable groups having a stake in public policy are relatively narrow. Therefore, a sample survey—even one with the special characteristics of the Citizen Participation Study—will not contain sufficient cases for analysis of those who have a joint interest in a particular policy. In our survey, however, we are able to locate two sets of respondents for whom we might infer a stake in public outcomes: recipients of government benefits and parents of school-aged children.

Another source of issue engagement is citizens' deeply held views on controversial matters. The issues that arouse passion are many and varied. Many issue controversies—conflicts over, for example, the siting of a public housing facility or an incident of alleged police brutality—are sufficiently localized that, even though tempers run high, a national survey cannot register the elevation of the political temperature. Throughout American history, however, issues have periodically arisen that generate passion on a more widespread basis.[1] Often, the issues that elicit this kind of depth of commitment have a cultural or moral dimension: nativism, abolition, and temperance in the nineteenth century; civil rights

---

1. For an analysis of the ebb and flow of passionate issues in the American public see Samuel P. Huntington, *American Politics: The Promise of Disharmony* (Cambridge, Mass.: Harvard University Press, 1981). Joseph R. Gusfield's analysis of the temperance issue gives a template for understanding a large number of deeply divisive, non-economic issues in American politics. See *Symbolic Crusade: Status Politics and the American Temperance Movement* (Urbana, Ill.: University of Illinois Press, 1963).

and Vietnam in the twentieth. Sometimes, however, the issues are economic: free silver a century ago; tax revolts in recent years. At the time our survey was conducted, in the spring of 1990, the issue that generated this kind of heat on a national basis was abortion. As we saw in Chapter 3, a remarkable proportion of all activity on national issues—in particular, protest activity on national issues—was focused on the single issue of abortion.

If issue engagements—based on having either a stake in what the government does or deep commitments on a controversial issue—operate independently of other participatory factors in fostering participation, we would expect to see the consequence in activity directed toward the particular policy concern that is the subject of the issue engagement. That is, we would anticipate deeply held views on pornography to have an influence on the likelihood of contacting a public official about pornography, but not on the likelihood of contacting a public official about international trade or the city's failure to collect the garbage.[2] The effect on participation of having passionate views on an issue might or might not be perceptible when it comes to overall activity. Whether we could detect a boost to overall activity from intense issue commitments would depend on two factors: the size of the impact of the issue engagement on the relevant issue-specific activity, and the extent to which activity devoted to that particular issue figures importantly in a citizen's overall bundle of issue-based participation.

Fortunately, we have information about the issues and problems behind participation and can target our inquiry on activity that is specific to the policy matter of an issue engagement. Therefore, in investigating the extent to which—over and above the effects of other participatory factors—issue engagements influence activity, we shall, whenever possible, focus upon participation directed at

---

2. In some cases, strong commitments on a particular issue might lead citizens to become active on what they consider to be a related issue. For example, citizens who are extremely concerned about crime might decide to fight a state-wide tax cap referendum so that there would be extra funds to build prisons or to help communities to hire more police. In this case, strong views on crime would lead, quite reasonably, to increased activity about taxes.

the particular issue with which the individual is engaged rather than upon overall activity.

Government Services and Political Activity

The sheer number and variety of government programs imply both that everyone has a stake in what the government does and that many of the issue publics affected by government policies are so narrow that they cannot be located in a sample survey. As we indicated, we were able to identify in our survey two relatively large groups for which we could reasonably infer a stake in government policy: recipients of means-tested government benefits and parents of school-aged children. Because they benefit from services provided by the government with respect to basic welfare or schooling, what the government does is relevant to the lives of the members of these two groups: recipients of mean-tested benefits are affected by government policies with regard to, for example, the medical procedures covered by Medicaid or the regulations governing eligibility for food stamps; parents of school-aged children are affected by levels of local spending on education or federal mandates for bilingual education or mainstreaming of disabled students.[3] Moreover, issues involving basic human needs or education figure quite importantly on citizens' participatory agendas. Therefore, not only can we find enough cases for analysis of two groups having a stake in government policy, but there is enough activity on the subjects of basic human needs and education that we can investigate whether an issue engagement that grows out of benefiting from a particular government policy is linked to activity with respect to that policy.

We begin by asking whether the issue engagement deriving from being a policy beneficiary has an impact on overall activity. Table 14.1 reports the results of a regression in which the participation factors from the Civic Voluntarism Model—along with two addi-

---

3. Educational policy is less relevant to the small minority of parents whose school-aged children do not attend public schools. Unfortunately, we have no way of locating these respondents.

Table 14.1 Predicting Overall Participation by Participatory Factors and Stake in Government Policy: OLS Regression

Variable	B	SE B	Beta
PARTICIPATORY FACTORS			
Education	.22	.02	.20**
Income	.06	.01	.11**
Job Variables	.10	.02	.11**
Organization Variables	.12	.02	.11**
Church Variables	.15	.02	.14**
Political Interest	.30	.02	.29**
STAKE IN GOVERNMENT POLICY			
Receipt of Means-Tested Benefits	.00	.05	.00
School-Aged Children	.09	.07	.04*
(Constant)	−.86	.14	
R^2		.41	

* Significant at .05 level.
** Significant at .01 level.
Note: Age, gender, race and ethnicity also included in the equation.

tional measures of issue engagement, receipt of means-tested benefits and status as the parent of a school-aged child[4]—are used to predict overall activity. The data for the effects of non-political institutions—workplace, organization, or church—are organized according to a somewhat different scheme from that used in earlier chapters. There we aggregated across participatory factors analytically. We combined into a single index measures of the civic skills exercised in the three institutional domains and, similarly, we created a single measure of recruitment attempts across the domains. Here we aggregate within particular domains, creating separate measures for job, organization, and church effects. Each index is the additive sum of the number of civic skills and recruit-

---

4. The measure of means-tested benefits is the number of programs (AFDC, food stamps, housing subsidies, or Medicaid) from which the respondent or an immediate family member living in the household benefits. (See Appendix B.16.b.) The variable for school-aged children is the number of the respondent's children (including step- and adopted children) over four years of age living in the household. (See Appendix B.14.)

ment attempts (being asked to vote and being asked to take some other political action) from that institution.[5] This allows us to assess the effects of the various non-political institutions—workplace, organizations, and church. Since these institutions relate differently to the issue engagements in which we are interested in this chapter, it is useful to distinguish them from one another.

The results of the regression, reported in Table 14.1, are familiar. They demonstrate the workings of the Civic Voluntarism Model. The new components, the two measures of having a stake in government policy, contribute little additional explanatory power.

As we have mentioned, however, if we are concerned about the impact of issue engagement, we should consider, rather than overall activity, activity that is targeted to the particular issue in question. The verbatim discussions of the issues and problems that led to activity permit us to locate issue-based activity directed toward problems of basic human needs and educational concerns.[6] We can undertake an analysis parallel to that presented in Table 14.1, omitting the measure of overall activity and substituting in its place measures of the amount of issue-based activity on these two subjects.[7] The results are shown in Table 14.2. The top portion of the table, which contains the data for activity on the subject of basic human needs, and the bottom portion, which contains the data for activity animated by educational issues, show similar patterns. Several of the participatory factors that have shown

---

5. For this measure, see Appendix B.8.e.

6. As in previous chapters, issues of basic human needs include references to various government benefits (welfare, AFDC, food stamps, housing subsidies, Social Security, Medicare, and Medicaid); unemployment (either as an economic issue or in terms of the respondent's own circumstances); housing or homelessness; health or health care; poverty or hunger; aid to the handicapped or handicapped rights. Educational concerns include references to educational issues such as school reform, school voucher plans, and so forth; problems or issues related to schooling of family members; guaranteed student loans.

Both sets of issue concerns were cited relatively frequently in conjunction with issue-based activity. Thirteen percent of those who gave us a codeable response about the issues and problems associated with activity mentioned an issue involving basic needs, and 15 percent mentioned an issue involving education.

7. The dependent variable is the number of political activities for which a respondent mentioned an issue or problem that fell into one or the other of these two categories of issues. See Appendix B.3.

Table 14.2 Predicting Issue-Based Activity by Participatory Factors and Stake in Government Policy: OLS Regression

A. Activity on Basic Human Needs	B	SE B	Beta
PARTICIPATORY FACTORS			
Education	.01	.01	.05*
Income	.00	.00	.03
Job Variables	.01	.00	.06*
Organization Variables	.02	.00	.07**
Church Variables	.01	.00	.03
Political Interest	.01	.00	.07**
STAKE IN GOVERNMENT POLICY			
Receipt of Means-Tested Benefits	.04	.01	.07**
(Constant)	−.07	.03	
R^2		.03	
B. Activity on Education	B	SE B	Beta
PARTICIPATORY FACTORS			
Education	.03	.01	.10**
Income	.00	.00	.03
Job Variables	.02	.01	.08**
Organization Variables	.04	.01	.11**
Church Variables	.02	.01	.07
Political Interest	.02	.01	.08**
STAKE IN GOVERNMENT POLICY			
School-Aged Children	.11	.02	.09**
R^2		.09	

* Significant at .05 level.
** Significant at .01 level.
Note: Age, gender, race and ethnicity also included in the equation.

consistent capacity to predict activity are less powerful when it comes to activity around these two specific issues. The important point, however, is that having a stake in a particular policy—in this case, either receiving means-tested government benefits or having school-aged children—has a strong additional impact on the likelihood of being active on issues related to that policy, over and above how well an individual is endowed with the other factors that foster political participation. Thus, issue engagements that derive from having an interest in what the government does with respect to some issue can play an independent role in generating activity about that issue.[8]

The results in Table 14.2 provide an interesting perspective on a comment made to us by several readers. They suggested that being on welfare is such a demeaning and demoralizing experience in American society that recipients of means-tested benefits would naturally have low rates of activity. These data suggest that, on the contrary, receiving means-tested benefits actually gives a boost to issue-based activity with respect to concerns about basic human needs. However, since recipients of means-tested benefits are otherwise so poorly endowed with participatory factors, the lift given by their issue engagement leaves them still a very inactive group.

The Politics of Passionate Issue Commitment

Earlier in the chapter we suggested a second source of issue engagement that might impel citizens to engage in issue-based activity: intense concern about some policy matter. As we indicated, almost any issue can become the object of passionate commitment—the local schools, scientific creationism, Pentagon cost overruns, human rights abroad. To investigate the implications of passionate issue commitments for political participation, however, we need to find an issue generating sufficient heat on a national basis that its effects are perceptible in a sample survey. As we mentioned, at the time our survey was conducted, the controversy over abortion fit this description.[9] To characterize abortion as an issue about which feelings run deep is not, however, to argue that it is necessarily either the issue that the largest proportion of Americans

---

8. For further analysis and a discussion of gender differences in relation to involvement with educational issues, see Kay Lehman Schlozman, Nancy E. Burns, Sidney Verba, and Jesse Donahue, "Gender and Citizen Participation: Is There a Different Voice?" *American Journal of Political Science* 39 (1995): 267–294.

9. Discussions of the politics of abortion, with particular emphasis on the role of the public in the debate, include Kristin Luker, *Abortion and the Politics of Motherhood* (Berkeley: University of California Press, 1984); Malcolm L. Goggin, ed., *Understanding the New Politics of Abortion* (Newbury Park, Calif.: Sage Publications, 1993); and Barbara Hinkson Craig and David M. O'Brien, *Abortion and American Politics* (Chatham, N.J.: Chatham House, 1993).

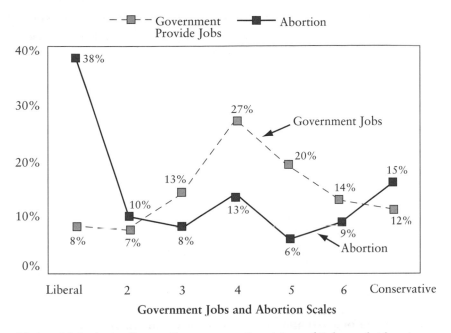

Figure 14.1 Attitudes on Government Provision of Jobs and Abortion.

mention when asked to name the most important issue or problem facing the country or the issue that is mentioned most frequently in connection with issue-based activity. A number of issues, including the perennial concerns about the economy and taxes, are more likely to be cited in polls and, as we saw in Chapter 3, to have been mentioned more often among the issues associated with participation. What we shall investigate is whether extreme views on abortion operate on their own to increase activity. For contrast, we shall consider the role of views on the economy.

Public opinion data confirm the impression created by media images of massive demonstrations on the subject of abortion and violence at abortion clinics: abortion is an issue about which many Americans have strong views.[10] Figure 14.1, which uses two seven-

---

10. Students of public opinion traditionally distinguish between direction of opinion (that is, whether a respondent is pro or con) and intensity of opinion (that is, how much a respondent cares). Since we do not have a direct measure of intensity, we are forced to use location on an issue scale as a surrogate for intensity.

point scales to compare the distribution of opinion on two issues, government provision of jobs and abortion, shows a striking contrast.[11] With respect to attitudes toward government provision of jobs, opinion is relatively centrist: 60 percent of respondents are clustered in one of the three middle categories. In contrast, when it comes to abortion, opinion is polarized: a majority, 53 percent, chose one of the positions at either end of the scale, and only 27 percent located themselves in one of the three moderate categories.[12] It is important to note, in addition, that although opinion on abortion is clustered at the ends of the issue continuum, it is not balanced. More than twice as many respondents registered extremely pro-choice views as registered extremely pro-life views. In short, attitudes on abortion are polarized in a way that attitudes on government provision of jobs are not.

Attitudes on public issues are often related to the factors that foster participation—those well endowed with the resource of money, for instance, have distinctive views on economic policy. This linkage of particular issue positions and the general participatory factors has consequences for the messages that are communicated through participation. When it comes to the issue of abortion, the relationship between attitudes and participatory factors is especially complex. We have seen both that education has a powerful effect on participation and that activity in religious institutions provides an alternative, though weaker, route to participation for those who are less well endowed with socioeconomic resources. As shown in Figure 14.2, views on abortion are related in contradictory ways to these two participation-enhancing factors. Although education and attendance at religious services are not significantly related to each other, they have opposite relationships to attitudes on abortion: support for pro-life positions rises with church attendance and falls with educational attainment.[13]

---

11. Question wordings are in Appendix B.6.b and d.

12. The contrast is informative, but ought not to be overinterpreted. The particular distribution on an issue depends heavily on the form of the question. One frequently used set of questions about abortion asks whether abortion should be permitted under various conditions. This battery shows the public to be more centrist in opinion than does the seven-point scale used in the Citizen Participation Study.

13. For data on the religious roots of pro-life positions and the support for pro-choice

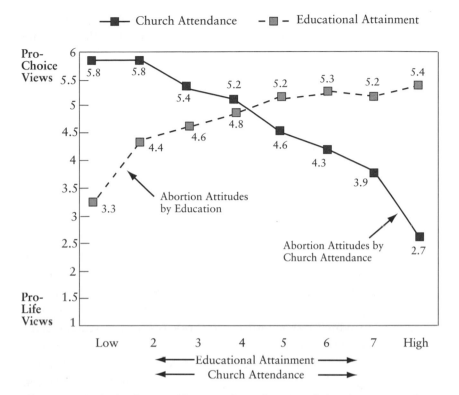

Figure 14.2 Attitudes on Abortion by Educational Attainment[a] and Church Attendance.[b]

a. For definitions of 8 levels of educational attainment, see Appendix B.10.a.

b. The lowest 2 categories (never and less than once a year) of a 9-category religious attendance measure have been combined. For definitions, see Appendix B.2.b.

positions among the more highly educated and other advantaged groups, see Donald Granberg and Beth Wellman Granberg, "Abortion Attitudes, 1965–1980: Trends and Determinants," *Family Planning Perspectives* 12 (1981): 250–261; James L. Guth, Corwin E. Smidt, Lyman A. Kellstedt, and John C. Green, "The Sources of Anti-Abortion Attitudes: The Case of Religious Activists," in *Understanding the New Politics of Abortion,* ed. Goggin, chap. 2; and Elizabeth Adell Cook, Ted G. Jelen, and Clyde Wilcox, *Between Two Absolutes: Public Opinion and the Politics of Abortion* (Boulder, Colo.: Westview Press, 1992). Robert Huckfeldt, Eric Plutzer, and John Sprague ("Alternative Contexts of Political Behavior: Churches, Neighborhoods, and Individuals," *Journal of Politics* 55 [1993]: 365–381) show that exposure to fellow parishioners increases pro-life attitudes and that this is amplified by frequent church attendance.

Each of these relationships has, as we shall see, consequences for the way in which abortion views are communicated through the participatory process.

ATTITUDES ON ABORTION AS A PARTICIPATION FACTOR

What are the consequences for participation of the fact that, at the time of the Citizen Participation Study, Americans had deep and polarized convictions about abortion? We can compare the role of views on abortion with views on government provision of jobs—a perennial issue in American politics about which, as we have seen, views were not polarized at the time of our survey—as participatory factors leading to political activity. To do so we create measures of the strength of opinion on these issues by "folding" the attitude measures so that those at either end of the scale (who take the most liberal *or* the most conservative position) are high on the scale. We then incorporate these measures into the Civic Voluntarism Model. Table 14.3 presents the results of a regression in which participatory factors—resources, recruitment, and political interest—are used in concert with the folded attitude measures to predict overall activity.[14] The contrast between the influence of economic and abortion attitudes is quite clear. When other participatory factors—including a general interest in politics—are taken into account, having extreme attitude positions on government provision of jobs has no independent effect on activity, but having extreme opinions on abortion does. Thus, the data suggest that a strong view on the abortion issue is another example of an issue engagement that, on its own, fosters political participation. It is interesting to note in this context that analyses (not reported in the table) demonstrate that having extreme views on abortion has an effect on time-based activity, but not on the giving of political money, a form of participation for which family income is, overwhelmingly, the most important factor.

We have seen that the participation-enhancing effect of having extreme attitudes on abortion is sufficiently strong to be registered on a measure of overall activity. However, we have argued that, if

---

14. We use the condensed specification described above.

Table 14.3 Predicting Overall Activity by Participatory Factors and Extreme Attitude Positions: OLS Regression (abortion and government provision of jobs scales "folded")

	B	SE B	Beta
PARTICIPATORY FACTORS			
Education	.23	.02	.22**
Income	.06	.01	.11**
Job Variables	.09	.02	.10**
Organization Variables	.12	.02	.08**
Church Variables	.18	.02	.15**
Political Interest	.31	.02	.30**
EXTREME ATTITUDE POSITIONS			
On Abortion	.10	.02	.07**
On Government Provision of Jobs	−.01	.02	−.00
(Constant)	−1.05	.15	
R^2		.42	

* Significant at .05 level.
** Significant at .01 level.
Note: Age, gender, race and ethnicity also included in the equation.

issue engagements act as an independent force in mobilizing activity, they would do so for activity that is grounded in the issue that is the subject of the engagement rather than for activity in general. We can investigate this contention by returning to the verbatim reports about the issues or problems that led to activity and using measures of the number of participatory acts for which the subject was either abortion or, for purposes of comparison, issues of basic human needs.[15] Table 14.4 reports regression analyses explaining these two kinds of issue-based activity. The explanatory variables are the participatory factors—resources, recruitment, and political interest—as well as the extremity of attitude positions on, respec-

---

15. Given that the attitude item focused on government provision of jobs, we felt it appropriate that the issue-based activity in the dependent variable focus on issues of basic human needs. We did, however, undertake a parallel analysis in which the dependent variable was issue-based activity where the subject matter was the economy (or the economy or taxes). When this alternative formulation is used, the results are unchanged: attitudes toward government provision of jobs have no independent effect.

Table 14.4 Predicting Issue-Based Activity by Participatory Factors and Extreme Attitude Positions: OLS Regression (abortion and government provision of jobs scales "folded")

	Activity on Basic Human Needs			Activity on Abortion		
	B	SE B	Beta	B	SE B	Beta
PARTICIPATORY FACTORS						
Education	.01	.01	.05*	.03	.01	.10**
Income	.00	.00	.02	.01	.00	.06**
Job Variables	.01	.00	.05*	−.01	.01	−.04
Organization Variables	.02	.01	.07**	−.00	.01	−.00
Church Variables	.01	.01	.02	.04	.01	.13**
Political Interest	.01	.00	.06**	.03	.01	.10**
HAVING EXTREME ATTITUDE POSITIONS						
Government Provision of Jobs	.01	.01	.03			
Abortion				.04	.01	.10**
(Constant)	−.10	.04**		−.30	.05**	
R^2		.03			.08	

* Significant at .05 level.
** Significant at .01 level.
Note: Age, gender, race and ethnicity also included in the equation.

tively, the economy and abortion. For activity on issues of basic human needs, having extreme attitudes on the economy has no impact. When it comes to activity on abortion, however, having extreme views on abortion has a strong independent effect—once again, over and above that of general political interest.[16]

The consequences for participation of deeply held views on a particular issue need not be the same on both sides of the issue. The power of extreme attitudes on abortion to increase activity

16. To be certain that we were observing a difference in the effect of attitudes in two different issue domains and not something special about the people who have extreme views on abortion, we undertook an analysis parallel to that reported in Table 14.4 using the abortion attitudes as an explanatory variable in an equation for predicting activity on issues of basic human needs. Our purpose was to make sure that those with strong abortion views were not simply more active on all issues. With activity on issues of basic human needs as the dependent variable, the coefficient for abortion attitudes is zero.

might vary depending upon whether those attitudes are pro-choice or pro-life. To investigate potential asymmetry in the impact of intense views on abortion, we repeated the analysis in Table 14.4 using two measures of abortion attitudes, one measuring pro-life and the other measuring pro-choice position. Extreme opinions on both sides of the issue are, on their own, significant predictors of abortion-related activity. Nonetheless, the impact of pro-life attitudes on activity is more than twice as large as that of a pro-choice position.[17]

In short, the data show how a passionate issue commitment can mobilize citizens to activity over and above the workings of the other factors in the Civic Voluntarism Model. The other factors in the model are, however, still relevant. As it does for activity in general, education predicts activity on abortion. Church-based factors also have a strong effect in fostering abortion-related participation. The ideological impacts of these two factors, as one would expect from the data in Figure 14.1 and as we discuss more fully below, are in opposite directions. The effect of education is to bring in an activist population that is more pro-choice; the effect of religious factors is to enhance the number of pro-life activists.[18]

PRAYER IN THE PUBLIC SCHOOLS

We can shed additional light on this process by considering an issue that would seem to have many affinities with abortion,

---

17. The beta weights—which are, in each case, significant at the .01 level—are .16 and .07 respectively. Other studies confirm that those with pro-life views are less numerous but more intense in their positions. A 1989 Gallup poll found 32 percent of the public in favor of, and 62 percent opposed to, overturning *Roe v. Wade*. However, three-quarters of the former—in contrast to 43 percent of the latter—felt "extremely" or "very" strongly on the issue. In addition, abortion opponents are twice as likely to have written a letter on the subject and one and a half times as likely to have contributed money on the issue. See Craig and O'Brien, *Abortion and American Politics*, pp. 270–272. See also Jacqueline Scott and Howard Schuman, "Attitude Strength and Social Action in the Abortion Dispute," *American Sociological Review* 53 (1988): 785–793.

18. In their discussion of the political cues given by clergy, Welch, Leege, Wald, and Kellstedt indicate that, overall, there is more focus on abortion and sexual matters than on economic matters. They also show variation among denominations, with mainline Protestant clergy more likely to mention issues of the economy. In contrast, Catholic and evangelical Protestant clergy are more likely to focus on abortion and sexual behavior. See Michael R. Welch, David C. Leege, Kenneth D. Wald, and Lyman A. Kellstedt, "Are the

prayer in the schools. Like abortion, school prayer is an issue with moral and religious overtones. Like abortion, school prayer is an issue on which public opinion is relatively polarized. When we asked respondents to place themselves on a seven-point scale ranging from the position that "public schools should be allowed to start each day with a prayer" to the position that "religion does not belong in the public schools," 52 percent chose one of the two extreme categories.[19] In addition, as with views on abortion, religious involvement and educational attainment work in opposite directions with respect to attitudes on prayer in the schools: frequent church attendance is associated with support for school prayer; higher levels of educational attainment with opposition to school prayer.[20] Thus, there are many similarities between school prayer and abortion that might suggest that they would function similarly in fostering issue-based activity.

In fundamental respects, however, school prayer and abortion differed as issues at the time our survey was taken. School prayer simply did not get as many people incensed as abortion did.

Sheep Hearing the Shepherds? Cue Perceptions, Congregational Responses, and Political Communication Processes," in Lyman A. Kellstedt and David C. Leege, *Rediscovering the Religious Factor in American Politics* (Armonk, N.Y.: M. E. Sharpe, 1993), p. 239.

19. Opinion on the issue of prayer in the schools arrayed itself as follows:

Oppose prayer						Favor prayer
17%	7	5	16	9	10	35%

We should note that, in contrast to abortion where opinion is clustered on the liberal or pro-choice side of the issue, opinion on school prayer is clustered on the conservative or pro-prayer side of the issue.

20. If we conduct an analysis for school prayer parallel to that reported in Figure 14.2, we find relationships between attitudes on school prayer and education and religious involvement almost identical to those for abortion. The mean scores on the school prayer attitude scale (with a higher score indicating greater favorability to school prayer) for groups defined by their level of education and religious attendance are as follows:

	Low	2	3	4	5	6	7	High
Educational Attainment	3.7	2.6	2.4	2.2	1.8	1.7	1.8	1.6
Religious Attendance	1.1	1.2	1.6	1.8	2.4	2.7	3.1	4.2

Moreover, in contrast to abortion, prayer in the schools was not an issue that figured importantly on the public's participatory agenda. Our survey registered 345 instances in which a respondent mentioned abortion as the subject of issue-based participation and 82 in which a respondent mentioned abortion as the subject of a protest.[21] In contrast, prayer in the schools was mentioned only 3 times across all activities and never in relation to a protest. The result is that, while attitudes on abortion have an independent effect on overall political activity, attitudes on prayer in the schools do not. We repeated the regression that showed abortion attitudes on their own to influence overall activity, substituting views on school prayer for views on abortion. We found that, in contrast to attitudes on abortion which have a highly significant effect on activity, attitudes on prayer in the schools have no effect.[22]

In drawing a contrast between two issues engaging a moral dimension, one of which, abortion, raised the political temperature at the time of our survey in a way that the other, school prayer, did not, we do not mean to suggest that it is in any way inevitable that the two issues should function so differently in animating activity. Given the right configuration—for example, a controversial Supreme Court decision, attention from the media, or efforts by political leaders to mobilize the public around the issue—school prayer might become the object of intense citizen activity and play the independent role in fostering activity that abortion did at the time of our survey.

A GLANCE BACKWARD: THE WAR IN VIETNAM

Issues that raise public passions come and go in American politics. Had we conducted our survey twenty-five years earlier, we would have made sure to ask about an issue about which there was

---

21. These are unweighted numbers, i.e., the actual times the issue came up in our interviews. This seems the appropriate figure for this purpose. The weighted numbers are 256 and 37 respectively.

22. The regression coefficient is .007 and the beta is .005. Of course, we could not undertake an analysis for school prayer parallel to that reported in Table 14.4. That is, we could not assess whether attitudes on school prayer function independently in stimulating activity on the subject of school prayer, for there is barely any activity on school prayer to explain.

intense public conflict on a national basis, the war in Vietnam. Like abortion at the time of our survey, Vietnam had, at that time, a prominent place on the national political agenda and was the subject of widespread protest activity. Moreover, just as pro-life activists have a readily available institutional infrastructure that can facilitate political mobilization—conservative Protestant and Catholic churches—the doves on Vietnam were able to use college campuses as the institutional base for anti-war activity.

The 1972 National Election Study contains measures, including seven-point scales on attitudes toward both the Vietnam war and government provision of jobs, roughly equivalent to the ones we have used to analyze the abortion issue. In order to assess whether intensity of opinion on the war in Vietnam had an independent impact on political activity, we used these to replicate, insofar as possible, the analysis in Table 14.3. The results, which are remarkably similar to those presented earlier about abortion, are shown in Table 14.5.[23] Not surprisingly, the socioeconomic variables of educational attainment and income are significant predictors of political activity. More important for our purposes, having extreme views on government provision of jobs is not significantly related to participation but having extreme views on the Vietnam War is.[24] The data confirm the role that an issue arousing deep

23. The variables are fairly similar to those from the Citizen Participation Study. Education and income are standard survey items. The "job" measure is a variable based on the respondent's occupational category. Unfortunately, the survey included no information about activity in religious institutions. As we did with the abortion scale, in order to measure intensity, we "folded" two seven-point attitude scales, the standard NES item about "government provision of jobs" that was used in the Citizen Participation Study as well and a "Hawk-Dove" scale on what to do about Vietnam. The dependent variable is an activity scale based on seven acts: voting, campaign work, contributing campaign money, membership in a political organization, writing a letter to an official, trying to persuade someone how to vote, and attending a political meeting or rally. Note that this participation scale gives relatively greater weight to electoral activity than does the scale of overall activity that is derived from the Citizen Participation Study. The equation also includes dummy variables for age, gender, and being Black or Latino.

24. We carried out a parallel analysis on data from the 1968 election when, if anything, emotions on Vietnam were even stronger. In that analysis, the intensity of attitudes on Vietnam makes some difference, but the effects are not statistically significant. Even though the conflict over the war in Vietnam was especially intense in 1968, we would not expect attitudes on the war to have mobilized citizens to activity—at least as measured by the scale

Table 14.5 Predicting Overall Activity by Participatory Factors and Extreme Attitude Positions on Vietnam and Government Positions on Jobs: OLS Regression (Vietnam and government provision of jobs scales "folded")

	B	SE B	Beta
PARTICIPATORY FACTORS			
Education	.33	.04	.33**
Income	.22	.04	.15**
Job Category	.05	.03	.05
EXTREME ATTITUDE POSITIONS			
Vietnam	.07	.03	.06*
Government Provision of Jobs	.03	.03	.02
(Constant)	−.18	.26	
R^2		.19	

* Significant at .05 level.
** Significant at .01 level.
Note: Age, gender, race and ethnicity also included in the equation.
Source: American National Election Study, 1972.

feelings within the public can play in fostering participation. If we had the capacity to undertake this kind of analysis at appropriate moments throughout American history, we would expect to find similar political mobilization around various other issues.

We have contended that the participatory effects of intense issue commitments would be manifest with respect to activity directed at the issue in question. Unfortunately, the 1972 NES did not inquire about the issue content of activity. However, we can deepen our understanding of the way in which attitudes on the war in

derived from the NES, which gives special weight to electoral activity and includes no measure of protest. Although many citizens believed the war in Vietnam to be the "overriding issue" in 1968—that is, the issue on which they were willing to base their vote—the major party presidential candidates in that year, Richard Nixon and Hubert H. Humphrey, offered little choice on the issue. Better measures of non-electoral participation, especially protest activity, might have yielded different results. For an analysis of the role of Vietnam as an issue in 1968, see Sidney Verba and Norman H. Nie, *Participation in America: Political Democracy and Social Equality* (New York: Harper and Row, 1972), pp. 106–108.

Vietnam functioned in stimulating activity on the issue with reference to a study undertaken in 1967, which asked about various activities specifically related to the issue of Vietnam: writing a letter, protesting, or trying to change someone's mind about the subject. It is, as we have argued, such issue-specific activity that would be most likely to be affected by strong views. As reported, the results demonstrate the joint effects of socioeconomic forces and issue engagements in fostering participation.[25] As we have seen with respect to other issues, the association between attitudes toward the war in Vietnam and other characteristics—in particular, socioeconomic status—had implications for the messages communicated to policymakers through various forms of participation. Those higher on the SES scale, as well as men and Whites, tended to have more hawkish views on Vietnam. Since these are groups that tended also to be more politically participant, it is not surprising that those who engaged in the mainstream activity of writing a letter about the war tended, on average, to be more hawkish in their views than the population as a whole. In contrast, when it came to protest about the war, an activity that is less mainstream than writing letters, the activists were overwhelmingly dovish. Presumably, the intense issue commitment of the doves acted as an independent factor in enhancing the participation of citizens who might otherwise not have been active.

Deeply held convictions about abortion and the war in Vietnam seem to work similarly as factors that, in themselves, operate to enhance issue-based participation. It is noteworthy, however, that similarity in the structure of the relationships is not paralleled by similarity in content. With respect to abortion, the thrust of socioeconomic factors is to increase participation from (pro-choice) liberals while issue commitments operate in a contrary fashion to enhance activity from (pro-life) conservatives. With respect to Vietnam, the forces worked in the opposite direction ideologically. Socioeconomic forces augmented letter-writing among (hawkish) conservatives on the issue while issue engagements stimulated (dovish) liberals to protest.

---

25. Sidney Verba and Richard A. Brody, "Participation, Policy Preferences, and the War in Vietnam," *Public Opinion Quarterly* 34 (1970): 325–332.

ISSUE ENGAGEMENT AND PARTICIPATORY PROFILES

We can enrich our understanding of how issue engagements work together with other participatory factors by considering more closely the characteristics of several issue constituencies. We turn to the four groups we were able to identify whose participation is generated, at least in part, by their issue engagement: recipients of means-tested benefits, parents of school-aged children, and those in the most extreme pro-life and pro-choice categories in their attitudes on abortion. Table 14.6 presents extensive data about the political resources, general political engagement, political recruitment, and political activity of these issue publics. Although it contains a lot of numbers, it offers a snapshot of the participatory factors commanded by several groups and their consequent activity. Let us consider these four groups.

In comparison with the public at large, the *beneficiaries of means-tested government benefits* are in many ways distinctive. Recipients of means-tested benefits are, not unexpectedly, less well educated and less well off financially. Although they attend church regularly, they exercise very few civic skills in non-political institutions and are relatively uninterested in and uninformed about politics. It is, therefore, not surprising that recipients of means-tested benefits are, of the groups profiled in Table 14.6, by far the least active in politics. Although more than half of their participation is directed at issues of basic human needs, there just is not very much of it. The lift given to their participation by their interest in issues of basic human needs is insufficient to overcome their other resource deficits.

These data shed light on the earlier finding from Chapter 7 to the effect that recipients of means-tested benefits are so much less active than recipients of non-means-tested benefits such as Social Security or veterans' benefits. The two groups differ substantially in terms of socioeconomic status, with consequent disparities with respect to the factors that foster participation. Receipt of means-tested benefits does not, of itself, depress activity.

Those in the other group whose issue engagement derives from having a stake in a particular policy, *parents of school-aged children,* stand in sharp contrast to recipients of means-tested benefits. Parents of school-aged children are relatively advantaged in terms

Table 14.6 Issue Engagement and Participation: Profile of Four Groups (averages or percentages)

	All Respondents	Receive Benefits	Have School-Aged Children	Pro-choice	Pro-life
RESOURCES					
Education: years	13.2	10.8	13.4	13.9	11.8
Family income	$40,300	$21,200	$45,300	$44,000	$31,100
High-level job[a]	26%	3%	28%	28%	13%
Civic skills	2.4	.9	3.1	2.4	2.1
Attend church regularly[b]	49%	49%	60%	30%	81%
POLITICAL INTEREST SCALE	5.8	4.9	5.9	5.8	5.5
RECRUITMENT					
On the job	13%	5%	19%	15%	11%
In an organization	22%	13%	26%	26%	18%
In church	23%	17%	31%	17%	34%
POLITICAL ACTIVITY					
Number of activities	2.1	1.2	2.3	2.3	1.8
Contributions to politics	$66	$8	$80	$81	$36
ISSUE-SPECIFIC ACTIVITY					
% of group members engaging in act on their[c] issue		12%	21%	8%	23%
% of group's total issue-based activity devoted to their[c] issue		53%	43%	11%	58%

a. High-level jobs are in the top two categories of the job level variable. See Appendix B.11.b.

b. 2–3 times a month or more.

c. For those receiving means-tested benefits, "their" issue is human need; for those with children in school, the issue is education; for those who are pro-life or pro-choice, the issue is abortion.

of education and income. On average, they are likely to exercise civic skills on the job, at church, and in non-political organizations, and they are relatively interested in and informed about politics. It follows from this profile that, compared to recipients of means-tested benefits, they would be much more politically participant and more likely to engage in a political act directed at the government program from which they benefit. Nonetheless, their activity is less concentrated on this issue: that is, a smaller proportion of the participation of parents of school-aged children is devoted to issues surrounding education. Moreover, the issue-based activity of these two groups of policy beneficiaries differs in an another way as well. When recipients of means-tested benefits get involved in the politics of basic human needs, it is ordinarily on behalf of narrow concerns relevant to themselves and their families. Of their contacts on the subject, fully 76 percent were particularized. In contrast, when it comes to parents of school-aged children, only 18 percent of their contacts about educational matters concerned only themselves or their children.

In many ways—their levels of education, income, political interest and information, and participation—those in the most *extreme pro-choice* category in their attitudes on abortion resemble the parents of school-aged children. In two respects, however, those with extreme pro-choice attitudes differ from parents of school-aged children. First, they are much less likely to go to religious services regularly. In addition, although an active group, those with pro-choice views do not focus their activity on the issue of abortion. Of the four issue publics profiled in Table 14.6, they are the least likely to engage in an issue act inspired by the issue that defines the group. Even more striking is how low a proportion of the issue-based activity of the pro-choice group is dedicated to abortion.

The much smaller group with attitudes at the opposite end of the abortion scale is very different. Those with *pro-life attitudes* are neither especially advantaged in socioeconomic terms nor particularly interested in or knowledgeable about politics. Moreover, they are relatively inactive in politics. Where they are distinctive is in their level of church attendance, which is remarkably high, and in the extent to which they concentrate on the issue of abortion when they do take part. The fact that 58 percent of their issue-based activity is directed at the issue of abortion makes those with extreme pro-life attitudes the closest to a single-issue constituency of the groups in Table 14.6.

Considering these four constituencies illustrates how issue engagements work together with the other factors in the Civic Voluntarism Model—resources, political engagement apart from particular issues, and recruitment—to produce distinctive participatory profiles. For a group that has a stake in a government policy or a deep commitment on a particular issue, the level of the group's activity and the concentration of that activity on the particular issue depend both upon the strength and centrality of its issue engagement and upon the size of its stockpile of other participatory resources. Thus, those with pro-life attitudes are not especially advantaged with respect to participatory factors—except for those deriving from religious activity. Nevertheless, public opinion data cited earlier in the chapter indicate that they care intensely about the issue of abortion. Hence, although their overall level of participation is not particularly high, they are very active when it comes to abortion. In contrast, those with pro-choice views are more numerous and relatively well-endowed with the factors that foster participation. However, because the issue of abortion figures less importantly in the bundle of their participatory concerns, they combine a high rate of overall participation with much more limited involvement with respect to abortion.

If we had the data to focus on smaller issue publics—for example, physicians, pharmaceutical executives, prisoners' rights or anti-smoking advocates—we would, undoubtedly, find groups with still different configurations of participatory factors and levels of activity. What we have seen, however, is that issue engagements are only one piece of the puzzle. For a group that is resource-deprived, issue engagements go only so far in elevating a depressed level of participation. For a group that is well-endowed with participatory resources, issue engagements can give an additional participatory push. Thus, political participation is deeply enmeshed with the substance of politics. Yet the way in which political issues and conflicts are manifest in participatory input also depends fundamentally upon the structure of participatory factors having their origins outside politics.

Conclusion

In this chapter we have introduced a final component to the Civic Voluntarism Model, one that adds another dimension to our understanding of the process of participation in the United States. We have seen that issue engagements from having either a stake in what the government does or deep feelings about some issue can function as an independent force in stimulating participation.

By incorporating issue engagements into the model, we bring politics back in as well. That is, we have located the origins of most of the factors that foster participation in experiences outside politics—at home, in school, on the job, at church, and in non-political organizations. With this step we have demonstrated that political activity also has roots in political issues and conflicts. It is not our enterprise to investigate where issue engagements come from—how government actions create attentive constituencies of those affected by policies or why certain issues generate deep passions while others do not. What matters for us is that what happens in politics has implications for who is active in politics.[26] In Chapter 16 we return to this theme and show how participation factors such as resources and general political engagement interact with the particular issue engagements of citizens to shape what the government hears on various subjects.

---

26. Thus, this analysis complements Rosenstone and Hansen's analysis of the role of strategic elites in generating citizen activity. See Steven J. Rosenstone and John Mark Hansen, *Mobilization, Participation, and Democracy in America* (New York: Macmillan, 1993), esp. chaps. 2, 4, and 6.

15

From Generation to Generation:
The Roots of Participatory Factors

The Civic Voluntarism Model focuses on several sets of activity-enhancing factors: resources, political engagement, and the experience of being exposed in a non-political setting to attempts at direct political recruitment. We have located the roots of these various factors in non-political institutional affiliations. In this chapter we probe more deeply into their origins by tracing the complex processes by which the characteristics acquired at birth and early experiences in family and school ramify throughout the life course, generating participatory factors and, ultimately, political activity. We will demonstrate that the participatory process is rooted in the basic structures of American society.

We outline a four-step process, summarized in Figure 15.1. The process begins with characteristics present at the outset: in particular, sex, race or ethnicity, and parents' educational attainment. In the first step, we investigate how these characteristics are related to pre-adult experiences at home and in school, especially to formal education and to political socialization by family and school. Educational attainment and exposure to politics while growing up, in turn, affect the placement of the individual in various adult institutions: in a job, in organizations, and in religious institutions. Institutional location, then, affects the acquisition of the various factors that foster participation. Finally, as we have already shown,

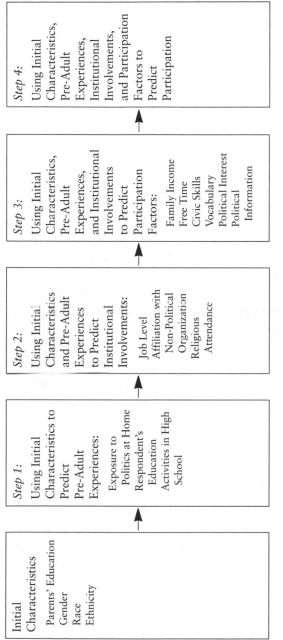

Figure 15.1 The Roots of Participatory Factors.

these participatory factors affect the amount and kinds of political activity.

To depict this chain of interrelated processes is a task of daunting magnitude. We do not aspire to explain fully every single participatory factor. For example, we leave to students of social stratification the full explanation of family income. Still, we are able to highlight significant aspects of the accumulation of participatory factors from generation to generation and within the individual's own life.

This enterprise raises the usual questions about the imputation of causality. To tackle the intellectual problem we have set for ourselves, longitudinal data gathered throughout the life-cycle of an individual would be far preferable to the cross-sectional data that we have. This means that we shall, as always, need to exercise caution and be clear about the uncertainty associated with the inferences that we make. Furthermore, because a number of our measures involve retrospective reconstructions of experiences that may have taken place decades ago, we need to be cognizant of the extent to which assessments of the past are distorted by the vagaries of memory or the lens of subsequent commitments and events. Nevertheless, what we find out about the processes by which participatory factors are stockpiled is so interesting and plausible that, exercising due caution, we feel it appropriate to make causal connections.

Two Central Themes:
Intergenerational Transmission and Education

In our analysis, we pay special attention to two aspects of this multi-stage process: the importance of intergenerational transmission and the crucial role of education. The two are closely related and, together, play an important role in the process by which some citizens come to be active while others do not.

INTERGENERATIONAL TRANSMISSION
We are concerned with the legacy of past generations in various ways: one involves the transmission of social class across genera-

tions; another the transmission of more direct political cues. These processes have been investigated extensively in the social sciences, the former in the field of social mobility,[1] the latter in the field of political socialization.[2] We consider both and find that we can distinguish their effects on future activity. With respect to the transmission of social class, we begin with the socioeconomic status of the parents, which we measure in terms of parental education. Although those who study social stratification differ in the extent to which they find that social background determines life chances, there is no doubt that circumstances of initial social advantage or disadvantage have consequences for ultimate educational attainment, occupational choice, and income level. In terms of political socialization, we are interested in the implications of exposure to politically relevant stimuli in the family early in life—having politically involved parents or being exposed to political discussion at home—for the propensity to become active in politics as an adult.

We consider another form of intergenerational influence as well. Both parental religious attendance and parental education have an impact on religious commitments, which are in turn related to political activity. These parental characteristics are also related to residential mobility in later life, which has an effect on political activity in the community. This constitutes a third route for intergenerational transmission.

---

1. Important works in a vast literature include Peter M. Blau and Otis Dudley Duncan, *The American Occupational Structure* (New York: Free Press, 1967) and David L. Featherman and Robert M. Hauser, *Opportunity and Change* (New York: Academic Press, 1978).

2. Works on political socialization have dealt with the transmission of general orientations toward the legitimacy of the political system, more specific attitudes such as political ideology or partisan identification, as well as with the propensity to be politically engaged and active. The literature is extensive. For general accounts see Richard E. Dawson, Kenneth Prewitt, and Karen S. Dawson, *Political Socialization: An Analytic Study,* 2nd ed. (Boston: Little Brown, 1977); Stanley Allen Renshon, *Handbook of Political Socialization: Theory and Research* (New York: Free Press, 1977); and Kenneth P. Langton, *Political Participation and Learning* (North Quincy, Mass.: Christopher Publishing House, 1980). For works particularly relevant to our concern with experiences during adolescence, see M. Kent Jennings and Richard G. Niemi, *The Political Character of Adolescence: The Influence of Families and Schools* (Princeton: Princeton University Press, 1974); and Jennings and Niemi, *Generations and Politics: A Panel Study of Young Adults and Their Parents* (Princeton: Princeton University Press, 1981).

THE ROLE OF EDUCATION

The emphasis upon the consequences for future participation of school experiences leads to a second major theme, the crucial role of education. All studies of political activity emphasize the strength of the relationship between formal education and participation.[3] This chapter presents a complex analysis that gets inside that relationship. As we shall see, education plays multiple roles vis-à-vis participation. Indeed, education enhances nearly every single one of the participatory factors: those who are well educated have higher incomes and exercise more civic skills; they are more politically interested and informed; they are more likely to be in institutional settings from which they can be recruited to politics.

The impact of education is both direct and indirect. The direct effects happen in the school. Both in the classroom and in extra-curricular activities, students learn communications and organizational skills. They may also absorb civic values and develop an interest in politics. In addition, education has an indirect influence on participation. Educational attainment is the most powerful determinant of the kinds of jobs people get. Since occupational level, in turn, has a substantial influence on the incomes they earn, the civic skills they practice on the job, and the kinds of networks with which they become involved, educational attainment thus has an indirect impact on the acquisition of several crucial political resources.[4] In addition, education affects level of activity in organizations and, to a lesser extent, religious institutions and, therefore, the opportunities for the exercise of civic skills and for political recruitment. All of these processes work together, with the result that those with more education accumulate more of the resources and motivations that foster activity.

---

3. The central role of education is stressed in much of the socialization literature. See especially Langton, *Political Participation and Learning*. In their analysis of voting turnout, Wolfinger and Rosenstone emphasize the key role of education in determining who votes. They cite various ways in which education affects turnout—among them, providing skills and facilitating the acquisition of information. Education also increases the gratification derived from voting. See Raymond E. Wolfinger and Steven J. Rosenstone, *Who Votes?* (New Haven: Yale University Press, 1980).

4. "The best available predictor of a young man's eventual status or earnings is the amount of schooling he has had." Christopher Jencks et al., *Who Gets Ahead: The Determinants of Economic Success in America* (New York: Basic Books, 1979), p. 230.

The Variables in the Chain

Because the analysis in this chapter is complicated, involving not only the many variables treated earlier but some new ones as well, let us begin by introducing the variables in sequence before we delineate the chain of connections.

INITIAL CHARACTERISTICS

The first set of variables in the chain of participatory factors are measures of characteristics acquired at birth. We focus on the same ones to which we pay attention when we consider adults: social class, race or ethnicity, and sex. We measure social class of origin by the average number of years of schooling of the respondent's parents.[5] An adult's social class is, of course, not fixed at birth. Indeed, a significant component of the American ideology is the possibility of upward mobility. Still, social class origins constitute a factor having long-term consequences for later life. Given the central place of education in both explanations of participation and the measurement of social class, parental educational attainment provides a useful proxy for parental social class and a good starting point for the chain of connections posited here. Although it is a retrospective measure, we have considerable confidence that respondents know, and report fairly accurately, their parents' education. Moreover, it is, quite obviously, antecedent to later experiences.

Sex and race or ethnicity are also established at birth.[6] These characteristics obviously have the basic features of causally prior factors: temporal priority and immutability. However, their implications for human behavior are dependent upon the social interpretation of their meaning. Hence, the nature and extent of the effects of sex and race or ethnicity on the factors that facilitate political participation are not fixed but, instead, can vary with changing circumstances and changing times. In short, although

---

5. See Appendix B.18.a.

6. In this chapter these will be measured, as usual, by using dummy variables for being female (rather than male), and for being Latino or for being African-American (rather than "other"—mostly, Anglo-White).

race, ethnicity, and sex cannot vary over the life course of the individual, their meaning for the factors associated with political activity can.

YOUTH EXPERIENCES

From these initial characteristics, we move to three sets of variables reflecting experiences at home and school while growing up. We focus first on the family, considering the extent to which the respondents were exposed to politically relevant stimuli at home— whether, at the time when respondents were sixteen, their parents were politically active and there were discussions of politics at home.[7] These measures present no problems of temporal priority. However, there is reason to be concerned that they may not be accurate reports of the past. Those who are currently active might well be more likely to report past exposures—because they are unconsciously harmonizing memories of home with their present commitments or because they were more sensitive to the political cues at the time they were growing up. We cannot eliminate this possibility and should, thus, view any effects on participation of politics at home with particular caution. However, when we consider the data later in the chapter, the pattern of effects of these variables is sufficiently compelling as to suggest that we are tapping a real phenomenon.

Education and Educational Experiences. As we have already indicated, education is the key to much of the analysis in this chapter. As a vehicle through which parental social class operates to affect future participatory life, education links backward to the previous generation. Moreover, it links forward in several ways to enhance the likelihood that an individual will become active. One of the main goals of this chapter is to sort out the multiple implications of education for participation.

In spite of the large volume of data confirming the relationship between educational attainment and political participation, there have been relatively few empirical inquiries as to *why* schooling

---

7. Jennings and Niemi, *Generations and Politics,* show that parents who are active are more likely to produce children who are active. For the questions about parental activity, see Appendix B.18.b.

fosters activity. In order to investigate what it is about educational experiences that promotes future political participation, we included a series of items in our questionnaire. The list covered a variety of ways in which schooling might affect political involvement.[8] We asked whether:

> The respondent had taken any courses that required students to pay attention to current events;
>
> Students in the respondent's high school were concerned about current events and politics;
>
> Students in the respondent's high school were encouraged to debate and make up their own minds about current events;
>
> Students in the respondent's high school were allowed to complain if they thought something was unfair;
>
> The respondent was concerned about current events and politics;
>
> The respondent was active in school sports;
>
> The respondent was active in school government;
>
> The respondent was active in other school clubs or activities.

In short, these questions asked about the civic culture of the school, the political engagement of its students and of the respondent, and the extracurricular activity of the respondent. However, it is important to recognize that respondents' experiences reflect not only their own tastes and commitments but also the opportunities offered by the school. In order to take courses requiring attention to current events, there must be such courses in the curriculum. In order to get involved in school activities, there must be sports programs and clubs to join.

We used the answers to these questions in a regression analysis with the overall scale of political activity as the dependent variable.[9] The analysis is not intended to be an explanation of partici-

---

8. For the full questions, see Appendix B.10.b.

9. Although we do not report the coefficients in Table 15.1, we also included the respondent's age, educational attainment, and the "initial characteristics" (parents' education, gender, race, and ethnicity). The control for age is useful to eliminate generational effects. We carry it along in the current analysis. At later stages in the analysis, controlling for age controls as well for life-cycle effects which are irrelevant at this point since we are considering high school experiences. There is more to the impact of age than the analysis in this chapter can reveal—but that must wait for future research. The control for education

Table 15.1 Predicting Overall Participation by High School
Experience: OLS Regressions (among high school
graduates)

Variable	B	SE B	Beta
Respondent cared about current events	.31	.06	.13**
FELLOW STUDENTS			
Cared about current events	−.11	.06	−.04
Encouraged to debate	.06	.05	.02
Had a chance to complain	−.09	.06	−.03
RESPONDENT'S ACTIVITIES IN HIGH SCHOOL			
Civics course	.25	.08	.06**
High school government	.21	.04	.13**
Clubs	.10	.03	.07**
Sports	−.07	.03	−.05*
(Constant)	.13	.22	
R^2		.25	
Sample size		2,146	

* Significant at .05 level.
** Significant at .01 level.
Note: Also in the equation are age, parents' education, gender, race and ethnicity, and the respondent's ultimate educational achievement.

pation, a task to which we return at the end of this chapter. Rather, we use the analysis to help us choose which variables to carry along as the argument unfolds. The data, which are presented in Table 15.1, indicate how closely each of these experiences relates to later political activity. Not surprisingly, respondents' retrospective reports on how much they cared about current events while in high school are strongly related to adult activity. This measure is the one most likely to be tainted by backward projection of current views and is, thus, not entirely trustworthy. Nevertheless, it is a useful indicator of a general taste for politics. The other aspects of high school experiences are more interesting. The data

is useful in ensuring that the results are not a function of education in general. The data are for those who completed high school, so that all respondents had an equal chance to experience the high school effects. If the analysis is replicated for all who attended high school, whether or not they finished, the results are similar.

suggest that the most important predictive variables are not those that measure the attributes of the school—the extent to which fellow students were politically involved or to which the school encouraged students to debate current events or permitted them to complain. Rather, the variables most closely related to subsequent participation are those that measure the activity of the respondent as a high school student—in particular, involvement in high school government, but also involvement in other clubs and activities—though not activity in high school sports. In addition, having taken a course that includes discussion of current events—an experience that is shared by 79 percent of high school graduates and that may reflect either a decision by the respondent or a requirement by the school—is related, though somewhat less strongly, to future activity.[10]

That activity in school government or school clubs is such a strong predictor of later political activity fits nicely with our emphasis on the role of civic skills as a resource for politics, for these activities would presumably develop communications and organizational skills. Indeed, the fact that actual participatory experiences appear to be the most important school effect is a significant finding for understanding civic education. To writers like Tocqueville, local governments and voluntary organizations are "schools of democracy," not because they give formal instruction in democratic governance but because they give opportunities to practice democratic governance. At least as far as our data suggest, American high schools have a similar effect, not by teaching about democracy but by providing hands-on training for future participation.

With respect to the measures of experiences in high school, we must, however, repeat some of the same concerns raised when we discussed respondents' memories of their homes. The questions are retrospective and allow a good deal of backward projection. In addition, even if the responses are accurate depictions of high

---

10. The regression coefficient for taking a civics course is quite high, but, in this case, the beta weights are probably a better measure of the relative power of the variables in Table 15.1. The measure of civics course involvement is a dichotomy, while the measures of involvement in clubs or student government have four categories running from "not at all active" to "very active."

school experiences, there is the danger of an omitted variable; that is, that some unmeasured taste for activity is responsible for both activity while in high school and subsequent political participation. In spite of these concerns, we are given some encouragement by the fact that the variables do not all behave in the same way. Taking part in school sports does not predict future activity in the way that participation in high school government or clubs does; indeed, athletic participation is negatively related to subsequent political involvement. Moreover, other factors that might be expected to have an equally strong impact on political participation—for example, fellow students who are interested in politics or a school atmosphere conducive to debate or complaint—do not. In short, although we must interpret these data with caution, they present an interesting indication of how early experiences affect later civic life.

In the analysis that follows, we shall use three variables that derive from early experiences: exposure to political stimuli in the family; educational attainment; and, as a measure of both early interest in being active and organizational and communications skills, high school activity, a combination of the measures of activity in high school government and other high school clubs.[11]

INSTITUTIONAL INVOLVEMENTS

As adults, individuals enter the institutional realms of the workplace, organizations, and churches. The sorting process by which adults end up in institutions represents a series of constrained choices, choices shaped by the kinds of variables we have been discussing—the characteristics with which one is born as well as early experiences at home and in school. The measures of institutional affiliation are ones that, having been used extensively in our

---

11. Although taking a civics course is positively related to later political activity in Table 15.1, for several reasons we are not including it in our analysis. First, since four out of five report taking such a course, the measure does not discriminate well among respondents. In addition, the characteristics associated with high school activities are closer to our theoretical interest in the acquisition of communications and organizational civic skills. Finally, the civics course variable, unlike the measures of high school activity, does not remain a significant predictor of later activity once other adult variables are added to the analysis. Thus, given the necessity of simplifying our model as we move along, it seemed wise to use the high school activities variable only.

analysis, are familiar: job level, affiliation with non-political organizations, and frequency of religious attendance.

PARTICIPATORY FACTORS

As demonstrated by the earlier analysis, these institutional affiliations are the source, in turn, of various factors that influence the
amount and kinds of political activity. The factors we shall consider are the ones introduced in preceding chapters. However, in
order to simplify a complex analysis, we use some summary measures. Let us enumerate these factors.

Resources. We focus on family income and civic skills. As before, we simplify the analysis by using a summary of the three
different skill measures—skills practiced on the job, in non-political organizations, and in church. In addition, we use the measure
of vocabulary skill as a general measure of cognitive and communications ability.[12]

Political Engagement. We use two measures, political interest
and political information, as measures of affective and cognitive
engagement. As we argued in Chapter 12, where we originally
discussed these variables, political information may also legiti-
mately be considered as a resource. We believe it indexes both
engagement and skill.[13]

Institutional Recruitment. As in Chapter 13, we sum the number of requests for political activity on the job, in non-political
organizations, and in church to create a scale measuring exposure
to institutional recruitment.

The Data Analysis

Our data analysis involves a series of OLS regressions in which
the variables from each step are used to predict the variables at
the succeeding step. As we develop the analysis suggested by

---

12. We do not consider free time as a resource at this point in the analysis but shall
consider it later in the chapter. The roots of free time are different from those associated
with the factors we are discussing here.

13. We omit the efficacy and partisanship measures as part of the simplification of the
analysis. Unlike political interest and information, neither variable was significant in the
two-stage least squares analysis. (See Chapter 12, Table 12.6.)

Figure 15.1 we add new variables into the equations. At any stage the full effects of any variable on a dependent variable are its direct effect at that stage plus any indirect effects through other variables that appear at earlier stages in the model. Thus, we use the four initial background characteristics (parents' education, sex, race, and ethnicity) to predict youth experiences (education, high school participation, and politics at home). At the next step, we use these seven variables (the four initial background variables plus the three pre-adult variables) to predict each of the institutional affiliation variables. For example, the full impact of parents' education on institutional variables such as job level is its direct effect in the regression predicting job level plus any indirect effects from the preceding steps in the analysis, such as the effect that parents' education might have on the respondent's job level through the impact of parents' education on the respondent's education.[14] Before turning to the analysis of the data, we offer some comments on our choice of statistical method.

CAUSAL DIRECTION, TRIANGULAR SYSTEMS, AND OLS REGRESSION

The basic analytical method in this chapter is ordinary least squares (OLS) regression analysis, which we described in Chapter 10. At this point we need to put it into the context of the long causal chain we are exploring in this chapter, a chain that runs from characteristics acquired at birth to current political behavior. Our use of this technique is based on the assumption, one we consider reasonable, that we are estimating a recursive, triangular system.

A *triangular* system is one in which the arrows linking variables in a chain of causality all go in one direction—as they do in Figure 15.1. Variables earlier in the chain, such as "initial characteris-

---

14. Consistent with what we have done in the previous chapters, we carry additional controls as we move through the chapter. These are controls for age (through a set of dummy variables), gender, race or ethnicity, being Catholic, speaking English at home, and citizenship. These controls have little effect on the results and are not reported in the tables. Since they make no sense for understanding pre-adult experiences, we add controls for whether the respondent is working or retired later in the chapter. Since employment status interacts with job level in relation to some of the participation factors, we shall deal with it explicitly.

tics," affect later variables, such as "participation factors," but these later variables do not affect the earlier ones. This assumption seems reasonable for the four-stage process illustrated in Figure 15.1. In some instances—for example, the impact of parents' educational attainment on that of the respondent and, in turn, the impact of the respondent's educational attainment on a participation factor such as income—the assumption seems straightforward. For other connections—for example, the purported causal link between civic skills and political participation—where the causal direction might be more ambiguous, the analyses and discussion in Chapters 9, 11, and 12 provide evidence for the assumption about the direction of causality.[15] In short, we think it appropriate to consider this a triangular causal system.

The analysis depends on a second basic assumption: that the omitted variables that are incorporated in the error terms in the equations implied in Figure 15.1 are not correlated with one another. When error terms are not correlated, a triangular system is said to be *recursive*. One way to increase our confidence that the omitted variables are not correlated is to include in each equation a set of explanatory variables that is as comprehensive as possible. Another approach is to estimate the model using two-stage least squares regression to correct for correlated error terms as well as for simultaneous causation. We have done this in earlier chapters for analyses that are part of the overall Civic Voluntarism Model and have demonstrated that the results for OLS and 2SLS are very similar. We do the same for the extension of the model across generations in this chapter.

PRE-ADULT EXPERIENCES

To begin, we use the four initial background characteristics to predict the respondent's political exposure at home, educational attainment, and activity in high school. Table 15.2 presents the results of OLS regressions. Not unexpectedly, parents' education has a large and significant effect on all three dependent variables:

---

15. A more technical discussion of this issue can be found in Henry Brady, Sidney Verba, and Kay Lehman Schlozman, "Beyond SES: A Resource Model of Participation," *American Political Science Review* 89 (1995): 271–294.

Table 15.2 Predicting Pre-Adult Experiences by Initial Characteristics: OLS Regressions (standardized regression coefficients)

Predicting:	Politics at Home	Education	High School Activity
INITIAL CHARACTERISTICS			
Parents' Education	.27**	.42**	.22**
Female	.00	−.06**	.07**
Black	−.01	−.05**	.02
Latino	−.06*	−.10**	−.05*
R^2	.08	.23	.08
Sample size	2,517	2,517	2,517

* Significant at .05 level.
** Significant at .01 level.

exposure to political stimuli at home, respondent's education, and activity in high school. The other initial background characteristics (being female rather than male and African-American or Latino rather than Anglo-White) have more moderate but still significant negative effects on the respondent's ultimate educational attainment. Table 15.2 shows the beginning of a complex process. In subsequent steps we shall distinguish the paths from parents' education through the respondent's education, politicization in the home, and activity in high school. Each influences political activity, although through different processes.

INSTITUTIONAL INVOLVEMENTS

Table 15.3, which contains the predictive equations for the three institutional affiliations, carries the analysis forward to the next step. Many of the results shown there repeat material presented in Chapter 11, where we considered who gets high-level jobs, who joins organizations, and who attends church.

Job. Understanding the location of the individual in the work force implies two considerations: whether or not the individual is working and, if so, at what kind of a job. The first two columns of Table 15.3 contain the relevant data: the left-hand column shows the determinants of work force participation; the second column contains—for those with jobs—data about the factors

Table 15.3 Predicting Institutional Involvements by Initial Characteristics and Pre-Adult Experiences: OLS Regression (standardized regression coefficients)

Predicting:	Work Force Participation	Job Level[a]	Affiliation with Non-Political Organization	Religious Attendance
INITIAL CHARACTERISTICS				
Parents' Education	−.04*	.02	.05*	−.06**
Female	−.22**	−.12**	.01	.12**
Black	.01	−.06**	−.03	.08**
Latino	−.01	−.01	−.07**	.01
PRE-ADULT EXPERIENCES				
Education	.11**	.57**	.25**	.02
Politics at Home	−.03	.00	.04*	.05**
High School Activity	.02	.06**	.12**	.15**
R^2	.35	.47	.16	.09
Sample size	2,517	1,652	2,514	2,517

* Significant at .05 level.
** Significant at .01 level.
a. Among working respondents.

associated with having a high-level job.[16] Clearly, the main predictor of work force participation is being male rather than female, with education also increasing the likelihood of being employed. Among those working, by far the most important determinant of job level is the respondent's educational attainment. In addition, with education taken into account, women and, to a much lesser extent, Blacks are likely to be in jobs requiring less education and training. Thus women are more likely both to be out of the work force and, when working, to occupy lower positions than men who share their educational attainment. It is interesting that, taking into account the respondent's education, there is no direct effect of parents' education on the job level of the respondent. Parental influence on job success appears to be transmitted through its effect on the respondent's educational attainment.

---

16. The measure of working is a trichotomy: not working, working part-time, and working full-time. The measure of job level—which is explained in Chapter 10—is based on the education and on-the-job training it requires.

To simplify our analysis, as we move forward through the argument, we retain measures of work force participation and job level. However, we report only the coefficients for job level. Ordinarily, the work force participation variable has no effect. Where it does, we comment on it.

Non-political Organizational Affiliation. Education is the single best predictor of affiliation with a non-political organization. The other substantial effect comes from having been active in high school, presumably reflecting both skills obtained as a high school activist and a propensity for activity.

Church Attendance. Consistent with what we have seen, church attendance is the exception to the strong association between education and institutional affiliation. While education plays a strong and significant role in relation to jobs and organization, it has no effect on religious attendance. With respect to church attendance, we see in Table 15.3 the familiar pattern whereby—other things being equal—women and Blacks are active. As with organizational involvement, activity in high school is related to attendance at religious services. In addition, parental education is negatively related to the respondent's church attendance. We return to the secularizing effect of having well-educated parents at the end of this chapter.

Overall, the pattern of predictive variables for institutional involvements varies from institution to institution. No single variable has a powerful impact on affiliation across all three domains of adult non-political involvement. Educational attainment, so critical for job level and organizational involvement, has no role when it comes to attending church. The youth exposure variables—which affect organizational and church involvement, but not job level—appear to lead to a broader social involvement by the individual. We turn now to the forward links to participatory factors.

Participatory Factors

The data in Table 15.4 show the predictive equations for the six participatory factors we have used before. The full effect of the various predictive variables involves as well the indirect impact of the variables shown in Tables 15.2 and 15.3. Because the data are complex, let us highlight the major points.

THE DOMINANT ROLE OF EDUCATION

Education is the prime factor in most analyses of political activity. The data in Table 15.4 help us to understand why. Education has a significant direct role with respect to each of the participation factors. It affects the acquisition of skills; it channels opportunities for high levels of income and occupation; it places individuals in institutional settings where they can be recruited to political activity; and it fosters psychological and cognitive engagement with politics. Scholars have sometimes asked why education is so important when it comes to political participation. Is it skills, psychological engagement, being in a network of recruitment, or the good job and income to which it provides access? Table 15.4 makes clear the answer: All of these are components of the role of education in participation. Moreover, the direct impact of education is compounded by its indirect effects. Let us consider the role of education with respect to each of the participatory factors.

Education and Income. Education is the prime mover when it comes to the economic position of the individual. It is a dominant force in determining income, which, as we saw in Chapter 12, is a crucial political resource especially when it comes to the increasingly important activity of making campaign contributions. As shown in Table 15.4, education has direct consequences for income. In addition, as indicated in Table 15.3, education influences income indirectly through its impact on job level.

Education and Vocabulary Skill. As we might expect, education is closely related to vocabulary skill. In this case, the direction of causality is ambiguous but, for our purposes, irrelevant. It is not clear whether education develops vocabulary, or whether people with good verbal skills stay in school. With respect to our enterprise, it is not necessary to assign causal priority. As we saw in Chapter 11, cognitive ability is a prime resource for politics—as it is for many other forms of endeavor.

Education and Civic Skills. Education develops civic skills. Not only does schooling itself foster communications and organizational skills, but educational attainment is also a principal factor

Table 15.4 Predicting Participatory Factors by Initial Characteristics, Pre-Adult Experiences, and Institutional Involvements: OLS Regressions (standardized regression coefficients)

Predicting:	Family Income	Civic Skills	Vocabulary	Recruitment	Political Interest	Political Information
INITIAL CHARACTERISTICS						
Parents' Education	.07**	.03	.09**	-.03	.03	.04*
Female	-.05**	-.03	.06**	.00	-.10**	-.20**
Black	-.02	-.01	-.12**	.02	.01	-.12**
Latino	-.03	.03	-.02	-.03	-.06**	-.09**
PRE-ADULT EXPERIENCES						
Education	.19**	.13**	.38**	.13**	.12**	.28**
Politics at Home	.03	.02	.00	.00	.16**	.06**
High School Activity	.10**	.08**	.07**	.08**	.17**	.09**
INSTITUTIONAL INVOLVEMENTS						
Job Level	.08**	.21**	.05*	.02	.05*	.03
Non-Political Organization	.09**	.32**	.09**	.10**	.11**	.12**
Religious Attendance	-.02	.21**	-.05**	.27**	.07**	.01
R^2	.20	.53	.33	.18	.23	.32
Sample size	2,422	2,489	2,489	2,489	2,480	2,489

* Significant at .05 level.
** Significant at .01 level.

in the exercise of civic skills in adult institutions. In this regard, education plays both a direct and an indirect role. As we have said so often, without being on the scene, one cannot practice civic skills in a non-political setting. As we saw in Table 15.3, those with higher levels of education are more likely to have high-level jobs or to be in organizations—though not to attend church services. Furthermore, the data in Table 15.4 indicate that, even taking into account affiliation with institutions—that is, with measures of institutional affiliation in the equation—education plays a major direct role in determining who has opportunities to exercise skills.[17] Thus, it has dual implications for the exercise of civic skills—placing individuals in institutional positions from which skills can be acquired and affecting the likelihood that they will develop skills once they are there.

Education and Institutional Recruitment. The main effects on institutional recruitment are, as one might expect, the measures of involvement in those institutions. (The apparent anomaly in Table 15.4 is the absence of an effect for job level on the recruitment measure. The main effect on recruitment on the job is being employed, not the kind of job one has. The beta weight for the measure of work force participation, in the equation but not reported, is .09, significant at .001.) However, in a pattern analogous to that discussed for the antecedents of political skills, education has both an indirect and a direct influence on processes of political recruitment in non-political institutions. The data in Table 15.3 demonstrated the consequences of educational attainment for occupational level and organizational affiliation (though not for church attendance). Those presented in Table 15.4 indicate that, as with civic skills, education has a direct impact on political recruitment among those affiliated.

Education and Political Interest and Information. Table 15.4

---

17. Education affects the acquisition of civic skills on the job and in organizations, but not in church. If we look at the measures of skills acquired in each of the three domains separately, rather than at a composite skill measure as in Table 15.4, we find that education has a substantial and statistically significant effect on the acquisition of skills on the job and in organizations—even controlling for affiliation. The beta weights are .14 and .07 respectively (both significant at the .01 level). The beta weight for church skills is an insignificant .02.

confirms a finding from Chapter 12: education fosters political engagement. Educated citizens are more likely to be interested in and, especially, informed about politics. Several other correlates of political interest and information are also worth noting. Pre-adult experiences influence political engagement in adulthood. Activity in high school is associated with both political interest and information. While it has no direct effect on other participatory factors, political stimulation at home has a significant impact on political information and, especially, political interest. In addition, voluntary involvements are related to political engagement. While church attendance increases political interest, affiliation with a non-political organization enhances both political information and, especially, political interest.

In short, these data highlight the multiple paths by which education influences the development of the factors that foster participation. Education has a direct impact of varying strength on each of the six factors summarized in Table 15.4. Through its influence on job level and organizational involvement, education has additional indirect consequences for all of these factors.

Education and the Growth of Participation: A Note. We should make clear that, in placing education at the center of the understanding of participation and in specifying its multiple effects of activity, we are not arguing that aggregate changes in the level of education of the population will be associated with commensurate changes in the aggregate level of participation. It is well known that, over the past generation, increasing educational attainment has not been accompanied by parallel increases in political activity. In fact, over the period there has been unambiguous erosion in an important, although atypical, form of participation, voting.[18]

There have been numerous attempts to explain this, including the decline in strength of the political parties and disillusionment with candidates.[19] Another possibility is that when it comes to

---

18. Richard A. Brody called attention to this in "The Puzzle of Political Participation in America," in *The New American Political System,* ed. Anthony King (Washington, D.C.: American Enterprise Institute, 1978), pp. 287–324.

19. See, for instance, Richard A. Brody, "The Puzzle of Participation"; Paul R. Abramson and John H. Aldrich, "The Decline of Electoral Participation in the United States," *Ameri-*

participation, it is relative position in the educational hierarchy that counts. Thus, at any moment in time, education plays a significant role, but over time it does not lead to more activity.[20] We cannot solve this puzzle. What is important from our perspective is that at any moment in time, education plays a major role in determining who is active and who is not. Indeed, at the same time as education has been going up and turnout going down, the strong relationship between education and activity has remained remarkably steady.[21] These data suggest that the long-term structural relationship between education and activity is unlikely to change.

The Parental Legacy

Among the most fascinating data in Tables 15.2, 15.3, and 15.4 are those that delineate the various paths by which initial background affects the accumulation of participatory factors. Perhaps the main road for the intergenerational transmission of political involvement is parents' education. Its principal effect on the participation factors listed in Table 15.4 is indirect—through the

---

can Political Science Review 76 (1982): 502–521; Lee Sigelman, et al., "Voting and Non-Voting: A Multi-election Perspective," American Journal of Political Science 29 (1985): 749–765; Ruy A. Teixeira, Why Americans Don't Vote: Turnout Decline in the United States, 1960–1984 (New York: Greenwood Press, 1987); Carol A. Cassel and Robert C. Luskin, "Simple Explanations of Turnout Decline," American Political Science Review 82 (1988): 1321–1330; Warren E. Miller, "The Puzzle Transformed: Explaining Declining Turnout," Political Behavior 14 (1992): 1–43; and Ruy A. Teixeira, The Disappearing American Voter (Washington, D.C.: The Brookings Institution, 1992).

20. See Norman H. Nie, Jane Junn, and Kenneth Stehlik-Berry, Education and Citizenship in America (Chicago: University of Chicago Press, forthcoming).

21. In an equation predicting an overall scale of political activity (with income and age in the equation), the standardized coefficient for education is .33 in 1967, .37 in 1987, and .38 in 1990. (The 1967 coefficient is calculated from the data from the survey used in Sidney Verba and Norman H. Nie, Participation in America [New York: Harper and Row, 1967]; the 1987 coefficient is from the National Opinion Research Center's General Social Survey of that year; and the 1990 data come from the Citizen Participation Study.) Similar findings are reported in Jan E. Leighley and Jonathan Nagler, "Socio-Economic Bias in Turnout: 1964–1988: The Voters Remain the Same," American Political Science Review 86 (1992): 725–737. They find that although voting has gone down, the relationship between voting and socioeconomic class has stayed the same. See also Nie, Junn, and Stehlik-Berry, Education and Citizenship in America.

education of the child. Still, its consequences for the respondent's educational attainment imply that it deserves some credit for the multiple educational effects just discussed. Over and above the impact of parents' education on the respondent's education and, through educational attainment, on job level, it has a direct effect on the respondent's income—which presumably reflects the intergenerational transmission of wealth as well as opportunities. In addition, parental education has a moderately strong direct effect on vocabulary skills and a somewhat weaker one on political interest and information.

An especially interesting stream of intergenerational transmission is the one that runs through respondents' political exposures while young. Parents' education has a strong effect on the likelihood that respondents will be exposed to political stimuli in the home and active in high school. In turn, those early political exposures have long-term implications. They are strongly associated with interest in politics. Indeed, exposure to politics at home and involvement in school activities are the strongest predictors of political interest. A distinction between these two variables is noteworthy: activity in high school is positively related to the acquisition of civic skills, but exposure to politics in the home has no effect. This difference would suggest that one probably learns organizational and communications skills more effectively by doing than by watching—that is, by taking part in high school government and clubs than by observing politically active parents and listening to political discussions at home.[22]

The data confirm the existence of two paths from characteristics of one generation to the acquisition of the factors that foster political participation in the next. The starting point of each one is the education of the parents, and respondents' educational attainment figures importantly in both. One path is more or less socioeconomic. The main effect along this path is the impact of parents' education on respondents' education and from there to the job and income levels that they ultimately attain. The second path runs through political stimulation in the home and school.

---

22. That we find such differential effect among early experiences also lends credence to our belief that the retrospective questions about school and family do not all represent a projection backwards of the current state of the respondent.

Well-educated parents are more likely also to be politically active and to discuss politics at home and to produce children who are active in high school. Growing up in a politicized household and being active in high school are associated with political engagement as an adult.[23]

The data to this point illustrate a complex process of the accumulation of participatory factors. The family plays a major role by channeling the next generation into socioeconomic positions and into institutions associated with those positions. Through this process, resources for political activity are acquired. The family also provides direct political stimuli, which in turn arouse political interest. Although there are many links from the family to the participatory factors, the key link is education. Education, in turn, has much of its impact through involvements with non-political adult institutions.

The Origins of Free Time

To round out our analysis, we consider one last resource, free time. As we saw in Chapter 10, it has a somewhat different origin from other resources. Unlike other resources, free time is not rooted in such stratification variables as educational or occupational level. Instead, it is related to life circumstances, especially work and family commitments. Table 15.5 presents the results of an OLS regression that repeats the analysis in Table 10.1 but adds the variables in the life-course model that were used to predict the other participation factors.[24] The addition of the new variables leaves the earlier results unchanged. What affects the availability of free time is having a job (rather than the kind of job), children (especially pre-schoolers), and having a working spouse. In addition, all else being equal, women have less time than men.[25]

---

23. Unfortunately, we did not ask questions analogous to those just discussed about the religious affiliation and activity of respondents' parents. We were able, however, to ask such a question in a smaller follow-up survey. We refer to parents' religious commitments later in the chapter.

24. The analysis in Table 15.5 also contains the variables for age and other demographic characteristics carried as controls for the other analyses in this chapter.

25. Since the single greatest consumer of otherwise free time is paid work, and since women are less likely than men to be in the work force and less likely to work long hours

Table 15.5 Predicting Free Time by Initial Characteristics, Pre-Adult
Experiences, Institutional Involvements, and Family
Variables: OLS Regression (standardized regression
coefficients)

INITIAL CHARACTERISTICS	
Parents' Education	.01
Female	−.10**
Black	.01
Latino	.00
PRE-ADULT EXPERIENCES	
Education	−.01
Politics at Home	−.02
High School Activity	−.03*
INSTITUTIONAL INVOLVEMENTS	
Working	−.51**
Job Level	.01
Retired	.11**
Non-Political Organization	−.01
Religious Attendance	−.04*
FAMILY VARIABLES	
Married	−.01
Pre-school Children	−.15**
School-Aged Children	−.08**
Working Spouse	−.09**
R^2	.53
Sample size	2,436

* Significant at .05 level.
** Significant at .01 level.
Note: Age, Catholic religious preference, citizenship, and English skill in the equation.

Explaining Participation

The final stage, quite obviously, is to assess the impact on political
activity of the variables in the preceding steps. The analysis is
presented in Table 15.6. The data show the direct effects on overall

if they are, as we pointed out in Chapter 10, women do not, on average, have less free time
than men. However, since women continue to do a disproportionate share of the housework
even if they are employed, they have less leisure than men do with other factors, including
work force participation, controlled. For elaboration of this theme, see Table 10.2 and the
accompanying discussion.

Table 15.6 Predicting Overall Participation by Initial Characteristics, Pre-Adult Experiences, Institutional Involvements, and Participatory Factors: OLS Regression (standardized regression coefficients)

INITIAL CHARACTERISTICS	
Parents' Education	.04*
Female	−.03*
Black	.02
Latino	.03
PRE-ADULT EXPERIENCES	
Education	.12**
Politics at Home	.04**
High School Activity	.08**
INSTITUTIONAL INVOLVEMENTS	
Job Level	−.03
Non-Political Organization	.01
Religious Attendance	−.01
PARTICIPATORY FACTORS	
Family Income	.09**
Free Time	−.02
Civic Skills	.14**
Vocabulary	.05*
Recruitment	.13**
Political Interest	.24**
Political Information	.12**
R^2	.45
Sample size	2,404

* Significant at .05 level.
** Significant at .01 level.
Note: Age, Catholic religious preference, citizenship, working, retired, and English skill in the equation.

participation of the variables discussed earlier. Since they resemble the results of the analyses contained in Chapters 12 and 13, these results should be quite familiar. With the exception of free time (which, as we shall soon see, becomes significant when corrected for measurement error), each of the participatory factors just discussed—family income, civic skills, vocabulary skill, political interest and information, and institutional recruitment—is a powerful predictor of activity. In contrast, the institutional involvement variables introduced in the preceding step are not significant once the politically relevant residues of institutional exposure—the exercise of civic skills and requests for political involvement—have been taken into account. By incorporating measures of demographic background and pre-adult experiences—including activity in high school, a possible measure of a long-term taste for politics—the analysis provides a challenging test of the model presented earlier. Nonetheless, the results show unambiguously that the Civic Voluntarism Model—based on resources, engagement, and recruitment—holds.

Interestingly, once their intervening effects on subsequent variables are taken into account, the initial characteristics have almost no direct influence on participation. With other factors controlled, neither being African-American nor being Latino has a direct impact on activity; having well-educated parents has a small positive effect and being female a small negative effect. We should underline what this finding means. The analysis reported in Table 15.6 does not imply that groups defined by their race or ethnicity, gender, and parental educational attainment are identical in their levels of participation. Quite the contrary. As we have seen in earlier chapters, there are group differences of varying magnitude with, on average, men and Anglo-Whites somewhat more active than women, African-Americans, and, especially, Latinos. What this analysis does is to explain how these attributes are linked to activity. Social class, race or ethnicity, and gender are related in complicated ways to the participatory factors that shape activity. The absence of direct effects does not reduce the significance of these groups for politics or the political implications of the fact that the government hears more from some people, and some kinds of people, than from others.

Finally, the continuing direct effect of exposure to politics in the family and involvement in high school is striking. Over and above their effects on political activity through political interest, these factors have direct consequences for participation. Once again, this suggests the multiple roles that the family and school experiences play in bringing individuals into politics, indirectly by shaping opportunities to acquire education, jobs, and income and more directly by providing political stimulation.[26]

---

26. We must, however, repeat the caution that the measure of exposure to politics as a

We have cautioned repeatedly about the difficulties in making causal inferences from cross-sectional data in which some of the explanatory variables—for example, a respondent's recollections of parental political activity or level of political interest—are possibly the result rather than the cause of that which is to be explained, political participation. As we have done previously, we replicated the OLS analysis using two-stage least squares regression with the six participatory factors from the last step of the causal chain as explanatory variables and the variables from earlier steps in the causal chain and other prior variables as instruments.

Table 15.7, which presents the data, reinforces our earlier conclusions. With two exceptions, all the participatory factors are significant predictors of activity. Civic skills retain their impact even with additional variables entered into the analysis. Income and education also are significant. Once the measure of free time is corrected for unreliability through 2SLS, it becomes a significant factor for participation. Furthermore, the two measures of engagement, political interest and political information, have significant consequences for political activity. In short, then, the Civic Voluntarism Model based on measures of resources—time, money, and skills—and political engagement hold up quite well as an explanation of political participation.

The two variables that are not significant are vocabulary skill and institutional recruitment. We are not sure why the former does not have a significant effect on activity—except that several other variables in the model overlap with vocabulary skill. With respect to institutional recruitment, we are uncertain. An inventory of our instruments suggests that we do not have as effective instrumental variables in relation to institutional recruitment as we have for the other measures. This means that the two-stage least squares results may underestimate the importance of institutional recruitment. On the basis of the strength of the results from the OLS analysis, we suggest, cautiously, that it makes sense to retain institutional

---

child may be contaminated by current political involvement. Hence, we would not want to overemphasize the residual effect of exposure to politics at home.

Table 15.7 Predicting Overall Participation: Two-Stage Least Squares Analysis

	B	SE B	Beta
RESOURCES			
Education	.13	.03	.12**
Vocabulary	.01	.02	.02
Family Income	.05	.01	.09**
Free Time	.04	.01	.10**
Civic Skills (sum)	.11	.03	.16**
Citizenship	.72	.09	.07**
POLITICAL ENGAGEMENT			
Political Interest	.50	.05	.49**
Political Information	.11	.06	.13*
RECRUITMENT			
Recruitment (sum)	.04	.14	.02
(Constant)	−2.55	.19	
R^2		.37	
Sample size		2,389	

* Significant at .05 level.
** Significant at .01 level.

Note: Instruments for the 2SLS are: citizenship, education, vocabulary, speaking English at home, family income, working, retired, job level, non-political organizational affiliation, religious attendance, Catholic, number of children under eighteen, preschool children, gender, spouse working full or part-time, Black, Latino, education of parents, age, and (from the screener) political interest, political information, and partisan strength.

recruitment in the model. In a model as complex as this, we can, perhaps, be grateful that we have so few puzzles remaining.

OTHER MODES OF POLITICAL PARTICIPATION

Our analysis thus far has concentrated on overall activity. However, as we have seen, making financial contributions and going to the polls are forms of political activity that have distinct origins. Chapter 12 demonstrated that making contributions depends on having money and on little else; voting depends upon political engagement—being politically interested and, to a lesser extent, informed—and requires little civic skill. Table 15.8 confirms that these findings hold up when measures of initial background characteristics and pre-adult experiences are included in the model.

When we repeated the analysis of overall activity reported in Table 15.6 for these two modes of participation, we found, once again, that what matters most for making political contributions is family income and what matters most for electoral turnout is political engagement, especially political interest. In each case, other variables are also significant. However, they are much less important.

Of particular note is the role of education. Though education is generally considered to be the dominant single variable in relation to participation, it is insignificant for voting and for making contributions. We believe that this tells something additional about education, but what we learn from Table 15.8 is *not* that education is unimportant. Rather, we learn the way in which it is important. For political contributions, income is the dominant variable. Education is not irrelevant, however, since it plays a major role in determining income, directly and through occupation. For voting, political interest is dominant. But again education is important as a main source of political interest. (See Table 15.4 as well as the discussion in Chapter 12.) To repeat, we have not found education to be irrelevant; instead we have specified the different effects of education upon activity. The effect on contributions is through the socioeconomic path of job and income. The effect on voting is through the development of political interest.

Sub-Groups and Origins of Participation

The model we have developed appears to be a powerful one for predicting political activity across the public as a whole. However, the Civic Voluntarism Model should be relevant for significant sub-groups of the population as well. We repeated the analysis reported in Table 15.6—predicting overall activity—for the various groups we have considered throughout this book: men, women, African-Americans, Latinos, and the poor. The results are presented in Table 15.9. Since there are several different groups, a complex model, and a smaller case base for several of the groups, there is some variation in the standardized regression coefficients and levels of significance for particular variables across the groups. Overall, however, the basic analysis holds. The measures of institutional involvement do not, by and large, predict participation.

Table 15.8 Predicting Time-Based Acts, Voting, Contributions, and Political Discussion by Initial Characteristics, Pre-Adult Experiences, Institutional Involvements, and Participatory Factors: OLS Regressions (standardized regression coefficients)

	Time-Based Acts	Voting	Political Contributions	Political Discussion
INITIAL CHARACTERISTICS				
Parents' Education	.03	−.01	.02	.02
Female	−.02	.01	−.03	−.08**
Black	.02	.02	.01	.02
Latino	.03	−.02	.03	−.00
PRE-ADULT EXPERIENCES				
Education	.06*	.03	.04	−.02
Politics at Home	.02	.05*	.03	.06**
High School Activity	.09**	.06**	.03	.02
INSTITUTIONAL INVOLVEMENTS				
Job Level	−.05*	−.01	−.00	.00
Non-Political Organization	.03	.02	−.02	.03
Religious Attendance	−.04*	.10**	−.03	−.06**
PARTICIPATORY FACTORS				
Family Income	.05*	.04*	.30**	.04*
Free Time	.01	−.03	.05*	−.03
Civic Skills	.17**	.00	.04	.01
Vocabulary	−.01	.04*	−.03	.00
Recruitment	.13**	.05*	.01	.05**
Political Interest	.21**	.26**	.06**	.53**
Political Information	.06**	.12**	.02	.11**
R^2	.24	.36	.14	.43
Sample size	2,404	2,300	2,404	2,404

* Significant at .05 level.
** Significant at .01 level.

The participatory factors—in particular, political interest and the civic skills developed in recruitment attempts at institutions—that are at the heart of our model are quite potent.

The results in Table 15.9 are crucial for our argument. For one thing, they show that our model is quite robust; it holds for the public and it holds for significant social groups. In addition, the fact that the model holds for these groups is important for the

Table 15.9 Predicting Overall Participation for Sub-Groups of the Population: OLS Regressions (standardized regression coefficients)

	Men	Women	Blacks	Latinos	Poor
INITIAL CHARACTERISTICS					
Parents' Education	.03	.05*	.01	−.06	.04
Female			.03	−.11**	−.00
Black	−.01	.05*			.03
Latino	.03	−.03			.06
PRE-ADULT EXPERIENCES					
Education	.13**	.11**	.19**	.07	.26**
Politics at Home	.02	.06*	.01	.03	.03
High School Activity	.09**	.07**	.08*	−.01	.14**
INSTITUTIONAL INVOLVEMENTS					
Job Level	−.05	.01	.00	−.01	.01
Non-Political Organization	−.02	.05	−.06	.09*	.03
Religious Attendance	−.03	.00	.00	.01	.06
PARTICIPATORY FACTORS					
Family Income	.07**	.11**	.06	.12**	.03
Free Time	−.09*	.01	−.02	.00	−.10
Civic Skills	.15**	.13**	.26**	.14*	.04
Vocabulary	.05	.05	.01	.05	−.03
Recruitment	.14**	.12**	.17**	.20**	.16**
Political Interest	.26**	.23**	.22**	.21**	.18**
Political Information	.13**	.10**	.08*	.10*	.16**
R^2	.43	.46	.49	.48	.41
Sample size	1,156	1,248	452	343	425

* Significant at .05 level.
** Significant at .01 level.

impact of the participatory process on representation. As we saw earlier in Chapters 7 and 8, how well a group is represented depends on the overall activity rate of the group as well as the characteristics of the activists drawn from the group. That the participatory process we have described works *within* social groups means that this process determines not only the average activity level of a group but which group members become active. The same process that determines the level of activity for poor people or for Latinos determines which poor people and which Latinos are likely to be the activists. If the process produces a bias in what is communicated across the public as a whole, it may produce a similar bias within groups in terms of what activists from the group communicate. We return to this point in the next chapter, where we consider the implications of the participatory process for the representation of politically relevant characteristics.

Youth Variables and Participation: A Summary

Our data show complicated paths from experiences as a youth to political activity. Because the analysis in this chapter has involved so many variables and such complex results, it may be useful to summarize the ways in which education, involvement in high school activity, and political stimulation in the home affect participation. We present such a summary analysis in Table 15.10, which shows the effects of these pre-adult experiences—both directly and through other variables—on political activity.

Consider the various effects of *education*. As we have seen, its greatest single effect is direct.[27] However, the effects of education on participation through the impact that education has on institutional location and on a wide range of the participatory factors, when added together, are even more substantial than education's direct effect. The table illustrates the various ways in which education influences participation by increasing institutional involve-

---

27. The figures for direct effects are the standardized regression coefficients for the effects of education, activity in high school, and politics at home on activity after one has controlled for their effects via other variables. The effects of education, activity in high school, and home politics on activity through other variables are calculated as the sum of the effects of the various paths through these other variables to activity. An example should make this clearer. Take the effect of education on activity that runs through affiliation with a non-political organization (the path *education > organization > activity*). This effect is the sum of the standardized regression coefficient for the effect of education on organizational affiliation multiplied by the standardized coefficient for the effect of organizational affiliation on activity *plus* the seven additional three step paths from education to organization to participatory factors to activity (for instance, *education > organization > civic skills > activity*). The three step paths are the product of the coefficients for each step. Note one feature of the way we sum these indirect effects that differs from the standard way of so doing. In the previous example, the three step path *education > organization > civic skills > activity* could be counted as the effect of education through civic skills or through organization. We count it as an effect through organization since the social process we are describing involves the effects of education; and the proximate effect of education is to get one into organizations (or a good job), which then has further consequences.

Table 15.10 Education, High School Activity, Government and
Politics at Home: Direct Effects on Overall Political
Activity and Effects through Other Variables

	Education	High School Activity	Politics at Home
DIRECT EFFECT	.12	.08	.04
Effects Through Institutional Involvements:			
Job	.01	.00	.00
Non-Political Organizations	.03	.02	.00
Church	.00	.01	.00
Effects Through Participatory Factors:			
Income	.02	.01	.00
Free Time	.00	.00	.00
Civic Skills	.02	.01	.00
Vocabulary	.02	.00	.00
Recruitment	.02	.01	.00
Political Interest	.03	.04	.04
Political Information	.03	.01	.01
TOTAL EFFECTS THROUGH OTHER VARIABLES	.18	.11	.05
TOTAL EFFECT	.30	.19	.09

ment (especially voluntary association involvement), by raising socioeconomic status (especially income), by enhancing civic skills, and, most strongly, by fostering political interest and information.

The overall impact on political activity of participation in *high school activities* is quite substantial though less than that of educational attainment. About half of the effect of this measure is direct and the other half through various participatory factors—the strongest of these effects being via the development of political interest. The socioeconomic path from high school activities through job and income is quite small.

Political stimulation in the home also has consequences for political activity. It has, however, less effect on political activity than either education or high school activities. The data in Table 15.10 help us to understand why. Its direct effect is smaller. Its effect through the development of political interest is substantial—similar to the effects of educational attainment and high school activity through interest. Political stimulation at home, however, has minimal effect through the other possible paths. The political involvement of the parents can, thus, be passed on to the child, but its overall influence on political activity cannot match the multiple effects of education.

The data in Table 15.10 are for the overall measure of political activity. If we were to consider political contributions rather than overall activity, we would find, not surprisingly, a simpler pattern for the impact of youth variables. Education has the largest effect. Most of this is through income, with much less running through other paths.[28] Thus, in contrast to the multiple roles played by education in stimulating overall political activity by, for example, fostering the development of civic skills or political interest, when it comes to making political contributions, it is the economic effects of education—determining job opportunities and influencing earnings—that are central.

Family, School, Job, Organization, and Church: The Role of Institutions

Citizens move through many institutions during the life course. Our analysis has highlighted the way in which these institutions provide the factors that foster participation, a process that begins in the family and continues through adult institutional involvements. In Table 15.11 we summarize these institutional effects, showing the direct and indirect impact that they have on activity. We begin with the effect of parental education on political activity. The effects are substantial, but largely indirect. The main indirect effect (data not shown in Table 15.11) is through the link between parental education and respondent's education. Of the .22 indirect effect on activity deriving from parental education, more than half (.13) goes through the educational level of the child and about a

---

28. The total effect of education on giving political contributions is .13, of which .04 is direct and .09 indirect. Of the latter, .06 is via income.

Table 15.11 Direct, Indirect, and Total Effects of Pre-Adult and
Adult Institutional Involvements on Overall Activity

	Direct Effect	Indirect Effect	Total Effect
INITIAL CHARACTERISTICS			
Parents' Education	.04	.22	.26
PRE-ADULT EXPERIENCES			
Respondent's Education	.12	.18	.30
High School Activity	.08	.11	.19
Politics at Home	.04	.05	.09
INSTITUTIONAL INVOLVEMENTS			
Job[a]	.02	.05	.07
Non-Political Organization	.01	.11	.12
Religious Attendance	−.01	.08	.07

a. This includes the effects of working, job level, and retired.

fifth (.04) goes through the high school activity of the child. In
addition, there is a .03 indirect effect through political discussion
at home.[29] The data show how significant effects on activity run
from generation to generation. The main way they do so is via the
education that educated parents provide for their children, but
maintaining a stimulating political environment around the dinner
table helps as well.

The second section of Table 15.11 contains the summary of the
direct and indirect effects of pre-adult experiences—repeated here
from Table 15.10 for comparison purposes. The powerful role of
education still stands out, but it is interesting to note that its role

---

29. The smaller remaining effects run through income and engagement. The direct and
indirect effects of parents' education are calculated in a manner similar to that in Table
15.10. The effect of parents' education on activity through the respondent's education is
calculated as the product of the standardized coefficient for the effect of parents' education
on respondent's education and the *total* effect of education on activity. For instance, the
path *parents' education > respondent's education > job level > income > activity* is
considered to be a component of the effect of parents' education on activity through
respondent's education, not a component of the effect of parents' education on activity
through job level or income. Again, this makes the most substantive sense in this context.
The effects of parents' education through other participatory factors are calculated as the
sum of those effects that do not run through respondent's education.

is only slightly larger than the role of parental education—largely, of course, because of the link between the two.

The third section of Table 15.11, in turn, provides summaries of the effects of the three adult institutions. As we know from our analyses of the way these institutions function in relation to political activity, their effects are largely indirect through the various participation factors that come later in the chain. Table 15.11 allows us to compare the relative importance of these three institutions. Non-political voluntary associations play a larger role than job or religious institutions. The effect of such associations is almost equal to the combined effect of job and religion—underlining their central role in American democracy. It is interesting, further, that the role of job and religious involvement is equal. Finally, we can note that the sum of the three institutional effects is about equal to the effect of parental education.

One of the main themes of our book has been the way in which the political behavior of Americans is rooted in the non-political world. Table 15.11 provides data—comparing various non-political institutions—on how deep these roots are.

Roots in the Community and Religious Attendance

Our analysis of the factors that foster participation has omitted a potentially important one: ties to the local community. We might expect that roots in the community—living in one place for a long time, owning a home, and having children in the local schools—would enhance the resources and motivation for political activity. Roots in the community would, presumably, increase concern about local issues, connections to others in the community, and knowledge about local political customs, leaders, and controversies. The importance of long-term residence in the community has often been noted in relation to voting turnout. Highly mobile citizens are less likely to vote.[30] Furthermore, community attachment is likely to enhance various other forms of participation.[31]

---

30. See Wolfinger and Rosenstone, *Who Votes?*, chap. 3.
31. See the studies cited in Lester Milbrath and M. L. Goel, *Political Participation: How*

Table 15.12 Predicting Participation by Roots in the Community: OLS Regressions (standardized regression coefficients)

	Overall Participation	Local Participation	National Participation
Years in community	.05**	.11**	.06**
Home ownership	.06**	.09**	.02
School-aged children	−.03	.01	−.07**
R^2	.45	.33	.31
Sample size	2,399	2,399	2,399

* Significant at .05 level.
** Significant at .01 level.
Note: Other participatory factors and control variables in the equation.

From the perspective of the model we have developed in this chapter, the role of close ties to the community is particularly intriguing. We use three measures: the number of years the respondent has lived in the community, whether or not the respondent is a homeowner, and whether the respondent has school-aged children.[32] We entered these three variables into the equation used to produce Table 15.6—that is, the equation to predict overall participation on the bases of the variables from each of the steps of the model developed in this chapter. Because the effect of community attachment is likely to be felt most strongly in conjunction with local activity, we also repeated the analysis for local and national political participation.[33]

Table 15.12 reports the effects of these variables measuring community rootedness on overall activity, as well as on local and national activity. Because the effects of the other variables in our model do not change in any significant way, we report only the coefficients for the explanatory variables measuring community rootedness. The data make clear that length of residence in the

---

and Why Do People Get Involved in Politics?, 2nd ed. (Chicago: Rand McNally College Pub. Co., 1977), p. 113; and Steven J. Rosenstone and John Mark Hansen, *Mobilization, Participation, and Democracy in America* (New York: MacMillan, 1993), pp. 157–159.

32. See Appendix B.14 and 17 for the questions.
33. For the local and national participation scales, see Appendix B.1.1.

Table 15.13 Predicting Roots in the Community: OLS Regressions

	Years in Community	Home Ownership
Parents' Education	−.07**	−.01
Female	.04*	−.02
Black	.07**	−.11**
Latino	−.04*	−.04*
Respondent's Education	−.12**	.03
Politics at Home	.01	.04
High School Activity	−.05**	.07**
R^2	.32	.10
Sample size	2,489	2,499

* Significant at .05 level.
** Significant at .01 level.
Note: Age, Catholic religious preference, working, retired, English skill, and citizenship in the equation.

community and home ownership are positively related to political activity, especially activity directed toward local matters.[34]

As with the other variables that foster participation, we can ask about the origin of community attachment. What kinds of people are likely to remain in one place? To be homeowners? Consistent with our earlier analysis, we seek the answers in the characteristics that are with the respondent at birth—gender, race or ethnicity, and parents' education—as well as experiences at home and in school. These are, of course, not the only possible determinants of ties to the community, but they are the variables that are relevant to our model of the origins of political participation. Table 15.13, which repeats the analysis in Table 15.3, shows the relationship between these early experiences and the two measures of community rootedness that affect participation, years in the community and home ownership.

---

34. In addition, there are differences across various participatory acts in the impact of these measures of community rootedness. They have no effect on giving money, a moderate effect on time-based acts, and—as we would expect—a strong effect on voting turnout. The coefficients of a combined measure of years in the community and home ownership on contributions, time-based acts, and voting are .03, .05, and .11 respectively.

The data on length of residence in the community are particularly interesting. Those who have educated parents and who are themselves well-educated are more mobile and less rooted in their communities. Thus, ties to the community can represent an alternative—indeed, one of the only alternatives—to the dominant force of education and the other socioeconomic stratification variables associated with it.[35] Insofar as long residence in the community enhances the likelihood of participation—and we saw in Table 15.12 that it does—we have found a rare case in which the impact of education on political activity is negative. Education is associated with mobility and job enhancement and many of the resources valuable for participation. At the same time, however, it loosens the community ties that foster activity—especially local activity. Education does not, of course, depress home ownership. This effect is by no means as substantial as the many participation-enhancing effects of education, but it is noteworthy because this particular indirect effect of education in dampening activity is so unusual.

The role of parental education is especially striking. Having highly educated parents confers many advantages. It sets a person on a course toward civic involvement—as well as economic advancement. It also increases geographical mobility: the children of educated parents are more likely to leave home and move elsewhere. While mobility may create job opportunities, it does undermine the community attachment that plays a role in enhancing community involvement.

A NOTE ON RELIGION AND INTERGENERATIONAL TRANSMISSION

Parents provide an additional legacy beyond the educational opportunities they present to their children. At various places in this book, we have stressed the role of religious involvement as an

---

35. In her study of participation in a small Vermont town, Jane J. Mansbridge shows how the long-term resident farmers use that status—and the special skills and respect that accompany it—to counterbalance the skills and self-confidence of the newer, articulate newcomers who have moved to Vermont from New York and other large cities. *Beyond Adversary Democracy* (New York: Basic Books, 1980), chap. 9.

alternative path to political activity, one not connected to the usual stratification variables that structure political participation. Just as families can transmit an educational heritage to their offspring, so might they transmit a religious one. If involvement in a religious institution is influenced by parental involvement, we would then have an alternative form of intergenerational transmission.

Unfortunately, although we asked respondents about the educational attainment of their parents in our original survey, we did not ask about their parents' church attendance. In a smaller follow-up survey, we were able to re-interview a random sample of about one-quarter of our original respondents and ask them to recall whether, at the time they were growing up, their parents went to church regularly. Not unexpectedly, respondents whose parents were regular churchgoers are much more likely to attend church regularly themselves. Compared with those whose parents rarely attended religious services, those whose parents attended church almost every week or more frequently are twice as likely both to be regular church attenders themselves and to be active in their churches beyond attendance at services. Having highly educated parents, however, decreases slightly the likelihood that the respondent will become a church attender.[36] Since those respondents whose parents were churchgoing are, themselves, more religiously involved as adults, they obtain the opportunities for the development of civic skills and institutional recruitment in their churches.

Parental churchgoing is also related to community rootedness. Those whose parents were regular church attenders are likely to stay in their communities. On average, the children of church-attending parents report 6.5 more years of residence in their communities than do the children of parents who did not attend church.[37] In short, there appears to be a cluster of characteristics

---

36. Controlling for age and the respondent's education, the relationship between parents' and respondent's church attendance is .18 (significant at .001 level, N = 507), while the relationship between parents' education and respondent's church attendance is −.06 (significant at the .05 level).

37. The relationship holds up, even taking the educational level of both parents and the respondent into account.

that counterbalances, at least in part, the force of education—both parents' and respondent's—in fostering participation. Families with less education and families that attend church pass on a legacy of community attachment as well as church involvement, offering an alternative path to activity—especially locally based activity.

In light of this discussion, it makes sense to introduce the data on community rootedness into the analyses used to generate Tables 15.10 and 15.11 in order to reassess the effects of the respondent's and parents' education on participation. We can calculate the indirect effect of education on local political activity through education's influence on years in the community. The result is a small diminution of political activity with increased education—a coefficient of about −.01, which is about half the size of the indirect positive effect of education through its impact on income or information. A similar calculation—parallel to that used for Table 15.11—shows parental education (both through its direct effect on years in the community and through its indirect effect via education on years in the community) to have a negative effect on local activity of roughly the same magnitude, −.01. Once again, this is not a major impact, but an interesting counterbalance.

Similar calculations can be made for the influence of parental churchgoing on activity.[38] The impact of parents' religiosity on political participation is all indirect. Most of it comes through the effect of parental religious involvement on the respondent's church attendance and the impact, in turn, of church attendance on the kinds of church-based activity that lead to the exercise of civic skills and to institutional recruitment. An additional increment also derives from the impact of parental religious attendance on length of residence in the community and the effect of the latter, in turn, on activity. The impact is very small: the effect on overall participation of parental church attendance is about one-tenth the magnitude of that of parental education.[39] Nonetheless, in spite of

---

38. We use the overall measure of activity here since church attendance does not influence local and national activity differently.

39. If we calculate the effects of parental church attendance on political activity exactly as we did for parents' education, as reported in Table 15.11, we find a total effect of .028, which is about one-tenth the size of the figure reported for parental education.

the small size of the effect, the process we have described represents a different, and quite independent, way in which participation can be transmitted from generation to generation. Parental religious involvement, not connected to the educational attainment of the child or to the consequent socioeconomic advantages of educational attainment, thus constitutes a separate path to activity.

From Generation to Generation: A Summary

We have seen several processes by which one generation has an influence on the political activity of the next. One is grounded in the reproduction of social status, the way in which socioeconomic position is passed from generation to generation. A second involves political socialization, the more direct transmission of political orientations. Our data show that both processes are at work, and that both have significant effects on political activity. In addition, we have located other processes associated with religious commitment and roots in the community.[40] Indeed, we can isolate four intergenerational processes. Three begin with the educational level of the parents, and the last with the religious attendance of the parents. Two of the processes reinforce the social stratification of political participation across the generations and two provide a very partial counterweight to that stratification.

Parental education and the socioeconomic path to political activity: Highly educated parents pass on their advantage to children mostly because their children tend also to be highly educated and, thus, to have high-level jobs, to be affluent, and to affiliate with organizations. These effects, in turn, enhance all the factors—resources, engagement, and recruitment—that foster political activity.

Parental education and political socialization in the home: In

---

40. For an analysis that shows similar effects, see Darren E. Sherkat and T. Jean Blocker, "The Political Development of Sixties' Activists: Identifying the Influence of Class, Gender, and Socialization on Protest Participation," *Social Forces* 72 (1994): 821–842. They find that parents influenced the future protest potential of their children both by direct political socialization and by influencing their future academic careers. Parallel to what we find here, Sherkat and Blocker also show the contrasting influences of educated parents, whose children were more likely to protest, and religious parents, whose children were less likely to do so.

addition, parents who are educated are more likely to expose their children to politics—by taking part in politics themselves and by discussing politics at the dinner table—which has an impact on future political activity by enhancing political interest later in life.

Parental education and community roots: Respondents with highly educated parents and high levels of education themselves are less likely to remain in the community, which, in turn, reduces the community ties that foster activity. In this way, parental educational attainment reduces slightly participation in local politics.

Parental church attendance, respondent's church attendance, and community roots: Parents who attend church are likely to have children who do likewise, which, in turn, puts them in a position to acquire civic skills and to be recruited to politics. In addition, churchgoing parents have children who are more likely to maintain roots in the community, which also enhances slightly their later activity.

Conclusion

This chapter has presented a complex analysis that attempts to tie together the various strands of our argument about the social sources of political activity. There is no single path to political participation. The factors associated with political activity—resources, political engagement, and institutionally based political mobilization—derive from economic position in the labor force, from involvement with voluntary associations and religious institutions, and from families and schools. At the outset, the family of origin plays a significant role, setting the broad boundaries of the individual's educational and occupational opportunities and providing exposure to political stimuli and to religious institutions. Experiences in school build upon the foundation laid at home. Later on, jobs and economic position produce resources; affiliation with secondary institutions produces resources, fosters political engagement, and provides exposure to requests for political activity; and the structure of the family created in adulthood influences the availability of free time.

These data enable us to give a fuller account of the process by which citizens become political activists. First of all, the data underscore the stratified process by which those who enter the world with socioeconomic advantages are in a position to acquire resources that foster political participation. The analysis also illustrates the cumulative nature of the process of resource acquisition—advantage building on advantage. Critical to this process is education. Those with high levels of education are in a position to stockpile additional resources beyond those acquired in school. Moreover, we demonstrate how this process extends across generations, with parental education providing an important initial condition in the process of resource accumulation.

The process is clearly biased in favor of those with early advantage. However, opportunity is not entirely foreclosed to those whose original socioeconomic endowments are meager. For one thing, the connections posited here represent a series of probabilistic relationships that, although sometimes fairly strong, are far from deterministic. Having well-educated parents is certainly a boon to obtaining a good education, but intergenerational transmission is far from perfect. In addition, we have specified alternative paths to political activity that are not as dependent on socioeconomic position and the resources that it confers. One such path is political and derives from parental political involvement. A lively political atmosphere at home—in which politically active parents discuss politics around the dinner table—leads to politically interested children and, in turn, to political activity.

Another alternative path involves attachment to the community. Deep roots in the community are associated with participation in local politics. Respondents with churchgoing parents reap some compensatory benefits for participation: they are more likely to stay in the community and, like their parents, to attend church. Moreover, church involvement can provide civic skills and opportunities for political recruitment to those who might otherwise be resource-poor. These alternative effects on participation are quite small in magnitude and, thus, fall far short of fully counterbalancing the impact of various forces in stratifying participatory input. Nevertheless, they are noteworthy because they are contrary to what we ordinarily expect.

Participation, Representation, and Democracy

To achieve a full understanding of how the participatory process elaborated in Part III produces participatory representation as described in Part II, we need to take a final step. The factors that affect participation are also related to the politically relevant characteristics of citizens. Part IV ties our concern with the factors that produce participation to our concern with the representation of politically relevant attributes through the participatory process. In Chapter 16 we demonstrate how the various factors that foster participation operate to affect what and from whom the government hears about a variety of politically relevant characteristics— including actual circumstances, preferences on a variety of issues, and civic orientations. Finally, Chapter 17 summarizes what we have found and relates our findings to the nature of political conflict and the quality of public life in American democracy.

16

The Participatory Process
and the Sources
of Representational Distortion

This inquiry has had two underlying themes, one descriptive and one explanatory: we have described who is politically active on behalf of what policy concerns; and we have explained why citizens take part in politics. That is, on the presumption that it matters for politics what and from whom public officials hear, we have linked participation to the politically relevant characteristics of members of the public and demonstrated the extent to which activist publics are representative of the public as a whole in terms of their opinions, demographic characteristics, needs for government action, and participatory agendas. In addition, we have analyzed how experiences at home and in school, on the job, at church, and in non-political organizations lead citizens to acquire the wherewithal and the desire to participate. Clearly, however, these two themes are interrelated. The process by which citizens come to participate produces the representational bias we have described. Therefore, in this chapter we bring together these two strands of analysis—connecting the various factors that foster participation to the politically relevant characteristics represented through activity.

Putting the Parts Together:
Representation and the Process of Participation

In a sense we have told our story backwards—giving away the denouement early on. In Part II we described the outcomes of the

463

participatory process by relating measures of political participation to a variety of politically relevant attributes and demonstrating that, in many critical respects, activists differ from the public at large. Because participants are not representative—in their policy preferences and, especially, their demographic characteristics and political needs—activists communicate, implicitly and explicitly, a distorted set of messages to public officials. The extent of this participatory bias varies with the nature of the activity and with the particular politically relevant characteristic of the activists. As a group, voters are more representative of the public than are contributors. Activists are more representative with respect to their issue positions than with respect to their receipt of means-tested government benefits, and more representative with respect to their gender than with respect to their family incomes. Because citizen activity functions not only to communicate information to public officials about citizens' interests, preferences, and needs but also to generate pressure on them to respond, these participatory biases matter for democracy.

In Chapters 9 through 15 we developed the Civic Voluntarism Model, an explanatory model of the process by which individuals come to take part politically. We linked measures of political participation to a set of factors that foster it—especially resources, but also political engagement and institutional recruitment. In addition, we illustrated the way issue engagements can generate participation over and above what would be predicted on the basis of resources, generalized political engagement, and civic skills. We delineated the roots of various participatory factors—tracing their origins back to earlier experiences in the family and in school and to adult involvements at work, in religious institutions, and in non-political organizations. We also indicated detailed paths among the forward links: different participatory factors are differentially important for different modes of participation.

We have, thus, considered three sets of variables: measures of politically relevant characteristics, participatory factors, and political activity. However, we have looked at them in pairs—establishing links, first, between politically relevant characteristics and activity and, later, between participatory factors and activity. We wish now to bring all three together in order to examine how the participatory factors that determine political participation affect, in turn, the representation of politically relevant characteristics of activist publics. In other words, we shall investigate how the *process* by which people come to participate affects the *substance* of what is communicated through that participation.

Let us elaborate what we mean by this project. The factors that beget participation—education, family income, religious activity, political interest, and the like—are themselves or are related to politically relevant characteristics. For example, those with high family incomes are, not surprisingly, much less likely to receive means-tested government benefits and somewhat less likely to be African-American or Latino; those with high levels of education are likely to have liberal opinions on civil rights issues and to be relatively tolerant of unorthodox opinions; those who exercise politically relevant skills in church are less likely to be Catholic and, therefore, Latino. Because politically relevant characteristics are bundled with participatory factors, the participatory process brings into politics citizens with distinctive views, needs, and demographic characteristics.

Although we have taken great pains to establish the causal connections between participatory factors and activity, when it comes to the relationships between participatory factors and politically relevant characteristics, correlation will suffice. Let us illustrate. We have seen that African-Americans and Latinos have, on average, lower levels of education or family income. Obviously, neither education nor income causes being Black or Latino. Yet, because education and income are such powerful predictors of participation, Blacks and Latinos will be underrepresented within participant publics—a fact with significant potential implications for politics—even though neither being African-American nor being Latino has, in and of itself, consequences for participation. The fact that being African-American or Latino is related to variables such as education and income that are causally related to activity means, in turn, that there are disproportionately fewer participatory messages coming from these groups. Similarly, regular church attenders tend, as we have seen, to have conservative views on social issues like school prayer and abortion. We do not know whether going to church tends to instill conservative views or whether social-issue conservatives tend, selectively, to attend religious services. Whichever way, the fact that church activists tend to develop civic skills in church and, thus, all things being equal, to be more active in politics has consequences for the messages that activists send on social issues.

As usual, we look at the issue broadly and then consider finer variations. We have made consistent efforts to distinguish among modes of activity, among participatory factors, and among politically relevant characteristics: to demonstrate that different kinds of participation spring from different participatory factors and that different participant publics—voters, protesters, contributors, and so on—present different degrees and kinds of bias with respect to politically relevant characteristics. Therefore, in conducting this enterprise, one of our principal goals will be to decompose the participatory process into its components and to assess how each participatory factor contributes to participatory distortion. The multiple factors that produce activity are related to politically relevant characteristics in ways that are sometimes complementary, sometimes contradictory. For example, education and income sometimes work in tandem to bring into politics activists with particular attributes; on other occasions, however, they work at cross-purposes, activating citizens with opposing characteristics. Even when these contrary processes cancel each other out, yielding a group of participants that is representative with respect to some politically relevant characteristic, dissecting the process will help us to understand why policymakers hear what they do from citizens. Ordinarily, however, the net effect of these intertwined processes is some degree of participatory distortion. The analysis in this chapter will clarify the extent and direction of that distortion.

A summary of the themes of Parts II, III, and IV of this book is presented diagrammatically in Figure 16.1.

Analyzing the Participatory Process and Participatory Distortion

To assess how the participatory process affects the information communicated by participants, we must move to a new mode of analysis. In Part II, we described numerous examples of participa-

Part II: The Effect of Participation on Representation

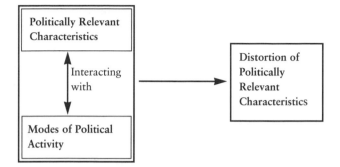

Part III: The Origins of Political Activity

Part IV: The Origins of Participatory Distortion

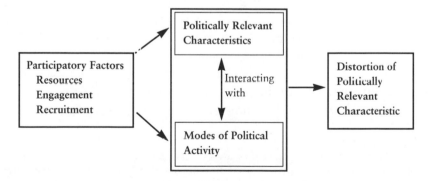

Figure 16.1 The Three Stages of Analysis.

tory distortion but were not then prepared to say anything about their source. The Civic Voluntarism Model developed in Part III began the task of understanding the source of participatory distortion by showing the effects of participatory factors on political activity. Now we add another connection, the relationship of the participatory factors to politically relevant characteristics. Our goal is to show how participatory factors create participatory distortion by influencing the correlations between activism and politically relevant characteristics that produce that distortion. A participatory factor has this effect if it is related both to activity and to a relevant characteristic. Income, for example, is positively related to political contributions and to conservative economic views. By being related to both, income creates a substantial participatory distortion.

We begin our analysis with the "difference" measure of participatory distortion—a measure first introduced in Chapter 6. This is an index of the difference between the average of the characteristic for the activist group and the average of the characteristic for the public at large.[1] If, for example, activists have more conservative opinions than the public at large on some issue, the messages sent to decision makers are distorted in a conservative direction. The amount of that distortion is captured in the difference measure, which we label the Index of Total Distortion. If activists and the public at large have the same average opinions, the Total Distortion Index is zero. As we show in detail in Appendix C, distortion occurs in this example when opinions (or any other politically relevant characteristic) and activism are correlated with one another.

We then break total distortion into its constituent parts by providing an index of the contribution of each participatory factor to total distortion. These indices, when added together, contribute

---

1. Strictly speaking, the measure of overall distortion is this difference measure standardized by being divided by the standard deviation of the characteristic being studied. This measure is fully described in Appendix C.3, where we also discuss its (close) relationship to the Logged Representation Scale and other measures used in Chapters 6–8. See also Henry E. Brady, Sidney Verba, and Kay Lehman Schlozman, "A Framework for Measuring the Fairness of Political Participation and Representation" (paper delivered at the Annual Meeting of the Political Methodology Group, Madison, July 1994).

to the net impact of the participatory factors.[2] Although it is often the case that any one participatory factor has a relatively small effect on distortion, the several factors in our model can have a cumulative effect in one direction, resulting in a large distortion. It is also possible that, instead of cumulating in a particular direction, participatory factors can produce distortions in opposite directions. In this case, their effect is real but the net participatory distortion may be zero or near to zero. We shall demonstrate that a substantial share of participatory distortion can be explained by the participatory factors described in earlier chapters. In our model, this means that the sum of the indices for these factors alone is close to the total distortion. The statistical model, including the measures we use and their properties, is described in detail in Appendix C.4.

By showing how the basic components of the participatory process in America—for example, the stratification of socioeconomic resources or the special role played by religious institutions—influence who takes part and what they communicate through their activity, this model rounds out our analysis of the participation process. Since the participation factors have their origins in the basic social and economic institutions of society, the analysis deepens our understanding of the way in which the fundamental non-political structures of American society are engaged with politics.

As much as this analysis can tell us, it is deficient in one respect. In Chapter 6, we argued that what matters for participatory representation is not simply activists' attitudes on a set of pre-selected issues in a survey but the actual subjects they address when they take part. For this reason, over the course of this inquiry, we have often considered issue-based activity for which we can specify the policy concerns on the minds of participants. Unfortunately, for many of the issues where there is *sufficient* activity for statistical analysis, it is impossible to ascertain the *direction* of activity. When

---

2. As is always the case in this kind of analysis, other unobserved factors included in the "error terms" of the Civic Voluntarism Model and the model for politically relevant characteristics also explain some of the total distortion. This means that the sum of the impacts of just the participatory factors will usually differ from the total distortion, but this difference will be completely attributable to the contribution of the error terms. For more details of the measures we use and their properties, see Appendix C.

a participant indicates that "welfare" or "housing" was the issue or concern behind the activity, we cannot discern—even from seemingly related attitude scales—whether the respondent wants the government to be more involved or less involved in solving the problem. Therefore, we cannot deal with participatory agendas in the way we have been able to elsewhere. Abortion is the sole issue for which we can be assured of the direction of activity from an associated attitude item. We consider political activity surrounding abortion later in this chapter.

THE VARIABLES IN THE MODEL

As we have indicated, the model of participatory distortion is based on three sets of variables: politically relevant characteristics, modes of participation, and participatory factors. Although these concepts should, by now, be familiar, let us specify what falls under each of these rubrics.

Throughout this inquiry we have construed *politically relevant characteristics* quite broadly to include any attribute of an individual that would be germane to public policy or other government action. Thus, any characteristic of a participant—including demographic attributes—would be politically relevant if deemed noteworthy by a public official at whom activity is directed.[3] We consider the impact of the participatory process on the representation of politically relevant characteristics drawn from several domains. The first is economic policy, not just attitudes on economic issues but also actual economic needs. This is, of course, an area of concern that has consistently been important in our discussion. The second is another issue area that is fundamental to American politics, attitudes on policies toward minorities. Third, we consider a social issue that generated considerable heat at the time of our study: abortion. Finally, we examine the way in which the participatory process affects the democratic quality of the participant population; that is, whether it brings into politics a set of activists who are politically informed and tolerant of unpopular

---

3. Chapter 6 contains a more extended discussion of the nature of politically relevant characteristics.

opinions. These are clearly politically relevant characteristics of some significance to contemporary American politics.

The *modes of political activity* are, as usual, the forms of participation through which activists convey information to policy-makers and hold them responsible for what they do. We have seen that political acts vary in terms of who engages in them. Therefore, we focus not only on overall activity but also on particular acts with distinctive profiles: making political contributions, voting, and protesting. Note that, because we are interested in the bias associated with participatory input, all our measures are measures of the *amount* of participation—number of acts, number of protests attended, or number of dollars contributed.

The *participation factors*—resources, political engagement, and recruitment networks—influence the likelihood of becoming active. As we have said, when participatory factors are related to politically relevant characteristics, then activists will not be representative of the public. The factors used in this analysis derive, as we would expect, from the Civic Voluntarism Model. However, for the sake of parsimony, we use a somewhat more limited set.

The model includes a number of variables familiar from our extended exposition of the Civic Voluntarism Model: education, family income, and political interest. In discussions of political behavior, education and family income are usually treated as more or less equivalent, both components of socioeconomic status. We have already seen that, although both are significant predictors of participation, they function somewhat differently in fostering activity. This chapter demonstrates that, when it comes to the impact on participatory distortion, they are not alternative measures of the same underlying explanatory variable but are, instead, quite different in their effects.[4]

The data for the effects of non-political institutions are aggregated as measures of the effects of the three institutional domains (workplace, non-political organizations, and religious institutions) rather than as measures of the different kinds of factors (civic skills

---

4. As usual, we include in the analysis certain background variables that are useful as controls: gender, race, ethnicity, and age. In the few cases where they are of substantive significance, we will comment on them.

and recruitment) acquired in those institutions. Our reasoning is the same as that spelled out in Chapter 14, where we aggregated the measures in this alternative way. We are dealing with the representation of politically relevant characteristics through activity; and different institutions—particularly religious institutions—relate differently to politically relevant characteristics. Thus, we use three institutionally based measures, the additive sum of the number of civic skills and recruitment attempts (being asked to vote and being asked to take some other political action) on the job, in a non-political organization, and at church.[5]

PARTICIPATION FACTORS, POLITICALLY RELEVANT CHARACTERISTICS, AND PARTICIPATORY DISTORTION: A CLARIFICATION

The logic in this chapter is somewhat complex. Variables that have appeared in one place in our earlier analysis appear in another place in this analysis. For instance, the measure of need—receipt of means-tested benefits—appeared as an independent variable in Chapter 14, where we used it to explain participation. In this chapter, it appears as a dependent variable and is dealt with in terms of the extent to which people with need are over- or under-represented in the participatory process.

In our analysis, we have distinguished between *participatory factors* (which cause participation) and *politically relevant characteristics* (which are germane to public policy or other governmental actions). What adds to the complexity is that the same characteristic can be a participatory factor, it can be a politically relevant characteristic, or it can be both. Let us give some examples:

Politically Relevant Characteristics but not Participatory Factors: Race and views on economic policy are politically relevant characteristics but not participatory factors. It matters for political outcomes whether African-Americans or those with distinctive views on economic policy are over- or underrepresented among activists. When other factors are taken into account, however, these characteristics do not themselves lead to political activity.

---

5. For this measure, see Appendix B.8.e.

Participatory Factors but not Politically Relevant Characteristics: Civic skills and political interest are participatory factors but not politically relevant characteristics. Exercising civic skills or being interested in politics leads to participation. Nevertheless, political controversies do not pit against one another groups divided on the basis of differences in their level of civic skills or political interest.

Politically Relevant Characteristics and also Participatory Factors: Income is both a politically relevant characteristic and a participatory factor. On one hand, income plays a major role in generating participation, especially when it comes to making contributions; on the other, it matters for political outcomes whether the affluent are over- or underrepresented among activists. In addition, in Chapter 14 we considered two examples of issue engagements that have this dual role: receipt of means-tested benefits and having a strong opinion on abortion.

The fact that some politically relevant characteristics are also participatory factors and that others, although not participatory factors themselves, are related to participatory factors complicates the logic of argument substantially. Nevertheless, what makes our analysis more complex also goes to the heart of why we bother to study political participation. It is because the factors that cause participation are themselves—or are linked to—attributes to which policymakers pay attention that participatory inequalities matter for politics. The analytical project of this chapter is to probe how the factors that cause activity operate to produce distortion in what and from whom public officials hear.

Economic Matters

One of the basic fault lines of politics in America—and every other developed democracy, for that matter—has been economic conflict. Moreover, as we have made clear, income is not only the subject of political contention, but it is an essential resource for taking part politically, especially for making contributions. Therefore, a consistent concern in this volume has been the citizen politics of economic matters. Chapter 7 showed that those who are strapped financially or who receive means-tested government benefits are less well represented among the activists. Moreover, although the differences are considerably smaller, those with conservative positions on economic policy are somewhat better represented. In addition, Chapter 12 demonstrated the fundamental role of resources—income itself as well as resources like job skills that accrue disproportionately to the financially well-off—in generating participation. Clearly, this finding about the nature of the participatory process helps us to understand the earlier one about participatory distortion with respect to economic matters. We can refine this understanding further by bringing together information about activity, participatory factors, and various economic characteristics.

ATTITUDES ON ECONOMIC POLICY

We begin by considering the way in which attitudes about economic policy are represented through the participatory process. The measure of economic attitudes is a scale formed by adding the scores on two seven-point questions: one asking about government provision of jobs and a good standard of living and one about government cuts in services, even in areas such as health and education, in order to reduce spending.[6] These questions, of course, do not measure all aspects of economic attitudes. However, conflict over the appropriate role of government in providing assistance with respect to such basic needs as health or jobs has long divided conservatives from liberals—and Republicans from Democrats—in America. Figure 16.2 reports the results. Since we use figures of this sort throughout this analysis, it is important to see what it contains. Each of the two sections of Figure 16.2 is devoted to a paired relationship between a politically relevant characteristic and a measure of political activity. For both sections of the figure, the politically relevant characteristic is attitudes on economic issues measured so that higher scores indicate conservative attitudes (or opposition to government programs) and lower scores indicate liberal ones (or support for government programs). In the top portion the measure of participation is overall activity; in the

---

6. See Appendix B.6.b for wording of questions.

Distortion of Economic Attitudes through Overall Participation

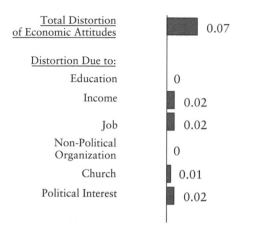

Distortion of Economic Attitudes through Political Contributions

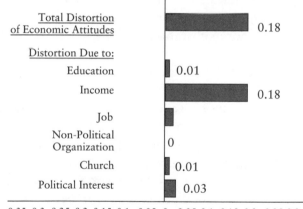

-0.35 -0.3 -0.25 -0.2 -0.15 -0.1 -0.05 0   0.05 0.1 0.15 0.2 0.25 0.3 0.35

Towards Liberal Attitudes ◄——— Distortion ———► Towards Conservative Attitudes

Figure 16.2 Distortion of Economic Attitudes through Overall Participation and Political Contributions.

bottom portion it is the amount of money given to electoral campaigns and other political causes.

For each analysis, we report the total participatory distortion. Note that, because we have divided by the standard deviation of the characteristic in question, these indexes have been standardized and, thus, can be compared to one another. The resulting measure is a dimensionless quantity, analogous to a standardized regression coefficient (beta weight), that should be interpreted in a manner analogous to the interpretation of a beta weight.[7] The index of participatory distortion can be positive or negative, with zero implying the absence of participatory distortion. Thus, the index of .07 in the top portion of Figure 16.2 suggests that overall political participation is biased to a quite modest degree in a conservative direction when it comes to attitudes on economic matters. The index of participatory distortion of .18 in the lower section of the figure indicates that the conservative distortion is considerably greater when it comes to participation through financial contributions. These results are, of course, familiar. When we used the Logged Representation Scale in Chapter 7, we found that the distortion with respect to economic attitudes is limited for activity in general, but more substantial when it comes to giving political money.

What Figure 16.2 adds to what we already knew derives from the coefficients showing the partial effects on participatory distortion of each participation factor.[8] Like the indexes of overall distortion, these coefficients can be positive or negative, with zero signifying that the participatory factor in question produces no distortion. Once again, they can be compared across analyses and interpreted in a manner analogous to the interpretation of a beta weight. As a rough guide, a coefficient of .04 or better may be considered to be substantively significant and worthy of attention.[9]

Consider overall political participation in relation to economic

---

7. For further discussion, see Appendix C.3.

8. The coefficients for the various participatory factors are designed so they can be added to produce the net result of effects of the various factors. In fact, if we were to report the coefficients for all variables used in the analysis as well as the error terms, they would sum to the overall participatory distortion.

9. For discussion, see Appendix C.4.

attitudes. Figure 16.2 indicates how several participatory factors—family income, job- and church-related factors, and political interest—contribute to this conservative tilt by each giving a tiny push in a conservative direction. None of these effects is substantial, and the outcome, as we saw in Chapter 7, is only a small tilt toward economic conservatism from overall activity.

The bottom portion of Figure 16.2, in which economic attitudes are paired with political contributions, presents a more dramatic illustration of how the participatory process can operate to produce bias in participatory input. In this case we see a more substantial impact of the participation factors, an impact that derives almost solely from the influence of family income, which dwarfs the effects of the other factors. We have seen how strongly family income affects contributions. In addition, the affluent are more conservative on economic issues,[10] with the result that, working through political contributions, family income creates a sizeable distortion in a conservative direction. Thus, Figure 16.2 illustrates the consequences for the representation of politically relevant characteristics of the participatory process we have explicated. Because political participation arises, at least in part, from resources that are differentially available to the more advantaged groups in American society, participatory input—especially political money—is skewed in a conservative direction with respect to attitudes on economic matters. The main driving force in relation to these attitudes is family income.

DEMOCRATS AND REPUBLICANS

These results are underscored if we consider the way the participatory process works within each of the parties. Democrats and Republicans differ fairly substantially in their views on economic policy, with Democrats further to the left.[11] Each party raises a

---

10. If we divide the public into quintiles based on their attitudes on economic matters, those respondents in the left-most quintile average $34,000 in family income while those in the far right quintile average $47,000.

11. Dividing the public into quintiles based on their economic attitudes, we find that 28 percent of the Democrats, but only 9 percent of the Republicans, are in the left-most quintile. At the other end of the scale in the right-most quintile, we find 30 percent of the Republicans, but only 10 percent of the Democrats.

substantial amount of money, the bulk from its more affluent affiliates.[12] It is, thus, interesting to examine whether the participatory process for political contributions produces distortion within the parties—in particular, whether the relation between family income and contributions and between family income and economic views tilts the contributions in both parties in a conservative direction. Figure 16.3 shows the workings of this process in relation to campaign contributions and economic attitudes for Democrats and Republicans taken separately.[13] The analysis is parallel to that in the bottom portion of Figure 16.2 except that distortion is measured within each of the partisan groups. Among Republicans, the process works decisively to bias political contributions in a conservative direction. Family income plays the main role, but other factors—including education, political interest, and job- and church-related factors—push in the same direction. In sum, Republicans are generally more conservative than the public as a whole; the result of the participatory process is that Republican contributions are even more conservative than the Republican rank and file.

For Democrats, the pattern is very different. The index of participatory distortion indicates that, in contrast to what we saw for Republicans, Democratic contributions are not biased in either direction.[14] This result is particularly striking in view of the fact

---

12. The correlation between family income and the amount contributed to politics is strong for both parties but is, in fact, somewhat stronger for Democrats (.41) than for Republicans (.32).

13. We consider as partisans both those who identify with the party or Independents who indicate that they "lean" in the direction of that party. The results are essentially unchanged if leaners are omitted.

14. In view of the longstanding concern with the extent to which party elites and activists in each of the parties are representative of the partisan rank and file, this is an especially noteworthy finding. On this issue, see Herbert McClosky, Paul J. Hoffman, and Rosemary O'Hara, "Issue Conflict and Consensus among Party Leaders and Followers," *American Political Science Review* 58 (1960): 406–427; Norman H. Nie, Sidney Verba, and John R. Petrocik, *The Changing American Voter* (Cambridge, Mass.: Harvard University Press, 1976); Jeanne Kirkpatrick, *The New Presidential Elite: Men and Women in National Politics* (New York: Russell Sage Foundation, 1976), especially chap. 10; John S. Jackson, III, J. C. Brown, and Barbara Leavitt Brown, "Recruitment, Representation, and Political Values: The 1976 Democratic National Convention Delegates," *American Politics Quarterly* 6 (1978): 187–212; John S. Jackson, III, J. C. Brown, and David Bositis, "Herbert McClosky and Friends Revisited: 1980 Democratic and Republican Elites Compared to the

Distortion of Economic Attitudes through Political Contributions
(Among Democrats)

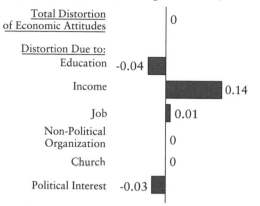

Distortion of Economic Attitudes through Political Contributions
(Among Republicans)

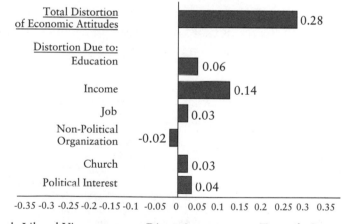

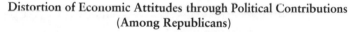

Figure 16.3 Distortion of Economic Attitudes through Political Contributions for Democrats and Republicans.

that income, which is so strongly related both to contributions and to conservative views, plays a role among Democrats equivalent in direction and magnitude to that among Republicans. That is, although Republicans and Democrats differ markedly in their positions on economic matters, the effect of income as a participatory factor operates within both parties to lend a distinctly conservative tilt to political contributions. However, the effect of income in distorting Democratic contributions in a conservative direction is counterbalanced by the effects of other variables—most notably, education and political interest. Thus, in both parties the more affluent have more conservative economic views. Among Republicans, those with high levels of education and political interest are also more conservative. Among Democrats, educational attainment and political interest are associated with economic liberalism.[15] To summarize, although the partisans have very different views on economic issues, the effect of income for both Republicans and Democrats is to skew contributions to the right. For Republicans the conservative bias introduced by family income is reinforced by the effects of other variables that push in the same direction. For Democrats other variables play a compensating role, with the result that Democratic financial contributions are representative when it comes to attitudes on economic issues.

Mass Public," *American Politics Quarterly* 10 (1982): 58–180; Warren E. Miller and M. Kent Jennings, *Parties in Transition: A Longitudinal Study of Party Elites and Party Supporters* (New York: Russell Sage Foundation, 1986), chap. 9.

15. The relationship of education and income to economic views in the two parties is intriguing. The following are the results of a regression in which the scale of economic attitudes is the dependent variable (a negative score on the scale is more liberal, a positive score, more conservative). The independent variables include the job-, organization-, and church-related factors as well as the controls for age, gender, race, and ethnicity. In addition, we have included four variables measuring the interaction between education or income and being a Republican or a Democrat. The pattern is quite striking. In each party the affluent are more conservative as are, among Republicans, the well-educated. In contrast, among Democrats the well-educated are more liberal.

Variable	B	SE B	Beta	Significance
Democrat*Income	.01	.01	.05	.08
Democrat*Education	−.04	.01	−.15	.00
Republican*Income	.02	.01	.09	.00
Republican*Education	.04	.01	.16	.00

ECONOMIC NEED

When we discussed the nature of participatory representation in Chapter 6, we pointed out that preferences on political issues are not the only, and probably not the most important, set of messages communicated through participation. We indicated that other politically relevant characteristics—including actual economic circumstances and, even, demographic characteristics—convey information to public officials and argued that those who are invisible in the participatory process are more likely to be ignored by policymakers. Chapter 7 demonstrated that the economically needy are, indeed, underrepresented among activists to an extent that is much more pronounced than any distortion in attitudes about economic issues—even though, as we saw in Chapter 14, by creating a stake in government policy, receipt of means-tested government benefits actually raises levels of activity somewhat beyond the low levels that result from this group's deficits of other participatory factors. The underrepresentation of the needy is especially pronounced when it comes to financial contributions to politics.

Figure 16.4, which presents data about the effects of the participatory process on the representation of people with actual economic need, clarifies how this result comes about. The measure of economic need is a combined scale based on whether or not an individual reported having to cut back on necessities and whether or not a member of the immediate family living in the household receives means-tested government benefits.[16] Figure 16.4 shows a process driven by socioeconomic factors. Because the economically needy are disadvantaged with respect to education and, of course, family income—two significant factors in generating political activity—they are underrepresented in participation. The effect is substantial for overall activity but is especially dramatic for political contributions, where the usual strong effect of income is manifest. Note as well the impact of political interest: the economically needy are not only disadvantaged with respect to education and income, they are also less politically interested, a fact that contributes to participatory distortion.

---

16. See Appendix B.16.a and b. We experimented with a number of versions of this scale since it can be constructed in many ways. The results were virtually identical each time.

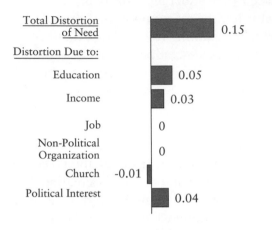

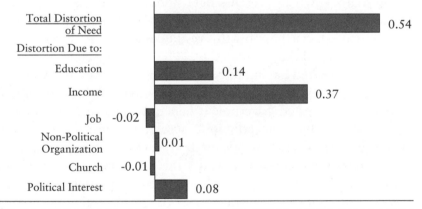

Figure 16.4 Distortion of Economic Need through Overall Participation and Political Contributions.
Economic need = need to cut back on necessities and receipt of means-tested benefits.

TIME AND MONEY

Earlier, we contrasted giving time and giving money to politics as means of citizen involvement. The amount of money given to politics, we noted, was tightly constrained by the need to have the relevant resource—money. And that resource was concentrated in the hands of the advantaged. The number of hours given to politics was less constrained: those who were disadvantaged could still have their voices heard by devoting time and effort. It is useful to consider the contrast between the dollars and the hours given to politics in the context of the present analysis, and that for two reasons. One reason is substantive. We want to illustrate the way in which these contributions of money and time interact with the participatory factors to distort the messages sent about economic attitudes and about need. The other reason is methodological. We are concerned about whether the distinction between overall activity and political money illustrated so starkly in Figures 16.2 and 16.4 might not be an artifact of the difference between the distributions of the two activity measures. Political contributions have a much larger relative standard deviation than overall activity. Since the number of hours given to politics has a relative standard deviation similar to that for political contributions, this comparison would take that into account.[17]

The data on political contributions have already been presented in Figures 16.2 and 16.4. The important role of income in relation to the number of dollars given skews political contributions in a conservative direction and effectively locks out of that mode of activity those who are truly needy. If we perform a parallel analysis of the number of hours given to politics, we find results quite similar to those for overall activity. Various socioeconomic factors tilt the messages communicated through the hours given to politics

---

17. The reader will remember that total time is the sum of hours for campaign work, informal activity, and participation on boards. Appendix C.3 shows that the total distortion equals the product of the correlation between the political activity and the politically relevant characteristic and the relative standard deviation of the political activity. The relative standard deviation is the quotient of the standard deviation of the activity and its average. As shown in Table C.1 in Appendix C, the relative standard deviation is only .77 for overall participation but 5.01 for political contributions. The relative standard deviation of 4.24 for total time given to political activities is similar to that for political contributions.

in a somewhat conservative direction, but the effects are not very great and are a lot less than the tilt communicated through political money. The effect of the various factors on the representation of the needy through political hours is much stronger—as it is for the case where the activity measure is overall activity. But, again, the effect is far less than the effect through political dollars. This makes clear that the results are not an artifact of the distributions of the variables. It also shows, once again, how significantly different are political contributions and time given to politics as modes of activity.[18]

PROTEST AND ECONOMIC MATTERS

Because protest is an activity that is less demanding in terms of resources and that has historically been associated with movements among the dispossessed, it deserves a closer look in this context. Nevertheless, as we saw in Chapter 7, the affluent are actually more likely than the poor to have reported attending a protest—although the differences among income groups with respect to protest are much less pronounced than they are for mak-

---

18. It is useful to go one step further. We showed in Chapter 7 that, among those who gave some time to politics, the poor and the affluent gave about as many hours. In contrast, among those who gave some money, there was a sharp difference between the poor and the affluent in how many dollars they gave. If we rerun the analyses in Figures 16.2 and 16.4 and look at the effect of the participatory factors on the distortion of economic views and need through giving time or giving money *among those who give time or money,* we find the following: When it comes to the distortion effect of political hours on economic attitudes, education has no distorting effect and income a very small one in a conservative direction. For political hours and economic need, education has a small effect in favor of those with need and income a small effect in favor of those without need. The resulting total distortion in relation to need is close to zero. In other words, among those who become active and give some time to politics, the participatory factors bring into politics economic liberals and conservatives as well as the needy and the not-needy with rough proportionality.

This is not the case when it comes to giving money. Among the contributors, income plays a major role in tilting economic views in a conservative direction (education pushes the other way but not as strongly) and an even stronger role in tilting the participatory input away from the needy (and, here, education adds a bit to the push in that direction). The differences are striking. The effect of income on attitudes through political time is .01 (in a conservative direction); the effect of income on the representation of actual economic need through political time is .02 (away from the needy). The parallel figures for the impact of income through political contributions is .09 and .20. In sum, the tight link between income and contributions has significant consequences for what is communicated through political contributions.

ing political contributions. Furthermore, we found an unusual pattern for the representation of attitudes and needs through protest: among protesters, those with liberal opinions on economic matters are overrepresented, but those who are disadvantaged with respect to their actual economic circumstances are underrepresented.

The role of the participation factors in producing this outcome, shown in Figure 16.5, is different from what we have seen so far. With respect to attitudes on economic issues, the top portion of the figure shows the seemingly contradictory circumstance in which, insofar as the participatory factors have any effect, they give a modest push to the right; yet the index of overall distortion (−.33) shows a substantial tilt in a liberal direction. How can protesters lean so decisively to the left when the participatory factors that make a difference—income, job-related factors, and political interest—have the opposite impact? Part of the answer rests with two variables that have been included in the model but not reported (because they ordinarily have no effect once the other variables are taken into account): race and age. Compared to the population at large, African-Americans and the young are more likely both to take part in protests and to have liberal economic attitudes. These two variables (both of which are included in the analysis for Figure 16.5 but not reported there) counterbalance somewhat the opposing effects of other participatory factors: the coefficient for being African-American is −.05 and for being young is −.03, each pushing the protesting population in a liberal direction. Still, our explanation based on participatory factors does not account for the liberalism of protesters very well.[19]

The differences among modes of activity with respect to the distortion of attitudes on economic issues are worth underlining. Making contributions is the form of participatory input that tilts most distinctively to the right, a result that derives, not from any special propensity of conservatives to give money to politics, but from the fact that contributions are related to affluence and the well-off tend also to be conservative. Protests, in contrast, lean left. In this case, the result rests, not on the operations of the

---

19. In fact, the distortion from the error term in this instance is about the same size as the index of participatory distortion.

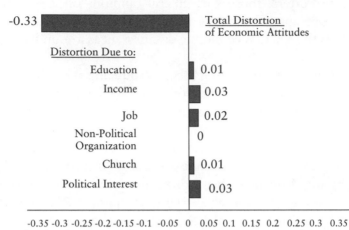

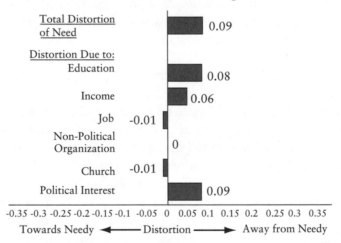

Figure 16.5 Distortion of Economic Attitudes and Economic Need through Protest.

Economic need = need to cut back on necessities and receipt of means-tested benefits.

factors that ordinarily foster participation, but on a linkage between being liberal and taking part in protest activity. Voting shows
still another pattern. Voters tend to be slightly more conservative
than the public at large. The index of participatory distortion,
which is .06, is comparable to that for overall activity. However,
in contrast to the circumstance of overall activity—for which a
number of the individual factors contributed to participatory distortion—this modest conservative tilt is not the result of the impact of the participatory factors in the model.[20]

Finally, we should consider the lower portion of Figure 16.5,
which reports workings of the participatory process in relation to
protest and actual citizen need. The pattern is quite different—and
less complex. The needy are underrepresented among protesters.
And the individual factors that contribute to this result—education, income, and political interest—all work to diminish the representation of the needy among protesters. Once again, other
factors not reported in the figure play an opposing role. Being
African-American and being young (for which the coefficients are
−.04 and −.08 respectively) operate to offset the impact of socioeconomic advantage and political interest. However, when it comes
to actual economic circumstances, the full effect of the participatory process works against the recruitment to protest of those most
in need.

Government Assistance to Minorities

The same model can be applied to the issue of views on government efforts to assist minorities. Our survey contained separate
questions about whether the government ought to help Blacks or
Latinos or whether members of these groups should help themselves.[21] The results of the analysis—for respondents who are not
themselves Black or Latino—are presented in Figure 16.6. The

---

20. The coefficients for education, income, and the job-, organization-, and church-related factors are all zero. For political interest the coefficient is .01.

21. We constructed a scale by adding the answers to two seven-point scale questions
about government aid to Blacks and to Hispanics. See Appendix B.6.c. Analyzing the two
scales separately produces a similar pattern for each question.

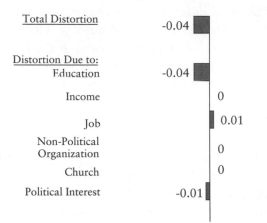

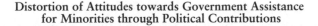

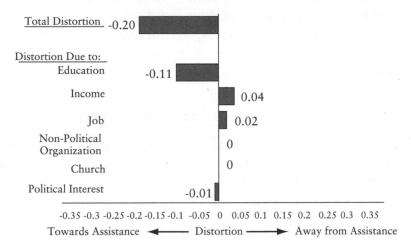

Figure 16.6 Distortion of Attitudes toward Government Assistance for Minorities through Overall Participation and Political Contributions (among non-minority respondents).

participatory process has a weak distorting effect in a liberal direction when it comes to overall activity; as usual, the distorting effect is stronger when it comes to giving money. The role of education in bringing in activists with liberal views on these issues is unambiguous. It is particularly interesting in terms of explaining the skew in opinions represented through political contributions. Ordinarily, it is income, which is associated with conservative views and is the most important factor in predicting political giving, that has the most substantial distorting effect. In this case, the leftward push given by the impact of education more than compensates for the rightward tilt introduced by the effects of income. Thus, education and income—both indicators of socio-economic status and ordinarily treated as surrogates in social science analysis—need not have the same effect when it comes to the distortion of politically relevant characteristics through participation.

The Participatory Process among Minorities and the Poor

When we discussed representation through participation in Chapter 6, we noted that there is more than one source of participatory distortion. Most obvious is the one we have been discussing: the over- or underrepresentation among activist publics of those with particular politically relevant characteristics. Our analysis demonstrates how political disadvantage accrues to the socioeconomically disadvantaged through the participatory process. Political activity underrepresents those who favor government programs for disadvantaged groups and those who would most benefit from such programs because they are less well endowed with the factors that foster participation. Participatory bias can also be introduced if the active members of a politically relevant group are not representative of less active fellow group members with respect to some other characteristic that is germane to politics. In this way, a group can be doubly disadvantaged by the participatory process—if they are, on average, less active and if group activists do not accurately represent their needs and preferences. We noted in Chapters 7 and 8 that the activists from disadvantaged groups—the poor, African-Americans, and Latinos—tend to be somewhat less supportive of government aid for their group and, even more so, to be drawn from group members who are less needy economically.

The analysis of the participatory process in this chapter makes clear why. The same biasing processes that operate within the population as a whole work within disadvantaged groups to distort the messages coming through their activity. That is, the participatory factors that lend a conservative tilt to the attitudes or the needs communicated through activity by the public as a whole—income and, sometimes, education, political interest, and other factors—also operate within disadvantaged groups so that group activists send more conservative messages on policy and, even more so, communicate a less needy image.

Figure 16.7 presents data for three groups—those with low incomes (family incomes under $20,000), African-Americans, and Latinos—on the representation of attitudes toward government aid to their own group through participation. With respect to views on government assistance to Blacks, Black political activists are quite representative of all Blacks. For low-income respondents and, much more so, for Latinos, there is distortion through the participatory process of views on government aid for the group. For Latinos, each of the factors, especially political interest, adds modestly to the participatory distortion of attitudes away from support for government efforts on behalf of Latinos. Thus, the data show how Latinos, who are already disadvantaged politically by low rates of activity, are further disadvantaged by the fact that the small cadre of Latino activists does not accurately represent Latino opinion.[22] This is a finding that might seem to contradict the apparent liberalism of many Latino public officials—for example, the Latinos in Congress, most of whom are liberal Democrats. It is critical to recall, however, that these data are about citizen activists, not government officials, and that generalizations about the latter might not hold for the former.

Figure 16.8 offers even more dramatic evidence for the way in

---

22. As noted in Chapter 8, this is not due to the impact of more conservative Cuban-American respondents. The relationship holds even if Cuban-Americans are not included in the analysis. See the discussion in Chapter 8 of the representativeness of Latino activists.

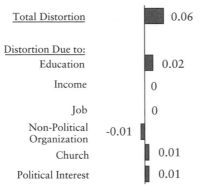

Distortion of Economic Attitudes (Among the Poor)

Total Distortion — 0.06

Distortion Due to:
Education — 0.02
Income — 0
Job — 0
Non-Political Organization — -0.01
Church — 0.01
Political Interest — 0.01

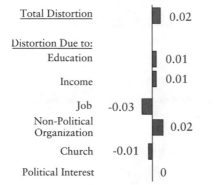

Distortion of Attitudes towards Government Assistance to Blacks (Among Blacks)

Total Distortion — 0.02

Distortion Due to:
Education — 0.01
Income — 0.01
Job — -0.03
Non-Political Organization — 0.02
Church — -0.01
Political Interest — 0

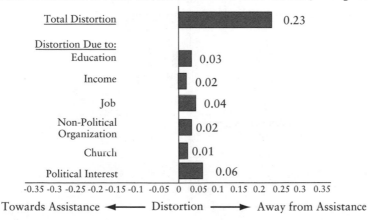

Distortion of Attitudes towards Government Assistance to Latinos (Among Latinos)

Total Distortion — 0.23

Distortion Due to:
Education — 0.03
Income — 0.02
Job — 0.04
Non-Political Organization — 0.02
Church — 0.01
Political Interest — 0.06

-0.35 -0.3 -0.25 -0.2 -0.15 -0.1 -0.05 0 0.05 0.1 0.15 0.2 0.25 0.3 0.35

Towards Assistance ◄——— Distortion ———► Away from Assistance

Figure 16.7 Distortion of Economic Attitudes and Attitudes toward Government Assistance for Blacks and Latinos through Overall Participation (among poor, Black, and Latino respondents).

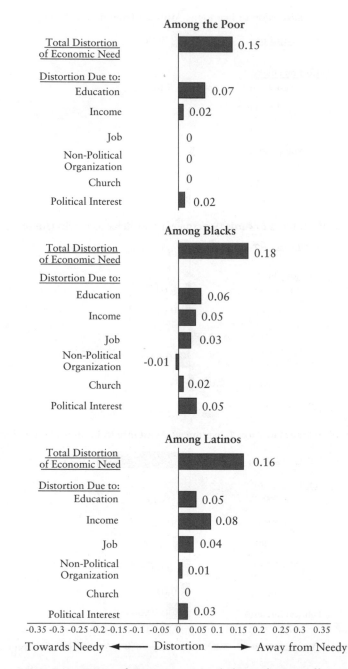

Figure 16.8 Distortion of Economic Need through Overall Activity.

which the participatory process can multiply disadvantage. Here we report the process as it affects the representation of the needy. Within all three groups—low-income respondents, African-Americans, and Latinos—the process operates to underrepresent those who have the greatest economic need. In particular, education but also income and political interest all work together to bias activity away from group members who are most needy. In short, then, the process that operates to underrepresent the disadvantaged among activists also operates to underrepresent among disadvantaged activists those who have the greatest economic need.

Representing Preferences and Needs: A Summary

These data—which touch on two of the enduring sources of division in American politics, economics and race or ethnicity—enrich our understanding of how the participatory process operates to produce the distortion described in Chapters 7 and 8. When participatory factors are associated with politically relevant characteristics—and they often are—then the result is participatory bias. This outcome follows even when the politically relevant attribute—for example, being Black or Latino—does not itself cause activity. The over- or underrepresentation of politically relevant groups among participants implies that public officials hear more from some kinds of citizens than from others and thus jeopardizes the democratic norm of equal protection of interests.

Central to the process is the role of income, which functions simultaneously as a powerful predictor of activity, especially when it comes to contributions, and as the object of ongoing political conflict. One of the consequences of the crucial role played by income is that, if there is distortion with respect to some politically relevant characteristic for overall activity, the distortion will be more pronounced for political contributions. We found no instance in which the participatory input through contributions represents the public—its views, demographic characteristics, or economic needs—more accurately than does overall participation. Also related to the multiple functions of income in the participatory process is the fact that activist publics are always more representative in terms of their attitudes than in terms of their policy-relevant circumstances and needs. Furthermore, education and income, both components of socioeconomic status and ordinarily treated as twins in social science analysis, sometimes function in opposition when it comes to the introduction of participatory distortion.

Also noteworthy in the process is the role of political interest. On one hand, political interest is unambiguously an indicator of engagement. On the other, as we saw in Chapter 15, the roots of political interest are, at least in part, in socioeconomic factors—in having educated parents, a good education, and a high-level job, as well as in organizational membership. The process that produces greater participation for the advantaged also produces greater political interest. Hence, although an index of *wanting* to take part, political interest is also related to *being able* to take part. Therefore, political interest also works to reduce the representation of the needy.

Passion, Participation, and Representation

Thus far in this chapter, we have shown that participatory factors have a major impact on what is communicated through participation, tilting the communication of needs and political attitudes in one direction or another. In Chapter 14 we considered the way in which another participatory factor—issue engagement deriving from deep commitment on some political subject—generates political activity. One of the most powerful issue engagements is related to the subject of abortion. Those who have strong views about abortion are more likely to be active, with strong pro-life attitudes having an even more pronounced effect than pro-choice attitudes. We can now explore this matter further. As we shall see, issue engagement on abortion has an independent effect on participatory distortion, but the effect works itself out in the context of the other factors in the Civic Voluntarism Model.

What we have learned so far would suggest contradictory hypotheses with respect to the representation of opinions about abortion through participation. On one hand, the general participatory factors should tilt activity in a pro-choice direction. In particular, the well-educated tend to be both pro-choice and active in politics. Hence, we would expect the overrepresentation of pro-choice views among activists. On the other hand, although extreme opinions on abortion, whatever the direction, act as an independent force in fostering political activity, pro-life attitudes are an even more potent form of issue engagement than are pro-choice views. On this basis, we would expect the underrepresentation of pro-choice views. By sorting out this complex set of relationships, we shall learn a good deal about the way in which participatory factors like education, income, and political interest interact with extreme attitudes on a powerful issue like abortion to shape the communication of citizen preferences.

Indeed, when it comes to overall participation, those with pro-choice views—who are, on average, endowed with higher levels of education and other participatory resources—participate at somewhat higher rates than those on the pro-life side of the issue. Those in the most pro-choice category of the seven-point attitude scale represent 38 percent of respondents. They are, however, responsible for 41 percent of all political acts (including votes) and 46 percent of all campaign dollars. In contrast, those in the most pro-life category on the seven-point scale constitute 15 percent of respondents and are responsible for 12 percent of all political acts and 8 percent of the campaign dollars. In short, overall activity, especially campaign giving, is tilted slightly in the pro-choice direction.

These figures, of course, refer to overall activity, not necessarily to activity directed at the issue of abortion. However, we can use the verbatim responses, in conjunction with the seven-point attitude scale on abortion, to locate activity specifically on the subject of abortion and to distinguish pro-choice from pro-life participation.[23] When we focus exclusively on activity on the subject of

---

23. In relation to many issues, including abortion, it is impossible to discern the respondent's view from the mere mention of an issue as being associated with activity. For example, from the brief phrases recorded by interviewers we cannot tell whether the respondent who contacted a public official about "welfare" or "public housing" wants the government to be doing more or less about it.

When an individual said that the issue associated with an act was "abortion" without the kind of embellishment that would allow us to distinguish pro-life from pro-choice activity, we used the seven-point attitude scale to infer the direction of opinion. In order

abortion, the bias that we observed for overall activity reverses direction. The 38 percent of respondents in the most pro-choice attitude category are responsible for 34 percent of the abortion activity, while the 15 percent of respondents in the most pro-life category are responsible for nearly twice their share of the abortion activity—29 percent. If we consider all those expressing pro-life or pro-choice views in response to the attitude item, instead of just those in the most extreme category, we find that the minority on the pro-life side produce a majority of the activity—that is, 45 percent of all activity inspired by the issue of abortion comes from the 57 percent of respondents who are pro-choice, and 51 percent of all abortion activity comes from the 31 percent of respondents who are pro-life. As we saw in Chapter 14, those with pro-choice opinions, a relatively participant group overall, are active on behalf of a broad agenda of policy concerns of which abortion is only one. Those with pro-life opinions, in contrast, are much more likely to concentrate their participatory firepower on the single issue of abortion.

The difference between the two attitude groups on the issue of abortion can be illustrated even more clearly if we consider protests. At the time our survey was conducted, abortion was by far the single most frequent subject of protest activity: 45 percent of the protests on an issue that affected the nation as a whole were about abortion.[24] Figure 16.9, which contains data on protest activity by people at various points on the seven-point abortion scale, shows the proportion who reported having taken part in a protest on any issue as well as the proportion who reported having protested on abortion. As we saw earlier in the chapter, liberals are, on average, more likely than conservatives to engage in pro-

---

to check the legitimacy of this approach, we considered 126 abortion activists (a group that represents roughly two-thirds of all abortion activists) who indicated the direction of their commitment in their open-ended answers: for example, "I participated in an abortion march—pro-life" or "It was about a woman's right to choose an abortion, which I favor." We were reassured to discover that, in all but one case, the opinion expressed in response to the seven-point attitude scale—an item that was in a very different part of a long interview—is consistent in direction with the verbatim description of the abortion activity. (The one discordant case involves a rather convoluted description of the issue that may not mean what it seemed at first reading to mean.)

24. See Chapter 3 for a discussion of these data.

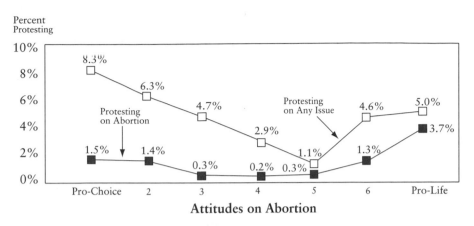

Figure 16.9 Protest on Any Subject and Protest on Abortion by Attitudes toward Abortion.

test. Figure 16.9 illustrates this. When it comes to protesting in general, those at the pro-choice end of the scale are more active. However, when we consider protests about abortion, we find that the pattern is reversed: those at the pro-life end of the spectrum were more likely to have reported taking part in a demonstration about abortion. Of the protesters in the most extreme pro-life category on the abortion attitude scale, 74 percent indicated that the issue was abortion. The analogous figure for those in the most extreme pro-choice category, a group with a diverse set of participatory concerns, is 18 percent. Once again, among political activists pro-choice views outnumber pro-life views. Nonetheless, opponents of abortion focus their activity much more narrowly on that single issue.

PARTICIPATORY DISTORTION AND THE ISSUE OF ABORTION
We can round out the abortion analysis by using the technique developed at the beginning of this chapter to show how the various participatory factors combine to shape the communications sent through various forms of activity. The use of this technique will highlight the way in which the participation factors in the Civic Voluntarism Model affect the communication of the abortion views of the American public. In Figure 16.10 we contrast the way the process works in relation to overall political activity and abor-

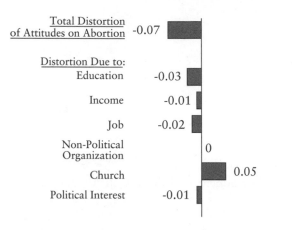

Distortion of Attitudes on Abortion through Overall Participation

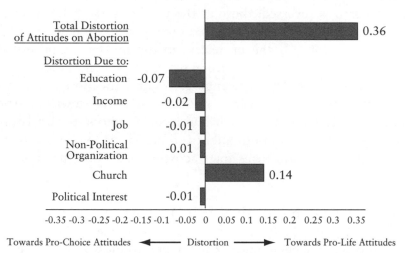

**Distortion of Attitudes on Abortion through Participation
on the Issue of Abortion**

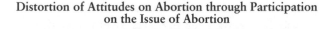

Figure 16.10 Distortion of Attitudes on Abortion through Overall
Participation and Participation on the Issue of Abortion.

tion views with the way the process works in relation to activity
directly on abortion. The top part of the figure shows the analysis
of overall activity and abortion views—that is, the extent to which
various participatory factors generate political activity from those
at one end or another of the abortion attitude continuum.

The data in Figure 16.10 show a circumstance in which the
principal factors producing participatory distortion work in opposite directions. The data in the top portion of the figure confirm
that socioeconomic factors—in particular, education—operate to
tilt the activist public in a pro-choice direction. Participatory factors anchored in religious institutions—that is, the civic skills
developed in the course of church-based activity and requests for
activity originating in church—push in the opposite direction,
bringing into politics participants who are disproportionately pro-
life. The net effect of these contradictory forces, however, is a
slight distortion in a pro-choice direction for overall political participation.

When it comes to participation that is specifically on the subject
of abortion, the bottom portion of Figure 16.10 shows a very
different result. Once again, participatory factors rooted in socioeconomic status, especially education, and participatory factors
derived from religious institutions operate in contrary directions
in producing distortion. In this case, however, total distortion is
very substantial—and is in a pro-life direction. That is, activity on
the subject of abortion comes very disproportionately from activists with pro-life attitudes, an outcome that reflects not only the
effects of civic skills developed in and requests for activity originating in religious institutions but also the fact that, as we saw in
Chapter 14, strong views on the subject of abortion, especially
pro-life views, are themselves a factor that boosts activity.

These findings illustrate how participatory factors and related
politically relevant characteristics work together in complicated
ways to shape the messages sent to public officials through participation. Although they are differentially relevant for different
forms of activity, the participatory factors discussed in Chapter 12
all operate to enhance participation. However, these factors work
in different, and sometimes contradictory, ways to produce distortion. What matters is not simply which politically relevant char-

acteristic is at stake (say, economic needs or attitudes toward government assistance to minorities) or which participatory factor is at work (say, income or political interest). Rather, the institutional origins of a participatory factor also have consequences for distortion. Civic skills and requests for activity in different settings may operate similarly in fostering participation. However, when it comes to distortion it matters whether institutionally derived participatory factors come from the workplace, non-political organizations, or religious institutions. Civic skills developed in church or requests for participation arising in church have the consequence of mobilizing to politics activists with distinctively pro-life attitudes on abortion.

Participation and the Good Citizen

So far, our focus on participatory distortion has been animated by a concern that inequalities in activity among politically relevant groups potentially jeopardize equal protection of interests in a democracy. However, we can approach from another perspective the question of how the participatory process works to bring into activity citizens with particular characteristics.

One of the dreams of philosophers of democracy has long been rule by the virtuous, and the ideal of participatory democracy has been a process of decision making in which enlightened citizens would reason together in the formation of public policy. Those taking part in this process would be informed—that is, knowledgeable about government and the issues confronting it. And they would be tolerant—that is, willing to consider and debate the views of others, even unpopular or unorthodox views. They would bring to the discussion concern not merely for their own individual interests, but for the common good. This process would not only involve good citizens, it would create them: mutual discourse among informed citizens would enlighten them and deepen their understanding of their common purposes.[25] In short, because tak-

---

25. That citizens ought, through participation, to bring more than their own narrow self-interests into the political process is a theme stressed by many writers including Jean-Jacques Rousseau, John Stuart Mill, and James Bryce. See John Stuart Mill, *Consid-*

ing part in political life would educate citizens about their shared interests and about the workings of democracy, this kind of democracy would be self-reinforcing.

We have already discussed some respects in which American activists come closer to this ideal than popular descriptions would suggest. As we saw in Chapter 4, citizen activists do not describe their activity simply in terms of a quest for individual benefits. Rather, they cite the gratification of performing a civic duty or influencing government policy in order to make the community a better place to live. Furthermore, the actual policy issues they mention in connection with their activity are often directed at goals that transcend narrow self-interest. Citizens can, thus, bring into politics a commitment to the betterment of the community.

Our survey contains measures that permit us to investigate the civic orientations of activists and how the participatory process affects the representation of these civic orientations. One, which has already been discussed, is information about politics. The other is tolerance of unorthodox opinions.[26] Figure 16.11 presents data on the association between political participation and political information or tolerance. As we saw in Chapter 12, political information and activity go hand in hand. With levels of information, activity (as measured by number of participatory acts) rises dramatically. The data for tolerance are less striking. As tolerance increases, so too does activity. However, the relationship is not as strong as that between information and participation. Nevertheless, activist publics are both better informed and more tolerant

---

erations on Representative Government (New York: H. Holt and Company, 1873); James Bryce, The Hindrances to Good Citizenship (New Haven: Yale University Press, 1909); and J. J. Rousseau, The Social Contract, in The Social Contract and Discourses, trans. G. D. H. Cole (London: J. M. Dent, 1973). For a vigorous contemporary argument see Benjamin R. Barber, Strong Democracy: Participatory Politics for a New Age (Berkeley and Los Angeles: University of California Press, 1984). For examples of this process in action, see Jane J. Mansbridge, Beyond Adversary Democracy (New York: Basic Books, 1980).

26. Other possible measures of "good citizenship," discussed in Chapter 4, cannot be used in this analysis because they are questions that were asked of participants only. These would include items about the civic gratifications attendant to activity or the nature of the policy concerns that animate activity. The tolerance measures are adapted from standard civil liberties questions used in various studies. For the tolerance and information measures, see Appendix B.7.c and d.

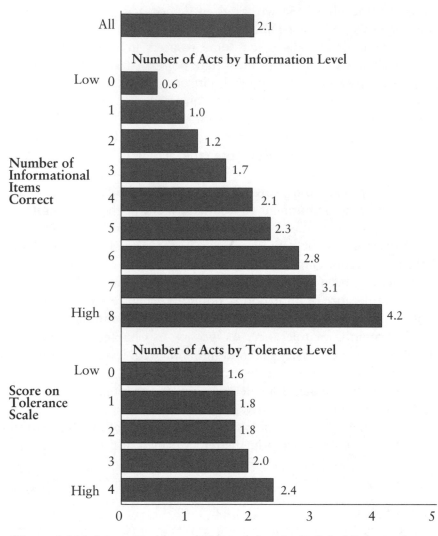

Figure 16.11 Mean Number of Political Acts by Political Information and Tolerance.

than the public as a whole.[27] This analysis cannot establish whether political information and tolerance are causes or consequences of activity. We surmise that they are both. In fact, however, the causal order is not our concern in this context. Rather our goal has been to ascertain whether informed and tolerant citizens are overrepresented among activists. Clearly, they are.[28]

INFORMATION, TOLERANCE, AND THE PARTICIPATORY PROCESS
How is this result, the overrepresentation of informed and tolerant citizens among activists, achieved through the participatory process? Given the significance of education for participation and the strong associations between education and both political information and tolerance, we would expect it to play a key role in the process. As shown in Figure 16.12, there is substantial participatory distortion in the direction of the better informed especially with respect to political contributions. Along with political interest—which, of course, derives in part from education—education is critical to bringing into politics a more informed participant population. Even when it comes to financial contributions, for which family income usually has the predominant role, the impact of education approaches that of income. The data in Figure 16.13 show similar results for tolerance. The bias in the direction of the tolerant is considerable—though not as great as in the direction of the informed. Education—in this case, not coupled with interest—again carries the greatest weight for overall activity and substantial weight for financial contributions to politics.

These data lend a somewhat different interpretation to the way in which the participatory system distorts the politically relevant

---

27. In part the difference may result from the measures used: the tolerance scale is shorter and does not discriminate as well. The lowest and highest categories of the information scale contain 3 percent of the cases each. In contrast, for the tolerance scale 20 percent are in the lowest category and 47 percent in the top. If we were to categorize information so that it roughly matched the distribution of the tolerance scale (by grouping together the 19 percent who answered correctly two or fewer questions and the 43 percent who answered five or more correctly) we would find a mean activity score of 1.1 at the bottom and 2.8 at the top. This difference is not as dramatic as what we saw for the entire information scale. Still, it is about twice as large as the difference associated with the tolerance scale.

28. Considering individual political acts shows similar differences.

Distortion of Information Level through Overall Participation

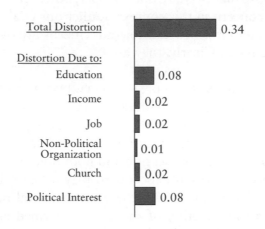

Distortion of Information Level through Political Contributions

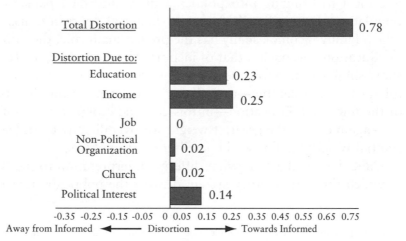

Figure 16.12 Distortion of Information Level through Overall Participation and Political Contributions.

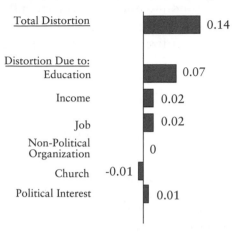

Distortion of Tolerance Level through Overall Participation

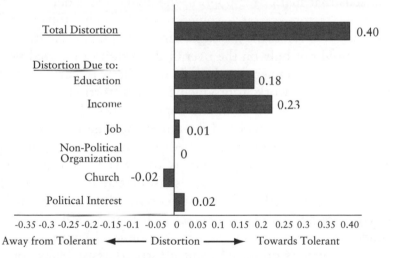

Distortion of Tolerance Level through Political Contributions

Figure 16.13 Distortion of Tolerance Level through Overall Participation and Political Contributions.

characteristics of citizens. Overrepresentation of the educated, affluent, and politically interested produces a skewed picture of the public. When it comes to economic matters—in particular, actual economic circumstances—and race or ethnicity, the result is distortion that threatens to jeopardize equal protection of interests among citizens. Yet, the impact of the participatory process is to reinforce another democratic ideal: the desirability of a participant public committed to the democratic process. It brings into politics citizens who are—compared with the public as a whole—informed, tolerant, and committed to activity for the community.

Conclusion

In this chapter, we have shown how the participatory factors of the Civic Voluntarism Model work to shape citizen input into the political process. Taking off from the fact that the multiple factors that foster participation are themselves, or are related to, attributes of citizens that matter for politics, the analysis has demonstrated how these factors operate—sometimes in tandem, sometimes in opposition—to affect the messages sent through participation. We have focused not only on the overall distortion of selected politically relevant characteristics but also on the way particular participatory factors work in producing that distortion. In so doing we have shed light on both the representational outcomes described in earlier chapters and the nature of American politics.

According to a liberal model of American democracy, the principal role of citizen participation is to transmit information to public authorities about activists' self-interested objectives. This chapter demonstrated a consistent pattern when it comes to the participatory politics of self-interest. Whether we are considering attitudes on the economy, actual economic circumstances and needs, or opinions on government efforts to assist Blacks or Latinos, the process operates to bias participatory input in the direction of the needs and preferences of the advantaged. Especially significant in producing this outcome is the role of income as a participatory factor that operates consistently to produce distortion toward conservative opinions and the underrepresentation of the needy. Interestingly, in the consistency of its effect in generating distortion, income contrasts with education—a variable with which it is ordinarily paired as an indicator of socioeconomic status. These patterns are especially pronounced when it comes to political giving in contrast to overall activity. For each politically relevant characteristic examined, the total distortion was greater for contributions than for overall activity.

This chapter pointed to another pattern with quite different implications for the meaning of citizen participation democracy. At the same time that the participatory process operates to bias the messages sent through political activity in the direction of the advantaged, it brings into politics a set of activists who are better informed and more tolerant of unpopular opinions. Thus, while the process exacerbates political inequality, it may enhance the quality of political discourse and democratic governance.

The politics of ideals reflects the fact that not all citizen activity is in the pursuit of self-interested objectives. Citizens are also committed to views of what the government should do on matters that are not directly of material self-interest to them.[29] The participatory system as a communicator of such views was illustrated by our analysis of the abortion issue and the way in which commitments on that issue—on either side, but with greater force from the pro-life side—affect what is communicated to the government. The shape of participatory communications, in this case, depends on the nature and intensity of the issue commitment as well as the location of those who are committed in the institutional structures of society.

Finally, we have seen how the participatory process shapes the quality of democratic discourse. In this view, the crucial aspect of democracy is not so much the outcome in terms of how well needs, interests, or passionate ideals are communicated, but the process by which this occurs—a process that should involve well-informed citizens engaged in open discussion.[30] As our analysis shows, the

---

29. The politics of self interest and ideals are, of course, difficult to distinguish at times. Individuals are likely to conflate the two. But it is clear that there is much activity whose goal is some state of society or the world that cannot, in the ordinary use of the term, be considered to be in the narrow self-interest of the activist.

30. The liberal, individualistic approach is associated with various versions of rational choice theory (for which references were given in Chapter 4) as well as with the work of such figures as John Rawls, *A Theory of Justice* (Cambridge, Mass.: Harvard University Press, 1971). The argument for a stronger democracy is made most vigorously in Barber, *Strong Democracy*.

participatory process has an effect on the nature of the democratic debate, bringing into politics a set of more informed and more tolerant citizens who are closer to the civic ideal.

Participation, thus, performs many functions: it communicates interests and needs; it communicates citizens' commitments on issues beyond self-interest; and it affects the quality of democratic discourse. How well does it do all three? In communicating the needs of the more affluent few more effectively than those of the rest of society, the participatory process creates a polity far from the ideal of equal consideration for all. In the communication of the non-self-interested commitments of portions of the citizenry, the participatory system is responsive, as it ought to be, to the concerns of the public. Whether the result is thought to be good for democracy may depend on the issue and the observer's own views on it as well as the nature of the discourse and debate that is generated. A politics of passionate commitment is a responsive politics, but it can also be a dangerous and divisive one. Finally, it is interesting to note that the same participatory process that privileges the needs and concerns of the more advantaged members of society also brings in a citizenry that is more informed and tolerant.

17

Conclusion:
Voice and Equality
in Democratic Participation

We stated at the outset that meaningful democratic participation requires that the voices of citizens in politics be clear, loud, and equal: clear so that public officials know what citizens want and need, loud so that officials have an incentive to pay attention to what they hear, and equal so that the democratic ideal of equal responsiveness to the preferences and interests of all is not violated. Our analysis of voluntary activity in American politics suggests that the public's voice is often loud, sometimes clear, but rarely equal.

Participation in America: Lively and Varied

Americans who wish to take part in politics have many participatory options available. They can attempt to affect government policy directly by communicating their wishes or indirectly by influencing who holds public office. They can get involved on the local, state, or national level. They can act on their own or with others. They can engage in forms of activity that require inputs of time or forms that require inputs of money.

Participation in America can be loud. If they are active beyond voting, activists can multiply the volume of their activity by participating in several different ways or by increasing their investment of time or money—attending more than one demonstration,

509

making several contacts with public officials, devoting substantial time to an electoral campaign or community effort, or writing bigger checks.

The voices of activists can be clear. Although the vote is singularly ill-suited for conveying precise instructions to policymakers, citizens engage in many kinds of participation that permit them to send clear messages to governing officials. Collectively, those messages encompass a dazzling number of issues and contradictory preferences. Nevertheless, the individual who chooses to become involved in any of a number of information-rich activities has the opportunity to speak in detail.

The participatory system also appears to be open. Significant legal barriers to the equal participation of all citizens were lowered during the 1960s. Although non-citizens are not permitted to vote, of course, we found little evidence that legal impediments impede political action. Furthermore, although there is anecdotal and case study evidence to the contrary, we did not find evidence of abstention resulting from fear. When asked, those who refrain from politics cited many reasons for their inactivity, but few indicated that they thought political participation would get them into trouble.

Beyond the absence of barriers created by law or intimidation, the system appears to be open to citizens who become excited about one issue or another. Those whose life circumstances create a stake in some policy or whose values and beliefs lead to engagement on some issue can and do become active on that subject. Activity may depend in large part on resources, generalized political engagement, and recruitment—the participatory factors at the heart of our Civic Voluntarism Model—but the citizen who becomes aroused will often speak up beyond what those factors would predict.

In short, participation in America is lively and varied. Public opinion studies have documented an increase in the number of citizens who believe that the government is out of touch and unresponsive.[1] Still, citizens seem not to have given up on participa-

---

1. For a good overview of the data on the decline of confidence in government, see Stephen C. Craig, *The Malevolent Leaders: Popular Discontent in America* (Boulder, Colo.: Westview Press, 1993), pp. 10–17.

tion. Moreover, as we saw in Chapter 4, active citizens do not deem their participation to be ineffectual: among activists, substantial majorities reported that they received satisfactory replies to their contacts, that the protest they attended made a difference, or that their campaign work swayed at least some votes. Clearly, a survey like ours does not permit us to judge whether activists overstate the efficacy of their participation and, if so, by how much. Many of them may be deluding themselves or seeking to please the interviewer. Nonetheless, for many of the activities we consider, it is entirely plausible to believe that taking part made a difference, especially when we compare these activities to casting a ballot—the political act on which political scientists have focused most often when discussing the ineffectiveness of the individual citizen. Besides, even if citizens overestimate their clout, it is important that they miscalculate on the high rather than the low side. Although citizens may believe that, in general, they have little voice, they do not report feelings of impotence with respect to their own activity. It is often argued that a benign consequence of participation is to bolster the legitimacy of the regime. The way in which the participants surveyed interpret their own experiences as activists substantiates this claim.

An Unequal System

As expressed through political participation, the voices of citizens may be loud and clear, but they are decidedly not equal. The voices of certain people—and people with certain politically relevant characteristics—are more resonant in participatory input. The consequences of unequal participation for what is communicated through political activity are complex and have formed one of the main themes of this volume. Whether participatory inequalities imply distortion in the messages sent to policymakers depends upon both the politically relevant characteristic and the mode of political activity we are considering. We have seen that, in terms of their policy preferences, those who take part are not very different from those who do not. However, when it comes to economic circumstances, needs for government assistance, or participatory agendas—the actual issues that animate activity—the discrepancies are much more substantial. In addition, we have seen the variation across activities in the extent of participatory distortion. Voters are relatively representative of the public. In terms of other forms of participation—acts that can be multiplied in their volume and that have the capacity to communicate more information— distortion in participatory input is more substantial. It is especially pronounced for political contributions. Indeed, when we investigated the extent of participatory distortion for a series of politically relevant characteristics, in each case we found it to be markedly greater for contributions than for other forms of activity.

Because the extent of participatory distortion depends upon the particular political act and the particular politically relevant characteristic in question, it is impossible to assess in the aggregate how biased is the set of messages communicated through citizen participation. The political battles over how votes should be counted make clear that the principle of political equality is not simple even when it comes to voting. However, the matter becomes many times more complicated when we move beyond the aggregation of votes to the aggregation of participatory acts that involve differing volume and various metrics—letters sent, dollars donated, or hours devoted. The complexities increase exponentially when we add consideration of the myriad politically relevant characteristics— preferences on a range of issues, actual circumstances and needs, even demographic characteristics—about which information is conveyed through participation. In short, across the totality of political input it is impossible to specify what one person, one vote would look like.

Nonetheless, whatever the difficulties of establishing a benchmark for aggregate participatory equality, we must recognize a systematic bias in representation through participation. Over and over, our data showed that participatory input is tilted in the direction of the more advantaged groups in society—especially in terms of economic and educational position, but in terms of race and ethnicity as well. The voices of the well-educated and the well-heeled—and, therefore, of those with other politically relevant characteristics that are associated with economic and educational privilege—sound more loudly.

With due allowance for the complexities of measuring aggregate participatory inequality and, therefore, of making comparisons, there is evidence that the situation is exacerbated for politics in America. Inequalities in activity seem to be more pronounced in the United States than in other democracies.[2] Moreover, they seem to be more pronounced with respect to political rather than non-political participation. Our data show that rates of activity of the advantaged and disadvantaged differ least in the religious domain and most when it comes to politics. Since politics is the realm for which democratic norms seem to promise a level playing field, this is a somewhat ironic finding.

THE ROOTS OF POLITICAL ACTIVITY AND POLITICAL INEQUALITY

An important part of our intellectual project has been to go beyond description of the participatory system in America in order to analyze the social forces that shape it. The process that produces participatory inequalities is multi-faceted, with no single factor responsible for the outcomes we have delineated. Moreover, although political factors play an important role in shaping what and from whom the government hears, the overall contours of the participatory process are not an accident of which party is in power or what is on the national agenda.

Political activity is firmly grounded in American social structure; that same social structure is also the prime source of the inequality in activity. The factors that foster participation—resources, generalized political engagements, and recruitment—are acquired in the basic institutions of society: families, schools, jobs, voluntary associations, and churches. The constrained choices individuals make about the way to engage these institutions have implications for their bundles of participatory resources. Depending upon the level of their educational attainment, the extent of their commitment to the labor force and the kinds of jobs they hold, the number and kinds of organizations with which they get involved, the kinds of churches they attend and the level of activity in ancillary educational, charitable, and social activities within those churches, individuals stockpile different amounts and different mixes of par-

---

2. See Sidney Verba, Norman H. Nie, and Jae-on Kim, *Participation and Political Equality: A Seven Nation Comparison* (Cambridge: Cambridge University Press, 1978), especially chap. 4.

ticipatory resources. The process is in many ways cumulative. Those with greater resources at the outset collect more as their resource endowments allow them to move into institutional positions conducive to further resource acquisition. The same processes create political engagement and place individuals in recruitment networks.

THE SPECIAL ROLE OF EDUCATION

Education is central to this sequence. Circumstances of initial privilege have consequences for educational attainment which, in turn, has consequences for the acquisition of nearly every other participatory factor: income earned on the job; skills acquired at work, in organizations, and, to a lesser extent, in church; psychological engagement with politics; exposure to requests for activity. We have been able to trace these processes, demonstrating the impact of family of origin on educational attainment and the ramifications of educational attainment throughout adulthood. Educational attainment has implications not only for the kinds of resources individuals accumulate but also for the kinds of citizens they become. Educated citizens are much more likely to be informed about politics and tolerant of unpopular opinions.

Analysts of the American educational system characterize its contributions to American society in several ways. Some stress its role in producing a skilled and competent work force. Others focus on its contribution to the creation of a citizenry committed to the ideals of democracy. For still others, of a more critical posture, it is a means of reproducing social stratification from one generation to the next. Our analysis makes clear that education functions in each of these ways: training workers, preparing citizens, and transmitting social class across generations. And in all three capacities—not only in transmitting social class—educational differences beget participatory inequalities.

Time, Money, and Inequality

A recurring theme in our investigation of the participatory process has been the contrast between time and money and the relationship between these forms of input and participatory inequality. Time and money figure in complex ways in our analysis. First, one or the other is essential for every form of activity. Each of the many participatory options available to citizens in America requires at least some time or some money. As the two essential media of participatory input, time and money thus both become resources for participation.

However, as resources for participation, time and money differ in significant ways. First, unlike time, money is a politically relevant characteristic—the over- or underrepresentation of which has potential political consequences—as well as being among the factors that foster participation. We have pointed out many times that politics in the United States and elsewhere frequently involves conflict between the more and less economically advantaged. It does not, in contrast, involve conflict between the harried and the leisured. Moreover, affluence is related to other politically relevant characteristics—for example, gender, race, and ethnicity—in a way that leisure is not. Time and money also differ in their distribution in ways that have implications for the way they operate as resources for participation. With due allowance for the difference in metrics between hours and dollars, time is less unevenly distributed among individuals than is money. Because each of us has no more than twenty-four hours in a day and because free time cannot be placed in the bank where it can draw interest until it is needed, compared with the poorest person, the richest in terms of time is not nearly as well off as the richest in terms of money.

Finally, time and money also differ in their relationship to participation. As we saw in Chapter 12, available free time is a much less potent predictor of activity that entails giving time than is family income in relationship to activity that entails giving money. Put another way, this means that time and money differ in the extent to which their absence constrains the ability to take part. There may be truth to the adage that if you want something done, ask a busy citizen. However, our analysis demonstrates the absurdity of applying this logic to political money. If you want a contribution, you should most definitely not ask a poor person.

CONTRIBUTING AS A POLITICAL ACTIVITY

In short, money has distinctive characteristics as a resource for activity: it is itself an attribute relevant for political conflict; it is unevenly distributed; and it is strongly related to the ability to make political contributions. Taken together, these characteristics of money as a political resource are responsible for the fact that making political contributions is singular as a form of participation. In the first chapter, we introduced the concept that the vote—a mode of political action on which political scientists, for good reason, have lavished a good deal of attention—is atypical among political acts. Our analysis has borne out that contention. However, it has also shown that donating money to political campaigns and causes is in many ways exceptional as a mode of participation.

One way in which contributing is distinctive is that it is, in spite of federal and state regulations, the single form of participation for which the volume of input varies most substantially among activists. We have pointed out many times that the vote is the only kind of activity for which there is mandated equality among those who take part. All other forms of participation permit an activist who has the will and the wherewithal to increase the amount of participatory input. Making contributions is at the other end of the continuum with respect to this dimension, the act for which those who do anything at all differ most in how much they do.

Making financial contributions is also unusual in the configuration of participatory factors that predict it. Whether we consider the predictors of overall political activity or a particular political act such as voting, many factors matter, and one that consistently matters a great deal is political interest. When it comes to making contributions, however, the pattern is very different. A single factor, family income, is overwhelming, and the effect of political interest, while statistically significant, is dwarfed by the impact of family income. This means that political contributions originate very disproportionately from the very well-off and that, in comparison to other activist publics, contributors are not especially interested in politics. Not only are the poor very substantially underrepresented when it comes to contributions, but even middle-income groups donate substantially less to politics than would be expected on the basis of their share of the population.

The variability of the volume of dollars given to politics, the strength of the single factor of family income in predicting contributions, and the association between family income and other politically relevant characteristics such as policy preferences, economic needs, or race work in concert to produce a circumstance such that participatory distortion is more pronounced for making contributions than for other kinds of activity. Across a variety of politically relevant characteristics examined in Chapter 16, we saw over and over that the representation of citizen attributes was less accurate through contributions than through overall participation. To the extent that our focus on participatory inequality derives from a concern with its implications for the democratic promise of equal responsiveness to all citizens, what this means is that a more skewed set of implicit and explicit messages is sent through participation when the medium is money than when the medium is time. Thus, with respect to those aspects of an activity that speak most directly to issues of participatory representation, making financial contributions presents the greatest challenge.

Making contributions is exceptional among political acts in other ways as well. For example, as we saw in Chapter 5, patterns of recruitment are unusual for contributors. Compared with requests for any other kind of activity, requests for donations are more common; they are more likely to come from strangers; and they are less likely to be met with assent. In addition, as an activity, making contributions is singular in terms of its meaning to activists. We saw in Chapter 4 that this is not an especially satisfying way to take part. When we discussed the gratifications attendant to various forms of voluntary activity, we noted that activities undertaken alone seem to provide fewer benefits than those undertaken in the company of others and that modes of participation requiring an input of time furnish greater benefits than those in which the investment is money. Although the particular mix of gratifications from contributing depends upon the beneficiary—a candidate or a political issue, party, or work-related organization—making contributions is not an especially rewarding way to take part. In addition, contributors are the exception to the overall tendency for activists to feel effective. They are less likely than those who engage in other forms of participation to think that their activity made much difference. Only a third of the campaign contributors indicated that their contributions affected some voters, and less than 4 percent indicated that their donations affected many voters. In contrast, of those who gave time rather than money to a campaign, three-quarters indicated that their campaign work swayed some votes and 16 percent that their work swayed a large number of voters.

In an oft-cited observation, the late Jesse Unruh, once Speaker of the California Assembly, called money "the mother's milk of politics." Our data seem to tell another story. From the point of view of the citizen rather than the politician, making contributions is, for those with the requisite resources, more like the junk food of participation, a relatively easy form of involvement that provides a certain number of empty participatory calories but relatively little in the way of lasting nutrition.

All of these findings about the ways in which contributing is distinctive as a form of activity gain resonance when viewed in the context of the longitudinal studies of participation reviewed in Chapter 3. We discussed the fact that there is disagreement as to whether, along with turnout, other forms of participation have declined over the past generation. Whatever puzzles there may be concerning the trajectory of participation over the past few decades, there was an unambiguous increase in the amount of money donated to politics over the period from the early 1970s to the late 1980s. What this means is that the mode of participation that has increased most substantially not only is the one that is most skewed in its origins and most distorting in its outcomes, but is one that provides activists with relatively few gratifications. These are findings with implications for participatory practice.

Religious Institutions and Participatory Equality

The effect of most of the social structural factors in our analysis is to overrepresent the advantaged in participatory input. This process is most evident with respect to the role of family income in making contributions. It is also apparent in the multiple paths through which education enhances activity: those with high levels of education are likely to get jobs that pay well and provide opportunities for the exercise of civic skills; to affiliate with organizations and to practice skills in that context as well; and to be interested in and informed about politics. Since parents' educational attainment has a significant impact on that of their off-spring, the process by which participatory factors are accumulated stretches across the generations. Thus, a series of processes operate to reinforce one another in producing unequal participatory outcomes.

Our analysis has, however, turned up certain examples of contrary tendencies that operate systematically to bring into politics those who are less advantaged. We saw, for example, that community attachment can play a limited equalizing role. Those who have long resided in the community tend to be more active in local politics. Since those who are locally rooted tend, on average, not to have well-educated parents and not to be especially well educated themselves, this process can act as a slight counterbalance to the overwhelming weight of socioeconomic status.

Religious institutions play a much more important role in potentially enriching the stockpile of participatory factors for those who are otherwise disadvantaged. Like other non-political institutions of adult life, churches provide exposure to requests for political activity and—in the context of activities with no demonstrable political content whatsoever—opportunities for the development of skills that are transferable to politics. We have seen that the workplace is particularly rich in opportunities for the development of skills. However, skill opportunities at work accrue disproportionately to those in jobs requiring high levels of education or on-the-job training. In contrast, opportunities for the exercise of skills are apportioned much more democratically in church, with the result that someone with a job demanding minimal training who is religiously active is likely to have more chance to develop skills at church than on the job. Thus, because churches serve as a locus for attempts at citizen recruitment to politics and provide chances to practice politically relevant skills, religious activity has the potential to act as a compensatory factor for participation, partially offsetting the impact of socioeconomic advantage.

RELIGIOUS INSTITUTIONS AND AMERICAN EXCEPTIONALISM

The significance of religious institutions for our analysis of political participation goes beyond the relatively egalitarian way they function in providing a site for political recruitment and the development of civic skills. We have seen evidence from several perspectives of the depth of the religious commitments of contemporary Americans. Americans give more of themselves—devote more time, energy, and money—to religious activity than to either secular non-political or political activity. Moreover, their involvement in religious institutions sets Americans apart from citizens of many other developed democracies. This can be viewed as another way in which American politics and society are distinctive, and it dovetails with other aspects of American exceptionalism—in particular, the traditional weakness of American unions, their failure to enroll a large share of American workers, and the further attenuation of their membership and power over the past two decades.

The unusual institutional configuration characteristic of American society has important consequences for the outcomes with which we are concerned.[3] We have argued that the civic skills developed in the non-political institutions of adult life are more or less fungible. That is, they function similarly in facilitating political activity no matter in which venue they were developed. From this perspective the strength of religious institutions compensates for the weakness of labor unions. We saw in Chapter 13 that a blue-collar worker is more likely to practice civic skills in church than in a union—not because American unions are particularly deficient as skill-builders, but because so few American blue-collar workers are union members and so many are church members. In short, if the less advantaged are not developing skills on the job (as the well-educated do) or in unions (as blue-collar workers elsewhere might), they may be doing so in church. Hence, because churches can pinch-hit for unions in providing skills, we might conclude that the weakness of American unions has no implications for the representation of the needs and preferences of the less well-off in American politics.

Nonetheless, there is an additional perspective that must be considered. Churches and unions are not simply politically neutral

---

3. E. E. Schattschneider captures the way in which particular configurations of institutions can have an impact upon the representation of interests and, thus, political outcomes in the concept of the "mobilization of bias" in *The Semisovereign People* (New York: Holt, Rinehart and Winston, 1960), chap. 2.

developers of skills; they are institutions with political concerns of their own. It has long been a part of the union mission to represent the less advantaged in the halls of government.[4] Although religious institutions sometimes take on this function—the Catholic Church, for example, often acts as an advocate for the poor[5]—the economic needs of the less well-off rarely top their lists of political priorities. Thus, when a church makes institutionally based attempts to mobilize the flock for political action, or when it gets involved directly in politics, the policy matter at stake is relatively unlikely to be an economic agenda focused on the less advantaged. Over the years churches in America have embraced many issues ranging from temperance to civil rights. At this juncture religious institutions are active on behalf of a wide range of issues and diverse points of view. However, the center of gravity of the religious agenda in politics is a conservative concern with social issues, with a particular focus on advocacy of pro-life views on abortion. Indeed, as we saw in Chapter 16, the weight of religious factors in stimulating participation is to distort citizen activity on abortion in a pro-life direction. While the particular issue bias generated by religious institutions is not inevitable and is likely to continue to change over time, churches are unlikely to substitute for unions in bringing the economic needs and preferences of the less advantaged to the attention of public officials.

Issue Engagements: The Wild Card of Participatory Inequality

The Civic Voluntarism Model encompasses a variety of factors that are enduring aspects of American society. Although we have noted that community attachment and religious engagement act as a partial counterbalance, most of these ongoing factors operate to exacerbate participatory inequalities and to mute the voices of

4. To give but one example, Theodore J. Lowi points to the importance of unions in the frozen coalition that materializes over and over in support of liberal positions on redistributive issues in "Distribution, Regulation, and Redistribution: The Functions of Government," *World Politics* 16 (1964): 677–715.

5. See Allen D. Hertzke, *Representing God in Washington: The Role of Religious Lobbies in the American Polity* (Knoxville: University of Tennessee Press, 1988), pp. 36–37.

the disadvantaged. In addition to the long-term components of the model, however, there are short-term factors: issue engagements that derive from having a stake in a particular policy or strong views on a particular issue. As we saw in Chapter 14, issue engagements stimulate political activity beyond the workings of the Civic Voluntarism Model.

In contrast to the more or less standing decision embodied by the Civic Voluntarism Model, issue engagements constitute a wild card with respect to their impact on participatory stratification. Their consequences for the representation of publics otherwise not well represented through participation are not fixed and stable. It depends upon whom the issue engages. The examples of issue-engaged publics that we reviewed in Chapter 14 present hybrid results. Of those mobilized by their stake in government policy to activity beyond what we would expect on the basis of the continuing factors encompassed by the Civic Voluntarism Model, parents of school-aged children are a relatively privileged group and recipients of means-tested government benefits are most definitely not. As for an issue engagement growing out of a strong commitment on the issue of abortion, the results are similarly mixed. Strong views on either side of the issue of abortion tend to raise activity, with pro-life views having particular force. In contrast to those on the pro-choice side of the spectrum, those on the pro-life side tend to be less advantaged when it comes to the resources that foster participation.

As issues come and go, they mobilize to politics different issue publics. Because the issues that engender issue engagements are many and transitory, it is impossible to assess their net effect in reinforcing or counteracting the unambiguous impact of the structural factors in the Civic Voluntarism Model in creating participatory distortion. Nevertheless, the additional boost given to activity by an issue engagement is a small increment to a level of activity shaped more fundamentally by long-term factors.

Race, Ethnicity, Class, and Participation

Our concern with the representation of politically relevant characteristics in participatory input has led us to a concern with race and ethnicity. Our analysis has shown that a pattern long known for African-Americans obtains for Latinos as well. Both groups, but especially Latinos, are less active in politics than Anglo-Whites. However, when the factors that foster participation are taken into account, the differences disappear. Thus, neither being Black nor being Latino itself reduces participation. Rather, it is the fact that both groups are less well endowed with the factors that foster participation that is responsible for the participation gap on the basis of race and ethnicity. Principal among these factors is the elaborated cluster that is associated with socioeconomic status: education, family income, and skills exercised on the job and in organizations. As is well known, class differences between groups result in disparities in participation.

We cannot conclude our explanation of the association between race or ethnicity and participation simply with a consideration of socioeconomic differences. Being Black or being Latino is connected to other characteristics—of which religion is the most important example—that affect participation. We saw that Latinos— a mostly Catholic group, in spite of significant recent defections to evangelical Protestant churches—are relatively unlikely to have the chance to develop civic skills in the context of church activity. African-Americans, in contrast, are affiliated with Protestant churches that are especially rich in opportunities for the development of civic skills. This religious difference—which we attributed to structural differences between Protestant and Catholic congregations—widens the class-based deficit in activity still further for Latinos. The addition of church-based factors broadens our understanding of disparities in activity between groups based on race or ethnicity by incorporating a participatory factor that is not grounded in class differences. Moreover, this is a factor that is related to ethnic or racial identity. The religious experiences of these groups contribute significantly to what it means to be Black or Latino in America.

The meaning of the participation gap between Anglo-Whites, on one hand, and African-Americans and, especially, Latinos, on the other, does not end with the understanding that these differences stem not from race or ethnicity per se but from participatory factors, most of which are rooted in class differences. Just as important as recognizing that inequalities in activity are not a function of being Black or being Latino is the *fact* of those inequalities. In Chapter 6 we made the argument that public officials are aware of who is paying attention to what they do and, therefore, that our understanding of politically relevant attributes must encompass demographic characteristics, particularly characteristics woven as deeply in the American political fabric as race or ethnicity. We have seen in Chapter 8 that these are groups with distinctive political preferences and participatory agendas: they differ in their opinions on public matters, and, when they are active, they are concerned with a different mix of issues. Hence, it makes a difference if participatory messages to policymakers underrepresent input from African-Americans and Latinos. Since these are minorities in the first place, their participatory underrepresentation becomes that much more important. In short, finding the roots of the differences in activity between Anglo-Whites and African-Americans or Latinos in characteristics other than race or ethnicity does not vitiate the political significance of those participatory differences.

Resources, Rational Choices, and the SES Model

By providing a general interpretation of the way in which resources, political engagements, and recruitment operate to foster participation, the Civic Voluntarism Model is relevant not only to the nature of American politics but also to the theory of political participation. As we discussed in Chapter 9, the two dominant academic approaches to understanding participation are rational choice theory and the SES model. It is not an accident that the former is called a "theory" and the latter a "model." Rational choice theory rests on the cost-benefit calculations made by a potential activist. Its strength is its deductive elegance. Its weaknesses are empirical and political. It predicts that few people will be active when, in fact, many are. And, by treating individuals as more or less interchangeable units differing only in their tastes, it makes few interesting predictions as to which ones will be active; therefore it is irrelevant to a question about participation with significant political implications: whose voice is loud and clear in politics?

The SES model, in turn, makes empirical predictions of unambiguous power and political relevance; nevertheless, its theoretical underpinnings are weak. Among the most reliable generalizations in political science—verified over the years for many polities—is that those high on the socioeconomic scale are more active in politics. The fact that the better-off are more active has important political implications for the messages sent to policymakers through participation and, thus, for who benefits from government policy. However, the SES model lacks a solid theoretical interpretation as to why those high on the socioeconomic scale are so unambiguously overrepresented in participatory input.

Our emphasis on resource constraints—that is, on the cost side of the cost-benefit calculation—helps to compensate for the shortcomings of both approaches, improving the predictive capacities and enhancing the political relevance of rational choice theory and buttressing the theoretical power of the SES model. Empirical studies of participation in the rational choice tradition have typically looked at the benefits accruing to activists and drawn the sometimes tautological inference that, if there is activity, there must be sufficient benefits to justify the effort. By taking seriously the costs of participation and taking into account how resource differences among individuals constrain their ability to meet these costs, we render the rational choice perspective predictive of a stratified pattern of political activity.

By specifying the factors that facilitate participation and showing how those factors relate to one another, the Civic Voluntarism Model provides an explanation as to why those with high socioeconomic status are more politically active and, thus, fortifies the SES model theoretically. In pursuing this theme we have detailed the mechanisms by which SES is translated into participation—not simply for overall activity but for particular modes of involvement. We have demonstrated that what is true for voting cannot be generalized to other forms of activity. Similarly, a unique configuration of factors—actually, a single factor, family income—predicts financial contributions to politics. We have noted the central position of educational attainment in the participatory process and traced its influence on multiple factors that foster activity including income, civic skills acquired at work, in non-political organizations, and at church, and political interest. By specifying how the components of socioeconomic status operate to enhance various forms of participation, we made clear that education and income are not simply interchangeable: the narrow and powerful effect of income on political contributions contrasts sharply with the broader role of education.

Participation and Democratic Governance

What is the meaning of what we have found for how we are governed? Any understanding of the role of participation in democracy must begin with an understanding that public officials act for many reasons, only one of which is their assessment of the state of what the public wants and needs. And, although the information communicated to them through the medium of participatory input is biased in systematic ways, policymakers have other ways of learning about what citizens want and need from government. They can, for example, pay attention to the media or they can monitor public opinion polls. Polls have the advantage that, if carefully constructed, they convey a representative slice of opinion. However, the survey respondent is confronted with a pre-selected menu of issues framed in pre-digested terms. In contrast, participatory input—at least the forms that permit the communication of relatively precise messages—allows citizens to indicate their priorities and to state their views in their own terms. Besides, as discussed in Chapter 1, the few systematic studies that exist buttress the conclusion that emerges from case studies and journalistic accounts, that what policymakers hear from citizens influences what they do. In short, participation matters and, therefore, unequal participation matters.

UNINTERESTED OR UNABLE?
What if those who are mute are opting out by virtue of their lack of interest rather than being kept out by virtue of their lack of resources? There is evidence that the political quiescence of the disadvantaged represents a choice. We saw in Chapter 12 that those with low levels of education and family income express less interest in politics and less taste for political discussion. In addition, like their better-heeled and better-educated counterparts, they

devote more in the way of time, energy, and money to religious activity than to political activity. However, in the case of the disadvantaged the gap between what is rendered unto politics and what is rendered unto religion is especially pronounced. Hence, we might conclude that the disadvantaged prefer to devote their resources to church rather than to political pursuits and that we do not need to worry about their underrepresentation in citizen participation. Viewing the participatory inequalities as the result of choice rather than resource constraint might alter the meaning we give to them.

This interpretation is, of course, compatible with findings about lower levels of political interest among the less well-off. However, it needs to be placed in the context of certain other findings. First, we saw in Chapter 15 (Table 15.4) that political interest is, unlike an individual's preference for chocolate or vanilla, not simply a matter of taste. Instead, along with other measures of political engagement such as political information and efficacy, political interest derives from the same process we have been describing and is deeply influenced by the same socioeconomic factors—in particular, education—that produce participation. Therefore, if the less advantaged are less interested in politics, or are otherwise less politically engaged, these predispositions reflect resources as well as choice. Furthermore, political interest or engagement can go only so far in overcoming resource deficits. We saw in Chapter 12 (Figure 12.1) that, among activists who are politically interested and efficacious, there is no systematic relationship between family income and the average number of hours devoted to campaign activity. However, campaign giving among engaged activists is highly stratified by income, with the most affluent givers contributing, on average, nearly fifteen times what the least affluent donate and more than three times what those in the next most affluent group donate. Thus, the ability to take part, especially when it comes to making donations, is related to much more than political interest.

We must also recall a quite different perspective on these matters. We saw in Chapter 6 that, when it comes to politics, Americans do not subscribe to a "just desserts" understanding of inequality. That is, in the economic domain, Americans construe unequal rewards as fair returns to the talented and industrious. In politics, however, the expectation shows greater deference to equality of results. Surveys show overwhelming support for the idea of equal government responsiveness to all citizens. According to this point of view, the principles of democracy dictate that no one should be ignored; even if all differences in participation were volitional—and, clearly, they are not—unequal treatment by government would not be justified. In short, if the ultimate concern is equal governmental treatment of all, it is possible to treat as a red herring the issue of whether the underrepresentation of the disadvantaged in participatory input represents the exercise of free choice.

PARTICIPATION AND THE COMMON GOOD

Implicit in our investigation have been alternative understandings of the meaning of citizen participation in a democracy. In one conception of democracy, politics is the arena for the working out of the self-interested claims of citizens. According to this view of the meaning of democracy, participatory inequalities matter because they jeopardize equal protection of interests. Our findings about participatory distortion along the major fault lines of political conflict in America—class, race, social issues—suggest that the participatory system does a very imperfect job of representing the politically relevant characteristics of citizens.

There is another conception of democracy embedded in our discussion for which our findings are germane. According to this vision, a democracy in which self-interested citizens compete for benefits is inadequate. In a fuller participatory democracy, political activity becomes a mechanism whereby citizens engage in enlightened discourse, come to understand the views of others, and become sensitized to the needs of the community and nation. Thus educated, they transcend their own interests to seek the public good.

Few concepts are as fraught with the possibilities for misinterpretation as the "common good," and we would not presume to assess the extent to which the participatory system as discussed here achieves something that might be characterized as the common good. Even when the public good is conceived as something more than the summation of individual preferences, there are competing conceptions of the good of all. Nevertheless, some of our findings are relevant to this understanding of democracy. In discussing the reasons they became active, participants make clear—to an extent we found surprising—that they think of themselves as acting for the common good. This does not mean that they do not also use their participation as a vehicle for furthering their own narrow interests or, to make the analytical task more complicated, that they do not sometimes construe what is good for themselves as being good for the country. Still, in a cynical era in which self-interested rhetoric is the norm, we were impressed with the level of respondents' concern for the common good and the extent to which they believed their activity to be motivated by it.

From the point of view of a concern with participatory democracy, it is worth noting that the same education-driven process that operates to overrepresent the advantaged among activists also works to bring into politics participants who are better informed and more tolerant of unpopular opinions. Thus, at the same time that the well-educated have politically relevant characteristics that distinguish them from their less well educated—and less active—compatriots, they also have characteristics that make them conform to participatory democratic notions of the good citizen. And a participatory system that overrepresents their interests also overrepresents the politically informed and tolerant.

A participatory democratic perspective might take the point one step further, however. A participatory system in which the effect of education is to draw in as activists those who are politically informed and tolerant may deprive those with fewer financial and educational advantages of the developmental opportunities that accompany participation. To the extent that participation creates democratic citizens by fostering political learning, interest, and tolerance, the gains in terms of democratic civility from a participatory system that is biased in favor of the privileged may be overstated.

PARTICIPATION AND DEMOCRATIC MALAISE

We live in an era of widespread political dissatisfaction. Democratic malaise—skepticism about what government can accomplish and distrust of politicians—is a theme often remarked by journalists and confirmed by public opinion polls and electoral returns. Clearly, this citizen orientation is not our principal concern. Still, we were led to query how what we have learned about citizen participation fits together with this tendency.

Citizens complain that politicians are out of touch and unresponsive. And they complain that politicians are unfair, paying attention to some parts of the public—especially, to special interests—rather than to ordinary folks. In short, they complain of inadequate voice and unequal voice. Unfortunately, these two ideals—effective voice and equal voice—do not necessarily reinforce each other. Indeed, there may be a tradeoff between them. The mode of participation for which participatory input approaches equality is, of course, voting. More citizens vote than engage in any other political act; unlike all other kinds of activists, voters are limited in terms of how many votes they can cast; and the electorate is the activist public that is most representative of the population at large. However, from the perspective of the individual voter, going to the polls is the least effective way to take part. As we have said many times, the vote is singularly limited in its ability to communicate detailed information about needs and preferences. While electoral outcomes can have substantial effects on policy, the individual voter almost never makes a difference. It would not matter if the voter had stayed home. We have seen that, with the exception of contributors, those who engage in relatively demanding forms of activity—who, for example, contact public officials or attend protests—feel that their participation makes a difference. Yet, in comparison with voting, participatory input from other acts—acts that are capable of being multiplied in volume and conveying more information—is much less equally distributed. In short, stronger citizen voices may imply less equal citizen voices.

Our data touch on the theme of democratic malaise in another respect as well. One of the political puzzles of our age is why substantial increases in the principal factor that drives political participation, education, have not yielded commensurate increases in participation. Electoral turnout has, of course, unambiguously declined over the past few decades. It is customary to explain this trend in terms of voter alienation. That is, counteracting the effects of rising levels of education and other changes such as less stringent residency requirements is the overwhelming impact of distrust and cynicism. Thus, democratic malaise is seen to be a factor with massive consequences for citizen participation.

Our evidence suggests that it might be useful to turn this formulation on its head by speculating that recent developments with respect to participation also have implications for citizen dissatisfaction. Although longitudinal data do not tell an unambiguous story about the changing frequency of various forms of participation, it seems clear that making financial contributions has assumed greater prominence in the mix of citizen activities. Among activities, contributing is far from the most rewarding; compared with other activists, contributors garner relatively few gratifications, especially of a social sort, and are less likely to feel that what they did had an impact. Thus, the activity that has gained in significance is one that is relatively unlikely to leave activists feeling satisfied.

At the same time, the increasing importance of contributing as a form of participation is likely to feed public dissatisfaction with politics. To the extent that, other than going to the polls, all forms of activity can be construed as forms of multiple voting, Americans are much more skeptical about participatory inequalities that are rooted in money than about those that are rooted in time. As we pointed out in the first chapter, nobody complains that it is unfair if the candidate who fields the most, or the most active and effective, campaign workers wins the election. And nobody worries that victorious candidates will be captured by their volunteers, adjusting their comportment in office to the wishes of the workers who made the campaign tick. However, we hear these concerns about financial contributions all the time: that money buys elections and money buys public officials. Whatever the legitimacy of these concerns—and scholars differ in their assessments—there is no doubt that the public is cynical about the growth in campaign spending. In short, a participatory system in which money plays a more prominent role is one unlikely to leave either activists or the citizenry at large feeling better about politics.

These considerations suggest that the extensive journalistic and scholarly debate surrounding political finance should be broadened to encompass additional issues. The controversy involving the use of money in politics engages a variety of normative concerns ranging from whether the process as currently constituted gives too much power to special interests, whether it costs too much, and whether it confers an undue advantage upon incumbents. The debate is rarely framed in terms of the extent to which a money-based politics contributes to skepticism about politics among citizens or undermines the ability of the less well heeled to take part on an equal footing with those who are better off and thus jeopardizes equal protection of interests. Our discussion suggests that these issues are relevant to the discourse surrounding political finance.

The Future of Participatory Equality

In comparison with other democracies, political conflict in America has traditionally been less deeply imbued with the rhetoric of class. In recent years, however, references to class seem to have become even less common in our political vocabulary than at any time since the New Deal, a circumstance that we could, speculatively, attribute to a number of developments over the past decade or two: the success of the Republican Party in defining itself as the party of the common folk; the erosion of the membership and power of labor unions; the emphasis upon multiculturalism; the declining appeal of Marxist social analysis as an intellectual tool; and changing occupational structures and the concomitant reduction in manufacturing employment. Nevertheless, the argument in this volume makes clear that, despite the absence of references to class in our political discourse, when it comes to political participation, class matters profoundly for American politics.

The fact that data over a two-decade period show the relationship between education and activity to be virtually unchanged in strength suggests that the long-term structural aspect of the Civic Voluntarism Model is unlikely to lose its relevance. To the extent that patterns of participation—whose voice is heard and whose voice is muted—are based in fundamental institutions of American society, the overall contours of American political activity are not likely to change rapidly. The society as a whole may become better educated or more affluent. However, so long as inequalities in education and income persist—and income inequality in America has become more pronounced of late—so long as jobs continue to distribute opportunities to practice civic skills in a stratified manner, then individuals will continue to command stockpiles of participatory factors of very different sizes and, thus, to participate at very different rates.

These features define the banks through which participation is channeled. What flows through will be determined by more proximate political factors ranging from the emergence of new issues to the strategic calculations of political elites. With changing issues and circumstances will come new issue publics, not all of them privileged. Nonetheless, because political participation is so deeply rooted in the essential structures of American society, we can expect that the voices heard through the medium of citizen participation will be often loud, sometimes clear, but rarely equal.

Citizen Participation Sample

Our data come from a two-stage survey of the voluntary activity of the American public. The first stage consisted of 15,053 telephone interviews of adult (18 years or older) Americans conducted by the Public Opinion Laboratory of Northern Illinois University and the National Opinion Research Center (NORC) during the last six months of 1989. These short telephone interviews were between 15 and 20 minutes in length, and they provided a profile of political and non-political activity, as well as basic demographic information. At this stage respondents were selected randomly from phone exchanges matched to the primary sampling units of the NORC national, in-person sampling frame. This clustered phone sample was designed to be representative of the American population. Within each household, adults were chosen at random using a Kish table.

To select respondents for a second stage of in-person interviews, the sample of 15,053 was first reweighted to adjust for the fact that the screener had yielded a slightly disproportionate share of women. The sample was then stratified by race and ethnicity (Black, Latino, and "all other") and by level and type of political participation. Blacks, Latinos, and political activists were oversampled, with weights ranging from 1 for the inactive Anglo-Whites to 16 for highly active Latinos. In the spring of 1990, NORC conducted in-person interviews of an average length of almost two hours each with 2,517 of the original 15,053 respondents. Most of the data used in the book come from the longer in-person reinterview, but at times we have used the data from the initial telephone survey. The data from the telephone survey and the follow-up in-person reinterview have been deposited at the Interuniversity Consortium for Political and Social Research at the University of Michigan. A codebook is available for each survey along with extensive information on sampling and other technical matters.

Throughout the book, we refer to tests for statistical significance. In the analysis of a complex stratified survey like the in-person follow-up, the correct methods for statistical inferences depend not only upon the weights used to construct the sample but also upon the specific statistical technique used, the population considered, and the question being asked. We explored the possibility of using complex statistical procedures[1] that have been developed to deal with these problems, but we came to the conclusion that a simpler approach would be adequate for our needs. For most of our analyses, we have been concerned with the entire adult population of the United States or with subgroups within the population. For these situations, we have reweighted our sample to make it representative of the entire population by using the reciprocal of the initial sampling weights and by setting the effective sample size to the number of interviews, 2,517. This is a standard approach with complex datasets. Reweighting by the reciprocal of the sampling weights ensures statistically unbiased estimates of means, regression coefficients, and other standard statistics. Setting the sample size to the number of interviews and then calculating standard errors as if the sample were a simple random sample has been shown by Kish and Frankel[2] and many others to produce reasonable standard errors for typical analytical techniques.

A very conservative lower bound on the actual standard errors can be computed by taking the simple random sample obtained from our data after dropping from each oversampled stratum the "extra" cases that come from oversampling. When we do this, we have a simple random sample of about 1,000 embedded within our larger sample. The standard errors for this sample would be 1.59 (or the square root of 2,517 divided by 1,000) larger than what we estimate. This is an exceptionally conservative estimate because it throws away all the information from the 1,517 remaining cases in the oversampled strata. This is clearly a foolish waste of information, but it is especially foolhardy when a sample was designed to increase statistical power by oversampling the groups of interest.

In fact, for many of the subgroups that we examine, such as samples of activists or minorities, we have effective samples that are at least several times *greater* than the numbers obtained when we reweight to produce a representative sample. For Latinos, for example, our reweighted sample appears to have 141 respondents, but we actually interviewed 375 Latinos, and our effective sample size using the exceptionally conservative method described above is around 350 cases—about two and one-half times the number in our reweighted sample. We have undertaken numerous calculations like these and have come to the conclusion that the standard procedure suggested by Kish and Frankel provides a reasonable and accurate approach to calculating standard errors.

Notes

1. An extensive discussion of these matters is in C. J. Skinner, D. Holt, and T. M. F. Smith, *Analysis of Complex Surveys* (New York: John Wiley and Sons, 1989).

2. Leslie Kish and Martin Frankel, "Inference from Complex Samples (with Discussion)," *Journal of the Royal Statistical Society* (1974), B36, 1–37.

Questions and Variables

The following Appendix contains the actual question wording for the variables used in the book. It also contains descriptions of constructed variables. The Appendix also contains discussions of the decisions made in constructing variables. Full information on interviewer instructions or on coding categories is not included, nor are the codes for the constructed variables. Fuller documentation, including the computer code used to construct variables, is available from the authors.

In cases where a variable is used as a basic categorization in a table or figure, we provide the frequencies. The frequencies are for the weighted sample—except for cases where unweighted frequencies are suitable, in which case we supply both. (See Appendix A for a discussion.) Other frequencies can usually be calculated from information on tables and figures. The full data are available from the Interuniversity Consortium for Political and Social Research of the University of Michigan.

Actual question wordings are in italics.

1. Political Activity

1.A: VOTING

In the additive scale of overall political activity and in the descriptive analyses of characteristics of voters, a voter is defined as someone who voted in the 1988 presidential election. A Vote Scale is used as a dependent variable in regression. It is constructed by adding the questions on national and local elections, with each question given a value of 0 through 4 (0 = never, 4 = all). The scale runs from 0 to 8.

Are you currently registered to vote?

In talking to people about elections, we find that they are sometimes not able to vote because they're not registered, they don't have time, or they have difficulty getting to the polls. Think about the presidential elections since you were old enough to vote. Have you voted in all of them, in most of them, in some of them, rarely voted in them, or have you never voted in a presidential election?

Now, thinking about the local elections that have been held since you were old enough to vote, have you voted in all of them, in most of them, in some of them, rarely voted in them, or have you never voted in a local election?

Thinking back to the national election in November 1988, when the presidential candidates were Michael Dukakis, the Democrat, and George Bush, the Republican, did you happen to vote in that election?

Frequency of voters: Voted in 1988 presidential election: N = 1,763.

1.B: CAMPAIGN WORK

Since January 1988, the start of the last national election year, have you worked as a volunteer—that is, for no pay at all or for only a token amount—for a candidate running for national, state, or local office?

(Thinking about the campaign to which you gave the most time and effort), What office was the candidate running for?

Did you work in the general election, in a primary, or both?

About how many weeks were you active in the campaign?

During the time you were active in that campaign on average about how many hours per week did you give to the campaign?

During the campaign, [in the 1988 election year] did you communicate to the candidate or to someone involved in running the campaign your views on an issue of public policy—for example, about what you wanted the candidate to do when in office?

How much did your own work in the campaign contribute to the number of votes (the candidate/the ticket) got—a great deal, some, or very little?

Frequency, Campaign Workers (Those who did any work in 1988 election): N = 213, unweighted N = 419.

1.C: CAMPAIGN CONTRIBUTIONS

(We have been talking about campaign activity.) Now we would like to talk about contributions to campaigns. Since January, 1988, did you contribute money—to an individual candidate, a party group, a political action committee, or any other organization that supported candidates?

In your best estimate, about how much money in total did you contribute since January, 1988? Just give me the letter from this card.

Think of your largest contribution to a single candidate or organization. Was that contribution to one particular candidate or was it to an organization supporting many candidates?

(For contributions to a candidate) What office was the candidate running for?

During the campaign, did you communicate to the candidate or to someone involved in running the campaign your views on an issue of public policy—for example, about what you wanted the candidate to do when in office?

How much did your own contribution in the campaign contribute to the number of votes (the candidate/the ticket) got—a great deal, some, or very little? A similar set of questions was asked for those who contributed to an organization. In addition, organization contributors were asked:

Was the organization a party organization, a political action committee, or what?

Was this organization one that was associated with your work? Was it one that was organized around a particular issue, was it a general liberal or conservative organization, was it a PAC associated with a particular politician, or what?

Was it organized by a union, a company or firm, a trade association, a professional association, or what?

Frequency, Campaign Contributors (Gave any money in 1988 election): N = 595, unweighted N = 795.

1.D: COMMUNITY ACTIVITY

Now some questions about your role in your community. In the past two years, since (CURRENT MONTH) have you served in a voluntary capacity—that is, for no pay at all or for only a token amount—on any official local governmental board or council that deals with community problems and issues such as a town council, a school board, a zoning board, a planning board, or the like?

What kind of board or council is that—that is, what is it about?

Have you attended a meeting of such an official local government board or council in the past twelve months?

Do you attend these meetings regularly or have you attended only once in a while?

What kind of board or council is that—that is, what is it about?

Aside from membership on a board or council or attendance at meetings, I'd like to ask also about informal activity in your community or neighborhood. In the past twelve months, have you gotten together informally with or worked with others in your community or neighborhood to try to deal with some community issue or problem? (If you have mentioned this activity elsewhere, perhaps in connection with your church or synagogue, or an organization or a local campaign, don't repeat it here.)

Frequencies: Informal activity: N = 427, unweighted N = 528; Board Membership: N = 76, unweighted N = 167.

1.E: CONTACTING

Now, I want to ask you a few questions about contacts you may have initiated with government officials or someone on the staff of such officials—either in person or by phone or letter—about problems or issues with which you were concerned. Please don't count any contacts you have made as a regular part of your job.

In the past twelve months, have you initiated any contacts with a federal elected official or someone on the staff of such an official: I mean someone in the White House or a Congressional or Senate Office?

What about a non-elected official in a federal government agency? Have you initiated a contact with such a person in the last twelve months?

What about an elected official on the state or local level—a governor or mayor or a member of the state legislature or a city or town council—or someone on the staff of such an elected official?

And what about a non-elected official in a state or local government agency or board? Have you initiated a contact with such a person in the last twelve months?

I'd like to ask you a few questions about your most recent contact with a public official. What was that official's title or position?

Thinking still about this contact, did you get a response or were you ignored?

Were you satisfied with the result?

How much difference did <u>your particular contact</u> make—a great deal, some, a little, or no difference?

Frequencies: Any contact: N = 855, unweighted N = 1,011.

1.F: PROTESTING

In the past two years, since (CURRENT MONTH), have you taken part in a protest, march, or demonstration on some national or local issue (other than a strike against your employer)?

Was this in the last twelve months?

Did the protest make any difference? That is, did the protest, march, or demonstration accomplish a lot, something, not too much, or did it backfire?

How much difference did your own participation make in the outcome of the protest, march, or demonstration?

Frequencies: Took part in a protest: N = 144, unweighted N = 295.

1.G: POLITICAL ORGANIZATION

Respondents were shown a list of 16 types of membership organizations and 4 additional types of non-membership organizations. The list is found in Chapter 3, Table 3.4. For each type on the list, the respondent was asked a series of questions about the nature of affiliation. A person is counted as an affiliate of a political organization if he or she belongs to or contributes to at least one organization that the respondent describes as taking political stands.

We may have underestimated the extensiveness of involvement with organizations that take stands in politics. Our strategy was to ask about only one organization in each category for which a respondent indicated membership or contribution. For example, a respondent who is on the board of the local senior citizens' center would probably have chosen to report on that activity over membership in the American Association of Retired Persons. However, the latter is deeply embroiled in public controversies while the former might concentrate on the direct delivery of services. For this category at least, this respondent would have been recorded incorrectly as having no politically salient organizational involvement. Forty percent of those who reported that none of the organizations with which they were involved took stands in politics (representing 15 percent of respondents indicating organizational involvement and 12 percent of all respondents) had multiple organizational affiliations in at least one category.

Are you a member of . . . (READ ITEM)

Not counting any membership dues, have you contributed money in the past twelve months (since CURRENT MONTH) to any organization of this type?

Now I'd like to ask you a few questions about each kind of organization you are involved with. (First/Next ORGANIZATION TYPE) How many such organizations are you involved with?

What is the name of the organization?

Have you attended a meeting of the organization in the past twelve months?

Are there sometimes political discussions on the agenda of these meetings?

Do people at these meetings sometimes chat informally about politics or government?

Do you consider yourself an active member of the organization—that is, in the past twelve months have you served on a committee, given time for special projects, or helped organize meetings?

In the past five years, have you served on the board or been an officer of the organization?

Does this organization sometimes take stands on any public issues— either locally or nationally?

Does this organization fund or provide charitable or social services to benefit people who are not members of the organization?

Thinking about the past 12 months, including membership dues, about how much money did you contribute to the various organizations and charitable and social service activities we've just discussed? Just give me the letter from this card.

If you average across the last twelve months, about how many hours per week did you give to work for all of the various organizations and charitable and social service activities we've just discussed?

Frequency: Affiliated political organization: N = 1,210, unweighted 1,331.

1.H: POLITICAL MAIL CONTRIBUTIONS

How often do you receive requests through the mail asking you to donate to political organizations, political causes, or candidates?

In the past twelve months, have you sent any money in response to such mail requests?

Over the past twelve months, about how much money in total have you contributed to political organizations, political causes, and candidates in response to such mail requests? I don't mean all you have given to such causes. Just in response to such mailed requests. Just read me the letter on the card.

1.I: OVERALL ACTIVITY INDEX

The components of the additive scale are as follows: voting in the 1988 national election; working as a volunteer for a candidate running for national, state, or local office; making a contribution to an individual candidate, a party group, a political action committee, or any other organization that supports candidates in elections; contacting government officials; taking part in a protest, march, or demonstration; working informally with others in the community to deal with some community issue or problem; serving in a voluntary capacity on any local governmental board or council (for example, a school or zoning board), or attending meetings of such a board or council regularly; and being a member of or giving money to a political organization. One point was given for each act. The scale runs from 0 to 8.

The various items of the Overall Index are all positively related to each other, as the following correlation matrix shows:

Correlation Coefficients of Items in Overall Participation Scale

	Campaign Work	Campaign Money	Contact	Protest	Community Board	Informal Community	Political Organization
Vote	.15	.28	.22	.04	.10	.13	.26
	P= .00	P= .00	P= .00	P= .03	P= .00	P= .00	P= .00
Campaign Work		.27	.21	.13	.16	.13	.18
		P= .00	P= .00	P= .00	P= .00	P= .00	P= .00
Campaign Contribution			.26	.15	.13	.15	.37
			P= .00	P= .00	P= .00	P= .00	P= .00
Contact				.15	.16	.23	.31
				P= .00	P= .00	P= .00	P= .00
Protest					.08	.10	.16
					P= .00	P= .00	P= .00
Community Board						.15	.12
						P= .00	P= .00
Informal Community							.19
							P= .00

Cronbach's α = .6192

Time frames for the activities: The time frames for the various acts differ somewhat. For voting, campaign work and campaign contributions, it is activity within the most recent election year (1988). For contacting, informal community activity, and political organization affiliation, it is within the past year. For board or meeting attendance and protesting, it is within the past two years.

We were interested in the impact of the time frame that we chose on the extent to which we capture people who move in and out of activity. Although a few political activities, such as serving on a local board, are ongoing, most are intermittent. In order to probe the extent to which citizens move in and out of political activity, we asked also about activity in the previous five years, with the following results:

Proportion of the Public Reporting Activity in the Past Five Years

	Percent	Ratio 5 years/one year
Campaign work	10	2.3
Board membership	9	2.5
Contact	34	1.4
Protest	6	1.5

Not unexpectedly, expanding the time frame produces more activists. It does not, however, increase five-fold the proportion of activists, indicating that those active in any particular year are likely to be active in others. Otherwise, each year would bring us a new set of activists and a larger accumulation of activists by the end of a five-year period.

Frequencies: Overall Activity:

Number of Acts	Weighted	Unweighted
None	422	429
1	662	521
2	499	388
3	429	398
4	267	316
5	158	260
6	59	144
7	19	52
8	2	8

1.J: TIME-BASED ACTIVITY INDEX

This is the same as the Overall Activity Index minus campaign contributions and voting.

1.K: POLITICAL MONEY

This is measured by the sum of the amount contributed to candidates or to groups (parties or PACs) supporting candidates in the period between the beginning of the presidential electoral cycle in January 1988 and the time of the interview in spring 1991, and the amount contributed to political organizations, causes, and candidates in response to direct mail requests in the twelve months preceding the interview.

There may be some overlap between the two measures. However, the correlation between the two measures is only .33. (As shown in Chapter 7, the gratifications from contributing to work-related PACs work are quite different from those for contributing to a PAC associated with a political cause.)

1.L: LOCAL AND NATIONAL ACTIVITY

The local and national participation scales are sums of the following acts:

Local: voting in most or all local elections, campaign work for a candidate for local office, campaign contributions for a candidate for local office, contacting a local official, protesting on a local issue, membership or attendance at local board meetings, working informally with people in the community, membership in a political organization whose main activity is on the local level.

National: voting in most or all presidential elections, campaign work for a candidate for national office, contributions to a national candidate, contacting a national official, protesting on a national issue, membership in a political organization whose main activity is on the national level.

2. Non-Political Activity

2.A: CHARITABLE WORK AND CHARITABLE MONEY

The following questions were asked on the screener interview. Because a great deal of charitable effort emanates from religious institutions, we specifically asked about donations of time or money other than those made in church. There is, probably, a good deal of overlap between the activity referenced by these questions and that covered in the extensive section on voluntary organizations in the follow-up interview. See 2.c below.

(Aside from activity associated with (your/a) church or synagogue, (In/in) the past twelve months, since (INTERVIEW MONTH), did you spend any time on charitable or voluntary service activities—that is, actually working in some way to help others for no monetary pay?

If you average across the past twelve months, about how many hours per week did you spend?

(Aside from contributions to (your/a) church or synagogue, (In/in) the past twelve months, since (INTERVIEW MONTH), did you contribute any money to charitable or voluntary service activities and organizations?

2.B: RELIGIOUS ACTIVITY AND AFFILIATION

Now on a different subject, what is your religious preference? Is it Protestant, Catholic, Jewish, some other religion, or no religion?

(If Protestant) What specific denomination is that, if any?

Now I would like to ask you a few questions about your religious activity. How often do you attend religious services?

Do you belong to or are you a member of a church, synagogue or other religious institution in this or a nearby community?

When you attend services do you usually go to the same congregation or parish?

Aside from attending services, in the past twelve months have you been an active member of your (church/synagogue)—I mean, have you served on a committee, given time for special projects, or helped organize meetings?

In the past five years, have you served on a board or held an official position in your (church/synagogue)?

In your best estimate, about how much money do you contribute to your religion every year not including school tuition? Just give me the letter from this card.

If you average across the last twelve months, about how many hours per week did you give to (church/synagogue) work—aside from attending services? IF NECESSARY PROBE: For example, participating in educational, charitable, or social activities or in other church affairs.

How often do you watch religious programs on television?

Have you sent in a contribution to a religious program in the last twelve months?

About how much money in total have you sent to such religious programs in the past twelve months? Just read me the letter on the card.

> Frequencies:
> Religious preference:
> Protestant N = 1,516
> Catholic   N = 648
> Religious Attendance:
> Never   315
> Less than once a year   139
> Once or twice a year   300
> Several times a year   315
> About once a month   174
> 2–3 times a month   235
> Nearly every week   524
> More than once a week 263
> Worked in church: N = 609
> Church affiliated (church member or attends same church once a month or more): N = 1,728

2.C: NON-POLITICAL ORGANIZATION AFFILIATION

Non-political organizational affiliation is defined parallel to the measure of political organization affiliation (see Appendix B.1.g) except that the respondent is affiliated with at least one organization that does *not* take political stands. In analyses of respondents affiliated with a non-political organization, we define them as anyone who is a member of, or a contributor to, an organization that does not take stands on public issues. For regression analyses, the measure is a trichotomy: not affiliated, affiliated, and attends meetings.

The amount of non-political activity that is found in a survey depends on the nature of the questions asked. For this reason, estimates of this activity vary widely. Data from the Current Population Survey conducted about the time of our survey report about one in five Americans as having worked without pay for an institution or organization at some time during the year ending May 1989.[1] In contrast, a survey for the Independent Sector conducted by the Gallup Organization in 1990 finds that 54 percent of the public did volunteer work in the twelve months prior to the survey.[2] The difference is partially a reflection of the difference in questionnaire administration and in the questions themselves. The CPS asks one person in a household to estimate the activities of others and use the data to arrive at their estimates. As they report, this can lead to an underestimate of what others do. Also, the Independent Sector asks a much more elaborate set of questions about specific activities that tends to jog the respondent's mind.[3]

Our own approach was closer to that of the Independent Sector. We asked, in fact, about a wider range of activities specifying many types of organizations and probing more specifically for religious based participation. Our findings are closer to Independent Sector's. Fifty-four percent of our sample reported some volunteer time for a non-political organization or a charity in the past month, exactly the Independent Sector figure. Adding those who reply positively about activity within the framework of their churches, our total goes up to 63 percent.

For a discussion of differences in cross-national measures of non-political activity, see Chapter 3, footnote 31.

Frequency: Affiliated with non-political organization: N = 1,704.

3. The Subject of Activity

For each of the political activities in which individuals reported engaging, they were asked whether there was some specific issue and whom it affected. The distinction among activities that were particularized and those with a more general referent is based on the first question (below) about whether the referent of the act was the respondent (or his or her family) or a broader group. If a respondent said that the activity affected both the respondent or the respondent's family and others, the follow-up question was used to place those who said that the activity was aimed at a personal or family issue into the particularized category. If a respondent reported being active more than once in a particular type of activity, the follow-up question about the issue was asked about the most recent activity.

Thinking about this (activity), were there any issues or problems ranging from public policy issues to community, family, or personal concerns that led you to engage in it? What were they? [Record verbatim]

Thinking about the (first) issue you mentioned, that is (READ FIRST ISSUE ABOVE), which of these categories best describes who was affected by the problem?

Only myself or my family
Only other people, but not myself or my family

Myself or my family, as well as others like us
All people in the community
All people in the nation or all people in the world

(If both family and others), Was your [activity] aimed at dealing with the problem for you and your family only, or were you trying to deal with it for other people as well?

4. Reasons for Activity

For each activity, the respondent was shown a list of reasons for the act. The list of reasons was adjusted when a particular reason made no sense for an act. If a respondent reported being active more than once in a particular type of activity, the follow-up question about the issue was asked about the most recent activity. For organizational activity, the questions refer to the organization to which the respondent gave most time or money—or, if these were different, the one that was most important to the respondent.

Here is a list of reasons people give us for campaigning or other activity. Thinking about the time when you decided to become active in the campaign, please tell me if each of these reasons was very important, somewhat important, or not very important in your decision to become active in the campaign. How about: (SHOW LIST BELOW)? DO NOT READ STATEMENTS.

I found it EXCITING.
I wanted TO LEARN ABOUT POLITICS AND GOVERNMENT.
The chance TO WORK WITH PEOPLE WHO SHARE MY IDEALS.
The chance TO MEET IMPORTANT AND INFLUENTIAL PEOPLE.
The chance TO INFLUENCE GOVERNMENT POLICY.
MY DUTY AS A CITIZEN.
I AM THE KIND OF PERSON WHO DOES MY SHARE.
The chance TO FURTHER MY JOB OR CAREER.
The chance FOR RECOGNITION FROM PEOPLE I RESPECT.
I might want to GET A JOB WITH THE GOVERNMENT someday.
I might want TO RUN FOR OFFICE someday.
The chance TO BE WITH PEOPLE I ENJOY.
I DID NOT WANT TO SAY NO TO SOMEONE who asked.
I might want TO GET HELP FROM AN OFFICIAL on a personal or family problem.

The chance TO MAKE THE COMMUNITY OR NATION A BET-
TER PLACE TO LIVE.
The chance TO FURTHER THE GOALS OF MY PARTY.

5. Reasons for Inactivity

Respondents who engaged in no political act beyond voting were asked
the following.

Here is a list of reasons people give us for not being very active
politically. Please tell me if each of these reasons is very important,
somewhat important, or not very important in explaining why you are
not very politically active. How about: [The opening part of the question
was different for those who were never active and those who were once
active. For analysis, answers of both kinds of inactives were combined].

I find that AS ONE INDIVIDUAL, I DON'T FEEL I CAN HAVE
AN IMPACT.
I am afraid that I might GET INTO TROUBLE *by getting in-*
volved in politics.
I find that POLITICS IS TOO COMPLICATED *for me to under-*
stand.
I find POLITICS UNINTERESTING AND BORING *compared to*
other aspects of my life.
I think I SHOULD TAKE CARE OF MYSELF *and my family be-*
fore I worry about the welfare of the community and nation.
Given the many pressures in my personal life, I simply DON'T
HAVE ENOUGH TIME *for politics.*
I just NEVER THOUGHT ABOUT BEING INVOLVED.
I think that POLITICS IS A DIRTY BUSINESS, *and don't want to*
have anything to do with it.
I think that what I get out of political participation is NOT WORTH
THE TIME AND TROUBLE *I would have to put into it.*
I feel it's NOT MY RESPONSIBILITY *to participate.*
The really IMPORTANT THINGS *that affect my life* HAVE
NOTHING TO DO WITH POLITICS.
IT'S NOT MY PLACE *to be involved in politics.*
I find I DON'T LIKE *the people.*
I feel BURNED OUT.

*I find that POLITICS CAN'T HELP ME WITH MY PERSONAL
    OR FAMILY PROBLEMS.
There just AREN'T ANY GOOD CAUSES ANYMORE.*

6. Attitudes on Political Issues and General Ideology

Respondents were asked to locate themselves on the following seven-point scales.

6.A: GENERAL IDEOLOGY

*We hear a lot of talk these days about liberals and conservatives. Here
is a scale on which the political views that people might hold are arranged
from extremely liberal—point 1—to extremely conservative—point 7.
Where would you place yourself on this scale?*

6.B: ECONOMIC ATTITUDES

*Some people feel that the government in Washington should see to it
that every person has a job and a good standard of living. Suppose these
people are at one end of the scale at point number 1. Others think that
the government should just let each person get ahead on his or her own.
Suppose these people are at the other end, at point 7. And, of course,
some other people have opinions somewhere in between at points 2, 3,
4, 5, or 6. Where would you place yourself on this scale?*

*Some people feel that the government should provide fewer services,
even in areas such as health and education in order to reduce spending.
Other people feel it is important for the government to provide many
more services even if it means an increase in spending. Where would you
place yourself on this scale?*

In various analyses, these two items are combined as a single scale of
economic attitudes by adding them together. In some cases we look at
liberals and conservatives on economic matters. We define liberals as
those who were on the liberal side of the scale on both economic items
or on the liberal side on one and in the middle on the other. Conservatives
are those who were on the conservative side of the scale on both items
or on the conservative side on one and in the middle on the other.

6.C: AID TO WOMEN AND MINORITIES

*Some people feel that the government in Washington should make
every effort to improve the social and economic position of Blacks.
Others think that the government should not make any special effort to*

help Blacks because they should help themselves. Where would you place yourself on this scale?

Some people feel that the government in Washington should make every effort to improve the social and economic position of women. Others think that the government should not make any special effort to help women because they should help themselves. Where would you place yourself on this scale?

And what about Hispanic-Americans? Some people feel that the government in Washington should make every effort to improve their social and economic position. Others think that the government should not make any special effort to help Hispanics because they should help themselves. Where would you place yourself on this scale?

6.D: SCHOOL PRAYER AND ABORTION

Some people think public schools should be allowed to start each day with a prayer. Others feel that religion does not belong in the public schools but should be taken care of by the family and the church. How do you feel about this?

Some people feel that a woman should always be able to obtain an abortion as a matter of personal choice. Others feel that, by law, abortion should never be permitted. Where would you place yourself on this scale?

7. Civic Orientation

7.A: POLITICAL INTEREST

The political interest scale is the sum of the answers to the following questions about local and national interest, with "very interested" coded as 4 and "not at all" as 1. The scale runs from 2 to 8. The two items are closely related; the Pearson correlation is .54.

We also use a question on interest from the screener as an instrument in some 2SLS regressions.

Thinking about your local community, how interested are you in local community politics and local community affairs? Are you Very interested, Somewhat interested, Slightly interested, or Not at all interested?

How interested are you in national politics and national affairs?

Screener question:

How interested are you in politics and public affairs? Are you very interested, somewhat interested, only slightly interested, or not at all interested in politics and public affairs?

7.B: POLITICAL DISCUSSION

The political discussion scale is the sum of the answers to the following questions about local and national discussion. The scale runs from 2 to 10.

How often do you discuss local community politics or local community affairs with others? Is it Every day, Nearly every day, Once or twice a week, Less than once a week, or Never?

How often do you discuss national politics and national affairs with others?

7.C: INFORMATION

Respondents were asked the following information questions. The information scale is based on the number of correct answers, from 0 to 8. The Cronbach's alpha is .66.

We want to know how well known the different governmental leaders are around here. If you happen to know, what are the names of the United States Senators from (STATE WHERE R LIVES)? (WRITE IN THE NAMES THE RESPONDENT GIVES.)

Could you tell me the name of the Congressman or Congresswoman from this district? Do you happen to know his or her name? (WRITE IN THE NAME THE RESPONDENT GIVES.)

We are interested in how much people know about American government. On average over the past few years, did the federal government spend more money on the National Aeronautics and Space Administration (NASA) or Social Security?

Does the Fifth Amendment to the American Constitution mainly guarantee citizens protection against forced confessions, or mainly guarantee freedom of speech?

Who was mainly behind the increased use of primary elections in the United States to choose candidates: party "bosses" who can use them to control nominations, or reformers who want the voters to choose party candidates themselves?

When people talk about "civil liberties," do they usually mean the right to vote and run for office, or freedom of speech, press and assembly?

Which is the major difference between democracies and dictatorships: that democratic governments allow private property, or that democratic governments allow citizens to choose their representatives freely?

Two screener questions are used as instruments in some analyses.

Now, I have just a few questions about your knowledge of politics and your feelings about government.

How old do you have to be to vote for President?

Which party has more members in the United States House of Representatives—the Democrats or the Republicans?

7.D: TOLERANCE

The scale of tolerance is the sum of the "tolerant" answers to the following questions.

There are always some people whose ideas are considered bad or dangerous by other people. Consider someone who is openly homosexual. If some people in your community suggested that a book he or she wrote in favor of homosexuality should be taken out of your public library, would you favor removing this book or not?

What about someone who believes that Blacks are genetically inferior? If some people in your community suggested that a book he or she wrote arguing that Blacks are genetically inferior should be taken out of your public library, would you favor removing this book or not?

Or consider someone who advocates doing away with elections and letting the military run the country: should he or she be allowed to or not?

And what about someone who is against all churches and religion? If such a person wanted to make a speech in your community, should he or she be allowed to or not?

7.E: PARTISANSHIP

The following questions were used to identify Democrats and Republicans, as well as strength of identification. The partisan strength scale has 7 categories: strong Democrat, weak Democrat, Democratic leaners, independents, Republican leaners, weak Republicans, strong Republicans. A screener question on partisanship is used as an instrument in some 2SLS analyses.

Generally speaking, do you usually think of yourself as a Republican, a Democrat, an Independent, or what?

Would you call yourself a strong (Republican/Democrat) or not a very strong (Republican/Democrat)?

Do you think of yourself as closer to the Republican or Democratic Party?

Screener question:

Generally speaking, do you usually think of yourself as a Republican, a Democrat, an Independent, or what?

Would you call yourself a strong (Republican/Democrat) or a not very strong (Republican/Democrat)?

Do you think of yourself as closer to the Republican or Democratic Party?

7.F: POLITICAL EFFICACY

The political efficacy scale was the sum of the answers to the following four questions, with 1 point given for "none" and 4 points given for "a lot." Cronbach's alpha is a respectable .79.

If you had some complaint about a <u>local government</u> activity and took that complaint to a member of the local government council, do you think that he or she would pay a lot of attention to what you say, some attention, very little attention, or none at all?

If you had some complaint about a <u>national government</u> activity and took that complaint to a member of the local government council, do you think that he or she would pay a lot of attention to what you say, some attention, very little attention, or none at all?

How much influence do you think someone like you can have over <u>local government</u> decisions—a lot, some, very little, or none at all?

How much influence do you think someone like you can have over <u>national government</u> decisions—a lot, a moderate amount, a little, or none at all?

8. Political Recruitment and Stimuli

8.A: RECRUITMENT BY ACTS

Recruitment questions about being asked to be active were posed in relation to the following activities: campaign work and/or contribution, contacting, protesting, and community activity (service on a board, attendance at board meetings, or informal activity). The questions were asked of all respondents, whether they had been active in that manner or not.

Aggregating the requests for political activity posed some difficulties because of the way we counted requests for campaign work and requests for campaign money. We should make clear how we arrived at these figures. When we enumerated the activities for which our respondents had been recruited, we considered campaign work and campaign contributions to be separate activities, thus yielding a score from zero to five for these two activities plus contacting, protesting, and community activity. In doing so, we may have undercounted the total number of activities for some of our respondents because our data may incompletely capture instances in which a respondent received both requests for campaign work and requests for campaign money during the past year.

Respondents who indicated that they had received more than one request for campaign involvement in the past year were asked to elaborate only on the most recent request; "Think of the most recent such request: was this to work or to contribute money (or both)?" Over three-quarters of the 33 percent of our respondents who received requests for campaign involvement got more than one such request. Of this group, 79 percent—or 20 percent of the whole sample—indicated that the most recent request was for either work or a contribution but not both. Because we queried only about the most recent request, it is possible that a prior request was for the other form of campaign involvement. For example, a respondent whose most recent request was for campaign work might have received an earlier one for financial assistance. In such a case we undercounted the total number of activities for which the respondent was recruited. Counting the two forms of campaign involvement as a single activity, thus producing a scale that runs from zero to four, raises to 3 percent the proportion of respondents who received requests to do all the activities.

In the past twelve months have you received any request <u>directed at you personally</u> to take part in (activity named)?

Did this happen once or more than once?

Think about the person who made (this/the most recent such) request. Was this someone you knew personally?

Was this person either a close friend or relative?

Was this someone who knows someone you know?

Was this someone whose name you recognized?

How much do you remember about him/her? Is that A lot, Some, A little, or Nothing at all?

We are interested in learning about the kinds of people who ask others to take part in (activity named). Think about the person who made this request. Please look down this list and tell me, if you know: Was the person who made the request . . .

male or female?

White, Black, Hispanic, or Asian-American?

a Republican or a Democrat?

a neighbor?
a member of your profession or occupation?
someone who works where you work?
someone in a supervisory position over you at work?
someone of your religious background?
someone who belongs to an organization you belong to?

Did you respond positively to the request—I mean, did you take the action requested?

8.B: RECRUITMENT IN INSTITUTIONS

The following questions were asked about the job, religious institution, and the respondent's main voluntary organizations. The measures are combined for regression analyses into a measure of institutional recruitment: the sum of the number of times an individual was asked either to vote or to take some other political action on the job, in church, or in a non-political organization. The scale runs from 0 to 6.

In the past five years, did someone in authority on the job, in church, or in your organization ever suggest that you:

personally vote for or against certain candidates in an election for public office?

take some other action on a political issue—sign a petition, write a letter, or get in touch with a public official?

8.C: EXPOSURE TO POLITICAL STIMULI IN CHURCH

Over the past five years, have you been to a meeting in your (church/ synagogue) about some local or national <u>political</u> issue or problem?

Over the past five years, has anyone in your (church/synagogue)—a member of the clergy or someone in an official position—ever suggested that you vote for or against certain candidates in an election?

8.D: EXPOSURE TO POLITICAL STIMULI IN NON-POLITICAL ORGANIZATIONS

Two measures of organizational stimuli were used: exposure to informal discussion about politics at a meeting of a non-political organization, and having political issues on the agenda of a non-political organization. For the relevant question wordings see sections 1.g and 2.c above.

8.E: SUMMARY MEASURES OF INSTITUTIONAL EFFECTS

These are the sum of the number of civic skills exercised in each of three domains—job, non-political organization, and church—plus the sum of the two institutional recruitment questions for each domain (8.b and 9.a in this Appendix). Since there are four possible skills but only two possible recruitment attempts in each domain, the skill variables weigh twice as much in the measure. The results of analyses where this measure is used are the same if we weigh skills and recruitment equally.

9. Civic Skills

9.A: ADULT CIVIC SKILLS

Respondents were asked about opportunities to practice civic skills in three domains: job, organizations, and in church/synagogue. The job skill questions were asked of those who were employed. The questions about skills practiced in an organization were asked about the respondent's "main" organization—the one to which the most time or money was given or, if different, the one the respondent considered most important. We used only skills acquired in non-political organizations in our analysis. The church skill questions were asked of those who were active members of their churches in the past year or served on a church board in the past 5 years or gave 2 or more hours to their church.

Skill questions were asked only of the respondent's "main" organization as defined above. If the respondent's main organization was political but the respondent was affiliated with one or more non-political organizations, this might mean we would underestimate the skill opportunities in non-political organizations. To correct for this, we imputed non-political organizational civic skills to those whose main organization was political and who were affiliated with non-political organizations. The imputation was based on the number of non-political organizations and their level of activity in those organizations.

A note on the estimate of church skills: We asked the skills questions of all employed respondents (i.e., all respondents who reported that in the week preceding the interview they worked full or part time or were temporarily absent from a job for a reason such as illness or vacation) and of all respondents who indicated giving any time or money to an organization. However, pre-testing showed that nominal church members who neither attend services nor are active in their churches resented the detailed church questions. They answered with comments to the effect that they had just told us that they never set foot inside the church of which they are a member, so why were we asking if they make speeches there. To meet this objection, we asked the detailed church questions (including skill questions) only of respondents who indicated having been active in church over the past twelve months, having been on the board or served as an officer over the past five years, or devoting at least two hours each week to church-based educational, social, or charitable activity.

This approach solved one problem but created another. Analogous data about involvement in non-political organizations suggest that, while active organization members are much more likely to exercise civic skills than inactive ones, even inactive organization members do so occasionally. Hence, filtering out inactive church members resulted in the underestimation of the skills exercised in church. If we make the assumption that the exercise of civic skills in church conforms to the same patterns as in non-political organizations, we can make the rough estimate that the average number of skills practiced in church would rise from .44 to .53 among all respondents and from .64 to .77 among church members. This brings the averages for skills exercised in church closer to the figures for non-political organizations, but does not affect the overall findings that the workplace is especially rich in opportunities for the practice of civic skills and that organizations provide somewhat more opportunities than religious institutions.

The four skill questions in each domain are added to create a scale of civic skills acquired at work, in non-political organizations, and in church. In some analyses, all of the civic skill items are added to form an overall measure of civic skills.

The civic skill items have several attractive features consistent with the conclusion that they measure the acquisition of transferable skills. For one thing, in each domain the four items form similar Guttman scales (with differences explainable by variations in chances to perform the skill from one domain to another), indicating that they measure something common across institutions, not something specific to a particular institution. In addition, one other activity—contacting a government official—that was included in the list asked in each domain (but which we did not consider to be an opportunity to gain a civic skill as much as an actual political act) does not scale with the other activities when a number of different methods are used. This is true whether one uses Cronbach's alpha as a criterion, loadings or communalities in a factor analysis, or the coefficient of determination for a Guttman scale. For example, the *lowest* loading for the four items in factor analyses of each domain is .527 while the loadings for contacting are .279, .446, and

.385, which strongly suggests that contacting does not belong with the others. This, too, is consistent with the hypothesis that these activities are a common set.

Despite these virtues, it is still possible to worry whether civic skills are truly developed at the workplace, in non-political voluntary organizations, or in religious institutions. This problem is addressed later in Appendix D, and in more detail through the development of a learning model for civic skills in another publication[4] where we show that there is a single dimension of civic skills underlying the various measures of civic skills (i.e., the three measures of adult skill-acts, educational attainment, vocabulary score, and English language ability), that people develop adult civic skills through their involvement in the institutions of adult life, and that the nature of the institution itself affects the number of skills exercised there even after controlling for individual attributes which might affect the performance of skill acts. This supports the notion that we are observing a real process of skill development within institutions, not merely the consequences of the attributes people bring with them.

The civic skill questions are as follows:

Here is a list of things that people sometimes have to do as part of their jobs (are asked to do as part of their involvement with organizations/part of their church activities). After I read each one, please tell me whether or not you have engaged in that activity in the last six months as part of your job. Have you . . .

Written a letter?
Gone to a meeting where you took part in making decisions?
Planned or chaired a meeting?
Given a presentation or speech?

9.B: VOCABULARY SKILLS

Respondents were asked to choose the correct synonym for 10 words. The vocabulary scale is based on the number of correct answers. Because this scale is used by the National Opinion Research Center for multiple studies, we cannot list the words.

The vocabulary test may not be a very good measure of verbal ability for a very small fraction of our sample. The 1.8 percent of the sample who sometimes or always speak another language at home besides English or Spanish (and therefore did not have the choice of being interviewed in their own language) might have done better if they had been interviewed in their native language. Our results, however, are not affected by excluding these people, so we have left them in our analysis.

Thorndike and Gallup describe this test as a "test of verbal intelligence . . . [which assesses] the nature of past learning and not the ability to make novel adaptations."[5] The mean of 6.20 (with standard deviation of 2.15) on our vocabulary score is close to the mean of 6.51 (with standard deviation of 2.25) reported by Alwin for the 1989 GSS, which covered a slightly different population.[6]

9.C: ENGLISH SPOKEN AT HOME

The measure of English skill was based on the language spoken at home ranging from no English, to English and another language, to only English. English was scored as 3, English plus another language as 2, and another language as 1.

What language do you usually speak at home—English or something else?

10. Education

10.A: EDUCATION LEVEL

The main education variable used is an 8-category variable with the following categories: grammar and less, some high school, high school graduate, some college, college graduate, some graduate work, master's degree, and professional degree. At times, other categorizations are used as indicated in the text. The following questions were used to create the categorization.

What is the highest grade of regular school that you have completed and gotten credit for? (IF NECESSARY, SAY: By regular school we mean a school which can be counted toward an elementary or high school diploma or a college or university degree.)

Did you get a high school diploma or pass a high school equivalency test?

Do you have any college degrees—that is, not including degrees from a business college, technical college, or vocational school?

What is the highest degree that you have earned?

Frequency: Basic Educational Categorization:

Grammar and Less	122
Some HS	249

HS Grad/GED	902
Some College	615
College Grad	328
Some Grad Work	93
Master's	146
PhD/Prof	62

10.B: EXPERIENCES IN HIGH SCHOOL

How concerned were the students in your high school about current events and politics—were they Very concerned, Somewhat concerned, or Not at all concerned?

How about you? Thinking again about high school, how concerned were you about current events and politics?

Thinking still about high school, did you have any courses that required you to pay attention to current events?

Was there a lot of encouragement for students to debate and <u>make up their own minds</u> on current events, was there some encouragement, or was there none?

Was your school the kind of place where students could talk to or complain to someone in authority about something they thought was unfair, or was your school the kind of place where it was better not to complain to someone in authority?

I will now ask you about a few activities in which people sometimes get involved while in high school. First, how active were you in high school sports?

How active were you in school government?

How active were you in other school activities—such as school clubs or the student newspaper?

11. Occupation

11.A: WORK STATUS AND OCCUPATION

Work status is measured by a trichotomy of not working, working part-time, and working full-time. Occupation was coded from an open-ended question. For some analyses we use a dummy variable for being retired or not.

Last week, were you working full-time for pay, working part-time for pay, going to school, keeping house, or something else?

What kind of work (do you/did you) normally do? That is, what (is/was) your job called?

Frequencies: Employment status

Not working	846
Part time	256
Full time	1,415

11.B: JOB LEVEL

The job level variable is based on the amount of education and on-the-job training needed for the respondent's job. It has 5 levels. The lowest level jobs require no more than a high school diploma and no more than one month of on-the-job training for mastery. At the other end of the scale (level 5) are jobs requiring either a college degree and at least two years of training on the job or a graduate degree. Although the job level classifications are based on what respondents told us rather than upon objective assessments, examination of actual cases suggests that respondents make judgments fairly accurately. Examples of occupations at each level include:

1. Dishwasher, janitor, cashier
2. Bank teller, mail carrier, machine operator
3. Electrician, machinist, construction inspector
4. Insurance agent, engineer, elementary school teacher
5. Physician, architect, attorney

(In general) How much formal education does somebody need to do a job like (yours/the one you had)—no special formal education, a high school diploma, technical school, a college degree, a graduate degree, or what?

How long does a person have to spend in training on the job to be able to handle a job like yours?

Frequencies: Job Level (among those working):

Lowest	237
2	493
3	419
4	228
Highest	293

12. Race and Ethnicity

We consider African-Americans, Latinos, and others. Our categories are based on the designations respondents chose. In addition we distinguish among Latinos on the basis of place of origin. The small number of respondents who identified themselves both as Latino (or Hispanic or another designation such as "Chicano") and as African-American (or Black) were asked which they considered themselves mostly, Hispanic or Black, and were so categorized.

Do you consider yourself Hispanic or Latino?

Is your background Mexican, Puerto Rican, Cuban or something else?

What is your race? (Which category best describes your racial background?)

(If both Black and Hispanic) What do you consider yourself mostly, Hispanic or Black?

Frequencies: Race and ethnicity:

	Weighted	Unweighted
Anglo-White	2,073	1,606
African-American	233	477
Latino	141	370

13. Income

For analysis purposes, family income is used. For descriptive analyses, income is usually divided into 6 categories: under $15,000, $15–34,999, $35–49,999, $50–74,999, $75–124,999, and over $125,000.

About 8 percent of the sample refused to provide their income in response to our question. For descriptive analyses, we consider these as missing values. In order not to lose cases for regression analyses, we estimated the income of those respondents on the basis of their answer to the income question on the screener interview (for those who provided that information on the screener). We also used the screener interview data to create an income measure corrected for unreliability. This variable is used in regressions.

Which of the income groups listed on this card includes the total 1989 income before taxes of all members of your family living in your home? Please include salaries, wages, pensions, dividends, interest, and all other income.

Frequencies: Income levels (uncorrected measure):

Under $15,000	445
$15–34,999	826
$35–49,999	487
$50–74,999	360
$75–124,999	143
Over $125,000	65

14. Marital Status, Spouse Working, and Children

Are you currently married, living in a marriage-like relationship, widowed, divorced, separated, or have you never been married?

Is your (husband/wife/partner) currently working full-time for pay, working part-time for pay, going to school, keeping house, or something else?

How many children do you have <u>living at home</u> with you? Please include step- and adopted children living in your household.

(If one child) Is this child under age 5?

(If more than one) How many of these children are under age 5?

What is the age of the youngest child you have living at home with you?

15. Free Time

The measure is based on a series of questions about the time spent by the respondent on necessary activities in an average day. Free time is calculated as the time remaining after necessary activities are subtracted from 24 hours.

We would have been able to generate more precise data if we had asked respondents to keep time budgets instead of asking about a typical day, but this would have been too complicated and costly in a survey designed to cover a wide range of concerns. In fact, the results based on our approximations accord very well with the results contained in the literature on time use.[7]

We did not ask about "free time" directly because pre-testing indicated that this concept had no clear-cut meaning to respondents, whereas the time spent working, doing household work, studying, and sleeping seemed meaningful to them. We concluded that there would be much more error in an ambiguous query about free time than in the total error across all of our easily understood questions. The questions about necessary activities follow:

We would like to ask you a few questions about other ways you spend your time, that is, how you divide your hours among various activities.

About how many hours per day do you spend on necessary work for your home and family including cooking, cleaning, taking care of children or other relatives, shopping, house and yard chores, and so forth? About how many hours in total do you spend in an average day on such necessary activities for home and family?

About how many hours do you spend on gainful employment in an average day, including commuting and work that you take home?

About how many hours do you spend studying for a degree or enrolled in courses for a degree in an average day?

About how many hours of sleep do you average a night?

16. Needs and Program Participation

16.A: ECONOMIC NEED

The Economic Need scale is the sum of positive answers to the following.

These days, many people have been feeling a financial pinch. Here is a list of actions that some people find are necessary to make ends meet. Over the past twelve months have you or any members of your immediate family living with you had to take any of these actions in order to make ends meet? Just read me the letters.

Put off medical or dental treatment
Delayed paying the rent or making house payments
Cut back on the amount or quality of food
Worked extra hours or took an extra job

Frequencies: Number of needs mentioned:

None	1,373
1	530
2	355
3	173
4	85

16.B: PROGRAM PARTICIPATION

Respondents were asked about participation in eight programs. The measure of "means-tested benefits" is the sum of positive answers about food stamps, subsidized housing, Medicaid and public assistance such as AFDC, General Assistance, General Relief, or Supplemental Security Income (SSI). The measure of "non-means-tested benefits" is the sum of positive answers to Social Security payments, veterans' benefits, Medicare, and guaranteed student loans.

There are many benefit programs sponsored by the federal, state, and local government. Please tell me if you or any family member in your household currently receives . . .

Social Security Payments
Veterans' Benefits
Food Stamps
Subsidized Housing
Medicare
Medicaid (Green Card)
Guaranteed Student Loans
Public Assistance such as AFDC/ADC, General Assistance, General
   Relief or Supplemental Security Income (SSI)

Frequencies: Receiving non-means-tested benefits: N = 737; receiving
means-tested benefits: N = 227.

16.C: POLITICAL PARTICIPATION IN RELATION TO BENEFITS PROGRAMS

For each program in which the respondent reported being active, the
following questions were asked.

In the past five years, have you taken into account the position of a
candidate in relation to (PROGRAM) in deciding how to vote?

In the past five years, have you contacted a government official to
complain about (PROGRAM)?

In the past five years, have you given a campaign contribution based,
at least in part, on your concern about (PROGRAM)?

Do you belong to any organization concerned about (PROGRAM)?

16.D: COMBINED NEED AND MEANS-TESTED BENEFITS SCALE

This measure is a simple scale based on needing to cut back necessities
and receiving means-tested benefits. It is scored as 0 if the respondent (or
a member of the immediate family in the household) neither had to cut
back on necessities (that is, put off medical or dental treatment, delay
paying the rent or making house payments, or cut back on the amount
or quality of food) nor receives means-tested benefits. It is scored as 1 if
the respondent cut back, and 2 if the respondent receives means-tested
benefits.

17. Community Roots

How long have you lived in your present city or town?

[From screener] Where you live now; do you or your family own your
own home or pay rent?

18. Family of Origin

18.A: PARENTS' EDUCATION

Parents' education is measured by summing the educational categories of both parents. If there is information for only one parent, then this is counted twice. The scale runs from 2 to 14.

Which of the categories on this card best describes the highest educational level your father completed and got credit for? If you were raised by a stepfather or some other male relative, please answer for that person.

Which of the categories on this card best describes the highest educational level your mother completed and got credit for? If you were raised by a stepmother or some other female relative, please answer for that person.

18.B: POLITICAL EXPOSURE IN FAMILY OF ORIGIN

This is measured by the sum of the categories in the following questions.

At the time you were sixteen years old, how frequent were political discussions at home? Were they frequent, did they happen sometimes, or almost never?

When you were sixteen, how active was your mother in politics or in the affairs of the community—very active, somewhat active, or not active at all?

When you were sixteen, how active was your father in politics or in the affairs of the community—very active, somewhat active, or not active at all?

19. Miscellaneous

19.A: AGE

Respondents were asked for their year of birth. For regression analyses, age is categorized into six categories, five of which are entered as dummy variables. The six categories are: under 25, 25–34, 35–44, 45–54, 55–65, and 65 and over. The 45–54 category is omitted in regression analyses.

19.B: CITIZENSHIP

In regression analyses, citizenship is a dummy variable.
Were you born in the United States?
[If not born in US] Are you an American citizen?

Notes

1. See Howard V. Hayghe, "Volunteers in the U.S.: Who Donates the Time?" *Monthly Labor Review* 114 (1991): 17–23.

2. See Virginia Ann Hodgkinson and Murray S. Weitzman, "Giving and Volunteering in the United States: Findings from a National Survey" (Washington, D.C.: Independent Sector, 1990).

3. See Hayghe, "Volunteers in the U.S.," p. 19.

4. See Henry E. Brady, Sidney Verba, and Kay L. Schlozman, "Beyond SES: A Resource Model of Political Participation," *American Political Science Review* 89 (June 1995): 271–294.

5. See Robert I. Thorndike and George H. Gallup, "Verbal Intelligence of the American Adult," *Journal of General Psychology* 30 (1944): 75–85.

6. Duane F. Alwin, "Family of Origin and Cohort Differences in Verbal Ability," *American Sociological Review* 56 (1991): 625–638, 628, Table 1.

7. Martha S. Hill, "Patterns of Time Use," in *Time, Goods, and Well-Being,* ed. F. Thomas Juster and Frank P. Stafford (Ann Arbor: Institute for Social Research/ University of Michigan Press, 1985).

Measuring Representation
and Distortion

1. Participatory Distortion and the Logged Representation Scale

Throughout this book, we have used a definition of representation that is sufficiently broad to encompass a variety of different meanings. We have taken representation to be the process whereby a politically relevant characteristic or concern is communicated to decision makers through political activity. We use the terms "politically relevant characteristics," "characteristics," and "concerns" interchangeably in this Appendix. The terms refer to the full range of subjective and objective attributes of an individual that may be of political relevance. Our examples of such politically relevant characteristics will often be particular attitudes, but the analytic techniques can be applied equally well to demographic characteristics that are politically relevant or to needs. For a discussion of politically relevant characteristics and their role in our model, see Chapter 6. These characteristics or concerns are at the heart of our model of representation since they are that which is represented.

Our definition of the process of representation covers a number of different approaches to representation[1] because we allow politically relevant characteristics to include many possibilities such as opinions, attitudes, identities, and demographic attributes and because we construe communications broadly to include political acts carrying only small bits of information such as voting and political acts sending a strong and explicit message such as protesting.

There are many ways to evaluate the representativeness of acts that communicate information about politically relevant characteristics, but we have used a very simple measure. Representativeness depends upon the degree to which activists have the same characteristics as the general population. The measures of participatory distortion discussed in Chapter 6 and used in Chapters 7 and 8 are of this kind.

COMPARING AVERAGE CHARACTERISTICS

These measures of participatory distortion can be defined more formally with a little mathematical notation. The population of citizens is assumed to be described by some politically relevant characteristic (C)—an attitude, a party preference, a demographic characteristic, whatever—for some level of activity (A). For the moment, we assume that A can be split into activists (A = a) and non-activists (A = n), but C can be any measure for which it makes sense to take an average. Thus, C could be whether someone favors or opposes a measure, and it might be coded as one for those favoring the measure and zero otherwise. In this case, the average of C over the population would be the fraction of the population favoring the measure. Or C could be a seven-point attitude scale for which the average would be the mean scale value for the population. Or C could be a demographic characteristic such as race scored one if the person is Black and zero otherwise. Then the average would be the fraction of the population that is Black.

Using this notation, the average characteristic of those people in the population can be expressed as E(C) where "E" is the expectation or average of the quantity in parentheses.[2] We can express the average characteristic of the activists as E(C|a) where "E(C|a)" is read as the expectation or average of C for the activists "a".[3] It seems reasonable, given our notions of representation, to compare E(C|a) with E(C). If they are the same, then the average characteristic of the activists is the same as that of the average citizen and we have undistorted representation by the activists. If these averages are different, then we have participatory distortion in one direction or another depending upon which quantity is bigger.

This approach has the drawback of requiring us to report E(C|a), the fraction of those with each characteristic among the activists, *and* E(C). This is done in the first two columns of Table 7.2 in Chapter 7 for two different politically relevant characteristics—attitudes about government provision of jobs and about government spending for services. This table reports a lot of numbers—probably too many for easy interpretation.

A "DIFFERENCE" MEASURE OF DISTORTION

One solution proposed in Chapter 6 is to compute the following "difference" measure of participatory distortion (D_c) for characteristic C:

$$(1) \qquad\qquad D_c = E(C|a) - E(C).$$

The measure D_c has been used by Wolfinger and Rosenstone[4] and many others. It also appears as the "Difference" column in Table 7.2 in Chapter 7 in a situation where A = a is voting and where C is either governmental provision of jobs or government spending for services.

We can apply this measure to the example in Chapter 6 where the characteristic is favoring or opposing the referendum and the activity is being an activist for or against it. In this example, 40 percent of the population in a town favor the referendum ($E(C) = 40\%$)[5] but a larger percentage, 50 percent, of the activists are in support ($E(C|a) = 50\%$). The "difference" measure of participatory distortion is $D_c = 50\% - 40\% = 10\%$.

The measure D_c is very appealing because it directly compares the average characteristics communicated to decision makers by activists [$E(C|a)$] with the average characteristic in the population [$E(C)$]. The difference between these is an obvious measure of distortion. This measure also has the virtues that it is simple and it does not require C to be dichotomous, but it has the defect, mentioned in Chapter 6, of having upper and lower bounds that depend upon the characteristics of the population no matter what the characteristics of the activists.

COMPARING AVERAGE ACTIVITY

Other measures are also possible. Assume that C is a set of categories for which the typical one is denoted by lowercase "c". Also assume that we are considering just one activity (e.g., political contacting) and making comparisons across different characteristics. Unlike the situations considered above, the activity does not have to be dichotomous, although its average level, E(A), will be constant for each comparison because we are considering just one activity. It seems sensible in this case to consider the average level of activity for those with characteristic c, which is $E(A|c)$. If representation is proportional and no characteristic is under- or overrepresented, then $E(A|c)$ should be constant from one category to another—the average level of activity should be equal across the categories.[6] If representation is not proportional and varies with the characteristic then $E(A|C)$ will not be constant across categories.

This measure of average activity for various characteristics is used repeatedly in Chapters 7 and 8 in Figures 7.1–7.3, 7.6–7.8, 8.1, 8.4, and 8.5 and in Tables 8.1–8.5 and 8.7. The major characteristics considered include those describing economic condition (family income, economic attitudes, economic needs, advantaged and disadvantaged, and receiving means-tested benefits), race or ethnicity, and gender. A number of different measures of activity are employed, but the point of these tables and figures is to consider variations in the average level of activity across characteristics for just one activity at a time.

In some figures and tables, levels of activity for many different activities are compared across a set of standard demographic or socioeconomic categories. Table 8.1, for example, does this for race or ethnicity and citizenship, and it shows what fraction of Anglo-Whites, African-Americans, Latinos, and Latino citizens engage in eight different political activities. Figure 8.4 considers these eight activities by gender. In Figure 7.2, the percentage of those engaging in an activity among the poor and the percentage among the rich are reported for the same eight activities. We find that the fraction of activists is always less for the poor, demonstrating that the poor are underrepresented compared to the rich. Most tables and figures of this type deal with political activity, but some deal with secular non-political (Table 8.3) or religious activity (Tables 8.4 and 8.5) or both (Figure 8.5). One deals with all three at once (Table 8.7). Some figures show how the mean number of political acts varies across one characteristic with a number of categories (Figures 7.1 and 8.1) and other figures show how the mean number of political acts varies across several characteristics (Figures 7.7 and 7.8). Finally, there are presentations of average activity level (such as time, money, frequency) for specific activities by single characteristics (Table 8.2, Figure 7.3, and Figure 7.6).

These figures and tables are very useful because they present information directly on the major concern of our study—voluntary activity, especially political participation. They are also useful because for any specific activity, variations in the level or amount of activity across different categories of the same characteristic suggest that there is inequality in representation. They do have the defect, however, that it is difficult to compare across activities. What should we make, for example, of the fact that 25 percent of Anglo-Whites report campaign contributions and 5 percent report protesting whereas 22 percent of African-Americans report campaign contributions and 9 percent report protesting? We need a measure that allows us to compare across activities as well as across characteristics for one activity.

REPRESENTATION RATIOS AND THE LOGGED
REPRESENTATION SCALE

We can develop a useful measure for comparing across activities and characteristics in the special case where both A and C are dichotomous as in the referendum example. In this case, let A = a denote an activist, and let C = c denote favoring the referendum. Of course, any A or C can be dichotomized so that the measure we discuss here can always be used, but the value of the measure may depend upon the way in which A and C are dichotomized.

With A and C as dichotomies, the cross-tabulation of A and C is a two by two table. The entire table can be summarized by three numbers such as the two marginal percentages—the percentage of activists [E(A)] and the percentage of the population with the characteristic [E(C)]—and one other number such as the percentage of the activists with the characteristic [E(C|a)] or the percentage of those with the characteristic who are activists [E(A|c)]. These last two numbers come from taking percentages in the table either by rows or by columns and taking the percentage in the cell for activists who have the characteristic. A third possibility is to report E(AC), which is the total percentage of those who are activists and who have the characteristic.

Although three numbers are required to summarize a two by two table, we have already seen that we do not usually need to report as many as three to study representation. If we wish to compare representation through different modes of activity for *one* characteristic, then we can get by with reporting just the average of the characteristic for different activities E(C|a) because the overall average of the characteristic E(C) will not change, and we do not really care about the average size E(A) of the activist populations. If we also want to compare across characteristics, then it makes sense to standardize E(C|a) by E(C). Previously we showed that we can do this by taking the difference between these two quantities, but the ratio also seems sensible as long as E(C) is not zero—and it will not be zero in any but a trivial and uninteresting case where no one in the population has the characteristic. Hence we define the ratio R(C):

(2) $$R(C) = E(C|a)/E(C).$$

This ratio measure shows up in the right-most column of Table 7.2.[7]

Conversely, if we wish to compare the representation of a number of different dichotomous characteristics, say group memberships, for *one* activity, then we can get by with reporting just the average activity level for different characteristics $E(A|c)$ because the average activity level $E(A)$ will not vary for this one activity and we do not really care about the relative size $E(C)$ of the groups. If we also want to report across activities then it makes sense to standardize the average activity level for a characteristic $E(A|c)$ by the average activity level in the population $E(A)$. Once again the ratio seems sensible as long as $E(A)$ is not zero—and it will not be zero in any but a trivial and uninteresting case where no one in the population performs the activity. Hence we define the ratio $R(A)$:

(3) $$R(A) = E(A|c)/E(A).$$

In the two by two case, it is easy to show that $R(C)$ and $R(A)$ are *identical* to one another,[8] and both are equal to $E(AC)/[E(A)E(C)]$.[9] Hence, in this case we can define the *representation ratio* R_{AC} for two by two tables as simply:

(4) $$R_{AC} = R(C) = R(A) = E(AC)/[E(A)E(C)].$$

The representation ratio R_{AC} is useful if we wish to report across both activities and characteristics at the same time[10] as in Figure 7.9 where we compare eight political activities to three notions of economic difficulty (being poor, receiving means-tested benefits, or having to cut back on necessities). This measure is appropriate because it is "standardized" by both the average level of activity $E(A)$ and average characteristic $E(C)$ in the population. The only problem with the representation ratio is that it ranges asymmetrically going from zero to infinity with equality of representation when $R_{AC} = 1$. A somewhat more suitable measure is the Logged Representation Scale (LRS) discussed in Chapter 6:

(5) $$LRS = \log[R_{AC}].$$

This measure ranges symmetrically from minus infinity to plus infinity with equality of representation at zero.

Because there are several equivalent definitions of the LRS, it can be understood in several different ways. One way is to say that the LRS is the logarithm of the ratio of the fraction of activists with the characteristic over the fraction of people in the population with the characteristic. In the referendum example, it is the logarithm of the fraction of activists who favor the referendum over the fraction of the population that favors the referendum. This is the logarithm of 50 percent over 40 percent or $\log[1.25] = .097$. An LRS of zero indicates that activists have exactly the same likelihood of having a characteristic as members of the population as a whole. Negative values indicate that the characteristic is underrepresented among the activists compared to the population as a whole, and positive values indicate that the characteristic is overrepresented.

STATISTICAL SIGNIFICANCE

It is not hard to develop statistical tests for all the measures discussed in this section, but a few tricks are required. In all cases, we are estimating population averages such as $E(C|a)$ by sample averages for which the statistical issues are well-developed and elementary. The calculation of the standard error for difference measures such as $[E(C|a) - E(C)]$ or $[E(A|c) - E(A)]$ does pose a small problem because the sample used to construct the estimate of the conditional expectation $E(C|A)$ or $E(A|c)$ is nested within the sample used to construct the estimate of the unconditional expectation $E(C)$ or $E(A)$, and standard difference of means tests are not applicable in this situation. This presents a few problems for obtaining the standard error of the measure, but these problems can be overcome through careful bookkeeping.[11] The statistical significance of the LRS can be approached easily by noting that the important hypothesis of equal representation implies an LRS of zero and this is equivalent to independence in a two by two table. The standard chi-square statistic is a ready-made test for this purpose.

Despite the fact that it is not difficult to construct standard errors and tests of significance for our measures of representation, we have chosen not to clutter our tables with these extra numbers. We have, however, been careful not to mention differences where they are insignificant, and where we do discuss differences, it is usually obvious that they are large enough to be statistically significant. Moreover, since many of our tables include percentages of those active by some characteristic, it is relatively easy to compute the standard errors for them by employing well-known results about the standard errors of percentages and the discussion in Appendix A about the sample and sample weights.

2. Participatory Distortion and Groups

ARE THERE DIFFERENCES OF OPINIONS ACROSS GROUPS?

Using the LRS and other measures of participatory distortion, we show in Chapters 7 and 8 that political activists are more conservative than the general public about governmental assistance to Blacks or Latinos and about government provision of jobs.[12] This suggests that activists distort public opinion in ways that may affect these groups. This inference immediately raises other questions. What are the views of those groups putatively affected by these distortions toward conservative opinions—namely the poor, Blacks, or Latinos—on these issues? Are they more like the activists or more like the general public? And what about the activists from among these groups? Are their attitudes like those of their group, like activists in general, or what?

These questions suggest we should specify in more detail the relationship between two types of politically relevant characteristics, opinions and group membership. To do this, we must distinguish between these two types of characteristics. For simplicity, we will continue to denote opinions and other concerns by C, but we will denote group membership by G and particular groups by the lowercase g.

As a first step toward answering the questions posed above, we looked for differences in opinions or issue concerns between the general population and groups defined by economic need, race or ethnicity, and gender. We looked for differences in two ways. First, we compared average opinions on various questions for the population $[E(C)]$, the group $[E(C|g)]$, and the activists within the group $[E(C|g,a)]$. In Figure 7.10 we compare the average opinions on two economic issues for the whole population, for the group of poor respondents, and for the activists within the group of poor respondents. Figure 8.3 presents the results for opinions on governmental assistance to Blacks and Latinos for the whole population, for Blacks and Latinos as groups, and for the activists among Blacks and Latinos. These data show clearly that average opinions on these issues for the overall population are different from those of the groups and that the average opinions of the groups also differ from those of their activists.

The second approach we used to study differences in opinions was to consider the issues activists mentioned as their major reasons for undertaking activities such as protesting and contacting that are especially well-suited to communicating information. After categorizing issue responses (C) into a set of categories (c), we reported the fraction of all activists engaging in these information-rich activities who gave each issue response. These are the probabilities $p(C = c|a)$ where c is the response category and a is the information-rich activity. We also reported the same type of information but for members of particular groups (such as the disadvantaged in Table 7.3, Anglo-Whites, African-Americans and Latinos in Table 8.6, and men and women in Table 8.8). This amounts to reporting $p(C = c|a,g)$. From these data, we concluded that activists in general and activists who are members of particular groups often have significantly different issue agendas.

DECOMPOSING PARTICIPATORY DISTORTION

All the measures introduced in the preceding section seem individually interesting and important, but when taken together, they can easily produce a sense of information overload and confusion. To tame this menagerie of measures, we have been aided by a mathematical model that shows how the measures are related to one another for any given (dichotomous) activity, any opinion or characteristic (not necessarily dichotomous), and any classification of the population into a set of mutually exclusive and exhaustive groups.

Starting with politically relevant groups, we want to account for how their concerns are represented through political activity. The net result of representation will be more or less distortion, call it $D_c(g)$, for any group in the population. This measure can be thought of as the group's contribution to the total distortion, D_C, defined in equation (1). For any set of mutually exclusive and exhaustive groups within the population, it seems reasonable to think of overall distortion as the weighted average of these group distortions where the weights are the relative sizes of the groups. For example, overall distortion for attitudes on government aid to Blacks as expressed through, say, political contacting about the issue is the sum of the group distortions for Blacks and Whites and the Rest of the population—each weighted by the appropriate proportion of the population:

$$(6) \qquad D_C = p(Blacks)^*D_c(Blacks) + p(Whites)^*D_c(Whites) \\ + p(Rest)^*D_c(Rest),$$

where $p(Blacks)$, $p(Whites)$, and $p(Rest)$ indicate the proportion of the population that is Black, White, and the Rest (these should always sum to one) and $D_c(Blacks)$, $D_c(Whites)$, and $D_c(Rest)$ are the distortions for each of the three groups.

As it stands, this equation is not very interesting because it tells us nothing about how to calculate each of the group distortions, and it is always possible to choose values for the group distortions that will satisfy the equation.[13] What is needed is an interesting and calculable definition of group distortions that will simultaneously satisfy equation (6). A definition that sheds some light on the many measures we have introduced for understanding participatory distortion would be especially welcome.

MEASURING PARTICIPATORY DISTORTION IN A GROUP

The concerns of groups can be distorted either because their activists provide a distorted view of the group's concerns or because the members of the groups are not active. In two unpublished papers,[14] we have proposed that participatory distortion, $D_c(g)$, for a group g can be broken down into these two fundamental effects expressed in the following equation:

$$(7) \quad D_c(g) = R_{AG} [E(C|a,g) - E(C|g)] + [R_{AG} - 1] [E(C|g) - E(C)].$$

The difference in the first term of this equation between the average of the concerns of the group's activists $[E(C|a,g)]$ and the average of the group's concerns $[E(C|g)]$ captures the effect of distortion from the group's activists. The representation ratio for the group $[R_{AG}]$ measures its activism, and this amplifies or mutes distortion from the group's activists in the first term above. In the second term, a higher than average level of activism on the part of the group (indexed by a representation ratio greater than one) will amplify the group's concerns $E(C|g)$ to the degree that they differ from those of the overall population $E(C)$. A lower than average level of activism (and a representation ratio less than one) will mute the group's concerns.

This definition of $D_c(g)$ has a number of attractive properties. First, if we calculate each group distortion from (7), then we can show that (6) will always be true. This suggests that (7) is a meaningful definition of group distortion. Second, and possibly more important, equation (7) suggests that distortion through participatory activity from a group with respect to some politically relevant concern (C) is dependent upon three familiar and plausible factors:

(i) Representation of the Group Among Activists: The extent to which group members are over- or under-represented among activists (measured by the representation ratio R_{AG} for the group) affects group distortion.

(ii) Representation of the Group Characteristic or Concerns by its Activists: The difference in the concerns expressed by the activists in the group and group members as a whole $[E(C|a,g) - E(C|g)]$ also affects group distortion. If the concern is an opinion on some issue, then this would be the degree to which the opinions of the group's activists are

different from, in fact, the degree to which they distort, the opinions of the group itself.

(iii) Extremity of the Concerns of the Group Compared to the Concerns of the Population as a Whole: Finally, the difference between the group's concerns and those of the population as a whole $[E(C|g) - E(C)]$ matters. This difference tells us how far the average concern for the group is from the average for the overall population. If the concern is an opinion, then this measures the extremity of the group's opinions compared to those of the general population.

By considering each of the terms in (7) we can see the multiple ways in which participatory distortion for a group can come about. The first term on the right-hand side of (7) is the contribution to distortion that can come from group activists who provide a distorted view of the group's concerns. The second term on the right is the contribution to distortion that can result from the inactivity or hyperactivity of the group.

For example, if group members are proportionately represented among activists—that is, if the group's representation ratio is 1—the group deviation from the population mean on some politically relevant charac teristic will not contribute to group distortion because the group has a proportional complement of activists to represent its characteristics or concerns. In this case the second term on the right will be zero. Group distortion can, however, still result if activists drawn from a group are not representative of the group as a whole with respect to that characteristic. Thus, we might expect Blacks to be more liberal than the population as a whole when it comes to attitudes on government provision of jobs $[E(\text{Govt.Jobs}|\text{Black}) - E(\text{Govt.Jobs}) < 0$, assuming negative numbers are more liberal]. If Blacks are proportionally represented among contactors about government provision of jobs (the representation ratio $R_{\text{Contactors,Blacks}}$ is one), then this deviation alone will not contribute to any distortion in what government officials hear from Blacks about government provision of jobs through contacts. However, if Blacks who contact about government provision of jobs are even more liberal on the subject than all Blacks $[E(\text{Govt.Jobs}|\text{Black Contactors}) - E(\text{Govt.Jobs}|\text{Black}) < 0]$, then their contacts will send public officials a set of messages that is skewed in a liberal direction.

Conversely, even if Black contactors about government jobs are representative of all Blacks in their views on government jobs $[E(\text{Govt.Jobs}|\text{Black Contactors}) - E(\text{Govt.Jobs}|\text{Blacks}) = 0]$ so that the first term on the right is zero, group distortion will result from the deviation of Blacks from

the population in their attitudes on government provision of jobs
[E(Govt.Jobs|Blacks) − E(Govt.Jobs) ≠ 0] if Blacks are over- or underrep-
resented among those who contact about government provision of jobs
[$R_{\text{Contactors, Blacks}} \neq 1$].

The representation ratio can be seen as an amplifying or muting factor
depending upon whether it is above or below one. As an amplifying
factor, the higher the representation ratio rises above one, the more group
deviations from the population average (in this case Black liberalism on
the issue of government provision of jobs) contribute to group distortion
$D_c(g)$ and the more distortions created by activists who fail to represent
more quiescent group members (in this example, differences between the
attitudes on government provision of jobs of Blacks who contact and
Blacks as a whole) contribute to group distortion. These effects could
conceivably cancel one another out as when more moderate group activists ameliorate the extreme opinions of their rank and file group members, but they can also reinforce one another as when more extreme group
activists accentuate the extremity of their group members. As a muting
factor, the representation ratio reduces the impacts of group deviations
from the population mean and it reduces the impact of group activists
who differ from their group.

USING THESE MEASURES

This model allows us to show the cumulating impacts for groups of
being underrepresented and of having activists that are more conservative
than the group itself. In Figure 7.10, we show that poor respondents are
more likely to have liberal attitudes on economic issues than the general
population, and we show that poor activists are in between these two
groups. Figure 7.9 shows that the poor are underrepresented in their
political activity so the representation ratio is less than one for them.
Using equation (7), we can easily see that the attitudes of the poor are
systematically distorted in the conservative direction for two reasons:
their activists are more conservative than the poor themselves (the first
term of (7)), and the poor are underrepresented compared to the rest of
the population so that their more liberal economic views are not represented with the same force as the views of the remainder of the population
(the second term of (7)). In Figure 8.3 we show that these same processes
are at work for attitudes on government help to Blacks and Latinos, but
that they work much more strongly for Latinos because Latino activists
tend to be substantially more conservative than Latinos as a whole.

3. Measuring the Volume of Messages

DEFINING AND MEASURING MESSAGES

The messages that representatives hear from their constituents matter. Those who are not active cannot send messages. Those who are very active can send multiple messages. This can lead, as we showed above, to distortions in the transmission of the public's concerns by those activists who communicate with decision makers.

In this section, we develop a general framework for thinking about messages that extends what we have done in previous sections. We assume that the amount of message sending is measured by the level of activity, A. This activity can be described in terms of hours given, money contributed, or the frequency of action. We assume that the content of the messages also matters, and it is measured by the politically relevant characteristic C. This could be a demographic characteristic, a political attitude, or any measurable characteristic of the person.

Using this notation, we define a message as $M = AC$. This functional form for the relationship among M, A, and C amounts to a strong assumption about the way people's activities and concerns interact to produce messages. A multiplicative form is not the only way this might happen. Maybe dollars, acts, or hours have diminishing marginal impacts so that M should be equal to C times the logarithm of A. Or maybe some other functional form is more appropriate. Lacking any clear-cut guidance on the issue, the multiplicative form seems like a good starting place.

The multiplicative form makes it easy to calculate messages. If, for example, a person writes ten letters promoting the government provision of jobs (scored as one) instead of the status quo (scored as zero), then M is ten times one or ten. If this person gives one hundred dollars for the same purpose, then M is 100. If the person's concern is scored as minus two on some scale, then a 100 dollar contribution would lead to minus 200 dollars in messages.

After calculating the messages (and non-messages) from everyone in the population, their distribution is obviously of great interest, and it seems useful to think about comparing the distribution of the message described by M with the distribution of C, the characteristic or concern of people in the population. These distributions can be described as histograms or frequency plots with the value of the message (for M) or the concern (for C) along the horizontal axis and the frequency or probability of the message or concern along the vertical axis. There is no reason why M and C must have the same shape or the same location on the horizontal axis. Differences in location indicate that activity amplifies or mutes people's concerns. Differences in shape indicate how activity distorts these concerns. In this section, we develop a framework for thinking about how to compare these features of the two distributions.

If everybody engages in one and only one act (A = 1), then clearly messages and characteristics will be the same, and decision makers will be sent messages that provide an undistorted view of people's characteristics. Even if activity is constant, but not one, it seems reasonable to say that participation provides an undistorted version of characteristics, although it might provide an amplified or muted version of them depending upon whether the constant is greater or less than one. The level of activity, then, can be thought of as the volume or noisiness of the messages. Volume is probably important in ensuring that decision makers pay attention to citizens—certainly a volume of zero is unlikely to exert much influence—but here we focus upon comparing the shape of M with the shape of C. In order to facilitate a comparison of M and C in these simple cases with A constant, it seems sensible to divide M by the constant A to adjust for the muting or amplifying effects of activity. More generally, when A might vary, it seems reasonable to divide M by E(A), the average volume of activity to form:

(8) $M^* = M/E(A) = AC/E(A)$.

This will ensure that M^* and C will be in the same units and that they can be easily compared with one another.

As mentioned above, both M^* and C are random variables with a range of values and probabilities attached to each value. They can be displayed using a histogram or probability plot. This is not a very convenient way to summarize data because it requires two figures for each pair of activities and characteristics. We have only done this once in this book, and we have done so with respect to the very interesting case of abortion attitudes and protesting. Figure 14.1 shows how attitudes in the general population on abortion are heavily weighted toward the liberal position—38 percent of the respondents placed themselves at the most liberal position on a seven-point scale and only 15 percent placed themselves at the most conservative position. This histogram for C can be compared with the histogram for M in Figure 16.8, which shows the percentage taking part in a protest on any issue and the percentage taking part in a protest specifically on abortion by attitudes on abortion. We find that while protest activity in general is more heavily weighted toward the liberal pro-choice side, protest explicitly on abortion is heavily weighted toward the conservative pro-life side. Explicit protests on abortion distort the public's opinion on the issue toward the pro-life side.

THE AVERAGE DISTORTION OF MESSAGES

Although the abortion and protest example demonstrates that the entire distributions of M and A may be of interest, in most cases we just need a summary measure of the shape of a distribution. The obvious approach is to compare the average or expectation of C with that of M^*. Thus, we take the expectation of (8), and we use the basic result that the expectation of a product equals the product of the expectations plus the covariance (Cov) between the two variables:

$$
(9) \quad E(M^*) = E(AC)/E(P) = [E(A)E(C) + \text{Cov}(A,C)]/E(A)
$$
$$
= E(C) + \text{Cov}(A,C)/E(A).
$$

If $E(M^*)$ and $E(C)$ were the same, we would say that the activity A did not lead to messages M^* that communicated a distorted average position on the characteristic C. This will happen if A and C do not co-vary with one another; that is, if $\text{Cov}(A,C)$ is zero in (9). This makes a great deal of intuitive sense. Consider the case where A and C co-vary with one another because a protest concerning abortion is much more likely for a person who is pro-life and against abortion than for a person who is pro-choice and in favor of legal abortion. This will cause the messages sent through protests to be more pro-life than is the sentiment in the population. This is the message of Figures 14.1 and 16.8.

The difference between $E(M^*)$ and $E(C)$ seems like an excellent measure of mean message distortion D_M:

$$
(10) \quad D_M = E(M^*) - E(C) = \text{Cov}(A,C)/E(A).
$$

This measure has the advantage of being very easy to compute, but it appears to proliferate measures. How does it relate to some of the other measures we have already defined? For example, how does it relate to D_C defined by equation (1)? It turns out that in the case of dichotomous participation (the condition under which (1) was defined), (1) is a special case of (10).[15]

Do the terms on the right-hand side of (10) make intuitive sense? Does it seem reasonable to omit $E(C)$ from (10)? The direct impact in (10) of the covariance between activity and characteristics follows because it is the interaction of the two, such as higher activity people having more of some characteristic, that is the primary source of distortion. The inverse impact of the average level of activity is most easily understood by comparing what would happen at zero and at very high or infinite levels of activity. At zero levels of activity, distortion would be infinite or undefined because no one would be sending messages. This is exactly what (10) implies. At infinite levels of political activity, distortion would be zero because any variance in activity levels would be small compared to the average level of activity.[16] Finally, there is no reason why E(C) should be in the formula for D_M because a change in the average characteristic should not matter unless it interacts somehow with level of activity.

A STANDARDIZED MEASURE OF THE DISTORTION OF MESSAGES

One of the nice features of D_M is that it is in the same units as the characteristic C. This makes it especially useful for comparing distortion across different activities for the same characteristic. In fact, we noted the same advantage for D_C. But we also noted that D_C was not very good for situations where we wanted to compare across different characteristics because its metric would probably be different from one characteristic to another. This led us to define the representation ratio (R_{AC}) for the case of dichotomous activity and dichotomous characteristics. This ratio provided a standardized measure by taking the ratio of E(AC) and [E(A)E(C)], but it also required that E(A) and E(C) be non-zero. Both E(A) and E(C) will be non-zero for dichotomous activity and characteristics in all except trivial and uninteresting cases. At this point, however, we do not want to be limited to the assumption of either dichotomous activity or dichotomous characteristics, so we must find another way to develop a standardized measure.

An obvious approach, similar to what is done with standardized regression coefficients or beta-weights, is to divide D_M by the standard deviation of the characteristic to get a new measure D_M^*:

(11) $$D_M^* = \text{Cov(A,C)}/[\text{E(A) StdDev(C)}],$$

where StdDev(C) is the standard deviation of C. The standard deviation of C will always be positive (except in trivial and uninteresting cases), and it will make D_M^* a dimension-less quantity that can be compared across different characteristics as well as different activities. We use D_M^*

extensively throughout Chapter 16, and it appears on Figures 16.2–16.8, 16.10, and 16.12–16.13 as the "Total Distortion." We can get a better sense of what this measure means by multiplying the top and bottom by the standard deviation of A and rearranging the terms:

$$(12) \qquad D_M^* = \frac{Cov(A,C)}{StdDev(A)\,StdDev(C)}\,\frac{StdDev(A)}{E(A)}.$$

The first term on the right is the correlation between activity and concerns, and it ranges from minus one to plus one. The second term is the relative standard deviation (or coefficient of variation) for A. This can range from zero to infinity. For example, if A is a dichotomous activity with $E(A) = \pi$ (so π is the proportion who engage in the activity), then the relative standard deviation is equal to the square-root of $(1-\pi)/\pi$. If everybody participates, then π is one, the relative standard deviation is zero, and there is no distortion. If nobody participates, then π is zero, the relative standard deviation is infinity, and there is infinite distortion. But these are extreme cases, and they vastly overestimate the range of the relative standard deviation and consequently of D_M^*. Even if only 5 percent of the population participates in a dichotomous activity, the relative standard deviation will be merely 4.35. For the activities in our survey, the values of the relative standard deviation are shown in the right-most column of Table C.1. They range from a low of .66 for voting to a high of 5.01 for total political contributions. Note that our overall measure of the number of political acts has a value of only .77. These data suggest a maximum range for D_M^* between minus five and plus five, but these bounds are still very loose and exaggerated.

What, then, constitutes a significant distortion?[17] There are several different ways to calibrate this measure. One approach is to consider dichotomous activities and to remember that in this case, D_M is equal to D_C. If we go one step farther and assume dichotomous characteristics as well, then D_M is the proportion of the activists with the characteristic minus the proportion of the population with the characteristic. The standardized measure D_M^* is just D_M divided by the standard deviation of the characteristic. For any characteristic, we would probably consider a five percent difference between the activists and the population to be somewhat significant, a ten percent difference to be significant, and a fifteen percent difference to be highly significant. If about fifty percent of the population has the characteristic, then D_M^* will be ±.10 for the five percent difference, ±.20 for the ten percent difference, and ±.30 for the

Table C.1 Relative Standard Deviations for Basic Political Activities

	Mean E(A)	Standard Deviation σ_A	Relative Standard Deviation $\sigma_A / E(A)$
EIGHT INDIVIDUAL POLITICAL ACTS			
Campaign Work	.08	.28	3.29
Campaign Contribution	.24	.42	1.80
Contact an Official	.34	.47	1.39
Protest	.06	.23	4.06
Member of Board or Attend Meetings Regularly	.04	.20	4.73
Informal	.17	.38	2.21
Vote	.70	.46	.66
Member of Political Organization	.48	.50	1.04
AVERAGE NUMBER OF EIGHT ACTS	2.11	1.63	.77
MONEY AND TIME FOR ACTIVITY			
Political Time (hours/week)	.93	3.92	4.24
Political Contributions	$66.16	$331.16	5.01

fifteen percent difference. The sign of D_M^* will depend upon whether the difference between activists and the population is in favor of the activists or the general population. The total distortions reported in the figures in Chapter 16 cover this range and beyond. Political money and economic need (Figure 16.4) lead to a total distortion of .54; protest and economic views (Figure 16.5) produce a distortion of −.33; messages about abortion and abortion attitudes (Figure 16.10) lead to a distortion of .36; and political money and information (Figure 16.12) leads to a whopping distortion of .78.

Another approach is to consider what we might expect for the correlations between activities and characteristics and to see what that implies for distortion. Correlations of .3 or higher in absolute value are often considered quite impressive for the social sciences. Because many of our activity measures are highly skewed, it seems likely that their correlations with less highly skewed attitude and demographic variables will be less than this. Indeed, if we peek at the data we find that even political interest and education, the two strongest predictors of political activity, are typically correlated between .10 and .30 with all political activity measures except the total number of acts with which they are correlated about .45. If we multiply these numbers by the appropriate relative standard deviations, we obtain *upper bounds* for distortions of somewhere between .30 and .90. These are, indeed, some of the larger distortions we obtain in Chapter 16. Our sense is that values of D_M^* over .10 imply a substantial amount of total participatory distortion and should be taken seriously. Values as large as .30 are extremely large and suggest a great deal of bias in the participatory system.

VARIANCES

The measures of total distortion described so far depend upon differences in average characteristics between activists and the general population, but an average is only a partial description of any distribution of characteristics. In some cases, such as with protest on the abortion issue, other aspects of the distribution are of interest.[18] Public opinion is very polarized on the abortion issue. Construing total distortion in terms of deviations from the mean attitude of the population, we can imagine three possibilities in which there is no participatory distortion: abortion activity emanates proportionally from each of the attitude groups—pro-life, moderate, and pro-choice; abortion activity comes disproportionately from moderates, with those holding pro-life and pro-choice positions relatively quiescent; abortion activity emerges disproportionately from those with extreme pro-life and pro-choice opinions and moderates are relatively inactive. In all three cases, abortion activity represents accurately the mean opinion of the public. In the latter two cases, however, there is distortion with respect to the variance in opinion. This distortion would surely have implications for the nature of abortion politics. We would expect the politics of abortion to be very different depending upon whether most of the activity originates with moderates or with those at the extremes. This consideration is one of the reasons why we presented the entire histograms for abortion attitudes and protest activity on abortion in Figures 14.1 and 16.8.

GRAPHIC PRESENTATION OF DISTORTION

In Chapters 7 and 8 we present a number of "pie-charts"[19] in which we compare the proportion of each group in the population and their proportion weighted by their participation. This provides a way of seeing how large these groups will look to those decision makers who rely upon political participation to provide messages.[20] In these pie-charts we found that higher income groups and Anglo-Whites were much more visible through their participation than lower income groups and ethnic and racial minorities who participate much less.

These pie-charts were constructed straightforwardly by calculating a set of average standardized message levels $E(M_j^*)$ generated for each possible category j of the basic characteristic. Thus, for the six income categories in Figures 7.4 and 7.5, we constructed six different variables, $C_1, C_2, \ldots, C_6$, such that $C_j = 1$ if and only if a person has that income level. Then a separate $E(M_j^*)$ was constructed for each of these variables using equation (9). It can be shown that each one of these $E(M_j^*)$ equals the following:[21]

$$(13) \qquad E(M_j^*) = E(C_j) \, [E(A|C_j=1)/E(A)],$$

where $E(C_j)$ is the proportion of people in group j, $E(A|C_j=1)$ is the average activity level of those in group j, and $E(A)$ is the average activity level of the population. The ratio in brackets on the right-hand-side of (13) is simply the representation ratio for characteristic C_j (see equation (3)). If this ratio is one, then $E(M_j^*)$ is equal to the group's proportion in the population.[22] If the ratio is greater than one, then the group is overrepresented; if it is less than one then the group is underrepresented.

The proportions in the pie-charts are calculated by taking each $E(M_j^*)$ over the sum of all the $E(M_j^*)$. Each slice is then the fraction of the total messages coming from those with characteristic j. Because the sum of all the $E(M_j^*)$ turns out to be one,[23] the proportions in the pie-charts are given by (13) and they are equal to the group's proportion in the population times their representation ratio. The pie-charts consequently provide a visual representation of how the activity of a group magnifies or diminishes the volume of the group's messages compared to the volume if messages were strictly proportional to the group's characteristics.

4. Explaining Messages by Participatory Factors

A SIMPLE LINEAR MODEL FOR ACTIVITY AND CHARACTERISTICS

The preceding section provides a way to think about measuring the distortion, if any, in the way activity transforms concerns and characteristics into messages. In this section we explore how to evaluate the distortion that comes from the impact of factors affecting both activity and characteristics. We start with a linear regression model for both activity and concerns:

$$(14) \qquad A = \alpha + X\,\beta + \epsilon = \alpha + \Sigma_j\, X_j\, \beta_j + \epsilon,$$

$$(15) \qquad C = \gamma + X\,\delta + \psi = \gamma + \Sigma_j\, X_j\, \delta_j + \psi.$$

In these equations, the X_j are a set of factors (or independent variables) affecting activity and concerns, α and γ are constants or intercept terms, β_j and δ_j are slope coefficients, and ϵ and ψ are error terms.[24] We take equation (14) for activity to be the Civic Voluntarism Model described in Chapters 9–15 of the book, but it could be other models as well. Equation (15) has the same factors in it as the CVM because these provide a fairly exhaustive set of possible determinants of politically relevant concerns.

Total distortion D_M as defined in (10) will be affected by a change in an independent variable X_j if $E(A)$ or $Cov(A,C)$ is affected by the change. This could happen in two ways. First, a change in the mean of X_j will either increase or decrease the average activity level depending upon the sign of its coefficient because the mean of A is equal to $[\alpha + E(X)\,\beta]$.[25] Thus, an increase in education would increase the average level of participation, assuming that education is positively related to participation. Second, a change in the variance of X_j could affect the covariance between activity and concerns because X_j appears in both (14) and (15) and the covariance of A and C will depend upon the covariance of X_j in one equation with X_j in the other. The covariance of these two X_j is, of course, just the variance of X_j. Increases in the variance of X_j will occur when X_j is more unequally distributed in the population, and decreases in its variance will occur when X_j is more equally distributed.

The total impact of a change in any factor involves both these changes in the average level of political activity and in the covariance between activity and concerns. The Civic Voluntarism Model, however, is primarily a cross-sectional model explaining differences in people's participation at one point in time rather than a time-series model for explaining changes in the level of participation. Consequently, we feel that it is much more appropriate to use it to consider changes in the variance of independent variables rather than changes in their mean level. We feel confident, for example, that we can use the Civic Voluntarism Model to say something about what would happen if education were more equal or civic skills more equally distributed, but we do not feel very confident about using it to predict how participation levels would change if average educational attainment, for example, suddenly increased by four years.[26] For our purposes, then, we are less interested in changes in the mean of activity than in changes in the covariance of activity and characteristics brought about by changes in the variances of independent variables. From now on, we will always assume that participation stays constant as we consider the impact of changes in our independent variables.

PARTITIONING CAUSES OF PARTICIPATORY DISTORTION

Increases or decreases in distortion without changes in the level of political activity requires changes in the covariance of A and C. This covariance can be written in terms of covariances among the independent variables and the error terms for the linear models in (14) and (15):

$$(16) \quad Cov(A,C) = \Sigma_j \, \Sigma_k \, \beta_j \, \delta_k \, Cov(X_j,X_k) + \Sigma_j \, \beta_j \, Cov(X_j,\psi) + \Sigma_k \, \delta_k \, Cov(X_k,\epsilon) + Cov(\epsilon,\psi).$$

If the same independent variables appear in both (14) and (15), then the two middle terms on the right must be zero to satisfy the standard specification assumptions for linear regression.[27] In our empirical work we always include the same independent variables in both equations, but we will carry these terms along in our development here until it becomes absolutely necessary to drop them to make additional progress.

Now consider the following version of (16) which collects all the terms with β_h in them:

$$(17) \quad Cov(A,C) = \Sigma_h \, \beta_h \, [\Sigma_k \, \delta_k \, Cov(X_h,X_k) + Cov(X_h,\psi)] + \Sigma_k \, \delta_k \, Cov(X_k,\epsilon) + Cov(\epsilon,\psi).$$

One reasonable definition of the impact of X_h *through activity* might be that it is β_h times the term in brackets because β_h links X_h to activity. If we divide both sides of (17) by E(A) then the left-hand side becomes the unstandardized measure of distortion D_M, and it seems reasonable to define the distortion due to X_h through political activity, denoted by D_h^A, as β_h times the term in brackets in (17) divided by E(A):

$$(18) \quad D_h^A = \beta_h \, [\Sigma_k \, \delta_k \, Cov(X_h,X_k) + Cov(X_h,\psi)]/E(A).$$

By taking the summation over k and putting δ inside the covariance term in the expression above, we can easily show that this can be written as:

$$(19) \quad D_h^A = \beta_h \, [Cov(X_h,C)]/E(A),$$

and this is the distortion from X_h through β_h.

This definition of distortion from each independent variable provides a way to decompose the total distortion D_M into pieces due to each variable X_h in A and pieces due to the error term ϵ in A:[28]

$$(20) \qquad D_M = \Sigma_h \, D_h^A + [\Sigma_k \, \delta_k \, \mathrm{Cov}(X_k, \epsilon) + \mathrm{Cov}(\epsilon, \psi)]/E(A)$$
$$= \Sigma_h \, D_h^A + [\mathrm{Cov}(C, \epsilon)]/E(A).$$

Note that the "remainder" that is not explained by some D_h^A can be written as the covariance of C with the error term ϵ from the equation for A. This term will usually reduce to $\mathrm{Cov}(\psi, \epsilon)/E(A)$ if the same independent variables are in both equations. Equation (20) provides a straightforward way to interpret the distortion due to each variable. If a value of D_h^A is zero, then it seems reasonable to say that the distortion from X_h through activity is zero, and if the values of all D_h^A are zero, then it seems reasonable to say that there is no distortion from any X_h through activity.

The preceding paragraphs have developed a measure, D_h^A, of participatory distortion from a factor through political activity. We can develop a parallel measure of participatory distortion from a factor *through a characteristic* by collecting all the terms in δ_h in (16). This yields measures D_h^C that are very similar to those defined by (19):

$$(21) \qquad D_h^C = \delta_h \, \mathrm{Cov}(A, X_h)/E(A).$$

This can be thought of as the distortion of X_h through δ_h, and it provides another decomposition of D_M as follows:

$$(22) \qquad D_M = \Sigma_h \, D_h^C + [\Sigma_k \, \beta_k \, \mathrm{Cov}(\psi, X_k) + \mathrm{Cov}(\epsilon, \psi)]/E(A)$$
$$= \Sigma_h \, D_h^C + [\mathrm{Cov}(A, \psi)]/E(A).$$

This is parallel to (20) above.

ANOTHER MEASURE

The measures D_h^A and D_h^C each tell part of the story about the impact of X_h. One (D_h^A) tells the story about the impact of X_h through activity; the other (D_h^C) tells the story about the impact of X_h through characteristics. The total impact of X_h must take into account both of these. This suggests that we should add the two measures together, but this will lead to double-counting because the sum of *each* of these across the independent variables X_h (plus some covariances of the error terms) equals the total distortion D_M. A more useful overall measure is the average of D_h^A and D_h^C:

$$(23) \qquad D_h = [D_h^A + D_h^C]/2.$$

In the common situation where the errors ϵ and ψ in the basic equations for activity and characteristics are not correlated with the X_h, the total distortion can be written in terms of this new measure as:

(24) $$D_M = \Sigma_h D_h + [Cov(\psi,\epsilon)]/E(A).$$

Except for the covariance of the error terms, these new measures D_h will sum to the total distortion.[29] Moreover, each D_h gives a reasonable indication of how much X_h contributes to the distortion. Like our earlier measures, however, D_h is not standardized. Therefore, we divide it by the standard deviation of C to get:

(25) $$D_h^* = D_h/[StdDev(C)].$$

Then we can use (11) and (24) to write:

(26) $$\begin{aligned} D_M^* &= D_M/[StdDev(C)] \\ &= \Sigma_h D_h^* + [Cov(\psi,\epsilon)]/[E(P)*StdDev(C)]. \end{aligned}$$

The D_h^* are now dimensionless quantities that indicate the contribution of a participatory factor X_h to the total distortion. These quantities are reported in the figures in Chapter 16. Equation (26) shows that the D_h^* will sum to the total distortion except for the contribution of the last term resulting from correlated error terms across the two equations.

INTERPRETING THE D_h^*

Equation (26) provides the most help in interpreting the D_h^* because it shows that they can be thought of as components of the total distortion. Consequently, our earlier discussion about interpreting the total distortion is relevant with the qualification that the D_h^* provide information on the contribution of each participatory factor or independent variable. Furthermore, since we argued earlier that a total distortion D_M^* of .10 would be somewhat significant and a total distortion of .30 would be very significant, it seems reasonable to argue that D_h^* values equal to these numbers divided by the number of participatory factors X_h should be considered significant. Typically our regression equations have five to ten factors in them. This suggests that the lower bound for D_h^* values that would be considered significant would be in the range of .01 to .06.

We can, however, go beyond this useful observation by examining the meaning of the D_h^* in the special case where the participatory factors happen to be uncorrelated with one another. This is very unlikely to occur, but it provides the basis for a useful thought experiment. If the participatory factors are uncorrelated with one another and if they are uncorrelated with the error terms (as we have been assuming throughout this subsection), then we can write:[30]

$$(27) \qquad\qquad D_h^* = \frac{\beta_h \delta_h \, Var(X_h)}{StdDev(C)E(A)}.$$

In fact, this can be written as follows where β_h^* and δ_h^* are standardized regression coefficients or "beta weights":[31]

$$(28) \qquad\qquad D_h^* = \beta_h^* \, \delta_h^* \, \frac{StdDev(A)}{E(A)}.$$

This is very similar to what we obtained earlier for D_M^* in equation (12) except that the product of the standardized regression coefficients has replaced the correlation between A and C.

Equation (28) provides a useful basis for interpreting D_h^*. In most of our regressions, we have found that standardized regression coefficients of .10 or above were invariably statistically significant and substantively significant as well. The product of two such coefficients is .01. If the relative standard deviation ranges from one to five as in Table C.1, then D_h^* values starting in the range of .01 to .05 would be worth considering.

These two approaches for calibrating D_h^* yield convergent results. The lower bound on statistically and substantively significant values of D_h^* is somewhere between .01 and .06. In the main body of the book, we suggest a value around .04 as a very conservative threshold.

PROGRAMMING THESE MEASURES

We developed an SPSS matrix program that calculates D_M^* and all the D_h^* values for any set of activities A, characteristics C, and independent variables X_h. This program also produces a number of other useful measures. It assumes linear models as in (14) and (15), and it can deal with weighted data. This program produced all of the results in Chapter 16. The program does not produce information about the statistical significance of each measure, but this is certainly possible in principle.

5. Summary Statement

Our goal has been to develop a framework for measuring representation. We started by developing a number of different measures for describing participatory distortion that go beyond standard approaches that treat only dichotomous activities and dichotomous characteristics. We also sought measures that would allow for easy comparisons across different characteristics and different activities. We have suggested a number of these kinds of measures in this Appendix, and we use them throughout the book.

Knowing that there is participatory distortion is only the first step. We also want to trace it through the politically relevant groups (defined by politically relevant characteristics) that are such an important part of American politics. This was done by first breaking down participatory distortion into pieces due to each group, and then by showing how this group distortion could be expressed in terms of the activity or inactivity of its members and the possible distortion of the group's concerns by its activists. The resulting calculus allowed us, for example, to show that opinions on governmental help for Blacks are skewed in the conservative direction, and this is primarily because of the inactivity of Blacks and not the conservatism of Black activists.

After describing participatory distortion and breaking it down by groups, we then turned to asking how the factors that contribute to political participation affect participatory distortion. The Civic Voluntarism Model developed in Chapters 9–15 provided the starting place for doing this. In this Appendix we have described how this model can be used to identify the factors that contribute to participatory distortion. We have developed some measures for quantifying these effects, and we have calibrated these measures.

These techniques have been used throughout the book. They all come together in Chapter 16. Perhaps the best example of the entire framework is presented by Figures 16.6 and 16.7. In Figure 16.6, the total participatory distortion in attitudes toward minorities is broken down by various participatory factors. In Figure 16.7, these same attitudes are considered but the analysis is just for the subgroups. Thus, in this figure the "total" distortions that are reported are for the distortion within these groups which is the factor $[E(C|a,g) - E(C|g)]$ in equation (7). This analysis brings together the decomposition of distortion for groups and the decomposition of distortion for participatory factors.

Notes

1. It certainly seems to include accountability approaches and descriptive representation as defined by Hanna Fenichel Pitkin in *The Concept of Representation* (Berkeley and Los Angeles: University of California Press, 1967).

2. Formally, if C_i is an observation of C and there are I such observations, then E(C) equals $\Sigma_i C_i / I$. Alternatively, if p(C = c) is the probability that C equals c, then E(C) equals $\Sigma_{C = c} C\, p(C)$ or the weighted average over all possible values of C.

3. Formally, $E(C|a)$ is the conditional expectation of C given a. If $p(C = c|a)$ is the probability that C equals c for the activists a, then $E(C|a)$ equals $\Sigma_{C\,=\,c}C\ p(C|a)$.

4. Raymond Wolfinger and Steven Rosenstone, *Who Votes?* (Berkeley: University of California Press, 1980).

5. We get this percentage by assuming that C is scored one for those favoring the referendum and zero otherwise.

6. In *Mobilization, Participation, and Democracy in America* (New York: MacMillan, 1993), Steven J. Rosenstone and John Mark Hansen use a measure they call EQ to describe inequality in political participation across groups. This measure is the ratio of $E(A|c_1)$ for the characteristic c_1 at one end of a distribution (such as those with the lowest education) to the ratio $E(A|c_N)$ for those at the top end of a distribution (such as those with the highest education). Our consideration of $E(A|c)$ for many different values of c is an implicit use of this kind of measure. (Rosenstone and Hansen actually define EQ in terms of representation ratios like those defined in this Appendix in equations (2) through (4), but their definition of EQ amounts to the one given above.)

7. This measure is also identical to the "RATIO" defined by Rosenstone and Hansen, *Mobilization, Participation, and Democracy in America*, p. 291.

8. The proof relies upon noting that in this doubly dichotomous case with $A = a$ scored as one and $C = c$ scored as one and the other two possibilities as zero, $E(A|c)$ equals the probability of the event (a and c) divided by the probability of the event c. Hence, R(A) is [p(a and c)/(p(c)*p(a))]. Similarly, R(C) is [p(a and c)/(p(c)*p(a))]. This can also be written, in this dichotomous case, as $E(AC)/[E(A)*E(C)]$.

9. The proof is in the footnote above. This formula provides another interpretation of the representation ratio. If A and C are independent of one another, then $E(AC) = E(A)*E(C)$, so the representation ratio is unity in this case. The departure of the representation ratio from unity indicates the degree to which A and C are not independent of one another.

10. As noted in footnote 6, at the same time as we first developed our measure, Rosenstone and Hansen (*Mobilization, Participation, and Democracy in America*, pp. 293–296) proposed a somewhat different measure EQ of inequality in political participation for groups. This measure is defined as a ratio of representation ratios. If C has multiple categories, $c_1, \ldots, c_N$, then this measure amounts to the ratio of R_{AC} for C equal to some category c_1 and R_{AC} for C equal to category c_N. When $C = c_1$ then R_{AC} is equal to $E(A|c_1)/E(A)$ and when $C = c_N$ then R_{AC} is equal to

$E(A|c_N)/E(A)$. Thus the EQ measure amounts to $E(A|c_1)/E(A|c_N)$. Rosenstone and Hansen argue that "the representation ratios by themselves are sensitive to changes in each group's share of the population, meaning that the ratios cannot be used to make comparisons over time or across divisions of the population" (p. 296, note 8). Rosenstone and Hansen are correct in saying that representation ratios are sensitive to changes in each group's share of the population and EQ is not, but EQ is sensitive to how c_N is defined. More important, they overstate the case when they say that representation ratios cannot be used to make comparisons; representation ratios just make different comparisons than EQ. The differences follow from their definitions. For a category c_1 of interest, R_{AC} equals $E(A|c_1)/E(A)$ and EQ equals $E(A|c_1)/E(A|c_N)$. Both measures compare the activity level $E(A|c_1)$ of those with characteristic c_1 to a referent population. The representation ratio makes a comparison with the overall activity $E(A)$ in the population and EQ makes a comparison with the activity $E(A|c_N)$ of some group c_N. Although there is great merit in Rosenstone and Hansen's measure, we choose to standardize in terms of the whole population because we know of no obvious choice for c_N.

11. For a random sample of size I, the variance of the estimate of the measure $E(A|c) - E(A)$ is $\{[(I - 2I_c)Var(A|c)/II_c] + Var(A)/I\}$ where $Var(A)$ is the variance of A for the entire sample and $Var(A|c)$ is the variance of A for the I_c people in the sample with characteristic c. If $Var(A)$ equals $Var(A|c)$, then this formula reduces to $[(I - I_c)Var(A)/II_c]$, and the variance for the difference measure will be bigger than the variance for the estimate of $E(A)$ which is $[Var(A)/I]$ by the factor $[(I - I_c)/I_c]$. If 10 percent of the population has characteristic c then this is equal to nine; if 50 percent have the characteristic then it is one.

12. See Table 7.2 and Figure 7.7 for data on government provision of jobs and Figure 8.3 for data on government assistance to Blacks or Latinos.

13. Thus, once p(Blacks), p(Whites), and p(Rest) are given, we can simply choose D_C(Blacks), D_C(Whites), and D_C(Rest) to be equal to D_C, and the equation is satisfied but in a very uninteresting and uninformative fashion.

14. See Henry E. Brady, Sidney Verba, and Kay Schlozman, "Participation, Resources and Representation: How Citizen Attitudes are Distorted," paper presented at the Annual Meetings of the American Political Science Association, Washington, D.C., September 1993, and Henry E. Brady, Sidney Verba, and Kay Schlozman, "A Framework for Measuring

the Fairness of Political Participation and Representation," paper presented at the Annual Meetings of the Political Methodology Group, Madison, Wisconsin, July 1994.

15. The proof relies upon the result (used above) that $Cov(A,C)$ equals $E(AC) - E(A)E(C)$ and the fact that $E(AC)$ equals $E(C|A = a)E(A)$ when A is dichotomous. The result then follows by a little algebra.

16. Perhaps the impact of activity level is easiest to see in the case of a dichotomous form of participation. Then high activity—namely 100% participation—cannot cause any distortion because everyone is represented equally.

17. Here we are considering substantive significance—the extent to which the results are of some practical or scientific interest—and not statistical significance, which is the extent to which results can be considered the consequence of something more than chance.

18. For another discussion of a measure of participatory distortion that incorporates consideration of differences in variance, see Sidney Verba, Kay Lehman Schlozman, Henry Brady, and Norman H. Nie, "Citizen Activity: Who Participates? What Do They Say?" *American Political Science Review* 87 (1993): 303–318.

19. Figures 7.4 and 7.5 for political and non-political activities by income groups and Figure 8.2 for political activities by race and ethnic groups.

20. If decision makers follow the opinion polls, then they will get messages proportional to the size of the group. But most decision makers probably do rely upon messages communicated through political participation, and this will distort what they hear.

21. The first steps of the proof rely upon the definition of M_j^* and the fact that C_j is a dichotomous variable with values of zero and one to produce the following results:

$$E(M_j^*) = \Sigma_i \ A_i \ C_j \ p(A_i,C_j)/E(A) = \Sigma_i \ A_i \ p(A_i,C_j = 1)/E(A).$$

Then we use the definition of conditional probability to write $p(A_i,C_j = 1)$ as $p(A_i|C_j = 1)p(C_j = 1)$, we use the definition of conditional expectation for $E(A|C_j = 1)$, and we use the fact that $E(C_j) = p(C_j = 1)$:

$$E(M_j^*) = \Sigma_i \ A_i \ p(A_i|C_j = 1)p(C_j = 1)/E(A)$$
$$= p(C_j = 1) \ \Sigma_i A_i p(A_i|C_j = 1)/E(A) = E(C_j) \ E(A|C_j = 1)/E(A).$$

22. In this case, D_M will be zero because by equation (10) D_M equals $E(M_j^*) - E(C_j)$.

23. Each $E(M_j^*)$ equals $E(C_j)$ times the representation ratio for C_j. The representation ratio is equal to $E(AC_j)/[E(A)*E(C_j)]$ so that $E(M_j^*)$ equals $E(AC_j)/E(A)$. Therefore $\Sigma_j\ E(M_j^*)$ equals $\Sigma_j E(AC_j)/E(A)$. It is a simple matter to use the definition of the C_j to show that $\Sigma_j E(AC_j)$ equals $E(A)$ and $\Sigma_j\ E(M_j^*)$ must equal one.

24. We use a linear regression framework because it is simple and a reasonable starting place, but many other functional forms might be considered. Because participation is often dichotomous, a probit or logit setup might be appropriate, although we believe that the linear probability usually suffices quite nicely. A multiplicative form might make some sense, and it has interesting consequences. These approaches are discussed in more detail in our papers cited earlier.

25. This follows from an application of the well-known results that the expectation of a sum equals the sum of the expectations and that the expectation of a constant times a random variable is the constant times the expectation of the random variable.

26. As pointed out by Norman Nie, Jane Junn, and Ken Stelik-Berry, education may be not only a source of skills but also a filtering mechanism that restricts participation (and other activities) to those who have made it to the top levels. In this case, participation will not necessarily increase if everyone gets more education because participation will still be restricted to those at the (now more highly educated) top levels. See Nie, Junn, and Stehlik-Berry, *Education and Citizenship in America* (Chicago: University of Chicago Press, forthcoming).

27. The specification assumption is that the included independent variables are not correlated with the error terms.

28. Equation (20) follows from the definition of D_h^A in (18), the expression for $Cov(A,C)$ in (17), and the definition for D_M in (10).

29. This follows because in the case where the errors are not correlated with the X_h, we can write the decompositions of total distortion in (20) and (22) as follows:

$$D_M = \Sigma_h\ D_h^A + [Cov(\psi,\epsilon)]/E(A)$$

and

$$D_M = \Sigma_h\ D_h^C + [Cov(\psi,\epsilon)]/E(A).$$

If we take the average of these two equations then (24) in the text follows by using the definition of D_h in (23).

30. This result follows straightforwardly from the definition of D_h^* in

(25) in terms of D_h, the definition of D_h in (23) in terms of D_h^A and D_h^C, the definition of these two terms in (18) and (21), and the assumption that $Cov(X_j, X_k) = 0$ for j not equal to k.

31. The proof only requires remembering that a beta weight β_h^* equals β_h times the standard deviation of X_h divided by the standard deviation of A. Similarly δ_h^* equals the standard deviation of X_h divided by the standard deviation of C.

Specification of the Civic Voluntarism Model

The specification of the Civic Voluntarism Model (CVM) involves a number of complicated issues that are mentioned in the text and given fuller treatment in this appendix. The most fundamental claim of the CVM is that resources, political engagements, and recruitment through social networks are the basic sources of political participation. We elaborate this claim in three steps through Chapters 9–15. First, in Chapters 10 and 11 we show that resources, especially civic skills, come from the institutions in which people are involved as children and as adults. In Chapter 11, we are especially concerned with demonstrating that civic skills do not just covary with involvements in institutions, they are also the result of these involvements. Second, in Chapters 12 through 15 we trace out the causal mechanisms by which people amass resources, become politically engaged, and establish their positions in recruitment networks. Third, throughout these chapters we show how the CVM works in ways we would expect for different political acts. We perform separate analyses for different acts, and we consider specific measures of involvement such as amount of political contributions or amount of time. These elaborations of our model provide additional confirmation of it and require careful thinking about the proper specification. In this appendix we review some of the technical assumptions that are made.

D.1 Resources Come from Institutional Involvements

It seems relatively straightforward to show that time and money come from the circumstances of people's lives. Having a working spouse and pre-school children at home, for example, seem like reasonable and noncontroversial determinants of free time. Similarly, being highly educated and having a job are clearly closely related to people's income. In both these cases, it seems hard to argue that we have the causal order reversed. The situation, unfortunately, is not so clear-cut with civic skills. It is true that it seems unlikely that having civic skills causes people to be involved in religious institutions, non-political organizations, or high-status jobs, but it is possible that a common cause, say a taste for organizational involvement, causes people to be involved in some kinds of organizations and to have civic skills. For this reason, we were especially careful in Chapter 11 to control for as many factors as possible that might explain differences in civic skills.

In addition, in Table 11.7 we presented an analysis, of church members who also work at a job full or part time, that shows how the same kinds of individuals fare quite differently in different kinds of institutions. This table, modest though it seems, provides a very powerful demonstration that the same kinds of people obtain quite different skills depending upon their religious affiliations or job involvements. For example, we show that Catholics with high-status jobs exercise about two and a half times as many skills on the job as do Baptists with low-status jobs, but the high-status Catholics exercise only about one-quarter the number of skills in church as do the latter. Since we are looking at what happens to the same people in two different places, Table 11.7 strongly suggests that these are institutional effects and not differences in the people who choose to join the institutions.

This is an essential step in our argument, and we have considered it from another perspective in a published article.[1] There we have developed a simultaneous equation "Learning Model for Civic Skills" that estimates the extent to which skills are learned in institutions. This model distinguishes between skill-acts measured directly by questions about writing a letter, organizing a meeting, or giving a speech and the underlying civic skills which are people's abilities to do these things. We show in the article that involvement in institutions leads to undertaking skill-acts and that this in turn leads to the development of civic skills. These results along with those in Chapter 11 provide us with a strong belief that civic skills are, indeed, developed through institutional affiliations.

D.2 Specifying the Core Equation of the CVM

The core predictions of the CVM are tested in Chapter 12 by estimating an equation that explains the number of political acts performed by an individual in terms of the person's resources and political engagements. We construct this equation very carefully in Chapter 12 and in a related article,[2] but two important specification issues require more elaboration in this appendix. First, we use both ordinary least squares (OLS) and two-stage least squares (2SLS) to estimate the model, and we use somewhat different specifications of the model in each case. For the 2SLS estimates we also make assumptions about what constitutes legitimate instrumental variables. We explore these issues in this section. Second, we use a linear specification throughout the book, but we often talk as if resources and political engagement are both necessary conditions for participation. If both are really required, then a multiplicative specification might seem to make more sense. We discuss this issue in the last section of this Appendix.

ESTIMATING A RESOURCE VERSION OF THE CVM USING OLS AND 2SLS

The econometrician Edward E. Leamer warns us that "a fragile inference is not worth taking seriously."[3] Because we want to demonstrate the sturdiness of our results for the CVM, we present many different formulations of the model in Chapters 12–15. Our first approach, in Table 12.2, is a version including just institutional affiliations and resources as explanatory variables. We estimate this model using ordinary least squares (OLS) because we argued in Chapters 9 and 12 that one of the advantages of a resource explanation for political participation is that resources result from decisions about life circumstances, jobs, joining organizations, and attending church that are temporally and causally prior to political participation. This seems obviously true for family income and free time, and it seems very likely for adult civic skills developed at work, in church, and in non-political organizations. If so, resources can be considered exogenous in a regression model of political participation and OLS can be used, as in Table 12.2, to estimate the CVM with just institutional affiliation and resources as explanatory variables. Proceeding in this way, however, depends upon our faith in the exogeneity and reliability of the resource measures and our belief that we have included all of the relevant explanatory variables in the model. In subsequent versions of the CVM, we correct for the unreliability of the free time measure, we relax the assumption of exogeneity for some of the resources, and we add additional explanatory variables.

The regression reported in Table 12.2 already includes a measure of family income corrected for unreliability. A measure is unreliable when the reported value deviates from the true value because of random error stemming from factors such as the difficulty of providing accurate responses. The income and free time variables very likely suffer from this problem. The danger of unreliable measures is that OLS estimates of their coefficients will be biased in unpredictable ways.[4] For the family income measure we corrected for unreliability by using the screener family income question. The predicted value from a regression of the follow-up family income on the screener family income amounts to a measure of family income corrected for unreliability. (We used the screener value for family income in the small number of cases where only the screener value was available.) The family income measure that we use in all the regressions in the book, including the one reported in Table 12.2, is constructed in this way. Although a reasonable measure, family income measured in this way is clearly only an approximation of the money available to an individual to use for political or other contributions.

Because we had no screener measure of free time, we had to use another method to adjust for its unreliability. In Table 12.3 we use two-stage least squares (2SLS) to correct for the unreliability in free time and to correct for the possible endogeneity of civic skills. Endogeneity in our model refers to the possibility that a putative independent variable such as civic skills might be partly the result of political participation as well as the cause of activity. Two-stage least squares corrects for endogeneity by using instrumental variables that are correlated with the endogenous variables (in our case civic skills) but are not caused by political participation. (Instrumental variables of this type are called exogenous variables.) Two-stage least squares also corrects for unreliability by using instrumental variables that are correlated with the underlying true component of the unreliable measure (in our case free time) but are not correlated with the random error in the unreliable measure. Often the same instruments can solve both sets of problems as long as the instruments are exogenous and uncorrelated with the error in the unreliable measure.

In Table 12.3 we assume that the following socioeconomic and demographic variables are exogenous:

Citizenship, education, vocabulary, English at home, family income, Catholic, number of children under eighteen at home, preschool children at home, sex, spouse working full- or part-time, Black, Latino, education of parents, and age.

And we assume that the following variables for institutional affiliations are exogenous:

Working, retired, job level, organizational affiliation, and religious attendance.

It seems hard to imagine that any of the socioeconomic and demographic variables in the first list are determined by levels of political participation, so their exogeneity seems assured. It also seems likely that any error in them is uncorrelated with error in free time or civic skills. There is, however, one possible problem. Some of these variables may belong in our equation that explains political participation, in which case leaving them out would lead to a mis-specification of the equation. Indeed, we do include the first five of them (citizenship, education, vocabulary, English at home, family income) in our equation because there are good theoretical reasons to do so. We leave out the rest because we believe they are mediated by those variables included in the model. We have strong theoretical reasons, discussed in Chapters 9 and 12, for leaving most of them out. Perhaps the most problematic of these left-out variables is age. However, as we note, if age is included, the basic pattern of Table 12.3 remains.

The exogeneity of the institutional affiliations may be somewhat more controversial than the exogeneity of the socioeconomic and demographic variables, but we have presented arguments in Chapters 9–12 about why it seems unlikely that people would take a job, join a non-political organization, or attend church because of their political participation. Thus, there seem to be ample reasons for believing that these variables are exogenous. It also seems unlikely that errors in reports of affiliations would be mirrored by errors in reports of free time or civic skills.[5]

Of more concern is the possibility that these institutional affiliations should be included in our equation. If they are included as exogenous variables, then civic skills and free time remain significant and the coefficients of all of the institutional affiliations except being retired are very negative. These negative coefficients make little sense, so it seems reasonable to assume that the institutional affiliations should be dropped from the equation.[6]

ADDING POLITICAL ENGAGEMENTS TO THE CVM

The biggest defect of the version of the CVM in Tables 12.2 and 12.3 with only institutional affiliations and resources is that it leaves out measures of political engagement. Engagement with politics may be another necessary ingredient for some forms of participation. Engagement may also index a taste for politics and organizational life. If this taste for participation is correlated with both the accumulation of resources (most likely civic skills) and political participation, then omitting it from the model will yield biased and incorrect estimates. Although we have doubts about whether the process that leads to involvement in a church, job, or non-political organization has much to do with a taste for politics, we do believe that psychological engagement with politics matters for at least some forms of political participation. Consequently we must add political engagements to the CVM. This has the advantage of also controlling for a taste for politics—to the extent that our measures of political engagement measure this taste.

In Table 12.5 we use OLS to estimate the CVM with both civic skills and political engagements. The results are very strong, and they show that there are good reasons to include political engagements in the model. Yet OLS is even more suspect for estimating this model than for the CVM with just resources because there are ample reasons for believing that political interest and other engagement measures may be the result, rather than the cause, of political activity. In addition, attitudinal measures also suffer from substantial measurement error and unreliability.

Table 12.6 attacks these problems by using 2SLS for civic skills, the political engagement measures, and free time. All of the instruments described above are used again along with three variables from the screener survey: political interest, political information, and partisan strength. These three screener variables cannot be considered exogenous to our model for the same reason that their counterparts on the follow-up survey are not considered exogenous. There is every reason to believe that *past* political participation at least partly determined political interest, political information, and partisan strength on the screener. Although these screener engagements are endogenous in the CVM, they do have one useful property not shared by their cousins on the follow-up survey: They are *lagged* endogenous variables since they were measured six to twelve months earlier than the ones on our follow-up. Because they were measured before the participatory activities on our follow-up, screener engagements cannot be the result of *current* political participation. Lagged endogenous variables like these are called pre-determined variables, and they can serve the same purposes as exogenous variables. In addition, it seems likely that random errors from responses on the screener questions will be uncorrelated with random errors from responses to the follow-up questions. Thus they can serve as instruments in a 2SLS analysis.

In this way, the mutual causation between political engagements such as interest and political participation is disentangled by assuming that current participation depends directly upon current interest (and other factors, of course), and current interest, in turn, depends upon current participation and past interest. Past interest is measured by the question on a screener interview six to twelve months before the final interview. In this set-up, even if both interest items are measured with error, it can be shown that 2SLS provides consistent estimates for the participation equation. With these assumptions, we show in Table 12.6 that civic skills and political engagements (especially political interest and political information) still matter.

In Table 13.6 we go on to add institutional recruitment to the CVM, and we estimate the model using OLS. We show that institutional recruitment matters and that civic skills and political engagements matter as well. In Table 15.6 we present an OLS estimation of a slightly pared down version of the CVM, and in Table 15.7 we present the 2SLS version of this model.

The only slight disappointment in this process is the relatively weak showing of the institutional recruitment measure in the 2SLS estimation (but not the OLS estimation in Table 15.6). Our measure of recruitment, however, was designed to be very conservative (see footnote 2 in Chapter 13 and the discussion at that point in the text), and we have poor instruments for recruitment. This suggests that we should not take too seriously the fact that institutional recruitment failed to get over the final hurdle after making it go over so many others.

Only our result concerning free time appears to be truly fragile. Free time appears to have no impact in the OLS regressions, but it has a consistently significant impact in the 2SLS regressions. Which approach is correct?

One of the reasons free time has a substantial impact in the 2SLS regressions is that working and retirement are excluded from the equation and used as instruments to help correct for the unreliability in free time. We believe that this is the proper specification for the following reasons. In the OLS regression, free time appears to be insignificant when we include dummy variables for working and retirement in the equation because these two variables are so highly correlated with free time. But should we even include working and retirement in an equation that has resources in it? It seems likely that work increases participation through the development of skills (job skills and working are correlated at .61) and decreases participation by reducing free time (free time and working are correlated at −.63). These seem to be the main routes by which working could have an impact on participation. Hence, once job skills and free time are included in an equation for participation, working and retirement should be excluded. When we do include working in an OLS equation with job skills, free time, and many other variables, we find that it has a negative coefficient and that free time appears to have no impact. Yet, we can think of no significant consequence of working, other than its reduction of free time, that would cause its coefficient to be negative. Moreover, the estimated coefficients for working and for free time are strongly correlated (.61), suggesting that working is acting in place of free time. Thus, we believe that the 2SLS regression does a better job of representing the impact of free time than the OLS equation—both because it is a better specification and because it provides instruments for dealing with measurement error in the free time variable. Despite these arguments, the impact of free time is the most fragile of our results, and our ultimate reason for believing it is important is that there is strong evidence (reported in Chapter 12) that at the very least, free time matters for participation in time-based acts once the decision to participate is made.

All in all, our major results—the importance of family income, civic skills, education, and political engagement—for the CVM are not fragile. We have shown that the addition of plausible variables does not cause any of these effects to go away, and different estimation methods yield the same pattern of results. Our investigations do exactly what Edward Leamer argues we must do with empirical research:

> We must insist that all empirical studies offer convincing evidence of inferential sturdiness. We need to be shown that minor changes in the list of variables do not alter fundamentally the conclusions, nor does a slight re-weighting of observations, nor correction for dependence among observations, etcetera, etcetera.[7]

No matter what we do, it seems impossible to find a specification in which civic skills, education, family income, and political engagements do not matter.[8]

D.3 The Multiplicative Specification and Different Acts

At the beginning of Chapter 12 we say that "The resources of time, money, and civic skills make it easier for the individual who is predisposed to take part to do so. The various indicators of political engagement—for example, political interest and efficacy—measure that predisposition." This formulation of the CVM suggests an interactive or multiplicative specification between political engagements and resources. We have not, however, estimated an interactive specification. There are a number of reasons, some technical and some theoretical, why we have not done so.

The theoretical reason is that there may be some acts where differences in either resources or engagement do not matter very much. Political engagement, for example, seems to matter a great deal for voting, and resources are of little importance (see Table 12.8). Even those with little money, time, or civic skills can vote. At the other end of the scale, the resource of income explains most of the variation in political contributions, and political engagement is of secondary importance. We wanted to allow for the possibility that one or the other of engagements or resources would not be relevant for participation, and an interactive specification might have obscured this possibility.

The technical reasons interact with this theoretical concern. Even under the best of circumstances, we know that our measures of resources and engagements are only linear transformations of the true underlying measures of these quantities. We certainly cannot know what the true zero point is of a measure of political interest or civic skills. Under these conditions, it is a simple matter to show that even if we know that the true underlying relationship between engagements and resources is multiplicative, we must estimate a regression equation with a term that is linear in engagements and linear in resources as well as a term that is the product of engagements and resources. These linear terms arise from the need to deal with the unknown zero-point of the engagement and resource measures. Furthermore, only the sign of the interaction term can be predicted in these circumstances. It must be positive.

We have found, in fact, that a regression of this sort for overall participation using the sum of civic skills, political interest, and the interaction of the two, yields a statistically and substantially significant positive coefficient for the interaction term and a statistically significant negative coefficient for one of the two linear terms. This may seem to offer support for the interactive model, but the difficulty is that there is really no way we can be sure that the true underlying model in the metric of the measures we have is truly multiplicative. For example, suppose that when political participation, civic skills, and political interest are measured in a particular fashion, then participation is multiplicatively related to skills and interest. But also assume that the way we have actually measured political participation, civic skills, and political interest amounts to the logarithm of the measures in the multiplicative model. Under these conditions, our measured variables will be linearly related to one another.

Given these uncertainties, we must find a functional form that is robust enough to yield the right signs, if not the right magnitudes, under a variety of alternative specifications. Obviously the linear formulation will yield the correct result if the true model in the measured variables is linear. Problems only arise if the true model in the unmeasured variables is multiplicative, but we go ahead and estimate a linear version. In this case, it can be shown that if the underlying variables are ratio scales with a multiplicative relationship and if the observed variables are linear transformations of these scales, then estimating the linear form will produce the correct signs. This result, the theoretical point made above, and the ease with which linear equations can be estimated suggest that the linear model is the best way to estimate the CVM. Knowing as little as we do about the correct functional form, it seems best to stay with the simple linear formulations.[9]

Similar considerations apply to the way we have estimated models for particular acts. We have consistently used the linear probability model (without a Goldberger correction)—which is, in fact, a fancy name for ordinary least squares. This model is easy to estimate, easy to interpret, and arguably as robust as the standard logit and probit formulations.[10] To check our results, we have estimated some of our models with logit, but the results have not been significantly different. In short, we have focused more on presenting alternative specifications and discussing numerous possible threats to the validity of our results rather than trying to use fancy statistical estimation methods that might or might not be appropriate for our circumstances.

Notes

1. Henry E. Brady, Sidney Verba, and Kay Lehman Schlozman, "Beyond SES: A Resource Model of Political Participation," *American Political Science Review* 89 (1995): 271–294.

2. Ibid.

3. "Sensitivity Analyses Would Help," *American Economic Review* 75 (1985): 308.

4. See Christopher H. Achen, "Proxy Variables and Incorrect Signs on Regression Coefficients," *Political Methodology* 11 (1985): 299–316.

5. There might be some social desirability factor that would create correlated errors between these measures, but for reasons outlined in Appendix E, we think this is unlikely.

6. Being retired might be left in the equation, but its inclusion or omission makes very little difference. If civic skills are assumed to be exogenous and we estimate the model using OLS, then job level, organizational affiliation, and religious attendance are not statistically significant (see Table 12.1) and the coefficient of working is negative.

7. "Sensitivity Analyses Would Help," p. 308.

8. As well as the numerous specifications reported in Chapters 12–15 in this book, there are additional approaches—with a somewhat different dependent variable, some other independent variables, and somewhat different instruments—reported in Henry E. Brady, Sidney Verba, and Kay Lehman Schlozman, "Beyond SES: A Resource Model of Political Participation."

9. A brave empiricist might argue that we should have let the data tell us the correct functional form by estimating a flexible non-linear form. Our efforts to do this with simple models with only one resource and one engagement measure suggested that the data were not very revealing in this regard, and the complexity of estimating a non-linear model with many resources and engagements did not seem worth the effort to us.

10. Furthermore, none of the particular acts is measured as a dichotomy.

Measuring the Amount of Activity

Throughout this book we have relied upon responses to questions about political participation, organizational affiliations, and religious involvements. It is well known that responses to questions can vary dramatically depending upon the way the questions are worded,[1] and this may affect the results we obtain. Answers to questions about political participation can depend upon the specificity of the stimulus, the time period mentioned, and the context of the question. In addition, a number of authors[2] have noted that respondents typically overreport forms of participation like these because of a social desirability bias "in which cognitive dissonance can lead to a rather consistent distortion of memory in order to reinforce continued perception of oneself as a good citizen."[3] This raises two possibilities. Our results may differ from other studies because we used different question wordings, or, more generally, our results may be affected by social desirability bias.

Different Question Wordings

Most of the available data on political participation come from questions asked on surveys whose primary purpose is not the study of political participation. These studies usually use short batteries of items and abbreviated questions to inquire about participation. Since we focused on political participation, we developed detailed batteries of questions with extensive descriptions, particularly acts. This approach may increase the number of people claiming to engage in an activity, but there is good reason to believe that this method provides a closer approximation to the truth than short and often vague questions about political activity.

We know, for example, from comparing the screener data with the follow-up questionnaire that more detailed questions administered to the same people increase the amount of reported participation. Whereas 49 percent of screener respondents said they belonged to an organization when we asked a simple question about organizational membership on the screener, almost 80 percent of the respondents on the follow-up said they were associated with an organization when we presented a list of over twenty organizations. Turning to contacting, we found that when we used one question on the screener to ask whether people had contacted at any level in the past year, 26 percent said yes. On the follow-up questionnaire, we found that 34 percent of the same respondents reported contacting at the federal or local level in the last year. The two questions cover the same time period (one year), but on the follow-up, we asked whether people had contacted a "federal elected official or someone on the staff or such an official," "a non-elected official in a federal government agency," "an elected official on the state or local level," or "a non-elected official in a state or local government agency or board." By specifying four different targets for their contacting, we increased the number of people who said they contacted quite substantially.

Similar disparities arise when we turn to other questions. We find in our study, for example, that 24 percent of the population had contributed to an individual candidate, a party group, a political action committee, or any other organization that supported candidates between January 1988 and the interview in Spring 1990. This is a substantially larger figure than the 9 to 10 percent of the respondents on American National Election Studies who answer yes to either one or both of two questions about contributing to a party or a candidate,[4] but the question we ask covers a longer time period than the ANE questions, and it asks about a broader range of activities. Similarly, we find that 9 percent of our sample said that between January 1988 and Spring 1990 they had "worked as a volunteer . . . for a candidate running for national, state, or local office." This is more than the 4 to 5 percent who said yes to the ANE question "Did you do any (other) work for one of the parties or candidates during the campaign?" but our question covers a longer period of time and it explicitly mentions all levels of government.

These data suggest that responses about political participation vary a great deal depending upon the question wording. The differences we find make sense in terms of what we know about recall and question wording effects. We believe that the questions we use are better because they are explicit about time periods and activities.

Social Desirability Bias and Spurious Correlations

For at least one activity, voting, it is possible to obtain actual national turnout for 1988 and to compare it with the percentage of the respondents in the Citizen Participation Study who report having voted in that election. According to official election statistics, 50.1 percent of the voting-age population voted for President in 1988, but 71 percent of respondents report having voted. These figures strongly suggest that we have some bias, equal to the amounts found in other studies, in our reports of voting. It certainly seems possible that we also have biases in the reports of other activities.[5]

If these biases exist, do they create any problems for our multivariate analyses? Could social desirability bias invalidate the causal inferences we try to make from our data? For social desirability to create spurious multivariate results, it must operate in such a way that some subgroups are more prone to it than others.[6] Silver, Anderson, and Abramson apparently believe that this happens. They argue that "the tendency to overreport voting is related to respondent characteristics" so that "measures of the relation between respondent characteristics and self-reported voting will overestimate the strength of the relation between the dependent and independent variables."[7] They reject earlier findings that validated and self-report measures of voting yield the same results.[8]

We believe that the evidence, especially Silver, Anderson, and Abramson's finding that "vote expectation is a powerful filter for the effects of general political attitudes on vote overreporting,"[9] is more consistent with a simple model of self-reporting that does not assume a subgroup of people especially prone to social desirability bias. When an interviewer asks a question about political participation (often substantially after the fact), a respondent forms a sense of the likelihood of having performed the act based upon the relevant clues or considerations. He or she exaggerates this likelihood by some random amount that is independent of his or her characteristics.[10] If the resulting likelihood is above some threshold, the respondent says that he or she performed the activity. Those who actually are more likely to have in fact performed the act (and perhaps did so, but not in the period asked about by the interviewer) are more likely to go over the threshold and to report they did it because of the exaggeration factor. Those who are less likely to have done it are less likely to go over the threshold even though they add in the same exaggeration factor.

Hence, we tend to find that overreporters look a lot like truthful reporters—although maybe just somewhat less educated, interested in politics, and so forth because it is these people who are closest to the threshold. This is exactly what has been found in the literature cited earlier. Volgy and Schwarz, for example, find that "those who claim to participate and those who actually do participate have a good deal in common, . . . both undocumented and documented participants may come from a similar 'pool' of potential activists"[11] and Silver, Anderson, and Abramson find that "Americans who are more concerned about the outcome of the election are also more likely to overreport voting."[12] These results are consistent with a model in which social desirability bias affects all respondents to some extent. More generally, several studies that have either devised experimental manipulations to increase social desirability or looked for factors in the interview situation that would have increased social desirability have failed to find any effects.[13] These studies suggest that differential social desirability may be a phantom.

As an empirical test of our theory, we examined some data from the 1990–1993 National Election Studies panel to see if those who overreported voting in 1988 (through a retrospective question asked in 1990) were likely to do the same in 1990. If overreporters are especially prone to social desirability bias, then they should be much more likely to overreport than self-reported voters who did vote in 1988. If everyone is prone to social desirability bias and overreporters are simply closer to the threshold where they can make mistakes than are members of other groups, then overreporters should only be somewhat more likely to overreport again in 1990. The second hypothesis appears to be correct, with percentages of overreporting of 36.9 percent for 1988 overreporters and 27.8 percent for those self-reported voters who did vote in 1988. Moreover, the 1988 overreporters were quite likely to vote in 1990 (52.5 percent of them compared to only 26.1 percent of the 1988 validated nonvoters who also reported not voting), suggesting that they often do vote. In short, the evidence is consistent with the assumption that social desirability bias is uncorrelated with specific characteristics of the respondents. This means that it would not bias our results (except for the intercept of our regressions because of general overreporting).

Furthermore, if social desirability does exist and some people are more prone to it than others, it will be a problem for multivariate analyses only if it causes crucial variables to be correlated with one another. If there are *different forms* of social desirability and they are uncorrelated with one another—for instance, some think that church attendance is socially desirable and others think that voting is socially desirable—then social desirability is unlikely to cause spurious correlations. In fact, it is more likely to lead to an underestimation of the importance of some factors because of an error in variables situation. In such a case, social desirability would add random noise to many of our variables, probably reducing regression coefficients instead of inflating them.

Our analysis indicates that the creation of spurious relationships via social desirability is unlikely. Many of the basic variables in the Civic Voluntarism Model are not highly correlated with one another. Consider the crucial relationship between civic skills and participation. If this relationship is spurious because of a common social desirability factor, then the three measures of civic skills (in jobs, in non-political organizations, and in churches) should be significantly correlated. In fact, the correlations are .30 between job skills and organizational skills, .09 between job skills and church skills, and .29 between organizational skills and church skills. Since the lowest of these numbers is the upper bound on the possible amount of common social desirability bias, it is hard to believe that a correlation of .09 could account for all of our results. Similarly, the correlations between religious attendance and giving money or religious attendance and protesting are very low. These results make it unlikely that our results are spurious.

Summary

The fact that our detailed question wordings have led to estimates of political participation that differ from those obtained in other surveys is good reason to trust our measures at least as much, if not more, than those of other studies. We also believe that it is possible that reports of activities may be inflated in our data through a social desirability bias— although we suspect that in many cases we have done a better job of identifying true activity by asking very specific questions. Finally, we have shown that the dangers of spurious correlation are probably quite small.

Notes

1. See, for example, Norman Bradburn, Lance J. Rips, and Steven K. Shevell, "Answering Autobiographical Questions: The Impact of Memory and Inference in Surveys," *Science* 236 (1987): 157–161.

2. See, for example, Barbara A. Anderson and Brian D. Silver, "Measurement and Mismeasurement of the Validity of the Self-Reported Vote," *American Journal of Political Science* 30 (1986): 771–785; Kim Quaile Hill and Patricia A. Hurley, "Nonvoters in Voters' Clothing: The Impact of Voting Behavior Misreporting on Voting Behavior Research," *Social Science Quarterly* 65 (1984): 199–206; John P. Katosh and Michael W. Traugott, "The Consequences of Validated and Self-Reported Voting Measures," *Public Opinion Quarterly* 45 (1981): 519–535; Brian D. Silver, Paul R. Abramson, and Barbara A. Anderson, "The Presence of Others and Overreporting of Voting in American National Elections," *Public Opinion Quarterly* 50 (1986): 228–239; Brian D. Silver, Barbara A. Anderson, and Paul R. Abramson, "Who Overreports Voting," *American Political Science Review* 80 (1986): 613–624; Thomas J. Volgy and John E. Schwarz, "Misreporting and Vicarious Political Participation at the Local Level," *Public Opinion Quarterly* 48 (1984): 757–765; and Carol H. Weiss, "Validity of Welfare Mothers' Interview Responses," *Public Opinion Quarterly* 32 (1968): 622–633.

3. Don Cahalan, "Correlates of Respondent Accuracy in the Denver Validity Survey," *Public Opinion Quarterly* 32 (1968): 607–621.

4. The two questions are: "Did you give money to a political party during this election year?" and "Did you give any money to an individual candidate running for public office?" The 9 to 10 percent figure represents the number of people saying yes to either question.

5. Comparisons of survey data on church attendance with count based church attendance "suggest that Protestant and Catholic church attendance is roughly one-half the levels reported by Gallup," C. Kirk Hadaway, Penny Long Marler, and Mark Chaves, "What the Polls Don't Show: A Closer Look at U.S. Church Attendance," *American Sociological Review* 58 (1993): 741–752.

6. The exact way in which it must enter follows from Henry E. Brady, "The Perils of Survey Research: Inter-Personally Incomparable Responses," *Political Methodology* 11 (1985): 269–291.

7. "Who Overreports Voting?" p. 620.

8. Lee Sigelman, "The Nonvoting Voter in Voting Research," *American Journal of Political Science* 26 (1982): 47–56, and John P. Katosh and Michael W. Traugott, "The Consequences of Validated and Self-Reported Voting Measures," *Public Opinion Quarterly* 45 (1981): 519–535.

9. "Who Overreports Voting?" p. 617.

10. The process we describe is similar to the mechanism for answering

questions outlined in Scot Burton and Edward Blair, "Task Conditions, Response Formulation Processes, and Response Accuracy for Behavioral Frequency Questions in Surveys," *Public Opinion Quarterly* 55 (1991): 50–79.

11. "Misreporting and Vicarious Political Participation at the Local Level", p. 760.

12. "Who Overreports Voting?" p. 614.

13. Silver, Abramson, and Anderson, "The Presence of Others and Overreporting of Voting in American National Elections," and Stanley Presser, "Can Changes in Context Reduce Vote Overreporting in Surveys?" *Public Opinion Quarterly* 54 (1990): 586–593. The race of the interviewer may have an impact; see Barbara A. Anderson, Brian D. Silver, and Paul R. Abramson, "Effects of Race of the Interviewer on Measures of Electoral Participation by Blacks in SRC National Election Studies," *Public Opinion Quarterly* 52 (1988): 53–83.

Supplementary Tables

The following tables provide results that were omitted from the tables in the main part of the book to simplify the presentation. This supplementary information is identified by the table number in the text. Thus Table F.12.2 below contains additional information for Table 12.2 in the text. We have chosen to provide this information for all tables that are crucial in the development of the Civic Voluntarism Model. The computer code for these and all other tables in the text is available from the authors upon request.

Table F.12.2

	B	SE B	Beta
Working	−.09	.05	−.05
Retired	.45	.13	.09
Catholic	.05	.06	.01
Age 18 to 24	−.78	.12	−.14
Age 25 to 34	−.46	.09	−.12
Age 35 to 44	−.15	.09	−.04
Age 55 to 64	.00	.11	.00
Age > 64	−.19	.14	−.04

Table F.12.3

	B	SE B	Beta
Citizenship	.90	.20	.09
English at Home	.08	.10	.02

Table F.12.5

	B	SE B	Beta
Citizenship	.71	.18	.07
English at Home	.09	.09	.02
Working	−.05	.04	−.03
Retired	.42	.12	.08
Catholic	.08	.06	.02
Age 18 to 24	−.62	.11	−.11
Age 25 to 34	−.35	.09	−.09
Age 35 to 44	−.13	.08	−.04
Age 55 to 64	−.05	.11	−.01
Age > 64	−.25	.13	−.05

Table F.12.6

	B	SE B	Beta
Citizenship	.70	.19	.07
English at Home	.09	.09	.02
(Constant)	−3.57	.52	

Table F.12.7

Time-Based Acts:	B	SE B	Beta
Education	.06	.02	.10
Vocabulary	−.01	.01	−.03
Family income	.01	.01	.05
Job Level	−.03	.02	−.05
Non. Pol. Org.	.04	.02	.04
Religious Attend.	−.01	.01	−.02
Civic Skills (sum)	.07	.01	.20
Political Interest	.12	.01	.21
Pol. Information	.03	.01	.05
Political Efficacy	.05	.01	.13

Table F.12.7 *(continued)*

Partisan Strength	.01	.02	.01
Citizenship	.03	.12	.01
Free Time	.00	.01	.01
English at Home	.07	.06	.03
Working	−.06	.03	−.06
Retired	.18	.08	.06
Catholic	.04	.04	.02
Age 18 to 24	−.04	.07	−.01
Age 25 to 34	−.05	.06	−.02
Age 35 to 44	.03	.06	.01
Age 55 to 64	−.02	.07	−.01
Age > 64	−.26	.08	−.10
(Constant)	−1.09	.16	

Voting:	B	SE B	Beta
Education	.08	.04	.05
Vocabulary	.06	.02	.05
Family income	.03	.02	.04
Job Level	.00	.04	.00
Non. Pol. Org.	.09	.06	.03
Religious Attend.	.10	.02	.11
Civic Skills (sum)	.01	.03	.01
Political Interest	.41	.03	.25
Pol. Information	.16	.03	.12
Political Efficacy	.07	.02	.06
Partisan Strength	.45	.05	.16
Citizenship	3.55	.51	.13
Free Time	−.03	.01	−.05
English at Home	−.03	.16	−.00
Working	.17	.07	.06
Retired	.71	.20	.09
Catholic	.23	.10	.04
Age 18 to 24	−1.31	.19	−.14
Age 25 to 34	−.86	.14	−.15
Age 35 to 44	−.40	.14	−.07
Age 55 to 64	.44	.17	.05
Age > 65	.76	.21	.10
(Constant)	−2.22	.54	

Political Contributions:	B	SE B	Beta
Education	8.94	5.05	.05
Vocabulary	−3.80	3.13	−.03
Family income	27.84	2.00	.30
Job Level	.67	4.96	.00

Table F.12.7 *(continued)*

Non. Pol. Org.	−8.09	7.70	−.02
Religious Attend.	−3.19	2.17	−.03
Civic Skills (sum)	5.69	3.18	.05
Pol. Interest	11.59	3.97	.07
Pol. Information	3.99	3.51	.03
Political Efficacy	1.12	2.49	.01
Partisan Strength	12.15	5.89	.04
Citizenship	16.13	37.59	.01
Free Time	3.26	1.64	.05
English at Home	−.12.69	18.04	−.02
Working	2.40	8.79	.01
Retired	−3.43	25.54	−.00
Catholic	−6.75	12.48	−.01
Age 18 to 24	−19.80	23.42	−.02
Age 25 to 34	9.07	18.23	.01
Age 35 to 44	18.60	17.99	.03
Age 55 to 64	12.93	22.27	.01
Age > 64	32.19	26.59	.04
(Constant)	−188.53	51.43	

Political Discussion:	B	SE B	Beta
Education	.01	.03	−.01
Vocabulary	−.01	.02	−.02
Family income	.03	.01	.04
Job Level	.02	.03	.01
Non. Pol. Org.	.07	.04	.03
Religious Attend.	−.04	.01	−.06
Civic Skills (sum)	.02	.02	.02
Political Interest	.65	.02	.54
Pol. Information	.12	.02	.12
Political Efficacy	.02	.01	.03
Partisan Strength	.07	.03	.03
Citizenship	.22	.21	.02
Free Time	−.01	.01	.02
English at Home	.04	.10	.01
Working	.03	.05	.02
Retired	.14	.14	.02
Catholic	.10	.07	.02
Age 18 to 24	.15	.13	.02
Age 25 to 34	.14	.10	.03
Age 35 to 44	.20	.10	.05
Age 55 to 64	.23	.12	.04
Age > 64	−.39	.15	−.07
(Constant)	.56	.28	

Table F.13.6

	B	SE B	Beta
Age 18 to 24	−.62	.11	−.11
Age 25 to 34	−.36	.09	−.10
Age 35 to 44	−.14	.08	−.04
Age 55 to 64	−.03	.10	−.01
Age > 64	−.18	.12	−.04
Retired	.42	.12	.08
Working	−.08	.04	−.05
English at Home	.04	.08	.01
Citizenship	.76	.18	.08
Catholic	.07	.06	.02
(Constant)	−2.38	.24	

Table F.15.6

	B	SE B	Beta
Parents' Education	.04	.02	.04
Female	−.11	.06	−.03
Black	.14	.09	.02
Latino	.18	.13	.03
Education	.13	.02	.12
Politics at Home	.05	.02	.04
H.S. Activity	.07	.02	.08
Job Level	−.03	.02	−.03
Non. Pol. Org.	.02	.04	.01
Religious Attend.	−.01	.01	−.01
Family income	.05	.01	.09
Free Time	−.01	.01	−.02
Civic Skills (sum)	.09	.02	.14
Vocabulary	.04	.01	.05
Recruitment	.25	.03	.13
Political Interest	.25	.02	.24
Pol. Information	.10	.02	.12
Age 18 to 24	−.75	.11	−.13
Age 25 to 34	−.40	.09	−.11
Age 35 to 44	−.14	.08	−.04
Age 55 to 64	−.01	.10	−.00
Age > 64	−.11	.12	−.02
Catholic	.09	.06	.02
English at Home	.10	.10	.02
Citizenship	.82	.18	.08

Table F.15.6 *(continued)*

Retired	.39	.12	.07
Working	−.08	.04	−.04
(Constant)	−2.09	.26	

Table F.15.7

	B	SE B	Beta
Citizenship	.72	.19	.07
English at Home	.09	.09	.02

Index